SPEECH COMMUNICATION:

A REDEMPTIVE INTRODUCTION

-SECOND EDITION-

DONALD H. ALBAN JR.

SPEECH COMMUNICATION:

A REDEMPTIVE INTRODUCTION

-SECOND EDITION-

DONALD H. ALBAN JR.

Associate Professor of Communication Studies

LIBERTY UNIVERSITY

Kendall Hunt
publishing company

Cover design: Paul Segsworth
Interior design: RJS Design Studio

Unless otherwise indicated, all Scripture quotations in Part I are taken from the Holy Bible, New Living Translation (NLT), copyright © 1996, 2004, 2007 by Tyndale House Foundation. Used by permission of Tyndale House Publishers, Inc., Carol Stream, Illinois 60188. All rights reserved.

Unless otherwise indicated, all Scripture quotations in Part IV are taken from the King James Version of the Bible.

Scripture quotations marked (ESV) are from The Holy Bible, English Standard Version® (ESV®), copyright © 2001 by Crossway, a publishing ministry of Good News Publishers. Used by permission. All rights reserved.

Profiles in Part IV are reprinted with permission from their respective copyright holders: The Estate of James R. Adair (Adair, LeTourneau, McGuirl, Poland), Greg Asimakoupoulos (DeHaan, Field, Haugen, Schoendoerfer), Christin Ditchfield (Vicki Caruana), Grace Fox (Anderson, Bish, Chamberlain-Froese, McKnight, Richardson), Vicki Huffman (Dick Wright), Jews for Jesus (Block), John W. Kennedy (Barna, Beiler, Blessman, Cathy, Causey, Damadian, Elzinga, The Great Passion Play, Green, Hardin, Hoekstra, Hofman, Olasky, Ramsey, Staver, Thomas, Spielman, Ware), Marlo Schalesky (Phillip Johnson), Ben Taylor (Parkening), Worldwide Challenge (Struecker), Karen Spears Zacharias (Baehr, Dorminy, McClary, Ortega, Strobel).

Job descriptions adapted from the Bureau of Labor Statistics, U.S. Department of Labor, Occupational Outlook Handbook, 2010-11 Edition. Available on the Internet at http://www.bls.gov/oco. Public domain.

Cover image: © istockphoto / Robert Churchill

www.kendallhunt.com
Send all inquiries to:
4050 Westmark Drive
Dubuque, IA 52004-1840

To my wife and soul mate, Evangeline, an authentic lover of God
whose compassionate heart regularly reminds me that
redemption is something to be lived,

and

To my parents, Donald and Joanne,
whose lifetime of serving others has taught me much more
about redemptive communication than words alone can relay.

CONTENTS

PART 1
REDEMPTIVE COMMUNICATION: BASIC PRINCIPLES

2

PART 2
PUBLIC SPEAKING:
A PRIMER FOR REDEMPTIVE COMMUNICATORS

3

PART 3
COMMUNICATION VOCATIONS: PUBLIC PLATFORMS FOR REDEMPTIVE COMMUNICATORS

4

PART 4
REDEMPTIVE COMMUNICATORS: PROFILES FROM ACROSS THE JOB FIELDS

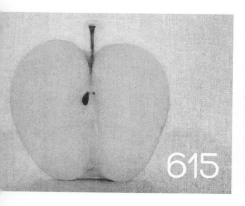

615

777

859

APPENDICES

PREFACE
TO THE SECOND EDITION

This edition of *Speech Communication: A Redemptive Introduction* is a significant revision of the book's first edition, one made largely in response to feedback from professional peers. I would be remiss to begin this edition without thanking these esteemed colleagues for suggesting helpful additions and deletions, for recommending clarifications, for highlighting typos, and for otherwise contributing to the improvement of the textbook's quality and usefulness. I am particularly indebted to my Liberty University COMS 101 online instructional colleagues and my residential COMS 101 graduate student assistants (and Mrs. Carla Sloan, who supervises the GSA team) for their thoughts as we used the text to instruct several thousand students since the first edition's publication. I thank the university's College of General Studies administrators (Drs. Emily Heady, Bruce Bell, and Yaw Adu-Gyamfi and Associate Dean Wayne Patton) for their supportiveness of this project. I am especially grateful to those outside of Liberty who have made helpful suggestions—most notably, my former doctoral instructor and dissertation chair, Dr. Jack Keeler of Regent University, whose especially detailed and insightful feedback has been most valuable. A special thank you to Mr. Curtis Ross of Kendall/Hunt, who proposed this project nearly two years ago, for his supportiveness throughout the publishing process and for his help in gathering constructive suggestions from colleagues at other institutions. I thank Mrs. Evangeline Alban, a top-notch Liberty University Online instructor and, most of all, the love of my life, without whose constant encouragement and patience this project never would have happened.

The most obvious change to this edition of the text, to anyone who has seen the first edition, is its considerably slimmer size. Largely because of its thick paper stock, the first edition, in its initial form at least, weighed a whopping 5.5 pounds! What a load that proved to be for those of my COMS 101 students who attempted each week to carry the book up three long flights of stairs to the master session classroom. If they succeeded, they deserve medals! The book's size and weight generated justified complaints from students and statements of wonder from peers in my field who evaluated the text during the 2012 National Communication Association conference in Orlando. We have remedied this problem in this edition by using a thinner quality paper stock and by removing about 200 pages of secondarily significant content from the book.

Content-wise, the most notable change is that I have reorganized the book's contents to give it a stronger initial emphasis, after its introductory section on communication, on the principles and practices of effective public speaking and a secondary emphasis on the vocational platforms through which students can exercise their calling to be redemptive communicators. As noted, I have removed about 200 pages of content, mostly from the "Job Fields for Redemptive Communicators" section that, in this edition, I have re-titled "Communication Vocations: Public Platforms for Redemptive Communicators." To enhance the work's uniformity, the new edition blends together the content of my separately published textbook, *Created for Connection*, and the Makay et al. *Public Speaking* materials, into a single unit with one table of contents, one index, and one series of sequentially developed chapters. I also have added several additional supplemental articles to this edition—articles by content experts and instructors that give students additional helpful insights into themes that the main material presents only generally. Finally, this edition of the text includes an end-of-chapter workbook feature that gives instructors a set of optional resources for helping students assimilate and apply the principles presented in the reading materials.

INTRODUCTION

What should I do with my life? Which occupation should I choose? Which major will prepare me to enter it? What meaningful difference, if any, would it make in my life and in the lives of others, if I were to go in this direction? Which skills must I develop in order to make this kind of meaningful difference?

If you are like many thoughtful college students, this set of questions hounds you as each semester passes, especially during your first year or two of study. With so many options to consider in today's world, choosing your field is no easy task, and this shows in the typical collegian's experience. About 80 percent of students enter college uncertain of their major, and nearly half change their major at least once, according to research.[1] Even after completing a degree, many college graduates remain uncertain about their calling in life. More than ever, they founder as they contemplate their next step. Indeed, a recent study by the National Association of Colleges and Employers reports that the Class of 2011 had "the largest percentage of graduates aiming to avoid the work force *and* to avoid graduate/professional school than any class in recent memory."[2]

Why today's young people struggle with finding direction in life puzzles those who investigate such trends. Some scholars believe it is at least partly the result of stiflingly strong parental involvement in this generation's growing-up and decision-making experiences. Others suggest it is the immobilizing result of this generation's strong focus on achievement and the potentially overwhelming pressure to succeed that accompanies it. Whatever the cause of the indecisiveness may be, one thing is certain—it is not because this generation lacks a desire to make a difference in the world. To the contrary, researchers describe this generation as "motivated, goal-oriented, assertive, and confident. They want to make a difference."[3]

With this phenomenon in mind, I have written this introductory communication text-book for Christian college students in a format that not only acquaints them with basic communication principles and with the communication field, but also helps them develop a clearer sense of what it takes to make a difference in the world and which vocational paths they could follow in order to make this happen. Although it is true, as is commonly suggested, that students should consider their interests and abilities when charting their course in life, they also must heed a larger question that can enrich and give abiding direction to these interests and abilities and help them make a truly meaningful difference—What makes anything I do significant or valuable?

In a social world like ours, answering this question requires us to consider the people in our lives and our motives for interacting with them as we do. Whatever else it may be, a job is a platform for communicating with a certain set of people in a specific way for the purpose of satisfying a specific need or set of needs, whether these needs are theirs or ours and whether the needs are physical, social, cognitive, aesthetic, financial, spiritual, or something else.

Although collegians must consider their personal interests and needs when charting their course in life, this book brings into this analysis the historic Christian premise that God created us to express authentic love for Him by living in a state of *communis* (the Latin term from which we derive "communication") with Him and with each other. The Bible, the foundational statement of Christian doctrine, teaches that humans corrupted this plan by resolving to live life autonomously on our terms rather than on God's terms. Rather than leaving us in our self-imposed state of exile, God, because of His unyielding love for us, Self-sacrificially made our restored *communis* with Him possible through His redemptive work on the cross. The Bible teaches that an authentic Christian is someone who receives this gift by acknowledging his or her corruption, by recognizing Christ's atoning work as his or her only hope for restoration, and by resolving to live in a way that mirrors God's original intent for his or her life.

To appreciate this principle as it relates to communication, Christian collegians must understand that authentic Christian commitment touches every aspect of the redeemed person's life, including his or her choice of a major or job field. Whatever else it may be, a career is a means to another end, whether this end is happiness, security, or social utility. This authentic Christian is someone who quests, above all, to do everything "for the glory of God" (1 Cor. 10:31, NLT). If a job field is significant to him or her, he or she understands that it is not merely because the field promises to deliver happiness, security, or social utility. What gives the field its ultimate worth is its potential as a platform for interacting with people in a way that honors God by promoting what He values in this world. By seeing one's career choice in this light, the Christian collegian begins to understand what it takes to make an enduringly meaningful difference in the world. He or she also begins to understand why developing public communication skills is valuable and why communication, as a major and as an job field, is a great option for students who want to realize their calling in a way that touches many lives.

As an expression of this rationale, this textbook, in Part I, presents communication as a multifaceted information-exchange process through which people attempt to establish meaningful connections with God and with each other. After defining communication and surveying its diverse forms, Part I contrasts a Biblically Christian view of communication's purpose with several autonomous counterpoints and briefly makes a case for the former's preeminence. The section culminates by challenging Christian students to engage the world as redemptive communicators—as people, that is, who see the world as God intended it to be and who interact with others in a way that, above all, promotes His redemptive purpose for human lives.

With this as the presented primary motive for developing communication skills, Part II of this textbook helps students develop the formal oral communication skills that students will need in order to be effective, regardless of which major they pursue or which career path they follow. Integrating portions of Makay, et al.'s *Public Speaking: Choices for Effective Results*, this section instructs students in such fundamental principles of effective speech construction as audience analysis, research, documentation, and information organization. This section also helps students develop the ability to present such information orally to an audience in an effective way.

The book's Part III invites students to consider communication as an academic and professional specialization through which they can put these communication principles into practice in a public way that redemptively impacts many lives in a redemptive way. Using information from the Bureau of Labor Statistics, this section highlights several communication-related job fields, providing timely descriptions of the field's work, the credentials it requires, the compensation it involves, and its outlook for the future.

The book's Part IV helps students better understand how someone in any of many job fields, and not just in communication, could use the job as a platform for interacting with other people in a way that promotes something that God values. Departing from the didactic style of earlier sections, Part IV cultivates this awareness by challenging students to analyze profiles of real people who have used their diverse occupations—religion, education, media, law and government, business and finance, the arts, medicine, math and science, engineering, and the military—in this redemptive way.

This unique introduction to communication challenges Christian students to make a faith-integrated career choice—a choice that is ultimately valuable because it can enable them to make an enduringly meaningful difference in the world through their interactions with other people. As well, it teaches them the communication skills they will need as they quest, through their careers, to engage their world in a redemptive way.

—Donald H. Alban Jr., PhD

---

[1] http://dus.psu.edu/md/mdintro.htm

[2] http://www.naceweb.org/uploadedFiles/NACEWeb/Research/Student/student.pdf

[3] http://www.csulb.edu/divisions/students2/intouch/archives/2007-08/vol16_no1/01.htm

PART 1

....

REDEMPTIVE COMMUNICATION:

BASIC PRINCIPLES

A REDEMPTIVE PRAYER

God be in my head, and in my understanding;
God be in mine eyes, and in my looking;
God be in my mouth, and in my speaking;
God be in my heart, and in my thinking;
God be at mine end, and at my departing.

–The Sarum Primer (1538)

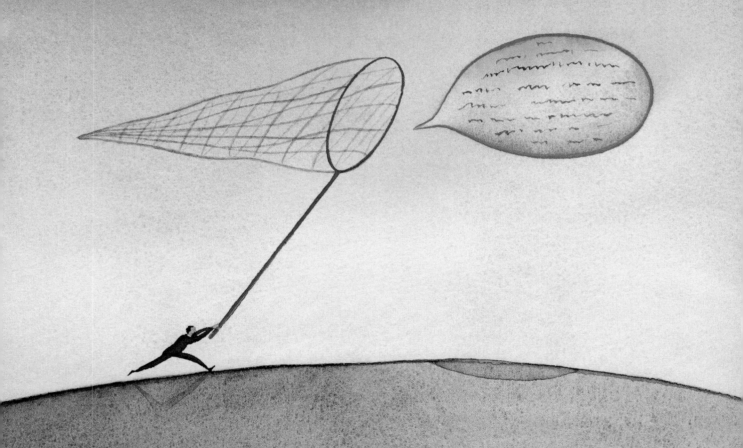

CHAPTER 1 >>

1 COMMUNICATION: WHAT IS IT?

OVERVIEW

We begin this study by considering what communication means. This chapter presents the word's literal meaning and then explains how this definition can be misunderstood unless further developed. After proposing a working definition of "communication," we evaluate the process through which communication takes place. Blending concepts from a couple of classic communication theories, we review several major elements in this process and explore the way they work together to cause communication to occur. We then consider factors that can prevent communication from happening.

❯❯A CLOSER LOOK

On a cool, overcast Good Friday morning not long ago, I sat in my office at Liberty University—a large, thriving, Christian institution located in central Virginia—contemplating what steps I might take to determine whether my introductory-communication-theory students were truly learning the content I had directed them to study throughout the semester. With only minutes to go before the scheduled beginning of my next session with them, I quickly decided that, at the very least, these students should be able to define one of the most basic terms to which their study had been devoted—communication. Moments later, I hastily grabbed my computer bag, bolted out the door, and strode down the stairs and across a courtyard to the classroom where our session was scheduled to begin.

© 2012 by Stockbyte.
Used under license of Thinkstock.

How do you define communication? Would your class-mates define it the same way? What makes a definition of the term a good one?

After entering the classroom and positioning myself behind the lectern, I prepared my computer equipment for the session and then, as had been my custom, called the class to order with an opening word of prayer. After briefly addressing several course-related administrative matters, I asked the approximately 60 students to pull out a piece of paper. A few scattered groans sounded throughout the classroom as students prepared for what several of them apparently feared would be yet another pop quiz over the assigned reading for the day.

"Hey! Don't worry. This is not a quiz . . ." I assured them, hoping to put minds at ease. "But, I do have an important question for you to think about, one that I'd like you to answer in writing. You have spent nearly an entire semester studying communication theory. Now I would like you to tell me in your own words—what does the term *communication* mean? A few students almost immediately set their pens to paper and hastily began to write. A few others stared blankly into empty space, as if locked in deep thought, before reviving and carefully etching the first words of their apparently pensive descriptions. Most students had completed their writing two minutes later; so I collected their work and placed it in my briefcase to review later that day.

Hours later, while sitting in my home office on a rainy afternoon, I perused the students' responses and noted, with some pleasure albeit not much surprise, that in a basic way at least, their descriptions of the concept were quite similar. Most had presented communication as a way in which people do exchange or can exchange information with each other. Although the respondents generally agreed with this basic idea, they were less unified in their appraisals of what, beyond this, the concept of communication involves. Some students painted communication in the broadest terms imaginable, presenting it as a phenomenon that, although applicable to humans, is not necessarily limited to them. As one young scholar put it, "Communication is the exchange of information between people, animals, and things." A few of her peers similarly portrayed communication broadly, but characterized it more concisely as something uniquely human. "Communication is everything that exists between people" one wrote. "It is the process of people sharing information with each other," penned another. Several other students were even more specific. Communication, they claimed, is not merely the exchange of information among people, but the shared understanding that can result when the exchange occurs.

As I pondered these distinctions and others like them among the dozens of submitted definitions, I was impressed by the fact that, although a professor's preliminary clarification of key terms does not totally eliminate differences in student understandings of the terms' meanings, taking this step is nonetheless an essential starting point in the study of any subject. I have observed during my years of teaching that presenting foundational definitions early in a course at least moves students closer to shared understandings of what they are studying and enables them to evaluate the study's content in a more meaningful, focused way.

Accordingly, I submit that it behooves us at the beginning of an introductory communication text like this one, to consider what communication is. Defining this core idea, as precisely and practically as possible, is the primary goal of this opening chapter. In the pages that follow, I further this goal, first, by considering the literal meaning of "communication" in the light of the language that produced it, and then by reviewing the elements that work together as a process to make communication possible. After defining communication and showing how it comes into existence, we review a series of terms that scholars often use to distinguish different types of communication that enrich one's study of the topic. Knowing these types can help students develop a clearer sense of the communications area that most interests them as they prepare to be skillful communicators in their personal lives, church lives, academic lives, and careers.

❯❯ THE ROOTS OF COMMUNICATION

One of the best places to go when trying to define an English word is to the word's roots, which often come to us from other languages like Latin, French, and German. Our word "communication" derives from the Latin term *communis*, which means common, general, universal, or public.[1] The presence of commonness, or of something shared, is a distinguishing feature of communication. Without the former, the latter does not exist. A communicative state exists when two or more people share or come to share a perception, an idea, a feeling, an attitude, or a value, among other applications. The same basic idea appears in several English words that resemble "communication" because they, too, derive from *communis*. A *community* or *commune*, for example, is a group of people who share something, whether physical space or common ideals, interests, or beliefs. A *common* or *commissary* is a place that people share or where they gather for a shared experience or type of experience. A *communion* service in church is an experience in which Christians assemble to focus as one on the significance of Christ's death. If you were to break down "communication" even further, you would note as well the root *unis* in this term, from which we derive such English words as "unity," "united," and "uniform." The core concept once again is the idea of oneness. When a person believes, feels, values, or acts as one with another person, *communis* exists.

Before considering an official definition of "communication," we should note, in the light of the literal meaning of communis, that your study of communication can be approached in at least two ways, both of which are utilized and encouraged as major thrusts of this book. The *expositional* approach identifies, analyzes, and attempts to explain the existence of attitudes, values, beliefs, feelings, or behaviors that unify people as a whole or that come to unify particular groups of people. Lots of things can bring and/or hold people

Our word "communication" derives from the Latin term *communis*, which means common, general, universal, or public.

together as units. Individuals might be unified, for example, by an apparently universal belief, such as belief in the law of gravity, or by an isolated but shared belief (e.g., that the earth is flat), conviction (e.g., that abortion is murder), appreciation (e.g., for classical music), or behavior (e.g., their subscription to the same magazine), among many other possibilities. The expositor is someone who identifies the things that unify groups and then explains how the unifiers came to have the mobilizing influence that they have. Among the other questions an expositor may attempt to answer while analyzing a group are the following: Are the points that unify this body something that is unique to this body or are they something that unifies people as a whole? Where did this unifier come from? Questions like these can be answered in a variety of ways, and it shows in the sometimes radically different explanations that expositors offer in their quest to make sense of what they observe. As later chapters explain, an expositor's worldview—his or her most basic beliefs about the way things are—can especially impact the way he or she approaches such questions and the types of answers he or she offers in response to them.

People are like a Pastry Display. Although we differ from one another in many respects, we are uniform in other respects. As an *expositor*, the student of communication tries to make sense of our uniformities, explaining such constant features in human communication as the widespread human sense that things in the world ought to be a certain way.

As a partly expositional project, this book focuses, starting in Chapter 3, on one trait that appears to unify people as a whole, rather than just an isolated group of people—the longing for something supremely meaningful outside ourselves that nothing in this world is apparently capable of perfectly satisfying. We will consider in that chapter how a Biblically Christian worldview accounts for this constant, human yearning in a way that is not only sensible, but demonstrably preferable to alternative explanations. At the very least, this account provides a rich starting point for expositing human behavior, including human communicative behavior. As will be explained, this approach to making sense of human experience begins with the human realization, as Augustine expressed it in words directed to God, that "thou hast made us for thyself and restless is our heart until it comes to rest in thee." Whatever else the human drive to connect with others through communication may be, it is fundamentally a response to this most basic of all human desires.

The *rhetorical* approach to the study of communication, which this project also utilizes and encourages, is similar to the expositional approach but it has a different objective. Whereas exposition aims to identify and to explain the existence of commonalities that already unify people, rhetorical analysis strives to identify and to explain the communicational steps people take in their various quests to establish points of oneness with others. To be more precise, the rhetorical approach concentrates especially on how communicators deliberately use information, particularly verbal information, in their quests to convince others to adopt their own attitudes, values, beliefs, feelings, or behaviors. People can be very creative in their uses of information for rhetorical purposes. First-year college students might notice this when coursework requires them to evaluate such diverse, rhetorically charged texts as speeches, essays, visual or musical works, movies, or plays. Sometimes the text's apparent purpose is to inform or to persuade. Other

© 2012 by John Foxx.
Used under license of Thinkstock.

People are like a Flock of Birds. As a *rhetorical* critic, the student of communication tries to make sense of how people use their communications as tools for establishing points of oneness with each other.

times its apparent purpose is to entertain. Whatever its apparent purpose may be, each text has as its overarching goal the creation of a connectedness of some sort between the text's creator and/or performer and its recipients. Showing that the text's creator and/or performer tries to do this and explaining why he or she does so is the expositor's task. Showing how he or she tries to do this and assessing whether he or she does so successfully is the rhetorical analyst's task.

How, then, shall we define *communication*? As you might anticipate, the answer to this question depends partly on whether we take the expositional or the rhetorical approach to making sense of human behavior. Because the expositor's primary focus is on making sense of existing connections among people, he or she will be less directly concerned than the rhetorical analyst with understanding how these links come about in everyday experience. Even so, the expositor cannot completely avoid questions about *how* people achieve unity through their interactions with each other. In order to explain why people quest for connections with each other, the expositor will presuppose that this drive is caused by something. Whether the assumed cause is God, genetics, social influences, a combination of these, or something else, the expositor necessarily considers whether this cause continues to drive human quests for connection. Whatever his or her conclusion may be, the expositor must be prepared to justify this answer in a way that involves some consideration of rhetorical questions.

Similarly, a rhetorical analyst cannot explain how humans achieve connection without considering expositional questions. If the rhetorical analyst considers the variety of ways humans build connections with each other, he or she must also consider what causes humans to do this and what impact, if any, this cause continues to have on human connection-building practices. A sufficient definition of "communication," then, addresses both expositional and rhetorical issues. It presents communication not only as a state of unity that exists among people in general and/or particular groups of people, but as something that has a cause. Not only does it identify this cause; it proceeds to consider what impact, if any, this cause continues to have on quests for personal connection. If the definition holds that the cause continues to drive these quests, it will explain how this impact works and how it manifests itself in the individual communicational situations that expositors and rhetorical analysts alike try to explain.

❯❯ COMMUNICATION DEFINED

Communication, for the purpose of this project, is the transmission of meaningful information from one person or group of persons *(the sender)* to another person or group of persons *(the recipient)* in a way that generates shared attitudes, values, beliefs, feelings, or behaviors between the sender and recipient. This definition, which blends concepts from twentieth-century theorists Claude Shannon and Warren Weaver[2] and Wilbur Schramm[3], implies several important points about communication that are explained in the paragraphs that follow:

• Communication is personal.
• Communication requires a message sender.
• Communication requires a message recipient.

- Communication requires the encoding, transmission, and decoding of a message.
- Communication produces a state of unity.
- Communication attempts can fail for a variety of reasons.

▲Communication Is Personal

Indeed, what distinguishes communication from other information-sending processes, like photosynthesis or magnetics, is the fact that its sending and receiving agents are persons. Unlike animals, plants, and moon rocks, people are fundamentally spiritual beings. This means they are intelligent and are capable of living without bodies. This view of personhood implies that although humans are the most obvious example of persons, the term may be applicable as well to other spiritual beings, whether they are angelic, demonic, or divine. As such, these beings, too, qualify as potential senders and/or receivers in the communication process. Chapter 3 explains the importance of this view of personhood in the Biblically Christian worldview, which recognizes God as the Creator Who, through a series of communicative acts, set the world into motion and Who continues to send intelligible information to persons via His creation and via His Word.

© 2012 by Hemera.
Used under license of Thinkstock.

Communication requires a sender.

▲Communication Requires a Message Sender

A communicative message may be sent by one or more persons. Sometimes a sender, acting alone, crafts and channels a message to the recipient, as typically happens when you say something to your roommate in an informal face-to-face conversation. The message may be intentional, such as when you purposefully say "What time is it?" to him or her. The message also may be unintentional, as when your subconscious frown informs your roommate that you are angry. On occasion, we work with others to craft and to send a communicative message, as happens when we work with peers to present a group project to the class or when a publishing team works together to create and circulate a print or digital publication with a message or set of messages for its intended readership. In any case, a message must have a sender in order to be a message. If it has no sender, it may be informational, but it is not a message in the personal sense that our definition of "communication" requires.

▲Communication Requires a Message Recipient

If you think to yourself late one night, *I wish my roommate would turn off the light so I could get some sleep!*, but you keep the thought to yourself, you obviously have formed an idea, but this alone does not create communication. If you write the thought on a piece of paper, but you keep the paper to yourself and do not show it to your roommate, this veiled expression of the thought does not create communication. If you say aloud, *Apaga la luz!*, but your roommate does not understand Spanish, communication still has not been achieved. Communication occurs only if the expressed thought *(the message)* is received and understood and this, of course, can happen only if there is a recipient. The existence of a *potential* recipient does not create communication. The existence of an *actual* recipient—a person who, in fact, perceives and accurately decodes the message's meaning in a way that creates a unity of understanding—is what gives communication its existence.

© 2012 by Ron Chapple Studios.
Used under license of Thinkstock.

Communication requires a recipient.

▲Communication Involves Encoding, Transmitting, and Decoding

Implicit in the preceding descriptions is the fact that the sender's attitude, value, belief, or feeling must be encoded, transmitted, and decoded by the recipient. Encoding is the sender's act, whether intentional or unintentional, of expressing his or her attitude, value, belief, or feeling in a tangible form, one that a recipient can perceive and decode in a way that results in shared understanding. Humans generally encode their messages in forms that recipients can receive through one or more of the senses. A spoken message is meant to be heard. A written message is meant to be seen. A pat on the back is meant to be felt. A spray of perfume is meant to be smelled.

Whether humans can exchange meanings in extrasensorial ways, such as via intuition, is questionable. Whether God communicates with humans via sensory channels and, if so, whether He uses only these means for communicating with humans are questions for theologians to debate. Some have argued, quite convincingly, that God does reveal information to people without channeling it through their senses. Natural law theorists, for example, support this idea by observing that people everywhere enter the world with some awarenesses already intact. Among these, some of them say, is the principle of noncontradiction—which holds that *A* cannot at the same time be *non A* (e.g., that something cannot at the same time be both true and false). As will be explained in Chapter Four, Biblically Christian theologians, too, believe that some divinely instilled human knowledge precedes sensory experience. They point for support to Biblical passages that indicate God has impressed certain awarenesses, such as an awareness that human life has a purpose, on the human heart without using sensory media to place them there (e.g., see Eccl. 3:11 and Rom. 2:14–15).

The amount of time that passes between a message's encoding, transmission, and decoding can vary. In our face-to-face interactions, the process is nearly instantaneous, with only a millisecond passing between the time when the sender says something and when the recipient hears and makes sense of it. On occasion, though, lots of time may pass before the process is complete. While doing research toward my master's degree during the mid-1990s, I visited an archive at the University of Oxford in England, where I was permitted to review 200-year-old publications that appeared to be relevant to my research topic. Although the creators of these documents could not have known that I would read their work some day, they functioned nonetheless as senders of information that they encoded in print and that I, many years later, received and decoded in a way that effected understanding. On other occasions, we may receive a message one day but not consciously notice or make sense of it until a day or two later when its meaning occurs to us. Perhaps you heard your parents asking you to call them within the next day but you did not really grasp their words, even though your memory retained them, until a day later when the words came back to haunt you.

Just as time is not necessarily a barrier to communication, neither is the physical distance that separates a sender and recipient. I spent my earliest days in the jungles of western Brazil, where my parents worked among tribal people groups, some of whom had no formal written language. For members of these tribes, communication was a mostly oral practice that took place while participants were within range of each others' voices or faces. Except for simple systems of signs that are used in rituals or to mark their property claims, most of these people groups lacked other means for sending information to each other. To this day, many still have no written language, nor do they have the print, electronic, or digital media that enable people in Western cultures to communicate with each other from virtually anywhere on earth, even from outer space, in either real or delayed time. For the technologically dependent Westerner, the stark reality of daily life in an oral culture is unfathomable until experienced for an extended period of time.

▲Communication Produces a State of Unity

As noted, communication is achieved when the recipient understands the attitude, value, belief, or feeling that the sender encoded and transmitted, whether intentionally or unintentionally. This unity of knowledge, or of understanding, may produce or help to produce additional unities between the sender and recipient, such as shared beliefs, feelings, attitudes, desires, intentions, or ways of acting. If you see a friend crying and infer from this and surrounding observations that she has lost a parent to cancer, this understanding (a unity of knowledge), might produce additional unities between you and her such as shared feelings of sadness and a shared desire for comfort.

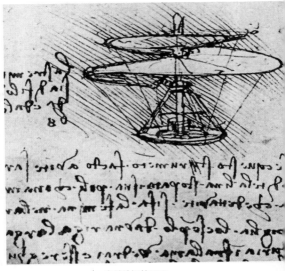

Communication is not always instant. The time that passes between a message's encoding and decoding can range from milliseconds to millennia. Leonardo da Vinci may have written these words 500 years ago, but the communication process can be completed today if a receipient reads and understands them.

The idea that people are capable of forming unities of this type is a tough idea for some critics to accept. Because nobody experiences life in exactly the same way as someone else, they object, no two people can ever come to view or to understand anything in exactly the same way. While this point may seem sensible at first, a closer look exposes several cracks in this way of thinking. First, this objection to the possibility of shared perspectives is self-discrediting. Let us suppose, for the sake of argument, that it is true that no two people can come to see something in exactly the same way. If this is so, as the critics argue, an important question emerges—how did these critics, despite supposedly being incapable of seeing the world as others see it, somehow manage to escape their standpoints in order to compare other human perspectives and to conclude that no two are alike? Indeed, how did they, despite their supposedly inescapable isolation, somehow become capable of knowing that shared perspectives are impossible to attain? While it is sensible to suppose that people do not always see things in exactly the same way, it is questionable to argue, as these critics do, that people are incapable of seeing at least some things in the same way.

A second problem with the critics' objection is that it recklessly supposes that all human knowledge is experience based. This is a blind assumption, for it dismisses without justification the possibility that humans enter the world with the shared knowledge of at least some things already intact and not contingent on what experience teaches us. We already have considered, among the possibilities for this type of shared knowledge, such widespread human awarenesses as the notion that something cannot, at the same time, be both true and not true and the notion that humans exist for a purpose.

A third problem with the critics' objection is their assumption that differences of perspective prevent people from sometimes seeing and responding to the same things. If my wife and

I are driving down the highway, we have slightly different perspectives since we are riding in different seats. Although our vantage points may differ slightly, either of us can see the road's boundaries from where we are sitting and, if necessary, can steer the car in a way that avoids the boundaries and gets us to our destination. We may not see the road in exactly the same way, but our shared recognition and understanding of some things (e.g., boundaries) can keep either of us moving down the road in the same direction, toward the same intended destination.

This is not to say that those who doubt the possibility of shared perspectives are entirely wrong. Our observations tell us that people often see things in very different ways, and this sometimes leads to misunderstandings and conflict. Indeed, if people saw all things identically, communication would be as constant a feature of human experience as breathing and circulation and not something to be created through encoding, transmitting, and decoding processes. In reality, lots of barriers can prevent communication from coming about. We consider some of these in the final section of this definition chapter.

▲Communication Attempts Can Fail for a Variety of Reasons

When we say communication is the result of a successful transmission of meaningful information from a sender to a recipient, we imply that attempts to communicate may not always be successful. These failures occur for several reasons that we pause to consider before moving into this definitional chapter's next section. The term for factors that can disrupt meaningful transmissions of information between senders and potential recipients is "noise," and it comes in several varieties.

Physical Barriers

Lots of things in the material world can prevent a sender's message from making its way to the receiver. A speaker's voice might not reach potential recipients because they are deaf, because they are out of the voice's range, or because another sound, like background noise, drowns out the speaker's voice. A visual impairment might prevent someone from reading a street sign, from seeing a friend's smile, or from reading words on a computer screen. Media malfunctions might block the transmission of messages via e-mail, text messaging, cell phone, webcast, or broadcast. Natural elements, like fire, water, moths, or decomposition might consume or render unreadable an ancient manuscript, a tombstone inscription, an antiquarian book, an old greeting card, an audio recording, or an improperly stored film. The passing of outdated media technologies might prevent a recipient from receiving messages via outdated media like 8-track or reel-to-reel tapes. Given enough time and a little imagination, one could conjecture thousands of situations in which physical factors like these could prevent the successful transmission of meaningful information from a sender to a recipient.

Linguistic Barriers

Sometimes the obstacle that prevents a message's transmission from one person to another

Physical Barriers
Sight and sound barriers can prevent a recipient from receiving a message.

has nothing to do with material factors. Instead, the breakdown may occur because of differences that exist between the sender and the receiver's language systems. *Language*, for the purpose of this study, denotes the system of verbal and nonverbal symbols that senders and recipients use to encode and to decode expressions of attitudes, values, beliefs, or feelings. This tool for finding common ground with others can be both an asset and a liability. Positively, language enables people, through the use of the same or similar symbolic systems, to exchange meaningful messages in a way that results in mutual understanding. Negatively, language use can create misunderstanding because of differences that distinguish two or more people's language systems. The greater these differences, the greater the potential for misunderstanding between them.

Linguistic Barriers For communication to occur, the recipient must understand the meaning's signified by both the sender's verbal and nonverbal language.

In a world of nearly 7,000 documented verbal languages, imagining situations in which linguistic differences complicate attempts to communicate is not too difficult a task for most people.[4] Your personal experiences with miscommunication probably provide a rich reference point for the study of this topic. We know that speakers of radically different languages, like English and Mandarin Chinese, will face obvious challenges if each speaks to the other in a language he or she does not understand. To bridge their divide, they will need to learn the other's language, to use a translator, or to use an alternative language system, whether a formal verbal one like French or German or an informal nonverbal one that consists of little more than gestures and/or facial expressions.

Even within a single verbal language system, like English, verbal differences exist that can create misunderstandings. The differences between American English and British English illustrate this point. What an American calls a "cookie," a Briton calls a "biscuit." What an American calls "soccer," a Briton calls "football." What an American calls a "truck," a Briton calls a "lorry." What Americans call "pants," a Briton calls "trousers." What Americans call an "attorney" or "lawyer," Britons call a "barrister." Despite inconsistencies like these, Americans and Britons are usually able to converse with each other with little difficulty, but their verbal differences can create misunderstandings and function as barriers to communication.

As an important aside, labels like American English and British English are actually somewhat misleading because language differences do not stop at the national level. Some differences are regional. I still recall the confusion that I once experienced at a grocery store in southern West Virginia, while attending college there during the late 1980s. Shortly after I entered the store, a clerk whom I had never met approached me and asked, "Would you like a poke?" *What a weird question!* I thought. *Why would you ask to jab a complete stranger with your finger?* After politely declining, I walked away perplexed. Days later the mystery dissolved when I learned from a friend that a "poke" is merely a local term for what I call a "shopping bag."

One additional point must be made about linguistic barriers to communication. Language systems are not just verbal. People routinely use nonverbal signals like facial expressions, gestures, movement, proximity, touch, volume, tone, pitch, pauses, silence, artifacts like clothing styles, eyewear styles, and jewelry, and other nonverbal cues to encode and transmit messages to others. Just as differences in verbal language can result in misunderstandings, so can differences in nonverbal language. The American's thumbs-up and A-OK hand gestures may mean something positive in America, but they are seen as obscene gestures in other parts of the world. Repeatedly turning the head side-to-side means "no" in North America, but in parts of South Asia it means "yes." Making eye contact with and smiling at strangers in rural Indiana may be a friendly gesture, but in Navajo American culture may be seen as disrespectful and in New York City it may be seen as threatening. Being an effective communicator, then, requires the sender and recipient to be mindful of the fact that nonverbal cues do not always signify what they have learned to think they mean.

Belief Barriers

Another type of obstacle that can prevent senders and recipients from establishing mutual understanding is their differences of belief about each other. What they assume about people in general, about people like each other, or about people with each other's individual histories can skew their interpretations of each other's communicative behaviors and messages and result in misunderstanding.

© 2012 by almagami.
Used under license of Shutterstock, Inc.

Belief Barriers
Differences in their most basic assumptions about life can prevent people from understanding each other.

As Chapter 3 explains, a person's view about people in general profoundly impacts the way he or she makes sense of the world and responds to it. Are people basically good, evil, or neither? Are they selfish or selfless by nature? What motivates them to act toward other people as they do? A recipient with a generally positive view of and attitude toward people might see the sender's motives as they really are, or else see them as something better intentioned than they really are. Conversely, the recipient with a generally negative view of and attitude toward people might see the sender's motives as they really are, or else see them as something more sinister than they really are.

Sometimes a recipient misunderstands the sender's communicative message because of false preconceptions he or she has about people like the sender or about a person with the recipient's individual history. The human tendency to form careless beliefs about people based on their features or group identities is called "stereotyping." People can be stereotyped and their message meanings and motives can be misunderstood for many reasons—their age or physical features, their economic, educational, or marital statuses, or their ethnic, racial, national, regional, linguistic, or religious identities, among other possibilities. What makes a stereotype potentially damaging is that its assumption about someone is based on an uninformed hunch rather than on credible evidence. As such, a stereotype is distinguishable from an "informed generalization." Unlike a stereotype, an *informed generalization* is an educated speculation about the sender's motives and message meanings, one that is based on credible evidence that these are, in fact, very likely what you suppose they are.

QUESTIONS FOR ANALYSIS

To be an effective communicator, you must be a good thinker who clearly and compellingly expresses your ideas to others in audience-appropriate ways. This requires you to form your most basic ideas about a topic before you ever write or say anything about it. The questions that follow invite you to do just this.

Prepare written responses to the following questions, as instructed. Be ready as well to present your answers to your classmates if your instructor requires you to do so.

• As this chapter explains, "communication" can be defined in lots of ways. Using credible, published sources, locate and compare three to five distinct definitions of "communication." Write them down. Be sure to quote them accurately and to document your sources properly.

• Next, write a 100- to 200-word response in which you, first, explain how the three to five definitions resemble each other and, second, explain how they differ from each other and from this chapter's definition.

• Evaluate this chapter's definition of "communication." What are its strengths? What are its weaknesses? If you were asked to improve it in one way, by adding, subtracting, or modifying something, what would you change? Present answers to each of these questions and explain the reasoning that justifies the answers in a 100- to 200-word written response.

• Recall an incident in which you or an acquaintance experienced a communication breakdown because of a verbal linguistic barrier. Chronicle this incident in a 150- to 250-word response.

• Recall an incident in which you or an acquaintance experienced a communication breakdown because of a nonverbal linguistic barrier. Chronicle this incident in a 150- to 250-word response.

• This chapter questions the statement that no people can see the same thing because the statement is self-discrediting. If the statement were true, the person making the statement would have no way of knowing that it is true since, by his or her own admission, he or she could never gain access to what other people see for the purpose of determining this. What do you think? Take a position and support it in a well-reasoned, clearly explained 150- to 250-word response.

• Historian Louis Gottschalk once said:

> Only part of what was observed in the past was remembered by those who observed it; only a part of what was remembered was recorded; only a part of what was recorded has survived; only a part of what has survived has come to the historians' attention; only a part of what has come to their attention is credible; only part of what is credible has been grasped; and only a part of what has been grasped can be expounded or narrated by the historian.[5]

"Communication" can be defined in lots of ways.

With this quotation in mind, and in the light of what this chapter says about barriers to communication, provide examples of three physical, three linguistic, and three different belief obstacles that might prevent an historian from receiving and understanding information in an historical text.

• This chapter discusses stereotyping as a potential obstacle to communication. Provide three examples of stereotypes and explain, after each, how it could prevent communication from occurring.

ENDNOTES

[1]Lewis, Charlton T, and Hugh M. Kingery. *An Elementary Latin Dictionary: With an Appendix of Names of Persons and Places Met in the Latin Authors Commonly Studied in the First Two Years of the College Course.* New York: American Book Co, 1918. 147–148. Print.

[2] Shannon, Claude E, and Warren Weaver. *The Mathematical Theory of Communication.* Urbana: University of Illinois Press, 1949. Print.

[3] Schramm, Wilbur. "How Communication Works." *The Process and Effects of Mass Communication.* Urbana: University of Illinois Press, 1954. 3-26. Print.

[4] Gordon, Raymond G. and Barbara F. Grimes, *Ethnologue: Languages of the World.* Dallas: SIL International, 2005.

[5]Gottschalk, Louis. *Understanding History: A Primer of Historical Method.* New York: Alfred E. Knopf, 1969, 45.

BIBLIOGRAPHY

Kennedy, George A. *Comparative Rhetoric: An Historical and Cross-cultural Introduction.* New York: Oxford University Press, 1997.

Mattelart, Armand. Susan Emmanuel, Trans. *The Invention of Communication.* Minneapolis: University of Minnesota Press, 1996.

Rogers, Everett M. *A History of Communication Study: A Biographical Approach.* New York: Free Press, 1994.

Schiller, Dan. *Theorizing Communication: A History.* New York: Oxford University Press, 1996.

Schramm, Wilbur. "How Communication Works." *The Process and Effects of Communication.* Ed. Wilbur Schramm. Urbana: University of Illinois Press, 1954. 3–26.

Schultze, Quentin. *Communicating for Life: Christian Stewardship in Community and Media.* Grand Rapids, MI: Baker Academic, 2000.

Shannon, Claude E, and Warren Weaver. *The Mathematical Theory of Communication.* Urbana: University of Illinois Press, 1949.

Strom, Bill. *More than Talk: Communication Studies and the Christian Life.* Dubuque, IA: Kendall/Hunt Publishing, 2005.

HONOR STATEMENT: I, the undersigned student, hereby declare before God, before the school, and before the professor that I have read Chapter 1 in its entirety, that I have completed the following exercise with help from no other sources, and that I neither have shared nor will share this work with anyone.

Signature: _____   Date: _____

SHORT ESSAYS

1. As this chapter explains, "communication" can be defined in lots of ways. Using credible, published sources locate and compare three to five distinct definitions of "communication." Write them down. Be sure to quote them accurately and to document your sources properly.

_____

_____

_____

_____

_____

_____

2. Next, write a 100- to 200-word response in which you, first, explain how the three to five definitions resemble each other and, second, explain how they differ from each other and from this chapter's definition.

_____

_____

_____

_____

_____

_____

_____

_____

_____

_____

_____

_____

_____

3. Evaluate this chapter's definition of "communication." What are its strengths? What are its weaknesses? If you were asked to improve it in one way, by adding, subtracting, or modifying something, what would you change? Present answers to each of these questions and explain the reasoning that justifies the answers in a 100- to 200-word written response.

_____

_____

_____

_____

_____

_____

_____

_____

_____

_____

_____

_____

_____

_____

_____

_____

4. Recall an incident in which you or an acquaintance experienced a communication breakdown because of a verbal linguistic barrier. Chronicle this incident in a 150- to 250-word response.

_____

_____

_____

_____

_____

_____

_____

_____

_____

_____

_____

_____

_____

5. Recall an incident in which you or an acquaintance experienced a communication breakdown because of a nonverbal linguistic barrier. Chronicle this incident in a 150- to 250-word response.

_____

_____

_____

_____

_____

_____

_____

_____

_____

6. This chapter questions the statement that no people can see the same thing because the statement is self-discrediting. If the statement were true, the person making the statement would have no way of knowing that it is true since, by his or her own admission, he or she could never gain access to what other people see for the purpose of determining this. What do you think? Take a position and support it in a well-reasoned, clearly explained 150- to 250-word response.

7. Historian Louis Gottschalk once wrote:

> "*Only part of what was observed in the past was remembered by those who observed it; only a part of what was remembered was recorded; only a part of what was recorded has survived; only a part of what has survived has come to the historians' attention; only a part of what has come to their attention is credible; only part of what is credible has been grasped; and only a part of what has been grasped can be expounded or narrated by the historian.*" [1]

With this quotation in mind, and in the light of what this chapter says about barriers to communication, provide examples of three physical, three linguistic, and three different belief obstacles that might prevent an historian from receiving and understanding information in an historical text.

_____

_____

_____

_____

_____

_____

_____

_____

_____

_____

_____

_____

_____

_____

_____

_____

_____

[1] Gottschalk, Louis. *Understanding History: A Primer of Historical Method*. New York: Alfred E. Knopf, 1969, 45.

8. This chapter discusses stereotyping as a potential obstacle to communication. Provide three examples of stereotypes and explain, after each, how it could prevent communication from occurring.

_____

_____

_____

_____

_____

_____

_____

_____

_____

_____

_____

_____

_____

_____

_____

_____

_____

_____

_____

_____

_____

CHAPTER 2 >>

2 COMMUNICATION: HOW DOES IT HAPPEN?

OVERVIEW

This chapter breaks communication into several categories that people should know in order to more fully appreciate the vital role it plays in the human experience and in their lives. It begins with an overview of major verbal and nonverbal forms through which people channel meaningful information to others and concludes with a brief review of terms that distinguish communicational situations from each other.

❯ A CLOSER LOOK

Now that we more clearly understand what communication is, what makes it happen, and what can prevent it from happening, we turn our attention to a series of terms that scholars use to distinguish various types of communication from each other. Several of these terms appeared in the previous section. Knowing what they mean can increase not only your knowledge of communication's many forms, but also your appreciation for the vital role this phenomenon plays in the human experience and in your life.

❯ THE FORMS OF COMMUNICATION

© 2012 by msaunder1972. Used under license of Shutterstock, In

As noted in the section in Chapter 1 about communication's encoding process, people use many verbal and nonverbal forms to express themselves to others. Verbal expressions, by definition, involve the use of words. A *word*, as one source aptly puts it, is "a sound or a combination of sounds, or its representation in writing or printing, that symbolizes and communicates a meaning."[1] Nonverbal expressions, by contrast, involve the use of meaningful symbols other than words for expression. In the paragraphs that follow, we briefly survey these major classifications of communicative message forms.

If we say someone kicked the bucket to indicate the person died, which figurative language form are we using?

▲ Verbal Messages

People use a variety of verbal forms to get information across to each other. Whether spoken, written, or printed, words or combinations of words are *literal* if they are used forthrightly to signify the person, place, thing, idea, action, or state of being that the words or combination of words evidently symbolize. If you announce to family members in an e-mail that your neighbor "bought the farm," "kicked the bucket," or "bit the big enchilada," and mean that your neighbor actually bought a farm, kicked a bucket, or bit a big enchilada, you are speaking literally. At other times the words are *figurative* because they are used to signify a secondary meaning that is not obvious when the words are taken at face value. If you say your neighbor "bought the farm," "kicked the bucket," or "bit the big enchilada," and mean through these nonliteral expressions that the neighbor died, you are speaking figuratively.

Literal expressions are forthright. They say what they mean and have no hidden meanings. Figurative expressions come in many forms. The following list defines and provides examples of several especially common figurative forms:

Metaphor (*A is B or substitutes B for A*): A common figurative form, a metaphor identifies one thing in a way that symbolically stands for another thing.

A mighty fortress is our God.—Martin Luther
You are a mist that appears for a little time . . . —James 4:14, ESV
Time is a physician which heals every grief.—Diphilus

My love is like
a red, red rose.
–Robert Burns

© 2012 by Lynn Whitt.
Used under license of Shutterstock, Inc.

A simile explicitly
compares two
otherwise dissimilar
things, usually via the
modifiers "like" or "as."

Simile (*A is like or as B*): A simile explicitly compares two otherwise dissimilar things, usually via the modifiers "like" or "as."

My love is like a red, red rose.—Robert Burns
He was as idle as a horse doctor in Detroit.—Anonymous
A face that looks like it had worn out four bodies.—Anonymous

Synecdoche: This figurative form alludes to something by either highlighting only one aspect of it or something broader that includes it.

Washington *as a reference to America's federal government*
Hollywood *as a reference to America's film industry*
Threads *as a reference to clothing*

Euphemism: A euphemism is the use of a mild term in place of a harsh term to relay the same basic idea in a more tasteful form.

Pro-choice *instead of* pro-abortion
Passed away *instead of* died
Restroom *instead of* bathroom

Dysphemism: The opposite of a euphemism, a dysphemism is the use of a harsh term instead of a mild term for an intended effect.

Ambulance chaser *instead of* lawyer
Rug rat *instead of* small child
Dinosaur *instead of* old person

Overstatement: Also called "hyperbole," overstatement is the use of exaggerated terms for emphasis but not for literal meaning.

I am so hungry I could eat a horse.
He has a million things to do today.
We are so happy we could jump to the moon.

Understatement: The opposite of overstatement, understatement is the use of terms to diminish the seriousness or intensity of something.

It was an interesting day.—George W. Bush recalling 9/11
It's no big deal. He only had a heart attack.
Hitler had a little problem with Jews. (He murdered 6 million.)

Idiom: An idiom is a combination of words that means something different than the words' literal meaning.

Business has hit the rocks *lately (reached a low point).*

Idioms drive me crazy (frustrate me).
You will do well if you play your cards right (act correctly).

Personification: To personify is to ascribe human qualities to something that is not human.

The trees of the field shall clap their hands.—Isaiah 55:12, ESV
The stars in the sky looked down where He lay.—Martin Luther
The wind is a playful child.—Katherine Mansfield

Paradox: A paradox is a statement that appears to be self-refuting but that is, in fact, true or possibly true.

The more things change, the more they stay the same.
I shut my eyes in order to see.—Paul Gauguin
You are absolutely unique. Just like everyone else.—Margaret Mead

When evaluating a message's verbal content, a recipient will infer its meaning based on observations of not only the words (the text), but also the circumstances surrounding the encoding of the words (the context). Who is the speaker? Who is the audience? What is the topic? What is the setting? Which words were used? How were they stated? A recipient's answers to questions like these will impact how he or she interprets the words' meanings.

Because of their relevance, two additional important terms are noteworthy at this point. A word or phrase's literal meaning is sometimes called its *denotative* meaning. This is the meaning of the word or phrase according a dictionary or other recognized authoritative sources. A word or phrase's *connotative* meaning, by contrast, is the secondary meaning a recipient takes it to have when used in a particular situation. Sometimes the connotative meaning matches the denotative meaning; other times it does not. When it does not match, it is often because the sender's nonverbal cues indicate that the word or phrase should not be taken literally.

▲Nonverbal Messages

Whether literally or figuratively expressed, verbal messages play a vital role in the transmission of meanings from the sender to the receiver. Even so, verbal messages are less significant than nonverbal messages in human communication. A classic study by psychologists Albert Mehrabian and Susan Ferris, years ago, indicated that as much as 93 percent of communication is nonverbal. According to the study, 55 percent of communication involves facial expressions, 38 percent involves nonverbal vocal qualities, and only 7 percent involves verbal content.[2] Other researchers, during the decades since then, have estimated that about 80 percent of communication is nonverbal.

© 2012 by Akihito Yokoyama.
Used under license of depositphotos.

Nonverbal messages, by definition, involve the use of symbols other than words for meaningful expression.

Nonverbal messages, by definition, involve the use of symbols other than words for meaningful expression. People try to send messages, including information about themselves, to each other in lots of nonverbal ways—smiling, waving, hugging, whispering, standing close to someone, keeping breath fresh with chewing gum, wearing clothes of a certain color and style. We even use our material possessions to make statements about ourselves that we hope others will notice. I recall being puzzled at a funeral service several years ago when a relative with a basic service-oriented job showed up for the procession in a luxury vehicle that workers in his field typically cannot afford. Several days later I learned that although he had presented the car as his own, he had actually borrowed it from a wealthy friend, apparently to create a more favorable impression of himself on family members. Before chuckling at people who do this, contemplate how often each of us does the same thing, in different ways, every day. We choose many of the things we wear or display in public not merely because they are practically useful, but because we think they will create ideas about us, in the minds of others, that we consider to be favorable.

Whereas verbal information comes to us principally through the senses of sight and sound, nonverbal information can come to us through virtually any of the five senses. To witness this, walk through a large grocery store sometime. The product manufacturers and the store present their products to you as they do for one basic purpose—to get you to buy them. As you walk the aisles, notice the persuasive messages that come to you through your eyes as you view store signs and product labels. Listen to the messages that channel to your ears through the music and voices on the store's speaker system. Consider the appeals to taste that occur at the product-sampling displays. Observe the appeals to smell on the scratch-n-sniff products on some of the shelves. Finally, notice the subtle appeals to touch on the packaging of products like toilet paper, which use words like "soft" to compel passersby to feel the product, to be impressed, and to buy it.

Just as words like "metaphor," "simile," and "personification" denote distinct types of verbal messages, a terminology exists that enables us to distinguish the different types of nonverbal messages and to consider how they work together, along with verbal messages, to impact interpretations of a message's meaning. Scholar Judee Burgoon has created perhaps the most recognized "typology," or classification system, for this purpose. Definitions and descriptions of her categories of nonverbal communication follow:

Vocalics

A person's use of volume, tone, pitch, accent, speaking pace, and silence can profoundly impact a recipient's interpretation of his or her message and motives. Throughout our lives, we learn which combinations of these qualities communicate specific meanings to certain audiences under certain circumstances. We also learn that the same vocalic features may mean one thing to one audience but something very different to another audience. One learns, for example, that the hushed tones that communicate love to a spouse might communicate insecurity or weirdness if directed to a stranger. We learn as well that although cheering loudly may relay enthusiasm at a football game, it may imply disrespect or immaturity if sounded during a church service or a class session. We come to know, too, that what passes as a normal accent in New York City may come across as

> A person's use of **VOLUME,** tone, pitch, accent, s p e a k i n g p a c e , and silence can profoundly impact a recipient's interpretation of his or her message and motives.

Any given bodily movement can be read in diverse ways by multiple recipients.

something strange or suspicious in southern Mississippi, and vice versa. Learning what vocalic nuances like these represent in the minds of one's potential audiences is vital for a would-be communicator, for unless one gains this proficiency, he or she will be ill-prepared to use vocalics in a way that establishes mutual understanding with an audience.

Kinesics

We generally place body language in three categories (gestures, facial expressions, and eye contact). Think for a moment about the many ways people use bodily movement to send information to each other: standing, sitting, kneeling, bowing, lying down, crying, jumping, skipping, dancing, shaking, moving the mouth, the tongue, or the lips, winking, squinting, hugging, hitting, kicking, spitting, clapping, waving, pointing, motioning with the hand, head, or foot, and so forth. Experience teaches us that our bodily movements, or in some situations the absence of bodily movements, is by default a statement that, taken alone, may relay a message or that, when combined with verbal information, may relay a blended message. A simple wink of the eye can be meaningful by itself. It can also transform words that, when taken alone are shocking, into a lighthearted statement that is offered in jest. A crossing of the arms can be meaningful by itself. It can also transform words that, taken alone imply friendliness, into a statement of apparent resentment.

Any given bodily movement can be read in diverse ways by multiple recipients. The key to effective kinetic communication is knowing which movements signify which meanings to which audiences, especially audiences with whom the sender aims to establish shared understanding. The prolonged eye contact through which a Midwesterner might signify friendliness might be received as invasive and rude among Navajo Indians in the Southwest. Miscommunications like these can result when senders neglect to speak in a kinetic code the recipient understands.

Proxemics

People send information to each other through their use of space. We become upset when someone cuts in line, tailgates us, or stands too close to us, or when a stranger parks his car on our yard without permission, because these behaviors violate rules concerning the use of space that we expect others to respect. In face-to-face interaction, our use of space implies something about the nature of our relationship with the other. Anthropologist Edward Hall made this point during the 1960s when he popularized the notion that people have invisible public, social, personal, and intimate zones that they expect other people to recognize and respect. In American culture, he suggested, the public space, which is 10 feet or more away, is where we generally expect strangers to stand during interaction. Social space, which is 4 to 10 feet away, is where we permit acquaintances who are not necessarily friends to stand. Personal space, which is 1.5 to 4 feet away, is where friends or comfortable acquaintances are permitted to position themselves in relation to us. Intimate space, which is zero to 1.5 feet away, is reserved for our closest relations.

The measurements for these zones are culturally relative. Some cultures, like those of southern Europe, the Arab world, and Latin America, have comparatively smaller personal/intimate space ranges than North Americans. Northern European and Asian cultures share the American cultural tendency to be more personal-space conscious. Cultural differences of this type can be defined not just by geographic variables, but also by the race and sex of the group. Researchers Teresa J. Rosegrant and James C. McCroskey have shown that males establish greater interpersonal distance from each other than females do from each other and that blacks and whites establish greater interpersonal distance from each other than they do when speaking to someone of the same race.[3]

Interpersonal interactions are just one setting in which proxemics can impact communication. Proxemics extends to consider, as well, the broader concept of personal property and what happens in communication when people violate each other's property-related expectations. A telemarketer might violate your sense of personal space by giving you an unwanted phone call. A friend might violate the same sense by posting an obnoxious message as an announcement on your social-networking site. A dorm mate might play his or her music too loudly and violate the supposed right to enjoy your room in silence. As with vocalics and kinesics, a would-be communicator must consider his or her audience's proxemic standards when developing a plan for interacting with them. One's failure to do so can adversely affect his or her attempt to establish shared understanding with that audience.

Haptics

Communication can be impacted as well by touch, or by the lack thereof, among people. Touch can include lots of things—hugging, kissing, tickling, pinching, scratching, slapping, punching, kicking, grasping, holding, squeezing, patting, or shaking, and so

Communication can be impacted as well by touch, or by the lack thereof, among people.

forth. How the touching is interpreted will depend on the situation in which it occurs and on the significance attached to it by the observer. Punching a stranger in a traffic jam may be more acceptable in one part of the world than it is in another part. In American culture, doing this is likely to been seen as a negative expression of anger or frustration, although punching an opponent in the boxing ring may be seen as a positive expression of competitiveness. Whether touch is acceptable in any culture is determined by the relationship of the people involved, the parts of the body that touch, how long they touch, the purpose of the touching, and other factors. A person's decision not to touch another is meaningful as well, although it may be viewed alternatively as perfectly appropriate or as expressive of coldness or indifference.

As with previous nonverbal forms, haptics is culturally relative. What might be regarded as acceptable touching behavior in one region might be regarded as unacceptable elsewhere. Whereas opposite-sex handshakes are permissible in American culture, they are not acceptable in Arab culture. Although same-sex handholding is acceptable as an expression of friendship among males in Arab culture, this is generally unaccepted in American culture. Being aware of and respecting norms like these obviously increases a sender's likelihood for success in achieving his or her communication goals.

Chronemics

This nonverbal communication form concerns time as a communicative factor. The timing of our message transmissions to others can profoundly impact the recipient's reading of it. For example, students often assume a professor should respond to their e-mails or grade their work within what they assume is a reasonable timeframe. Whether the professor does so can impact the student's impression of the professor and, by extension, of anything else he or she has to say. Professors, too, may form their impressions of students partly in response to whether the student submits his or her work on time. The same principle applies in the workplace. Prospective employers and existing bosses alike expect us to respond to their communications in a timely fashion. For some, this means immediately while, for others, it means within 24 hours. Whether a person satisfies this expectation can profoundly impact the employer's impression of him or her and influence the way the employer responds to his or her future communications.

© 2012 by SVLuma.
Used under license of Shutterstock, Inc.

Chronemics refers to the human use of time to make meaningful statements to each other.

What qualifies as a timely response depends partly on the unspoken rules of the culture in which the communication occurs. *Monochronic cultures* view time in a highly structured manner, reducing life to a series of tasks that are generally accomplished, one at a time, in a designated sequence. Northern European and American culture are this way. Because of their structured nature, cultures like these tend to be more task oriented and less tolerant of deviations from the schedule than others. Breaking from the schedule without having good reason for doing so is generally viewed as a negative in these settings. So is lateness.

Adjusting to a monochronic culture can be a challenge for international students who come to America from less schedule-oriented *polychronic cultures*. They quickly learn after beginning studies in American universities that a late assignment submission in a monochronic culture is considerably more likely not to be accepted or more likely to be penalized for lateness than would be the case in a polychronic setting. Although they might not realize it, students from polychronic cultures, by submitting their work after deadline, might be sending a message to their professor that they are undisciplined or incapable of satisfying university-level academic standards.

On the other hand, the monochronic American businessperson or missionary may struggle when adjusting to life in a polychronic cultural setting. He or she may be frustrated when a native colleague shows up two days late for a scheduled task, as might be the norm in that setting. Although this may be unacceptable in the United States, the American must be careful not to send the wrong message to the native by protesting the lateness. Whether they realize it or not, the American who protests local norms like this may actually create the impression among polychronic locals that he or she is impatient, unfriendly, or hostile. Understanding and accommodating his or her audience's chronemic standards will help him or her be effective in realizing his or her goals in that setting.

Chronemics factors involve more than just whether a person is on time according to the standards of a given culture. This category also concerns the impact of time variables on the meanings people associate with other communicational expressions. Whether two people acted appropriately in a given situation may depend, at least partly, on whether their conversation, their hug or kiss, their eye contact, and so forth. were too long or too short by the culture's standards for people with the relationship that they share. In mainstream American culture, you may perceive disinterest in the person whose eye contact is too brief and eccentricity in the person whose eye contact is too lengthy. As with the other nonverbal message forms, the rules that distinguish what it too long and what is too short are to some extent culturally relative, so a person should make sense of another person's chonemic behavior in the light of the cultural standards that have impacted the meanings that person has come to associate with this dimension of human behavior.

Physical Appearance

Although Aesop may have been correct when he observed that appearances are often deceiving, it is also true, in words taken from Scripture, that "man looks on the outward appearance" (1 Sam. 16:7, ESV). If people judge books by their cover and products on the shelf by their labels, they certainly judge people, at least initially, based on their physical features.

Research consistently demonstrates that a person's physical features can affect how people respond to him or her.

- Attractive people earn 5 to 10 percent more than average-looking people, according to a 1994 study.[4]
- Men who are more than 6 feet tall are 50 percent more likely to be married or have a long-term relationship with a woman than men who are shorter than 5 feet 5 inches, according to a 2005 study.[5]
- Highly obese women earn 24 percent less than thin women, according to a 2002 article.[6]

Not surprisingly, because physical attractiveness can significantly impact the way people respond to each other, people spend lots of money on products and procedures that are designed to make them more beautiful. Americans are expected to increase their spending on cosmetic surgical procedures to $2.6 billion by the year 2014.[7] These procedures include reshaping, implants, lifts and tucks, liposuction, injections, dermal resurfacing, laser treatments, injectable products, equipment, disposables, biological materials, and polymers. Moreover, Americans' spending on cosmetic and toiletry products, which exceeded $47 billion in 2008, is projected to continue its yearly increase through the year 2019.[8]

Although there are obvious limitations to what we can do to change our looks, doing what we can to enhance our appearance in the eyes of a target audience can promote the

Americans are expected to increase their spending on cosmetic surgical procedures to $2.6 billion by the year 2014.

realization of our communication objectives. While definitions of attractiveness are to some extent culturally relative, they are similar across cultures in a number of basic ways. For example, a recent study indicated that the distance between a woman's eyes and her nose is recognized across cultures as determinative of whether her face is considered appealing. According to this 2009 study, a female face is viewed as attractive if the distance between her mouth and eyes is about 36 percent of the face's length and if the distance between her eyes is approximately 46 percent of the face's width.[9] Research about what makes a male face physically attractive is less conclusive than this, although one prominent study, from 1990, indicates a female preference for male faces with large eyes, prominent cheek bones, a large chin, and a big smile.[10]

Nonetheless, definitions of physical attractiveness are culturally relative to some extent. For example, whereas obesity is generally regarded to be a detractor from beauty in North America and Northern Europe, it is commonly considered to be an attractive quality, especially as a female feature, in parts of Africa, Asia, Latin America, and the Pacific Islands. Whether a physical feature is universal or culturally desirable, one thing about physical attractiveness is clearly established—it is a nonverbal factor that can impact the way a recipient responds to a sender.

Artifacts
People send lots of information about themselves to others via the material objects through which they express their identities. Regardless of whether intended, a sender transmits lots of information about himself or herself through his or her displays of clothing, headwear, eyewear, footwear, jewelry, makeup, badges, ribbons, buttons, tattoos, masks, makeup, hair coloring, and scents. People also sometimes use their material possessions to make statements to others. The funeral story that I shared earlier demonstrates how someone used another person's expensive car in an attempt to make himself look more accomplished than he feared people would believe him to be. People use messages on personalized license plates or use clothing that publicly links them with a popular brand and all that it apparently represents for the same general purpose.

People send lots of information about themselves to others via the material objects through which they express their identities.

Unlike physical appearance, which generally concerns a person's natural traits, artifacts as a category accounts for how people use material objects in a way that says something about their attitudes, values, beliefs, and feelings. Your choice of clothing alone can send lots of messages that impact the way people respond to you. Which colors do you wear? Which styles do you choose? Which name brands or symbols do you display? What do your colors, styles, and name brands or symbols say about you to your particular audience? Is this the kind of statement you want to make to them? If not, how should you modify your attire so it will send the right kind of message to them?

Whether we like it or not, people form their initial impressions of us based largely on nonverbal factors like these. These first assessments can have lasting consequences, so it behooves us to be mindful of the way we present ourselves to others, not just in what we say but in how we say it. As this section demonstrates, your communications can be profoundly impacted by the way you use your voice, your movements, the space around you, your time, the way you appear, and the way you use material objects to make statements about yourself.

This chapter, so far, has identified several major verbal and nonverbal devices that people use when they interact with each other. These message filters, and others like them, enable people to exchange meaningful messages in a communicative way. Because of differences between senders' and recipients' language systems, though, people sometimes assign different meanings to the same message. Effective communication requires a sender to gain an understanding of variables like these that exist in the communication process. Armed with such an awareness, the responsible communicator is someone who studies his or her audience to determine what he or she must do in order to encode the message meaningfully.

❱❱THE MODES OF COMMUNICATION

Before moving into a study of communication's origin, purpose, value, and potential, we must familiarize ourselves with one additional way of looking at communication. Whereas the previous section reviewed verbal and nonverbal forms that messages sometimes assume, this section briefly reviews several types of communicational situations and presents the terms commonly used to differentiate them. These situations are generally distinguished from each other by the number of people involved in the interaction, by the purpose of their interaction, by whether their interaction is immediate, and by the role, if any, that media play in the interaction. You should note that although communication scholars generally acknowledge these categories, they do not always agree about the precise meanings of the terms that distinguish them from each other.

▲Interpersonal Communication

This term applies to situations in which people socially interact, usually in a face-to-face environment, but possibly also in real-time virtual environments like through interactive radio, phone, and computer programs. What makes the situation interpersonal is not so much the number of participants as it is the real-time interactive nature of their encounter. *Dyadic communication*, a subconcentration of this category, denotes interpersonal interaction that takes place between two people.

Unless you live in complete isolation, you experience interpersonal communication almost every day. It happens when you're having an informal conversation with friends, family, classmates, neighbors, fellow church attendees, business associates, or with strangers. The conversation might be face-to-face or else be mediated by phone, computer, or another interactive medium.

▲Group Communication

This communicational situation occurs when three or more people come together for a common purpose, whether formally, as in a work group, or informally, as in social situations. Anytime three or more people come together for a common purpose and can

Unless you live in complete isolation, you experience interpersonal communication almost every day.

interact and influence each other in the exercise of this purpose, a group communication situation exists. *Small group communication* refers more specifically to situations in which a group of three to ten people advance the group's purpose in a largely but not necessarily exclusively informal manner.

You may have experienced group communication if you have been part of a work team, a sports team, a support group, a Sunday school class, or a committee. If the experience involved three or more people whose interactions advanced realization of a common purpose, it qualifies as a group communication situation.

In public communication, a speaker formally addresses a group of typically 10 or more individuals in a face-to-face environment where interactivity is possible but generally not practiced.

▲Public Communication

This term and *public speaking* are often used interchangeably, as if they mean the same thing. This is a mostly valid assumption, although some communication scholars include variations of mediated and mass communication in their definitions of this category. In public communication, a speaker formally addresses a group of typically 10 or more individuals in a face-to-face environment where interactivity is possible but generally not practiced. The face-to-face quality distinguishes this mode from mediated communication. The potential for interactivity distinguishes it from mass communication. Although you likely experience this communicational mode less frequently than you experience interpersonal or group communication, you may recall being in situations that clearly link to this category. Perhaps you listened to a pastor give a sermon, a teacher give a lecture, an administrator give school announcements, or a best man pay tribute to a groom.

▲Mediated Communication

This communicational mode concerns situations in which senders use technologies to channel messages to recipients, whether synchronously or asynchronously. *Synchronous transmissions* take place in real time. *Asynchronous transmissions* do not take place at the same time. The media through which the messages channel are diverse, but they can be broadly classified as written, printed, electronic, or digital. When you use a pen, a printing press, a keyboard, or a radio tower to channel meaningful information to someone, you are engaging in mediated communication.

▲Mass Communication

When people use a media technology to distribute information to a large group of physically detached people, they engage in mass communication. People use a variety of media types for this purpose. Possibilities include billboards, mass mailings, newspapers, magazines, website postings, e-mails, podcasts, and radio or TV broadcasts.

▲Other Recognized Modes

Scholars use additional terms to denote other types of communications and communicational situations. *Organizational communication* highlights situations in which people interact as members of large networks, like businesses. *Family communication*, as one might expect, considers the unique interactions that take place among people who are related by marriage, birth, or adoption. *Intercultural communication* considers situations in which individuals from significantly different people groups, each of these with a distinguishable identity, interact with each other. These are but a few of the many terms that people use to distinguish different modes of communication.

▲Less Recognized Modes

Unlike its mainstream alternatives, this textbook assumes that we have no reason for not supposing that personal beings other than humans are real and that they are justifiably factored in analyses like this one as potentially if not actually communicative. Moreover, one could reasonably argue that such beings do exist—leading philosophers and theologians have compellingly argued this point over the centuries—and that they are rightly factored, therefore, in studies such as this one. Accordingly, we conclude this definitional chapter with a review of several communicational types that standard communication texts do not consider.

The term *spiritual communication* denotes any situation in which fundamentally spiritual beings—that is, intelligent, moral beings who are capable of living without bodies—send meaningful messages to each other. Examples of this in the Biblically Christian tradition include message exchanges between God and humans, between God and angelic or demonic beings, between humans and angelic or demonic beings, and between angelic or demonic beings and each other. Technically, human-to-human message transmissions fall into this category, too, since humans are fundamentally spiritual beings.

© 2012 by Mikael Damkier.
Used under license of Shutterstock, Inc.

Divine revelation refers to situations in which God, whether directly or indirectly, imparts meaningful messages to humans.

Spiritual communication exists in several varieties. *Divine revelation* refers to situations in which God, whether directly or indirectly, imparts meaningful messages to humans. In Christian tradition, divine revelation assumes two basic forms. *General revelation* refers to the nonverbal messages that God has imprinted on human consciousness or that come into human consciousness in response to what God discloses through nature. *Special revelation* refers to the messages that God discloses supernaturally through His Holy Spirit or through Scripture via the agency of the Holy Spirit. It also includes His Biblically documented disclosures of information to humans via channels like miracles, dreams, soundings, appearances, and so forth.

Religious expression, by contrast, is the human attempt to connect with God, or with something apparently ultimately fulfilling like Him, especially but not exclusively through such overtly "religious" message forms as meditation, prayer, chanting, singing, reciting, dancing, fasting, almsgiving, body decoration, self-punishment, sacrifices, and so forth. A Biblical worldview sees a religious motivation not just in these expressive forms, but in virtually all human conduct, since it holds that human behavior is driven, to a large extent, by a longing to reconnect with the God Whose communion we were created to enjoy, yet from Whom we have estranged ourselves. In religious expression, understood in this broader sense, a person attempts to satisfy this longing by adopting and exhibiting attitudes, beliefs, and behaviors that he or she believes will plug this void. This quest for a God-like connection can appear in the person's pursuit of almost anything that seems capable of providing ultimate fulfillment—knowledge, wealth, power, fame, love, respect, sex, or amusement, to name but a few possibilities. Some people even turn to formal religion or to morality, rather than to God Himself, to fill the void. In any of these cases, a person's ultimate passion shows itself in the way he or she does live. Whatever else your life may be, it is fundamentally a religious expression, since it manifests your sense that something of ultimate worth exists and that it is worth pursuing.

© 2012 by Dmitriy Shironosov.
Used under license of Shutterstock, Inc.

Religious expression, by contrast, is the human attempt to connect with God, or with something apparently ultimately fulfilling like Him, especially but not exclusively through such overtly "religious" message forms as meditation, prayer, chanting, singing, reciting, dancing, fasting, almsgiving, body decoration, self-punishment, sacrifices, and so forth.

Redemptive criticism is a term for the attempt to make sense of human communicative behavior and specific human communications in the light of divine revelation. You may recall the terms *exposition* and *rhetoric* from Chapter 1. As was noted, the expositor tries to explain why people share certain attitudes, values, beliefs, feelings, or behaviors. He or she does this by explaining mysteries like the widespread human longing to connect with God or something God-like. The redemptive expositor aims to show how this yearning gives shape to human communications and tries to explain why the longing exists and why it works as it does, in the light of what divine revelation says about it. As a rhetorical analyst, however, the redemptive critic also considers how people find redemption and what role, if any, communication plays in the process. The critic considers, too, how the redeemed life functions as a message to others and how it impacts or can impact other people.

Redemptive communication resembles religious expression, but it differs from it in a major way. Whereas *religion* is the human attempt to connect with God or with something God-like, redemption is the state of having actually connected with God in the God-centered way that enables one to start seeing things as He sees them and relating to them as He relates to them. The redemptive communicator is one who submits to the realization that the God of Scripture is, in fact, the creator and sustainer of the universe and that everything in it, therefore, including communication, must be understood and engaged in the instructive light of what His *divine revelation* says about it. This God-centered stance not only gives shape to his or her definition of communication, but also frames his or her understanding of what motivates people to communicate and impacts his or her own communication practices.

Now that we have a basic understanding of what communication is and how it works, we turn our attention to a series of interrelated questions that must be engaged if we are to appreciate the practical value of studying and practicing it. As you will see, people's differences of belief at the most basic level can help to steer them toward very different conclusions about matters like these. In contrast to disappointing alternatives, a Biblically Christian approach to communication provides a rich starting that avoids many of the pitfalls that beset so many of its alternatives.

To be an effective communicator, you must be a good thinker who clearly and compellingly expresses your ideas to others in audience-appropriate ways. This requires you to form your most basic ideas about a topic before you ever write or say anything about it. As the questions at the end of the preceding chapter, the queries that follow invite you to do just this.

Prepare written responses to the following questions, as instructed. Be prepared as well to present your answers to your classmates if your instructor requires you to do so.

• Words are powerful communicational tools. Consider the following wisdom from James 3: 2–10:

> If we could control our tongues, we would be perfect and could also control ourselves in every other way. We can make a large horse go wherever we want by means of a small bit in its mouth. And a small rudder makes a huge ship turn wherever the pilot chooses to go, even though the winds are strong. In the same way, the tongue is a small thing that makes grand speeches. But a tiny spark can set a great forest on fire. And the tongue is a flame of fire. It is a whole world of wickedness, corrupting your entire body. It can set your whole life on fire, for it is set on fire by hell itself. People can tame all kinds of animals, birds, reptiles, and fish, but no one can tame the tongue. It is restless and evil, full of deadly poison. Sometimes it praises our Lord and Father, and sometimes it curses those who have been made in the image of God. And so blessing and cursing come pouring out of the same mouth. Surely, my brothers and sisters, this is not right!

Drawing from your personal experience, write a 200- to 300-word essay in which you describe the power of words to be destructive and to be constructive.

• Bring a product, as packaged for sale on a store shelf, to your next class session. Analyze it and be prepared to explain to your classmates how its creator blends verbal and nonverbal elements in a quest to make the product more appealing to prospective buyers and more likely to be sold. Among the variables you should consider are word choice, the number of words, the font, size, color, placement, and relative size of the words, colors or symbols that appear elsewhere on the packaging, and so forth. If the product maker's goal is to use these variables to motivate people to buy it, how well did the maker do? Which variables work, and why? Which variables could work better, and why?

• Share three examples of a strange regional word or expression that you or a friend has encountered during your lifetime. Be sure for each of these to identify your hometown or region and where you were when you encountered the strange expression. Who said it? What was his or her home region? What did you think when you first heard the expression? How did you learn the intended meaning of the strange expression? Which term do people from your home region use for the same thing?

• In a paragraph or two, answer the following questions about your use of artifacts to send people information about yourself: a) Which colors or clothing items do you like to

The Bible discusses the power of our words: "And the tongue is a flame of fire. It is a whole world of wickedness, corrupting your entire body. It can set your whole life on fire, for it is set on fire by hell itself."

wear? Which do you not like to wear? b) Why do you like or not like them? Which ideas or feelings do or might they communicate to other people?

• Write a 200- to 300-word response to the following statement by Cornelius LaPide, a seventeenth-century Jesuit priest, about the face's tendency to show what is truly in a person's heart:

> The face, therefore, is the image of the heart, and the eyes are the mirror of the soul and its affections. One finds this principally in tumultuous and vile men who conceal their badness for a long time, but when they are distracted and unaware, it suddenly appears in their face and eyes. Therefore, the face and the eyes indicate the joy or sadness of the soul, its love or hatred; so also, honesty or treachery and hypocrisy.

You may agree, partly agree, or disagree with this observation. In either case, state your position, clearly and succinctly, and back it with supportive information, such as illustrations or examples from your personal experience or that of someone else.

"The face, therefore, is the image of the heart, and the eyes are the mirror of the soul and its affections."
- Cornelius LaPide

ENDNOTES

[1] McArthur, Tom. *Living Words: Language, Lexicography, and the Knowledge Revolution.* Exeter: University of Exeter Press, 1998. 43.

[2] Albert Mehrabian and Susan R. Ferris, "Inference of Attitudes from Nonverbal Communication in Two Channels," *Journal of Consulting Psychology*, 31.3 (1967): 248–252.

[3] Teresa J. Rosegrant and James C. McCroskey, "The Effects of Race and Sex on Proxemic Behavior in an Interview Setting," *Southern Speech Communication Journal*, 40 (1975): 408–419.

[4] Daniel S. Hamermesh and Jeff E. Biddle, "Beauty and the Labor Market," *American Economic Review*, 84.5 (1994): 1174–1194.

[5] Nicolas Herpin, "Love, Careers, and Heights in France," *Economics and Human Biology*, 01 (Jan. 2005).

[6] Elizabeth Kristen, "Addressing the Problem of Weight Discrimination in Employment," *California Law Review*, 90.1 (2002): 57–109.

[7] "Cosmetic Surgery Products: U.S. Industry Study with Forecasts for 2014 & 2019," *The Freedonia Group*, (Dec. 2010): accessed 9 May 2011. http://www.freedoniagroup.com/brochure/27xx/2712smwe.pdf

[8] "Perfumes, Cosmetics, and Other Toilet Preparations," Highbeam Business, n.d., accessed 9 May 2011, http://business.highbeam.com/industry-reports/chemicals/perfumes-cosmetics-other-toilet-preparations

[9] University of Toronto, "New 'Golden Ratios' for Female Facial Beauty," ScienceDaily, 17 (Dec. 2009), accessed 9 May 2011.

[10] Michael R. Cunningham and Anita P. Barbee, "What Do Women Want? Facialmetric Assessment of Multiple Motives in the Perception of Male Facial Physical Attractiveness," *Journal of Personality and Social Psychology*, 59.1 (1990): 61–72.

BIBLIOGRAPHY

Verbal Communication

Akmajian, Adrian, Richard A. Demers, and Robert M. Harnish. *Linguistics: An Introduction to Language and Communication*. Cambridge, MA: MIT Press, 1979.

Austin, J. L. *How to Do Things with Words*. Cambridge, MA: Harvard University Press, 1975.

Fasold, Ralph W., and Jeff Connor-Linton. *An Introduction to Language and Linguistics*. Cambridge, UK: Cambridge University Press, 2006.

Finch, Geoffrey. *Word of Mouth: A New Introduction to Language and Communication*. New York, NY: Palgrave Macmillan, 2003.

French, Peter A., and Howard K. Wettstein. *Figurative Language*. Boston, MA: Blackwell Publishers, 2001.

Fromkin, Victoria, and Robert Rodman. *An Introduction to Language*. Fort Worth, TX: Harcourt Brace Jovanovich College Publishers, 1993.

Ortony, Andrew. *Metaphor and Thought*. Cambridge: Cambridge University Press, 1979.

Trask, R. L. *Key Concepts in Language and Linguistics*. London: Routledge, 1999.

Nonverbal Communication

Andersen, Peter. *Nonverbal Communication: Forms and Functions*. New York: McGraw-Hill, 1999.

Armstrong, David F., William C. Stokoe, and Sherman Wilcox. *Gesture and the Nature of Language*. Cambridge: Cambridge University Press, 1995.

Burgoon, Judee K., Laura, K. Guerrero, and Kory Floyd. *Nonverbal Communication*. New York: Allyn & Bacon, 2009.

Ekman, Paul and L. Erika Rosenberg (Editors). *What the Face Reveals*. Oxford: Oxford University Press, 1998.

Emmorey, Karen and Judy S. Reilly (Editors). *Language, Gesture, and Space*. Mahwah, NJ: Lawrence Erlbaum Associates, 1995.

Feldman, Robert S. and Bernard Rimé (Editors). *Fundamentals of Nonverbal Behavior*. Cambridge: Cambridge University Press, 1991.

Hickson, Mark I. III and Don W. Stacks. *Nonverbal Communication: Studies and Applications* (2nd ed.). Dubuque, IA: Wm. C. Brown Publishers, 1989.

Knapp, Mark L. and Judith A. Hall. *Nonverbal Communication in Human Interaction*. Fort Worth, TX: Holt, Rinehart and Winston, 1992.

Leathers, Dale. *Successful Nonverbal Communication: Principles and Applications*. New York: Allyn & Bacon, 1997.

Mader, Thomas F. and Diane C. Mader. *Understanding One Another*. Dubuque, IA: Wm. C. Brown Publishers, 1990.

Malandro, Loretta, Larry Barker, and Deborah Ann Barker. *Nonverbal Communication* (2nd ed.). New York: McGraw-Hill, 1989.

Remland, Martin. *Nonverbal Communication in Everyday Life*. New York: Houghton Mifflin, 1999.

HONOR STATEMENT: I, the undersigned student, hereby declare before God, before the school, and before the professor that I have read Chapter 2 in its entirety, that I have completed the following exercise with help from no other sources, and that I neither have shared nor will share this work with anyone.

Signature: _____ Date: _____

SHORT ESSAYS

1. As Words are powerful communicational tools. Consider the following wisdom from James 3: 2–10:

"If we could control our tongues, we would be perfect and could also control ourselves in every other way. We can make a large horse go wherever we want by means of a small bit in its mouth. And a small rudder makes a huge ship turn wherever the pilot chooses to go, even though the winds are strong. In the same way, the tongue is a small thing that makes grand speeches. But a tiny spark can set a great forest on fire. And the tongue is a flame of fire. It is a whole world of wickedness, corrupting your entire body. It can set your whole life on fire, for it is set on fire by hell itself. People can tame all kinds of animals, birds, reptiles, and fish, but no one can tame the tongue. It is restless and evil, full of deadly poison. Sometimes it praises our Lord and Father, and sometimes it curses those who have been made in the image of God. And so blessing and cursing come pouring out of the same mouth. Surely, my brothers and sisters, this is not right!"

Drawing from your personal experience, write a 200- to 300-word essay in which you describe the power of words to be destructive or to be constructive.

_____

_____

_____

_____

_____

_____

_____

_____

_____

_____

_____

_____

2. Bring a product, as packaged for sale on a store shelf, to your next class session. Analyze it and be prepared to explain to your classmates how its creator blends verbal and nonverbal elements in a quest to make the product more appealing to prospective buyers and more likely to be sold. Among the variables you should consider are word choice, the number of words, the font, size, color, placement, and relative size of the words, colors or symbols that appear elsewhere on the packaging, and so forth. If the product maker's goal is to use these variables to motivate people to buy it, how well did the maker do? Which variables work, and why? Which variables could work better, and why? Record your thoughts about this in the space below.

_____

_____

_____

_____

_____

_____

_____

_____

_____

_____

_____

_____

_____

_____

_____

_____

_____

_____

_____

_____

3. Share three examples of a strange regional word or expression that you or a friend has encountered during your lifetime. Be sure for each of these to identify your hometown or region and where you were when you encountered the strange expression. Who said it? What was his or her home region? What did you think when you first heard the expression? How did you learn the intended meaning of the strange expression? Which term do people from your home region use for the same thing?

_____

_____

_____

_____

_____

_____

_____

_____

_____

_____

_____

4. In a paragraph or two, answer the following questions about your use of artifacts to send people information about yourself:

   a) Which colors or clothing items do you like to wear? Which do you not like to wear?
   b) Why do you like or not like them? Which ideas or feelings do or might they communicate to other people?

_____

_____

_____

_____

_____

_____

_____

_____

5. Write a 200- to 300-word response to the following statement by Cornelius LaPide, a seventeenth-century Jesuit priest, about the face's tendency to show what is truly in a person's heart:

> "The face, therefore, is the image of the heart, and the eyes are the mirror of the soul and its affections. One finds this principally in tumultuous and vile men who conceal their badness for a long time, but when they are distracted and unaware, it suddenly appears in their face and eyes. Therefore, the face and the eyes indicate the joy or sadness of the soul, its love or hatred; so also, honesty or treachery and hypocrisy."

You may agree, partly agree, or disagree with this observation. In either case, state your position, clearly and succinctly, and back it with supportive information, such as illustrations or examples from your personal experience or that of someone else.

_____

_____

_____

_____

_____

_____

_____

_____

_____

_____

_____

_____

_____

_____

_____

_____

_____

_____

CHAPTER 3 »

3 COMMUNICATION: WHY DOES IT MATTER?

OVERVIEW

In this chapter, we consider why communication is significant. A person's answer to this question is influenced by his or her worldview, his or her most basic beliefs about the world as it really is. This chapter reviews a couple of autonomous (humanly devised) approaches to making sense of things and pauses to consider their limitations. We then review how Biblically Christian thinking answers the same basic questions and how these answers enhance its merits as an alternative to human-centered models.

❯❯A CLOSER LOOK

As has been explained, communication is the transmission of meaningful information from one person or group of persons (the sender) to another person or group of persons (the recipient) in a way that generates shared attitudes, values, beliefs, feelings, or behaviors between the sender and recipient. People use verbal and nonverbal forms like the ones presented in the previous chapter, sometimes intentionally and other times unintentionally, to create these shared understandings.

Important as these basic concepts are, they merely set the stage for larger questions that the serious student of communication must consider before exploring what it takes to excel as a communicator. Among these more basic questions are the following: Where did communication come from? What is its purpose, if indeed it has a purpose? What meaningful difference can it make in individual lives and in the world? What, if anything, makes a communicative act or a communicational message moral or good? What, if anything, makes it immoral or evil? Unless it factors foundational questions like these, the study of communication has little value.

A person's answers to questions like these, about communication's significance, will be powerfully influenced by his or her *worldview*—an individual's most basic assumptions about the way things truly are. Your worldview is a composite of your beliefs about human origin (where we came from), human nature (what makes us human), human purpose (why we are here), and human destiny (where we are going). It also involves your beliefs about moral values (the rightness or wrongness of things) and aesthetic values (the desirability or undesirability of things). Most thinking people have at least a basic set of answers to these questions, and these answers impact what they value in life and how they interact with other people. These beliefs are so basic to your way of viewing life that you instinctively just assume them unless something presses you to critically evaluate or to justify them.

What is your worldview? Your behavior does more to answer this question than the words you offer when you are asked to state your beliefs.

❯❯WORLDVIEWS AND THE VALUE OF COMMUNICATION

What is your worldview? Your behavior does more to answer this question than the words you offer when you are asked to state your beliefs. A person who professes to be a follower of Jesus but who lives in a way that contradicts what Jesus taught may profess the Christian worldview, but this person's behavior may imply that his or her worldview is more hedonistic than it is Christian. Indeed, a worldview is the belief system that you practice in daily life, not just the set of belief statements that you offer when asked to do so. If the beliefs a person professes contradict the beliefs he or she actually practices, one may reasonably infer from this that the person is hypocritical, delusional, or else ignorant of his or her true belief system. A hypocrite is someone who is aware of and content to live with an inconsistency between the belief system he or she professes and the one he or she

© 2012 by Zastol'skiy Victor Leonidovich. Used under license of Shutterstock, Inc.

If your parents warned you to avoid the wrong crowd or to avoid watching certain types of TV programming when you were young, they likely did so because they recognized the powerful impact one's socialization experiences can have in fashioning what one becomes.

practices. A delusional person is someone who does not know that such an inconsistency exists because he or she chooses to disbelieve in its existence, even though this person has reason for believing that it does. An ignorant person is someone who does not know that such an inconsistency exists because he or she has no reason to know that it exists.

People whose walk and talk are inconsistent are often unaware of this disconnect because they thoughtlessly assume that they truly believe in what they say they believe. Blind assumptions of this type can harm them in a number of ways. Besides preventing them from seeing themselves as they really are, this misconception can persuade those who notice the inconsistency that they are untrustworthy because of it. Biblically Christian thinking recognizes an even greater potential consequence of inauthentic statements of belief: "Just as you can identify a tree by its fruit, so you can identify people by their actions. Not everyone who calls out to me, 'Lord! Lord!' will enter the Kingdom of Heaven. Only those who actually do the will of my Father in heaven will enter" (Matt. 7:20–21).

How does a person's worldview develop? Several factors contribute to this. Perhaps the most obvious of these is his or her lifetime of *socialization*—the person's history of interactions with people whose input helps to shape the way he or she sees and acts toward the world. Parents, spiritual leaders, teachers, friends, and media personalities are the most obvious examples of these influential others. Through formal and informal interactions with other people, we derive our verbal and nonverbal languages, our behavioral patterns, our group and individual identities, and many of our values and beliefs. If your parents warned you to avoid the wrong crowd or to avoid watching certain types of TV programming when you were young, they likely did so because they recognized the powerful impact one's socialization experiences can have in fashioning what one becomes.

A second factor that may impact a person's worldview development is *physical constitution*—the bodily dynamics, like neurological and biochemical processes, that help to shape the individual's personality and, by extension, his or her openness to certain types of ideas, feelings, and behaviors. Volumes of scholarly research affirm that a person's physical constitution can impact his or her levels of aggressiveness, agreeability, sociability, and impulsiveness, among other belief-expressive behaviors. The research also shows that when a person's physical constitution changes, his or her personality can change, too. Perhaps you have witnessed such a transformation in someone who has suffered a brain injury or whose brain arteries have hardened (a condition called "atherosclerosis") as he or she has aged.

A third factor that may impact a person's worldview development is his or her *spiritual constitution*. While mainstream communication scholars disregard this as a factor in someone's worldview development, Biblically Christian thinking does not. The Bible teaches that people enter the world in a state of spiritual brokenness. Although we are inclined to seek something God-like, we are not inclined, on our own, to seek for God himself (see Rom. 3:9–26). Despite this tendency, God, in ways not necessarily understandable to humans, can open a person's eyes to otherwise indiscernible spiritual truths and use this revelation to transform a person's understanding of life's purpose and the right approach to living (see John 6:37–40, 44, 63–65). Thus, divine intervention, no less than socialization and physical constitution, can impact a person's worldview development and the communicative behaviors that flow from it.

Worldviews can be distinguished from each other in lots of ways. At the most basic level, worldviews can be broken into two major categories. *Autonomous worldviews* are systems of belief that people develop on their own, primarily in response to what human standards have taught them to deem believable or acceptable. The autonomist's defining belief, in words from the ancient Greek philosopher Protagoras, is that "Man is the measure of all things." A *theocentric worldview*, by contrast, recognizes that God, the timeless, changeless source and sustainer of the universe and the source of all knowledge, discloses otherwise indiscernible foundational truths through Scripture, and that these otherwise hidden disclosures rightly frame and give direction to human quests to make sense of anything, including communication.

Friedrich Nietzsche.

In their quests to determine what is believable, acceptable, or true, autonomists test beliefs through the use of several types of human-centered proof standards. Rationalistic and empirical truth standards, for example, hold that a belief, feeling, or behavior is unacceptable if it is illogical or if it is at odds with what common human observations tell us is true. To the rationalistic/empirical mind, Biblical accounts of miracles—such as Jesus's feeding of the 5,000 with five loaves and two fishes, or His walking on water (Mark 6)—are difficult to accept since these accounts go against commonly observed, supposedly unchangeable laws of physics.

Pragmatic truth standards, by contrast, hold that a belief, feeling, or behavior is acceptable if it simply "works" for the person who holds it, regardless of whether it logically consists with anyone else's experiences and standards. The twentieth-century libertarian Ayn Rand expressed this way of thinking when she claimed that "man must be the beneficiary of his own moral actions" and that the "actor must always be the beneficiary of his action and that man must act for his own rational self-interest."[1] Many pragmatists deny the idea that people come to know things in exactly the same way, so they reject the use of supposedly objective criteria, like rationalistic or empirical rules, for the purpose of determining whether a person's beliefs, feelings, or behaviors are acceptable. What matters to these pragmatists, at least in theory, is that individuals are free to discover or to create truth for themselves without being sidetracked by other people's standards. To the pragmatist, others' moral standards are little more than tools for manipulating other people, or what nineteenth-century nihilist Friedrich Nietzsche's more cynically called "the best of all devices for leading mankind by the nose."[2]

> To the pragmatist, others' moral standards are little more than tools for manipulating other people, or what nineteenth-century nihilist Friedrich Nietzsche's more cynically called "the best of all devices for leading mankind by the nose."

Utilitarian truth standards, like pragmatic ones, hold that a belief, feeling, or behavior is acceptable if it "works," but differ radically from pragmatists in how they determine what works. For the utilitarian, a belief, feeling, or behavior that works is one that promotes the greatest good not for the individual, but for humanity as a whole. As Jeremy Bentham, an eighteenth-century formulator of this model, put it, "Ethics at large [for the utilitarian] may be defined as the art of directing men's actions to the production of the greatest possible quantity of happiness, on the part of those whose interest is in view."[3] For a modern example of how utilitarian thinking works, one can review the writings of Peter Singer, a controversial ethics professor at Princeton University. Like a pragmatist, he rejects universal moral rules, such as the Biblical teaching that all human life is valuable. Instead, he uses utilitarian logic to argue, shockingly, that killing some birth-defected babies is morally justified for utilitarian reasons. The following quote illustrates how his thinking operates: "When the death of a disabled infant will lead to the birth of another infant with better prospects of a happy life, the total amount of happiness will be greater if the disabled infant is killed. The loss of happy life for the first infant is outweighed by the gain of a happier life for the second. Therefore, if killing the hemophiliac infant has no adverse effect on others, it would, according to the total view, be right to kill him."[4] This is the utilitarian thinking in its rawest form.

Before presenting the theocentric approach's truth standard and contrasting it with the autonomous standards just presented, we must briefly review a couple of the autonomous approach's especially prominent worldview traditions—physical determinism and social constructionism. In doing so, we contrast what these subsystems say about human origin, purpose, destiny, and values and consider the implications of these views for their adherents' answer to this chapter's guiding question, "Why does communication matter?"

❯❯ AUTONOMOUS WORLDVIEWS AND COMMUNICATION

How many worldviews are there? Scholars differ in their answers to this question. Dennis McCallum, in his book *Christianity: The Faith That Makes Sense*, identifies five systems—physical determinism, pantheism, theism, spiritism and polytheism, and postmodernism. David Noebel, in his book *Understanding the Times*, highlights six—Christianity, Islam, secular humanism, Marxism, cosmic humanism, and postmodernism. Anthony Steinbronn, in his book *Worldviews: A Christian Response to Religious Pluralism*, lists seven systems—Buddhism, Confucianism, Hinduism, Islam, tribalism, modernism, and a Biblical view. In the latest edition of his *The Universe Next Door*, a work that has sold more than 300,000 copies since its first edition, James Sire profiles nine worldview traditions—Christian theism, deism, physical determinism, nihilism, existentialism, Eastern pantheistic monism, New Age spirituality, postmodernism, and Islamic theism.

Obviously, some of these works are more meticulous than others in their approach to parsing the world's major, basic belief systems. Despite differences, each of these treatments, and others like them, helpfully demonstrates how our fundamental assumptions about the world impact the way we distinguish things that matter from things that do not matter. Rather than pointlessly deeming one of these treatments to be better than the others—each affords an interesting, informative approach to the topic—I reduce their distinctions to two clearly distinguishable, autonomous classifications and then contrast these with their theocentric alternative. My goal in an introductory text

How many worldviews are there? Scholars differ in their answers to this question.

like this one is not to catalog every autonomous way of thinking or every worldview subsystem, but briefly to describe the overarching systems—physical determinism and social constructionism—that have most profoundly impacted Westerners' ways of thinking about life and about the significance of anything in life, including communication.

▲Physical Determinism

The late astronomer Carl Sagan's quip that "the Cosmos is all that is or ever was or ever will be" aptly expresses this belief system's guiding assumption.[5] Physical determinists see the universe as a self-created, self-sustaining machine, consisting of material particles and processes and nothing more than these, that invariably follows the course that physics has blindly programmed it to follow. Everything that happens, this view holds, happens because nature has programmed it to occur. History follows an inevitable course, and nothing can alter this.

Physical determinism denies the existence of a separate spiritual realm and of a Creator Who can alter history's course as He wills.

Physical determinism denies the existence of a separate spiritual realm and of a Creator Who can alter history's course as He wills. The beliefs that God or spiritual beings exist and that life has an overarching spiritual purpose, it maintains, are little more than biochemically conditioned illusions that the human brain creates to enable people to cope with the harsh realities of a hostile world. These determinists hold that although the universe appears to be an infinitely complex yet remarkably functional machine, it was not intelligently created. As one prominent evolutionary biologist reportedly expresses this, "It is all accident, all a matter of chance. No reason, no end, no purpose at all."[6]

This view has become increasingly popular in Western culture since the beginning of the Enlightenment in the seventeenth century, when European scholars began to investigate and to explain the world independently, inspired but not necessarily guided by Biblical precepts. Ironically, a number of this movement's early trailblazers were outstanding Christians who aimed, through their direct investigations of the material world, simply to use their logical and observational powers to better understand the universe they realized God had created. They visualized their task, in words commonly attributed to astronomer Johannes Kepler, as being simply to "think God's thoughts after Him."

Buoyed by these trailblazers' discoveries and successes, emboldened new scholars emerged during the centuries that followed who saw in the human powers of observation and reasoning the key to answering questions not just about the physical universe's elements and operations, but about virtually anything. The Biblical precepts that inspired and framed many of their predecessors' investigations ceased to be revered as divinely disclosed and rightly authoritative, and were themselves subjected to rationalistic and empirical truth standards for the purpose of judging their validity. The new thinkers recognized human experience as most people know it or can come to know it through observation as the standard for determining whether something is believable. Thus, they produced works like Thomas Jefferson's *The Life and Morals of Jesus of Nazareth*, a New Testament that retained Jesus's moral teachings but removed references to His miracles. This human-centered way of making sense of the world gradually emerged as the accepted way of determining whether something is true, not just among intellectuals but among people in general. It remains especially popular today in scientific circles, where quests for understanding typically disregard Biblical precepts to explain the world, including such God-initiated earthly wonders as human communication.

Why then do people communicate as we do? Inspired by ideas that biologist Charles Darwin popularized during the mid-nineteenth century, physical determinists assume the drive to survive is fundamentally what moves individuals to interact with each other. As these theorists see it, human history is primarily the story of people working with or struggling against nature and each other in each individual's quest for self-preservation. Nature, they say, has somehow wired people to operate in this way. Physical determinists believe an individual instinctively communicates with other individuals to establish connections that boost his or her likelihood for survival. This, in a nutshell, is the naturalist's explanation of what makes human communication significant. It is seen as little more than a lifeline in a turbulent Darwinian ocean in which only the fittest survive. When they sink beneath the waters and drown, this view supposes, they simply cease to exist. As noted earlier, there is no spiritual afterlife in the physical determinist's way of seeing things.

"Everything is determined, the beginning as well as the end, by forces over which we have no control."
- Albert Einstein

One more point about physical determinism is noteworthy in this brief description because of its relevance to communication. Physical determinists hold that people are essentially machines—that because they are wired to behave as they do, they are unable to choose their actions freely or to determine what they will become. Instead, these theorists posit, people become only what genetic and environmental variables combine to dictate that they shall become. Determinists dismiss a person's belief that he or she is free to define his or her own destiny as a biochemically induced illusion. As the eighteenth-century philosopher Benedict de Spinoza expressed this fatalistic notion, "In the mind there is no absolute or free will; but the mind is determined to wish this or that by a cause, which has also been determined by another cause, and this last by another cause, and so on to infinity."[7] More recently, Albert Einstein expressed the same assumption in the following words: "Everything is determined, the beginning as well as the end, by forces over which we have no control. It is determined for the insect as well as the star. Human beings, vegetables, or cosmic dust, we all dance to a mysterious tune, intoned in the distance by an invisible piper."[8]

A critical look at this way of thinking is in order at this point. If the universe and all it comprises is an accident with no overarching purpose, as physical determinists assert, then people can have no more value, significance, or purpose than mice, fleas, or amoeba, because each is a product of the same accidental yet supposedly self-directed creative process. Physical determinism assigns humans no special status or significance in the universe. Thus, people's religious rituals and their charitable acts toward others are seen as biochemically programmed quests for self-preservation that have no eternal value. Human abuses, too—whether genocide, rape, or child molestation—are trivialized as little more than culturally relative, socially unaccepted acts in the ongoing struggle among living beings for survival. Physical determinism does not see the abuse of another person as being wrong in the principled, absolute sense that theocentrists do when they criticize the abuse as wrong.

Physical determinism is autonomous because it begins with the blind rationalistic/empirical assumption—and it is just an assumption—that people can credibly believe only in that which common experience deems objectively believable. If most people can see, hear, smell, taste, or feel something, it is sufficiently believable for the physical determinist. He or she then tries to make sense of this something by examining and explaining it as if it were a purely physical phenomenon.

Charles Darwin.

Darwin himself, in a letter to a Harvard biologist, admitted that his attempt to explain life's origin in purely naturalistic terms relied heavily on guesswork: "I am quite conscious that my specula-tions run quite beyond the bounds of true science."

This way of thinking is questionable for a couple of reasons. First, physical determinists can offer no physical evidence—the only type that counts, they say—to support their belief that everything in existence is entirely physical and that there is no separate spiritual dimension. This is a faith-based assumption, not a scientifically provable premise. Darwin himself, in a letter to a Harvard biologist, admitted that his attempt to explain life's origin in purely naturalistic terms relied heavily on guesswork: "I am quite conscious that my speculations run quite beyond the bounds of true science."[9] Second, physical determinists can offer no physical evidence to support their assumption that humans' sense perceptions give accurate pictures of things as they really are. Even if we assume that our sense perceptions are demonstrably accurate, determinists fail to show why we should also assume, as they do, that our senses can actually grasp and that our brains can accurately process the volume of data one would need in order to formulate accurate answers to the questions we autonomously explore. This, too, is a faith-based assumption.

Because it rests on speculations like these, physical determinism is not the obviously best way of looking at the world that its proponents believe it to be. Many people who recognize this have compared physical determinism to its worldview alternatives and have criticized it for being one of the worst belief systems, mainly because its portrayal of human existence is so bleak and its ethical implications for it are so dark. Indeed, this system's logic has been used throughout modern history to justify racism, sexism, and even mass murder. Peter Singer, who has argued for euthanasia, admits such evils are a consequence of atheistic naturalistic thinking::

The view that [voluntary euthanasia] can never be right gains its strongest support from religious doctrines that claim that only humans are made in the image of God, or that only humans have an immortal soul, or that God gave us dominion over the animals—meaning that we can kill them if we wish—but reserved to himself dominion over human beings.

Reject these ideas, and it is difficult to think of any morally relevant properties that separate human beings with severe brain damage or other major intellectual disabilities from nonhuman animals at a similar mental level.[10]

This treatment of naturalism is necessarily brief in a text like this one. Suffice it to say, for these reasons as well as for others that have been explained in greater detail by other critics, that physical determinism falls short as a model for making sense of human origin, nature, purpose, and destiny and, therefore, as a framework for explaining human communication.

▲Social Constructionism

If *physical determinism* places too strong an emphasis on physical factors as shapers of what people do and what they can become, social constructionism places too heavy an emphasis on each person's unique experiences as determinative of what he or she can do or become. Like physical determinism, social constructionism is autonomous because it appeals primarily to humanly devised standards, rather than divine precepts, in its attempt to answer questions about human origin, nature, purpose, and destiny. However, unlike physical determinists, who use a rationalistic and empirical truth standard when validating or invalidating answers to such questions, social constructionists typically use a pragmatic truth standard. This is so because constructionists reject the ideas, popular among physical determinists, that people can come to see the world in the same way, despite their different conditioning experiences.

Social constructionists assume that because each person experiences the world in a unique way, no two persons can come to see the world in exactly the same way, no matter how hard they try to do so. They believe a person becomes what his or her socializing experiences precondition him or her to become. Whatever else it may be, a person's way of communicating is seen as an artifact of these unique experiences and is deemed appropriately interpreted as little more than this.

What motivates people to communicate as they do? Social constructionists provide a variety of answers to this question. Many of them share the Darwinian notion that human behavior is motivated primarily by the drive to survive. Some place a greater emphasis on the Nietzschean idea that human behavior is fundamentally motivated by the individual's appetite for power. Others subscribe to the Marxist idea that human behavior is primarily conditioned by the person's status in the ongoing struggle between society's haves and its have-nots. Some adopt the Freudian notion that human behavior is driven, above all, by sexual impulses. Still other constructionists are more agnostic about questions like these and assert that we cannot know whether human behavior has a primary motive or, if so, what the motive might be.

Existentialism

Social constructionists also disagree with each other about the question of whether people are free to choose their behaviors and their destinies. Two recent subtraditions—*existentialism* and *postmodernism*—are noteworthy for their contrasting views about this. Existentialists believe that although the material world may exist in a fixed form, with all its particles and processes, it is nonetheless removed from us, and we cannot have direct contact with it. All we can know about the world, they say, is what our perceptions tell us about it. Whether our perceptions of it are accurate or not, existentialists believe we come to see the world as we do by the people who influence us through socialization. They believe this neither has to be nor should be so, arguing that individuals are radically free to take control of their minds, to break away from stifling social influences, and to free themselves to see the world in authentic, uninhibited, self-directed ways. This movement's dislike for other individuals' socializing influences on our ways of thinking is aptly expressed in the late, leading twentieth-century existentialist Jean-Paul Sartre's famous literary line: "Hell is other people!"

To the existentialist, then, communication tends to be negative. It is like a rope in tug-of-war, with the influencers who have shaped your mind pulling to keep you positioned where their lifetime of tugging has taken you. The existential response to this situation is not simply for you to pull in the opposite direction, but for you to release the rope they have assigned to you and to stop playing their game. Only by ridding yourself of external influences can you live life authentically and freely, they say. For atheistic versions of existentialism, this requires one to drop religious ideals, such as belief in God, which are dismissed as externally imposed barriers to thinking freely and to realizing, consequently, that everything is meaningless. Sartre explained his rationale for this way of thinking in the following statement:

> Nowhere is it written that the Good exists, that we must be honest, that we must not lie; because the fact is we are on a plane where there are only men. Dostoievsky said, "If God didn't exist, everything would be possible." That is the very starting point of existentialism. Indeed, everything is permissible if God does not exist, and as a result man is forlorn, because neither within him nor without does he find anything to cling to. He can't start making excuses for himself.[11]

To attain this existential type of freedom, Sartre proposed, one must bravely endure the pain that comes with realizing, as he claimed to believe, that everything, including one's communications with others, is pointless. Nausea is Sartre's term for the psychological pain one feels upon authentically realizing this belief. He also used the term to title a literary work that he authored, a story in which the main character's realization that life is meaninglessness nauseates him in this existential way. Sartre's only remedy for this anxiety—if it can be called a solution—is self-actualization, which means doing what your raw impulses tell you to do without allowing your reasoning to get in the way.

Existentialism, like physical determinism, has been criticized for several reasons over the years. First, it is self-refuting. This system's thinkers—who argued that individuals should resist having their thoughts assigned to them by other people—attempted through their writings, ironically, to assign their own thoughts to other people. Thus, their walk simply did not match their talk, a glaring inconsistency that raises questions about the believability of the ideas they proposed. Existentialism has also been criticized for providing a bleak picture of human existence by giving people so little a reason for living

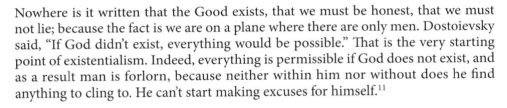

To the existentialist, then, communication tends to be negative. It is like a rope in tug-of-war, with the influencers who have shaped your mind pulling to keep you positioned where their lifetime of tugging has taken you.

and so little a motive for behaving ethically toward others. Sartre himself may have realized his system's flaws later in his life. In a 1974 interview, he offered a statement, in a published interview, that implies his worldview may have shifted by that point, late in his life: "I do not feel that I am the product of chance, a speck of dust in the universe, but someone who was expected, prepared, prefigured. In short, a being whom only a creator could put here; and this idea of a creating hand refers to God."[12]

Postmodernism

Like existentialism, postmodernism, the second social constructionist sub-tradition that we consider, assumes that people act as they do and become what they become primarily, if not exclusively, as a reaction to their lifetime of conditioning experiences. Postmodernists, who are also called "deconstructionists," are especially interested in the ways people use language to impact each other's ways of thinking, feeling, and acting. Many of these theorists share the existentialists' belief that the material world, if it is really there, exceeds our grasp. The only reality people can know, they say, is the one their minds construct in response to the world as language filters it to them.

How should one respond to his or her lifetime of conditioning experiences? Existentialists and postmodernists answer this question differently. Whereas existentialists urge people to rid themselves of their socially instilled ways of seeing the world and to follow their raw instincts instead, postmodernists focus elsewhere. Those with Marxist leanings explore how powerful people (the haves) use language and media as tools to suppress the weak (the have-nots) and call for solutions to this supposed problem. Those with feminist leanings investigate how men use language and media to dominate women and call for fixes to this. Many deconstructionists explore how other groups of haves (whether racially, ethnically, culturally, religiously, or politically defined) use language and media to exploit corresponding groups of have-nots and call for remedies to this. The goals for the postmodernist in any of these cases are twofold: 1) exposition—showing how social influencers can impact what people become and how privileged groups use this to promote themselves at others' expense and; 2) emancipation—promoting remedies for these supposed misuses of power. Deterministic deconstructionists devote themselves only to exposition, believing calls for emancipation to be pointless since, they believe, people inevitably become what their social conditioning has predisposed them to become.

Beneath these concerns are assumptions that clearly identify postmodernism as an autonomous, social constructionist tradition. As already noted, deconstructionists believe there is no real world out there waiting to be discovered. Reality, they propose, is something your mind constructs in response to the language-filtered and shaped perceptions that it gathers and synthesizes throughout your lifetime. You supposedly have no way of rising above these perceptions to access and to know for certain that anything outside you truly exists. Whatever you believe to be true, real, meaningful, and right or wrong, they say, is just a mindset that you have formed in response to your conditioning experiences. Because these perceptions are unique—no one, they assert, can experience and see life as another person does—you must respect the "fact" that each individual creates his or her own truth. Accordingly, postmodernists contend, you must not try to impose your view of the world and your values on other people. Deconstructionists are

Postmodernists, who are also called "deconstructionists," are especially interested in the ways people use language to impact each other's ways of thinking, feeling, and acting. Many of these theorists share the existentialists' belief that the material world, if it is really there, exceeds our grasp.

especially prickly about violations of this principle in situations in which members of traditionally empowered groups consciously or subconsciously "impose" their views of the world on members of traditionally disempowered minority groups, whether they are ethnically, racially, religiously, or politically defined.

To the postmodernist, communication is a weapon that can be used to promote good or evil. The good, as he or she imagines it, is the advancement of his or her postmodern ideals and values, including the works of exposition and emancipation. The evil, not surprisingly, is the disregard of these ideas and values and the imposition of one person's values on another or of a majority viewpoint on minorities through language and media. Postmodernists would not state this point about themselves so directly—to state anything so objectively, after all, would be contrary to the relativistic ideals they profess—but it is clearly the implication of what they write.

This brings us to a discussion of postmodernism's merits as a framework for making sense of communication, or of anything else for that matter. If one assumes, as postmodernists contend, that there is no world outside our perceptions, we must ask how one could possibly know that this is so. As G. K. Chesterton once observed, "We do not know enough about the unknown to know that it is unknowable."[13] If anything is unknowable, we could never learn that it exists and is unknowable unless this were revealed to us by one who, unlike us, has access to it. The same objection applies to postmodernism's contention that no two people see the world in exactly the same way. In order to say credibly that this is so, the postmodernist somehow must escape the supposedly inescapable prison of his own perceptions in order to compare its content with the content of other people's perceptions and to determine, consequently, that no two perspectives are alike. Postmodern theorists consistently fail to explain why we should assume that they somehow are exempt from the very limitations, such as this one, that they assign to everyone else.

Deconstructionists also fail to explain why anyone in a postmodern world should conduct himself or herself ethically toward others. If we assume that individuals create their own truth and their own morals in response to their unique perceptions, as postmodernists suggest, then we must ask whether it is fair to hold people accountable to a moral standard other than one's own. Such an idea has ominous implications, as the Oxford literary scholar C. S. Lewis observed in an essay that he penned while the Nazis threatened to overtake his British homeland during World War II:

> Out of this apparently innocent idea comes the disease that will certainly end our species (and, in my view, damn our souls) if it is not crushed; the fatal superstition that men can create values, that a community can choose its "ideology" as men choose their clothes. Everyone is indignant when he hears the Germans define justice as that which is to the interest of the Third Reich. But it is not always remembered that this indignation is perfectly groundless if we ourselves regard morality as a subjective sentiment to be altered at will. Unless there is some objective standard of good, overarching Germans, Japanese, and ourselves alike whether any of us obey it or not, then of course the Germans are as competent to create their

To the postmodernist, communication is a weapon that can be used to promote good or evil.

ideology as we are to create ours. If "good" and "better" are terms deriving their sole meaning from the ideology of each people, then of course ideologies themselves cannot be better or worse than one another. Unless the measuring rod is independent of the things measured, we can do no measuring.[14]

Postmodernists often argue that we must protect the beliefs and values of the have-nots from the supposedly corrupting, self-serving influence of the haves. However, if each person's moral values are personally constructed and if one person's values are not necessarily better than the next person's values, why must we protect the have-nots? Why should one not crush them instead if his or her personal values deem this appropriate? Deconstructionists provide no satisfactory answers to this question.

❯ THE LIMITATIONS OF AUTONOMOUS REASONING

As this chapter demonstrates, autonomous approaches to explaining human origin, nature, purpose, and destiny and to providing meaningful reasons for appreciating communication are plagued by serious limitations. Some of these problems are intellectual. Others are ethical. From a Biblically Christian standpoint, these problems, although intellectual and ethical on their surface, are fundamentally spiritual.

To understand this, one must recognize seven core principles that define the Biblically Christian worldview. First, the Bible reveals that God alone—the timeless, changeless source and sustainer of the universe and our creator—knows everything that can be known: "O Lord, you have examined my heart and know everything about me. You know when I sit down or stand up. You know my thoughts even when I'm far away. You see me when I travel and when I rest at home. You know everything I do. You know what I am going to say even before I say it, Lord. You go before me and follow me. You place your hand of blessing on my head. Such knowledge is too wonderful for me, too great for me to understand!" (Psalm 139: 1–6). Humans simply cannot attain the perfect knowledge that only God has.

The Bible reveals that God alone–the timeless, changeless source and sustainer of the universe and our creator–knows everything that can be known.

Still, God has made known or knowable to us essential facts about the universe He created and our place in it, facts that must be considered in our attempts to make sense of things. This is especially vital in attempts to make sense of ourselves and why we do the things we do. Perhaps the most illuminating Biblical passage about our limited ability to make sense of such things on our own is the book of Romans, especially its first two chapters. This epistle explains that "[People], through everything God made . . . can clearly see his invisible qualities—his eternal power and divine nature. So they have no excuse for not knowing God" (Rom 1:20). Even though people "know the truth about God because he has made it obvious to them" (v. 19), people "suppress the truth by their wickedness" (v. 18).

This highlights the fact that people are corrupted by autonomy and do not seek after the God by Whom and for Whom we were created. This self-centeredness traces back to our earliest history when our ancestors autonomously quested to "be like God, knowing both good and evil" (Gen. 3:5). This decision to chase an egotistical lie had enduringly adverse effects for humanity, for "When Adam sinned, sin entered the world. Adam's sin brought death, so death spread to everyone, for everyone sinned. Yes, people sinned even before the law was given. But it was not counted as sin because there was not yet any law to break" (Rom. 5: 12–13).

Thus, people live in a self-inflicted state of corruption, having divorced ourselves from the very One for Whom we were created and in Whose restored fellowship we find our completion: "No one is righteous—not even one. No one is truly wise; no one is seeking God. All have turned away; all have become useless. No one does good, not a single one. Their talk is foul, like the stench from an open grave. Their tongues are filled with lies. Snake venom drips from their lips. Their mouths are full of cursing and bitterness. They rush to commit murder. Destruction and misery always follow them. They don't know where to find peace. They have no fear of God at all" (Rom. 3:10–18).

© 2012 by Aliaksei Lasevich.
Used under license of Shutterstock, Inc.

"If I find in myself a desire which no experience in this world can satisfy, the most probable explanation is that I was made for another world."
- C. S. Lewis

Although our Creator has given us intelligence that we can use, despite our brokenness, to make sense of some things about the universe and our place in it, this intelligence is considerably limited in its potential reach: "My thoughts are nothing like your thoughts," says the Lord. "And my ways are far beyond anything you could imagine. For just as the heavens are higher than the earth, so my ways are higher than your ways and my thoughts higher than your thoughts" (Isa. 55:8–9).

Despite the stifling effects of our corruption, our sense that we are made for something perfect, unlike anything in this world, lingers in our souls. Indeed, although we do not long for God himself (cf. Rom. 3:11), a craving for this perfect something that eludes our grasp drives much of our behavior. We long to connect with it, not knowing what it is or where to find it. Instead of humbly acknowledging our limitations and turning for guidance to the all-knowing Creator Whose restored presence alone can fill this void, we often anesthetize the pain within us by chasing empty alternatives that, in some cases, temporarily create false feelings of satisfaction: "They traded the truth about God for a lie. So they worshiped and served the things God created instead of the Creator himself, Who is worthy of eternal praise! Amen" (Rom. 1:25). Among the God-made things that we worship is our corrupted human intelligence, which we sometimes centralize in our quests for worldview-related answers that simply exceed our fallen grasp—answers to questions about human origin, nature, purpose destiny, and values. We justify the answers that these generate using rationalistic/empirical, pragmatic, and utilitarian truth standards, among others that our minds devise, as if our minds could independently generate trustworthy answers despite their brokenness. In the end, though, these intellectual saviors disappoint and fail to deliver what we our souls truly desire. The logical implication of this pattern is clear, as C. S. Lewis explains: "If I find in myself a desire which no experience in this world can satisfy, the most probable explanation is that I was made for another world."[15]

The only real solution to this crisis begins when we sincerely acknowledge that on our own we are hopelessly autonomous, that our hearts and minds are helplessly impaired by this corruption, and that our only hope for escaping our brokenness and seeing anything as it truly is must be God-centered (theocentric) and God-initiated. Through His Son's redemptive death on the cross, God bridged the gap that separates us from Him and extended to us the offer of a cure for our brokenness, one that we receive when we humbly and repentantly centralize God's authority in our lives (cf. Psalm 51:16–18; John 1:12). When we surrender ourselves in this way, we commit to make sense of anything, including ourselves as communicators, and to conduct ourselves, communicatively or otherwise, in the instructive light of His revealed Word to us (cf. Psalm 119:105; 1 Thes. 2:13; 2 Tim. 3:16–17). The person who is thus redeemed does not become all-knowing like God. Nor does he or she necessarily become more knowledgeable about human experience. However, this transformation does give the person the corrective lens through which the human experience must be filtered if one hopes to avoid the logical shortsightedness and the ethical distortions that inevitably plague autonomous attempts to make sense of it.

The next chapter considers how this corrective lens impacts one's view of the world and of human communication. An authentically theocentric vantage point impacts not only the way one makes sense of communication, but also the way one practices it. As you contemplate this book's first three chapters and as you read through the fourth and fifth, I invite you to become a redemptive communicator—someone who sees the world as God, according to His revelation, intended it to be and who interacts with others in a way that, above all, promotes His redemptive purpose in their lives.

 QUESTIONS FOR ANALYSIS

- This chapter indicates that a person's worldview is not the beliefs he or she professes, but the beliefs his or her behavior suggests. State whether you agree or disagree with this statement in a 100- to 200-word response. Be sure to provide at least three different reasons, examples, illustrations, or other supportive material that clearly supports your stated position.

- Read the following two poems. Then, using relevant terms from this chapter, write a 200- to 300-word response that identifies the worldview that each of these compositions appears most to express. Be sure to justify your answers with clear, logical explanations so it is obvious how you arrived at your conclusions.

FROM "PARACELSUS"

Truth is within ourselves; it takes no rise
From outward things, whate'er you may believe.
There is an inmost centre in us all,
Where truth abides in fullness; and around,
Wall upon wall, the gross flesh hems it in,
This perfect, clear perception—which is truth.

A baffling and perverting carnal mesh
Binds it, and makes all error: and, to know,
Rather consists in opening out a way
Whence the imprisoned splendour may escape,
Than in effecting entry for a light
Supposed to be without.

—*Robert Browning (1812–1889)*

OPEN MY EYES THAT I MAY SEE

Open my eyes, that I may see
Glimpses of truth Thou hast for me;
Place in my hands the wonderful key
That shall unclasp and set me free.

Silently now I wait for Thee,
Ready my God, Thy will to see,
Open my eyes, illumine me,
Spirit divine!

Open my ears, that I may hear
Voices of truth Thou sendest clear;
And while the wave notes fall on my ear,
Everything false will disappear.

Open my mouth, and let me bear,
Gladly the warm truth everywhere;
Open my heart and let me prepare
Love with Thy children thus to share.

— *Clara H. Fiske Scott (1841–1897)*

• As mentioned in the chapter, Romans 1:25 states: "They traded the truth about God for a lie. So they worshiped and served the things God created instead of the Creator himself, who is worthy of eternal praise! Amen." The chapter highlights corrupted human intelligence as one of the God-made things that we worship instead of God himself. Make a list of at least five other God-like substitutes in human experience that people "worship" or serve rather than God himself. Explain why you placed each item on your list.

ENDNOTES

[1] Ayn Rand and Nathaniel Branden, *The Virtue of Selfishness: A New Concept of Egoism* (New York: Penguin Books, 1964), n.pag.

[2] Friedrich W. Nietzsche and H. L. Mencken, *The Antichrist* (New York: A. A. Knopf, 1920), 127.

[3] Jeremy Bentham, *An Introduction to the Principles of Morals and Legislation*, 1907, Library of Economics and Liberty, accessed 25 May 2011, http://www.econlib.org/library/Bentham/bnthPML18.html

[4] Peter Singer, *Writings on an Ethical Life* (New York: Harper-Collins, 2001), 189.

[5] Carl Sagan, *Cosmos* (New York: Random House, 1980), 4.

[6] *Gems from Martin Lloyd-Jones: An Anthology of Quotations from "The Doctor,"* (Colorado Springs: Paternoster, 2007), 76.

[7] Benedictus Spinoza and R. H. M. Elwes, *The Chief Works of Benedict De Spinoza* (London: G. Bell, 1889), 119.

[8] John Carey, *Eyewitness to Science* (Cambridge: Harvard University Press, 1997), 274.

[9] Neal C. Gillespie, *Charles Darwin and the Problem of Creation* (Chicago: University of Chicago Press, 1979), 2.

[10] Peter Singer, "Decisions about Death," *Free Inquiry* (Aug/Sept 2005): n. pag., accessed 28 May 2011, http://www.utilitarian.net/singer/by/200508--.htm

[11] Lawrence E. Cahoone, *From Modernism to Postmodernism: An Anthology* (Malden, MA: Blackwell Publishing, 2003), 171.

[12] Simon Critchley, *The Book of Dead Philosophers* (Carlton, Vic: Melbourne University Publishing, 2008), 252.

[13] Gilbert Keith Chesterton, *William Blake* (New York: Cosimo Books, 2005), 74.

[14] C. S. Lewis, *Christian Reflections* (Grand Rapids: Wm. B. Eerdmans, 1994), 73.

[15] C. S. Lewis, *Mere Christianity* (New York: Macmillan, 1986), 106.

BIBLIOGRAPHY

Blamires, Harry. *Recovering the Christian Mind: Meeting the Challenge of Secularism*. Downers Grove, IL: InterVarsity Press, 1988.

Blamires, Harry. *The Christian Mind: How Should a Christian Think*. Ann Arbor, MI: Servant Books, 1978.

Blamires, Harry. *The PostChristian Mind: Exposing Its Destructive Agenda*. Ann Arbor, MI: Vine Books, 1999.

Clark, Gordon Haddon. *A Christian View of Men and Things: An Introduction to Philosophy*. Jefferson, MD: Trinity Foundation, 1991.

Colson, Charles W., and Nancy Pearcey. *How Now Shall We Live?* Wheaton, IL: Tyndale House Publishers, 1999.

Geisler, Norman L. and William D. Watkins. *Worlds Apart: A Handbook on World Views*. Eugene, OR: Wipf and Stock Publishers, 2003.

Holmes, Arthur Frank. *All Truth Is God's Truth*. Grand Rapids, MI: Eerdmans Publishing, 1977.

Naugle, David K. *Worldview: The History of a Concept*. Grand Rapids, MI: W. B. Eerdmans Publishing, 2002.

Nash, Ronald H. *Worldviews in Conflict: Choosing Christianity in a World of Ideas*. Grand Rapids, MI: Zondervan Publishers, 1992.

Sire, James W. *The Universe Next Door: A Basic Worldview Catalog*. Downers Grove, IL: InterVarsity Press, 2009.

Sproul, R. C. *Lifeviews: Understanding the Ideas That Shape Society Today*. Old Tappan, NJ: F. H. Revell, 1986.

Weaver, Richard M. *Ideas Have Consequences*. Chicago: University of Chicago Press, 1984.

Wolterstorff, Nicholas. *Reason within the Bounds of Religion*. Grand Rapids, MI: W. B. Eerdmans Publishing, 1976.

NAME: _____   DATE: _____

HONOR STATEMENT: I, the undersigned student, hereby declare before God, before the school, and before the professor that I have read Chapter 3 in its entirety, that I have completed the following exercise with help from no other sources, and that I neither have shared nor will share this work with anyone.

Signature: _____   Date: _____

SHORT ESSAYS

1. This chapter indicates that a person's worldview is not the beliefs he or she professes, but the beliefs his or her behavior suggests. State whether you agree or disagree with this statement in a 100- to 200-word response. Be sure to provide at least three different reasons, examples, illustrations, or other supportive material that clearly supports your stated position.

_____

_____

_____

_____

_____

_____

_____

_____

_____

_____

_____

_____

_____

_____

_____

_____

2. Read the following two poems. Then, using relevant terms from this chapter, write a 200- to 300-word response that identifies the worldview that each of these compositions appears most to express. Be sure to justify your answers with clear, logical explanations so it is obvious how you arrived at your conclusions.

FROM "PARACELSUS"

Truth is within ourselves; it takes no rise
From outward things, whate'er you may believe.
There is an inmost centre in us all,
Where truth abides in fullness; and around,
Wall upon wall, the gross flesh hems it in,
This perfect, clear perception—which is truth.
A baffling and perverting carnal mesh
Binds it, and makes all error: and, to know,
Rather consists in opening out a way
Whence the imprisoned splendour may escape,
Than in effecting entry for a light
Supposed to be without.

—Robert Browning (1812–1889)

OPEN MY EYES THAT I MAY SEE

Open my eyes, that I may see
Glimpses of truth Thou hast for me;
Place in my hands the wonderful key
That shall unclasp and set me free.

Silently now I wait for Thee,
Ready my God, Thy will to see,
Open my eyes, illumine me,
Spirit divine!

Open my ears, that I may hear
Voices of truth Thou sendest clear;
And while the wave notes fall on my ear,
Everything false will disappear.

Open my mouth, and let me bear,
Gladly the warm truth everywhere;
Open my heart and let me prepare
Love with Thy children thus to share.

— Clara H. Fiske Scott (1841–1897)

_____

_____

_____

_____

_____

_____

_____

_____

_____

_____

_____

_____

_____

_____

3. As mentioned in the chapter, Romans 1:25 states: "They traded the truth about God for a lie. So they worshiped and served the things God created instead of the Creator himself, who is worthy of eternal praise! Amen." The chapter highlights corrupted human intelligence as one of the God-made things that we worship instead of God himself. Make a list of at least five other God-like substitutes in human experience that people "worship" or serve rather than God himself. Explain why you placed each item on your list.

_____

_____

_____

_____

_____

_____

_____

CHAPTER 4 >>

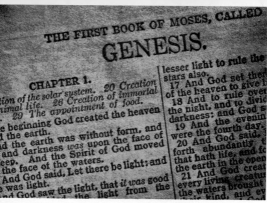

4

COMMUNICATION: A BIBLICALLY REDEMPTIVE ACCOUNT

OVERVIEW

A redemptive communicator is someone who views and practices communication in the light of what God discloses to us about it through His special and common grace.

❯❯A CLOSER LOOK

Unlike autonomous worldviews, the Biblically Christian worldview is a set of beliefs about human origin, nature, purpose, destiny, and values that people hold primarily in response to what God has revealed to be true, regardless of whether this revelation satisfies rationalistic, empirical, pragmatic, or utilitarian truth standards. Truth, the Biblically informed theist understands, is not a biochemical illusion or a social construction, but that which actually is the case, regardless of how it is perceived. As such, it is something to be discovered and to which people are accountable, regardless of whether they choose to believe it exists. The law of gravity, for example, is as true for the lunatic who tries to fly off a cliff as it is for the common person who carefully descends a stairway. Laws of ethics, too, are as true for those who deny or ignore them as they are for those who recognize and respect them. Physical laws like gravity are laws not because we recognize them, but because they are divinely fixed projections of God's creativity. Ethical laws are laws not because we see or believe them, but because they are divinely fixed projections of God's perfect character. Regardless of whether we like it, all people are accountable to the physical and ethical laws that God has instituted. Those who deny or disregard them must endure the consequences of doing so.

This realistic outlook frames the way Christians answer the questions that distinguish worldview systems from each other. Who are we? Where did we come from, why are we here, and where are we going? What relevance, if any, do the answers to these questions have for the way we live or should be living our lives now? What is right and what is wrong, and what makes it right or wrong? What should we desire and not desire in life, and why?

The Biblically Christian answer to these questions, not surprisingly, derives primarily from what God—the all-knowing, purposeful, truthful, and immutable source and sustainer of the universe and of human life—discloses through Biblical revelation. Christian theists recognize that God's Word, the Bible, is perfectly authoritative in anything that it addresses and that it rightly frames our quests to understand the universe and our place in it. Because its Author's knowledge and character are perfect and constant, His Word's truth claims are received as *fixed* (they do not change), *uniform* (they consist with each other), and *universal* in their sweep (they are true for all people at all times, even for people who deny or ignore them).

❯❯THE BIBLICALLY CHRISTIAN WORLDVIEW

Accordingly, as worldview scholar James Sire observes, Biblically Christian thinking recognizes the following revealed truths as foundational to our quests to make sense of anything, including human communication:

- God is infinite and personal, triune, transcendent and immanent, omniscient, sovereign and good.

- God created the cosmos *ex nihilo* to operate with a uniformity of cause and effect in an open system.

- Human beings are created in the image of God and thus possess personality, self-transcendence, intelligence, morality, gregariousness, and creativity.

Why did God place us here?

What is His purpose for humanity as a whole? What is His purpose for your life and for mine? What must you or I do in order to realize this purpose, and what are the implications of this for our communication practices?

- Human beings can know both the world around them and God Himself because God has built into them the capacity to do so and because He takes an active role in communicating with them.

- Human beings were created good, but through the Fall the image of God became defaced, though not so ruined as not to be capable of restoration; through the work of Christ, God redeemed humanity and began the process of restoring people to goodness, though some choose to reject that redemption.

- For each person death is either the gate to life with God and His people or the gate to eternal separation from the only thing that will ultimately fulfill human aspirations.

- Ethics is transcendent and is based on the character of God as good (holy and loving).

- History is linear, a meaningful sequence of events leading to the fulfillment of God's purposes for humanity.[1]

The last of these premises raises a series of interrelated questions that we must address in order to understand why Biblically Christian thinking regards communication to be significant. Why did God place us here? What is His purpose for humanity as a whole? What is His purpose for your life and for mine? What must you or I do in order to realize this purpose, and what are the implications of this for our communication practices?

In order to appreciate the Biblically Christian answer to these questions, one must understand the human drama for what it fundamentally is—the true story about our Creator, despite our rejection of Him and the corruption that resulted from it, graciously giving us a second chance to have the purposeful lives for which He originally created us. Detailed accounts of this Biblical story emerge from many creeds and catechisms that Christians have crafted over the centuries in their attempts to express this story accurately yet concisely. Rather than reciting one of these creeds at this point (see Appendix 1 for several noteworthy examples of these), I proceed in the following pages to summarize the Biblical drama in my own words, albeit with plenty of Biblical proof texts, in a way that sets the stage for our subsequent focus on how communication plays a part in this story.

© 2012 by Lentolo.
Used under license of Shutterstock, Inc.

Because of common grace, people can use communication to form personally meaningful connections with God and with each other and to do so in ways that manifest His true purpose for our lives.

❯❯ A BIBLICAL VIEW OF HUMAN PURPOSE

The physical universe and its components—living and nonliving, visible and nonvisible—were created (Gen. 1) by a personal God Who has intellect (Gen. 18:19; Ex. 3:7; Acts 15:18), emotion (Gen. 6:6; Psalm 103:8–13; John 3:16), and willpower (Gen. 3:15; Psalm 115:3; 2 Peter 3:9) for the purposes of displaying His glory (Psalms 8:1; 19:1 and Isa. 40:5), and inspiring the reverence that is rightly His alone (Isa. 43:7; Rev. 4:11). He set the physical world into motion and enables it to continue operating as it does (Neh. 9:6; Col. 1:17; Heb. 1:3).

Humans have intelligence, emotions, and freedom to choose what is right because God created us after His own likeness (Gen. 1:26, 27; Gen. 9:6; James 3:9). Although He disclosed His moral will to the first persons intellectually (Gen. 2:16, 17) and intuitively (Gen.3:8–11; Rom. 1:20), God granted them the freedom to decide whether they would comply with this perfect will. The first humans, in history's original expression of human autonomy, corrupted themselves by choosing not to comply (Gen. 3:6). Their sinful act polluted the course of human history. It alienated humans from their Maker and sentenced them to both physical death (Gen. 3:19; Rom. 5:12; 1 Cor. 15:22) and a spiritual death that would forever separate them from the One whose presence they were created to enjoy (Rom. 5:21; Eph. 2:1–5). Their sin's lethal effects corrupted not just the first humans, but every person, since everyone inherited the first humans' sinful nature (Job 14:1–4; Rom. 2:12–14) and its consequences (John 3:18, 36; Rom. 6:23; 1 Cor. 15:22). Sin estranged people not only from God, but also from each other by generating such relational cancers as greed, hatred, envy, murder, quarreling, deception, malicious behavior, gossip, and backstabbing (Rom. 1:29–30). Sin also afflicted the earth's environment with death and corrosion (Gen. 3:17–19; Isa. 24:3–6; 19–20 and Rom. 8:19–22).

Despite humanity's self-inflicted state of spiritual brokenness, God extends certain undeserved graces to people. Although all people are thus corrupted (Rom. 3:23) and deserve death because of it (Rom. 6:23), God extends *special grace* by offering humans a remedy for their spiritual alienation from Him. He made this possible by taking human form as Jesus Christ (John 10:30; 14:10; Phil. 2:5–8), Who was sinless (2 Cor. 5:21; Heb. 4:15; 1 Peter 2:22) and capable, therefore, of paying the penalty for human sinfulness that justice requires. Jesus paid this penalty through His death on the cross and thereby restored for humanity the hope of renewed spiritual life and of restored communion with God (Rom. 3:25, 26; 5:19). Though His redemptive work was sufficient for every human in history (John 3:16; Gal. 4:4, 5; 1 Tim. 4:10; 1 John 2:2), it ultimately benefits only those who by faith acknowledge His Lordship (Acts 16:31; Rom. 10:9) and submit to it repentantly (Acts 3:19;17:30, 31; Luke 13:2–5) before they die physically (Heb. 9:27; Luke 16:19–26).

Whereas God's special grace benefits only those who turn to Him in this manner, His common grace benefits believers and unbelievers alike. The term *common grace* denotes God's undeserved act of giving humans immeasurable blessings that they, because of their corruption, have no right to expect from Him. The most obvious example of this is the fact that God permits people, despite their sinfulness, to live physically for a while rather than experiencing the immediate death that they deserve. He also allows them to notice, explore, understand, and enjoy many life experiences in ways they could not appreciate were it not for His merciful restraint.

Human communication is possible because of common grace. Despite our sinfulness, people remain capable of receiving and making sense of communicative messages that God discloses through nature, through conscience, and especially through His Word. We

"There is no thumb-width of the entire domain of our human life of which the Christ, the Sovereign over everything, does not proclaim, 'It is mine!'"

–Abraham Kuyper

also can receive and make sense of messages from other people. Humans also remain capable of forming attitudes, values, feelings, and beliefs, encoding them in meaningful ways, and sending them to recipients who likewise remain capable of receiving the messages, deciphering them, and understanding their meanings. Because of common grace, people can use communication to form personally meaningful connections with God and with each other and to do so in ways that manifest His true purpose for our lives.

Anything true, honorable, right, pure, lovely, or admirable that humans experience is an expression of God's grace (Col. 4:8). Because He is gracious, our minds, although corrupted, are capable of conceptualizing God, self, sin, and the message of redemption that He offers us through Christ. Because God is gracious, our hearts, although darkened, can be stirred by His Spirit and freely choose to receive His Gospel. Because He is gracious, we can be spiritually redeemed and have restored communion with Him. Because God is gracious, spiritually redeemed people can relate to Him, to other people, and to the world as a whole in the God-centered manner His perfect standard requires, as He intended when He first made us. Indeed, the apostle Paul urges this in his epistle to the Colossians:

> Don't let anyone capture you with empty philosophies and high-sounding nonsense that come from human thinking and from the spiritual powers of this world, rather than from Christ. For in Christ lives all the fullness of God in a human body. So you also are complete through your union with Christ, who is the head over every ruler and authority. (Col. 2:8–10)

This, in a nutshell, is the Biblically Christian calling for human lives—to acknowledge that we are helplessly corrupted with autonomy and to find the only possible deliverance from this self-serving pit by repentantly surrendering to our Deliverer's rightful authority over every aspect of our being. True surrender to God's absolute authority is all-encompassing in its sweep. It recognizes, as the Dutch statesman Abraham Kuyper once put it, that "There is no thumb-width of the entire domain of our human life of which the Christ, the Sovereign over everything, does not proclaim, 'It is mine!'"[2] When we yield to this realization, God enables us to express His grace to others "in the full and vigorous prosecution of our life." The surrendered person understands that authentic God-centeredness is to permeate and to give color to "our feeling, our perception, our sensations, our thinking, our imagining, our willing, our acting, our speaking" and that it must "not stand as a foreign factor in our life, but must be the passion that breathes throughout our whole existence."[3]

How then does the surrendered person who aspires to love God in this way view communication's significance? Why should he or she value human interaction? How does God-centeredness impact the way he or she tries to make sense of human communicative behavior? How does it impact his or her own communicative practices? As the next chapter explains, the surrendered person realizes that God values communication because He created it for a purpose. Indeed, communication is the channel through which people can connect with Him and with each other in ways that mirror His original intent for us. Through communication we can promote many of the things He values in this world. God discloses this to us through Scripture—itself a communicative text through which He reveals foundational truths apart from which we can make little significant sense of ourselves.

Let us pause for a moment to contemplate what this means in daily life. First, Biblical precepts frame the way a surrendered person makes sense of communication—the way it works, the way people use it, the way it affects people, and so forth. This is not to say that these principles alone define the surrendered person's understanding of communication. Direct observation and reasoning, after all, are common graces through which God enables us to gain knowledge. Without these faculties, we could make little sense of anything, including what God discloses to us through Scripture. We must remember that observation and reasoning, although incapable by themselves of answering such overarching questions as where we came from and why we are here, are nonetheless common graces through which we can gather and interpret reliable information about the world and ourselves—information that becomes all the more meaningful when viewed in the light of what God reveals about who we are. Observation and reasoning may tell me that a shared longing for crisis resolution is what motivates people to listen to fairy tales or to watch movies, but Scripture tells me why people have such a longing for resolution in the first place (see Rom. 1:18–20). In this manner God's Word serves to enrich the surrendered person's understanding of what we otherwise merely observe in human communication.

The fact that God enables surrendered people, through Scripture, observation, and reasoning, to make sense of communication does not mean they always will arrive at the same conclusions about it. Only God sees anything perfectly, according to His Word. Although Scripture functions as a corrective lens that can help people make better sense of things, all people continue to struggle against our corruption's lingering effects. As the apostle Paul stated this, "Now we see things imperfectly as in a poor mirror, but then we will see everything with perfect clarity. All that I know now is partial and incomplete, but then I will know everything completely, just as God knows me now" (1 Cor. 13:12).

Biblical precepts affect not only the way the surrendered person makes sense of communication, but also the way he or she practices it. Such a person, for example, speaks truthfully yet lovingly (Eph. 4:15), graciously and attractively (Col. 4:6), deliberately (Prov. 10:19), and in a thankful, uplifting manner that promotes healing rather than harm (Prov. 12:18; Eph. 4:29; 5:4). He or she refrains from sending messages that are angry, bad, abusive, obscene, filthy, foolish, or cruel (Eph. 5:4; Col. 3:8). Such a person communicates in a way that promotes what God values in the world, whether justice for the wrongly oppressed (Isa. 1:16–17) or the redemption of spiritually lost human souls (Matt. 28:18–20), among other possibilities.

> We must remember that observation and reasoning, although incapable by themselves of answering such overarching questions as where we came from and why we are here, are nonetheless common graces through which we can gather and interpret reliable information about the world and ourselves.

Now that we understand in a basic way the distinguishing features of a Biblically Christian worldview, we turn our attention in this book's remaining chapters to a more detailed consideration of what it means to do anything in a genuinely Christian way. What does it mean to be authentically Christian in one's study and in one's practice of communication? How does someone make sense of a communicative text in an authentically Christian way? What does it mean to communicate in a way that promotes something God values? In order to answer these questions, we must first consider genuine love for God as the motive without which our attempts to understand anything in a Biblically Christian way fall short of their intended mark.

 ## QUESTIONS FOR ANALYSIS

- Review this chapter's definition of God's common grace. Then list five to seven specific examples of God-honoring common graces—not just the ones identified in the chapter—that God permits humans in general to experience despite the debilitating effects of our self-inflicted corruption. After listing these examples, be sure to explain why you believe each qualifies as a common grace in this chapter's sense of the term.

- A creed is a statement that encapsulates the essential elements of a specific belief system. See the Apostles' Creed and the Nicene Creed in Appendix 1, toward the end of this book. Analyze their individual statements. Then compose a 200- to 350-word response in which you explain how the wording in these historic statements of Christian faith highlights God's interest in communicating (connecting or reconnecting) with humans.

- Read the Laussanne Covenant, also in Appendix 1. Then write a 200- to 300-word response in which you explain how the wording in this document highlights God's interest in human-to-human communications. In which ways, if any, does God call people to communicate with each other?

- Read Dr. Arne H. Fjeldstad's article "God the Communicator" in Appendix 2. Then compose a 200- to 350-word response in which you answer the following: (a) According to the article, in which senses can God be considered a communicator? (b) According to the article, why should people—Christians in particular—care about communication?

ENDNOTES

[1] James Sire, *The Universe Next Door: A Basic Worldview Catalog* (Downers Grove: Intervarsity Press, 2009).

[2] Craig G. Bartholomew and Michael W. Goheen, *The Drama of Scripture: Finding Our Place in the Biblical Story* (Grand Rapids: Baker Academic, 2004), 220.

[3] Abraham Kuyper, *Lectures on Calvinism* (Grand Rapids: William B. Eerdmans, 1931), 5.

BIBLIOGRAPHY

Christianity Today, Inc., and Carl F. H. Henry. *Basic Christian Doctrines*. New York: Holt, Rinehart and Winston, 1962.

Calvin, Jean. *Institutes of the Christian Religion*. Philadelphia, PA: Westminster Press, 1960.

Erickson, Millard J. *Christian Theology*. Grand Rapids, MI: Baker Book House, 1983.

Erickson, Millard J., and L. Arnold Hustad. *Introducing Christian Doctrine*. Grand Rapids, MI: Baker Academic, 2001.

Geisler, Norman L. *Systematic Theology*. Minneapolis, MN: Bethany House, 2002.

Geisler, Norman L., and William E. Nix. *A General Introduction to the Bible*. Chicago: Moody Press, 1968.

Grudem, Wayne A. *Systematic Theology: An Introduction to Biblical Doctrine*. Leicester, England: Inter-Varsity Press, 1994.

Hodge, Charles. *Systematic Theology*. New York: C. Scribner, 1887.

Lewis, C. S. *Mere Christianity: A Revised and Amplified Edition, with a New Introduction, of the Three Books, Broadcast Talks, Christian Behaviour, and Beyond Personality*. San Francisco, CA: HarperSanFrancisco, 2001.

Packer, J. I. *Concise Theology: A Guide to Historic Christian Beliefs*. Wheaton, IL: Tyndale House, 1993.

Packer, J. I. *Knowing God*. Downers Grove, IL: InterVarsity Press, 1973.

Plantinga, Cornelius. *Engaging God's World: A Christian Vision of Faith, Learning, and Living*. Grand Rapids, MI: W. B. Eerdmans, 2002.

Stott, John R. W. *Basic Christianity*. Grand Rapids, MI: W. B. Eerdmans, 1971.

HONOR STATEMENT: I, the undersigned student, hereby declare before God, before the school, and before the professor that I have read Chapter 4 in its entirety, that I have completed the following exercise with help from no other sources, and that I neither have shared nor will share this work with anyone.

Signature: _____ Date: _____

SHORT ESSAYS

1. Review this chapter's definition of God's common grace. Then list five to seven specific examples of God-honoring common graces—not just the ones identified in the chapter—that God permits humans in general to experience despite the debilitating effects of our self-inflicted corruption. After listing these examples, be sure to explain why you believe each of these qualifies as a common grace in this chapter's sense of the term.

_____

_____

_____

_____

_____

_____

_____

_____

_____

_____

_____

_____

_____

_____

_____

_____

2. A creed is a statement that encapsulates the essential elements of a specific belief system. See the Apostles' Creed and the Nicene Creed in Appendix 1, toward the end of this book. Analyze their individual statements. Then compose a 200- to 350-word response in which you explain how the wording in these historic statements of Christian faith highlights God's interest in communicating (connecting or reconnecting) with humans.

_____

_____

_____

_____

_____

_____

_____

_____

_____

_____

_____

_____

_____

_____

_____

_____

_____

_____

_____

3. Read the Lausanne Covenant, also in Appendix 1. Then write a 200- to 300-word response in which you explain how the wording in this document highlights God's interest in human-to-human communications. In which ways, if any, does God call people to communicate with each other?

_____

_____

_____

_____

_____

_____

_____

_____

_____

_____

_____

_____

_____

_____

_____

_____

_____

_____

_____

_____

_____

4. Read Dr. Arne H. Fjeldstad's article "God the Communicator" in Appendix 2. Then compose a 200- to 350-word response in which you answer the following:

(a) According to the article, in which senses can God be considered a communicator? (b) According to the article, why should people—Christians in particular—care about communication?

_____

_____

_____

_____

_____

_____

_____

_____

_____

_____

_____

_____

_____

_____

_____

_____

_____

_____

_____

_____

_____

_____

© 2012 by Apostrophe. Used under license of Shutterstock, Inc.

CHAPTER 5 >>

5 COMMUNICATION: A BIBLICALLY REDEMPTIVE APPROACH

OVERVIEW

A redemptive communicator is someone who views communication through the lens of what God says about it and who, as an expression of authentic love for Him, interprets and crafts communicative texts in the light of what He values.

⟩A CLOSER LOOK

What makes communication valuable or significant? A person's worldview impacts the way he or she answers this question. As Chapter 3 indicated, a utilitarian determines whether a particular communication is significant by evaluating whether it promotes something that is in society's best interest. A pragmatist considers whether the particular communication is something personally meaningful for the individual communicator, regardless of how it affects other people. Unlike these humanly devised approaches to answering the question, the Biblically Christian standard considers whether the particular communication consists with God's timelessly, changelessly loving character as His Word defines it. The apostle John could not have stated it more clearly: "God is love . . ." (1 John 4:26).

God's love for us is a dominant theme throughout Scripture. Because He loves us, He created us, even though He knew we would corrupt ourselves. Because He loves us, He assumed earthly form as Jesus Christ and paid a costly price to remedy our spiritual corruption and to make possible renewed communion with Him. As the apostle John affirms, "God showed how much he loved us by sending his one and only Son into the world so that we might have eternal life through him. This is real love—not that we loved God, but that he loved us and sent his Son as a sacrifice to take away our sins" (1 John 4:9–10). Other Biblical passages affirm the same principle (John 3:16; Rom. 5:8).

The person who loves God yearns to please Him and expresses this by living in a way that honors His timeless precepts (John 14:15).

When we repentantly submit to His leadership and receive His liberation from our corruption, He enables us through His Holy Spirit, despite the lingering effects of our corruption, to reflect His love to others as we interact, or communicate, with them. Indeed, "God has given us his Spirit as proof that we live in him and he in us" for "God is love and all who live in love live in God, and God lives in them" (1 John 4:13, 16). If we love our spiritual brothers and sisters as we should, it is only because God's love has enabled us to do so (v. 19). Additionally, a person who professes to love God but who hates a spiritual brother or sister is a liar (v. 20). When we love each other as we should, God's love is perfectly expressed through us (v. 11). This love, Jesus said, makes a powerful communicative statement to those around us: "Your love for one another will prove to the world that you are my disciples" (John 13:35).

The person who loves God yearns to please Him and expresses this by living in a way that honors His timeless precepts (John 14:15). Foremost among these guiding principles, Jesus said, are two that encapsulate all the rest: "'You must love the Lord your God with all your heart, all your soul, and all your mind.' This is the first and greatest commandment. A second is equally important: 'Love your neighbor as yourself.' The entire law and all the demands of the prophets are based on these two commandments" (Matt. 22: 37–40). To love God, then, one must love other people, for as the apostle Paul explains, "If you love your neighbor, you will fulfill the requirements of God's law. For the commandments say, 'You must not commit adultery. You must not murder. You must not steal. You must not covet.' These—and other such commandments—are summed up in this one commandment: 'Love your neighbor as yourself'" (Rom. 13:8–9).

Communication is significant to the Biblically Christian thinker, then, because it enables people, through divine revelation, to understand and to embrace their God-appointed purpose and to fulfill this purpose through expressions of authentic love for Him and for

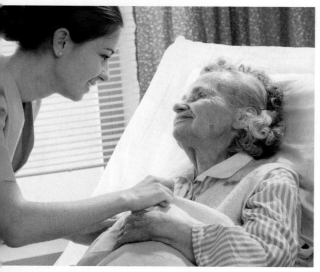

Communication is significant to the Biblically Christian thinker, then, because it enables people, through divine revelation, to understand and to embrace their God-appointed purpose and to fulfill this purpose through expressions of authentic love for Him and for each other.

each other. As important as this foundational concept is, it only raises another question that must be given extra emphasis in an instructional communication text like this one—how does authentically God-honoring love show itself in a person's communicational practices? Can someone express Godly love through the acts of receiving and decoding messages from others? Can he or she do so through the acts of encoding and sending messages to others? This book assumes that honoring God in these ways is possible. The question we must face, then, is a practical one—how can the study and practice of communication honor God? In the next two sections, we consider a couple of Biblically Christian responses to this question—redemptive criticism, which involves the receiving and decoding of messages, and redemptive communication, which involves the encoding and sending of messages.

❯ REDEMPTIVE CRITICISM

You may recall, from Chapter 1, that *redemptive criticism* is a term for the attempt to make sense of human communicative behavior and specific human communications in the light of divine revelation. This task involves an *expositional* and a *rhetorical* component. As previously noted, an expositor tries to explain why people share certain attitudes, values, beliefs, feelings, or behaviors. He or she does this by explaining mysteries like the widespread human longing to connect with God or something God-like. The redemptive expositor aims to show how this yearning gives shape to human communications and tries to explain why the longing exists and why it works as it does, in the light of what divine revelation says about it. As a rhetorical analyst, however, the redemptive critic also considers how people find redemption and what role, if any, communication plays in the process. The critic considers, too, how the redeemed life functions as a message to others and how it impacts or can impact other people.

As a redemptive critic, the God-lover is one with a passion for truth and truth telling who "speaks the truth in love" (Eph. 4:15) and who "rejoices whenever the truth wins out" (1 Cor. 13:8). As an expositor, this critic highlights "what is true, and honorable, and right, and pure, and lovely, and admirable" (Phil. 4:8) in his or her quests to describe things, including corrupted things, as they really are. When expositing human behaviors like communication, he or she goes beyond merely explaining how it works to emphasize its ultimate significance in the light of humanity's God-given purpose. With such an explanation as his or her goal, the critic recognizes and identifies God's common graces for what they are upon seeing them in a communicative text. Three such graces—humanity's widespread God-consciousness, purpose-consciousness, and ethical consciousness—present especially rich discussion points in the redemptive expositor's analysis.

▲ God-Consciousness

Writing more than a century ago, John Henry Newman eloquently observed that "God has so implicated Himself with [the universe], and taken it into His very bosom, by His presence in it, His providence over it, His impressions upon it, and His influences through it, that we cannot truly or fully contemplate it without in some main aspects contemplating Him."[1] This statement highlights the fact that, whatever else it may be, nature is a text through which God proclaims His existence and His divine qualities to all thinking people. The Old Testament affirms this communicational principle throughout the psalms, among other passages:

The heavens proclaim the glory of God.
  The skies display his craftsmanship.
Day after day they continue to speak;
  night after night they make him known.
They speak without a sound or word;
  their voice is never heard.
Yet their message has gone throughout the earth,
  and their words to all the world. (Psalm 19:1–4)

My wife and I recently came to appreciate this passage's depth during an escape to Virginia's Shenandoah Valley for our tenth anniversary celebration. As we sat alone one evening, on our secluded Bed & Breakfast's shadowed porch, we watched in speechless wonder as the sunset slowly cast its darkening amber glaze on the surrounding distant mountains. Far above us, one by one, twinkling stars announced their presence, piercing brilliantly through the descending blackness. As the wind lazily whispered its way through a field of nearby trees, a scattered chorus of crickets enriched our sense of the moment's magic with a symphony that lasted long into the night. I am reminded, during moments like these, of words from another psalm:

When I look at the night sky and see the work of your fingers—
  the moon and the stars you set in place—
what are mere mortals that you should think about them,
  human beings that you should care for them? (Psalm 8:3–4)

After raising these thoughts and others like them, the psalmist ends with a worshipful postscript that I have uttered many times while contemplating the wonders of God's world: "O Lord, our Lord, your majestic name fills the earth!" (Psalm 8:9).

The picture of nature as a common grace through which God expresses His existence and divine qualities to the world is not confined to the Old Testament. The apostle Paul affirms it throughout the New Testament, in statements he directs to both unbelievers (Acts 17:24) and believers (Rom. 1:18–32). God, through nature, has given all people reason to know of His existence, creativity, and power. Although this is so, His Word indicates that we are not inclined to seek after Him (Rom. 3:11). Still, as an expositor, the redemptive critic explains the human capacity to be awed by nature as a God-given clue to His existence and to the fact that the universe has a purpose.

The Redemptive Expositor: As an expositor, this critic highlights "what is true, and honorable, and right, and pure, and lovely, and admirable" (Phil. 4:8) in his or her quests to describe things, including corrupted things, as they really are.

▲Purpose-Consciousness

People seem always to be questing for something more than they already have—a something that perfectly satisfies their craving to live meaningful, purposeful lives. They thirst for a God-like something in their lives that can quell the inner longing for ultimate meaning that God, as a common grace, has placed in our hearts (Rom. 1:23–25). Because we are autonomously inclined, we often follow this urge down self-serving paths to earthly solutions that inevitably fall short. Among the God-like substitutes we pursue in our quest to quench this sense of soul-thirst are knowledge, wealth, power, fame, love, respect, or gratification through food, alcohol, drugs, sex, and other physically or psychologically pleasurable indulgences.

The Biblically redemptive critic understands that God is perfect, or holy (Psalms 18:30; 145:17 and 1 Peter 1:16), that He created people in His perfect image (Gen. 1:27), and that people, although they have corrupted this divine image through deliberate disobedience (Rom. 3:23; 5:12), remain vaguely aware of the fact that they exist for a purpose, even if they do not know what the purpose is or that it is God-given. Whatever else may motivate it, human behavior is driven fundamentally by a thirst to satisfy this God-given longing for significance. As Augustine of Hippo famously expressed this point, "O Lord, you have made us for yourself, and our heart is restless until it finds its rest in you."[2] Blaise Pascal echoed the same point, centuries later, in these words:

> What is it then that this desire and this inability proclaim to us, but that there was once in man a true happiness of which there now remains to him only the mark and empty trace, which he in vain tries to fill from all his surroundings, seeking from things absent the help he does not obtain in things present? But these are all inadequate, because the infinite abyss can only be filled by an infinite and immutable Object, that is to say, only by God Himself.[3]

To say the human yearning for purpose is foundational to our behavior is not to suggest that this is the only motive for human behavior. Abraham Maslow, a prominent twentieth-century psychologist, created a famous model—his Hierarchy of Needs—that, although limited by naturalistic assumptions, helpfully identifies other factors that motivate individuals to behave as they do. At the most basic level are physical needs, such as one's need for food, water, and air. If you cannot breathe, you likely will be motivated to behave in a way that gives you access to air. At the next level, people have safety needs, such as protection from physical forces, from disease, from other people, and so forth. When people buy insurance, lock their doors, or carry concealed weapons, their behavior is probably a response to their need for safety. Next, Maslow proposed, people have belongingness and love needs that motivate them to form and to maintain relationships. People also have esteem needs that may motivate them to buy expensive sports cars, to wear popular brands of clothes, or to take other steps that give them a sense of status or accomplishment. Finally, Maslow suggested, people have self-actualization needs—needs for personal growth and for realizing their potential—that may motivate them to do humanitarian work, to climb high mountains, and take other steps that give them a sense of personal fulfillment.[4]

The Polish anthropologist Bronislaw Malinowski proposed a similar model that identifies seven basic needs that motivate people, acting as groups more than as individuals, to conduct themselves as they do. The first of these, metabolism, denotes the human need for food, drink, and air. Reproduction references the human need for procreating. Bodily comforts is this model's term for the human need to protect people's bodies from distress or disrespect. People also have needs for safety, movement, growth, and health.[5] A person's behavior can be impacted by the drive to satisfy the needs of his or her family, community, culture, or other group in any of these areas.

The redemptive critic does not necessarily reject models like the ones Maslow and Malinowski proposed. To the contrary, these can actually be very useful tools for describing human behavior. If models like these are flawed, it is typically because they are short-sighted and omit from their analyses spiritual factors that influence human behavior. However, this does not discredit the fact that the models' other factors do actually influence human behavior. Because the redemptive critic's goal is to describe things as they truly are, including these factors in one's description of human communicative behavior may actually generate colorful details for his or her analyses.

Still, for an analysis of human behavior to be ultimately valuable, it must go beyond merely describing what direct observation tells us. It must also consider foundational questions about human origin and purpose and how this impacts the needs that seem to drive our behavior. If indeed the drives to physically survive, to belong, to self-actualize, and so on impact our behavior, as Maslow and Malinowski propose, why is this so? Why do people care whether they survive, belong, or realize their potential? As Chapter 3 explained, autonomous worldviews provide disappointing answers to questions like these—blind guesses that often wield dark implications and that insufficiently address more basic questions. For example, if physical survival, belonging, and self-fulfillment drive human behavior, as autonomous theorists commonly suggest, why do people—including people who seem to have it all—commit suicide? Why do people who apparently have everything sometimes choose to sacrifice everything, including their lives, their families, and their personal wants, for higher causes?

The Biblically redemptive critic understands that human behavior is driven by something deeper than what Maslow or Malinowski proposed. He or she knows, as Blaise Pascal put it, that "All men seek happiness. This is without exception. Whatever different means they employ, they all tend to this end. The cause of some going to war, and of others avoiding it, is the same desire in both, attended with different views. The will never takes the least step but to this object. This is the motive of every action of every man, even of those who hang themselves."[6]

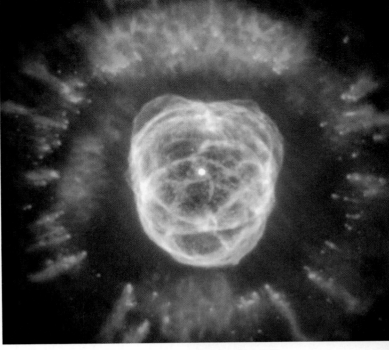

Eskimo Nebula, NASA
Courtesy of nasaimages.org

"God has so implicated Himself with [the universe], and taken it into His very bosom, by His presence in it, His providence over it, His impressions upon it, and His influences through it, that we cannot truly or fully contemplate it without in some main aspects contemplating Him."
–John Henry Newman

The Biblically Christian critic understands that the happiness for which people long is one that cannot be satisfied by anything in their surroundings, but only by the Infinite Someone by Whom and for Whose company they were created. C. S. Lewis explained the reasoning for supposing this in the following words:

> The Christian says, "Creatures are not born with desires unless satisfaction for those desires exists." A baby feels hunger: well, there is such a thing as food. A duckling wants to swim: well, there is such a thing as water. Men feel sexual desire: well, there is such a thing as sex. If I find in myself a desire which no experience in this world can satisfy, the most probable explanation is that I was made for another world. If none of my earthy pleasures satisfy it, that does not prove that the universe is a fraud. Probably earthly pleasures were never meant to satisfy it, but only to arouse it, to suggest the real thing. If that is so, I must take care, on the one hand, never to despise, or be unthankful for, these earthly blessings, and on the other, never to mistake them for the something else of which they are only a kind of copy, or echo, or mirage. I must keep alive in myself the desire for my true country, which I shall not find till after death; I must never let it get snowed under or turned aside; I must make it the main object of life to press on to that other country and help others to do the same.[7]

The last sentence in Lewis's observation succinctly states the redemptive critic's guiding vision. As an expression of authentic love for God and for others, he or she interprets everything—including the content of our communications—in the light of His revealed design and purpose for humanity. Whatever else may drive people to communicate, the redemptive critic sees in this motivation a God-initiated, God-sustained channel through which people can lovingly connect with Him and with each other, and thus realize the purpose for which He created them and for which they thirst.

▲Ethical Consciousness

God's common grace to humans shows not just in our God- and purpose-consciousnesses, but also in our humanity's innate general awareness that some things are right and that some things are wrong for people in general and not just for ourselves. Even the person who claims to believe that nothing is right or wrong for everyone, by making this very statement suggests that he or she does not really believe it, since the statement implies his or her belief that this view is the right one and that its alternatives are wrong. Such a person also betrays his or her stated view when he or she objects, on moral grounds, to thieves, reckless drivers, or anyone else who they feel has done them wrong.

God's Word discloses that humanity's ethical consciousness is divinely originated. As the apostle Paul observed, "Even Gentiles, who do not have God's written law, show that they know his law when they instinctively obey it, even without having heard it. They demonstrate that God's law is written in their hearts, for their own conscience and thoughts either accuse them or tell them they are doing right" (Rom. 2:14–15). Although their specific definitions of what is right or wrong may differ, people have a God-given awareness that a moral "oughtness" exists in the universe—that things should be a certain

"O Lord, you have made us for yourself, and our heart is restless until it finds its rest in you."
–Augustine of Hippo

way—and that we must uphold or promote it. This moral sense shows itself, among other ways, in the stories we hear and tell throughout our lifetimes. Whether expressed via fairy tales, personal anecdotes, song lyrics, stage productions, or movie scripts, our stories fixate on finding just solutions for problematic situations. The evil empire must be defeated. The underdog must win. The criminal must be caught and punished. When our stories lack what we recognize as just outcomes (outcomes that consist with our God-given sense of moral oughtness), we criticize them, sometimes passionately, for lacking the result that our Creator predisposes our hearts to crave.

This craving for justice, for the restoration of things as they were designed to be, makes a profound statement about our human nature. Why do we sense that something is wrong in the world or in a story? Why do we so strongly desire solutions for these crises? The redemptive critic recognizes this impulse as a statement about our divine design and purpose. J. R. R. Tolkien, the literary scholar and fantasy author, highlighted this idea throughout his work:

> We have come from God, and inevitably the myths woven by us, though they contain error, will also reflect a splintered fragment of the true light, the eternal truth that is with God. Indeed only by myth-making, only by becoming "sub-creator" and inventing stories, can Man aspire to the state of perfection that he knew before the Fall. Our myths may be misguided, but they steer however shakily towards the true harbour, while materialistic "progress" leads only to a yawning abyss and the Iron Crown of the power of evil.[8]

Stated another way, Tolkien's idea is simply this: the stories that we live, that we create, and that we communicate to others, although skewed by our corruption, manifest our awarenesses that God has created things to be a certain way and that at least some things in creation fall short of this ideal. Although polluted by our corruption, their subtexts consistently exhibit their creators' God-given longing for something better than the brokenness that defines our lives and our stories' plots. The redemptive critic shows, through exposition, how our craving for perfect solutions to problems exists because God, as an expression of His common grace, has placed within our hearts a yearning for redemption, for a restoration of righteousness that He alone can deliver. Were it not for His common grace, our yearning for liberation would be something far less than the clue to our true purpose that God designed it to be.

One must note that, although humanity's moral consciousness bears its Creator's imprint, it is not a perfect expression of God's moral will. Humanity's corruption has smudged this thumbprint and rendered it only generally reliable as evidence of our divine design and purpose. Our corruption shows, among other ways, in our failure to live up to the very standards that we know to be correct. Rather than relating to God and to each other in the selfless way He prescribes, humans are often self-centered and self-serving and inclined to suppress what moral sense He has given us.

The redemptive critic acknowledges this but puts it in a Biblical perspective. He or she recognizes our failure to live as we know we should as evidence that God has "abandoned [people] to their foolish thinking and let them do things that should never be done" (Rom. 1:28). The critic explains that our lives, consequently, have become "full of every kind of wickedness, sin, greed, hate, envy, murder, quarreling, deception, malicious behavior, and gossip." Apart from God's redemptive grace, we are "backstabbers, haters of God, insolent, proud, and boastful." We even "invent new ways of sinning, and . . . disobey [our] parents." Moreover, we "refuse to understand, break [our] promises, are heartless, and have no mercy." Even though we realize "God's justice requires that those who do these things deserve to die . . . [we] do them anyway. Worse yet, [we] encourage others to do them, too" (Rom. 1: 28–32).

The redemptive critic explains these vices as evidence of the corruption from which we long to escape. He or she explains that because human conscience is flawed as a guide for determining right and wrong, God has given the corrective lens of Scripture partly to provide the reliable definition about moral matters that people otherwise lack. "How can a young person stay pure?" the psalmist asks. "By obeying your word . . . I have hidden your word in my heart that I might not sin against you" (Psalm 119: 9, 11). The apostle Paul makes the same point about the ethical function of God's Word: "All Scripture is inspired by God and is useful to teach us what is true and to make us realize what is wrong in our lives. It corrects us when we are wrong and teaches us to do what is right. God uses it to prepare and equip his people to do every good work" (2 Tim. 3:16–17).

❯ REDEMPTIVE COMMUNICATION

How can one honor God in his or her practice of communication? The preceding section yields a partial answer to this question by showing how one can honor Him through the explanations he or she infers from the communicative behaviors he or she observes. The section that follows considers what it means to honor God when we behave as senders of messages toward others, whether we transmit the information verbally, nonverbally, or both. The primary focus here is on our communicative behavior toward people, rather than toward God. Suffice it to say, as we already have established, that one's expression of authentic love for God will flow through oneself to touch other people.

A person functions as a redemptive communicator when his or her verbal and/or nonverbal behavior manifests God's love to others in a way that promotes what God values in the world. Our words and actions indicate or communicate whether we love Him in this way. Jesus made this point as a rebuke to religious leaders who did the "right" things without being motivated to do so by an authentic love for God: "Whatever is in your heart determines what you say. A good person produces good things from the treasury of a good heart, and an evil person produces evil things from the treasury of an evil heart. And I tell you this, you must give an account on judgment day for every idle word you speak. The words you say will either acquit you or condemn you" (Matt. 12:34–37).

God values communication that manifests an authentic love for Him. Such a love shows itself not only through a God-centeredness in our stated attitudes, values, and/or beliefs, but also through our actions—whether actions toward God, toward others, toward ourselves, or toward the world. The prophet Micah emphasized this all-encompassing

© 2012 by courtyardpix.
Used under license of Shutterstock, Inc.

understanding of authentic faith in his oft quoted synopsis of life's purpose: "This is what he requires of you: to do what is right, to love mercy, and to walk humbly with your God" (Micah 6:8). The apostle Paul underscored the same idea in his instructive words to the Colossians: "Let the message about Christ, in all its richness, fill your lives. Teach and counsel each other with all the wisdom he gives. Sing psalms and hymns and spiritual songs to God with thankful hearts. And whatever you do or say, do it as a representative of the Lord Jesus, giving thanks through him to God the Father" (Col. 3:16–17).

Although God may use a person's wrongly motivated communications to promote His redemptive purposes, one's use of words alone is worthless. Jesus, quoting the prophet Isaiah, questioned people who "say they are mine" and who "honor me with their lips," but whose "hearts are far from me. And their worship of me is nothing but man-made rules learned by rote" (Isa. 29:13; cf. Matt. 15:7–9 and Mark 7:5–7). Indeed, without the love of God as its motive, speaking the right words or performing the right actions has little value in God's eyes for, as the apostle Paul observed, "if I gave everything I have to the poor and even sacrificed my body, I could boast about it; but if I didn't love others, I would have gained nothing" (1 Cor. 13:3).

The redemptive communicator, then, is someone who expresses an authentic love for God in visible ways. Yet, as vital an element as motivation is, redemptive communication involves something more than this. To function redemptively, a communicator's expressions must also promote something God values in this world. Because God is timeless and changeless, the things He values are constant. They do not change. We learn much about these eternal values through what He discloses about Himself in His Word, the Bible. Among the many things that He values and that the redemptive communicator, as an expression of authentic love for God, promotes through his or her communications are the following, each of which appears with specific Biblical references that disclose it:

- **God values His rightful authority over all things, including our bodies** (Ezek. 18:4; 1 Cor. 3:16–19; 6:18–20; 2 Cor. 6:16–17), **our minds** (Isa. 55:7; Rom. 12:2; 2 Cor. 10:5), **and His creation** (Ex. 9:29; 19:5; Deut. 10:14; 1 Chron. 29:11–12; Job 41:11; Pss. 24:1; 50:10–12; 89:11; 95:4–5; 1 Cor. 10:26).

- **God values truth as that which actually is the case** (Num. 23:19; Pss. 31:5; 33:4; 89:14; 111:7; 119:160; Isa. 65:16; Micah 7:20; John 8:31–32; 14:6; 17:17; 2 Cor. 4:2; 2 Thes. 2:10–12; 2 Tim. 2:15; Titus 1:2; 3 John 4; Rev. 15:3). *Truth sometimes can be legitimately applied in a variety of ways* (Rom. 14; 1 Cor. 8; Gal. 5:13–14).

- **God values His exclusive right to our worship** (Ex. 20:3–5; 34:14; Deut. 4:24; 5:9; 6:14–15; Isa. 43:21; 44:22–23; 45:5–6; Jer. 13:11; Matt. 21:12–13; 1 Pet. 2:9; Rev. 4:8–11; 15:3–4).

Even the person who claims to believe that nothing is right or wrong for everyone, by making this very statement, suggests that he or she does not really believe it, since the statement implies his or her belief that this view is the right one and that its alternatives are wrong.

© 2012 by SubbotinaAnna.
Used under license of Shutterstock, Inc.

"Even Gentiles, who do not have God's written law, show that they know his law when they instinctively obey it, even without having heard it. They demonstrate that God's law is written in their hearts, for their own conscience and thoughts either accuse them or tell them they are doing right" –Rom. 2:14-15

• **God values human life** (Gen. 1:26–27; 9:6; Ex. 20:13; 21:12, 22–25; Deut. 5:17; Prov. 6:16–17; 24:11–12; Amos 1:13; Acts 17:28–29; Rom. 1:29; James 2:11). *This includes preborn human life* (Isa. 44:24; 49:1–5; Jer. 1:5; Gal. 1:15–16), *older human life* (Lev. 19:32; Job 12:12; Prov. 16:31; Isa. 46:3–4), *and impaired human life* (Matt. 14:14; 15:30; 20:34; Luke 4:18; 7:22).

• **God values animal life, albeit less than he values human life** (Gen. 1:28, 31; 9:8–13; Ex. 23:5 and 12; Deut. 5:14; 25:4, Job 12:10; Pss. 36:6; 37:5–6, 28; 104:10–14 and 24–25; Prov. 12:10; 27:23; Jer. 12:4; Matt. 6:26; 10:29–31; Luke 12:6; 1 Cor. 3:16–17).

• **God values the earth** (Gen. 1:31; Deut. 10:14; Job 26:7–9, 11–14; Pss. 24:1; 89:11; 145:9; 1 Cor. 10:26; Col. 1:16–17). *He values humans' care of the earth* (Gen. 2:15; Ex. 23:10–11; Lev. 18:26–28; 25:2–5; Deut. 20:19).

• **God values justice** (Deut. 10:17–18; 2 Chron. 19:7; Pss. 9:8; 10:17–18; 11:7; 36:6; 45:6–7; 67:4; 75:2; 89:14; 97:2; 98:9; Prov. 21:3; Isa. 61:8–11; Amos 5:14–15, and 24; Micah 6:8; Matt. 5:6; Acts 17:31; 2 Thes. 1:5–6).

• **God values mercy** (Num. 14:18; Neh. 9:27; Job 20:19–20; Pss. 106:1; 107:1; 136:1–26; Isa. 54:7; Lam. 3:32; Amos 8:4–7; Micah 7:18; Matt. 5:7; 9:13; 12:7; 18:23–35; Eph. 2:4–7; 4:32; James 2:13; 1 Pet. 1:3).

• **God values humility** (Pss. 18:27; 147:6; Prov. 3:34; 27:2; Isa. 5:21; 66:2; Micah 6:8; Matt. 18:3–4; Luke 1:52; 14:7–11; 18:9–14; 22:24–27; Mark 9:35; Rom. 12:3; 1 Cor. 3:19; 13:4; 2 Cor. 11:30; 12:6–10; Gal. 6:14; Eph. 4:2; Phil. 2:1–11; Col. 3:12; James 4:6; 1 Pet. 5:2–6). *This humility shows, among other ways, when a person limits his or her freedom out of respect for another person's sensitivities* (Rom. 14; 1 Cor. 8; Gal. 5:13–14).

• **God values peace** (Ps. 34:14; 133; Isa. 2:1–5; 26:3; 55:12; Matt. 5:9; Rom. 12:18; 14:17–19; 2 Cor. 13:11; Gal. 5:22; Phil. 2:1–2; 2 Tim. 2:22; James 3:16–18), *although there are times when He authorizes war* (Deut. 20:1–4; Josh. 8:1–29; 2 Chron. 20:13–21; Ps. 144:1; Eccl. 3:8). *He loathes interpersonal discord* (Prov. 6:19; 18:6; 22:10; James 3:14–18).

• **God values honesty** (Lev. 19:13, 35–37; Deut. 25:13–16; Prov. 11:1–5; Micah 6:10–13; 7:2–4; Luke 3:12–14; 1 Cor. 6:10; Eph. 4:28; 1 Thes. 4:6).

• **God values self-control** (Prov. 16:32; 25:28; 1 Cor. 6:10; 9:24–27; Gal. 5:23; 1 Thes. 4:4–5; 1 Tim. 3:2, 11; Titus 1:8–9; 2:2, 12; 1 Pet. 1:13; 2 Pet. 1:6).

• **God values family** (Psalms 127 and 128; Prov. 20:6–7; 31:10). *He values reproduction* (Gen. 1:22–28; 9:1–7; Deut. 7:12–14; Ps. 113:7–9; 127:3–5).

• **God values monogamous, heterosexual marriage** (Gen. 2:22–24; Deut. 24:5; Prov. 5:18–19; 18:22; 19:14; Matt. 19:4–6; Mark 10:6–9; 1 Cor. 7:1–16; Eph. 5:22–23; Col. 3:18–19; Heb. 13:4). *He loathes divorce* (Matt. 5:32).

- **God values sexual purity. He loathes sexual activity that is premarital** (Matt. 19:19; Rom. 1:29; 1 Cor. 7:1–5), *adulterous* (Ex. 20:14; Matt. 5:18; Heb. 13:4), *homosexual* (Lev. 18:22; 20:13; Rom. 1:23–28; 1 Tim. 1:10), *or perverse* (Lev. 18:23; Rom. 1:23–28; 1 Cor. 5:1–8; 6:9–10; Gal. 5:19–21; Eph. 5:3; 1 Thes. 4:3–5; Jude 7). *This includes lust* (Job 31:1–12; Matt. 5:28–29; 1 Cor. 7:9; Col 3:5; 2 Tim. 2:22; 2 Pet. 2:14–16).

- **God values the church as an equipper of believers for doing God's redemptive work in the world** (Matt. 16:18; 1 Cor. 10:31–33; 12:12–26; Eph. 1:22–23; 2:19–22; 4:4–16; 5:25–32; Col. 1:17–20; 3:14–16; 1 Pet. 2:9–10).

- **God values government as an executor of His righteousness** (1 Kings 10:9; 2 Chron. 9:8; Amos 5:15–24; Rom. 13:1–7; 1 Tim. 2:1–4; Titus 3:1; 1 Pet. 2:13–17). *He values His authority over government* (Col. 2:10, 15; Eph. 1:20–22).

- **God values personal property rights** (Ex. 20:15; Lev. 6:1–7; 19:11–13; Deut. 5:19; Judg. 11:15; Prov. 22:28; Eccl. 5:19; Amos 3:10; Zech. 5:3–4; Matt. 19:18; 25:14–30; 1 Cor. 6:10; Eph. 4:28).

- **God values our faith in Him** (Gen. 15:6; Hab. 2:2; Matt. 17:20; 23:23; Mark 11:22; Luke 18:17; Rom. 1:17; 3:27–5:2; 10:6–10; Gal. 3:6–23; Heb. 11; James 2).

- **God values our love for others** (John 13:34–35; 15:12–17; Rom. 12:10; 16:16; 1 Cor. 16:20; 2 Cor. 13:11–12; Gal. 5:13–15; Eph. 4:2, 16; Phil. 1:9; Heb. 10:24; 1 Thes. 3:12; 4:9; 5:13; 2 Thes. 1:3; Heb. 13:1; 1 Pet. 1:22; 4:8; 5:14; 1 John 2:7; 3:10–11, 18; 4:7–21; Rev. 2:4).

- **God values our compassion for others. This includes the poor and oppressed** (Job 18:7; Isa. 58:7; Jer. 5:28; 22:16; Mal. 3:5; Matt. 4:23–25; 8:1–3; 9:1–8; 25:35; 1 Tim. 5:10; John 3:17), *children* (Matt. 18:1–14; 19:13–15; Luke 17:1–3; James 1:27; 2:6–9), *employees* (Isa. 58:6), *prisoners* (2 Chron. 28:15; Matt. 25:39), *widows and the fatherless* (Job 31:16–22; Jer. 5:28; Mal. 3:5; 1 Tim. 5:1–12), *strangers* (Mal. 3:5; Matt. 25:31–46), *and the sick* (Matt. 25:31–46).

- **God values our hospitality to others** (Lev. 19:34; Job 31:32; Isa. 58:7; Matt. 25:35, 38; Luke 10:30–37; 14:12–14; Rom. 12:13; Heb. 13:2; James 2:15–17; Titus 1:7–8; 1 Pet. 4:9).

- **God values our impartiality** (Acts 10:34; Rom. 2:11; Eph. 6:9). *He loathes prejudice against the poor* (Ex. 23:6; Job 18:8; James 2:2–9), *against employees* (Eph. 6:9; Col 4:1), *against foreigners* (Lev. 19:33; Deut. 10:17–19), *against people of different races/ethnicities* (Numbers 12; Rom. 3:9, 29–30; Gal. 2:11–16; 3:28), *or against the opposite sex* (Gen. 5:1–2; Gal. 3:26–29; Col. 3:18–19). *This does not disregard the fact, in the case of opposite-sex relations, that God assigns unique roles to males and females* (Gen. 3:16–19; 1 Cor. 11:3–10; Eph. 5:21–30).

- **God values human creativity that expresses truthful or righteous principles** (Ex. 31:1–6; 35:30–35; Psalm 150; 1 Cor. 14:26; Eph. 5:19–20; Col. 3:16).

- **God values sound reasoning that expresses truthful or righteous principles** (Isa. 1:18; Matt. 22:37; Mark 12:30; Luke 10:27; John 20:30–31; 2 Tim. 3:16–17; 1 Peter 3:15–16).

- **God values our attempts to liberate the wrongly oppressed via speech** (Ps. 82:3–4; Prov. 24:11–12; 31:8–9; Isa. 1:17; Jer. 22:3; Ezek. 33:8).

- **God values our attempts to communicate His gospel of forgiveness and redemption to those who do not know Him** (Pss. 67:1–2; 96:2–3; Isa. 49:6; 52:7; Matt. 5:14–16; 28:18–20; Mark 13:9–10; 16:15; Acts 1:8; Rom. 10:14–15).

- **God values our attempts to help others in their efforts to promote the things God values according to Scripture** (John 13:1–17; 1 Cor. 12:12–31; Gal. 5:13; Eph. 4:12; 6:2–22; Col. 4:7–8).

As explained in Chapter 2, *redemptive communication* resembles religious expression, but it differs from it in a major way. Whereas *religion* is the human attempt to connect with God or with something God-like, *redemption* is the state of having actually connected with God in the God-centered way that enables one to start seeing things as He sees them and relating to them as He relates to them. The redemptive communicator is one who lovingly submits to the realization that the God of Scripture is, in fact, the creator and sustainer of the universe and that everything in it, therefore, including our communication practices, must be understood and engaged in the instructive light of what His *divine revelation* says about it.

Consider for a moment the prescriptive implications of God's values for your approach to interacting with other people. Which communicational situations should you seek, and which should you avoid? Which topics should you discuss? What should you say about these topics? How should you say this? In the light of what Scripture discloses about God's eternal values, how should you view and what should you say about the following topics of our day?

abortion, infanticide, mercy killing, or euthanasia
abuse (child, elder, self, spousal)
addictions/codependency/eating disorders
air, land, space, or water pollution
animal abuse or vivisection
bioethics (cloning, eugenics, stem cell research)
birth or population control
crime (street, juvenile, gang, or white collar)
criminal justice (capital punishment, prison crowding, recidivism)
discrimination (ageism, ethnocentrism, racism, sexism)
ecology (climate change, pollution, littering)
education (underachievement or illiteracy)
false beliefs
famine, drought, or diseases

immigration
intellectual property (copyright, patent,
   trademark, plagiarism)
labor issues (child labor or sweatshops)
legal issues (government regulation of anything)
marriage (divorce, cohabitation)
poverty (welfare, world hunger, or homelessness)
   taxation
sex (premarital, extramarital, homosexual,
   pornographic)
slavery or human trafficking
substance abuse (drugs, alcohol)
war

The stories that we live, that we create, and that we communicate to others, although skewed by our corruption, manifest our awarenesses that God has created things to be a certain way and that at least some things in creation fall short of this ideal.

Remember, the spiritually redeemed individual understands, based on what God graciously discloses, that our supreme calling in the world is to honor God by seeing things in the light of His eternal plan and by lovingly promoting what He values in our communicative behavior toward others. This calling is not confined to one part of our lives. Rather, it applies to all of life. Whether as a family member, a friend, a church member, a student, a teacher, a citizen, an employer or employee, or in any other role, the redemptive communicator's goal is the same: "So whether you eat or drink, or whatever you do, do it all for the glory of God" (1 Cor. 10:31). Such a person understands that "the fear of the Lord is the beginning of knowledge" (Prov. 1:7), that "the wisdom of this world is foolishness to God" (1 Cor. 3:19), and that His wisdom is an essential foundation for ultimately significant communication. Indeed, as a Biblical writer put it, "from a wise mind comes wise speech; the words of the wise are persuasive" (Prov. 16:23).

❯❯ FINDING YOUR REDEMPTIVE FIELD

So where do you go from here? How can you fulfill your life's purpose by glorifying God as a redemptive critic and communicator? Questions like these could set the stage for communication textbooks of many types. Some of these could emphasize, in greater detail, what it means to be a redemptive critic and how to be a redemptive critic of specialized text or story types. Others could emphasize, in greater depth, what it takes to function as an effective sender of redemptive messages, whether in interpersonal, small group, organizational, public, or specific mediated communication contexts.

Because this textbook is written primarily as an introductory communication textbook, it is designed with two types of introductory communication courses in mind. The first is the introduction to public speaking course that students in many majors encounter during their first or second year of undergraduate study. The second is the introduction to communication course that many colleges or their communication programs require students to take, whether as a general education component or as a foundational component of the major.

As a text for introduction to public speaking courses at Christian colleges, this textbook, in the next section, teaches students what it takes to function as an effective sender and recipient of messages in a public communication context. Indeed, Part II is a public speaking primer. Reviewing the particulars of audience analysis, research, organization, and information presentational strategies, this 12-chapter section introduces students to an eight-step process that, if practiced, can help them achieve their informative or persuasive goals when directly addressing a live public audience. The section also helps students understand what it takes to work well with others to create effective small group presentations to public audiences.

As a text for introduction to communication courses, this book, in Part I, defines communication, explores how it works, and considers what makes communication's study or practice potentially significant or valuable. Building on this foundation, Part III introduces students to a variety of communication-related job fields that are worthy of consideration as they explore their future vocational options. These job field descriptions, which are adapted from the Occupational Outlook Index, can help students intelligently find a field that matches their individual interests and abilities and through which they can interact with other people in a way that makes a redemptive difference. Each job listing provides an overview of the job field, emphasizing the nature of its work, any qualifications or credentials required for one to practice it, the job field's current employment situation and its outlook for the future, and the earnings currently earned by practitioners in this field.

Part IV makes it clear, though, that communication occupations, although potentially more influential than their alternatives, are not the only vocational platforms through which a student can prepare to interact with others in a redemptive way. Indeed, this part of the book makes this point by profiling dozens of Christ-followers, representing a variety of job fields, who have used their vocations as platforms for advancing some of the things God values that we have highlighted in this chapter. As the profiles in this section demonstrate, one's ability to function as a redemptive communicator is neither defined nor limited by one's vocation or location. It is one's consecration—one's depth of devotion to loving God in an interactive way—that can make a redemptive difference in the world.

Whether you review this textbook as an introductory public speaking student or as an introduction to communication student, be reminded that you need not live the inferior life that autonomous motives for communicating with others promise to deliver. Rather, God calls you, through redemptive faith in Christ, to experience "life in all its fullness" (John 10:10) by submitting to His authority, receiving His forgiveness, embracing what He values, and interacting with other people in a way that manifests His timeless, changeless intentions for them and for you.

QUESTIONS FOR ANALYSIS

• This chapter indicates that God values our attempts to liberate the wrongly oppressed via speech (Ps. 82:3–4; Prov. 24:11–12; 31:8–9; Isa. 1:17; Jer. 22:3; Ezek. 33:8). If you could speak out to liberate one particular group of wrongly oppressed people (oppressed for something God's Word does not present as sinful), as an expression of authentic love for God, which group would you choose? Then describe three specific steps you can take during the next month to put this vision into action.

• This chapter also indicates that God values our attempts to communicate His gospel of forgiveness and redemption to those who do not know Him (Pss. 67:1–2; 96:2–3; Isa. 49:6; 52:7; Matt. 5:14–16; 28:18–20; Mark 13:9–10; 16:15; Acts 1:8; Rom. 10:14–15). Is it possible to do this without using words, as Francis of Assisi once suggested? Write a 100- to 150-word response in which you state and support your answer.

• Choose one profile of a redemptive communicator in a PART II chapter that highlights a vocational field that interests you. Using principles from the present chapter, explain in 100–150 words how the story subject functioned as a redemptive communicator in his or her story.

• Choose one additional profile and do the same thing the previous question asked you to do.

ENDNOTES

[1] John Henry Newman and Frank Miller Turner, *The Idea of a University* (New Haven: Yale University Press, 1996), 45.
[2] Augustine and Henry Chadwick, *Confessions* (Oxford: Oxford University Press, 1992).
[3] Blaise Pascal, *Thoughts* (New York: P. F. Collier and Son, 1910), 138–139.
[4] Abraham Maslow, *Motivation and Personality* (New York: Harper, 1954).
[5] Bronislaw Malinowski, *A Scientific Theory of Culture and Other Essays* (Chapel Hill: The University of North Carolina Press, 1944).
[6] Blaise Pascal, *Thoughts* (New York: P. F. Collier and Son, 1910), 136.
[7] C. S. Lewis, *The Complete C. S. Lewis Signature Classics* (New York: HarperCollins, 2007), 114.
[8] C. S. Lewis, and Walter Hooper, *On Stories: And Other Essays on Literature* (New York: Houghton-Mifflin-Harcourt, 2002), xiv.

BIBLIOGRAPHY

Baggett, David, and Jerry L. Walls. *Good God: The Theistic Foundations of Morality*. New York: Oxford University Press, 2011.
Feinberg, John S., Paul D. Feinberg, and Aldous Huxley. *Ethics for a Brave New World*. Wheaton, IL: Crossway Books, 1993.

Frame, John M. *The Doctrine of the Christian Life*. Phillipsburg, N.J.: P & R Publishing, 2008.

Geisler, Norman L. *Christian Ethics*. Grand Rapids, MI: Baker Book House, 1989.

Geisler, Norman L., and Ryan P. Snuffer. *Love Your Neighbor: Thinking Wisely about Right and Wrong*. Wheaton, IL: Crossway Books, 2007.

Heimbach, Daniel R. *True Sexual Morality: Recovering Biblical Standards for a Culture in Crisis*. Wheaton, IL: Crossway Books, 2004.

Moreland, James Porter, and Scott B. Rae. *Body & Soul: Human Nature & the Crisis in Ethics*. Downers Grove, IL: InterVarsity Press, 2000.

Mouw, Richard J. *Uncommon Decency: Christian Civility in an Uncivil World*. Downers Grove, IL: InterVarsity Press, 1992.

Schaeffer, Francis A. *The mark of the Christian*. Downers Grove, IL: Inter-Varsity Press, 1970.

VanDrunen, David. *Bioethics and the Christian Life: A Guide to Making Difficult Decisions*. Wheaton, IL: Crossway, 2009.

NAME: _____ DATE: _____

HONOR STATEMENT: I, the undersigned student, hereby declare before God, before the school, and before the professor that I have read Chapter 5 in its entirety, that I have completed the following exercise with help from no other sources, and that I neither have shared nor will share this work with anyone.

Signature: _____ Date: _____

SHORT ESSAYS

1. This chapter indicates that God values our attempts to liberate the wrongly oppressed via speech (Ps. 82:3–4; Prov. 24:11–12; 31:8–9; Isa. 1:17; Jer. 22:3; Ezek. 33:8). If you could speak out to liberate one particular group of wrongly oppressed people (oppressed for something God's Word does not present as sinful), as an expression of authentic love for God, which group would you choose? Then describe three specific steps you can take during the next month to put this vision into action.

_____

_____

_____

_____

_____

_____

_____

_____

_____

_____

_____

_____

_____

_____

_____

_____

_____

2. This chapter also indicates that God values our attempts to communicate His gospel of forgiveness and redemption to those who do not know Him (Pss. 67:1–2; 96:2–3; Isa. 49:6; 52:7; Matt. 5:14–16; 28:18–20; Mark 13:9–10; 16:15; Acts 1:8; Rom. 10:14–15). Is it possible to do this without using words, as Francis of Assisi once suggested? Write a 100- to 150-word response in which you state and support your answer.

_____

_____

_____

_____

_____

_____

_____

_____

_____

_____

_____

_____

_____

_____

_____

_____

_____

_____

_____

_____

3. Choose one profile of a redemptive communicator in a PART IV chapter that highlights someone who used or is using his or her vocational field to promote something that God values in this world according to Scripture. Using the present chapter, explain in 100–150 words how the story subject functioned as a redemptive communicator in his or her story.

_____

_____

_____

_____

_____

_____

_____

_____

_____

_____

_____

_____

_____

_____

_____

_____

_____

_____

_____

_____

_____

_____

_____

4. Choose another profile of a redemptive communicator in a PART IV chapter that highlights someone who used or is using his or her vocational field to promote something that God values in this world according to Scripture. Using the present chapter, explain in 100–150 words how the story subject functioned as a redemptive communicator in his or her story?

_____

_____

_____

_____

_____

_____

_____

_____

_____

_____

_____

_____

_____

_____

_____

_____

_____

_____

_____

PART 2

....

PUBLIC SPEAKING:

A PRIMER FOR REDEMPTIVE COMMUNICATORS

THE REDEMPTIVE COMMUNICATOR & PUBLIC SPEAKING

By Donald H. Alban Jr, PhD

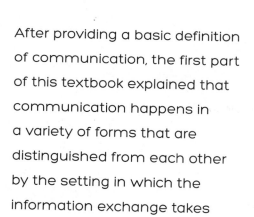

After providing a basic definition of communication, the first part of this textbook explained that communication happens in a variety of forms that are distinguished from each other by the setting in which the information exchange takes place, the number of participants it involves, and whether the exchange is direct or indirect, instant or delayed, and formal or informal. As the first chapter indicated, the most commonly recognized of these modes include the following:

>> 1. Interpersonal communication, which occurs when people socially interact, usually in a face-to-face environment, but possibly also in real-time virtual environments like through radio, phones or computer programs.

>> 2. Group communication, which happens when three or more people come together for a common purpose and interact and influence each other in the exercise of this purpose.

>> 3. Mediated communication, which results when senders use technologies to channel messages to recipients, whether synchronously or asynchronously.

>> 4. Mass communication, which takes place when people use a media technology to distribute information to a large group of physically detached people.

>> 5. Public communication, the primary focus of this book's second part, which occurs when a speaker formally addresses a group of typically 10 or more individuals in a face-to-face environment in which interactivity is possible but generally not practiced.

Now that we have defined communication, established its divine origin, and explained its redemptive purpose, we turn our attention in the remainder of this book to public speaking, a mode that enables us to address groups of people in a way that promotes what God values in this world. What does it take to be an effective public speaker? Prominent thinkers have debated this question since ancient times when Greco-Roman intellectuals like Plato, Aristotle, and Cicero made it a primary theme in their dialogues. Students in European and American cultures, too, have formally considered the same question since medieval times when oratory courses became a foundational emphasis in university-level liberal arts curricula.

How does one answer the question? Indeed, what does it take to be an effective public speaker? As you might expect based on the discussion of worldviews in Part 1, a person's answer to this question will be framed if not shaped by his or her most basic beliefs about human origin, nature, purpose, and destiny. To the physical determinist who believes life is little more than

TO THE BIBLICALLY-DIRECTED CHRISTIAN, PUBLIC SPEAKING IS PRIMARILY A MEANS, AMONG OTHERS, FOR EXPRESSING AUTHENTIC LOVE FOR GOD BY PROMOTING WHAT HE VALUES IN THIS WORLD.

© Bejamin J. Myers/Corbis.

a struggle to physically survive in a hostile world, public speaking may be valuable mainly as a tool for influencing others in a way that helps assure this outcome. To the pragmatist, public speaking may be little more than a means for influencing others in a way that helps assure the achievement of his or her individual goals or dreams. To the utilitarian, public speaking may be primarily a platform through which speakers can advance that which is in society's best interests. To the Biblically-directed Christian, public speaking is primarily a means, among others, for expressing authentic love for God by promoting what He values in this world. Whatever a person's worldview may be, a course in public speaking can give him or her valuable skills through which he or she can promote his or her overarching goal in life. >>

© Bettman/Corbis.

Be relevant. Know your audience –
its wants, its needs, its expectations,
and its sensitivities.

Regardless of which goal you're trying to promote through a speech presentation, you will be more effective in achieving if you take the strategic approach to constructing and delivering speeches that the rest of this book presents to you. This strategizing involves a number of vital steps—selecting an appropriate topic, developing effective purpose and thesis statements, discovering, selecting, and organizing credible supportive information, and presenting your thesis and supportive information to the audience in a clear and compelling way. If you carefully go through each of these steps in the process, you should be well prepared to deliver an effective speech to your audience.

As we move into the public speaking section of this textbook, I invite you to consider several basic guidelines for effective communication that, if applied to your speech construction and delivery, can enrich your attempts to engage audiences in a redemptive way. These principles resound in much of the instructional content that follows. You will note their significance as well if you take time to analyze great public speeches—such as Jesus' Sermon on the Mount (Matt. 5-7) and the Apostle Paul's speech to the skeptics in the Areopagus (Acts 17)—and observe how these presentations put these principles into practice. To make them more memorable, I present these principles in the form of an acrostic:

Be a REDEMPTIVE public speaker

R	Be relevant
E	Be educated
D	Be deliberate
E	Be ethical
M	Be methodical
P	Be passionate
T	Be transformational
I	Be interactive
V	Be versatile
E	Be eloquent

Be relevant. Know your audience—its wants, its needs, its expectations, and its sensitivities. Learn who they are—their age, sex, race/ethnicity, educational background, economic status, political and religious affiliation, etc. Discover what you can about their existing attitudes, values, and beliefs. Learn what you can about the setting and the circumstances in which you will address this audience. Having this information is a vital first step in the speech preparation process since, without it, you will have difficulty determining which topics and supportive information will impact them in the way you desire.

Be educated. Know not only your audience but also the world in which we live and the issues that affect your audience. Be a regular reader of local, national, and international news sites. This will help you become well versed in the social, political, and religious issues of the day. Enrich your ability to make sense of these issues by expanding your understanding of Biblical precepts and principles and consider their implications of these principles

for matters like these. Know not merely what you believe, but also why you believe it. Know not only what you disbelieve, but also why you disbelieve it. Expanding your knowledge is essential to this. The better versed about today's world you are, the better equipped you will be to relate God's values to the issues of the day in a redemptive, rhetorically effective way.

Be deliberate. Delivering an effective speech involves careful thought and planning. Be intentional about the process. Think through each step you take in preparing to present your speech. Ask yourself whether each step you are about to take is, in fact, the best option in the light of your ultimate goal in making the presentation. Do not hesitate to change your plans or to revise what you have already done when doing so serves to improve the overall quality of your presentation.

Be ethical. Pursue your information vigorously. Present it honestly. Properly credit your sources. Be charitable yet »

truthful when addressing your audience. From the beginning of the speech creation process to its end, do what is right, love mercy, and walk humbly with your God (Micah 6:8).

Be methodical. Be strategic as you approach the task, meticulously confirming, step by step, that you know your audience, that your topic is relevant to that audience, that you can clearly state a main point about that topic, that you can back your main point with supportive information from credible sources, that you can use structure your information in a logical sequence, and that you know how to present the information in a compelling way. Unless you deliberately follow a plan that addresses each of these steps, your speech is unlikely to as effective as possible.

Be passionate. Unless you really care about the topic you are addressing and the statement about it that you are going to make to your audience, you will have difficulty giving an effective presentation about it to your audience. To the extent that you can do so, then, choose your topic and formulate purpose and thesis statements that you can express from your heart and not merely from your head. Your audience is more likely to be moved by a presentation that comes from the head and the heart than by one that comes only from your head.

Be transformational. Remember that your role as a redemptive communicator is to interact with other people in a way that promotes something God values in this world. Your goal in any given speech, then, is not merely to inform or to persuade your audience about your topic but, in doing so, to equip and to inspire them to do something that achieves this goal. When considering your speech topic and formulating a thesis about it, then, consider the redemptive value or potential value of your various options and choose one that not only interests you, but also promotes something God deems good in this world.

Be interactive. As you present your speech, be attentive to your audience. Note whether your presentation is having its intended effect and, if not, adjust your presentation in an attempt to make your speech more effective. Such responsiveness is an essential quality for effective public speakers.

Be versatile. Different audiences require different types of presentations, so be prepared to address your topic and to make your statement about it using the verbal and non-verbal symbols that will help you achieve this as effectively as possible. The language you use when addressing a group of 8-year-olds obviously should differ from the language you use when addressing a group of adults. Adaptability, no less than responsiveness, is an essential quality of effective public speaking.

Be eloquent. Choose appropriate words that impact your audience in the specific way you desire. Use gestures, facial expressions, movement, volume, pitch, tone, and other presentational variables in a way that communicates your ideas and your passion to your audience in an effective way. This textbook provides guidelines for doing this that will serve you well if you follow them in the public speaking opportunities that you encounter during the days to come.

Whatever your goal in public speaking may be, the information you relay can impact a lot of people. Take this responsibility seriously. If you put this book's principles into practice, you will be well prepared to function as a public speaker who is both rhetorically skillful and redemptively motivated.

"Speech is a mirror of the soul:
as a man speaks, so is he."

- Publilius Syrus (c. 42 B.C.)

CHAPTER 6 >>

 6 GETTING STARTED ON YOUR FIRST SPEECH

EIGHT STEPS FOR PREPARING TO SPEAK

1. Decide on a Topic

2. Demonstrate Ethical Behavior Throughout the Process

3. Determine the General Purpose, Specific Purpose, and Thesis Statement

4. Define the Audience

5. Document Ideas Through Support and Sound Reasoning

6. Draft the Introduction, Body, and Conclusion

7. Develop the Language of the Speech with Care

8. Deliver Your Speech While Making Your Tension Work for You

SUMMARY

QUESTIONS FOR STUDY AND DISCUSSION

ACTIVITIES

REFERENCES

Adapted from *Public Speaking: Choices for Effective Results, Fifth Edition* by John Makay et al. Copyright © 2008.
Reprinted with permission of Kendall Hunt Publishing Co.

For some, speaking in public can be an exciting, adrenalin-producing activity, but for others, it is a dreaded experience to be feared. Whereas some will jump at the chance to perform in public, others will do just about anything to avoid standing, let alone speaking, before a group of people. A few years ago, there was a community fundraiser at a local restaurant. People gathered for a meal, a silent auction, and some entertainment. Those in charge of entertainment thought it would be fun to select some community members to provide the group with a rendition of the song "YMCA." Wendell, an enormously successful businessman, was chosen to participate. He stood up, opened his wallet, and took out $50, stating, "I won't do it, but I'll pay my way out." His money was welcomed, and Wendell was allowed to choose the person to replace him. He chose John, another successful businessman. John stood up, opened his wallet, and shelled out $50. John then selected Bob, a restaurant owner, who opened his wallet, frowned, showed the crowd he only had $2, and said, "I guess I'm in!"

© 2012 by Danomyte.
Used under license of Shutterstock.

Whether you embrace the opportunity for public speaking or feel the urge to run away, there are many things you can do to enhance your potential for success.

Think about your response to this situation. Some of you may have jumped at the idea of performing "YMCA." After all, most of the people knew each other, and the atmosphere was festive. But for those of you with real apprehension, the comfort of a friendly group is not good enough.

Lack of preparation time may have influenced Wendell and John's apprehension. Wendell confesses his dislike of public speaking, no matter what the circumstances. He admits that not having a college education, combined with his own poor perception of his speaking skills make public speaking one of the worst possible situations for him to endure.

Whether you embrace the opportunity for public speaking or feel the urge to run away, there are many things you can do to enhance your potential for success. Following is an overview of eight key steps you should follow when preparing and presenting a speech. This overview is particularly important for your first speech. Keep in mind that you will most likely move back and forth among the steps. The chapters ahead are designed to provide more detail so you may increase your knowledge about public speaking and your skill as a speaker and as a listener.

❯❯EIGHT STEPS FOR PREPARING TO SPEAK

1. Decide on a topic.
2. Demonstrate ethical behavior throughout the process.
3. Determine the general purpose, specific purpose, and thesis statement.
4. Define your audience.
5. Document your ideas through firm support and sound reasoning.
6. Draft the beginning, middle, and end.
7. Develop the language of your speech with care.
8. Deliver your speech while making your tension work for you.

GET REAL!
A HIDDEN KEY TO MEMORABLE PUBLIC SPEAKING

BY EVANGELINE F. ALBAN, M.A. (Instructor, College of General Studies, Liberty University)
& DONALD H. ALBAN JR., PH.D. (Associate Professor of Communication Studies, Liberty University)

You probably have attended events in which a singer performed for a crowd, whether at a concert hall, a ball game, at a community holiday celebration, or at a church. Maybe you heard the live performance on a TV, a radio, or a website instead. Which of these performances, if any, stands out in your memory as having been amazingly good? Which of them, if any, stands out as having been unbelievably bad? For most of us, recalling the unusually good or bad performances is simpler than remembering the ones (most of them, really) that were neither great nor terrible.

Think about a related question for a moment—which public speech or speeches, among the many that you've heard, whether in the classroom, in a chapel or convocation service, or in church, stand out in your mind as exceptionally good or exceptionally bad? What made the speech exceptional? Was it the speaker's effective or ineffective word choice or use of reasoning? Was it his or her skillful or unskillful use of gestures, facial expressions, or other movements to accentuate the message? Was it a visual or presentational aid that the speaker used during the speech? Was it a combination of all or several of these variables?

Whether you are a singer or a speaker, a key to success in your presentation to an audience is your belief in the presentation and in the message it represents. Without this, you might deliver a presentation that satisfies the audience's expectations, but it is unlikely that your message will linger in your audience's minds as something worth remembering. A textbook like this one cannot teach you to believe in your message—this is something that transcends the authors' ability and perhaps even yours. However, we do advise you to choose, when given freedom to do so, a message that you value, one that you can deliver to your audience from your heart and not merely from your mind.

The main point in all of this is that you must be real when addressing your audience. Your words must be authentic—they must express ideas that you truly believe. Your volume, pitch, tone, rate, accent, and inflection must be genuine—they must relay your true feelings about your message. So, too, must your facial expressions, your gestures, your bodily movements, and the aural or visual aids that you include in the presentation. Be real in what you say. Be real in how you say it.

When you talk with a friend, you use meaningful words to relay your ideas and feelings to him or her. You also smile, gaze, nod, blink, wink, squint, tap, touch, pat, clap, or use other bodily movements to relay your thoughts and feelings these during the conversation. You express yourself clearly, spontaneously, and naturally. You are real, and this is what makes the interaction something richer, more enjoyable, and more memorable than a dry information exchange. To be rich, enjoyable, and memorable, a speech, no less than a conversation, must be communicated clearly, spontaneously, and naturally. How would you feel if a friend, while conversing with you, would make no eye contact with you or smile at you? How would you react if the friend, during the same talk, were to speak passionlessly, monotonously, and awkwardly, with information gaps or logical lapses in his remarks that leave you bewildered? Remember, your speech audience will feel much the same way unless you speak to them in the intelligible, realistic way that is an essential quality of enjoyable conversations.

Being realistic about public speaking means you also must be accept the fact that a conversational audience and a speech audience, although similar in some ways, are inevitably different in other ways that you must anticipate as you prepare to interact with each. Unlike the former, a speech audience, in most situations, expects you to plan your remarks in advance, a step that involves topic and thesis selection, research, information selection, information organization, and presentation planning. A textbook like this one can help you make your way through this process in a productive way. If you are not careful, though, following this process too rigidly can generate a speech that although well researched and organized, is less than compelling because it seems impersonal, detached, and unrealistic to the audience. To avoid this, remember to respect the following pointers as you prepare your speech.

1. SPEAK EXTEMPORANEOUSLY

Although there are times when reading a speech to an audience is a good idea (see chapter 14), it is usually a better idea for you to speak to your listeners in a natural, conversational tone as you proceed, point by point, through your presentation. Imagine how strange it would seem if a friend, in conversation, were to read her remarks to you from a note card. Just as you would not read from notes while addressing a conversational audience, you should avoid reading from notes while addressing your speech audience, if you can help it.

2. TELL STORIES

When it is possible to do so, use stories—especially stories from your life—to impress your points on an audience. As the American youth novelist Madeleine L'Engle explained, "Stories make us more alive, more human, more courageous, more loving."[i] Why stories affect people in this way has intrigued scientists for years. One team of researchers, in a 2010 study, used brain scan data to document the power of stories to impact people in this way. The study's findings, as summarized by *Psychology Today,* are that "When you tell a story to a friend, you can transfer experiences directly to their brain. They feel what you feel. They empathize. What's more, when communicating most effectively, you can get a group of people's brains to synchronize their activity. As you relate someone's desires through a story, they become the desires of the audience. When trouble develops, they gasp in unison, and when desires are fulfilled they smile together. "[ii] As this relates to your speech planning, remember that "for as long as you've got your audience's

attention, they are in your mind. When you hear a good story, you develop empathy with the teller because you experience the events for yourself. This makes sense. Stories should be powerful."

3. BE INTERACTIVE

Research your speech audience in advance. Relate your message to them in the light of who they are. Personalize your message, relating it to them in practical ways. While speaking to them, make eye contact with audience members. Slightly elevate your eye brows. Smile. Move about naturally, and use gestures. Speak to them in friendly tone. These steps can do much to make you and your message seem more realistic and relevant to your audience.

4. USE MEMORABLE WORDS

Use concrete words and images to get your point across. Say what you need to say in order to relay an important point, but do so as concisely as you can. Use words that mean precisely what you intend to communicate. To do otherwise can confuse your audience and waste their time.

In summary, be real in what you say, be real in how you say it, and be realistic about satisfying the unique needs and expectations of your speech audience. With some careful thought and quality planning, you can put together a speech that your linger in your audience's minds as something worth remembering.

_____

[i]Chase, Carole F. "Words of Wisdom from Madeleine L'Engle." *The Writer* 2002: 26-8. ProQuest. Web. 25 May 2013.

[ii]http://www.psychologytoday.com/blog/you-illuminated/201106/why-sharing-stories-brings-people-together

1. Decide on a Topic.

A difficult task for students beginning the study and practice of public speaking is to select a topic. Some instructors will give you a topic and others will provide strict limits. If you can choose, however, often the best place to begin your search for a speech topic is yourself. When the topic springs from your own interests, you bring to it personal involvement, motivation, and the information necessary for a good speech.

For example, Courtney found herself preoccupied with choosing the topic for her informative speech. As she reflected on her possibilities, she thought about her two years' experience at a local day care center before college. She realized she could speak to her classmates about how working at a day care led to her decision to work with children as her vocation. She felt earning a degree in education would open more doors, and she stressed the notion of getting some experience through work or internship in one's area of interest before completing a major. Her speech was full of informative anecdotes and her enthusiasm made the speech highly effective.

Perhaps you have some interesting work experience to share with your class, or an amazing travel story, or maybe a life-changing service learning experience. In any case, if at all possible, choose your first speech topic from what you know best.

If no ideas come to you when thinking about a speech topic, try the following. Write down two or three broad categories representing subjects of interest to you, and divide the categories into parts. You might begin, for example, with the broad areas of politics and sports. From these general topics useful lists will emerge.

If you choose a speech topic that interests you, the audience may come to share your enthusiasm for it.

Politics
1. Campus politics
2. Political corruption
3. Contemporary political campaign tactics

Sports
1. Learning from participation in sports
2. The challenges facing student athletes
3. Why NASCAR races are increasingly popular

As your list of choices grows, you will probably find yourself coming back to the same topic or a variation of it. For example, "Football after college" could be added to "The challenges facing student athletes." Perhaps your brother played college football, and then attempted to join a professional football league. You could talk about his experiences, including successes and failures. Now you have your topic.

Do not assume, however, that any topic is relevant. Before choosing a topic, make sure you know the amount of time you have to speak, your level of knowledge about the topic, and the needs of your audience. A five-minute speech is not supposed to last ten minutes; it is not even supposed to last six. In some public situations, you may be in danger of getting cut off if your speech is too long. If you have a wealth of information, you need to determine what must be left out. If you do not have much knowledge about the topic, recognize where you need to do research, or choose another topic. If you know about the background of your audience, you can decide what information is most relevant and how much time should be spent on each point.

2. Demonstrate Ethical Behavior Throughout the Process.

A consideration of ethics is important in virtually all aspects of speech development, including, but certainly not limited to, how you approach a topic, where you get information, how you edit or interpret information, word choice, and distinguishing between your own ideas and those which need to be cited. Plagiarism, which involves using other's work, words, or ideas without adequate acknowledgement, has never been easier than it is today, according to Plagiarism.org. Add the ability to send files and share information via computers to the overwhelming amount of information available through the Internet, and the potential for engaging in unethical behavior is enormous.

Ethics are being discussed within the context of many disciplines, including medicine, psychology, business, and communication. It is relatively easy to find stories in the newspaper concerning ethical issues. According to communication professor Bert Bradley, "Speakers have ethical responsibilities which must be accepted if rhetoric is to play its most meaningful role in communication" (Bradley 1998, 47). That said, government officials have failed to speak truthfully until forced to do so, deception continues to be uncovered in the nation's business practices, and students, when questioned anonymously, admit to what can be described as wide-spread cheating.

On August 24, 2006, the Associated Press reported that "Allegations of criminal wrongdoing and ethical lapses among lawmakers are coloring a handful of competitive House and Senate races across the country this midterm election year." In October 2004, pop culture's Ashlee Simpson was derided for using a pre-recorded vocal track for a performance on Saturday Night Live. Certainly, politicians and pop stars are not the only ones engaging in unethical behavior. During the early months of 2006, Oprah Winfrey brought to task James Frey, author of the book *A Million Little Pieces*. On national television, Frey admitted to making up part of his "memoir," and his publisher discussed how the firm was duped. More than 3.5 million people bought Frey's book assuming it was non-fiction.

During the early months of 2006, TV hostess Oprah Winfrey exposed author James Frey for making up part of his memoir.

These abuses have heightened our sensitivity to the need for honesty from all sources, including public speakers. Speakers may have different values and beliefs based on family, cultural, and educational backgrounds, but many ethical standards are considered universal.

Freedom of speech is a fundamental right in our democracy, and implied in this freedom is the speaker's responsibility to avoid deceiving others. As you think critically about your topic, your audience, supporting material, and so on, remain concerned for the welfare of others. Use accurate and current information, rely on sound reasoning, and present a speech that is your own, based on your independent research and views. Remember to cite sources and to quote and paraphrase correctly when you present information or ideas that are not your own.

3. Determine the General Purpose, Specific Purpose, and Thesis Statement.

The time you spend preparing your speech may be of little value if you do not determine what you want your speech to accomplish. At the beginning, you should clarify the general and specific purposes of your speech. Then determine which statement will be the expression of your main idea; that is the thesis statement for your speech.

General Purpose

There are three general purposes for speeches: to inform, to persuade, and to entertain or inspire. If you want to explain the differences between a scooter and a motorcycle, the general purpose of your speech would be "to inform." If you hope to make people laugh after eating a good meal, your general purpose is "to entertain." If you want people to choose a hybrid for their next car, you are attempting "to persuade."

Keep in mind, however, that it is difficult to deliver a speech that is just informative or just persuasive or just entertaining. Often, in the perception of listeners, the purposes may converge or overlap. For example, as a speaker informs her audience about various options for eating a healthy breakfast each day, some audience members may interpret her speech as an attempt to persuade them to change their daily behavior.

Specific Purpose

Once the general purpose is set for your speech, determine the specific purpose. This is the precise response you want from your audience. The specific purpose also identifies who the audience will be. Specific purpose statements should be expressed as an infinitive phrase that includes the general purpose as well as the main thrust of your speech. Here are two examples of specific purposes:

1. To inform the class of differences between the operations of an on-campus political club and an off-campus political party
2. To persuade the class that requiring all college students to participate in service-learning projects benefits the student, college, and community

Because the specific purpose identifies the audience who will hear your speech, it guides you in speech preparation. A speech on health care reform given before a group of college students would be different than a speech on the same topic given before an audience of retirees. Obviously, the second audience has a much more immediate need for reform than the first group of listeners. The speech would be different because the older listeners usually feel a greater overall need to deal with health issues.

Thesis Statement

While the general and specific purpose statements set the goals for your speech, the thesis statement, or your core idea, focuses on what you want to say. The thesis statement distills your speech to one sentence, summarizing your main idea. According to James Humes, a corporate speech consultant, Great Britain's Prime Minister Winston Churchill once sent back a pudding because he said it had no theme. (Kleinfield 1990). A well-defined theme is critical to your speech's success. The thesis statement is the central message you want listeners to take with them. The following examples show how one moves from a topic to the thesis statement.

© 2012 by Renata Sedmakova.
Used under license of Shutterstock.

Great Britain's Prime Minister Winston Churchill once sent back a pudding because he said it had no theme.

Topic: Study abroad
General purpose: To inform
Specific purpose: To explain to my class what is involved in the study abroad options available to them at our university
Thesis statement: Students interested in earning college credit while studying abroad have several options that differ in terms of academic content, location, length of stay, potential number of credit hours, and cost.

Topic: Study abroad
General purpose: To persuade
Specific purpose: To convince my class that studying abroad will be a life-changing experience
Thesis statement: Studying abroad can be a life-changing experience because students gain knowledge in an academic area, face the unfamiliar, and interact with individuals from a different culture.

As you can see, although the topic is "study abroad," there are different aspects of studying abroad that one could address. The above example shows choices for an informative speech and persuasive speech. A speech with the general purpose to entertain could include humorous examples and illustrations of the trials and tribulations of studying abroad.

4. Define the Audience.

As stated throughout our book, public speaking is an audience-centered activity. Your reason for presenting a speech is to communicate your message to others in the clearest and most convincing way. When preparing your specific purpose you must define your audience. An effective speaker analyzes and adapts to the audience. This involves finding out as much as possible about your audience. What are their demographics (age, race, gender, religious affiliation, political affiliation, etc.)? What is their level of knowledge

EFFECTIVE PUBLIC SPEAKING
KEYS FOR CONNECTING WITH YOUR AUDIENCE

BY RANDALL P. PRUITT, PH.D. (Professor of Communication Studies, Liberty University)
& CLIFFORD W. KELLY, PH.D. (Professor of Communication Studies, Liberty University)

Have you ever asked yourself what would make you a better communicator?

The way we communicate affects almost everything we do. Our relationships with our families, our working relationships, and the success or failure we experience in our friendships with others are often connected to our ability to communicate. Your success as a public speaker, too, will be affected by your ability or inability to communicate.

What does it take to communicate effectively? Answering this question has been a challenge since the days when ancient Greek philosophers debated what it takes to be a successful public speaker. With the ceaseless rise of new technologies that enable people to interact in new ways, answering the question has become all the more challenging in recent years. Whether you are speaking face-to-face with a friend over a cup of coffee or tapping furiously on the keys of your smartphone, being successful in your interactions can be a challenge.

In the 1970s, two researchers from Cleveland State University began a scholarly discussion of what makes human communication effective. The work of professors Art Bochner and Cliff Kelly started a 30-year discussion of what it takes to develop the communication competence that one needs in order to be a successful communicator. Although they originally focused on what it takes to be competent in interpersonal conversations, their ideas are valuable to students of public speaking, too, since the keys to effective public speaking and good conversation are very similar. Here is a summary of Bochner and Kelly's five basic ideas:

1. EMPATHIC COMMUNICATION:
(the ability to take the role of the other person)
To be a strong communicator, it's important that we try to fully *understand* what the other person is feeling and thinking. Perhaps you've had the unpleasant experience of talking to someone who speaks only about himself or herself. This speaker-centered approach to conversing can leave listeners with the "What am I, chopped liver?" feeling. To avoid making this mistake when you are interacting with others, keep your radar tuned to your audience's needs and values and really *listen* to them. Take time to figure out where they are and meet them there. Everyone appreciates it when friends, family, and others take the time to understand and relate to us—and we should seek to do the same.

To be effective as a public speaker, you must have empathic insight into your audience's needs and values in order to speak to where they live. Empathy, research has shown, is the most essential communication skill in our arsenal and should be cultivated and be ever-present in our interactions with others, whether these are formal or informal. Analyzing the audience is vital to the speaker's success as a communicator.

2. DESCRIPTIVENESS:
(giving and receiving feedback)
There's an old story about the young man who takes out a quiet young lady on a date. The girl's father tells the young man to have his daughter home by 11:00 p.m. The young man, after a long and unsuccessful night of strained conversation, returns his date back home at 10:00 p.m., exhausted from the long silences and awkward moments.

Many of us have had the frustrating experience of trying to talk with someone who is unresponsive. We ask questions in an attempt to get to know the other person, but find ourselves getting few results. Bochner and Kelly suggest that successful relationships are more likely to occur when both people have a full and active exchange of responses. They also suggest that such *feedback* should be specific, concrete, and clear.

As public speakers, we are responsible to offer a clear and concrete message while remaining sensitive to the nonverbal and verbal cues of the audience. In effect, we seek to offer a sensible message while responding to feedback from our audience. There is no greater joy for a speaker than when he or she senses a strong or deep connection with the audience and presents a speech that meets them where they are.

3. OWNING FEELINGS AND THOUGHTS:
(taking responsibility)

A third suggestion for becoming a better (more competent) communicator is that we be willing to own the statements we make and to realize that we are *responsible* for the potential impact of what we say. We say what we truly believe in no uncertain terms.

In public speaking, owning our thoughts and feelings is crucial to the speech's success. The speaker's credibility is enhanced by the audience's perception of him or her as a person who is real and who is willing to say it like it is and to suffer the consequences for doing so. In addition, speakers are more credible when they use authoritative sources to show that they have done their homework and that their statements are informed conclusions rather than just thoughtless expressions of personal opinion.

4. SELF-DISCLOSURE:
(transparency and authenticity)

Perhaps you recall the scene from the movie *Shrek* where the ogre tries to explain to the donkey how both onions and ogres have layers. Unfortunately the donkey doesn't understand and ends the conversation by stating, "Oh, you both have layers! You know—not everybody likes onions." Shrek's attempt to talk about his inner and outer self highlights what Bochner and Kelly present as a fourth principle for healthy relationships—self-disclosure, vitally important to the formation, development, and growth of human relationships. Why? Because sharing your inner self permits the audience to know what you are feeling, thinking, or wishing.

Consider your own habits of disclosure and consider the people to whom you disclose, where and when you disclose to them, and how much you disclose to them. Self-disclosure is a valuable part of a relationship when it reflects transparent and authentic communication balanced with an awareness of what is appropriate and helpful in building the relationship.

The same principle holds true for each of us as public speakers. We should seek to be transparent in front of our audience, being as honest as is appropriate for the situation. This self-disclosure helps the audience to begin to trust you as a speaker, and this further enhances your credibility and personal connection with the audience. Research shows that speakers who disclose through personal examples and experiences are more persuasive then those who merely use impersonal data like statistics to support what they're saying. When you appropriately disclose your inner self to the audience, you *humanize* yourself to them and help them understand the practical importance of what you're trying to say.

5. BEHAVIORAL FLEXIBILITY:
(adaptability)

The fifth and final aspect of communicative competence concerns how flexible we are in the way we relate to others. Interpersonal communication experts will tell you that our ability to adapt and to work with a variety of people in a variety of ways and settings is vital to our ongoing success. In a day when advances in communication technology are bringing our diverse world closer together, our ability as individuals to be flexible in our everyday encounters becomes increasingly important.

As public speakers, our ability to *adapt* our message, our language, or our presentational style to our specific audience is vital to our success. You may have noticed that the best public speakers do well at adjusting their message and style to match audience reactions and moods. And this brings us right back to empathy, the first and most important skill. In order to be effective in adapting your speaking behavior to your audience, you must do well at reading the audience's response to your comments, and must know which adjustments are needed in order to stay connected with them throughout the speech.

_____

For More Information: These five competencies are based on the article, "Interpersonal Competence: Rationale, Philosophy, and Implementation of a Conceptual Framework," published in the November, 1974 issue of the journal *The Speech Teacher*. Subsequent work to discuss and develop a Christian framework for these principles of communication competency has been conducted by Kelly and Pruitt (2011).

about your topic? Is the audience there because they want to be? Do they lean toward your point of view, or away from it? Critical thinking skills are valuable here as you determine these parameters.

The initial way to approach your responsibility as an audience-centered speaker is to find answers to the following six pertinent questions.

What Does the Audience Know About Me?

Outside of the classroom, you may become a spokesperson for an issue, a cause, or an organization. Generally speaking, your audience will have some basic information about you. In college, characteristics such as age, gender, race, and level of education are easily known, but you may need to include relevant background information at the beginning of your speech. For example, if you wanted to talk about the problems associated with children of state and federal prisoners and your father worked in the prison system, it would be helpful to note this as you begin your speech.

What Does the Audience Know About My Specific Purpose?

The amount of supporting material you include and the extent to which you explain or elaborate are influenced by the expertise of your audience. If you are speaking to a group of cardiologists on the need to convince pregnant women to stop smoking, you can assume far greater audience knowledge than if you were to deliver the same message to a group of concerned citizens.

What Are the Audience's Views on My Topic and Purpose?

Attitudes can be more important than information in determining how your audience responds to a message. It is natural to expect some preconceived attitudes about what you are hoping to accomplish. The views of your audience should influence your choice of main points, the supporting material, and the way you develop your speech.

How Do Audience Members Define Themselves as an Audience?

Individuals who come together to listen to speeches often assume the cultural or organizational identity they share with the body of listeners. Is this a general group of college students? Conservatives? Music majors? At a city council meeting that addresses housing regulations in your community, you might be with several college students attending as tenants of rental property. At another city council meeting, you might gather with other college students because the council is discussing eliminating coffee shops from the city. Though the same people might be in the audience, how you identify or define yourselves differs from situation to situation. In one instance, you and the other college students identify yourselves as renters. In the second situation, you are with college students who are interested in expanded entertainment options.

How Does the Setting and Occasion Influence My Audience?

The setting may be an indoor gymnasium or an outdoor stadium. The occasion may be a graduation ceremony or a funeral service. It helps a speaker to plan carefully when she or he learns in advance what the general feeling is about the setting and the occasion for the presentation. We recall when a member of the clergy drifted off from his main message and began talking about his old family gatherings during a Christmas Eve service when his audience was expecting to hear about the story of the birthday of Jesus and what this event means in our present day. The congregation grew very restless. Remember that it is harder to reach a captive audience (those who are required to attend) than a voluntary audience (those who choose to attend). Students who attend a guest lecture on campus simply to obtain extra credit to boost their grade in a class may feel somewhat indifferent, if not bored, while those who chose to attend because of a keen interest in the speech and speaker will feel much differently. As a speaker, you need to obtain some helpful information about audience attitudes toward the setting and occasion that will bring everyone together for the speech.

What Other Factors Might Affect How the Audience Responds?

Are you the first speaker of the day? The last speaker? Are you speaking at a convention in Las Vegas at 8:00 a.m.? Were the participants out late? Are you one of six students to give a speech during graduation ceremony? Are you the school board representative giving a speech at graduation? If you have knowledge of any factor that may influence your listeners' attentiveness, you can plan in advance ways to increase the likelihood that they will listen carefully. You can shorten the speech, include more vivid examples, and/or work to make your speech even more engaging.

As time goes by, you get to know your classmates and their concerns. Use that information to create interest and engage their attention. Reflect on the six questions identified above and then adapt your topic, language, support, and delivery based on what you decide.

5. Document Ideas Through Support and Sound Reasoning.

Each point made before an audience should be backed up with reliable supporting information and sound reasoning. For example, if you want to persuade your audience that sales tax instead of real estate tax should be used to fund education, concrete evidence will be necessary to support your specific purpose. Later in the book we devote an entire chapter to research and supporting materials, but briefly, we want to point out five different ways that you can provide support.

Use Facts

Facts are verifiable. They hold more weight than opinions. If your specific purpose was to demonstrate how political campaigns have changed dramatically over the last several decades, you might include the following facts:

- In 1960 John Kennedy became the first presidential candidate to use his own polling specialist.
- In 1972 George McGovern pioneered mass direct-mail fundraising.
- In 1980 Jimmy Carter campaigned by conference phone calls to voters in Iowa and New Hampshire.
- In 1984 Ronald Reagan used satellite transmissions to appear at fundraisers and rallies.
- In 1988 a number of presidential hopefuls used videotapes to deliver their message to voters in the early primary states.

- In 1992 California Governor Jerry Brown introduced a 1-800 number for fundraising and answering questions.
- In 1996 candidates and prominent party supporters recorded one-minute phone calls that focused on issues believed to be important to voters.
- In 2007 Hillary Clinton established a website that included video snippets, news reports, an opportunity for blogging, and numerous ways to contribute to her presidential campaign.

These facts support the speaker's claim, and show how candidates have attempted to reach the masses over time. Keep in mind that you need to cite your sources as you provide the facts.

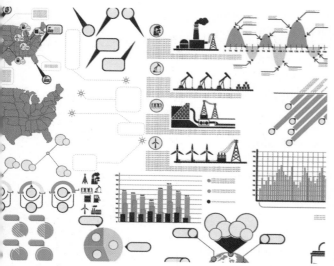

Statistics from reliable sources can add much credibility to your presentation.

Provide Statistics

Providing statistics can offer strong support to your speech. Statistics inform, startle, and convince. In trying to convince his audience about the dramatic increase in the use of the Internet in political campaigns, one student cited the work of Bruce Bimber and Richard Davis:

The number of Internet sites is in the tens of millions. A 2001 survey of Internet usage found that the top ten sites together attracted just under 17 percent of all Internet traffic. Despite the undeniable clout of some key businesses in delivering content on the Internet, this is a far different media environment than when Kennedy and Nixon squared off on the three networks in 1960 (2003).

Recognizing that Internet usage is increasing every day, a student giving a similar speech today could use statistics posted May 24, 2006 from "The Bivings Report." Survey results show that "ninety-six percent of this year's Senate candidates have active websites, while only fifty-five percent of candidates had websites in 2002" (www.bivingsreport.com). Statistics updated on June 30, 2006 reveal Internet users in the United States to be around 227,000,000, which reflects approximately seventy percent of the population (www.internetworldstats.com). These statistics provide useful support to the claim that technology has changed how candidates campaign. Keep in mind, however, that your speech should not be a laundry list of statistics.

Illustrate Using Examples

A third form of support is the use of examples to help illustrate a point or claim. Illustrations, especially detailed and current ones, help to clarify points and they may leave a lasting impression on your audience. If the purpose of your speech was "to convince the class that voters are influenced by information provided on the Internet," you might use the following illustration:

The use of computers by members of the general public has increased considerably in recent years. For example, my brother-in-law, Tom, and his friends purchased personal computers at some point before the last national campaign. Tom meets regularly with a group of friends who have retired after years of working in a nearby automobile plant. As they developed basic computer skills and surfed the Internet, they also began to pay attention to political news and advertisements. The information they gathered as individuals became subjects for their informal get-togethers leading up to the election. They reported to their friends and family members that the information from the Internet served as a strong influence on how they voted.

This example, along with other forms of support such as facts and statistics, can demonstrate to the audience the increasing use and effectiveness of the Internet in political campaigns. As an audience-centered speaker, you want to think of the best way to keep the attention of your audience, and provide support that is best suited to them. Chapter 6 will elaborate on the use of examples.

Figurative analogy: Studying abroad is like your first week in college. You're unfamiliar with the environment, you don't know the people who are around you, and you're not quite sure what to expect.

Include Testimony

A fourth form of support is the use of testimony, which involves quoting someone's experience or opinion. Testimony can be a powerful form of support because everyone pays attention to an expert. Courts of law frequently call on the testimony of expert witnesses; televised news programs broadcast the observations of experts on newsworthy stories; and, from time to time, even commercials provide the endorsement of experts rather than celebrities to confirm the reliability of a product or service. So to prove, reinforce, or clarify a point, a public or presentational speaker often links his/her contention with a statement of a recognized expert on a subject.

Construct Analogies

Using analogies is a fifth form of support. This involves making comparisons to clarify or prove a point. They lend support by encouraging listeners to think in a novel way. *Figurative* analogies compare different kinds of things, and *literal* analogies compare similar categories. If you compare an argument with a sporting event, you are using a figurative analogy, but if you compare one college with another college, you are using a literal analogy. For example, in a speech about studying abroad, a student could use the following figurative analogy.

Studying abroad is like your first week in college. You're unfamiliar with the environment, you don't know the people who are around you, and you're not quite sure what to expect. But as the week goes on, you start to make friendships, your environment becomes more comfortable, and you start to get into some kind of predictable routine. Keep in mind, anytime you have a new experience, you'll experience some uncertainty.

Then, the literal analogy:

> Studying abroad is similar to studying at this or any other university. You attend classes and take exams. You have a place to live, and dining options. You have to study, and you also have free time. The difference is, you're far from home, you aren't familiar with your environment, and people speak a different language.

6. Draft the Introduction, Body, and Conclusion.

If you spend days researching your first speech but only a few hours organizing your ideas, the result is likely to be a speech that fails to present your message in a focused way. To be effective, speeches require an easy-to-follow organizational plan that makes it possible for others to receive and understand your message. As you will see in Chapters Eight and Nine, the logical way to organize your speech is to divide it into three parts: the introduction, body, and conclusion.

As you draft your speech, lay it out into the three parts. Construct a comprehensive, full-sentence outline and work to tie the sentences into a coherent whole. Then, reduce these sentences to key words and phrases and transfer them onto speaker's notes, which will serve as your guide when you deliver your speech. A well-thought out, clearly constructed outline and speaker's notes will greatly increase the potential for success. The following paragraphs highlight important aspects to consider as you develop your first speech.

Introduction

The introduction should capture the attention and interest of your audience, establish your credibility as a speaker, and preview your speech. You can accomplish these aims in many ways, such as humorous anecdotes or a dramatic or startling statement.

Body

The body of your speech contains your key ideas and relevant supporting material. It is the most time-consuming aspect of speech development. Frequently, speakers work on the body before the introduction, because gaps in logic or information may be discovered as the body is developed. Main points should flow from the thesis statement. To be effective, the speech needs to follow some logical pattern. Chapter Six discusses organizing and outlining your ideas. You have at least five patterns of organization to consider: chronological, topical, spatial, cause and effect, and problem-solution.

Conclusion

Your concluding remarks have three purposes: (1) to reinforce the message, (2) to summarize the main points, and (3) to provide closure in some way that relates your message to your listeners' lives. Main ideas will be summarized. Your final thought may take the form of a quotation, a statement, or a question that reinforces or even broadens the purpose of your speech. The conclusion of a persuasive speech may also describe the specific actions you want your listeners to take.

7. Develop the Language of the Speech with Care.

An enthusiastic young woman looked out into the audience of almost 1,500 people on her graduation day and was overwhelmed with the spirit that marked this important occasion. A hush fell over the crowd as she began her address as president of the senior class: "You guys are all terrific! Awesome! This has been an awesome four years for us, right? Like, we have really made it! Wow!" As she proceeded, reflecting on the events of the past four years, her comments were laced with slang that may have been suitable for the coffee shop or gatherings with friends, but not for such a special occasion.

The words you choose to convey your message reflect your personality, your attitude toward your subject, occasion, and audience, and your concern for communicating effectively. Words are your primary vehicle for creating meaning. They set forth ideas, spark visions, arouse concerns, elicit emotions, but if not used carefully, produce confusion. The following four guidelines will help you choose your words with care.

Use Plain English
Let simple, direct language convey your message. Your audience should not need an interpreter. You could say "contusion" or "ecchymosis," but most audiences would find the word "bruise" clearer. Also, it is generally best to avoid the use of slang.

Remember That Writing and Speaking Are Different Activities
While in a written report the terms "edifice," "regulations," and "in the eventuality of," may be acceptable; in public speaking the words, "building," "rules," and "if," are far more effective.

Relate Your Language to Your Audience's Level of Knowledge
If you are describing drug testing in professional sports, do not assume your audience understands such terms as "false positives," "chain of custody," and "legal and individual safeguards." If you use these terms in your speech, you should define them in order to keep the message clear.

Use Language for Specific Effect
If your goal is to sensitize your audience to the plight of America's working poor, the following statement is not incorrect, but it may be ineffective: "Although millions of Americans work a full day, they cannot pay their bills or provide for their families."

For a more powerful effect, you might try the following alternative: "Millions of Americans come home each day, exhausted and covered with a layer of factory filth or kitchen grease. Their backbreaking labor has given them few rewards: They cannot pay their rent, buy shoes for their children, or eat meat more than once a week." Clearly, the second version paints memorable word pictures. We explain more about the power of language to create meaning in Chapter Ten. Keep your audience in mind as you choose effective language for communicating your ideas.

8. Deliver Your Speech While Making Your Tension Work for You.

As we noted earlier, you are not alone if you have some tension or anxiety about speaking in front of an audience. Most likely, you will engage in some in-class activities to help you feel more comfortable speaking in class. In the next several paragraphs, we first focus on delivery and then discuss how to make tension work for you.

Verbal and Nonverbal Delivery

Vocal elements of delivery include, but are certainly not limited to: volume, articulation and pronunciation, pacing, and avoiding "fillers." Nonverbal aspects include: eye contact, gestures, and movement. Your audience is not expecting perfection, but you do not want to create a situation where your lack of effective vocal and/or physical delivery keeps you from achieving your goals.

Your audience must hear you. No matter how convincing or eloquent your speech is designed to be, if you speak too softly your audience cannot hear your message and will not be able to respond. Be aware that your pace (rate of speech) may be slower in the comfort of your dorm room than it is in front of your class. Some nervous speakers unconsciously race through their speech. Normally rapid speakers should try to slow down. Varying your pace can aid in maintaining audience interest and draw attention to certain parts of your speech.

Proper articulation, the verbalization of distinct sounds, is important in formal speaking situations. Saying "hafta," "gonna," and "wanna" is discouraged. Also, if you have any question about the correct pronunciation of a word, check on it before your speech. When speakers mispronounce words, the audience may infer a lack of knowledge, interest, or preparation.

We also encourage you to avoid vocal fillers. In casual conversation, it is common to hear people say "you know," or "like," or "you know what I mean?" In front of a public audience, these pauses may be filled with "ah," or "um," or "er." Fillers can be awkward or distracting and should be reduced and, if possible, eliminated.

In addition to working on the verbal aspects of your speech, you need to tune in to the nonverbal aspects of your speech. Even if your verbal message is well developed and solidly researched, remaining frozen or slouching in front of your audience is likely to distract from what you intend to communicate. Look at your audience. Through eye contact a speaker can establish a connection with the audience. Your facial expression should match the tone of your voice. Speak conversationally, and use movement, nonverbal gestures, and appropriate facial expressions to provide meaning to your words as well as to gain and maintain your audience's attention. And do not forget, enthusiasm is contagious! For some, this is difficult, but choosing a topic that truly interests you and practicing your speech repeatedly can help greatly.

Strategies for Controlling Tension

The chances are slim of being "cured" of communication apprehension, to use an academic term. However, we can provide some help. One thing to consider is that a major symptom of "speech tension" is a physiological reaction. Most people experience three stages of physiological arousal immediately before and during the first few moments of a speech. The *anticipatory stage* takes place in the minutes before the speech—heart rates zoom from a normal testing rate of about 70 beats per minute to between 95 and 140. The *confrontational stage* is typically at the beginning of the speech, when heart rates jump to between 110 and 190 beats per minute. This stage usually lasts no more than thirty seconds and gives way to the *post-confrontational stage*. This final stage is when the pulse returns to anticipation levels or lower. Confrontation experienced in stage two is so strong that speakers may not perceive the decrease. As a nervous speaker, you may stop feeling nervous without realizing it. (Motley 1988).

© 2012 by StockLite.
Used under license of Shutterstock.

Speak conversationally and use eye contact and facial expression to hold your audience's attention.

Most fearful speakers experience the symptoms of a dry mouth and sweaty palms, and sometimes even heavy breathing. These symptoms are the body's "fight or flight" response. People who experience speech tension often feel the urge to withdraw (Run away! Run away!). We are not always aware of this desire. Even as we convince ourselves that we are not nervous, our nonverbal behavior may reveal our unconscious discomfort. Below are several strategies for controlling tension.

Many strategies are available for reducing anxiety. Ultimately, your goal is to channel this nervous energy into public speaking with self-confidence.

1. *Focus on your message and your audience, not yourself.* Keep your mind on your message and the best way to convey it to your audience. Always think of your audience as being on your side.

2. *Prepare!* Preparation sharpens your presentation and builds confidence. Start with a sound speech plan and then rehearse the speech aloud by yourself. Then practice in front of others to get the feel and response of an audience.

3. *Take several deep breaths.* Deep breathing has a calming effect on the body and mind. We have used this technique ourselves and find our students have used it with success as well. You can do this as you are waiting to speak. It also helps to take a final deep breath after you get in front of the audience and just before you speak. Try it!

4. *Realize that you may be your own worst critic.* Studies have shown that the amount of tension a speaker reports has little relationship to the amount of nervousness an audience detects. Even listeners trained to detect tension often fail to perceive it (Motley 1988, 47).

5. *Gain proficiency and confidence by choosing to speak*. Find opportunities to speak. Give "mini speeches" at meetings or in classes when discussion is invited. A colleague of ours conquered his considerable fear of public speaking before an audience and became a successful speaker in large lecture classes by volunteering to speak whenever a situation was convenient and available.

6. *Visualize your success as a speaker*. Creating powerful mental images of skillful performances and winning competitions is a technique that has been used for years by athletes who use visualization to help them succeed. This technique can also be used in public speaking. Visualize yourself speaking with confidence and self-assurance and imagine the sound of applause after your presentation (Ayers, Hopf, and Myers 1997).

7. *Release tension through assertive and animated delivery*. Here is where a nervous speaker may be caught between a rock and a hard place. Being nervous can inhibit your delivery, but assertive and animated delivery can provide a release from pent-up tension. So, if you are prepared to speak, you have practiced speaking out loud, and you focus on your audience, you will be able to gesture, use eye contact, and move—all means for releasing nervous energy.

We encourage you to try several of these suggestions during your first speech. You may not overcome your fear of speaking, but you may reduce it, and you may use your nervous energy productively. Keep in mind, nothing substitutes for preparation and practice. Just like when getting ready for a piano recital, choral concert, or a competitive sports activity, the more you practice, the more you learn, and the greater the likelihood of success.

❯SUMMARY

As public speaking instructors, we would prefer to cover everything in this text *before* you give a graded speech. However, we know that is not possible. That said, this chapter was designed to help you with your first speech as well as to provide a preview of the text. We have outlined eight steps for preparing to speak; each step involves reflection and decision-making. Remember to choose a topic you care about, engage in ethical behavior, determine the purpose of your speech and, as you develop your speech, use language that is appropriate and relevant to your audience. Focus on your audience. As you practice your speech, work on nonverbal aspects of delivery, such as eye contact, gestures, and movement. Find strategies to reduce tension and project enthusiasm and self-confidence.

QUESTIONS FOR ANALYSIS

1. What factors should you keep in mind when choosing a topic and framing a purpose for speaking?

2. Discuss with member of your class what is understood to be the relationships between a speaker's link to a topic, choice of a purpose, amount of information available, and the needs of the audience.

3. Although degrees of speech tension vary from speaker to speaker, most inexperienced speakers share common feelings of discomfort. What can you do to minimize your feelings of apprehension and make your nervous energy work for you rather than against you?

 # ACTIVITIES

1. Take an inventory of what you believe to be your own strengths and weaknesses as a public speaker and establish goals as well as expectations you intend to pursue as you participate in this course.

2. Make a list of the basic steps in preparing your first speech for class. Study your list to see how it relates to the steps featured in this chapter.

3. Prepare and deliver a five- to six-minute informative speech. Draw the topic from your own experiences or interests and not from one of your college courses.

REFERENCES

Ayers, J., T. Hopf, and D. M. Myers. 1997. Visualization and performance visualization: Application, evidence, and speculation. In J.A. Daly, J. C. McCroskey, J. Ayers, T. Hopf, and D.M. Ayers (Eds.), *Avoiding communication* (305–330). Cresskill, NJ: Hampton Press.

Bimber, B., and R. Davis. 2003. *Campaigning online: The Internet in U.S. elections*. New York: Oxford.

Bradley, B. 1988. *Fundamentals of speech communication*, (5th ed.) Dubuque, IA: Wm. C. Brown.

Esslinger, J.J. 1992. "National parks: A scenery of destruction and degradation." *In Winning orations of the interstate oratorical association*. WI: Mankato State University.

Motley, M. T. 1988. Taking the terror out of talk. *Psychology Today*, 46–49.

NAME: _____ DATE: _____

HONOR STATEMENT: I, the undersigned student, hereby declare before God, before the school, and before the professor that I have read Chapter 6 in its entirety, that I have completed the following exercise with help from no other sources, and that I neither have shared nor will share this work with anyone.

Signature: _____ Date: _____

SHORT ESSAYS

1. List and briefly describe, in order, each of the eight steps that this chapter presents as a guide for putting together an effective speech presentation. Use your own words to explain what each of these steps involves (200-300 words).

_____

_____

_____

_____

_____

_____

_____

_____

_____

_____

_____

_____

_____

_____

_____

_____

_____

_____

_____

_____

_____

_____

_____

_____

_____

_____

_____

_____

_____

_____

_____

_____

_____

_____

2. Explain in your own words the difference between a general purpose, a specific purpose, and a thesis statement (100-200 words).

_____

_____

_____

3. Describe in your own words some of the different ways that you can provide support for your message in a speech. Give an example of each that the textbook does not already present (100-200 words).

_____

_____

_____

_____

_____

_____

_____

_____

_____

_____

4. List and describe in your own words seven strategies, presented in the chapter, that you can use to channel nervous energy when preparing and presenting a speech. Propose two additional strategies that you would recommend and explain why you would recommend them.

_____

_____

_____

_____

_____

_____

_____

_____

HONOR STATEMENT: I, the undersigned student, hereby declare before God, before the school, and before the professor that I have read Chapter 6 in its entirety, that I have completed the following exercise with help from no other sources, and that I neither have shared nor will share this work with anyone.

Signature: _____   Date: _____

SPEECH PLANNING EXERCISE

One way to reduce communication apprehension is to speak about topics about which you are knowledgeable and passionate. Even so, students who understand this in principle can struggle to come up with such a speech topic. If you find yourself in this position, use a topic discovery list to stir your thinking. For this exercise, apply the following statements to yourself and then write down your responses. Then, using your responses as a guide, create a list of topics that might work for on informative speech and one that might work for a persuasive speech.

Topic Discovery Sheet

1. What I like to do in my free time is _____

_____

2. What most people don't know about me is _____

_____

3. The one thing I see happening today that really concerns me is _____

_____

4. A current event that has happened recently which makes me happy is _____

_____

5. If I could change one thing in my life it would be _____

_____

6. What l plan to do when I get out of college is _____

_____

7. The place I've visited that I enjoyed the most was _____

_____

8. The most important skill I someday will teach my kids is _____

_____

9. My favorite vacation was spent doing _____

10. The best decision I ever made was _____

_____

11. The worst decision I ever made was _____

_____

12. My hometown has changed during the last decade, mostly because of _____

_____

13. If I had a million dollars, I would use it to _____

_____

14. My favorite move is _____

_____

Now that you have identified some topics and issues, list some possible subjects for your speeches.

Informative topics

1.

2.

3.

4.

5.

Persuasive topics

1.

2.

3.

4.

5.

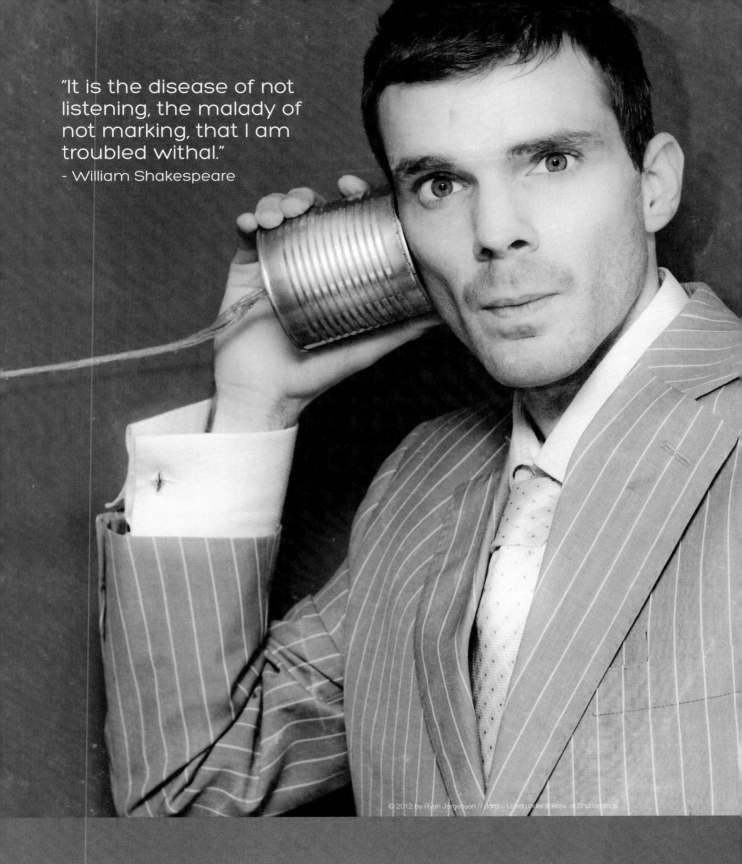

"It is the disease of not listening, the malady of not marking, that I am troubled withal."
- William Shakespeare

CHAPTER 7 »

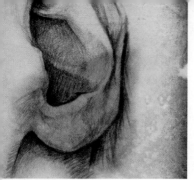

7 LISTENING TO AND EVALUATING SPEECHES

Adapted from *Public Speaking: Choices for Effective Results, Fifth Edition* by John Makay et al. Copyright © 2008.
Reprinted with permission of Kendall Hunt Publishing Co.

❯❯THE IMPORTANCE OF GOOD LISTENING SKILLS

As discussed in previous chapters, public speaking is an audience-centered process. Decisions made throughout this process, from topic selection to delivery, should focus on your listeners. One way to improve your chances of success is to approach the process from the listening side—that is, to work at developing better listening skills. These skills are essential for two different, but complementary, reasons:

© 2012 by Bettmann/Corbis.

Few who heard Kennedy's inaugural address recall the militant nature of his remarks; they focused on the inspirational message.

1. By understanding the needs of your listening audience, you will be able to develop and deliver speeches that have the greatest chance of communicating your intended meaning.

2. By understanding the factors affecting listening, you will be able to monitor your own listening habits and more effectively evaluate and criticize the speeches of others, including those of your classmates. There is a direct relationship between the quality of your listening and the quality of your speaking. *Good speakers use what they hear to analyze and respond to the needs of their audience, and to present information in a way that promotes communication.*

Despite the amount of time we spend listening, our ability to retain what we hear is limited. According to communication professor Ralph G. Nichols, a pioneer in listening research, immediately after listening to a speech, we can recall only half of what was said. After several days, only about twenty-five percent of the speech stays with us (Nichols 1961).

We can illustrate Nichols' findings by examining what people remember about John F. Kennedy's 1960 inaugural address. Although all who heard it when it was first delivered (or later on tape) remember these words, "And so, my fellow Americans, ask not what your country can do for you—ask what you can do for your country," few recalled the militant nature of Kennedy's remarks: "Let all our neighbors know that we shall join with them to oppose aggression or subversion anywhere in the Americas. And let every other power know that this hemisphere intends to remain master of its own house."

❯❯REFLECT ON HOW YOU LISTEN

Many people think of listening as a simple task that involves sitting back and giving the speaker your attention. As the following interchange suggests, listening is more complicated than it appears. As public speakers, we hope our message and meaning will be understood. As audience members, we may have other things on our minds—distractions, preconceived notions, prejudices, misunderstandings, and stress— and the message we receive may be much different from the message sent. The speaker (left-hand column) is a liberal activist from the 1960s. The listener (right-hand column) is a student in the new century.

SPEAKER

Around forty years ago, at about this time of year, I—and a whole lot of other committed students—spent a solid week—day and night—in the offices of our college president. Needless to say, we hadn't been invited.

We were protesters and proud of it. We were there because we believed the Vietnam War was wrong. We were there because we believed racism was wrong. We were there because we believed that women should be given the same opportunities as men.

Were we victorious? For about ten years, I thought so. Then something happened. The signs were subtle at first. Haircuts got shorter. The preppie look replaced torn jeans. Business became the major of choice.

In a flash—it happened that quickly—these subtle changes became a way of life. Campus life, as I knew it, disappeared. Revolution and concern for the oppressed were out, and conservatism and concern for the self were in.

From the point of view of someone who has seen both sides—the radical, tumultuous sixties and the calm, money-oriented eighties, nineties, and the new century—students of today are really forty-year-olds in twenty-year-old bodies. They are conservative to the core at the only time of life when they can choose to live free. I am here to help you see how wrong you are.

LISTENER

Here I am again—listening to another speaker who says he stormed his college administration building in the 60s. This must be a popular topic on the college speaking circuit. Maybe this guy will be different from the other three middle-aged radicals I heard, but I doubt it… The least they could do is turn up the air conditioning. It's so hot I can hardly breathe, let alone listen.

These guys keep talking about how they know the way and how we're all wrong… I wonder what he does for a living. I'll bet he hasn't saved any lives lately or helped the poor. He probably earns big bucks giving speeches on campus telling us how horrible we are… He looks like he spends a lot of time cultivating his hippie look. He must have slept in those clothes for a week. These guys all look the same.

He's harping on the same old issues. Doesn't he know the Vietnam War is ancient history; that African Americans have more opportunities than they ever had—I wish I could earn as much as Denzel Washington; that women are on the job along with men—I wish I could earn as much as Katie Couric … I guess I'll have a pizza for dinner. I should have eaten before I came. I'm really hungry.

Of course we're interested in business. Maybe he had a rich father who paid his tuition, but I don't. I need to earn money when I graduate so I can pay back my student loans.

Who does he think he is—calling us conservatives. I'm not a bigot. When I believe something is wrong, I fight to change it—like when I protested against ethnic cleansing overseas and flag burning right here.

I wonder when he'll finish. I've got to get back to the dorm to study for my marketing exam. He just goes on and on about the same old things.

❯REASONS AUDIENCES STOP LISTENING

You may see a bit of yourself in the speaker-listener example. Maybe you do not have this internal dialogue frequently, but most of us experience this occasionally. Based on the listening facts from Rankin and Nichols, it is clear that we spend much of our time listening. We can probably agree that listening is important, but research has shown that we do not retain much of what a speaker says. So, the question remains, why do we stop listening? There is no single answer to this question, but the six reasons listed below may strike a familiar chord. We stop listening:

Our environment determines how well we can listen.

▲When our attention drifts

Listeners drift in and out of a speech, thinking about the heat, their next meal, or an impending exam. Studies have shown that few of us can pay attention to a single stimulus for more than twenty seconds without focusing, at least momentarily, on something else.

▲When we are distracted

Our environment determines how well we can listen. In the speaker-listener example, the heat made it difficult to pay attention. Internal stresses—hunger, unresolved conflict, and concern about exams—are also distractions.

▲When we have preconceived notions

Before the speaker in the example above opened his mouth, the listener had already decided what the speaker stood for based on the speaker's appearance and on a stereotype of what sixties radicals stood for. Although in this case he was right—the speaker's views conformed to the listener's preconceived notions—he may be wrong about other speakers.

▲When we disagree

Although the speaker identified continuing social ills, the listener did not share his concerns. From his point of view, much more was right with the world than the speaker admitted—a perspective that reduced the listener's willingness and ability to consider the speaker's message.

▲When we are prejudiced or inflexible

Few African Americans are as famous or financially successful as Denzel Washington; few women earn as much as Katie Couric. Yet the listener based his reaction to the speaker's message on the premise that if one member of a group can succeed, all can. His prejudice prevented him from seeing the truth in the speaker's words.

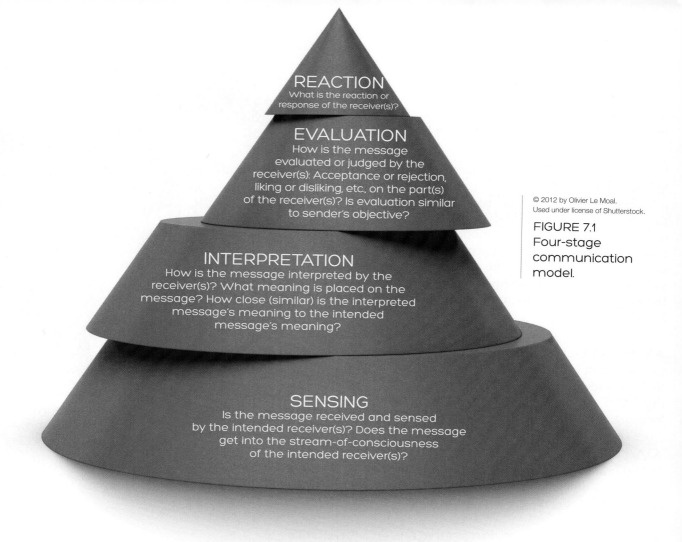

FIGURE 7.1
Four-stage
communication
model.

REACTION
What is the reaction or response of the receiver(s)?

EVALUATION
How is the message evaluated or judged by the receiver(s): Acceptance or rejection, liking or disliking, etc., on the part(s) of the receiver(s)? Is evaluation similar to sender's objective?

INTERPRETATION
How is the message interpreted by the receiver(s)? What meaning is placed on the message? How close (similar) is the interpreted message's meaning to the intended message's meaning?

SENSING
Is the message received and sensed by the intended receiver(s)? Does the message get into the stream-of-consciousness of the intended receiver(s)?

▲When we are faced with abstractions and form our own opinions

The speaker never defined the term "conservative." As a result, the listener brought his own meaning to the term, equating it with bigotry. This meaning may or may not have coincided with the speaker's intent.

As audience members, we know our purpose is to listen, think critically, and retain the central idea of the message. But think about what you do as you listen and why you stop listening. You may consciously or unconsciously tune the speaker out. You may focus on minor details at the expense of the main point. You may prejudge the speaker based on appearance. You may allow your own emotional needs and responses to distort the message, and so on. Later, we will provide specific tips for improving your listening skills, but first, we will discuss the elements of listening.

❯❯THE FOUR STAGES OF LISTENING

Think back to a time when, in an argument with one of your parents, you responded with, "I hear you!" You may have been correct. You *heard* your parent. It is possible, though, that you did not *listen* to your parent. American musical icon Paul Simon points to this problem in his song "The Sound of Silence," and if you listen to the lyrics, you will hear a reference to people "hearing without listening."

While hearing is the physical ability to receive sound, listening is a more complex process. Although listening seems to be instantaneous, it consists of several identifiable stages. Researcher Lyman Steil (1983) analyzes and explains listening in terms of four progressive stages: sensing, interpreting, evaluating, and responding (see figure 7.1, page 166). We move through these stages every time we listen, regardless of the situation. We may be part of a formal audience listening to a paid speaker, we might be engaged in conversation with a friend, or we might be home alone, listening to "things that go bump in the night." Listening can take place on several different levels which are characterized by different degrees of attention and emotional and intellectual involvement. At times, we only partially listen as we think about or do other things; other times we listen with complete commitment. The following is an elaboration of the four stages of listening.

1. Listening Starts When You Sense the Information from Its Source.

Listening begins with sensation, which requires the ability to hear what is said. Sight is also a factor, since the speaker's gestures, facial expressions, and the use of presentational aids communicate intent. Normally, the speaking voice is in the range of 55 to 80 decibels, a level that comfortably enables us to hear a speaker's words. Figure 7.2 shows how this level of sound compares with others in the environment.

As anyone who has tried to listen to a speech over the din of a car siren will realize, obstacles can—and often do—interfere with reception. These obstacles are known to communication theorists as "noise," which was discussed in Chapter One as part of the communication model. When your neighbor in the seat to your left starts coughing or when you are forced to sit at the back of a large, nonamplified auditorium, hearing is difficult, making concentrated listening impossible.

Noise takes other forms, such as environmental annoyances like uncomfortable chairs, stuffy rooms, or struggling air-conditioning systems. At times a remedy is possible. The speaker, for example, can ask the audience to move closer to the front and audience members can find more comfortable seats. When nothing can be done about noise, put yourself in the position of the speaker. Then work hard to listen to the message.

2. Listening Involves the Interpretation of Messages.

A second critical element in listening is interpretation, the phase in which you attach meaning to the speaker's words. As a listener, it is important to keep in mind that words

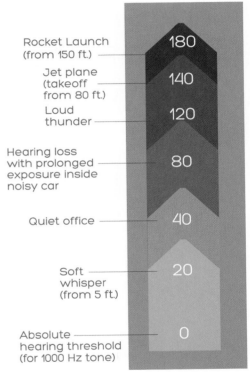

Rocket Launch (from 150 ft.) — 180
Jet plane (takeoff from 80 ft.) — 140
Loud thunder — 120
Hearing loss with prolonged exposure inside noisy car — 80
Quiet office — 40
Soft whisper (from 5 ft.) — 20
Absolute hearing threshold (for 1000 Hz tone) — 0

FIGURE 7.2
How loud are the sounds around us?

have different meanings to different people and that we interpret words based on subjective experiences. According to communication professor Paul G. Friedman, "When listening we can only hope to know what a speaker actually is thinking and trying to convey. Often, our attempts at `mind reading' … are inaccurate" (1986, 12)

Our ability to interpret what we hear is influenced by emotional and intellectual barriers that get in the way of the speaker's intended message. We may hear specific words that offend us, or we find a statement or message repugnant. These barriers are forms of semantic or psychological noise. Novelist David Leavitt (1989) explains how emotional barriers prevented him from dealing with the topic of AIDS many years ago. A homosexual, Leavitt found any mention of AIDS so threatening that he shut off his ability to listen:

> The truth was that AIDS scared me so much I wanted to block it out of my mind. When AIDS came up in a conversation, I'd change the subject. When a frightening headline leaped out at me from the pages of the newspaper, I'd hurriedly skim the article, and, once assured that it described no symptoms I could claim to be suffering from myself, turn the page. Only later … did I recognize the extent to which I was masking denial with self-righteousness (30).

In this case, the psychological mechanism of denial caused the listening obstruction. A college student who is $40,000 in debt due to loans and maxing out credit cards may consciously "tune out" a classmate's persuasive speech on credit card debt in order to avoid thinking about the future. A zoning board member might unconsciously stop listening after two of five citizens have spoken in favor of a petition. An expert on public health can hardly sit still as he listens to a lecture on asbestos removal. After a few minutes he realizes that he and the speaker have completely different views on removal procedure safety. Instead of listening to the rest of the information, he fumes over this difference of opinion.

Whether emotional and intellectual barriers are the result of an unwillingness to deal with real-world problems, a refusal to take advice, or a difference of opinion, the result is the same: Listening is obstructed, interpretation skewed, and communication prevented.

3. Listening Involves Evaluating the Message.

Evaluation requires that you assess the worth of the speaker's ideas and determine their importance to you, particularly when listening to a persuasive message. You must decide whether you share the speaker's point of view and, if not, why not? Research has shown that when we perceive speakers as trustworthy, competent, reliable, highly regarded by others, dynamic, sociable, and similar to ourselves, we are more likely to evaluate them positively than when we see them in negative or less acceptable ways. (Berlo, Lemert, and Mertz 1969)

It is a mistake to assume that we judge these messages solely on their own merits. Research shows that our assessment is influenced by how the message fits into our value system.

According to Friedman (1986) "This results from the human preference for maintaining internal consistency among personal beliefs, feelings, and actions" (13). We agree with messages that are consistent with other beliefs we have, and we disagree with messages that conflict with our beliefs.

This tendency was first described by psychologist Leon Festinger (1957) in his theory of cognitive dissonance. Essentially, the theory argues that we seek internal consistency between attitudes and behaviors. If we do not like a colleague and that person acts badly, we experience consistency between attitude and behavior. If someone we do not like acts in a sincere, friendly manner, we experience inconsistency.

When inconsistency exists, we experience mental stress. To reduce the stress, we are forced to change one or more of our attitudes or behaviors so that the inconsistency is reduced or eliminated. For example, assume you are a school board member who holds a high opinion of the school superintendent, until he angrily tells you to "Shut up!" during a meeting with administrators and other board members. You may experience dissonance because you cannot reconcile your previous esteem for this person with your new feelings of being disrespected. Dissonance disappears when your overall impression is consistent. In this case, you have a choice. You either rationalize the inappropriate behavior and go back to having a high opinion of the school superintendent ("He was under a lot of stress; he didn't mean it."). Or, you change your opinion of the person ("Someone who behaves this way in a formal meeting should not be leading our district."). Thus, as listeners, we seek information consistent with what we already know; we accept ideas more readily if they are linked to our values and commitments.

To preserve psychological balance, we often reject conflicting ideas and retain our original point of view. According to Friedman (1986, 13) this rejection can take many forms, including the following.

Shoot the messenger.
If you are a member of a college fraternity, you may reject the notion that any fraternity found guilty of a hazing violation should be banned from campus. You may criticize the speaker as uninformed or as someone who was never able to get into a fraternity himself.

Rally 'round the flag.
Listeners who disagree with a speaker's message may seek the support of others who share their point of view—in this case, other fraternity members. Shared support provides comfort and reassurance. However, it does not necessarily mean that you are right.

What the speaker says is not what you hear.
Although the speaker may focus on hazing violations that put pledges in physical jeopardy, you hear him say that all violations—even minor infractions—should result in the fraternity being banned.

Convince yourself that the speaker's message has nothing to do with you.
Even when opinions collide, you may convince yourself that you and the speaker are

talking about two different things.

Don't think about it and it will go away.

If, as a fraternity member, you took part in several unpleasant hazing incidents, listening to the speech may force you to question what you have done. To avoid the emotional discomfort that goes with this soul-searching, you may unconsciously block messages with which you do not agree.

Although these methods may seem extreme, we all rely on one or more of them at one time or another. Those who use them excessively—individuals who are threatened by any difference of opinion—are considered dogmatic and authoritarian (Ehrlich and Lee 1969).

4. Listening Involves Responding to the Speaker's Message

Feedback is also part of the listening process. In a conversation, the roles of listener and speaker change regularly. As the listener, you can interrupt the speaker, ask questions, engage in nonverbal behavior such as maintaining eye contact, touching, or hugging. At the mass media level, you may respond positively to a television series by watching it weekly or by purchasing a product that is advertised during the commercial. Listeners in a public speaking setting provide feedback in a variety of ways: laughing, smiling, nodding in agreement, cheering or booing, clapping, and questioning the speaker after the presentation is over. Listeners also provide feedback on a less conscious level, such as yawning, looking around the room, or whispering to the person next to you.

Effective speakers rely on and encourage feedback from their audience. They watch carefully for messages of approval or disapproval and adjust their presentations accordingly. We discuss audience feedback in detail in our chapter on the connection between the speaker and the audience.

❯❯EIGHT STEPS TO FINE-TUNE YOUR LISTENING SKILLS

As a skill, listening is notoriously undervalued. Philosopher Mortimer Adler (1983) uses the following sports analogy to describe why the act of listening is as important as the act of speaking: "Catching is as much an activity as throwing and requires as much skill, though it is a skill of a different kind. Without the complementary efforts of both players, properly attuned to each other, the play cannot be completed." The players involved in the act of communication are speakers and listeners, all of whom have a role in the interaction. In this section, we explain how you can improve your listening skills—and, therefore, the chances of meaningful communication—by becoming conscious of your habits and, when necessary, redirecting your efforts. Listening is a multi-stage process that can be improved in many different ways (Pudy 1989).

1. Get Ready to Listen.

Preparation is critical, especially when you have other things on your mind. Plan to make the effort to listen even before the speech begins, deliberately clearing your mind of distractions so you are able to concentrate on the speech.

2. Minimize Listening Barriers.

This step is more difficult than it sounds, for it often involves overcoming emotional and intellectual barriers to listening that we identified in preceding passages. Often, we need help in recognizing our listening "blind spots." As you talk with your classmates about each other's speeches, try to determine whether the message you received from a speaker was the same message they heard. If it was not, think about what the topic means to you; try to identify any reasons for your misunderstanding. It may be possible that you are the only one who accurately understood the speaker's message. Sometimes an entire audience misses the point. If a question-and-answer period follows the speech, you can question the speaker directly to make sure you have the right meaning.

© 2012 by Anatoliy Samara.
Used under license of Shutterstock.

Intentional listening is one of the most important communication skills one can develop.

3. Leave Distractions Behind.

Some distractions are more easily dealt with than others. You can change your seat to get away from the smell of perfume but you cannot make a head cold disappear. You can close the door to your classroom, but you cannot stop the speaker from rattling change in his pocket. Although dealing with distractions is never easy, you can try to put them aside so you can focus on the speaker and the speech. This task will become easier if you view listening as a responsibility—and as work. By considering listening as more than a casual interaction, you will be more likely to hear the message being sent.

4. Don't Rush to Judgment.

Resist the temptation to prejudge speakers. You may think about dismissing someone because "she's old," "he's conservative," or "he always dresses like a dork." As a listener, you have the responsibility to evaluate the content of the speech and not to jump to conclusions based on impressions of what you know about the speaker or how he or she looks.

Listeners have the tendency to prejudge topics as well as speakers. You may yawn at the thought of listening to one of your classmates deliver an informative speech about the "pickling process" or "stage make-up" until you realize that the topic is more interesting than you expected. You may not have an inherent interest in the topic, but that does not mean the speaker cannot be interesting or thought-provoking.

Some speakers save their best for last. They may start slowly and build a momentum of ideas and language. Your job is to listen and be patient.

5. Listen First for Content, Second for Delivery.

Both words and delivery impart meaning, and your public speaking class is designed to help you develop appropriate content and to deliver your speech in a meaningful way. But most of you have never participated in a speech tournament. Few of you have acted before. Your speaking engagements, for the most part, have been limited. Your job as a listener is to separate content from delivery, and focus first on the message.

Confronted with poor delivery, it is difficult to separate content from presentation. The natural tendency is simply to stop listening when speakers drone on in a monotone, deliver speeches with their heads in their notes, or sway back and forth. Delivery often has little to do with the quality of the speaker's ideas. Many of the speakers you will hear over the years will be in the position to address you because of their accomplishments, not their speaking ability. While a Nobel prize-winning scientist may be able to explain a breakthrough in cancer therapy, he or she may have no idea how to make eye contact with an audience. To avoid missing these speakers' points, look past poor delivery and focus on content.

6. Become an Effective Note Taker.

Each time a professor lectures or conducts a class discussion, you and your fellow students are expected to take notes. After years of note taking, this activity probably seems as natural as breathing; it is something you do to survive. Ironically, though you worked hard to develop this skill, it often disappears at graduation. Most people do not pull out a pad and pen when listening to a speech in the world outside the classroom. But note taking is as appropriate and necessary for nonstudents as it is for students. When you listen to a speech at a public event, a political rally, or on television, taking notes will help you listen more effectively. The following suggestions will help you improve your note-taking—and listening—skills:

© 2012 by wavebreakmedia ltd.
Used under license of Shutterstock.

After years of note taking, this activity probably seems as natural as breathing; it is something you do to survive.

- Create two columns for your notes. Write "Facts" at the top of the left-hand column and "Personal reactions/questions" at the top of the right-hand column. If the speaker does not answer your questions during the course of the speech, ask for clarification at the end. This is particularly important when someone is talking about something complex, such as a change in insurance coverage, taxes, or city development.

- Use a key-word outline instead of full sentences to document the speaker's essential points. If you get bogged down trying to write full sentences, you may miss a huge chunk of the message. At the end of the speech, the key-word outline also gives you a quick picture of the speaker's main points.

- Use your own abbreviations or shorthand symbols to save time. If you know that "comm" means communication, then use that. If you are not sure whether it means "communication," "communism" or "community," then the abbreviation is not working for you. We have seen students use up and down arrows instead of writing "increase" or "decrease." Use a system that works for you.

- Use diagrams, charts, scales, and quick-sketch images to summarize thematic concepts or theories. Smiley faces may seem trite, but they can express succinctly how you feel about a concept. A scale may be useful as someone presents the pros and cons of some issue.

- Use a numbering system to get down procedural, directional, or structural units of information. Numbering helps organize information, especially if the speaker did not organize the units of information for you.

- If, no matter how quickly you write, you cannot keep up, ask the speaker—verbally or nonverbally—to slow down. Be somewhat cautious with this last suggestion. Do not ask the speaker to slow down so that you might write full sentences. You are just asking the person to slow down for purposes of general understanding. If you are the only person who is experiencing difficulty, you may want to ask questions at the end, or make an appointment to fill in any gaps in understanding.

© 2012 by Hasloo Group Production Studio. Used under license of Shutterstock.

Do you tend to take "mental vacations" during class lectures?

7. Be an Active Listener.

One of the worst things about lecturing to 200 or more students is that some of them believe they cannot be seen because there are so many in the audience. So they talk to their neighbors, toss notes to their friends, slouch low in the seat, put their heads on their desks, or tuck into the cover of the hood on their sweatshirt. What these students do not know (surely you are not one of them!) is that we can see you and we want you to be engaged in the listening process.

As listeners, we have the ability to process information at the rate of about 400 words per minute. However, as most people talk at only about 150 words per minute, we have a considerable amount of unused thinking time to spare (Wolf et al. 1983, 154). This "extra time" often gets in the way of listening because we have the opportunity to take mental excursions away from the speaker's topic. It is natural to take brief trips ("I wonder what's for lunch?") but it can be problematic when they become major vacations ("Wow. Last night when I was talking to Suzy on the phone…and she said…..and then I said….and I couldn't believe it when she said….so I said…") To minimize the potential for taking a lengthy vacation while listening, experts suggest the following techniques:

- Take notes to keep your focus on the speech.
- Before the speech begins, write down any questions you have about the topic. As the speech progresses, determine whether the speaker has answered them.
- Apply the speaker's comments to your own experience and knowledge. This makes the message more memorable.
- Define the speech's thesis statement and main supporting points. This helps you focus on the critical parts of the speech.
- Decide whether you agree with the speaker's point of view and evaluate the general

performance. This keeps you engaged by focusing on the message and the speaker.

8. Provide Feedback.

Let speakers know what you think. Even in a large lecture hall, the speaker is aware of the audience and will establish eye-contact with members of the audience. Lean forward in your chair, nod your head, smile, frown. This kind of participation will force you to focus your attention on the speaker and the speech. Providing feedback at the various stages of a speech can be hard work, requiring total involvement and a commitment to fighting distractions.

❯❯EVALUATING PUBLIC SPEECHES

When you evaluate speeches, you engage in a form of feedback, a process that makes you a speech critic. As you consider the elements included in a speech and note the speech's strengths and weaknesses, you are taking part in a formal process of analysis and appraisal.

This formal process is not limited to the public speaking class. After virtually every speech the United States president gives, including the inaugural speech and the yearly State of the Union speech, politicians, rhetoricians, and media critics provide analyses. Over a decade ago, President Clinton received a grade in a syndicated column written by William Safire, a political columnist and former speechwriter. Safire is the author of numerous books and has distinguished himself as an expert on language.

Safire gave the president's speech good marks in terms of its theme (simple, direct, fitting); use of metaphor ("a season of service," "we force the spring"); hint of policy information; anaphora (communications and commerce are global; investment is mobile; technology is almost magical; and ambition for a better life universal); length (blessedly brief—fourteen minutes); historic resonance (echoes of Jefferson, Wilson, Roosevelt, Kennedy); turn of phrase ("anyone who has ever watched a child's eyes wander into sleep"); and delivery (his strong voice, confidence, demeanor, lack of flubs). The weaknesses he identified were with what he called "cheap shots" (The old "people are working harder for less"); ``fuzzy sacrifice" ("We must invest more in our own people [i.e., raise taxes] … and at the same time cut our massive debt"); "applause lines" ("There is nothing wrong with America that can't be cured by what is right with America"); and ``lift" (it never soared). Safire wrote: "I give it a B. Maybe he'll have another chance" (1993).

Outside of the classroom, chances are slim that you would receive a graded critique. Regardless, the point to keep in mind is that criteria are applied each time someone in an audience thinks about a speech, what it means, and what its value may be. As a participant in a public speaking course, you will be expected to criticize constructively your classmate's speeches. It is important that you note the constructive nature of this process.

As you criticize the strengths and weaknesses of speeches, keep in mind that your comments will help your classmates develop as speakers. Your remarks will help to focus their attention on areas that work effectively as well as areas that need improvement. All speakers need this feedback to improve the quality of their performance.

Unfortunately, many students feel reluctant to criticize their classmates' speeches. They may feel they are not experienced enough, they do not like the idea of having people critique their speeches, or they are simply unwilling to work at listening. These students do not view criticism as a skill in the same way they do public speaking. They do not realize that their public speaking success is measured by their ability to listen, speak, and critique.

© 2012 by auremar.
Used under license of Shutterstock.

Because student speakers are likely to feel vulnerable and defensive in the face of their classmates' criticism, it is important to put them at ease by pointing out first what was right with their speech.

CRITERIA FOR EVALUATING PUBLIC SPEECHES

While it is easy to say whether we enjoyed a speech or found it engaging, providing constructive criticism involves more work. The same criteria can be applied to a special occasion speech, an informative speech, or a persuasive speech. The following guidelines take the form of ten separate questions that analyze speeches in terms of their components. For our purposes, we examine content and delivery separately. However, these elements are parts of a unified whole that makes up the dynamic process of communication.

1. Was the topic appropriate for the assignment/audience?
2. Were the general and specific purposes clear?
3. Did the speaker make an effort to analyze the audience and adapt the speech to its needs?
4. Did the speaker use effective and relevant material to support the thesis statement?
5. Was the speech effectively organized?
6. Did the speaker use clear, interesting, and accurate language?
7. Did the speaker appear confident and self-controlled?
8. Was the quality of the speaker's voice acceptable?
9. Were the speaker's movement and gestures meaningful?
10. Did the speaker look for and respond to feedback?

Use these ten questions as a guide to evaluate your classmates' speeches. When you begin to offer criticism, try to be as substantive and concrete as possible. Instead of saying, "She was great," or "I certainly did not like his topic," say, "I liked the way she linked her own experiences as a lifeguard to the need for greater water safety," or "His discussion of the way accounting students are trained was irrelevant for an audience of nonaccounting majors."

Because student speakers are likely to feel vulnerable and defensive in the face of their classmates' criticism, it is important to put them at ease by pointing out first what was right with their speech. Then you can offer suggestions for improving their presentation. Instead of saying, "Your views on the link between electromagnetic fields and cancer were completely unsupported," you might say: "Your examples were clear and crisp when you talked about how common electric appliances, including coffee makers, emit potentially dangerous fields." Then you can add, "I don't think you were as clear when you started talking about how these fields can produce changes in body cells. More concrete examples would be helpful." Rather than saying, "Delivery needs work," you could write something more concrete, such as, "You had so much written on your note cards, you didn't look up. Perhaps having less on your note cards would make it easier to look at the class."

To encourage this type of criticism, many instructors ask students to use a speech evaluation form. This gives feedback to the speaker on a sliding scale and also gives listeners the opportunity to provide constructive comments. Try to provide as much written commentary as possible, for your explanations help speakers improve.

❯SUMMARY

Good listening skills are important for two reasons. First, by understanding the listening needs of your audience, you have a better chance of developing and delivering successful speeches. Second, an understanding of the factors affecting listening will enable you to monitor your own listening habits and help you to evaluate the speeches of others. Studies have shown that although we spend a great deal of time listening, most of us are not good listeners. Listening is a complex activity that involves four separate stages: you sense the information from its source through the physiological process of hearing; you interpret the message by attaching your own meaning to the speaker's words; you evaluate what your hear by judging the worth of the speaker's message and deciding its importance to you; and you respond to the speaker's message through feedback.

You can improve your listening skills by preparing yourself to listen, minimizing listening barriers and leaving distractions behind, by not making snap judgments, listening first for content and second for delivery, becoming an effective note taker, being an active listener, and by providing feedback.

In speech class, you will use your listening skills to evaluate the speeches of your classmates. It is important to learn the art of constructive criticism in order to encourage the speaker.

 QUESTIONS FOR ANALYSIS

1. What role do our emotions play in listening, and how are they related to our ability to think about and analyze a message? Can we suspend our feelings while listening to a speaker? Why or why not?

2. Why is preparation important in listening? How would you prepare to listen to:

    a. a speech on a topic about which you have strong, negative feelings?
    b. a political campaign speech delivered by a candidate you support?

c. a speech on a crisis that affects your life?

d. a lecture on a topic that interests but does not excite you?

3. From a listener's point of view, what is the relationship between the content and delivery of a speech? How does a dynamic delivery influence your opinion of the speaker's message? Compare this to your reaction to a flat, uninspired delivery.

4. Discuss the art of criticism as it pertains to public speaking. Why do so many people define criticism only in negative terms? Think of several well-known public speakers and evaluate the content and delivery of their messages.

ACTIVITIES

1. Attend a lecture, political event, or religious service with the intent of monitoring your own listening behavior. What barriers to listening do you notice as you attempt to follow the speaker's message?

2. Listen to a controversial speech in person or on a video cassette. Then, with the stages of listening in mind, jot down your thoughts and feelings at different times in the speech.

3. Write a brief paper (one to three pages) about a successful listening experience. Be certain to explain what made the experience successful for you.

REFERENCES

Adlet, M. J. 1983. *How to speak, how to listen*. New York: Macmillan.

Berlo, D. K., J.B. Lemert, and R. Mertz. 1969. Dimensions for evaluating the acceptability of message sources, *Public Opinion Quarterly* 33, 563–76.

Ehrlich, H. J., and L .D. Lee. 1969. Dogmatism, learning, and resistance to change: A review and new paradigm, *Psychological Bulletin*, 71, 249–60.

Festinger, L. 1957. *A theory of cognitive dissonance*. CA: Stanford University Press.

Friedman, P. G. 1986. *Listening processes: Attention, understanding, evaluation*, (2nd ed.), 6–15. Washington, DC: National Education Association.

Leavitt, D. 1989. "The Way I Live Now," *The New York Times Magazine*, July 9, 30.

Nichols, R. G. 1961. Do we know how to listen? Practical helps in a modern age, *Speech Teacher*, March, 118–24.

Pudy, M. 1989. Why listen? Speaking creates community. Doesn't it? The role of listening in community formation. *New York State Communication Association: New Dimensions in Communication: Proceedings of the 47th Annual New York State Speech Communication Association, III* (October 13–15) 71–76.

Rankin, P. T. 1926. "The Measurement of the Ability to Understand Spoken Language," unpublished Ph.D. dissertation, University of Michigan. *Dissertation Abstracts* 12 (1952), 847–48.

Safire, W. January 22, 1993. No spot on dean's list for Mr. Clinton, *The Toledo Blade*, 13.

Steil, L. K. 1983. *Listening: Key to your success*. New York: Random House.

Wolf, F. L., N. C. Marsnik, W. S. Taceuy, and R. G. Nichols. 1983. *Perceptive listening*. New York: Holt, Rinehart and Winston.

SHORT ESSAYS

HONOR STATEMENT: I, the undersigned student, hereby declare before God, before the school, and before the professor that I have read Chapter 7 in its entirety, that I have completed the following exercise with help from no other sources, and that I neither have shared nor will share this work with anyone.

Signature: _____   Date: _____

1. What are two reasons why listening is important in a public speaking situation. Use your own words to explain what this chapter says about this (100-200 words).

_____

_____

_____

_____

_____

_____

_____

_____

_____

_____

_____

_____

_____

_____

_____

_____

_____

_____

2. What are some reasons people stop listening? Use your own words to explain what this chapter says about this (100-200 words).

_____

_____

_____

_____

_____

_____

_____

_____

_____

_____

_____

_____

_____

_____

_____

_____

_____

_____

3. What are the four stages of listening, and what happens during each of these stages? Use your own words to explain what this chapter says about this (100-200 words).

_____

_____

_____

4. This chapter presents eight guidelines for becoming a better listening. Which four of these do you consider to be the most important? Be sure to explain your reasoning (200-300 words).

"Like hungry guests, a sitting audience looks."
- George Farquhar

CHAPTER 8 »

8

THE SPEAKER AND AUDIENCE CONNECTION

WHO ARE MY LISTENERS?
- Avoid the Age Gap
- Jettison the Gender Stereotypes
- Determine How Much Your Audience Knows
- Know the Group
- Recognize the Importance of Lifestyle Choices and Values
- Determine Why Your Audience IS an Audience

ARE THEY INTERESTED?
- What Are They Thinking?
- Using a Questionnaire
- Observe and Interview

CREATE THE LINK BETWEEN SPEAKER AND AUDIENCE
- Get to the Point Quickly
- Have Confidence: They Want to Hear Your Speech
- Be of the People, Not Above the People
- Connect with Your Listeners
- Make It a Participatory Event
- Examine Other Situational Characteristics

POST-SPEECH ANALYSIS

SUMMARY

QUESTIONS FOR ANALYSIS

ACTIVITIES

REFERENCES

"Hey professor, why don't you use some examples about cars?" This question was shouted from the back of the room during a workshop for supervisers at a large General Motors manufacturing plant. With frustration in his voice, the young critic was indicating that the speaker should link his ideas to the cultural context of his audience in order to connect with them; in this case, the automobile industry. Fortunately, the speaker had been raised in a family centered in the automobile industry. He himself had worked summers in a plant that produced parts for cars and trucks. The speaker was able to draw from his experiences and could share a considerable number of illustrations with his audience.

Whether in a large auditorium, a corporate board room, or a classroom, audiences are usually self-centered. Listeners want to know what they can learn from your speech or how they can take action that will, in some way, enhance their lives. If you solve listeners' problems, show that you understand what their needs are, and help them to achieve their goals, they will listen.

How do you prepare and deliver a speech that will mean enough to your audience to capture their attention and convince them to listen? Begin by learning as much as you can about your listeners so you can identify and focus on their concerns.

© 2012 by Joseph August / Shutterstock.com. Used under license of Shutterstock.

Presidents and other prominent politicians rely on professionals to write audience-appropriate speeches.

❯WHO ARE MY LISTENERS?

Peggy Noonan is well known for crafting the speeches of presidents and presidential candidates. When George H. W. Bush was about to accept the nomination of the Republican National Party, Noonan wrote the speech he delivered, and when he accepted the Republican nomination for president in 1988, she drafted that speech as well. As a top writer for Ronald Reagan, Noonan prepared the speech the president delivered after the 1986 *Challenger* disaster, in which American astronauts were tragically lost after a dramatic launch toward outer space. She also prepared the speech President Reagan delivered on the fortieth anniversary of D-Day. Noonan's writing was effective because she made sure her speeches and the men who delivered them were deliberately connected to the audiences she envisioned. She explains:

> I strived to make each [speech] special. I thought about the audience. I would think how happy they were to be near the president and how each deserved something special, something personal.... . I did not endear myself to the researchers when I asked them to go back again and again to find out who the leader of such and such an organization was and what his nickname was and has he ever met the President. And in the town where he's speaking, what are the people talking about, is there a local problem like a garbage scow nobody wants, does the local school have a winning team, what's the big local department store and are they hiring? Anything to make it seem as if someone had thought about this speech and these people (1989).

Finding out about the audience enabled Peggy Noonan to write speeches that were especially meaningful. You need not be a presidential speechwriter to understand your audiences in this way. All speakers can create a profile of their listeners by analyzing them in terms of key demographic and psychological characteristics: age, sex, level of knowledge, group membership, and shared values and lifestyles. The information that emerges from this analysis is the raw material for a successful speaker-audience connection. (Woodwad and Denton 2004)

▲Avoid the Age Gap

Is your audience filled with senior citizens or high school students, middle-aged executives or newly hired corporate recruits? By finding out the average age of your listeners, you can avoid being patronizing and condescending.

© 2012 by Artens.
Used under license of Shutterstock.

Learning about and relating to your audience is an essential first step in the speech preparation process.

Avoid assumptions about the average age of your audience. If you are speaking to a group of students, do not assume they will all be in your age bracket. Today, millions of nontraditional students are enrolled in four-year colleges. On any campus, you will meet forty-year-old sophomores seeking a new career or returning to school after their children are grown and sixty-year-old freshmen returning because they love learning.

Focus on your speech, not your age. Business consultant Edith Weiner started to deliver speeches to senior-level executives at the age of twenty-three. "I was much younger than people thought I was going to be," said Weiner. "When I got up to speak, they didn't know what to make of me." Weiner's response was to focus on her message. "If I did well in the first three minutes, not only did I surprise the audience, I created fans. Expectations were so low that when I came across as confident and funny and comfortable, the audience was hooked into the rest of my speech" (1989).

Avoid dating yourself with references or language. If you are addressing a group of teenagers on the topic of popular culture, talk about their current favorite rock group, not the New Kids on the Block. If you are addressing a group of middle-aged executives, do not assume that they know what college students are thinking.

▲Jettison the Gender Stereotypes

Today, a speaker must be inclusive to avoid unfairly categorizing or stereotyping members of the audience. Airlines no longer have "stewardesses," for example, but instead, use "flight attendants." "Car salesmen" have been replaced by "sales associates." Departments on college and university campuses are no longer headed by a "chairman" but rather by a "chair" or a "chairperson." For the most part, speakers should also avoid relying on the masculine pronoun and find ways to include men and women in their audiences.

Gender role differences do exist, however, and generalizations based on these differences are not necessarily wrong. Therefore, if you are addressing a group of young men who you know are likely to enjoy professional sports, it is fair to use a sports analogy to make your point—not because you are a fan but because talking about the Cleveland Browns or the Dallas Cowboys will help you connect with your listeners.

▲Determine How Much Your Audience Knows

Are the members of your audience high school or college graduates, experts with doctorates in the field, or freshmen taking their first course? Use this information to gear the level of your remarks to listeners' knowledge.

A speaker should avoid making reckless assumptions about his or her audience.

Do not assume that expertise in one area necessarily means expertise in others. For example, if you are a stockbroker delivering a speech to a group of scientists about investment opportunities, you may have to define the rules that govern even simple stock trades. Although the more educated your audience, the more sophisticated these explanations can be, explanations must be included for your speech to make sense.

Be careful about assuming what your audience knows—and does not know—about technical topics. Mention a server to people who know nothing about computers and they may be baffled. Define it for a group of computer experts and they will wonder why you were asked to speak to them. In both cases, you run the risk of losing your audience; people who are confused or who know much more about a subject may simply stop listening.

▲Know the Group

Are the members of your audience members of labor organizations or service clubs? Are they volunteers for a local or national organization? Are they politically liberal or conservative? Are they members of the Young Republicans Association? Are they active members of the Chinese Student and Scholar's Association on your campus? If the answer is yes to any of these questions, then the listeners belong to organized groups or party affiliations that may very well affect choices they make.

Listeners may identify themselves as members of formal and informal interest groups. An informal interest group may include YouTube watchers, Starbucks customers, and residents of an inner city neighborhood. A formal interest group may be those persons who belong to and are active with the Future Farmers of America or members of a LISTSERV on alternative treatments for Alzheimer's.

If you are addressing members of the Young Republicans, you can be sure the group has a keen awareness of political issues. Similarly, if you are addressing an exercise class at the local Y, you can be sure that physical fitness is a priority of everyone in the room. It

CROSSING THE CULTURAL DIVIDE
KEYS TO CONNECTING WITH OTHER HUMAN GROUPS

BY DAVID J. ALBAN, PH.D.

A few months after graduating from college during the mid-1990s, I boarded a large jetliner in Baltimore and flew half a world away to begin my teaching career in northern Africa—one of the most interesting and unusual places where I have lived. Leaving behind the familiarity and predictability of America, I entered a classroom filled with teenaged, Arabic-speaking students, aspiring to teach them well despite what I knew must be my very Americanized ways of seeing the world and of relating to them. During the months that followed, I learned through personal experience a lot about cultural differences and their potential for thwarting our attempts to communicate with people whose way of life differs radically from ours. My northern African adventure, along with other cross-cultural interactions that I've had since then, has given me several insights that I briefly share in this article for your benefit.

Culture, as one scholar, defines it is "the collective programming of the mind which distinguishes the members of one human group from another."i Think of it as the shared attitudes, values, and beliefs and ways of acting that unify a human group and distinguish them from other human groups. Some cultures, like the mainstream American and Canadian ways of life, strongly resemble each other. Others, like mainstream American and Arab cultures, differ radically from each another, and these differences can result in serious misunderstandings. Realizing this, the U.S. Army, in 2006, prepared American soldiers for deployment to the Arab world by advising them to avoid conduct there that is unacceptable in that cultural setting: Among the manual's points of advice were the following:

- Do not try and engage a woman in conversation unless you have been formally introduced.

- Do not stare at women or maintain eye contact.

- Do not ask an Arab questions about his wife or other female members of his family.

- Admitting, "I don't know" is distasteful to an Arab.

- Constructive criticism can be taken as an insult. Be careful not to insult [ii]

I became aware of cultural norms like these during personal conferences with my Arab students. When speaking to them, I expected them to make direct eye contact with me to indicate that they were paying attention. I soon discovered that while this may be an acceptable non-verbal way of interacting with people of the same sex in Arab culture, it was not acceptable for interactions with members of the opposite sex. I learned, too, that it is normal in Arab culture for males to express their friendship by publicly holding hands, an expression that connotes something very different in America.

You do not need to go to the other side of the world to encounter cultural differences like these. Years after my return to America, while serving as a school principal, I noted while questioning a student from a migrant family that he would gaze at the floor rather than look at my eyes while I spoke to him. Taking this as a sign of inattention or disrespect, I directed him to look at me when I speak to him. He fidgeted in obvious discomfort. At first, I read this as nonverbal confirmation that he had committed the wrongdoing about which I was questioning him. However, I changed my mind after speaking with another staff member, a liaison for migrant students who told me I had misunderstood the student's behavior. In the migrant's culture, the staff member told me, it is disrespectful to make direct eye contact with an authority who is correcting you. Thus, the student's shuffling was not his nonverbal confirmation of guilt, but rather his reaction to my directive for him to do something he considered disrespectful.

Incidents like these highlight the communication problems that can emerge when people with different backgrounds come together. In an increasingly diverse nation like the United States, learning to recognize and to navigate cultural differences is essential to your professional success, whether in education, healthcare, government, or business. Employers in these fields now routinely train their employees to be "culturally competent" so they can more successfully interact with people who represent a plethora of cultural backgrounds. In today's world, having cross-cultural communication skills is no longer optional. It is a necessity.

Communicating effectively across cultures does not come to us naturally. It requires constant, conscious effort. Here are several helpful principles to consider as you work to develop your skills in this area:

1. RESOLVE TO EXPLORE OTHER CULTURES.

Your culture's way of doing things or of expressing things is not necessarily the right way or the only way. Perhaps the reason we assume so is because we don't realize there are other ways or, if we do, because we don't know what the other ways are. Resolve to learn about other cultures and to address them in terms their constituents understand. Remember, as Albert Einstein once stated, "The measure of intelligence is the ability to change."

2. EXPOSE YOURSELF TO OTHER CULTURES.

Do not just resolve to learn about other cultures and to communicate with them. Place yourself in situations that expose you to these differences. Participate in an overseas study program. Go on a short-term mission trip with your church. Befriend immigrants in your local community. Volunteer to help a local Teaching English as a Second Language program. The opportunities for getting to know members of other cultures are plenteous. Interacting with them is the best way to learn their unique ways of looking at the world and to discover their peculiar communication practices.

3. SPEAK TO THE AUDIENCE USING THEIR COMMUNICATION STYLE.

As you learn the other group's culture, make sense of its members' communicative behavior in the light of what it signifies to its users. As you interact with them, express yourself in a communicative way that the audience understands. Make sure your tones, gestures, use of personal space, and word choice mean the same thing to your audience that they mean to you. Avoid using jargon, slang terms, and sarcasm since these subtler message forms can confuse your audience.

4. LOOK FOR VERBAL AND NON-VERBAL FEEDBACK.

One of the best ways to improve your ability to interact with your audience is by being attentive to their verbal and nonverbal responses to your messages. If your audience member appears to be confused by something you have said, do not ignore it. Ask questions to be sure your intended message is received and understood and to determine why your first attempt to send it did not succeed. Not all cultures will give you this kind of feedback since, for some of them, it may imply their disrespect for you. Still, you should always provide opportunities for constructive feedback.

5. EXPECT TO MAKE MISTAKES.

Learning a new culture can be as complicated as learning a new language, so you should not be surprised that you will commit your share of mistakes during this learning process. Accept this reality before the errors happen, and learn to laugh at yourself when you commit them. Show audience members that it's okay for them to laugh with you. When an audience knows you care enough about them to relate to them (or to attempt to relate to them!) in their language or style and that you do not take yourself too seriously, they often will be gracious as you continue to learn their culture's communicative norms.

As you encounter people from other cultures, whether in America or overseas, try to put these principles into practice. If you do, you will be well on the way to learning how to relate to them in terms they understand.

David J. Alban, Ph.D., is a secondary educational administrator in Michigan and a former cross-cultural educator.

© 2012 by Caitlin Mirra. Used under license of Shutterstock.

What an audience considers most important about the Hurricane Katrina tragedy may be influenced by its members' racial or ethnic features.

is important to know something about the group you are speaking before so you can adapt your message to their knowledge level or interests.

Some people identify themselves by their occupational group. It is important to know the types of jobs your listeners hold. The speaking occasion often makes this clear. You may be invited by a group of home builders to speak about the dangers of radon, or a group of insurance agents may ask you to talk about the weather conditions associated with hurricanes.

Occupational information can often tell you a great deal about listeners' attitudes. An audience of physicians may be unwilling to accept proposed legislation that would strengthen a patient's right to choose a personal physician if it also makes it easier for patients to sue for malpractice. A legislative speaker might need to find creative ways to convince the doctors that the new law would be in the best interests of both doctors and patients.

Knowledge of what your listeners do for a living may also tell you the type of vocabulary appropriate for the occasion. If you are addressing a group of newspaper editors, you can use terms common to the newspaper business without bothering to define them. Do not use job-related words indiscriminately, but rather, use them to your advantage.

Groups are often defined by socio-economic status. Do your listeners earn more than $100,000 a year or less than $30,000? The answer to this question may influence the nature of your speech and help you create common ground with your audience. When Rabbi Harold S. Kushner talks to groups about his book, *When All You've Ever Wanted Isn't Enough*, he learns the group's socioeconomic status in advance. He explains:

> Generally, if I'm addressing affluent business executives, I concentrate on the downside of economic success and on the spiritual nature of affluence. When the group is less affluent, I talk about learning to cope with economic failure and with the feeling of being left behind.

Religious background of the group may be a consideration. According to the article, "Where we Stand on Faith," many people in the United States consider themselves spiritual and religious (*Newsweek*, September 6, 2005, 48–49). Suppose your topic is in vitro fertilization, one of medicine's generally effective techniques to help infertile couples have children. Your presentation goes well, but the faces of your listeners suggest you hit a nerve. Without realizing it, you may have offended your audience by failing to deal with the religious implications of this procedure. Speakers rarely intend to offend their audiences, especially about religion. But when speakers fail to realize that religious beliefs may also define moral attitudes about issues like abortion, premarital sex, homosexuality, and birth control, they risk alienating their audience. Failing to acknowledge and address the religious beliefs of your listeners when your speech concerns a sensitive topic sets up barriers to communication that may be difficult to surmount.

Groups may identify themselves in terms of race and ethnicity. Long ago, the image of the United States as a melting pot gave way to the image of a rainbow of diversity—an image in which African Americans, Hispanics, Asians, Greeks, Arabs, and Europeans define themselves by their racial and ethnic ties as well as by their ties to the United States. Within this diversity are cultural beliefs and traditions that may be different from your own.

Even now, more than four decades after the most sweeping civil rights legislation in American history was passed by Congress and signed into law by the President, racial issues and differences spawn controversy. In 2005, Hurricane Katrina devastated much of the southeastern shoreline of America. Charges were made by a variety of leaders, essentially declaring that if the majority of the population of New Orleans had been white, there would have been much greater and quicker efforts to move citizens to safe places with ample food and water. If you deliver a speech on the topic of communication failures and the devastation of Hurricane Katrina, you need take into account the considerable problems faced by black citizens in New Orleans and along the southeastern shoreline. If you do not, you are likely to fail in achieving your specific purpose for your speech and you will make your presentation unacceptable to some of your listeners. This is not to suggest that you change your views if they are carefully conceived and supported. However, if your topic includes racial and ethnic issues that you fail to acknowledge during your speech, you can expect members of your audience to be offended.

Political affiliation of the group may be relevant. If you are fundraising for the homeless, you will probably give a different speech to a group with liberal beliefs than to a group of conservatives. Following are some variations.

To a group of political liberals:

> We are a nation of plenty—a nation in which begging seems as out of place as snow in July. Yet our cities are filled with poor citizens who have no food or lodging. They are the have-nots in a nation of haves. I ask for your help tonight because we are a nation built on helping one another escape from poverty. No matter how hard you work to cement your own success, you will never achieve the American Dream if one person is left on the streets without a home.

To a group of political conservatives:

> It is in your best interest to give money to homeless causes. I'm not talking about handouts on the street but money that goes into putting a roof over people's heads and into job training. In the long run, giving people dignity by giving them a home and training them for productive work will mean fewer people on welfare and lower taxes. Is it a leap of faith to see this connection or just plain common business sense?

Acknowledging political differences has been important in America since its founding. You will not compromise your values when you accept the fact that political differences exist. Rather, you will take the first step in using these differences as the starting point for communication.

Values separate the worthwhile from the worthless and determine what we consider moral, desirable, important, beautiful, and worthwhile.

▲Recognize the Importance of Lifestyle Choices and Values

Your lifestyle choices say a lot about you. If you choose to be a city dweller, living in a studio apartment twenty-two stories up, you probably have less inclination to experience nature than if you opt to live on a 50-acre farm in Vermont. If you put in 12-hour days at the office, your career is probably more important to you than if you choose to work only part-time. Lifestyle choices are linked to the attitudes, beliefs, and values of your listeners.

Attitudes are predispositions to act in a particular way that influence our response to objects, events, and situations. Attitudes tend to be long-lasting, but can change under pressure. They are often, but not always, related to behavior.

Beliefs represent a mental and emotional acceptance of information. They are judgments about the truth or the probability that a statement is correct. Beliefs are formed from experience and learning; they are based on what we perceive to be accurate. To be an effective speaker, you must analyze the beliefs of your audience in the context of your message. For example, if you are dealing with people who believe that working hard is the only way to get ahead, you will have trouble convincing them to take time off between semesters. Your best hope is to persuade them that time off will make them more productive and goal-directed when they return. By citing authorities and providing examples of other students who have successfully followed this course, you have a chance of changing their mind-set.

Values are deep-seated abstract judgments about what is important to us. Values separate the worthwhile from the worthless and determine what we consider moral, desirable, important, beautiful, and worth living or dying for. Free enterprise, free speech, hard work, and being part of a stable family are a few of the most important American values.

An audience of concerned students that values the importance of education might express this value in the belief that "a college education should be available to all qualified students" and with the attitude that "the state legislature should pass a tuition-reduction plan for every state college." If you address this audience, you can use this attitude as the basis for your plea that students picket the state capitol in support of the tuition-reduction plan. Understanding your listeners' attitudes, beliefs, and values will help you put your message in the most effective terms.

▲Determine Why Your Audience IS an Audience

Although an analysis of demographic characteristics, the first stage of audience analysis, will give you some clue as to how your listeners are likely to respond to your speech, it will not tell you anything about the speaking occasion, why people have come together as an audience, how they feel about your topic, or about you as a speaker. This information emerges from the second stage of audience analysis, which centers on the speaking situation.

Audiences are made of individuals drawn together in ways that create unity and a shared identity. This identity may be centered in roles, interests, group membership, ethnicity, or a combination of factors. For example, at the political conventions are held every four years. The audience comes together because of a shared commitment to a political perspective. Those in attendance represent their state, and they gather to vote for the presidential candidate they feel will best represent their interests and will conduct the most successful campaign against the other political party. They come into the convention with a shared political identity (Democrat or Republican), and the outcome of the convention is to create support (unity) for one candidate.

❯ ARE THEY INTERESTED?

Interest level often determines audience response. High school seniors are more likely than high school freshmen to listen to someone from the financial aid office at the local college discuss scholarship, grant, and financial aid possibilities. People who fly frequently are less likely to pay attention to the flight attendant's description of safety procedures than individuals who have seldom flown. We tend to pay attention to things that are timely and that we know will affect us.

Many topics do not guarantee the same degree of audience interest, especially if they have been used by other speakers.

▲ What Are They Thinking?

Experienced and successful professionals who frequently speak to audiences around the country collect information that will tell them who their listeners are and what they want and expect from their presentations. For example, Stew Leonard Jr. has delivered hundreds of speeches to corporate audiences about what makes his family's unusual supermarket (with petting zoo, entertainment, and employees in costume) in Norwalk, Connecticut a success. Leonard says he focuses on what the audience needs: "If I don't give them what they need, I am not doing my job. That's why I spend so much time learning about an audience before I speak. I start by sending out a questionnaire that asks the goals and objectives of the meetings and the challenges facing the company. I also like to learn as much as I can about the audience—the age of the people attending, how many males, how many females, their educational backgrounds, and so on." (1989)

Robert Waterman Jr., coauthor of the very successful book *In Search of Excellence*, indicates he spends a day or two before a speech observing his corporate audience at work. What he learns helps him address the specific concerns of his listeners (Kiechel 1987). Both Waterman and Leonard have achieved success as professional speakers, and both assume very little about the characteristics of their prospective audiences. Often, to analyze their audiences, they use questionnaires and observation—techniques that can be used successfully in the classroom.

▲ Using a Questionnaire

Public opinion polls are an American tradition, especially around election time. Pollsters Gallup, Harris, and Zogby ask Americans for their views on the candidates and issues. And when elections are over, pollsters try to find out what Americans think about such varied topics as U.S. foreign policy, church attendance, illegal drugs, and ice cream preferences. Their tool in these investigations is the questionnaire. Questionnaires also are used by market research companies to learn how the public might respond to a product and, every ten years, by the Census Bureau.

For audience analysis, a questionnaire can determine the specific demographic characteristics of your listeners as well as their perceptions of you and your topic. It can also tell you how much knowledge your listeners have about your topic and the focus they would prefer in your speech.

By surveying all your classmates, by sampling every fourth person in your dorm, or by calling selected members of your audience and asking them questions, you can find out information about your audience in advance. These methods are simple and effective. In addition—and depending upon the age of your intended audience—online survey creation and response tabulation companies like SurveyMonkey.com now make it easier to poll a group of people via the Internet.

The first step in using a questionnaire is designing specific questions that are likely to get you the information you need. Three basic types of questions are most helpful to public speakers: fixed-alternative questions, scale questions, and open-ended questions (Churchill 1983).

Fixed-alternative questions. Fixed-alternative questions limit responses to several choices, yielding valuable information about such demographic factors as age, education, and income. Fixed-alternative questions can offer many different responses, or they can offer only two alternatives (yes/no questions fit into this category). These questions can help you analyze the attitudes and knowledge of your prospective listeners. Here is an example of a fixed-alternative question focusing on attitudes:

> *Do you think all professional athletes should be carefully tested for drugs and steroids? (Choose one)*
> • Professionals should be carefully tested for drugs and steroids.
> • Professional athletes should be tested for the use of drugs and steroids in selected sports.
> • Professional athletes should never be required to test for drugs and steroids.
> • No opinion.

This type of question is easy to tabulate and analyze and, from the point of view of your audience, easy to answer. In addition, you can be fairly sure that if you asked the same question a second time, you would get the same answer (assuming, of course, that attitudes had not changed). These questions also give you standardized responses. That is, for everyone answering the question, the frame of reference is the same. If you ask people, "How many times a week do you eat out?" and do not supply possible responses, you may receive answers like "regularly," "rarely," "every day," and "twice a day." Answers like these are more difficult to interpret than answers guided by a fixed set of alternatives. Fixed alternative questions help avoid confusion. Ask people to describe their marital status and they may reply "unhappy." If you want to know whether they are single, married, widowed, or divorced, ask them the question and provide choices.

What is your marital status?
- Single
- Widowed
- Married
- Divorced

However, using fixed-alternative questions does have disadvantages. It may force people to respond to a question when they have no opinion or strong feelings, especially if you fail to include "no opinion" as a possible response.

Scale questions. Scale questions are a type of fixed-alternative question that ask people to respond to questions set up along a continuum. For example:

How often do you vote?
Always   Sometimes   Occasionally   Never

Although these responses could have been asked in the form of an ordinary fixed-alternative question, this format, placed at the top of a page, allows you to list different variables along the left margin. For example, you can ask people to use the scale to tell you how frequently they vote in presidential elections, congressional elections, state elections, and local elections.

Open-ended questions. In an open-ended question, audience members can respond however they wish. For example:

How do you feel about a twelve-month school year?
Why do you think the Japanese sell so many cars in the United States?

A variety of answers is possible for these questions. In response to your question about extending the school year, one respondent may write, "Keep the school year as it is," while another may suggest a workable plan for extending the year. Because the responses to open-ended questions are so different, they can be difficult to analyze. The advantage to these questions is that they allow you to probe for details; you give respondents the opportunity to tell you what is on their minds. Following are a few guidelines for constructing usable questions.

Avoid leading questions. Try not to lead people to the response you desire through the wording of your question. Here are two examples of leading questions:

Do you feel stricter handgun legislation would stop the wanton killing of innocent people?
Do you believe able-bodied men who are too lazy to work should be eligible for welfare?

These questions should be reworded. For example, "Do you support stricter handgun legislation?" is no longer a leading question.

Center your message on your listeners rather than concentrating on a prepared script.

Avoid ambiguity. When you use words that can be interpreted in different ways, you reduce the value of a question. For example:

> *How often do you drink alcohol?*
> • Frequently
> • Occasionally
> • Sometimes
> • Never

In this case one person's "sometimes" may be another person's "occasionally." To avoid ambiguity, rephrase the possible responses:

> *How often do you drink alcohol?*
> • More than once a week
> • At least once a month
> • Not more than once every six months
> • Never

Ask everyone the same questions. Because variations in the wording of questions can change responses, always ask questions in the same way. Do not ask one person, "Under what circumstances would you consider enlisting in the army?" and another, "If the United State were attacked by a foreign nation, would you consider joining the army?" Both of these questions relate to enlisting in the military, but the first one is an open question while the second is a closed question. The answers you receive to the first question have much more information value than the second, which could be answered "yes" or "no." If you do not ask people the same questions, your results may be inaccurate.

Be aware of time constraints. Although the results can help you determine interest, attitudes, and knowledge level, you do not want it to take too much time or be too complex. If your instructor allows you to pass out a questionnaire in class, make sure it takes only a few minutes to complete. You do not want to take too much time. Ask only what is necessary. Make sure the format fits your purpose.

▲Observe and Interview

You may find that the best way to gather information about a prospective audience is to assume the role of an observer. If you are to deliver a speech on weight control to a former smokers' support group, attend a meeting to determine how many members believe they are overweight and how much weight they have to lose. Then ask several people whether their weight problem is the result of their efforts to stop smoking or if they were overweight at other times in their lives. Similarly, if you are delivering a speech to corporate executives on ways to improve their written communication, ask for samples of letters, memos, and reports they have written in order to be personally familiar with their writing skills and styles.

The interviews you conduct during this process are likely to be less formal than the style of interview you use to gather information about your speech topic. When questions occur as you watch a group in action, ask people their thoughts and feelings. Their responses will help you analyze audience need.

❯❯CREATE THE LINK BETWEEN SPEAKER AND AUDIENCE

Unless they determine you have something relevant to say, it takes your listeners only seconds to tune out your message. You convince an audience your message has value by centering your message on your listeners and not locking into a prepared script. The following suggestions will help you build the type of audience connection that defines the reciprocal nature of public speaking.

Practice proper microphone technique, preferably in the actual setting.

▲Get to the Point Quickly

First impressions count. What you say in the first few minutes is critical. Tell your listeners how you can help them first, not last. If you save your suggestions to the end, it may be that no one is listening. Experienced speakers try to make connections with their listeners as they open their speeches. And, more importantly, they try to convey to their listeners the idea that the speech will be important to them.

▲Have Confidence: They Want to Hear Your Speech

It happens all the time. Speakers with relatively little knowledge about a subject are asked to speak to a group of experts on the subject. An educator may talk to a group of athletes about intercollegiate sports. A lawyer may talk to a group of doctors about the doctor-patient relationship. A politician may talk to a group of drug counselors about the problem of crack cocaine. When you feel your listeners know more than you do about your topic, realize they have invited you for a reason. In most cases, they want your opinions. Despite their knowledge, you have a perspective they find interesting. Athletes may want to learn how the college sports program is viewed by a professor; doctors want to hear a lawyer's opinion about malpractice; and drug counselors want to know what a politician will do, if elected, to relieve the drug problem.

▲Be of the People, Not Above the People

No one wants to listen to speakers who consider themselves more accomplished, smarter, or more sophisticated than their audience. If you convey even a hint of superiority, your listeners will tune you out. As a speaker, you will learn that modesty inspires confidence.

Humor can help you make this connection with your audience. Opening your speech with something that makes people smile or laugh can put both you and your listeners at ease. Humor encourages people to think of you as approachable rather than remote. Effective humor should be related in some way to the subject of your speech, your audience, or the occasion.

▲Connect with Your Listeners

Before management consultant Edith Weiner gives a speech, she learns the names of several members of her audience as well as their roles in the company. During her speech, she refers to these people and the conversations she had with them, thereby creating a personal bond with her audience. Connections can be made by linking yourself directly to the group you are addressing and by referring to your audience with the pronoun "you" rather than the third-person "they." The word "you" inserts your listeners into the middle of your presentation and makes it clear that you are focusing attention on them. Here is an example in a speech delivered by Jeffrey R. Holland, as president of Brigham Young University, to a group of early childhood educators:

> You are offering more than technical expertise or professional advice when you meet with parents. You are demonstrating that you are an ally in their task of rearing the next generation. In all that you do … however good your work, and whatever the quality of life parents provide, there is no comparable substitute for families. Your best opportunity to act in children's best interests is to strengthen parents, rather than think you can or will replace them (1988, 559).

▲Make It a Participatory Event

When a speaker invites the listeners to participate in her or his speech, they become partners in an event. One of the author's friends, a first-degree black belt in karate, gave a motivational speech to a group of college women at a state university in Michigan. At the beginning of her speech, and to the excitement of the crowd, she broke several boards successfully. She talked about her childhood, her lack of self-esteem, and her struggle to become a well-adjusted business woman. She used the phrase, "I can succeed" several times during her speech, and encouraged her audience to join in with her. By the end of her speech, the group, standing, invigorated and excited, shouted with her, "I can succeed!"

Another way to involve your listeners is to choose a member of your audience to take part in your talk—have the volunteer help you with a demonstration, do some role playing—and the rest of the group will feel like one of its own is up there at the podium. Involve the entire audience and they will hang on your every word.

▲Examine Other Situational Characteristics

When planning your speech, other situational characteristics need to be considered, including time of day, size of audience, and size of room. When speechwriter Robert B. Rackleff (1987) addressed his colleagues about the "art of speech writing," he offered this advice:

> The time of day affects the speech. In the morning, people are relatively fresh and can listen attentively. You can explain things more carefully. But in the late afternoon, after lunch …, the audience needs something more stimulating. And after dinner, you had better keep it short and have some fireworks handy (311–12).

Rackleff was reminding his listeners about the intimate connection between time of day and audience response. The relationship between physical surroundings and audience response is so strong that you should plan every speech with your surroundings in mind. Management consultant Edith Weiner says there is a vast difference between an audience of six people and an audience of dozens or even hundreds of people: In the first case, says Weiner, "I'm speaking with the audience," but in the second, "I'm speaking to the audience." The intimacy of a small group allows for a speaker-audience interchange not possible in larger groups. Small groups provide almost instantaneous feedback; large groups are more difficult to read.

Room size is important because it influences how loudly you must speak and determines whether you need a microphone. As a student, you will probably be speaking in a classroom. But in other speaking situations, you may find yourself in a convention hall, a small office, or an outdoor setting where only the lineup of chairs determines the size of the speaking space.

If you are delivering an after-dinner speech in your own dining room to ten members of your Great Books club, you do not have to worry about projecting your voice to the back row of a large room. If, on the other hand, you are delivering a commencement address in your college auditorium to a thousand graduates, you will need to use a microphone. And keep in mind, proper microphone technique takes practice, preferably in the auditorium in which you will speak.

❯POST-SPEECH ANALYSIS

As you know from your classroom experience, hearing what your audience thought of your speech can help you give a better speech the next time around. Realizing the importance of feedback, some professional speakers hand out post-speech questionnaires, designed to find out where they succeeded and where they failed to meet audience needs. At workshops, a feedback sheet is often provided that can be turned in at the end of the specific workshop or at any time during the day. As the speaker, you may choose to distribute questionnaires randomly to a dozen people or you may ask the entire audience to provide feedback. Valuable information often emerges from these responses, which enables speakers to adjust their presentation for the next occasion. Hypothetically, let us assume you delivered a speech to a civic organization on the increasing problem of drunk boating. You handed out questionnaires to the entire audience. From this procedure, you learn that your audience would have preferred a speech with fewer statistics and more concrete advice on combatting the problem. In addition, one listener suggested a good way to make current laws more effective, a suggestion you may incorporate into your next presentation.

Finding out what your audience thought may be simple. In your public speaking class, your fellow classmates may give you immediate, written feedback. In other situations, especially if you are running a workshop or seminar, you may want to hand out a written questionnaire at the end of your speech and ask listeners to return it at a later time. (A self-addressed stamped envelope will encourage a large response.) Here are some questions you can ask:

1. Did the speech answer your questions about the topic? If not, what questions remain?
2. How can you apply the information you learned in the presentation to your own situation?
3. What part of the presentation was most helpful? Least helpful?
4. How could the presentation have better met your needs?

To encourage an honest and complete response, indicate that people do not have to sign their names to the questionnaire.

❯❯SUMMARY

The most important relationship in public speaking is the relationship between speaker and audience. Learn everything you can about your audience, so you can meet its needs in your topic and your approach. Start by developing a profile of your listeners based on demographic and psychological evaluations. Learn the average age of your listeners, whether they are predominantly male or female, their educational level, and how much they know about your subject. Try to identify members of your audience in terms of their membership in religious, racial and ethnic, occupational, socioeconomic, and political groups. Lifestyle choices can tell you a great deal about audience attitudes, beliefs, and values.

Successful speakers define the expectations that surround the speaking occasion. They learn how much interest their audience has in their topic and how much their audience knows about it before they get up to speak. Audience analysis is accomplished through the use of questionnaires based on fixed-alternative questions, scale questions, and open-ended questions. Audience analysis can also be conducted through observation and interviews.

To ensure a speaker-audience connection, show your listeners at the start of your speech how you will help them; have confidence your audience wants to hear you, even if they are more knowledgeable than you are. Present yourself as fitting into the group, rather than as being superior to the group. Refer to people in your audience and involve your listeners in your speech. When your speech is over, try to determine your audience's response through a post-speech evaluation-questionnaire.

QUESTIONS FOR ANALYSIS

1. Why will a speech fail in the absence of audience analysis?

2. Can speakers be ethical and adapt to their audiences at the same time?

3. Does adaptation imply audience manipulation or meeting the audience's needs?

4. What underlying principles should you use to conduct an effective audience analysis?

5. From what you have learned in the chapter about listening, what steps can you take to ensure a positive speaker-audience connection?

ACTIVITIES

1. Focusing on the specific purpose of your next speech, analyze the students in your public speaking class who will be your audience. Conduct several in-depth interviews with your classmates. Circulate a questionnaire. Based on the information you gather, develop an audience profile. Write a three- to four-page paper describing the attitudes, values, interests, and knowledge of your listeners as they relate to your topic and you. Finally, outline a strategy of audience adaptation that will serve your interests and the interests of your listeners.

2. Before delivering another speech, give every member of your class, including your instructor, an index card on which a seven-point scale is drawn, with 1 being the most negative point on the scale and 7 being the most positive. Ask your classmates to register the degree to which your speech was relevant to them. If most of the responses fall below the scale midpoint, analyze how you could have prepared a more successful speech.

3. Select a recent speech you have attended or a famous speech about which you have read that exemplifies a successful audience adaptation. In a written paper, analyze the factors that contributed to the audience's positive response and present findings to your class. Conduct the same analysis for a speech that failed to meet the audience's needs.

REFERENCES

Churchill Jr., G. A. 1983. *Marketing research: Methodological foundations*, 3rd ed., (168–231). Chicago, IL: the Dryden Press.

Clanton, J. 1988. "Title unknown," *Winning orations of the interstate oratorical association*. Mankato, MN: Interstate Oratorical Association.

Griffin, J. D. "To Snare the Feet of Greatness: The American Dream Is Alive," speech delivered at Moorpark College, Moorpark, California, July 16, 1989. Reprinted in *Vital Speeches of the Day*. September 15, 1989, 735–36.

Holland, J. "Whose Children Are These? The Family Connection," speech delivered at the 1988 Conference for the Association of Childhood Education International, April 23, 1988. Reprinted in *Vital Speeches of the Day*, July 1, 1988, 559.

Kiechel III, W. "How to give a speech," *Fortune*, June 8, 1987, 179.

Kushner, H. S. October 13, 1989.

Leonard, S. October 3, 1989.

Noonan, P. October 15, 1989. "Confessions of a White House Speechwriter," *New York Times*, 72.

Rackleff, R. B. "The art of speechwriting: A dramatic event," delivered to the national Association of Bar Executives Section on Communications and Public Relations, September 26, 1987. Reprinted in *Vital Speeches of the Day*, March 1, 1988.

Weiner, E. October 10, 1989.

Woodwad, G. C., and R. E. Denton Jr. 2004. *Persuasion and influence in American life*, 5th ed. (173–174). Long Grove, IL: Waveland Press, Inc.

SHORT ESSAYS

HONOR STATEMENT: I, the undersigned student, hereby declare before God, before the school, and before the professor that I have read Chapter 8 in its entirety, that I have completed the following exercise with help from no other sources, and that I neither have shared nor will share this work with anyone.

Signature: _____   Date: _____

1. As a speaker, what do you need to consider when developing your speech in order to make an effective connection with your audience? (100-200 words)

_____

_____

_____

_____

_____

_____

_____

_____

_____

_____

_____

_____

_____

_____

_____

_____

_____

_____

2. When you think about the audience belonging to one or more groups, what kinds of categories of groups are there to consider? (100-200 words)

_____

_____

_____

_____

_____

_____

_____

_____

_____

_____

_____

_____

_____

_____

_____

_____

_____

_____

_____

_____

_____

_____

3. If you were to use a questionnaire to find out more about your audience, what types of questions do you need to consider? Explain each of these in your own words and provide two examples of each. (100-200 words)

_____

_____

_____

_____

_____

_____

_____

_____

_____

_____

_____

_____

_____

_____

_____

_____

_____

_____

_____

_____

_____

_____

_____

4. If you were to construct a questionnaire for your classmates in this course, in an attempt to better understand how to prepare a speech for them, which six questions would you present to them? Be sure to explain after each why you regard the question to be important for planning purposes. (100-200 words)

_____

_____

_____

_____

_____

_____

_____

_____

_____

_____

_____

_____

_____

_____

_____

_____

_____

_____

_____

When you need help,
consult your librarian.

CHAPTER 9 >>

9 RESEARCH AND SUPPORTING MATERIAL

Each speaker faces multiple decisions during the speech development process. Sometimes beginning speakers find selecting a topic to be the most difficult aspect of the process. You may feel relief when your instructor approves the topic you have chosen, but your work has just begun. After choosing a topic and developing the general and specific purposes of your speech, it is time for research and to develop appropriate supporting material. Credibility is crucial. To a large extent, your listeners will evaluate your speech on the amount and relevance of research conducted and the types of supporting material used. The extent to which a speaker is perceived as a competent spokesperson is considered speaker credibility. A person's background, set of ethics, and delivery are all part of speaker credibility. Message credibility, on the other hand, is the extent to which the speech is considered to be factual and well supported through documentation (Fleshler, Ilardo, and Demoretcky 1974). It is this second type of credibility that is the focus of this chapter. Through research, one can find sufficient, relevant, and timely supporting material which will enhance a speaker's message credibility.

With all the information available on the computer, it's a big job to decide what material to use and what to discard.

We live in an information society that produces far more information than we can use. Books are added to library collections on a regular basis, new information is found quarterly in journals, weekly in magazines, and daily in newspapers. Computers give us access to innumerable websites and ever larger databases. As a result of this galaxy of available information, one of your most important jobs will be to decide what is relevant and what is not, what you should incorporate into your speech and what you should discard. Setting limits on your own research requires that you stay focused on your specific purpose. Do what is required to give an effective presentation; do not allow yourself to be led down an interesting, but unrelated, path.

Research is the raw material that forms the foundation of your speech. It gives you the tools you need to expand your specific purpose into a full-length presentation. The raw material may include interviewing experts on your topic and locating print and web-based information. The result of this process is your knowledge of the topic.

Often, research can lead you to deliver a slightly different type of speech than you expected. As facts emerge, you may expand your speech in one place, streamline it in another, and take it apart to accommodate new information. Ultimately, you will piece it together in its final form.

The research process alone is not sufficient. You must determine how to use it most effectively. Supporting material is the information used in a particular way to make your case. For example, if you were preparing a speech to inform your class on services available in your community for individuals who are categorized as low income, your research process may lead you to an organization that specializes in debt consolidation, another that offers free or low-cost medical care, an agency that gives out food for low-income individuals, and a organization that supplies children with free school supplies. As you develop your speech, one of your points might be that "a variety of services are available in our community." For supporting material, these agencies provide examples of available services. As the types of supporting material can be quite varied, you must determine what is most suited to the topic and to your listeners.

❱❱DEVELOP A RESEARCH STRATEGY

Instructors rarely say, "Go! Prepare an informative speech." Instead, they establish parameters regarding topics, length of speech, minimum number of sources, and types of sources. What is the minimum number of sources required? How many different sources do you need? If you use three different issues of *Newsweek*, do they count as one source or as three? Can you use information from 1980 or 1990, or did your instructor say all material needs to be no more than five years old? Do you need both print and online sources? Does online access to a magazine count as a print source? Can you use all types of print sources? Does your instructor allow you to count an interview as a source? Can you use your family or yourself as a source? Before you begin to research your topic, make sure you know the constraints of the assignment as specified by your instructor.

This chapter focuses first on developing a research strategy. Supporting material will be discussed later in the chapter. Specifically, in developing your research strategy, you need to address the following aspects.

1. Analyze the audience
   (What are the needs, interests, and knowledge level of my audience?)
2. Assess your knowledge/skill
   (What knowledge or skill do I have in relation to this topic?)
3. Search print and online resources
   (Based on available resources, where and what will I find the most useful?)
4. Interview, if appropriate
   (Will this speech be helped by interviewing someone with personal knowledge or expertise about this topic?)

© 2012 by iStockphoto.
Used under license of Shutterstock.

Before you begin your topic research, make sure you know the parameters of the speech assignment.

Each of these aspects can be viewed as stages. The following section provides a look at each of these stages in greater detail.

1. Start (and End) with an Audience Analysis.

Throughout this book we stress the importance of connecting with your audience. Before you determine the general or specific purpose for your speech, consider your audience's needs. As explained in the previous chapter, a careful audience analysis gives you information about who they are and what they value. Understanding your audience helps you develop specific questions that can be answered as you follow your search strategy. For example, suppose you were planning an informative speech explaining prenuptial agreements. You may have some general questions about the topic, such as the following:

When do most people get married?
What are the statistics on the number of marriages and divorces each year?
Who benefits financially and who suffers as a result of a divorce?

What happens to property in divorce?
How expensive is an agreement?
Can people draw up the agreement without legal counsel?

To construct an effective speech that achieves its specific purpose, whether it is informative or persuasive, think about your specific audience. So, if you are working on a speech about prenuptial agreements, consider additional questions such as:

Considering the age of my audience, how much do they know about prenuptial agreements?
What do most people think about prenuptial agreements?
What might be this audience's greatest areas of concern or interest regarding the topic?

Do you have unique knowledge that would make an interesting speech topic?

Answering the more specific questions related to your audience helps you to determine the depth and breadth of information needed to answer your more general questions. By developing questions based on your understanding of the needs of your audience, you can increase the likelihood of establishing an effective speaker-audience connection. Reflect again on your audience after you have gathered information to determine whether or not you have collected enough material and if it is the right type of material to meet your audience's needs and interests.

2. Assess Your Own Knowledge and Skills.

Some students find topic selection difficult because they think they have nothing to offer or the class will not be interested. Upon reflection, however, you may find you have unique experiences or you have knowledge that others do not. Perhaps you were an exchange student, so you have had firsthand experience of another culture. Maybe you were raised by parents who spoke a different language, and you know what it is like to be bilingual. Maybe you live with an unusual disease.

Start your research process by assessing your own knowledge and skills. Most likely, you have direct knowledge or experience related to several topics. Your family may own a monument shop or a restaurant, and you grew up exposed to issues related to these professions. Maybe by the time you started college, you held one or more jobs, joined a political club, pursued hobbies like video games, or played sports such as soccer or rugby. You may know more about Jackie Chan movies than anyone on campus, or you may play disk golf. Examining your unique experiences or varied interests is a logical starting point for developing a speech.

Having personal knowledge or experience can make an impact on your audience. A student with Type I diabetes can speak credibly on what it is like to take daily injections and deal with the consequences of both low and high blood sugar. A student who works as a barista at the local coffee shop can demonstrate how to make a good shot of espresso. CAUTION: Remember the phrase, "Too much knowledge may be dangerous." Sometimes students want to share every detail with the audience, and that information can become tedious or overwhelming.

3. Search Print and Online Resources.

Once you have assessed your own knowledge or skills, it is time to search print and online resources for other supporting material. The computer provides a rich playing field that also complicates our lives. We have more choices, but we have to work harder to sift through them.

Your search may result in more questions, including the following: What information is most essential to this topic? What will have the greatest impact? How much background do I need to give? Utilizing a variety of sources is advantageous for a variety of reasons; different sources focus on research, philosophy, or current events. They may be part of a daily publication, or are contained within a one-time publication. Sources target different audiences. We suggest you examine and evaluate materials from various sources to select materials that will help you most.

Avoid wasting valuable time floating aimlessly in cyberspace or walking around the library. Instead, if you need direction, ask a librarian. Librarians are experts in finding both print and online information efficiently, and they can show you how to use the library's newest search engines and databases. With new online and print resources being added daily, using the expertise of a librarian can make your job as a researcher much easier.

If you are new to campus, and your instructor has not arranged a library tour for your class, consider taking a workshop on using the library. Your library's home page is helpful. Most college libraries belong to a "live chat" consortium on the web, where students may contact a librarian twenty-four hours a day. Also, you can try the Library of Congress online Ask-a-Librarian Service at www.loc.gov and click on "Ask a librarian."

4. Narrow Your Focus.

It is natural to start with a broad topic. But as you search, the information you find will help you move to a more focused topic, enabling you to define—and refine—the approach you take to your speech. Say you are interested in giving an informative speech about the use of performance enhancement drugs in sports. You need to narrow your topic, but you are not quite sure what aspects to consider. Choose a search engine, such as Google, Yahoo!, AltaVista, or Excite.

Try conducting a key-word search on Google for "drugs in sports." This is very general. The key-word search leads you to a list of records which are weighted in order of amount of user access. You may have more than a million records or "hits" from which to choose. Look for valid subject headings, and search more deeply than the first three or four records listed.

Results of the key-word search lead you to many possibilities, including "anabolic steroids." You find a website that addresses topics such as what they are, how they work, who uses them, how prevalent they are, the different types, drugs banned by the NCAA, and medical uses. Now you have other areas to pursue. Decide what aspects you want to cover that are relevant to the audience and can be discussed effectively within the given time constraints. Perhaps you are interested in who uses them, so you enter "Who uses anabolic steroids?" This leads you to a website on uses and abuses of steroids. You know you need to define what anabolic steroids are and to find out how they are used and abused. You can continue your research by examining both print and online resources for these specific aspects of performance enhancement drugs. Now you can develop a specific purpose statement and search for information to support it.

As you search for information, keep three aspects of research in mind: First, recognize the distinction between primary and secondary sources. Primary sources include firsthand accounts such as diaries, journals, and letters, as well as statistics, speeches, and interviews. They are records of events as they are first described. Secondary sources generally provide an analysis, an explanation, or a restatement of a primary source. If the U.S. Surgeon General issues a report on the dangers of smoking, the report itself (available from the U.S. Surgeon General's Office) is the primary source; newspaper and magazine articles about the report are secondary source material.

Second, there is a relationship between the length of your speech and the amount of time you must spend in research. Many students learn the hard way that five minutes of research will not suffice for a five-minute speech. Conventional wisdom suggests that for every one minute of speaking time, there is an hour of preparation needed. Whatever the length of the speech, you have to spend time uncovering facts and building a strong foundation of support.

Third, finding information is not enough; you must also be able to evaluate it (relevance, reliability, and so on), and utilize it in the most appropriate way in order to achieve your specific purpose. For example, your audience analysis may suggest that specific statistics are necessary to convince your audience. On the other hand, perhaps personal or expert testimony will be most persuasive. Overall, developing a research strategy is one of the most useful things you will learn in college.

© 2012 by Goodluz.
Used under license of Shutterstock.

Evaluating and using information appropriately is as important as finding it.

5. Specific Library Resources

In addition to providing access to computers for online searches, each library houses a variety of research materials, including books, reference materials, newspapers, magazines, journals, and government documents. Microfilm, specifically for archived newspapers may still be available, but the government has stopped producing microfiche. If information is not housed in your library, you can electronically extend your search far beyond your campus or community library through interlibrary loan. It may take two weeks or longer to process requests, so planning is especially important when relying on interlibrary loan.

Each library is different. One may not have the same databases or reference materials as another. Some libraries are depositories for your state, and it may be one of a few that receives state documents automatically.

Books

Historically, libraries have been most noted for their collection of books. Many universities have several libraries so students may access the large volume of books in general collections, archived collections, and specific collections. Using the library catalog is essential. Most libraries today have online computer catalogs, which contain records of all materials the library owns. In addition to identifying what books are available and where to find them, an online catalog will also indicate whether a particular book is checked out and when it is due back. Keep in mind that the library groups books by subject, so as you look in the stacks for a particular book, it makes sense to peruse surrounding books for additional resources.

General reference materials

At the beginning of your search, it may be helpful to start with one or more general reference resources, including encyclopedias, dictionaries, biographical sources, and statistical sources. Most likely, your time spent with these materials will be short, but these resources can provide you with basic facts and definitions.

Unlike some of our experiences in primary school, seldom does a student's research start and end with the encyclopedia. The World Book Encyclopedia is helpful if you are unfamiliar with a topic or concept. It can provide facts that are concise as well as easy to read and understand. Encyclopedias are either general or specialized. General encyclopedias (e.g., *The Encyclopedia Americana* and *Encyclopedia Britannica*) cover a wide range of topics in a broad manner. In contrast, specialized encyclopedias, such as the *Encyclopedia of Religion*, and the *International Encyclopedia of the Social Sciences*, focus on particular areas of knowledge in more detail. Over the last decade, there has been an explosion of discipline-specific encyclopedias. Articles in both general and specialized encyclopedias often contain bibliographies that lead you to additional sources.

Although encyclopedias are helpful as a basic resource, they generally are not accepted as main sources for class speeches. Use them to lead to other information. CAUTION: Do not fall into Wikipedia's web of easy access and understanding. Its legitimacy is questionable. Stephen Colbert, host of the TV show *The Colbert Report*, asked his viewers to log on to the entry "elephants" on Wikipedia.com to report that the elephant population in Africa "has tripled in the last six months." This online encyclopedia noted a spike in inaccurate entries shortly after the show aired. Most instructors discourage use of this online resource.

During your research, you may consult a dictionary when you encounter an unfamiliar word or term. They also provide information on pronunciation, spelling, word division, usage, and etymology (the origins and development of words). As with encyclopedias, dictionaries are classified as either general or specialized. It is likely you have used some general dictionaries such as the *American Heritage Dictionary* or the *Random House College Dictionary*. The dictionary is also just a click away. You might try Merriam-

General reference resources may be helpful as you begin your search for material.

Webster Online (www.m-w.com). Specialized dictionaries cover words associated with a specific subject or discipline, as in the following: *The American Political Dictionary, Black's Law Dictionary, Harvard Dictionary of Scientific and Technical Terms*, and *Webster's Sports Dictionary*. Many disciplines use their own specialized terminology that is more extensive and focused, and those definitions are found in their journals and books. CAUTION: Check with your instructor before beginning your speech with, "According to Webster's dictionary, the word _____ means…" As Harris (2002) notes in his book, *Using Sources Effectively*, "Generally speaking, starting with a dictionary definition not only lacks creativity but it may not be helpful if the definition is too general or vague" (35).

© 2012 by bondarchuk.
Used under license of Shutterstock.

Magazines and newspapers provide the most recent print information.

Biographical sources

Biographical sources, which are international, national, or specialized, provide information on an individual's education, accomplishments, and professional activities. This information is useful when evaluating someone's credibility and reliability. A biographical index indicates sources of biographical information in books and journals whereas a biographical dictionary lists and describes the accomplishments of notable people. If you are looking for a brief background of a well-known person, consult the biographical dictionary first. If you need an in-depth profile of a lesser-known person, the biographical index is the better source. Some examples of these sources are Author Biographies Master Index, Biography Index, the New York Times Index, Dictionary of American Biography, European Authors, World Authors, and Dictionary of American Scholars.

Statistical sources

When used correctly, statistics can provide powerful support. Facts and statistics give authority and credibility to research. Many federal agencies produce and distribute information electronically. The American Statistics Index (ASI) includes both an index and abstracts of statistical information published by the federal government. Try also the Index to International Statistics (IIS) and the Statistical Abstract of the United States. The online source LexisNexis touts itself as providing "authoritative legal, news, public records and business information" (www.lexisnexis.com).

Magazines, newspapers, and journals

Magazines (also known as periodicals) and newspapers provide the most recent print information. Once you identify ideas that connect with the needs of your audience, you can look for specific information in magazines and newspapers. General indexes cover such popular magazines and newspapers such as *Time, Newsweek, U.S. News & World Report, The New York Times*, and the *Chicago Tribune. The Readers' Guide to Periodical Literature* is an index available online as well as in print form. Other popular indexes include: the *New York Times Index, Wall Street Journal, Christian Science Monitor, Los Angeles Times, The Education Index, Humanities Index, Public Affairs Information Service Bulletin, Social Sciences and Humanities Index*, and *Social Sciences Index*.

Newspapers and magazines can be distinquished from journals in many ways. First, the frequency of distribution is different. While newspapers can be accessed daily, and magazines are either weekly or monthly, journals are usually quarterly publications. Second, authors of articles in newspapers and magazines are generally paid by their publisher, whereas authors of journal articles (usually referred to as "researchers" rather than "authors") are generally experts in their particular fields, and have submitted their article(s) on a competitive, reviewed basis. In general, the more prestigious the journal, the more difficult it is to get an article printed in it. Journals may have editorials or book reviews, but they generally focus on qualitative and quantitative research conducted by professionals—doctors, professors, lawyers, and so on. Third, magazines and newspapers are written for general audiences, whereas journal articles are written for a specific audience; an example would be faculty or graduate students interested in communication apprehension. Many journals can be accessed online, but not all are available electronically.

Fourth, and very importantly, journals focus on original, qualitative, and quantitative research. Much of the content in a journal is considered to be a primary source because it reports findings from research conducted by the author.

Government documents

Government documents are prepared by agencies, bureaus, and departments that monitor the affairs and activities of the nation. Documents are issued by the Office of the President, the U.S. Congress, the departments of Commerce, Agriculture, Education, Navy and Army, Indian Affairs, the Veterans' Administration, the Food and Drug Administration, and the FBI.

Through the U.S. Government Printing Office (GPO) one can find unique, authoritative, and timely materials, including detailed census data, vital statistics, congressional papers and reports, presidential documents, military reports, and impact statements on energy, the environment, and pollution. Consult the Monthly Catalog of United States Government Publications, which is available online.

6. Online Research

As stated earlier, your librarian can lead you to a variety of material. An enormous amount of databases exist, and one can approach web research in many ways. Without help of some kind, looking for information on the web is like upending the library in a football field and being given a pen light to search for information. The librarian can at least provide you with stadium lights.

Consider using online databases such as InfoTrac and EBSCO. According to InfoTrac College Edition's website (infotrac.thomsonlearning.com), more than 20 million articles from nearly 6,000 sources are available to you. The advantage of using this resource is that you may access cross-disciplinary, reliable, full-length articles. It is free of advertising and available twenty-four hours a day. EBSCO (www.ebsco.com) offers a similar service, and claims to be the most widely used online resource, with access to over 100 databases, and thousands of e-journals. By the time this book is printed, it is a sure bet that even more databases will be available.

7. Web Evaluation Criteria

Many students will start their research online. Computers are in dorm rooms, dorm halls, academic buildings, and the library. It may take only a few steps to access one. While there is nothing inherently wrong with this, we urge you to proceed with caution. Evaluating the credibility of your online resources is critical. The quantity of information available via the Internet is colossal, and includes highly respected research as well as pure fiction presented as fact. Seek information from competent, qualified sources and avoid information from uninformed individuals with little or no credentials. Ultimately, you are held accountable for the quality and credibility of the sources you use.

As you access each website, it is important to evaluate its legitimacy as a source for your speech. Susan Beck (1997) identifies five web evaluation criteria that serve as useful standards for evaluating online information.

1. Authority

Authority relates to the concept of credibility. As we know, virtually anyone can become a web publisher. A website that passes this first test contains information provided by an individual, group, or organization known to have expertise in the area.

Questions to guide evaluation include the following:
- *What type of group put up the site? (Educational institution? Government agency? Individual? Commercial business? Organization?)*
- *Can you identify the author(s)? (What is the organization or who is the person responsible for the information?)*
- *What are the credentials of those responsible?*

2. Accuracy

A website that is accurate is reliable and error-free. One aspect of accuracy is timeliness. If the last time the site was updated was two years ago and the site is discussing a bill before the legislature, then it is no longer accurate. One assumes more accuracy when it is clear that information is scrutinized in some way before being placed on the web. Accuracy is clearly related to authority, since the sites with greater authority are most likely to have mechanisms for determining how something becomes "site-worthy."

Questions to guide evaluation include the following:
- *Is the information accurate?*
- *Does the information confirm or contradict what is found in printed sources?*
- *Are references given to the sources of information?*

3. Objectivity

The extent to which website material is presented without bias or distortion relates to objectivity. As you examine the material, you want to determine if it is presented as opinion or fact.

Questions to guide evaluation include the following:
- *What is the age level of the intended audience? (Adults? Teenagers? Children?)*
- *Is the information on the site factual or an expression of opinion?*

- *Is the author controversial? A known conservative? A known liberal?*
- *What are the author's credentials?*

4. Coverage

Coverage refers to the depth and breadth of the material. It may be difficult to determine who the site is targeting. As a result, material may be too general or too specific. Determine if it meets your needs or if critical information is missing.

> Questions to guide evaluation include the following:
> - *What is the intended purpose of the site? (Educational? Informational? Commercial? Recreational?)*
> - *Who is the intended audience (General public? Scholars? Students? Professionals?)*
> - *Is information common knowledge? Too basic? Too technical?*
> - *Does information include multiple aspects of the issue or concern?*

5. Currency

Currency refers to the timeliness of the material. Some websites exist that have never been updated. Information may be no longer valid or useful. If you look for "Most popular books of the year," and find a site from 2003, that information is no longer current or relevant. Looking at birth rates or literacy rates from the past would not produce relevant information if you are looking for the most recent information.

> Questions to guide evaluation include the following:
> - *When was the site created?*
> - *Is the material recent?*
> - *Is the website updated?*

When using these five criteria to evaluate your online information, remember that all criteria should be met, not just one or two of the above. Accurate and current information must also be objective. If critical information is missing (coverage), no matter how accurate and current the information is, it should be eliminated as a source.

8. Interview, If Appropriate

Interviews are useful if you want information too new to be found in published sources or if you want to give your listeners the views of an expert. By talking to an expert, you can clarify questions and fill in knowledge gaps, and you may learn more about a subject than you expected. In the process, you also gather opinions based on years of experience. Look around your campus and community. You will find experts who can tell you as much as you need to know about thousands of subjects. You can get opinions about the stock market, the effect of different types of running shoes on the development of shin splints, race relations, No Child Left Behind legislation, ethanol, water or air pollution, or curbside recycling.

If you decide to interview one or more people, we offer the following four suggestions: *Contact the person well in advance.* Remember, you are the one who needs the information. Do not think that leaving one voice message is the extent of your responsibility. You may have to make several attempts to contact the person. Schedule a date and time to interview that leaves you with ample time to prepare your speech.

Prepare questions in advance. Make sure you know what topics need to be covered and what information needs to be clarified.

Develop questions in a logical order. One question should lead naturally to another. Place the most important questions at the top to guarantee that they will be answered before your time is up.

Stay within the agreed time frame. If you promise the interview will take no longer than a half hour, keep your word, if at all possible. Do not say, "It'll just take a minute," when you need at least fifteen minutes. Build in a little time to ask unplanned questions, questions based on the interviewee's answers or for clarification.

When you conduct an interview, make sure your questions develop in a logical order to get the information you need.

After reading this section on research, hopefully you are aware that it involves a significant time commitment. It is never too early to start thinking about your next speech topic and where you might find sources. Explore a variety of resources. Ask for help from your instructor or the librarian. Make sure you know the constraints of the assignment.

❯❯ CITING SOURCES IN YOUR SPEECH

Any research included in your speech needs to be cited appropriately in order to give due credit. If you interviewed someone, your audience should know the person's name, credentials, and when and where you spoke with him or her. If you use information from a website, the audience should know the name of the website and when you accessed it. For print information, the audience generally needs to know the author, date, and type of publication. Your credibility is connected to your source citation. Expert sources and timely information add to your credibility. Essentially, all research used in your speech needs to be cited. Otherwise, you have committed an act of plagiarism. Following are ways to cite sources in your speech. Consult with your instructor, however, as he or she may have specific concerns.

Example 1
Correct source citation. In their 1995 book on family communication, researchers Yerby, Buerkel-Rothfuss and Bochner argue that it is difficult to understand family behavior "without an adequate description of the historical, physical, emotional, and relational context in which it occurs."
Incorrect source citation. Researchers on family communication argue that it is difficult to understand family behavior without an adequate description of the historical, physical, emotional, and relational context in which it occurs.

Explanation. We need the date to evaluate the timeliness of the material. We need to know

CREDITING YOUR SOURCES
HOW TO CITE YOUR SOURCES PROPERLY IN A SPEECH

BY FAITH E. MULLEN, PH.D.
& WILLIAM L. MULLEN, PH.D.

In our experience of teaching public speaking to thousands of students, we have observed that many students do not take seriously every public speaker's responsibility to cite the sources of any information he or she includes in the speech. Sometimes this is simply because the student does not know any better. He or she just assumes that the information speaks for itself and it's not really necessary to put extra effort into identifying the source of the information and showing that the source is fair, accurate, and believable. Other students just assume that citing sources in a speech is a pointless technicality that may matter to a professor but that does not matter in the real world. Nothing could be farther from the truth. Failing to cite your sources properly, whether in a speech or in written work, is a potentially costly error since it can create the appearance of plagiarism—presenting the information of others as if it were your own. This ethical wrong can have serious consequences, whether automatic failure of an assignment or of the course or a permanent blight on your academic record. Thus, we must familiarize ourselves with recognized principles for source citation that, if implemented, will help you not only avoid this pitfall, but also enhance your credibility as a speaker.

There are three important questions to remember as you determine which information to cite during a speech—what, when, and why.

WHAT SHOULD BE CITED?

Always explicitly acknowledge the source of any supportive information in your speech (quotations, statistics, examples, illustrations, etc.) that you got somewhere else, whether from a website, a book or magazine, a broadcast, an interview, a lecture you attended, or anywhere else. The general rule of thumb, when citing sources, is to give your audience enough information to enable it to locate that source if its members wish to do so. Generally, it's okay to simply identify the source by name and the title, if any, of the work. Before using the information in your speech, you should determine on your own whether the information's source is credible. Do the source's name and credentials appear with the information? If not, you probably should not use the information in the

speech. However, if your research discloses that the source is indeed credible, be sure to cite the source's credentials when giving the information in your speech. Having said this, we encourage you, in your attempt to establish your sources' credibility, not to get bogged down in presenting unnecessary details about the sources. Presenting information that the audience does not really need will tend only to distract them from hearing the most important points in your speech.

WHEN SHOULD SOURCES BE CITED IN A SPEECH?

Always present the information about your source at the time when you're presenting the information that you've taken from that source. Don't commit the lazy error that too many students commit when they list their sources at the speech's beginning or its end without making it clear which information came from each. This may be appropriate on a speech outline, in which sources are listed on a bibliography or Works Cited page, but even in an outline, professors usually require students to use parenthetical citations or footnotes to link specific pieces of supportive information to the sources from which they derive. In the end, your audience should always know where you got any quotation, statistic, example, illustration, or other supportive information that you included in your speech.

WHY SHOULD SOURCES BE CITED VERBALLY IN A SPEECH?

There are two main reasons for verbally citing sources in a presentation. First, it is important to give credit to the originator of the information. In other words, citing sources is the ethical thing to do! Additionally, it is good to cite sources because it increases the credibility of the speaker. The speaker looks more credible in the eyes of the audience because it tells the audience they prepared and researched for the speech. The audience perceives that the speaker values them by presenting credible information to them. In return, the credibility of the speaker is enhanced, not reduced, in the minds of the audience.

Drs. Faith Mullen and William Mullen are Professors of Communication Studies at Liberty University, in Lynchburg, Virginia.

that this information was found in a book, as opposed to a television show, a newspaper, magazine, or other source. We need the authors' names so we know who wrote the information, and so we can find the book.

Example 2
Correct source citation. According to a personal interview last week with Diane Ruyle, principal of Danube High School, fewer students are choosing vocational classes than they were ten years ago.

Incorrect source citation. According to Diane Ruyle, fewer students are choosing vocational classes.

Explanation. We need to know why the person cited Diane Ruyle. As a principal, she ought to be able to provide accurate information regarding course selection. Adding "than they were ten years ago" gives the listener a comparison basis.

Example 3
Correct source citation. According to an Associated Press article published in *The New York Times* on August 9, 2007, "unlike in South Carolina, state laws in Iowa and New Hampshire require officials there to hold the first caucus and primary in the nation, respectively. "

Incorrect source citation. "Unlike in South Carolina, state laws in Iowa and New Hampshire require officials there to hold the first caucus and primary in the nation, respectively."

Explanation. First, if this is published information, it should be cited. Second, most of us do not know these facts, a citation is necessary. Otherwise, the speaker could be making this up. The date provided allows us to look up the source and shows us that the information is timely. No author was identified, and since Associated Press articles can be found in many newspapers, it is important to note this was found in *The New York Times*.

Example 4
Correct source citation. According to the current American Diabetes Association website, "Cholesterol is carried through the body in two kinds of bundles called lipoproteins— low-density lipoproteins and high-density lipoproteins. It's important to have healthy levels of both."

Incorrect source citation. Cholesterol is carried through the body in two kinds of bundles called lipoproteins—low-density lipoproteins and high-density lipoproteins. It's important to have healthy levels of both.

Explanation. This information is not common knowledge, so it should be cited. Many different organizations might include such information on their website, so it is important to note that it came from the American Diabetes Association (ADA). An audience would infer that the ADA is a credible organization regarding this topic. Using the word "current" suggests that one could find that information today on the ADA website, which reinforces the timeliness of the material.

In summary, remember that you do not need to cite sources when you are reporting your own original ideas or discussing ideas that are commonly held. You must cite sources when you are quoting directly or paraphrasing (restating or summarizing a source's ideas in your own words). You must also cite the source of an illustration, diagram, or graph. Providing the date of publication, date of website access, credentials of the source, and/or type of publication where applicable will allow the listener to evaluate the credibility of the information.

❯❯SUPPORTING YOUR SPEECH

Imagine a chef with a piece of steak, some cauliflower, and rice, the main ingredients for a dinner special. What the chef does with these raw materials will influence the response of the consumers. The chef decides whether to grill, broil, bake, steam, or fry. Different spices can be used for different results. Numerous possibilities exist.

The research you have gathered for your speech can be viewed as the raw material. Now you need to figure out how to organize and present the material in the most effective way for your audience. This is where the concept of supporting material applies.

Supporting material gives substance to your assertions. If you say that *Casablanca* is the best movie ever produced in Hollywood, you are stating your opinion. If you cite a film critic's essay that notes it is the best movie ever, then your statement has more weight. You may also be able to find data that indicates how well the movie did, and a public opinion poll that had it ranked as the top movie. These different resources provide support. Just about anything that supports a speaker's idea can be considered supporting material.

When developing your speech, you also have many decisions to make. Consider the following example:

Your public speaking professor has just given your class an assignment to deliver an informative speech on the problem of shoplifting. These two versions are among those presented:

Version 1
Shoplifting is an enormous problem for American retailers, who lose billions of dollars each year to customer theft. Not unexpectedly, retailers pass the cost of shoplifting onto consumers, which means that people like you and me pay dearly for the crimes of others.

Shoplifting is increasingly becoming a middle-class crime. Experts tell us that many people shoplift just for kicks—for the thrill of defying authority and for the excitement of getting away with something that is against the law. Whatever the reason, one in fifteen Americans is guilty of this crime.

Version 2
Imagine walking up to a store owner once a year and giving that person $300 without

getting anything in return. Could you afford that? Would you want to do that? Yet that's what happens. Every year, the average American family of four forks over $300 to make amends for the crimes of shoplifters.

Shoplifting is a big cost to big business. According to recent statistics from the National Association for the Prevention of Shoplifting, people who walk out of stores without first stopping at the cash register take with them more than $13 billion annually. That's more than $25 million per day. Their website claims that one out of eleven of us is guilty of this crime. To bring this figure uncomfortably close to home, that's at least two students in each of your classes.

Interestingly, shoplifting is no longer a poor person's crime. Hard as it is to imagine, many shoplifters can well afford to buy what they steal. Wynona Ryder received a great deal of unwanted press when she shoplifted $5,000 worth of merchandise at a Beverly Hills store in 2001.

Why do middle- and upper-income people steal? Psychologist Stanton Samenow, quoted in the July issue of *Life* magazine, offers some perspective:

> "Shoplifters will not accept life as it is; they want to take shortcuts. They do it for kicks" (Sawyer, Glenn Dowling 1988).

Although both versions say essentially the same thing, they are not equally effective. The difference is in the supporting materials.

▲Five Functions of Support
Support should strengthen your speech in five ways. Comparing Version 1 with Version 2 will help illustrate the value of supporting material.

1. Support is specific.
Version 2 gives listeners more details than Version 1. We learn, for example, how much shoplifting costs each of us as well as the financial burden retailers must carry.

2. Support helps to clarify ideas.
We learn much more about the reasons for shoplifting from Version 2. This clarification—from the mouths of experts—reduces the risk of misunderstanding.

3. Support adds weight.
The use of credible statistics and expert opinion adds support to the second version's main points. This type of support convinces listeners by building a body of evidence that may be difficult to deny. The testimony of Dr. Samenow is convincing because it is authoritative. We believe what he says far more than we do unattributed facts.

4. Support is appropriate to your audience.
Perhaps the most important difference between these two versions is Version 2's attempt to gear the supporting material to the audience. It is a rare college student who would not

care about a $300 overcharge or who cannot relate to the presence of two possible shoplifters in each class. Also, movie star Wynona Ryder's shoplifting is noted in Version 2. Students are familiar with her name, but college students would not be as familiar with an older famous person who has shoplifted, such as Bess Myerson, winner of Miss America in 1945 and actress on several television shows in the 1960s.

5. Support creates interest.

Although Version 1 provides information, it arouses little or no interest. Listeners have a hard time caring about the problem or becoming emotionally or intellectually involved. Version 2, on the other hand, creates interest through the use of meaningful statistics, quotations, and an example. When used properly, supporting materials can transform ordinary details into a memorable presentation.

Effective support is used to develop the message you send to your listeners. It is through this message that communication takes place between speaker and audience. In public speaking, you cannot separate the act of speaking from the message the speaker delivers. Supporting your message is one of your most important tasks as you develop your speech.

▲Forms of Support

Effective speeches generally rely on multiple forms of support. To give your speech greater weight and authority, at least five forms of support can be used. These include facts, statistics, examples, testimony, and analogies. Each of these forms of support will be discussed, and guidelines for using them will be presented.

Facts

Nothing undermines a presentation faster than too few facts. Facts are pieces of information that are verifiable and irrefutable. Opinions are points of view that may or may not be supported in fact. Too often, speakers confuse fact and opinion when adding supporting material to a speech. For example, while it is a fact that Forest Whitaker won the 2007 Academy Award for Best Actor, it is opinion to state that he is the best actor in Hollywood.

Facts serve at least three different purposes:

1. Facts clarify your main point.
They remove ambiguity, making it more likely that the message you send is the message your audience will receive.

2. Facts indicate your knowledge of the subject.
Rather than say, "The League of Women Voters has been around for a long time," report, "The League of Women Voters was founded in 1919." Your audience wants to know that you have researched the topic and can discuss specifics about your topic.

3. Facts define.
Facts provide needed definitions that may explain new concepts. If you are delivering a speech on "functional illiteracy," you may define the term in the following way:

While an illiterate adult has no ability to read, write, or compute, relatively few Americans fall into this category. However, some 27 million Americans can't read, write, compute, speak, or listen effectively enough to function in society. They cannot read street signs, write out a check, apply for a job or ask a government bureaucrat about a Social Security check they never received. Although they may have minimal communications skills, for all intents and purposes, they are isolated from the rest of society. These people are considered functionally illiterate.

In the above example, you anticipated the potential confusion between the terms "illiteracy" and "functional illiteracy," and you differentiated between these terms. While you defined this term for your public speaking class, if your audience was comprised of literacy coaches, this would not be necessary.

Guidelines for Using Facts

Carefully determine the number of facts to use. Too few facts will reveal that you spent little time researching, while too many may overwhelm your listeners. Sometimes, students want to impress their audience, or at least their instructor, with the amount of research completed for a particular speech. The desire to include all information may result in a "data dump," where facts are given in a steady stream with little or no connection to the speech or to each other. This results in an overload of information that is difficult to process.

To be effective, the number and complexity of your facts must be closely tied to the needs of your listeners. A speech to a group of hikers on poison ivy prevention may include practical issues such as identifying the plant and recognizing, treating, and avoiding the rash. However, if you are delivering a speech on the same subject to a group of medical students, a detailed explanation of the body's biochemical response to the plant is probably more relevant.

Make sure your meanings are clear. If you use words or phrases that have different meanings to you than they do to members of your audience, the impact of your speech is lessened. Misunderstandings occur when your audience attributes meanings to terms you did not intend. Think about the following words: success, liberal, conservative, patriot, happiness, good, bad, and smart. Collectively, we do not agree on the meanings of these words. One person may define success in terms of material wealth, while another may think of it in terms of family relationships, job satisfaction, and good health. When it is essential that your audience understand the meaning you intend, take the time to define it carefully as you speak.

Define terms when they are first introduced. The first time you use a term that requires an explanation, define it so that your meaning is clear. If you are talking about the advantages of belonging to a health maintenance organization, define the term the first time it is used.

Statistics

The second form of supporting material is statistics: the collection, analysis, interpretation, and presentation of information in numerical form. Statistics give us the information necessary to understand the magnitude of issues and to compare and contrast different points. Basic measures include the mean, median, and mode, which are generally referred to as descriptive statistics, because they allow us to discuss a set of numbers easily. The mean is calculated by adding all the numbers in a group and dividing by the number of items. It is the most widely used statistical measure. The median measures the middle score in the group. That is, half the values fall above it and half fall below. The mode is the value that occurs most frequently.

But statistics can be misleading. For example, if one were to examine the National League Baseball (MLB) salaries for 2005, one would find the average, or mean, salary for those players was $2,585,804 (http://asp.usatoday.com/sports/baseball/salaries). However, the highest salary went to San Francisco Giant's Barry Bonds who earned $22 million. Meanwhile, the median salary for all MLB players was $800,000. This means that half of the 439 players received more than $800,000 and half received less than that. In addition, the mode was $316,000. Twenty-six players received this amount. In this case, simply discussing these three statistical measures is not helpful, unless you want to make the point that salaries are not consistent. It might make more sense to discuss the range of salaries or look at a particular group of players' salaries. When using statistics in your speech, it is important to understand what they mean.

Include facts that will clarify the concepts you are describing in your speech.

Guidelines for Using Statistics

Be precise. Make sure you understand the statistics before including them in your speech. Consider the difference between the following statements.

A 2-percent decrease was shown in the rate of economic growth, as measured by the gross national product, compared to the same period last year.

The gross national product dropped by 2 percent compared to the same period last year.

In the first case, the statistic refers to a drop in the rate of growth—it tells us that the economy is growing at a slower pace but that it is still ahead of last year—while in the second, it refers to an actual drop in the gross national product in comparison to the previous year. These statements say two very different things.

It is critical that you not misinterpret statistics when analyzing the data. If you have questions, refer to a basic statistics text or another source that further explains the data. *Avoid using too many statistics.* Too many statistics will confuse and bore your audience and blunt the impact of your most important statistical points. Save your statistics for the places in your speech where they will make the most impact.

Round off your numbers. Is it important for your audience to know that, according to the Census Bureau's daily population projection on March 3, 2006, the U.S. population reached 298,228,575? The figure will have greater impact—and your audience will be more likely to remember it—if you round it off to "more than 298,000,000."

Cite your sources. Because statistics are rarely remembered for very long, it is easy for speakers to misquote and misuse them—often in a calculated way for their own ends. As an ethical speaker, you need to make sure your statistics are correct and you need to quote your sources. For example, if you were talking about the history of Girl Scout cookies, you could mention that during peak production of Girl Scout cookies, according to the Little Brownie Bakery website (www.littlebrowniebakers.com), one of two bakers for the Girl Scouts, 1,050,000 pounds of flour a week are used in production.

Use visual aids to express statistics. Statistics become especially meaningful to listeners when they are presented in visual form. Visual presentations of statistics free you from the need to repeat a litany of numbers that listeners will probably never remember. Instead, by transforming these numbers into visual presentations, you can highlight only the most important points, allowing your listeners to refer to the remaining statistics at any time. For example, in a speech extolling the virtues of graduate school, a graph displaying average salaries by degrees earned would be helpful.

Examples

Examples enliven speeches in a way that no other form of supporting material can. Grounding material in the specifics of everyday life has the power to create an empathic bond between speaker and audience, a bond strong enough to tie listeners to a speech and the speaker even after the example is complete.

Examples can be brief or extended, real or hypothetical, and narrative. Although examples differ in length, factual base, and source, their effectiveness lies in the extent to which they support the speaker's core idea.

Examples are brief or extended. Brief examples are short illustrations that clarify a general statement. If you made the following assertion: "Americans are more modest than Europeans," you could support it by using brief examples, such as, "If you take a walk on the beach in Italy or France, you should not be surprised to find women sunbathing topless. Also, many European countries, such as Sweden and Germany, have public saunas that are enjoyed by men and women—who are in the same sauna, sitting naked on their towels." Brief examples can be used effectively throughout a speech. Your decision to use them will depend on many factors, including the needs of your audience, the nature of your material, and your approach.

Extended examples are longer and richer in detail than brief examples. They are used most effectively to build images and to create a lasting impression on the audience, as can been seen in the following excerpt from a speech in 2006 given by Steven Darimont, candidate for sheriff in Coles County, Illinois. When making the point that money is spent unnecessarily on jail food, he stated:

© 2012 by violetkaipa.
Used under license of Shutterstock.

Use visual aids to express statistics. Statistics become especially meaningful to listeners when they are presented in visual form.

"Our food budget alone is at $140,000 and we will go over that by $12–15,000 this year. The sheriff has requested that (amount) be raised (an additional) $20,000, to $160,000 next year. The inmates currently get three hot meals a day. An example of this is breakfast: scrambled eggs, toast with butter and jelly, cold cereal with milk, hash browns, fruit, and juice. The Department of Corrections mandates only one hot meal per day, yet we feed three hot meals."

Providing more detail about the budget and the ample food choices creates a greater impact on the listener rather than saying, "We provide three hot meals a day, and we're going over budget."

Because of their impact, extended examples should not be overused or used at inappropriate points. As with other forms of support, they should be reserved for the points at which they will have the greatest effect: in clarifying the message, persuading listeners to your point of view, or establishing a speaker-audience relationship.

Examples are real or hypothetical. Sometimes the best examples are real, and come from your personal experience. By revealing parts of your life that relate to your speech topic, you provide convincing evidence and, at the same time, potentially create a powerful bond between you and your audience. Consider the student who has watched her mother die from lung cancer. The experience of hearing about the diagnosis, discussing treatment possibilities, and making final arrangements while her mother was alive can have a powerful effect on the audience. The words and emotion have great impact because the situation is real, not hypothetical, and the speaker provides a sense of reality to the topic. At times, it suits the speaker's purpose to create a fictional example, rather than a real example, to make a point. Although these examples are not based on facts, the circumstances they describe are often realistic and thus effective.

Hypothetical examples are useful when you want to exaggerate a point as Aaronson did. They are also useful when you cannot find a factual illustration for your speech. To be effective, they must be tied in some way to the point you are trying to illustrate.

It is important that your listeners know when you are using a hypothetical example and when you are not. Avoid confusion by introducing these examples in a direct way. You might start out by saying, "Imagine that you live next door to a college professor we'll call Dr. Supple," or "Let's talk about a hypothetical mother on welfare named Alice."

Examples can be in narrative form. Narratives are stories within a speech, anecdotes that create visual images in listeners' minds. In many ways, they take extended examples a step further by involving listeners in a tale that captures attention and makes a point—a story connected to the speaker's core idea. Many listeners love a good story, and when the speech is over, the narrative is what they remember.

Imagine Laura, a person who has traveled significantly, giving an informative speech on "The art of shopping outside the United States: Bartering made simple." She might include the following:

My husband and I were in Morocco shopping with my mother and my aunt. They stopped to speak with a shop owner about carpets and my husband and I went on. About forty-five minutes later, we walked by to see them STILL speaking with the shop owner. Now, though, all three were seated, and they were drinking hot, mint tea. We approached the shopkeeper and introduced ourselves. He proceeded to tell us how different my mother and aunt were from most American women. He said that American women will ask the price of something, and he'll throw out some high price. Then the women will offer a significantly lower price. He rejects that but comes down on his original high price. The American women, usually, will accept his second price, no matter how high! Not these women! My mom and aunt bartered back and forth with the shopkeeper about the price, never giving in! The shopkeeper said he really enjoyed negotiating with them; that they were both friendly and insistent. They didn't back down easily, and, according to the shopkeeper, they ended up paying a reasonable price for their carpet.

By their nature, narratives demand that listeners take an active part in linking the story to the speaker's main point. The story moves from beginning to middle, to end. Even if the speaker supplies the link after the narrative, audience members still make the connections themselves as they listen.

A narrative can be used anywhere in a speech. No matter where it is placed, it assumes great importance to listeners as they become involved with the details. Through the narrative, speakers can establish a closeness with the audience that may continue even after the story is over.

Guidelines for Using Examples

Examples add interest and impact. They should be representative because examples support your core idea only when they accurately represent the situation. No matter the type of example you use as supporting material, the following three guidelines will help you choose examples for your speeches:

Use examples frequently. Examples are often the lifeblood of a speech. Use them to make your points—but only in appropriate places. When using examples to prove a point, more than one example generally is needed.

Use only the amount of detail necessary. To make your examples work, you want to use only the amount of detail necessary for your audience and no more. The detail you provide in examples should be based on the needs of your audience. If your listeners are familiar with a topic, you can simply mention what the audience already knows. Interspersing long examples with short ones varies the pace and detail of your discussion.

Use examples to explain new concepts. Difficult concepts become easier to handle when you clarify them with examples. Keep in mind that although you may be comfortable with the complexities of a topic, your listeners might be hearing these complexities for the first time. Appropriate examples can mean the difference between communicating with or losing your audience.

Testimony

The word testimony may conjure a vision of witnesses in a court of law giving sworn statements to a judge and jury, adding credibility to a case. In public speaking, testimony has nothing to do with the law, but it has everything to do with credibility. When you cite the words of others, either directly or through paraphrasing, you are attempting, in effect, to strengthen your position by telling your audience that people with special knowledge support your position or take your side. Testimony can cite either experience or opinion. Also, short quotations may be an effective way to provide testimony.

In order to be effective, however, testimony needs to be used in its proper context. Purposefully distorting the testimony of an expert to suit the needs of your speech is misleading and unethical. Be honest to your source as well as your audience.

Narratives are stories within a speech, anecdotes that create visual images in listeners' minds.

Experience as testimony. Experience may be the most credible choice in some cases because someone was "on the scene." For example, hundreds of thousands of individuals were directly affected by hurricane Katrina. A student writer for the University of Texas at Austin newspaper interviewed Lorraine Brown about her personal experience during hurricane Katrina. The following account was printed in the September 6, 2005 issue of *The Daily Texan.*

At 5 a.m. on Monday, after floodwaters breached the New Orleans levees, Brown awoke to find water seeping into her house. 'I saw the water on my kitchen floor, and I picked up a mop and started mopping. But then I looked out the window and saw that the water was already up to here,' she said, holding her hand at her waist. 'It's lucky that I woke up at five, because by six the water would've been too high to get out.' She explained that the doors of her house swung outward and that she couldn't have pushed hard enough to overcome the weight of the water. 'I think about what if we woke up, and the water was already up over the house. Then it's just like a monster is outside, and there's nowhere to go.'

September 6, 2005 by Delaney Hall. *Copyright © 2005 by* The Daily Texan. *Reprinted by permission.*

Lorraine Brown's experience as one of the survivors of the hurricane provides vivid imagery that helps the listener recognize the terror that many experienced.

It is possible to use your own testimony when you are an expert. If you are writing a speech on what it is like to recover from a spinal cord injury, use your own expert testimony if you have suffered this injury. Similarly, if you are talking about the advantages and problems of being a female lifeguard, cite your own testimony if you are female and have spent summers saving lives at the beach. When you do not have the background necessary to convince your audience, use the testimony of those who do.

Opinion as testimony. In some circumstances, the opinion of a recognized authority may provide the credibility needed to strengthen your argument or prove a point. Jimmy Carter, former president, was an outspoken critic of the Iraqi War. At a news conference in July 2005, CBS News quoted him as saying, "I thought then, and I think now, that the invasion of Iraq was unnecessary and unjust. And I think the premises on which it was launched were false" (www. cbsnews.com). While he was clearly stating an opinion, Carter carried a certain amount of credibility, among his fellow political liberals at least, because he was speaking as a former president.

Short quotations. A short quotation is a form of testimony, but its purpose is often different. Frequently, short quotations are used to set the tone for a speech, to provide humor, or to make important points more memorable. If you were receiving the MVP award for football at your high school or college, you might start out with something like this:

Experience may be the most credible choice in some cases because someone was "on the scene."

> "Wow. I'm reminded of John Madden's words when he was inducted into the Pro Football Hall of Fame in 2006, 'And right now, I don't have, I got like numb, you know, a tingle from the bottom of my toes to the top of my head.' Yep. That's exactly how I feel."

Madden's quote is not the most articulate or insightful comment, but it certainly expressed the emotion the football player was feeling, and this quote would set an engaging tone for an acceptance speech.

Sometimes quotations are too long or too complicated to present verbatim. You can choose to cite the source but paraphrase the message. Instead of quoting the following description of the effect crack cocaine has on the body, it might be more effective to paraphrase.

Quote:
    According to Dr. Mark S. Gold, nationally known expert on cocaine abuse, founder of the 800-COCAINE helpline, and author of The Facts About Drugs and Alcohol, "as an anesthetic, cocaine blocks the conduction of electrical impulses within the nerve cells involved in sensory transmissions, primarily pain. The body's motor impulses, those that control muscle function, for example, are not affected by low-dose use of cocaine. In this way cocaine creates a deadening blockage (known as a differential block) of pain, without interfering with body movement" (Gold 1986, 36).

Paraphrase:
    According to Dr. Mark S. Gold, nationally known expert on cocaine abuse, founder of the 800-COCAINE helpline and author of The Facts About Drugs and Alcohol, cocaine blocks pain without interfering with body movement.

The second version is more effective when speaking to a lay audience who knows little about medicine, while the former is appropriate for an audience of science students or physicians.

© 2012 by Yuri Arcurs.
Used under license of Shutterstock.

Be sure to quote sources only if they are experts in the matters they address in the quote.

Guidelines for Using Testimony

Use only recognizable or credible testimony and quotations. At a time when media exposure is so pervasive, it is easy to find someone who will support your point of view. Before citing a person as an authoritative source, be sure that he or she is an expert. If you are giving a speech on the greatest movies ever produced, it would make sense to quote Roger Ebert, film critic and author of numerous books on the subject of film. However, he would not be the proper choice for a speech on the joys of collecting and trading baseball cards.

As you review expert testimony, keep in mind that the more research you do, the more opinions you will find. Ultimately, your choice should be guided by relevance and credibility of the source. The fact that you quote former Supreme Court Justice Sandra Day O'Connor in a speech on affirmative action is as important as the quote itself.

Choose unbiased experts. How effective is the following testimony if its source is the owner of the Oakland Athletics?

> There is no team in baseball as complete as the Athletics. The team has better pitching, fielding, hitting, and base running than any of its competitors in the National or American League.

If the same quote came from a baseball writer for *Sports Illustrated* you would probably believe it more. Thus, when choosing expert testimony, bear in mind that opinions shaped by self-interest are less valuable, from the point of view of your audience, than those motivated by the merits of the issues.

Identify the source. Not all names of your experts will be recognizable, so it is important to tell your audience why they are qualified to give testimony. If you are cautioning overseas travelers to avoid tourist scams, the following expert testimony provides support:

> According to Rick Steves, travelers should be wary of "The 'helpful' local: Thieves posing as concerned locals will warn you to store your wallet safely—and then steal it after they see where you stash it. Some thieves put out tacks and ambush drivers with their "assistance" in changing the tire. Others hang out at subway ticket machines eager to "help" the bewildered tourist buy tickets with a pile of quickly disappearing foreign cash" (www.ricksteves.com).

Without knowing anything about Rick Steves, your readers will have no reason to trust this advice. However, if you state his credentials first, you can establish the credibility of your expert. So instead, the speaker could start begin with, "According to Rick Steves, host and producer of the popular public television series *Rick Steves' Europe* and best-selling author of thirty European travel books, travelers should be wary of…"

Develop techniques to signal the beginning and ending of each quotation. Your audience may not know when a quote begins or ends. Some speakers prefer to preface quotations with the words, "And I quote" and to end quotations with the phrase, "end quote." Other speakers indicate the presence of quotations through pauses immediately before and immediately after the quotation or through a slight change of pace or inflection. It may be a good idea to use both techniques in your speech to satisfy your listeners' need for variety. Just do not make quotation signs with your fingers!

Analogies

At times, the most effective form of supporting material is the analogy, which points out similarities between what we know and understand and what we do not know or cannot accept. Analogies fall into two separate categories: figurative and literal. Figurative analogies draw comparisons between things that are distinctly different in an attempt to clarify a concept or persuade. Biology professor Paul Erlich uses an analogy of a globe holding and draining water to explain what he believed to be a world overpopulation problem. The following is an excerpt from a speech delivered to the First National Congress on Optimum Population and Environment, June 9, 1970:

> As a model of the world demographic situation, think of the world as a globe, and think of a faucet being turned on into that globe as being the equivalent of the birth rate, the input into the population. Think of that drain at the base of that globe— water pouring out—as being the equivalent to the output, the death rate of the population. At the time of the Agricultural Revolution, the faucet was turned on full blast; there was a very high birth rate. The drain was wide open; there was a high death rate. There was very little water in the globe, very few people in the population—only above five million. When the Agricultural Revolution took place, we began to plug the drain, cut down the death rate, and the globe began to fill up.

Regardless of whether he was right, his analogy is effective because it helps the audience understand the population explosion. It explains the nature of the problem in a clear, graphic way. Listener understanding comes not from the presentation of new facts (these facts were presented elsewhere in the speech) but from a simple comparison. When dealing with difficult or emotionally charged concepts, listeners benefit from this type of comparative supporting material.

Keep in mind that although figurative analogies may be helpful, they usually do not serve as sufficient proof in a persuasive argument. Erlich, for example, must back his analogy with facts, statistics, examples, and quotations to persuade his listeners that his analogy is accurate—that we are indeed in the midst of a population crisis.

A literal analogy compares like things from similar classes, such as a game of professional football with a game of college football. If, for example, you are delivering a speech to inform your classmates about Russia's involvement in the war in Afghanistan, the following literal analogy might be helpful:

> The war in Afghanistan was the former Soviet Union's Vietnam. Both wars were unwinnable from the start. Neither the Vietnamese nor the Afghans would tolerate foreign domination. Acting with the determination of the Biblical David, they waged

a struggle against the Goliaths of Russia and the United States. In large part, the winning weapon in both wars was the collective might of village peasants who were determined to rid their countries of the Superpowers—no matter the odds.

Literal analogies serve as proof when the aspects or concepts compared are similar. When similarities are weak, the proof fails. The analogy, "As Rome fell because of moral decay, so will the United States," is valid only if the United States and Rome have similar economic and social systems, types of governments, and so on. The fewer the similarities between the United States and Rome, the weaker the proof.

© 2012 by Alliance.
Used under license of Shutterstock.

Develop techniques to signal the beginning and ending of each quotation. Just do not make quotation signs with your fingers!

Guidelines for Using Analogies

Use analogies to build the power of your argument. Analogies convince through comparison to something the audience already knows. It is psychologically comforting to your listeners to hear new ideas expressed in a familiar context. The result is greater understanding and possible acceptance of your point of view.

Be certain the analogy is clear. Even when the concept of your analogy is solid, if the points of comparison are not effectively carried through from beginning to end, the analogy will fail. Your analogy must be as consistent and complete as in the following example:

In political campaigns, opponents square off against one another in an attempt to land the winning blow. Although after a close and grueling campaign that resembles a ten-round bout, one candidate may succeed by finding a soft spot in his opponent's record, the fight is hardly over. Even while the downed opponent is flat against the mat, the victor turns to the public and tells yet another distortion of the truth. "My opponent," he says, "never had a chance." Clearly, politicians and prize fighters share one goal in common: to knock their opponents senseless and to make the public believe that they did it with ease.

Avoid using too many analogies. A single effective analogy can communicate your point. Do not diminish its force by including several in a short presentation.

▶SUMMARY

Research gives you the tools you need to support your thesis statement. A solid research base increases your credibility. To begin your research strategy, assess your personal knowledge and skills. Then look for print and online resources. The librarian can lead you to valuable sources within the physical library as well as online. You may need to look up information in encyclopedias, dictionaries, books, newspapers, magazines, journal articles, and government documents. When using online resources, it is important to use website evaluation criteria and to question accuracy, authority, objectivity, coverage, and currency.

Supporting materials buttress the main points of your speech and make you a more credible speaker. Among the most important forms of support are facts—verifiable information. Facts clarify your main points, indicate knowledge of your subject, and serve as definitions. Opinions differ from facts in that they cannot be verified. Statistical support involves the presentation of information in numerical form. Because statistics are easily manipulated, it is important to analyze carefully the data you present.

Five different types of examples are commonly used as forms of support. Brief examples are short illustrations that clarify a general statement. Extended examples are used to create lasting images. Narratives are stories within a speech that are linked to the speaker's main idea. Hypothetical examples are fictional examples used to make a point. Personal examples are anecdotes related to your topic that come from your own life.

When you use testimony quotations, you cite the words of others to increase the credibility of your message. Your sources gain expertise through experience and authority. Analogies focus on the similarities between the familiar and unfamiliar. Figurative analogies compare things that are different, while liberal analogies compare things from similar classes. Literal analogies can often be used as proof.

QUESTIONS FOR ANALYSIS

1. How important is research in the preparation of most speeches? How can an audience tell whether a speech lacks a sound research base?

2. Why is it important that you conduct both an audience analysis and reflect on your own knowledge and skills when it comes to developing your topic?

3. When you are considering information you found on a website, how do you evaluate whether or not the information you found is appropriate to include as supporting material?

4. How can you best use the services of a librarian?

5. With the idea of a research strategy in mind, how will you determine the types and amount of support you will need to meet the specific purpose of your next speech?

6. Which supporting materials are most effective for clarifying a point and which are most appropriate for proof? Can some forms of support serve both aims? How?

7. In the hands of an unethical speaker, how can statistics and analogies mislead an audience? What is your ethical responsibility in choosing supporting materials?

ACTIVITIES

1. Tour the libraries at school and in your community. In a written report, compare the facilities and use your findings as a guide when you research your next speech.

2. For your next speech assignment, develop and follow a search strategy that includes both interviews and library research.

3. Analyze the connection between your choice of topic and your choice of support.

4. Select three different forms of support and assess the strengths and weaknesses of each as evidence in public speeches.

5. Include in your next persuasive speech as many different forms of support as possible. After your speech, hand out a questionnaire to determine which form of support had the most effect.

REFERENCES

Aaronson, R.J. "Air transportation: What is safe and needed." *Vital Speeches of the Day*, July 15, 1989.

Beck, S. "The Good, The Bad & The Ugly: or, Why It's a Good Idea to Evaluate Web Sources." 1997.

Erlich, P. June 9, 1970. Speech delivered to First National Congress on Optimum Population and Environment.

Fleshler, H., J. Ilardo, and J. Demoretcky. "The influence of field dependence, speaker credibility set and message documentation on evaluations of speaker and message credibility," *The Southern Speech Communication Journal* (Summer 1974): 389–402.

Glenn Dowling, C. "Shoplifting," *Life*, August 1, 1988, 33.

Gold, M.S. 1986. *The facts about drugs and alcohol.* New York: Bantam Books.

NAME: _____ DATE: _____

SHORT ANSWERS

HONOR STATEMENT: I, the undersigned student, hereby declare before God, before the school, and before the professor that I have read Chapter 9 in its entirety, that I have completed the following exercise with help from no other sources, and that I neither have shared nor will share this work with anyone.

Signature: _____ Date: _____

1. What is the difference between speaker credibility and message credibility?

_____

_____

_____

_____

_____

_____

2. What is the difference between research and supporting material?

_____

_____

_____

_____

_____

_____

3. When do you need to cite sources in a speech?

_____

_____

_____

_____

_____

_____

4. How does supporting material strengthen a speech?

_____

_____

_____

_____

_____

_____

5. Explain the difference between examples that are brief, extended, real, hypothetical, or narrative.

_____

_____

_____

_____

_____

_____

6. How does supporting material strengthen a speech?

_____

_____

_____

_____

_____

_____

_____

"We will draw the
curtain and show
you the picture."
- William Shakespeare

CHAPTER 10 >>

10 PRESENTATIONAL AIDS

Adapted from *Public Speaking: Choices for Effective Results, Fifth Edition* by John Makay et al. Copyright © 2008.
Reprinted with permission of Kendall Hunt Publishing Co.

Suppose an assignment in your class is one that really excites you, and makes you think of a speech topic that your audience will find provocative and controversial. Unlike many of the speeches you have heard, this one will tell a story your classmates will find difficult to ignore-or so it seems.

The topic is concerned with how so few of the college football and basketball program athletes ever graduate—a scandal that looms large in your own school. Recent articles in the student newspaper have criticized your school's athletic department for emphasizing winning over education. An editorial in last week's edition asked, "How can student-athletes practice forty hours a week and still go to class, study, and complete their assignments?" The answer is, they cannot. As you collect supporting material for your speech, you find statistics that tell a story of athletes not equipped to go professional, and not prepared for anything more than menial work. Here is part of the speech your classmates hear:

Instead of startling your listeners, too many statistics numb them. You may see several people yawning, many doodling, a few whispering.

> According to a study by the federal Governmental Accountancy Office, of the 97 colleges with Division 1-A basketball programs, considered the best in intercollegiate sports, 35—that's more than one third—graduate no more than 1 in 5 athletes; 33 graduate between 21 percent and 40 percent; 11 graduate between 41 percent and 60 percent; 10 graduate between 61 percent and 80 percent; and only 8 graduate between 81 percent and 100 percent.

> The graduation rates for football players on Division 1-A teams is little better. Of the 103 teams in this division, 14 graduate no more than 1 out of 5 players; 39 graduate between 21 and 40 percent; 31 graduate between 41 and 60 percent; 13 between 61 and 80 percent; and only 6 between 81 and 100 percent (Molotsky, *The New York Times*, September 10, 1989).

Instead of startling your listeners, these statistics numb them. You may see several people yawning, many doodling, a few whispering. You have no idea why until your classmates comment during the post-speech evaluation. The complaints are all the same: Your "can't miss" speech was boring and difficult to follow. Instead of stimulating your listeners, your long list of statistics put them to sleep.

Few of us think of speech making in visual terms—or find ways to reach our speaking goals by turning to presentational aids. In this example, an appropriately constructed visual aid could have helped you avoid saying so much in words. Despite the interest your listeners had in your topic before your speech began, the number and complexity of your statistics made it difficult for them to pay attention. By presenting some of your data in visual form, you could communicate the same message more effectively. Consider the difference when the following speech text is substituted for the text above and combined with figure 10.1 (see page 256).

> A study by the U.S. Governmental Accountancy Office, an arm of the federal government, shows that at some Division 1-A colleges, including those with the best

intercollegiate athletic programs, no more than 1 out of 5 basketball and football players graduate. As you can see, [speaker points to the figure] there are far fewer colleges with an 80 percent graduation rate than colleges graduating athletes at a rate of 20 percent or less. Although only 8 out of 97 colleges fit into the former group, 35 fit into the latter—and our college is one of them.

Numbers are still used, but not as many, and with the presentational aid, the audience gets a visual feel for the information and they are able to process the information for a little longer than if you just said the numbers.

This chapter focuses on the benefits of using presentational aids (frequently called visual aids). The different types of presentational aids are explored and criteria are given for their use and display. Based on the increasing use of PowerPoint for classroom presentations, a specific section on the creation/use of computer generated slides is included.

❯❯ FUNCTIONS OF PRESENTATIONAL AIDS

A decade ago, no one expected to see professional quality presentational aids for a class speech. As technology becomes more accessible, however, expectations have increased. Regardless of our advances in technology, we all expect to see effective presentations that communicate a message in a clear, direct manner.

Presentational aids function in a variety of ways. They are more than "add-ons." Your instructor may require you to use presentational aids not only to enhance the effectiveness of your speech, but also to learn how to work with them as you speak. Following are five functions of presentational aids.

▲ Presentational Aids Create Interest and Attraction

Have you ever seen a lotto billboard along side an interstate? As you approach it, you can see the jackpot amount increasing as the digital numbers change constantly. When a presentational aid is well prepared, little can compete with it to capture—and hold—audience interest. We live in a visual age. The images that surround us in the mass media make us more receptive, on conscious and unconscious levels, to visual presentations of all kinds. We are attuned to these presentations simply because they are visual—a phenomenon you can use to your advantage during a speech.

A student wanted to emphasize how fast the world's population is growing. During her speech, she accessed a website that keeps a digital tally of births, and kept the digital counter on the screen for about a minute. Then she made reference to the number of births that had occurred during that time frame. It kept the interest of the class.

A well-placed, professional-looking presentational aid will draw attention to the point you are trying to make or to the statistics you want the audience to process.

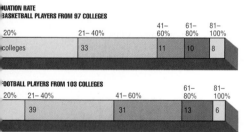

FIGURE 10.1
A visual aid can be an effective way to present statistics.

Our suggestions: In an effort to maintain interest and attention, try to limit each visual to one main point. Leave details out. Use as few words as possible. Be aware of spacing, and do not crowd the images. If there is too much information or the slide looks too "busy," you will lose attention and interest.

▲Presentational Aids
Make Complex Ideas Clear

Presentational aids have the power to clarify complex ideas. They are invaluable tools when explaining mechanical functions such as how a hot air balloon rises or how a computer stores information. They can help clarify complex interrelationships involving people, groups, and institutions. They can show, for example, the stages a bill must go through before it becomes a law and the role Congress and the president play in this process. Visuals reduce, but do not eliminate, the need to explain verbally the complex details of a process.

Presentational aids take the place of many words and, therefore, shorten the length of a speech. They do not replace words, and one or two statements are insufficient verbal support for a series of visual displays. But presentational aids and words in combination can reduce the amount of time you spend creating word pictures.

Remember, however, to keep your visuals simple. Speech consultants Karen Berg and Andrew Gilman (1989) explain, "When in doubt, simplify; eliminate extraneous material. If necessary, use an additional visual rather than burdening one with more information than it can efficiently transmit" (73).

▲Presentational Aids Make Abstract Ideas Concrete

Few of us enjoy abstractions. If you are delivering a speech on the effects of the 11 million gallon oil spill from the Exxon tanker on Alaska's Prince William Sound, it may not be enough to tell your audience that the spill was allowed to drift 470 miles in a period of 56 days. It is far more effective to refer to a map of the drifting spill that illustrates the extent of the spread on different days. Figure 10.2 shows the enormity of the disaster and eliminates any confusion audience members may have about its impact on the Alaskan coast.

Along with this visual, you explain:

> For three days after the Exxon tanker rammed into a reef on Alaska's Prince William Sound, the spill miraculously lingered near the ruptured hull. But officials were unable to take action. Instead they wasted this time—this precious time—arguing what to do. On day four, a powerful storm made their arguments academic as it spread the oil down the Alaskan coast where it drifted uncontrollably for 56 days and stained 470 miles of Alaska's pristine shore (*Newsweek*, September 18, 1989).

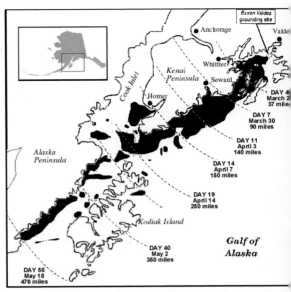

© Source: 1993 State On-Scene Coordinator's Report

FIGURE 10.2
The audience listening to a speech that includes explanations of where the oil spills took place needs to view a map with necessary detail included. In this figure, the words and the illustration work together to create meaning.

The image of the spill's movement provides us with a visual picture that makes the situation much more easily understood. Sometimes we need to see something in order to process it effectively.

▲Presentational Aids Make Messages Memorable

Did you review a news website this morning? What do you remember from it? Chances are, a photo comes to mind—the picture of a fireman rescuing a child from a burning building or the president of your university getting a pie in the face at the end of a fundraiser. You may have read the articles that accompanied these pictures, but the images are likely to have had the greatest impact.

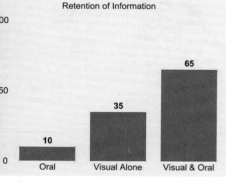

FIGURE 10.3
A simple bar graph can display information clearly so it is easier to understand.

The tendency for an audience to recall pictures longer than words gives speakers an important advantage. Research has shown, for example, that three days after an event, people retain 10 percent of what they heard from an oral presentation, 35 percent from a visual presentation, and 65 percent from a visual and oral presentation (www.osha.gov 2007). Using a simple bar graph to display this information makes it easier to understand these significant differences (see figure 10.3).

Presentational aids have persuasive power. Business speakers, especially those in sales, have long realized that they can close a deal faster if they use visual aids. A study by the University of Minnesota and the 3M Corporation found that speakers who integrate visuals into their talks are 43 percent more likely to persuade their audiences than speakers who rely solely on verbal images (Vogel, Dickson, and Lehman 1986).

▲Presentational Aids Serve to Organize Ideas

As with every other aspect of your speech, presentational aids should be audience-centered. They may be eye-catching and visually stimulating, but they do serve a more practical purpose. The flow and connection of a speaker's ideas are not always apparent to an audience, especially if the topic is complicated or involves many steps. Flow charts, diagrams, graphs, and tables can help listeners follow a speaker's ideas.

❯❯ GENERAL CRITERIA FOR USING PRESENTATIONAL AIDS

Your decision to include an aid should be based on the extent to which it enhances your audience's interest and understanding. The type of aid you choose should relate directly to the specific purpose of your speech and information you intend to convey. As you consider using a presentational aid, consider the following four general criteria.

▲Value to Presentation

Your instructor may require you to use a presentational aid for one or more of your speeches, but it does not mean that any aid is better than no aid. First and foremost, the aid must add value to your presentation. If you are bringing in a presentational aid just to meet the constraints of the assignment, it may not be effective. For example, if a student is giving a speech about the "cola wars," and brings in a can of Pepsi and a can of Coke, there is not much value to the presentation. We all know what they look like. But if the same student was giving a speech on the history of Coca-Cola, it would be interesting to see past Coke can designs or a lineup of all the various flavors available internationally.

So ask yourself, what is the purpose of the aid? To surprise? To entertain? To illustrate? To make some concept concrete? If you think your presentational aid will make your speech better, then it has value. If you think the audience will benefit from the visual aid, then it has value.

Consider both object and audience size.

▲Value of an Item

If the item is precious to you, think twice about bringing it to class. Maybe there will be a rain or snow storm. You might drop it. Someone might take it. You are taking a chance by bringing in an item that has either a high financial or sentimental value.

▲Ease of Transportation

Think about what may happen to your object during transportation. Is it a large poster you are trying to carry on a subway? Does it weigh forty pounds? Do you have to carry it with you all day? Is it bigger than a breadbox? Is it alive? You want to consider how difficult your aid will be to transport, as well as what you are going to do with it before and after your speech.

▲Size of Object and Audience

Imagine spending hours preparing a series of graphs and charts for a speech on low-impact aerobics. However, no one beyond the third row saw them. This violates the cardinal rule of presentational aids: To be valuable, they need to be visible. Whether you use a flip-chart or bring in an object of some kind, people in the back of the room need to see it. If they cannot read what is on the table or cannot see the pie chart clearly, the aid does not serve its purpose.

Consider both object and audience size. Showing an 8" x 10" picture of evangelist Billy Graham, would be appropriate in a small class but not in an auditorium. Bringing a coin to show the class is not helpful, unless the coin has little value, and each student can examine it. Students are better served by viewing an enlarged picture of the coin on a slide or poster. And, even if you bring in enough objects for everyone, you may lose their attention as they examine the object, drop it, or otherwise play with it during your speech.

❱❱ TYPES OF PRESENTATIONAL AIDS

Presentational aids fall into four general categories or types: actual objects, three-dimensional models, two-dimensional reproductions, and technology-based. Each of these will be described in greater detail.

▲Actual Objects

Actual objects are just that—actual. Students have unlimited options. A student who had been stricken with bone cancer as a child, a condition that required the amputation of her leg, demonstrated to her classmates how her prosthetic leg functioned and how she wore it. Not one of her listeners lost interest in her demonstration.

Another student, seeking to persuade her audience to pressure their members of Congress to support stricter toy safety regulations, brought to class a box filled with toys that could injure, maim, or even kill young children. Her demonstration was so persuasive that everyone signed the speaker's petition to encourage Congress to pass stronger toy safety legislation.

Yet another student, concerned about the vast amount of disposable diapers that linger in our landfills, brought to class a (heavy) week's worth of dirty diapers from one infant. In addition to having some shock value (students being grossed out), it left a powerful image to accompany her statistics about the "shelf life" of a dirty diaper, and the average amount of space diapers consume in a community landfill.

As these examples demonstrate, actual objects can be effective visual aids. Because you are showing your audience exactly what you are talking about, they have the power to inform or convince unlike any other presentational aid. In addition to the general criteria, when thinking about bringing an object to class, you need to be concerned with safety. Make sure the object you intend to use will not pose a safety risk to you or to your audience. Animals certainly fall into this category as well as chemicals and weapons. You may feel safe with your object(s), but that does not mean your classmates will feel safe. You think your little pet scorpion is adorable. It may terrify your classmates.

▲Three-dimensional Models

If you decide that an actual object is too risky, a three-dimensional model may be your best choice. Models are commonly used to show the structure of a complex object. For example, a student who watched his father almost die of a heart attack used a model of the heart to demonstrate what physically happened during the attack. Using a three-dimensional replica about five times the size of a human heart, he showed how the major blood vessels leading to his father's heart became clogged and how this blockage precipitated the attack.

Models are useful when explaining various steps in a sequence. A scale model of the space shuttle, the shuttle launch pad, and its booster rockets will help you describe what happens during the first few minutes after blast-off.

Some replicas are easier to find, build, and afford than others. If you are delivering a speech on antique cars, inexpensive plastic models are available at a hobby shop and take little time to assemble. But if you want to show how proper city planning can untangle the daily downtown traffic snarl, you would have to build your own scaled-down version

If your speech is about learning to play the violin, it would be good to bring your instrument along to demonstrate its features.

of downtown roads as they are now, and as you would like them to be—a model that would be too time-consuming and expensive to be feasible.

When considering using a three-dimensional model, you need to take into account the construction time and availability. It is possible you already have the model or you know where you can borrow one, so no construction time is needed. If, however, you need to create the three-dimensional model from a kit or your own imagination, you need to consider how much time it will take you to put it together. You do not want your construction time to take longer than your speech preparation.

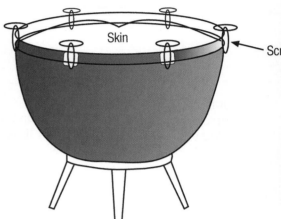

Skin

Scre

If the three-dimensional model is in your possession, availability is not an issue. If it is in your bedroom, attic, or garage in your hometown, you need to take travel time into account. If you have to sign your life away to borrow it, or if you have to plan six weeks or more ahead to access the model, it may not be worth your trouble. If the model is sold at the local Wal-Mart, then availability is not an issue.

▲Two-dimensional Reproductions

Two-dimensional reproductions are the most common visual aids used by speakers. Among these are photographs, diagrams and drawings, maps, tables, and graphs.

▲Photographs

Photographs are the most realistic of your two-dimensional visual choices and can have the greatest impact. For a speech on animal rights, a photo of a fox struggling to free his leg from a trap will deliver your message more effectively than words. If you are speaking about forest fire prevention, a photo of a forest destroyed by fire is your most persuasive evidence.

To be effective, photos must be large enough for your audience to see and using magazine or newspaper photos will not be as clear as a photo. If a photo is important to your presentation, consider enlarging it so the entire audience can see.

Caution: Although photographs are effective aids, avoid the negative impact. If a photograph truly offends or disgusts your audience, you have reduced the impact of your message.

▲Drawings and Diagrams

When you cannot illustrate your point with a photograph—or would rather not use one—a drawing is an adequate alternative. A drawing is your own representation of what you are describing. If you are demonstrating the difference between a kettledrum and a snare drum, a simple drawing may be all you need. If you want to extend your explanation to show how musicians are able to control the pitch of the sound made by a drum, your drawing must include more detail. The location of the screws used to tighten the skin of the drum must be shown as well as the relation between the size of the drum and the pitch of the sound.

FIGURE 10.4
A simple diagram can show how the parts of objects, such as this drum, interact.

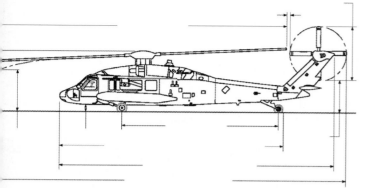

A detailed drawing showing the arrangement and relation of the parts to the whole is considered a diagram. Figure 10.4 (see page 261) is a simple diagram of a kettledrum. Labels are often used to pinpoint critical parts.

Avoid attempting a complex drawing or diagram if you have little or no artistic ability. Do not attempt to produce these drawings while your audience is watching. Prepare sketches in advance that are suitable for presentation. Keep your audience's needs—and limitations—in mind when choosing sketches. Too much detail will frustrate your audience as they strain to see the tiniest parts and labels. And when people are frustrated, they often stop listening. Imagine the glazed look in the audience's eyes in a basic speech course as they listen to someone using figure 10.5 to discuss the dimensions of the UH-60 Black Hawk helicopter.

FIGURE 10.5
An intricate line drawing will only serve to frustrate your audience as they strain to see the details. Keep illustrations simple.

▲Maps

Weather reports on TV news have made maps a familiar visual aid. Instead of merely talking about the weather, reporters show us the shifting patterns that turn sunshine into storms. The next time you watch a national weather report, pay attention to the kind of map being used. Notice that details have been omitted because they distract viewers from what the reporter is explaining.

When talking about Europe's shrinking population, do not include the location of the Acropolis or the Eiffel Tower. Too much detail will confuse your audience. Because your map must be designed for a specific rhetorical purpose, you may have to draw it yourself. Start with a broad outline of the geographic area and add to it only those details that are necessary for your presentation.

On election night 2004, many news programs showed a map of the United States that was divided into "blue states" and "red states." Blue states were those where the majority of voters chose John F. Kerry, and red states were those where the majority of voters chose George W. Bush. The map (see figure 10.6) gave a quick update on where the candidates stood. This map was so successful as a visual aid, that the concept of "blue states" and "red states" has become part of our political vernacular.

FIGURE 10.6
This map shows "blue states" and "red states", making it easier to get a quick update on each candidate.

▲Tables

Tables focus on words and numbers presented in columns and rows. Tables are used most frequently to display statistical data. When delivering a speech on the fat content of food where you note the types and percentage of fat in nuts, you could refer to a table similar to that shown in figure 10.7, page 263) This single table should be divided into two parts because it contains too much information to present in one visual. Keep in mind the audience's information absorption threshold—the point at which a visual will cease to be useful because it says too much.

	Saturated	Monosaturated	Polyunsaturated	Other
Chestnuts	18%	35%	40%	7%
Brazil Nuts	15%	35%	36%	14%
Cashews	13	59	17	11
Pine Nuts	13	37	41	9
Peanuts	12	49	38	6
Pistachios	12	68	15	5
Walnuts	8	23	63	6
Almonds	8	65	21	6
Pecans	6	62	25	7
Hazelnuts	6	79	9	6

FIGURE 10.7
The fat content of food is measured in a single table.

▲Charts

Charts help the speaker display detailed information quickly and effectively. Charts can summarize data in an easy-to-read format, they can illustrate a process, or they can show relationships among things. Flow charts are used to display the steps, or stages, in a process. Each step is illustrated by an image or label. If you are an amateur cartoonist, you might give a talk on the steps involved in producing an animated cartoon. Figure 10.8 displays a simple flowchart of the process one goes through when a lamp does not light. This visual shows your audience that there is a sequence, and one is dependent on the other.

Pictorial flow charts are also effective. You can draw the pictures yourself or, if your artistic ability is limited, you can use a series of carefully selected photographs from a variety of sources. Flow charts that depend on words alone should use short, simple labels that move the audience through the stages of a process. Figure 10.9 (page 264) shows how authority and responsibility are delegated in a corporation to meet organizational objectives.

Organizational charts reflect our highly structured world. Corporations, government institutions, schools, associations, religious organizations, and so on, are organized according to official hierarchies that determine the relationships of people as they work. You may want to refer to an organizational hierarchy in a speech if you are trying to show the positions of people involved in a project. By looking at a chart like that shown in figure 10.10 (page 264), for example, your audience will know who reports to whom.

▲Graphs

When referring to statistics or when presenting complex statistical information, a visual representation can be extremely effective because it has the ability to simplify and clarify. Statistics may be presented in numerous ways, including bar graphs, pictographs, line graphs, and pie graphs.

In a speech urging students to consider teaching the social sciences and humanities in college, you want to show, graphically, that our universities will face a serious shortfall of liberal arts professors well into the twenty-first century. As part of your speech, you tell your audience:

There were days back in the 1980s when having a Ph.D. in history or sociology or English literature or philosophy guaranteed little or nothing. Indeed, many people who aspired to teach the humanities and social sciences were forced into menial jobs just to survive. So great was the supply of potential faculty over the demand that a new phenomenon was created: the taxi-driving Ph.D.

Today, the story is different. As you can see in this graph, by 1997 three out of ten faculty jobs in the humanities remained unfilled and it hasn't been until now that the situation gets any better.

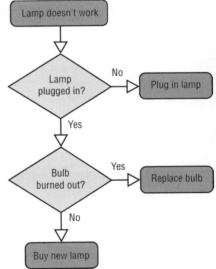

FIGURE 10.8
A simple flow chart of what to do if a lamp doesn't work.

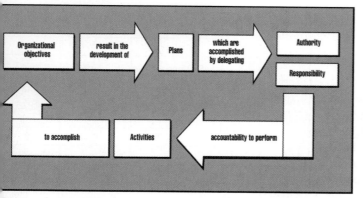

FIGURE 10.9
Flow charts can use blocked boxes and words to show how a corporation delegates authority and responsibility to achieve its objectives.

The visual referred to is shown in figure 10.11 (page 265), a bar graph of supply and demand projects for faculty members into the early part of the twenty-first century. The graph compares supply and demand figures for five-year periods and measures these figures in thousands. This type of graph is especially helpful when you are comparing two or more items. In this case, one bar represents the supply of potential faculty while the other represents the potential demand for faculty. To make the trend clear, you may want to color code the bars.

Pictographs are most commonly used as a variation of the bar graph. Instead of showing bars of various lengths comparing items on the graph, the bars are replaced by pictorial representations of the graph's subject. For example, if you are giving a speech on the effects of television on book sales, you can use a pictograph like that shown in figure 10.12 (page 265) to demonstrate the sales trend. The pictograph must include a scale explaining what each symbol means. In this case, each book represents 200 million books sold.

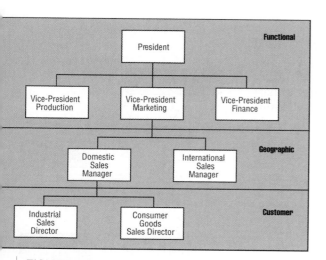

FIGURE 10.10
Almost every large group or company has an organization chart to illustrate the official hierarchy and lines of access.

When you want to show a trend over time, the line graph may be your best choice. When two or more lines are used in one graph, comparisons are also possible. Figure 10.13 (page 266) is a startling visual representation of the number of Irish immigrants entering the United States between 1820 and 1990. The tall peak in the graph represents the period of time when the potato famine was affecting the majority of Ireland. This simple graph could be used in a variety of speeches about Ireland and immigration.

Pie graphs, also known as circle graphs, show your audience how the parts of an item relate to the whole. The pie chart is one of the most popular and effective ways to show how parts of a whole are divided. The pie is used frequently to display the division of expenses or resources a speaker wants an audience to see. The most simple and direct way to demonstrate percentages graphically is with an accurate pie graph. In a budget presentation to the local school board, the chief financial officer displayed a series of pie graphs. He explained that revenue comes from three levels, federal, state, and local. Figure 10.14 (page 267) shows that taxes from local communities provide approximately half of the total revenue generated for the district. The federal government provides only ten percent, thus illustrating how dependent the school district is on local funding.

No matter what type of two-dimensional aid you choose, clarity is essential. It may happen that you create a two-dimensional aid that makes your audience think, "What does it mean?" Any presentational aid you use must clarify rather than confuse. If the aid contains too much information, your audience will be unable to process easily, and you may lose their attention. If you use graphs, pie charts, maps or tables, information

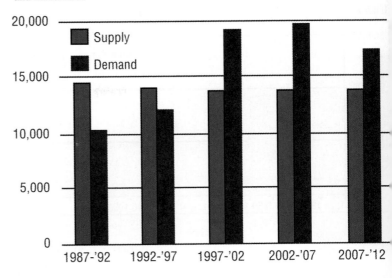

Faculty supply-and-demand projections in the social sciences and humanities

FIGURE 10.11
A speech to outline the projected need for new faculty as we face the next centurey can be enhanced by a bar graph such as this.

must be understandable. For example, if you have an x-axis and a y-axis, they should be clearly labeled so your audience knows what you are referring to quickly and easily.

DISPLAYING TWO-DIMENSIONAL PRESENTATIONAL AIDS

When you decide to use a line graph to illustrate the volatility of the market place, your next decision involves how to display the graph. Speakers have numerous options for displaying two-dimensional presentational aids. The amount of time used and money does not necessarily indicate the effectiveness of a presentational aid. Sometimes emphasizing important points on a flip chart or using prepared overhead transparencies will be perfectly acceptable. This next section focuses on how to display the two-dimensional aid. In particular, we discuss the benefits and disadvantages of using blackboards, large post-its, posters, and flip charts.

▲ Blackboard or Whiteboard

It is a rare classroom that does not have some type of board to write on, be it black, green, or white. The blackboard is the universal presentational aid. One advantage is that you know it is already in the classroom, so you cannot lose or damage it. A second advantage is that it involves no preparation time (other than the day of presentation). It is the easiest visual aid to use and involves the least amount of preparation time.

For the most part, however, the blackboard should be limited to serving as the back-up plan. If your poster is ruined, you cannot find an easel for your flip chart, or the computer is not available or is malfunctioning, then the blackboard may become Plan B.

The blackboard requires neat, legible handwriting. Seldom is it acceptable to write on the blackboard during the speech, but if you must, try to write as little as possible. Use key terms only. If possible, arrive early and complete most, or all, of your visual presentation in advance. If the board has a screen above it, and you write on the board before your speech, pull the screen down until time for your presentation.

In terms of disadvantages, the blackboard is generally viewed as less professional than other presentational aids and your audience may interpret your use of it as indicating you have not prepared sufficiently. Also, when writing on the blackboard during your speech, you must turn your back to your audience as you write. Turning from your audience is never a good idea, and writing on the board cuts into your valuable speaking time.

Books Sold — 1988 vs. 1998

FIGURE 10.12
Pictographs prove a twist on the traditional bar graph by using pictures or the items discussed to illustrate the "bar". The pictography should include an explanatory scale to explain what each symbol means, such as each book represents 200 million sold.

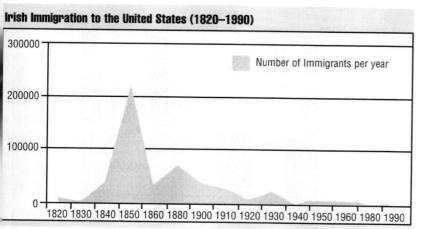

Irish Immigration to the United States (1820–1990)

Number of Immigrants per year

FIGURE 10.13
This is a graph of the number of Irish immigrants that entered the United States from 1820 to 1990. The climax of the migration was in 1851 when 221,253 Irish immigrants entered the United States. This was around the time when the potato famine was infesting the majority of Ireland. As the famine faded, the number of Irish immigrants decreased. It has gone up and down over time and is low today. This is because of the laws on European immigration. It takes many years before a citizen of Ireland can enter the U.S.

▲Poster Board

Even posters have changed over the years. We used to be limited to a white background, and they were somewhat flimsy. Then colors were introduced, then vibrant colors were added as possible options, and now we can use poster-sized foam board in different colors.

When your parents were in school, the clarity of a poster was dependent on the art skills of the student since posters were made by hand. If your university has an instructional materials office of some kind, you can make your own posters, using die-cuts (generally, Ellison die-cuts). These allow you to cut out letters and shapes to make the poster look more professional. Even better, a computer lab on campus or a photocopying facility will allow access to poster-sized computer-generated graphics.

One primary advantage to using a poster board is that it is relatively inexpensive, and most students have used them before. A second advantage is that poster boards are useful in a classroom where computer-generated technology is not available or difficult to access, and third, they can display any type of two-dimensional information.

Three specific disadvantages of using poster boards are first, not everyone has the time, talent, or patience to create a professional-looking poster. Second, displaying the poster may be a problem if you do not have an easel or a chalkboard with a chalk tray, and third, they may get damaged during transportation.

Many of you have already abandoned poster board because you have the opportunity to use computer-generated graphics in the classroom. For those who do not, posters are still a viable way to display two-dimensional information.

▲Flip Chart

Flip charts are still a popular method for displaying two-dimensional information. According to Laskowski (2006), since most presentations are delivered before small groups of thirty-five people or less, the flip chart is the perfect size. Flip charts give speakers the ability to show a sequence of visuals. Studies indicate that listeners are more likely to retain information when the chart is not completed fully in advance. Instead of coming with finished visuals, leave out a few key lines or words and fill them in as the audience watches. The process encourages listeners to perceive your visual as a product of your own expression—an identification important to developing the speaker-audience bond.

There are several advantages to using flip charts. The main advantage is that they allow for spontaneity. The speaker may add words or lines based on audience response. A flip chart can be prepared in advance or during your speech. Other advantages are that they do not require electricity, they are economical, and one can add color to them easily (Laskowski 2006).

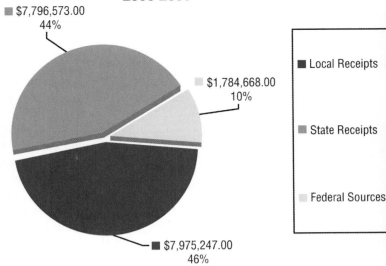

Education Fund Revenues 2005-2006

$7,796,573.00
44%

$1,784,668.00
10%

$7,975,247.00
46%

Total: $18,607,305.00

Legend:
- Local Receipts
- State Receipts
- Federal Sources

FIGURE 10.14
The pie chart
effectively illustrates
how parts of a
whole are divided.

Disadvantages to using flip charts are they may not be seen by all, and they may be distracting. Laskowski (2006) suggests avoiding yellow, pink, or orange markers, and sticking to one dark color and one lighter color for highlighting. Also, less expensive paper may lead to the marker bleeding through to the following page.

▲Repositional Note Pad

The large repositional note pad, most commonly known as a poster-sized Post-It, is a new breed of flip chart. Speakers can stick their presentational aid on a board or wall. These large sticky notes have useful application in group meetings where members brainstorm and then display the results on multiple pages around the walls. In your speech, you may want to have some pre-designed "Post-Its" that you stick on the board at different intervals for emphasis. These are most useful in classrooms lacking technology.

The two advantages to using poster-sized sticky notes are that you do not have to worry about chalk, tape, push pins, or staples, and you have tremendous flexibility. In addition to being able to stick just about anywhere, the speaker can write on it before or during the speech. The main disadvantage is that, as they are most likely hand-written, they may not look as professional as some other display techniques.

CAUTION:
In general, a flip chart belongs on an easel. It looks more professional than leaning it on a blackboard, pages can be turned with little difficulty, and it provides needed support. Be sure an easel or similar stand is available. Many speakers come prepared with elaborate poster-board-mounted visuals only to find that they have no place to display them. If you place the flip chart on the blackboard, make sure it is stabilized, and that pages can be turned without dropping the chart.

❯GENERAL SUGGESTIONS FOR USING PRESENTATIONAL AIDS

Do not let your presentational aid leave the lectern. When you pass things around the room, you compete with them as you speak. Your listeners read your handouts, play with the foreign coins, eat the cookies you baked, and analyze your models instead of listening to you. If handouts are necessary, distribute them at the end of the speech. When appropriate, invite people to take a close look at your displays after your speech.

Be aware of timing and pauses. Timing is important. Display each visual only as you talk about it. Do not force people to choose between paying attention to you and paying attention to your aid. If you prepare your flip chart in advance, leave a blank sheet between each page and turn the page when you are finished with the point. Cover your models with a sheet. Turn the projector off. Erase your diagram from the blackboard. Turn your poster board around. These actions tell your audience that you are ready to go on to another point.

Display your presentational aid, then pause two or three seconds before talking. This moment of silence gives your audience time to look at the display. You do not want to compete with your own visual aid. Try to avoid long pauses as you demonstrate the steps in a process. To demonstrate to his class how to truss a turkey, a student brought in everything he needed including a turkey, string, and poultry pins. He began by explaining the procedure but stopped talking for about five minutes while he worked. Although many members of the class paid attention to his technique, several lost interest. Without a verbal presentation to accompany the visual, their attention drifted to other things. Long periods of silence are not a good idea. Because most audiences need help in maintaining their focus, keep talking.

Make sure the equipment is working but be prepared for failure. Set up in advance. Make sure equipment is working before class, and know how to operate the equipment. Instructors are frustrated when time is wasted, and students will be bored if each speaker wastes valuable class time trying to figure out how the equipment works. Find out if the computer is equipped for a jump drive or zip disk. When things go wrong, you have to take responsibility for not being prepared.

Also, be prepared for equipment failure. What is Plan B? How much time are you willing to waste before you acknowledge that you cannot use the computer? Your audience may be sympathetic to your troubles, but we really do not want to hear you complain. Your presentation may be acceptable without the slide show. Perhaps you need to bring in a jump drive and a floppy disk. Maybe you want to use handouts or, as a back-up plan, write on the blackboard. The key here is the old Boy Scout motto, "Be prepared."

Use multimedia presentations only with careful planning and practice. Multimedia presentations can be effective, but they can be challenging. Gracefully moving from a flip chart to the computer to an overhead projector while maintaining audience interest requires skill that comes from practice and experience. Mixing media increases your chance that something will go wrong. You can mix media successfully, but careful planning and preparation is essential.

❯❯TECHNOLOGY-BASED PRESENTATIONAL AIDS

Often, speakers must communicate statistics, trends, and abstract information in a clear manner. Thirty years ago, teacher education programs stressed the importance of being proficient at changing light bulbs in all machines, threading a film projector, using a tape recorder, putting slides in the slide projector, and operating the overhead projector. My, how things have changed!

Virtually all classrooms have black or white boards, and an overhead projector. As funds become available and technology costs decrease, more and more classrooms will be technology-enhanced. Students will bring their jump drives to class and incorporate PowerPoint presentations into their speeches. This does not mean, however, that all previous technology is rendered useless. Instances still exist where a tape-recording or slide projector may make more sense than a computer-generated slide presentation. This next section discusses audio and projected images.

Audio and Projected Images

Seldom will the blackboard be your only option for a presentational aid. Depending upon the needs of your audience, the content of your speech, and the speaking situation, you may choose a presentational aid requiring the use of other equipment.

▲Audiotape/CD

Not all presentational aids are visual, and incorporating some audio clip into your speech is a simple task. If you are trying to describe the messages babies send through their different cries, using an audiotape or CD may be appropriate, just as it would for a discussion of contemporary music. Of course, in a technology-enhanced room, students can access music and many sounds on the computer.

Take care when using an audio clip. Time is an issue, and the clip can overshadow the oral presentation if it consumes too much time. The inexperienced speaker may not have the audiotape or CD set up at the right spot or the right volume, and recording quality may be an issue. Getting set up on the computer may take too much time. Students need to check the equipment to make sure it is working, the volume is set correctly, and that it is properly queued.

▲Traditional Slides

A slide projector is no longer easy to find because digital cameras allow us to put pictures into a PowerPoint slide presentation. However, slides may be available that show historical sites, art from a particular collection, or plant biology. Rather than convert existing slides, a speaker may use a slide projector on occasion. The advantages to using traditional slides are that the slides already exist, and your library may have an extensive slide collection. Clearly, the primary disadvantage is not knowing how to operate the slide projector. Another disadvantage is that slide projectors may be more difficult to find.

▲Overhead Projector

Using an overhead projector allows you to face your listeners and talk as you project images onto a surface. They may be used in normal lighting, which is an important advantage to the speaker. You can face your listeners and use a pointer, just as you would if you were using any other visual. If you choose to remain near the projector instead, you run the risk of talking down to the transparency you are showing rather than looking up at your audience. Unlike slides, transparencies can be altered as you speak, such as underlining a phrase for emphasis or adding a key word.

Marjorie Brody (2006), president of Brody Communications Ltd., provides several suggestions for using transparencies during your presentation, including: using 18- point font or larger so the audience can read the information, numbering the sheets so you stay organized, using color to add appeal, and using multiple overlays to communicate different ideas.

▲Film/VHS/DVD

In certain situations, the most effective way to communicate your message is with a film, video, or DVD. Films are rarely used because videotapes and DVDs are more convenient and more readily available. In a speech on tornadoes, showing a video of the damage done by a tornado is likely to be quite impressive. Showing snippets of a press conference or showing a movie clip to illustrate or emphasize a particular point can also be interesting and effective.

The novice speaker giving a five-minute speech may not edit the video carefully enough, however. The result may be four minutes of video and one minute to speak. If you choose an audio or video clip, practice with them, plan how to use them, and know how to operate the equipment. Know what to do if the equipment fails.

It is also possible to be upstaged by your video clip. Your visual presentation—rather than your speech—may hold center stage. To avoid this, carefully prepare an introduction to support the video clip. Point your listeners to specific parts so they focus on what you want rather than on what happens to catch their interest. After the visual, continue your speech, and build on its content with the impact of your own delivery.

When thinking about using any of the above projected images, do not forget to allow for sufficient set-up time. Check the equipment to make sure you can operate it and that it is in good working order. Remember also, a darkened room can disrupt your presentation if you need to refer to detailed notes, and if you want students to take notes, the room may be too dark.

© 2012 by Sergej Khakimullin.
Used under license of Shutterstock.

Presenting sensational visuals to the audience may be fun, but these visuals can easily distract the audience's attention from the point you're trying to make with the visuals.

▲PowerPoint Slides

Not all classrooms are technology-enhanced, but soon they will be. In April 2006, Microsoft estimated that it had 400 million PowerPoint customers worldwide. It claims that PowerPoint can improve the way "you create, present, and collaborate on presentations" (office.microsoft.com).

We agree that PowerPoint slides can be used effectively within the public speaking environment, but we will also provide some guidelines. Not everything is meant for a slide presentation. Imagine what the Gettysburg Address might have looked like when accompanied by PowerPoint as shown in figure 10.15 (page 271).

We have come to dedicate a portion of that field, as a final resting place for those who here gave their lives that that nation might live. It is altogether fitting and proper that we should do this. But, in a larger sense, we can not dedicate —we can not consecrate—we can not hallow—this ground. The brave men, living and dead, who struggled here, have consecrated it, far above our poor power to add or detract. The world will little note, nor long remember what we say here, but it can never forget what they did here. It is for us the living, rather, to be dedicated here to the unfinished work which they who fought here have thus far so nobly advanced. It is rather for us to be here dedicated to the great task remaining before us...

Peter Norvig, current Director of Research at Google, provides the example above as a parody, but he argues that a slide presentation may reduce the speaker's effectiveness, because "it makes it harder to have an open exchange between presenter and audience to convey ideas that do not readily fit into outline format" (Norvig, 2003, 343).

Presentation specialist Dave Parodi (2004) urges people to "awaken themselves to the power of a well-designed, well-structured, well-delivered presentation, and work as hard as they can to make it happen." Author of the article "Scoring Power Points," Jamie McKenzie (2000) notes that in the best case, PowerPoint "enhances and communicates a larger and deeper body of work and thought"; however, in the worst case, "students will devote more attention to special effects than they will spend on the issues being studied".

Similarly, in *Wired* magazine, presentation graphics guru Edward R. Tufte (July 2006), notes that PowerPoint is a competent slide manager and projector but bemoans the fact that speakers often use PowerPoint to substitute rather than supplement a presentation. He argues, "Such misuse ignores the most important rule of speaking: Respect your audience".

For those in the public speaking arena, these words have great instructional value. The speaker needs to act with the listener in mind. This is true in terms of designing and using presentational aids as well as the development and delivery of the speech.

▲PowerPoint Guidelines

In newspapers across the country, the Dilbert cartoon from August 16, 2000 depicted a co-worker collapsing from "PowerPoint poisoning" when he heard Dilbert announce "slide 397" (figure 10.16). Many of you can relate to this cartoon. You probably learned how to create a PowerPoint presentation well before you reached college. By now, you

Agenda
- Met on battlefield (great)
- Dedicate portion of field–fitting!
- Unfinished work (great tasks)

FIGURE 10.15
Not every speech is meant to be accompanied by a PowerPoint presentation.

FIGURE 10.16
Dilbert causes a PowerPoint tragedy.
© Scott Adams/Dist. by United Feature Syndicate, Inc.

Use visual aids to express statistics. Statistics become especially meaningful to listeners when they are presented in visual form.

have probably seen a hundred, if not a thousand, PowerPoint presentations.

Indeed, effective computer-generated graphics can have a great impact on your listeners. But the opposite is true, also. "Some of the world's most satisfying naps, deepest day dreams, and most elaborate notebook doodles are inspired by the following phrase, 'I'll just queue up this PowerPoint presentation,'" states Josh Shaffer, staff writer for the Raleigh, North Carolina, *News & Observer* (April 27, 2006).

Given the ubiquitous nature of computer-generated graphics along with the fact that careful audience analysis is crucial, the following guidelines are offered. Although these relate to computer-generated graphics, much of the following information applies to most presentational aids.

1. Make sure the presentational aid fits your purpose, the occasion, and your audience. Developing a specific purpose early on in the speech process is not just an exercise to keep you busy. Katherine Murray, author of more than forty computer books, offers the suggestion, "Start with the end in mind" (www.microsoft.com). Think about your speech from beginning to end. Make sure you are clear on the purpose of your speech. Do this before deciding on any presentational aid. Knowing what you are trying to accomplish should guide you in designing your PowerPoint presentation.

In addition to choosing a presentational aid that suits your purpose, you should also choose aids that are appropriate for the occasion. Certain situations are more serious or formal than others. Displaying a cartoon with little content or merit during a congressional hearing on the problems of the DC-10 aircraft diminishes the credibility of the speaker.

As you determine your purpose, ask yourself whether the visual support is right for your listeners, considering their age, socioeconomic backgrounds, knowledge, and attitudes toward your subject. Consider their sensibilities, as some listeners are offended by visuals that are too graphic. Pictures of abused children, for example, can be offensive to an audience not prepared for what they will see. If you have doubts about the appropriateness of a visual, leave it out of your presentation.

FIGURE 10.17A
What features make this an ineffective PowerPoint slide?

2. Emphasize only relevant points. Do not be "PowerPointless," a word coined by Barb Jenkins of the South Australia Department of Education Training and Employment, meaning, avoid "any fancy transitions, sounds, and other effects that have no discernible purpose, use, or benefit" (www.wordspy.com). The bells and whistles may be fun, but they can be annoying, or worse, distracting.

Tips on Traveling Abroad: Before You Go

- **Apply for passport**
- **Copy important documents**
- **Visit pharmacy**
- **Email itinerary**
- **Contact neighbor**
- **Pack; then Re-pack**

© 2012 by potowizard.
Used under license of depositphotos.

FIGURE 10.17B
What features make this an effective Power-Point slide?

We have all seen PowerPointless presentations. One slide has the words "The facts" on it…and that is all. A second slide says "The causes," and a third slide says "The solution." Maybe each slide contains a cute picture, or perhaps there is an elaborate template. Lacking content, they were unnecessary.

In your desire to create an attractive, professional slide presentation, do not forget the message. It is easy to find tips on general design, the number of words per slide, number of slides, images, transitions, color, and so on. But after you select the presentational aid that meets your purpose most effectively, think about what information needs to be on each slide.

Link only the most important points in your speech with a presentational aid. Focus on your thesis statement and main points and decide what words or concepts need to be highlighted graphically.

3. Implement the "Rule of Six." Use no more than six words per line, and no more than six lines per slide. Avoid using full sentences. This is an outline, not an essay. Make the text easy to read. Words need to be large enough, and do not think that using CAPITALIZED words will help. In addition to being a symbol for yelling when instant-messaging, it actually takes more effort to read words that are all capitalized. Try using 24-point type or larger. If the audience cannot read your slide, the message is lost.

Compare figure 10.17A (page 272) with figure 10.17B. Similarities include the title, points covered, and organization. However, figure 10.17A violates many rules of effective PowerPoint, including too many icons (too busy), full sentences, and small font size. Figure 10.17B is clear, simple, and professional. The template used would be appropriate for all slides used for a presentation on traveling abroad.

4. Select appropriate design features. Decisions need to be made regarding template, type of font, and color. The template, which provides color, style, and decorative accents may be distracting to your audience if you change it regularly. Use one template consistently. One can fritter away many minutes trying to determine what font-type (typeface) to use. In general, select something simple. While font-types may look fun, cute, or dramatic, they may also be hard to read, or distracting. Remember, keep your audience focused on the message; they may be distracted from the text if you have moving animations, and slides filled with "special effects."

Make sure the font-type and font-color complement the template. Rely on strong, bold colors that make your message stand out even in a large auditorium. In their article "About choosing fonts for presentations", Microsoft Office Online suggests, "To ensure readability, choose font colors that stand out sharply against the background" (Microsoft Office PowerPoint 2003). The words you place on the slide should not melt into the background color. Aim for contrast but keep in mind that the contrast you see on your computer screen may not exist on the projected screen.

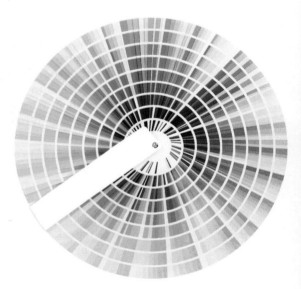

© 2012 by iStockphoto.
Used under license of Thinkstock.

FIGURE 10.18
Colors opposite each other on this wheel provide the most striking contrast for visual displays. Using an overhead projector during your speech gives you greater flexibility than many other visual aids.

The color wheel in figure 10.18 (page 273) will help you choose contrasting colors. You will achieve the strongest contrasts by using colors opposite one another. When these complements are combined, they produce distinct images. Blue and orange make an effective visual combination as do red and green, and so on. Colors opposite each other on this wheel provide the most striking contrasts for visual displays.

5. *Do not let your visual upstage you.* Keep in mind that your audience has come to hear you, not to see your presentational aids. If you create a situation in which the visual support is more important than the speaker or the purpose of the speech, you will have defeated your purpose.

With some exceptions, you will want to avoid using any presentational aid for the first few minutes. After you have set the tone of your speech and introduced your main idea you can turn to your first aid. Do not use a presentational aid to end your speech. Doing so eliminates the person-to-person contact you have built to that point by shifting the focus away from you.

6. *Preview and practice.* After creating your PowerPoint slides, run through them. Make sure slides are in the correct order, and that font-type, font-color, and font-size are consistent. Proofread and run spell check. Make printouts of your slides. Then practice the speech using your slides. According to a survey conducted by Dave Parodi (2003 (needs to be checked), the most annoying aspect of the PowerPoint presentation was when "The speaker read the slides to us." (Need more info. for references and need the page number after the quote here.)

One way to avoid sounding as though you are reading to the audience is through practice. Adding some type of presentational aid makes practicing even more important because you do not want to disrupt the flow of your speech.

During your practice session, focus on your audience, not your presentational aid. Many speakers turn their backs on the audience. They talk to the projection screen or poster instead of looking at the audience. To avoid this tendency, become familiar with your aid so that you have little need to look at it during your talk.

❯SUMMARY

Presentational aids serve many different functions in a speech. They help to create interest in your subject; they make complex ideas clear and abstract ideas concrete. They help make your message memorable; they help to organize you.

Presentational aids fall into four general categories including actual objects, three-dimensional models, two-dimensional reproductions, and technology-based visual aids. Two-dimensional reproductions include photographs, diagrams and drawing, maps, tables, and charts. Two-dimensional visual aids can be mounted on poster board and displayed on an easel or displayed on a flip chart, or on repositional note pads. Technology-based visual aids include slides, film, videotape and audiotape, overhead projections, and computer-generated images.

Effective presentational aids are simple; they use bold, contrasting colors and they are large enough for everyone to read with ease. To present effective aids, choose the points in your speech that need visual support; set up your presentation in advance; never let your presentational aids upstage you. Use multimedia presentations only if they are well planned and rehearsed. Avoid repeating what your audience sees in the visual and learn to display each aid only when you are talking about it. Focus on your audience, not your visual. Display your visual, then pause before talking, although you need to avoid long pauses during demonstrations. Do not circulate your presentational aids around the room. Choose visuals appropriate for the audience and occasion and rehearse your presentation.

 # QUESTIONS FOR ANALYSIS

1. What are the functions of presentational aids?
2. What are the different types of presentational aids?
3. What are the general criteria for using presentational aids?
4. What criteria must be met when thinking about particular presentational aids?
5. What should you know about displaying presentational aids?
6. What should you keep in mind as you design and develop a PowerPoint presentation?

 # ACTIVITIES

1. Plan to use presentational aids in your next speech. Spend enough time designing and preparing the visuals so they will have the impact you want.

2. Contact several business or professional speakers in your campus community or hometown. Based on what you have learned in this chapter, interview them about using visual aids in their presentations. Report your findings to your class, paying special attention to the similarities and differences in their approaches.

3. Locate individuals on your campus or in your community who produce presentational aids for speeches. Interview these specialists to learn the information they need to design effective aids and how much they cost. Consider both two-dimensional and technology-based visual aids and write a report on your findings.

REFERENCES

Berg, K. and A. Gilman 1989. *Get to the point: How to say what you mean and get what you want.* New York: Bantam.

McKenzie, J. 2000. "Scoring PowerPoints", From *Now On, The Educational Technology Journal,* Vol. 10, No. 1

Molotsky, I. "No more than 1 in 5 athletes graduating at many schools," *New York Times*, September 10, 1989, A1 and 46.

Norvig, P. Accessed August 12, 2007. "PowerPoint: Shot with its own bullets," *The Lancet*, Vol. 362, No. 9381, pages 343–344.

Vogel, D. R., G. W. Dickson, and J. A. Lehman. 1986. "Persuasion and the role of visual presentation support: the UM/3M study," commissioned by Visual Systems Division of 3M.

SHORT ANSWERS

HONOR STATEMENT: I, the undersigned student, hereby declare before God, before the school, and before the professor that I have read Chapter 10 in its entirety, that I have completed the following exercise with help from no other sources, and that I neither have shared nor will share this work with anyone.

1. What are the five functions of presentational aids?

_____

_____

_____

_____

_____

_____

_____

2. What are the four general criteria for presentational aids?

_____

_____

_____

_____

_____

_____

_____

3. Give examples of two actual objects you might use in a speech for the purpose of this class.
What are the advantages and the disadvantages of using actual objects like these as presentational aids?

_____

_____

_____

_____

_____

_____

_____

4. What are three-dimensional models? When might you use them in a speech?

_____

_____

_____

_____

_____

_____

5. If you were giving an informative speech about your hometown, your home state, or your home country, and you were asked to use three actual objects for the speech, which three would you use? Why?

_____

_____

_____

_____

_____

_____

6. If you were giving a how-to informative speech in which you show the audience, step-by-step, how to do something or to make something, which topic would you address? If you were required to use a two-dimensional object or two for the speech, which one(s) would you use? Why?

_____

_____

_____

_____

_____

_____

_____

7. Discuss the pros and the cons of using PowerPoint slides during a speech. What does the chapter say about this? Which additional thought or two would you add to what the book says?

_____

_____

_____

_____

_____

_____

_____

_____

_____

_____

_____

_____

"Let our advance
worrying become
advance thinking
and planning."
- Winston Churchill

CHAPTER 11 >>

11 ORGANIZING AND OUTLINING YOUR IDEAS

Adapted from *Public Speaking: Choices for Effective Results, Fifth Edition* by John Makay et al. Copyright © 2008.
Reprinted with permission of Kendall Hunt Publishing Co.

The organization of ideas in public speaking refers to the placement of lines of reasoning and supporting materials in a pattern that helps to achieve your specific purpose. Following a consistent pattern of organization helps listeners pay attention to your message. An organized speech with connected main points helps you maintain a clear focus that leads listeners to a logical conclusion. An organized speech flows smoothly and clearly, from introduction through body to conclusion.

Your introduction and conclusion support the body of your speech. The introduction should capture your audience's attention and indicate your intent, and the conclusion reinforces your message and brings your speech to a close. The body includes your main points and supporting material that supports your specific purpose and thesis statement. The introduction and conclusion are important, but audiences expect you to spend the most time and effort amplifying your main points.

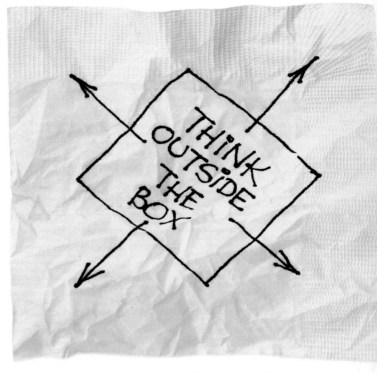

Based on your research, spend some time brainstorming to generate ideas for your speech.

It is easy to detect disorganized speakers. Their presentations ramble from topic to topic as they struggle to connect ideas. As a listener, you may be confused about what the speaker is trying to communicate. In the following example, a disorganized speaker addresses an audience on the topic of addictions:

> We are a nation of addicts. Not only are we addicted to drugs and alcohol—the substances usually associated with addiction—millions of us are also addicted to gambling, shopping, promiscuous sex, overeating, relationships that tear down our self-esteem, and even shoes.

> Before I explain how researchers view these addictions, I want to say something about the thousands of self-help groups that have sprung up across the nation to save addicts from themselves—groups like Debtors Anonymous, Women Who Love Too Much, and Neurotics Anonymous. Well, maybe I should start with a discussion of what an addiction is. According to Florida State University researcher Alan Lang, quoted in *U.S. News & World Report*, "There is no single characteristic or constellation of traits that is inevitably associated with addiction." There are about 2,000 addiction groups that hold meetings each week, up twenty percent from a year ago.

> Now let's get back to the concept of addiction. Can someone really be addicted to soap operas in the same way they are addicted to cocaine? According to Harvey Milkman, professor of psychology at Metropolitan State College in Denver and co-author of *Craving for Ecstasy*, "The disease concept may be applied to the entire spectrum of compulsive problem behaviors" (*US News & World Report* 1990, 62–63).

Listening to this speech is like watching a ping-pong ball bounce aimlessly across a table. You never know where the speaker will land next or what direction the speech will take.

If your ideas are organized, however, you will help your audience follow and understand your message.

❯❯ ORGANIZING THE BODY OF YOUR SPEECH

The body of your speech should flow from your introduction. Therefore, reflect first on your specific purpose and thesis statement. Since your specific purpose is a statement of intent and your thesis statement identifies the main ideas of your speech, referring to them as you determine your main points will help prevent misdirection. For example, consider a speech discussing how family pets help children with psychological problems. You might develop the following:

Specific purpose: To explain to my class how pets can provide unexpected psychological benefits for children with emotional problems by helping to bolster their self-esteem.

Thesis statement: A close relationship with a family pet can help children with emotional problems feel better about themselves, help therapists build rapport with difficult-to-reach patients, and encourage the development of important social skills.

Your thesis statement indicates your speech will address self-esteem, rapport with therapists, and the development of social skills. This suggests that there are many peripheral topics you will exclude, such as the type of pet, pet grooming tips, medical advances in the treatment of feline leukemia, how to choose a kennel when you go on vacation, and so on.

1. Select Your Main Points

Organizing the body of your speech involves a four-step process: selecting the main points, supporting the main points, choosing the best organizational pattern, and creating unity throughout the speech. Before you think about organizing your speech, you need to decide which points are essential. They must relate to your specific purpose and thesis statement. An audience analysis should help direct you in terms of what points you need to make and the extent to which you need to support them.

Usually you should limit your main points to no fewer than two and not more than five. If you add more, you are likely to confuse your listeners.

With your specific purpose and thesis statement clearly in mind, your next step is to generate a list of ideas consistent with the goals of your speech without critical evaluation initially. This stage is commonly known as brainstorming. Based on your research, write down ideas as they occur to you, using phrases or sentences. For purposes of illustration, consider the following:

Specific Purpose: To describe to my class the causes, symptoms, and treatment of shyness.

Thesis Statement: Shyness, which is an anxiety response in social situations that limits social interactions, may respond to appropriate treatment.

With your specific purpose and thesis statement clearly in mind, your next step is to generate a list of ideas consistent with the goals of your speech without critical evaluation initially.

Your brainstorming process for the topic of shyness might result in a list of possible main points that include, but are clearly not limited to, the following: symptoms of shyness, shyness and heredity, shyness as an anxiety response, physical and psychological indications of shyness, number of people affected by shyness, shyness and self-esteem, how to handle a job interview if you are shy, treatment for shyness, and what to do when your date is shy.

Upon reflection, you may realize that several of these points overlap, and others do not relate as much to your thesis statement and should be discarded. So, you make the following list of six possible important points: Symptoms of shyness, causes of shyness, treatment for shyness, number of people affected by shyness, shyness as an anxiety response, and shyness and self-esteem.

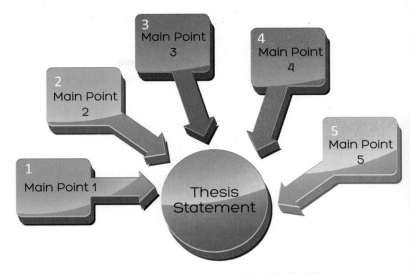

© 2012 Kheng Guan Toh.
Used under license of Shutterstock.

A thesis statement is the single-sentence statement of your speech's main idea—the idea your main points work together to develop or to support.

With six being too many main points to develop, you decide that "shyness as an anxiety response" describes a symptom of shyness and that "shyness and self-esteem" describes a cause. You decide that a discussion of the number of people affected by shyness belongs in your introduction. Your final list of main points may look like this: symptoms of shyness, causes of shyness, treatment for shyness.

Through this process, you transformed a random list into a focused list of idea clusters reflecting broad areas of your speech. Your main points should be mutually exclusive; each point should be distinct. In addition, each point should be important in expressing your thesis statement.

2. Support Your Main Points

After selecting your main points, use the supporting material you gathered to strengthen each main point. Fitting each piece of research into its appropriate place may seem like completing a complex jigsaw puzzle. Patterns must be matched, rational links must be formed, and common sense must prevail. When you finish, each subpoint should be an extension of the point it supports. If the connection seems forced, reconsider the match. Here, for example, is one way to develop the three main points of the speech on shyness. As you sit at your computer, you can expand phrases into sentences. So for now, you can begin to think in terms of the language of your speech.

Example

Main Point 1: *The symptoms of shyness fall into two categories: those that can be seen and those that are felt.*

Objective symptoms (symptoms that can be seen) make it apparent to others that you are suffering from shyness. These include blushing, dry mouth, cold clammy hands, trembling hands and knocking knees, excessive sweating, an unsettled stomach, and belligerence.

According to psychologist Philip Zimbardo, many shy people never develop the social skills necessary to deal with difficult situations (symptoms that are felt).

They may experience embarrassment, feelings of inferiority or inadequacy, feelings of self-consciousnes, a desire to flee, and generalized anxiety. They overreact by becoming argumentative.

Internal symptoms make the experience horrible for the sufferer.

―――――――――

Main Point 2: *Recent research has focused on three potential causes of shyness. Heredity seems to play a large part.*

Psychologists at Yale and Harvard have found that ten to fifteen percent of all children are shy from birth.—Dr. Jerome Kagan of Harvard found that shy children are wary and withdrawn even with people they know.

Shyness is also the result of faulty learning that lowers self-esteem instead of boosting self-confidence.

When parents criticize a child's ability or appearance or fail to praise the child's success, they plant the seeds of shyness by lowering self-esteem.

Older siblings may destroy a child's self-image through bullying and belittlement. Shyness is also attributable to poor social skills, due to never having learned how to interact with others, which leaves shy people in an uncomfortable position.

―――――――――

Main Point 3: *Shyness is not necessarily a life sentence; treatment is possible and so is change.*

In a survey of 10,000 adults, Stanford University researchers found that forty percent said that they had been shy in the past but no longer suffered from the problem. People who are extremely shy may benefit from professional therapy offered by psychiatrists and psychologists.

As you weave together your main points and support, your speech should grow in substance and strength. It will be clear to your listeners that you have something to say and that you are saying it in an organized way.

3. Choose the Best Pattern for Organizing Your Main Points

The way you organize your main points depends on your specific purpose and thesis statement, the type of material you are presenting, and the needs of your audience. As you develop your main points, you need to consider what you want to emphasize. Assuming you have established three main points, you need to choose your emphasis. You have three options. First, you may choose the *equality pattern*, which involves giving equal time to each point. This means that you will spend approximately the same time on each point as you deliver your speech. If the body of your speech was nine minutes long, each point would take about three minutes to develop.

A second option is to use a *progressive pattern*, which involves using your least important point first and your most important point last. If you choose to emphasize one point over another, the nine minutes of the body might be broken up into approximately one and a half minutes on the first point, three minutes on the second point, and four and a half minutes on the third point.

Your third option is to follow the *strongest point pattern*. In this case, your first point would take about four and a half minutes, the second point would be given about three minutes, and your final point would take approximately one and a half minutes.

The pattern you choose depends on your topic and audience. The equality pattern makes sense if you have three main points you think are equally strong and important. Some people believe that the progressive pattern is most effective, suggesting it is the first point listeners will be most likely to remember. This concept is known as the primacy effect. Others believe in the strongest point pattern, suggesting it is your last point listeners will remember most. This is the recency effect. There is general agreement, however, that your strongest argument, or the aspect you want to emphasize most strongly does not go in the middle of your main points.

In addition to organizing your main points by emphasis, it is important to have an overall organizational framework. A speaker has many choices in terms of how to organize his or her speech, but based on the specific purpose statement, one pattern of organization is generally more appropriate than the others. The seven effective patterns of organization we will cover are chronological, past-present-future, step-by-step, spatial, cause and effect, problem-solution, and topical.

Chronological Organization

In a chronological speech, information is focused on relationships in time. Events are presented in the order in which they occur. When developing your speech chronologically, you can choose to organize your ideas by starting at the beginning and moving to the present, then looking to the future, or going step-by-step.

To show how different organizational patterns affect the content and emphasis of a speech, we will choose a topic, establish different purposes for speaking, and show how the presentation differs when the organizational pattern is changed.

Topic: The civil rights movement.

Specific Purpose: To inform my audience of college students about certain crucial events that occurred in the civil rights movement between 1954 and 2007.

Thesis statement: The civil rights movement made dramatic progress from 1954 to 2007 as can be seen in events that occurred, legislature passed, and political involvement of African Americans.

In an informative speech on the civil rights movement, the speaker could include the following events:

1. The 1954 U.S. Supreme Court decision (*Brown vs. Board of Education*) made school segregation unconstitutional.
2. In 1955, Rosa Parks refused to give her seat to a white rider on a bus in Montgomery, Alabama. African Americans boycotted city buses for a year, and the courts ruled bus segregation unconstitutional.
3. In 1964, Congress passed sweeping civil rights law.
4. In 1984, the Reverend Jesse Jackson ran for president and became of powerful spokesperson at the Democratic National Convention.
5. In 2005, Edgar Ray Killen, member of the KKK and the ringleader of murdering civil rights activists Goodman, Chaney, and Swerner is convicted of manslaughter on the forty-first anniversary of the crimes.
6. In 2007, U.S. Senator Barack Obama easily became a leading contender for the Democratic nomination as a candidate for the presidency.

To be consistent, every event you analyze must be woven into the existing chronological outline.

In an informative speech on civil rights, you would likely include information about Rosa Parks' contributions to the cause.

Past-Present-Future Organization

Chronological order can also be used to construct a past-present-future organizational pattern. For example, if you were talking about the women's movement, you might have three points. First, you note that before the movement for women's equality, women's opportunities in the workplace were limited. Then you purport that today, greater opportunity is a reality, but women must cope with the dual responsibilities of career and home. Finally, you point out that you look forward to greater awareness from corporate America of women's dual roles and to accommodations that make the lives of working women easier. Using a past-present-future order allows a speaker to provide perspective for a topic or issue that has relevant history and future direction or potential.

Step-by-Step Organization

Chronological patterns can be used to describe the steps in a process. Here is a step-by-step description of how college texts are produced. Like the other patterns, the process shows a movement in time:

Step 1: The author, having gathered permissions for use of copyrighted material, delivers a manuscript to the publisher.

Step 2: The manuscript is edited, a design and cover are chosen, photos are selected, and illustrations are drawn.

Step 3: The edited manuscript is sent to a compositor for typesetting and set in galley and page proof form.

Step 4: The final proof stage is released to the printing plant where the book is printed and bound.

Spatial Organization

In speeches organized according to a spatial pattern, the sequence of ideas moves from one physical point to another—from London to Istanbul, from basement to attic, from end zone to end zone. To be effective, your speech must follow a consistent directional path. If you are presenting a new marketing strategy to the company sales force, you can arrange your presentation by geographic regions—first the East, then the South, then the Midwest, and finally, the West. If, after completing the pattern, you begin talking about your plans for Boston, your listeners will be confused.

Using space as the organizational key, our speech on civil rights takes the following form. Although the central topic is the same, the pattern of organization is tied to a different specific purpose and core idea:

Specific Purpose: To inform my audience of college students how the civil rights movement spread across the nation.

Thesis Statement: The civil rights movement spread from the cities and rural areas of the South to the inner-city ghettos of the North and West.

1. In places like Selma and Montgomery, AL and Nashville, TN, white brutality led to civil rights boycotts and protests.
2. Angry African Americans, pent up and hopeless in inner-city ghettos, rioted in Harlem, Newark, Chicago, and Detroit.
3. Riots took place in the Los Angeles ghetto of Watts, resulting in many deaths, far more arrests, and enormous losses from arson and looting.
4. In our 21st century we can easily see that African-Americans have become highly visible leaders in business, politics, education and religion, but the civil rights movement is still active, addressing issues of inequality and violence against minorities.

Persuasive speeches often present an audience with a problem and examine potential solutions.

Cause and Effect Organization

You may find that the most logical and effective way to organize is to arrange your main points into causes and effects. When using the cause and effect pattern, a speaker presents several causes of something, several effects of something, or both causes and effects of something. Here are the main points of our speech on civil rights arranged in a cause and effect pattern:

Specific Purpose: To inform my audience of college students how the suffering experienced by African Americans in the 1950s and 1960s created the environment for social change.

Thesis Statement: Racial discrimination in America during the 1950s and 1960s made sweeping social change inevitable.

Through the 1950s and early 1960s, discrimination prevented African Americans from using public accommodations, being educated with whites, riding in the front of buses, exercising their constitutional right to vote, being hired by corporations, and working for equal pay.

This pattern of discrimination resulted in landmark Supreme Court cases such as *Brown vs. Board of Education*, which declared separate but equal schools unconstitutional; the hugely successful march on Washington in 1963; and the passage in 1964 of the Civil Rights Act. With the cause and effect organizational pattern, the speaker can focus specifically on why something happened and what the consequences of the event or action were.

Problem-Solution Organization

A common strategy, especially in persuasive speeches, is to present an audience with a problem and then examine one or more likely solutions. For example, in a classroom speech, one student described a serious safety problem for women students walking alone on campus after dark. He cited incidents in which women were attacked and robbed and described unlit areas along campus walkways where the attacks had taken place. Next, he turned to a series of proposals to eliminate, or at least minimize, the problem. His proposals included a new escort service, sponsored and maintained by various campus organizations, the installation of halogen lights along dark campus walks, and the trimming of bushes where muggers could hide.

Occasionally, speakers choose to present the solution before the problem. Had this student done so, he would have identified how to provide effective security before he explained why these solutions were necessary. Many audiences have trouble with this type of reversal because they find it hard to accept solutions when they are not familiar with the problems that brought them about.

Let us turn, once again, to our speech on civil rights, this time arranging the material in a problem-solution pattern.

Specific Purpose: To persuade my audience of college students that, although the civil rights movement has reduced racial discrimination in many areas, the movement must continue to press for equality in education and employment.

Thesis Statement: The civil rights movement in America must remain strong and active because discriminatory patterns still exist in education and employment.

Problem: Discrimination in education and employment has perpetuated a culture of poverty and joblessness for millions of African Americans who remain second-class citizens despite the gains of the civil rights movement.

Solution: Joblessness, and the poverty that results from it, must be addressed through job training programs and by continuing to pressure corporations to hire minorities through affirmative action programs.

Here, the goal is to persuade an audience that a problem still exists and to have listeners agree about how it can be effectively handled.

Topical Organization

The most frequently used organizational system is not tied to time or space, problem or solution, or cause or effect, but, instead, to the unique needs of your topic. The nature and scope of your topic dictate the pattern of your approach.

© 2012 s_bukley / Shutterstock.com.
Used under license of Shutterstock.

Condoleezza Rice's appointment as U.S. Secretary of State could be a main point in a topical organizational pattern speech on civil rights.

Working within the confines of your topic, you determine a workable pattern. If you are delivering an after-dinner humorous speech on the responses of children to their first week of preschool, you can arrange your topics according to their level of humor. For example:

1. The school supplies preschoolers think are necessary to survive at school.
2. The behavior of youngsters at school when they do not get their own way.
3. Children's stories of their lives at home.
4. The reasons children believe their parents send them to school.

These topics relate to children and their first week at school, but there is no identifiable chronological pattern, so topical order makes sense. When organizing topically, think about how to link and order topics. Transitions can help the audience understand the connections and will be discussed in the following section.

The following example shows how a speech on the civil rights movement might be treated using a topical organizational pattern.

Specific Purpose: To inform my audience of college students about how the emergence of African American leaders in American politics and government influences the struggle for civil rights in our county.

Thesis Statement: The movement for civil rights is being waged from within the political establishment, and African Americans are achieving key positions in politics and in government.

Jesse Jackson became a leader in the Democratic party and succeeded in working within the system to register tens of thousands of African Americans to vote.

David Dinkins served as Mayor of New York City from 1990–1993.

Clarence Thomas was appointed to the U.S. Supreme Court by President George H. W. Bush in 1991, and in 2004 President George W. Bush appointed Condoleezza Rice to be secretary of state for the United States.

4. Create Unity Through Connections

Without connections, your main points may be difficult to follow. Your audience may wonder what you are trying to say and why you have tried to connect ideas that do not seem to have any relationship with each other. To establish the necessary connections, use transitions, internal previews, and internal summaries.

Transitions

Transitions are the verbal bridges between ideas. They are words, phrases, or sentences that tell your audience how ideas relate. Transitions are critical because they clarify the direction of your speech by giving your audience a means to follow your organization. With only one opportunity to hear your remarks, listeners depend on transitions to make sense of your ideas.

It helps to think of transitions as verbal signposts that signal the organization and structure of your speech. Here are several examples:

> *"The first proposal I would like to discuss…"*
> This tells listeners that several more ideas will follow.
> *"Now that we've finished looking at the past, let's move to the future."*
> These words indicate a movement in time.
> *"Next, I'll turn from a discussion of the problems to a discussion of the solutions."*
> This tells your listeners that you are following a problem-solution approach.
> *"On the other hand, many people believe…"*
> Here you signal an opposing viewpoint.

The following is a list of common transitional words and the speaker's purpose in using them.

Speaker's Purpose	Suggested Transitional Words
1. To define:	*that is to say; according to; in other words*
2. To explain:	*for example; specifically*
3. To add:	*furthermore; also; in addition; likewise*
4. To change direction:	*although; on the other hand; conversely*

5. To show both sides:	*nevertheless; equally*
6. To contrast:	*but; still; on the contrary*
7. To indicate cause:	*because; for this reason; since; on account of*
8. To summarize:	*recapping; finally; in retrospect; summing up*
9. To conclude:	*in conclusion; therefore; and so; finally*

(Makay and Fetzger 1984, 68)

Internal Previews and Summaries

Internal previews are extended transitions that tell the audience, in general terms, what you will say next. These are frequently used in the body of the speech to outline in advance the details of a main point. Here are two examples:

- I am going to talk about the orientation you can expect to receive during your first few days on the job, including a tour of the plant, a one-on-one meeting with your supervisor, and a second meeting with the personnel director, who will explain the benefits and responsibilities of working for our corporation.

- Now that I've shown you that "junk" is the appropriate word to describe junk bonds, we will turn to an analysis of three secure financial instruments: bank certificates of deposit, Treasury bonds, and high quality corporate paper.

In the second example, the speaker combines a transition linking the material previously examined with the material to come with an internal preview. Previews are especially helpful when your main point is long and complex. They give listeners a set of expectations for what they will hear next. Use them whenever it is necessary to set the stage for your ideas (Turner 1970, 24–39).

Internal summaries follow a main point and act as reminders. Summaries are especially useful if you are trying to clarify or emphasize what you have just said, as is shown in the following two examples:

- In short, the American family today is not what it was forty years ago. As we have seen, with the majority of women working outside the home and with divorce and remarriage bringing stepchildren into the family picture, the traditional family—made up of a working father, a nonworking mother, and 2-3 kids—may be a thing of the past.

- In sum, the job market seems to be easing for health care professionals, including nurses, aides, medical technicians, physical therapists, and hospital administrators. When summaries are combined with previews, they emphasize your previous point and make connections to the point to follow:

Previews are like game plans—they let listeners know what will come next in your presentation.

• In sum, it is my view that cigarette advertising should not be targeted specifically at minority communities. As we have seen, R. J. Reynolds test-marketed a cigarette for African Americans known as "Uptown," only to see it come under a barrage of criticism. What is fair advertising for cigarette makers? We will discuss that next.

Organization plays an important role in effective communication. The principles rhetoricians developed five centuries ago about the internal arrangement of ideas in public speaking have been tested by time and continue to be valid. Internal previews and summaries help the speaker create meaning with the audience by reinforcing the message and identifying what is coming next. Keep in mind that audience members do not have the opportunity to replay or to stop for clarification. Using transitions, previews, and internal summaries are tools a speaker can use to facilitate understanding and reduce the potential for misunderstanding (Clarke 1963, 23–27; Daniels and Whitman 1981, 147–160).

❯❯ CONSTRUCTING AN OUTLINE AND SPEAKER'S NOTES

Presenting your ideas in an organized way requires a carefully constructed planning outline and a key-word outline to be used as speaker's notes. Both forms are critical to your success as an extemporaneous speaker—one who relies on notes rather than a written manuscript. Your outline is your diagram connecting the information you want to communicate in a rational, consistent way. It enables you to assemble the pieces of the information so that the puzzle makes sense to you and communicates your intended meaning to your audience. Think of outlining as a process of layering ideas on paper so that every statement supports your thesis. It is a time-consuming process, but one that will pay off in a skillful, confident presentation (Sprague and Stuart 1992, 92).

Be familiar with the criteria for each speech assignment. Each instructor has his or her own requirements. Some may want to see your planning outline and speaker's notes while others may not. Instead of a planning outline, your instructor may ask you to turn in a full-sentence outline that includes points, subpoints, source citation, and reference page, but excludes statements about transitions or speech flow. The following discussion is designed to help you develop and, by extension, deliver, an effective speech. Your instructor will have specific ideas about the outline and note cards.

▲ The Planning Outline

The planning outline, also known as the full-content outline, includes most of the information you will present in your speech. It does not include every word you plan to say, but gives you the flexibility required in extemporaneous speaking.

When developing a planning outline, it is important to use a traditional outline format that allows you to see the interconnections among ideas—how some points are subordinate to others and how main ideas connect. In a traditional outline, roman numerals label the speech's main ideas. Subordinate points are labeled with letters and numbers.

Guidelines for Constructing a Planning Outline

The proper positioning of the main and subordinate points with reference to the left margin is critical, for it provides a visual picture of the way your speech is organized. Be consistent with your indentation. The main points are along the left margin, and each sub-point is indented. Each sub-sub-point is indented under the sub-point. This visual image presents a hierarchy that expresses the internal logic of your ideas.

The outline labels (introduction, body, conclusion) remind the speaker to give each section appropriate attention, focusing on the objectives of each section. These labels should be written in the left-hand margin of your outline.

Sample Planning Outline

Name:
Specific purpose:
Thesis statement:

Title of Speech

Introduction
    I. Capture attention and focus on topic
    II. Set tone and establish credibility
    III. Preview main points
Body
I. First main point
    A. First subordinate (sub-) point to explain first main point
        1. First sub-point/supporting material for first sub-point
            a. Sub-point that provides greater details or explanations
            b. Sub-point that provides more details, examples,
                or explanations to clarify and explain
        2. Second sub-point/supporting material for first sub-point
    B. Second subordinate (sub-) point to explain first main point
        1. First sub-point/supporting material for second sub-point
        2. Second sub-point/supporting material for second sub-point
            a. Sub-point that provides greater details or explanations
            b. Sub-point that provides more details, examples, or
                explanations to clarify and explain

II. Second main point
    A. First subordinate (sub-) point to explain second main point
        1. First sub-point/supporting material for first sub-point
            a. Sub-point that provides greater details or explanations
            b. Sub-point that provides more details, examples, or
                explanations to clarify and explain
        2. Second sub-point/supporting material for first sub-point
    B. Second subordinate (sub-) point to explain second main point
        1. First sub-point/supporting material for second sub-point
        2. Second sub-point/supporting material for second sub-point

III. Third main point
    A. First subordinate (sub-) point to explain third main point
    B. Second subordinate point to explain third main point
        1. First sub-point/supporting material for second sub-point
        2. Second subpoint/supporting material for second sub-point

Conclusion
I. Summary of main points
II. Relate to audience
III. Provide closure/final thought

References (on separate sheet)

Notice the particulars:

1. Your name, the specific purpose, thesis statement, and title of your speech are all found at the top of the page.
2. Each section (introduction, body, and conclusion) is labeled.
3. Each section begins with the Roman numeral "I."
4. Each level has at least two points. So if you have "I," minimally, you will see a "II." If you have an "A," minimally, you will see a "B." You should never have just one point or sub-point.
5. Each point is not developed identically. In some cases, there are sub-points and sub-sub-points. One point may need more development than another point.

A well-constructed planning outline ensures a coherent, well-thought-out speech. Using full sentences defines your ideas and guides your choice of language. Phrases and incomplete sentences will not state your points fluently, nor will they help you think in terms of the subtle interrelationships among ideas, transitions, and word choice.

Check with your instructor to see if you should have a regular planning outline or a full-sentence outline. A full-sentence outline requires that each point have one full-sentence. This means no sentence fragments, and no more than one sentence per point.

Include at the end of your planning outline a reference page listing all the sources used to prepare your speech, including books, magazines, journals, newspaper articles, videos, speeches, and interviews. If you are unfamiliar with documentation requirements, check the style guide preferred by your instructor, such as the *American Psychological Association (APA) Publication Manual* (online access at www.apastyle.apa.org), and the *Modern Literature Association (MLA) Handbook for Writers of Research Papers* (online access at www.mla.org).

Check with your instructor to see how detailed your source citation should be in the

Check with your instructor to see if you should have a regular planning outline or a full-sentence outline.

outline. Check to see if you should include last name, credentials, type of book (or magazine, journal, web page, etc.), year/date of publication?

Transitional sentences are valuable additions to your planning outline. They are needed when you move from the introduction to the body to the conclusion of the speech. They also link various main points within the body and serve as internal previews and summaries. Put these sentences in parentheses between the points being linked and try to use the language you may actually speak. When appropriate, include internal summaries and previews of material yet to come.

Here is an example of a planning outline that includes transitional sentences.

Sample Planning Outline with Transitional Sentences

Speaker's Name: Jim Doe

Specific Purpose: To provide a solution to the problem that marriageable young men outnumber marriageable young women.

Thesis Statement: Because there are far more unmarried men in their twenties than there are women in the same age group, young men often find it harder to meet eligible partners.

Title of Speech: Young women take control of the marriage pool

Introduction

I. It wasn't that long ago that sociologists were telling us that there were far more women of marriageable age than men.
   A. A report issued by the University of California at Berkeley told us that if we tried to match each woman born in 1950 with a man three years older, we would have millions of women left over.
   B. Neil G. Bennett, Patricia H. Craig, and David E. Bloom, researchers at Yale, predicted a lifetime of singlehood for college-educated women who postponed marriage into their thirties and forties.

II. New data from the U.S. Census Bureau suggests this trend has reversed itself for people in their twenties.
   A. For every five single young women in their twenties, there are now six single young men.
   B. Young women now have the advantage.

(Transition): Since I already see the men in my audience squirming and the women smiling, you must realize that the implications of this demographic shift are enormous.

Because there are far more unmarried men in their twenties than there are women in the same age group, young men today find it harder to meet eligible partners.

We will look at the problem men face from a number of different perspectives, including loneliness, pressure from corporations to marry, and the growing rivalry between older and younger men for the same women. At the end of the speech, we will examine some possible solutions.

Body

I. Before we begin, let's take a closer look at the hard data from the Bureau of Census.
  A. About twenty years ago there were 19.9 million men and 20.4 million women in their early twenties.
  B. However, there also were about 2.3 million more unmarried men in their twenties than unmarried women in the same age group.
     1. In part, this statistic is explained by the fact that women tend to marry older men, thus removing themselves from the marriage pool.
     2. Since the number of births in the United States fell by an average of 1.7 percent a year between 1957 and 1975, the men born in any given year outnumber the women born in the years that follow, making it even more difficult for men to find a mate.

II. The result is that an increasing number of young men find themselves without a date on Saturday night.
  A. These men are lonely.
  B. Young male college graduates also feel the pressure to marry in order to get the right job in corporate America.
     1. According to career consultants, many corporations view unmarried men in their thirties as oddballs.
     2. Corporations expect their young male managers to marry by the age of thirty.
  C. Young men resent older men who date younger women.
     1. According to William Beer, the deputy chairman of the sociology department at New York's Brooklyn College, young men feel that these older men are "poaching."
     2. Older men claim they are just following a traditional pattern.

(Transition): Why are younger women attracted to older men, especially with a glut of younger men to choose from?

III. Older men are perceived as more sophisticated.
  A. They have had more time to explore the world and their personal interests.
  B. "The older men that I have met have done so much after college … that I haven't done," said Martha Catherine Dagenhart, then a senior at the University of North Carolina at Chapel Hill.

IV. Older men have more money.
  A. A thirty-year-old man may have worked eight years longer than a twenty-two-year-old college graduate.

B. Many older men have money in the bank.

V. Older men are perceived as more powerful.
    A. An attractive woman in her twenties may be willing to have a relationship with a man in his forties if he's achieved a certain status in society.
        1. Often an executive will marry an assistant who sees him as a powerful person.
        2. Film stars and other major celebrities or prominence find themselves with women much younger then they are because of the power or status that goes with being a famous entertainer.
    B. Many older men cultivate an image of power and influence.

(Transition:) Now that we've examined the extent and implications of this phenomenon and looked at the reasons young women are attracted to older men, let's look at what eligible bachelors in their twenties can do.

Conclusion

I. One solution to this problem is that young men in their twenties date older women.
    A. Unmarried women over thirty still outnumber men in the same age group.
    B. Women have traditionally dated older men, so demographic realities may force men to consider doing the same.

II. Men can be less selective in their choice of mates.
    A. An "I'm not willing to settle" attitude may leave many men without a companion.
    B. Turning to the Internet is currently popular, in part because of the difficulty men may have in initiating a relationship with someone they do not know.

III. Men must learn to accept the fact that they no longer have a ready supply of eligible partners—a fact older women have struggled with for years.

References
Bradsher, K. "For every five young women, six young men." *New York Times*, (1990, January17), pp. C1 and C10.
Bradsher, K. "Young men pressed to wed for success." *New York Times*, (1989, December 13),
        pp. C1 and C12.
"Too late for Prince Charming?" (1986, June 2). *Newsweek*, June 2, 54–61.

A Brief Analysis of the Planning Outline
When applying a real topic to the boilerplate provided earlier, it is easy to see how the process unfolds. Note how transitions work, moving the speaker from the introduction of the speech to the body, from one main point to the next and, finally, from the body of the speech to the conclusion.

Remember, although the word "transition" appears in the outline, it is not stated in your speech. Transitions help connect listeners in a personal way to the subject being discussed. It also provides the thesis statement and previews the main points of the speech.

Notice that quotes are written word for word in the outline. Also, note the preview that is included at the end of the transition from introduction to body. Once stated, the audience will know the main ideas you will present.

As the outline proceeds from the first- to the second- to the third-level headings, the specificity of details increase. The planning outline moves from the general to the specific.

▲ Speaker's Notes

Speaker's notes are an abbreviated key-word outline, lacking much of the detail of the planning outline. They function as a reminder of what you plan to say and the order in which you plan to say it. Speaker's notes follow exactly the pattern of your planning outline, but in a condensed format.

Follow the same indentation pattern you used in your planning outline to indicate your points and subpoints. Include notations for the introduction, body, and conclusion and indicate transitions. It is helpful to include suggestions for an effective delivery. Remind yourself to slow down, gesture, pause, use visual aids, and so on. This will be helpful during your speech, especially if you experience speech tension.

Guidelines for Constructing Speaker's Notes

1. Avoid overloading your outline.

Many speakers feel that the more information they have in front of them, the better prepared they will be to deliver their speech. The opposite is usually true. Speakers who load themselves with too many details are torn between focusing on their audience and focusing on their notes. Too often, as they bob their heads up and down, they lose their place.

2. Include only necessary information.

You need just enough information to remind you of your planned points. At times, of course, you must be certain of your facts and your words, such as when you quote an authority or present complex statistical data. In these cases, include all the information you need in your speaker's notes. Long quotes or lists of statistics can be placed on separate index cards or sheets of paper.

3. Reduce your sentences to key phrases.

Instead of writing: "The American Medical Association, an interest group for doctors, has lobbied against socialized medicine;" write: "The AMA and socialized medicine." Your notes should serve as a stimulus for what you are going to say. If you only need a few words to remind you, then use them. For example, a speaker who had directed several high school musicals planned to discuss the various aspects of directing a high school musical. Her speaker's notes could include the key words "casting," "blocking," "choreography," "singing," and "acting." Little else would be needed, since she can define and/or describe these aspects of directing. However, under the key word "casting," she might include "when to cast," and "how to cast." Relevant quotes or perhaps a reference to a dramatic story would be included in the notes as well.

4. Include transitions, but in an abbreviated form.

If you included each transition, your notes would be too long, and you would have too much written on them. Look at one of the transitions from the previous speech about men and marriage:

(Transition): Since I already see the men in my audience squirming and the women smiling, you must realize that the implications of this demographic shift are enormous. Because there are far more unmarried men in their twenties than there are women in the same age group, young men today find it harder to meet eligible partners.

We will look at the problem men face from a number of different perspectives, including loneliness, pressure to marry from corporations, and the growing rivalry between older and younger men for the same women. At the end of the speech, we will examine some possible solutions.

Instead of these two paragraphs, your speaker's notes might look like this:

Men squirming/women smiling
More unmarried men than women
Problems: loneliness, pressure to marry, growing rivalry

If you practice your speech, these words should suffice as notes. Abbreviate in a way that makes sense to you. Each person will have his or her own version of shorthand.

5. Notes must be legible.

Your notes are useless if you cannot read them. Because you will be looking up and down at your notes as you speak, you must be able to find your place with ease at any point. Do not reduce your planning outline to 8-point and paste it to note cards. If you can type your notes, make sure they eare 14-point or larger. If you write your notes, take the time to write legibly. Think about this: You may have spent several hours researching, preparing, and organizing your speech. Why take the chance of reducing the impact of your speech by writing your notes at the last minute?

Following is an example of a set of speaker's notes. The transformation from planning outline to key-word outline is noticeable in terms of length and detail. Transitions, delivery hints, and the parts of the outline are emboldened.

Sample speakers' notes from the speech, "Young Women Take Control of the Marriage Pool":

Sample Speaker's Notes

(Introduction)

I. Sociology and the male/female dating ratio.
    A. Berkeley study: 3 million women born in 1950 will never have a mate
    B. Yale study

II. New Census Bureau data
    A. Ratio five single women to six single men in their twenties
    B. Advantage: women
(Look around room. Make eye contact. Slow down.)

(Men are finding it hard to meet mates. We will examine the problem and its implications.)

(Body)

(Slow down)

I. Closer look at data
    A. 19.9 million men, 20.4 million women in their twenties
    B. However, 2.3 million more unmarried men
        1. Women marry older men
        2. How declining birth rate affects pool of marriageable singles

II. Result for men: No dates
    A. Loneliness
    B. Pressure to marry from corporate America
        1. Unmarried "oddballs"
        2. Climb the corporate ladder: marry by thirty
    C. Young and old fight for same women
        1. William Beer, Brooklyn College sociologist: "Older men are poaching."
        2. Men are following tradition

(Why are younger women drawn to older men?)

III. More sophisticated.
    A. Time to explore interests and the world.
    B. *"The older men that I have met have done so much after college that I haven't done."*
    (Martha Catherine Dagenhart, senior at U. of NC at Chapel Hill.)

IV. More money
    A. Working longer
    B. Money in the bank

V. More powerful.
    A. Relationships based on status of man
        1. E.g., administrative assistant marries boss
        2. Stereotype: May-September marriages
    B. Older men cultivate the image of power

(Conclusion)

(Make eye contact during list)

I. Date older women
    A. Plenty of women over thirty
    B. Women have always dated older men

II. Be less picky
    A. "I'm not willing to settle."
    B. Try to meet someone through the Internet

III. Accept and adjust

A Brief Analysis of Speaker's Notes

Including your specific purpose and thesis statement in your speaker's notes is unnecessary. Speaker's notes follow exactly the pattern of the planning outline so you maintain the organizational structure and flow of your speech. The introduction, body, and conclusion are labeled, although it is possible you might only need the initial letters "I," "B," and "C" to note these divisions. Nonessential words are eliminated, although some facts are included in the speaker's notes to avoid misstatement. Delivery instructions help emphasize that your speech has implications to your listeners and can help personalize the message.

The more experience you have as a speaker, the more you will come to rely on both your planning outline and speaker's notes, as both are indispensable to a successful presentation.

❯❯SUMMARY

The first step in organizing your speech is to determine your main points. Organize your efforts around your specific purpose and thesis statement, then brainstorm to generate specific ideas, and finally, group similar ideas.

Your second step is to use supporting material to develop each main point. In step three, choose an organizational pattern. Arrange your ideas in chronological order, use a spatial organizational pattern, follow a pattern of cause and effect, look at a problem and its solutions, or choose a topical pattern. Your final step is to connect your main ideas through transitions, internal previews, and internal summaries.

As you develop your speech, your primary organizational tool is the planning outline, which includes most of the information you will present. The outline uses a traditional outline format, which establishes a hierarchy of ideas. The number of main points developed in your speech should be between two and five. The planning outline also uses complete sentences, labels transitions, and includes a reference list.

Speakers' notes, the notes you use during your presentation in an extemporaneous speech, are less detailed than the planning outline. They serve as brief reminders of what you want to say and the order in which you say it. They may include complete quotations and statistical data as well as important delivery suggestions. Speakers' notes are organized around phrases, not sentences, and they use the same format as the planning outline.

QUESTIONS FOR ANALYSIS

1. Match five speech topics with five different organizational patterns. Which pattern did you choose for each topic, and on what basis did you make your choice?

2. In public speaking, what functions are served by transitions and summaries? Can you think of several effective transitional statements to develop the speech topics from question number one?

3. Review the essential requirements for planning and key-word outlines. Why is it necessary to develop both outline forms, and why are both equally important in extemporaneous speaking? Explain the role each plays in different phases of a speech.

ACTIVITIES

1. Read a speech from Vital Speeches of the Day or from another collection. Outline the speech, identifying the specific organizational pattern or patterns the speaker has chosen. Write a paragraph examining whether the pattern chosen effectively communicates the core idea.

2. Write a specific purpose statement for a speech, then use three different organizational patterns to organize the speech.

3. Select a video from your library that contains a speech. Then listen to the speech to identify the organizational pattern. List the previews, transition, and summaries. Identify the core idea and its placement in the speech.

REFERENCES

Clarke, M. L. 1963. *Rhetoric at Rome: Historical survey*. New York: Barnes & Noble.

Daniels, T. D., and Witman, R. F. 1981. The effects of message structure in verbal organizing ability upon learning information. *Human communication research*, Winter, 147–60.

Makay, J., and R. C. Fetzger. 1984. *Business communication skills: Principles and practice* (2nd ed.). Englewood Cliffs, NJ: Prentice-Hall.

Sprague, J., and Stuart, D. 1992. *The speaker's handbook, 3rd ed*. San Diego, CA: Harcourt Brace Jovanovich.

Turner Jr., F. H. 1970. The effects of speech summaries on audience comprehension. *Central States Speech Journal*, Spring, 24–39.

SHORT ANSWER / SHORT ESSAY

HONOR STATEMENT: I, the undersigned student, hereby declare before God, before the school, and before the professor that I have read Chapter 11 in its entirety, that I have completed the following exercise with help from no other sources, and that I neither have shared nor will share this work with anyone.

Signature: _____   Date: _____

1. What are the three major sections of a speech, and what is the function of each?

_____

_____

_____

_____

_____

_____

_____

_____

_____

2. What is the purpose of brainstorming as you select your main points?

_____

_____

_____

_____

_____

_____

_____

_____

_____

3. What are the seven types of organizational patterns presented in the chapter? For each of these, provide an example of an informative speech topic one could address using this pattern. Explain why this pattern would work for that topic.

_____

_____

_____

_____

_____

_____

_____

_____

_____

_____

_____

_____

_____

4. Using the broad topic "fast-food chains," show how one could take each of the seven presented organizational patterns to make an organized presentation on some aspect of this general topic?

_____

_____

_____

_____

_____

_____

_____

_____

_____

5. What are transitions, internal previews, and internal summaries? Why are they important to the organization of your speech?

_____

_____

_____

_____

_____

_____

_____

_____

_____

6. Compare the planning outline and the speaker's notes. In which ways are they alike? In which ways are they different?

_____

_____

_____

_____

_____

_____

_____

_____

7. What should you keep in mind as you create your speaker's notes?

_____

_____

_____

_____

_____

_____

_____

_____

_____

_____

_____

_____

"The first ninety seconds.
They're absolutely crucial."
- Ron Hoff, public speaking consultant

CHAPTER 12 >>

12 INTRODUCING AND CONCLUDING YOUR SPEECH

Adapted from *Public Speaking: Choices for Effective Results, Fifth Edition* by John Makay et al. Copyright © 2008.
Reprinted with permission of Kendall Hunt Publishing Co.

Imagine your classmate is about to give a persuasive speech on intercultural communication, and is mulling over an almost unlimited number of ways to start. Consider the following three possibilities:

© 2012 by Studio DMM Photography, Designs & Art.
Used under license of Shutterstock.

The introduction and conclusion are bookends that hold your speech's content together.

- *Bonjour! Parce que ma presentation s'agit d'une question de la communication interculturelle, j'ai decidé de presenter completement en francais! D'accord? Bien. La communication interculturelle est un grand probleme dans l' Etats Unis et d'autres nations ont beaucoup souffert.* In other words, intercultural communication, or rather, lack thereof, is a huge problem that has plagued America as well as other foreign countries across the world….

- How many of you have finished your foreign language requirement for college graduation? How many of you feel that you are fluent in another language? Do you realize that it's not unusual for our European counterparts to speak four different languages? Intercultural communication, or rather, lack thereof, is a huge problem that has plagued America as well as foreign countries across the world….

- Intercultural communication, or rather, lack thereof, is a huge problem that has plagued America as well as foreign countries across the world…

Which beginning do you find most creative? Least creative? Most engaging? Least engaging? Which one would be the easiest to develop? The most difficult?

As you look at the above examples, a final question comes to mind. Are all three examples acceptable ways to begin a speech? The answer may certainly be "yes," but you need to keep in mind that the way you begin and end your speech is critical to your overall success. Expending effort on your introduction is time well spent.

This chapter approaches introductions and conclusions in relation to how your speech can make a lasting impression. Two topics will be considered: how to engage your audience at the beginning of your speech so they will be motivated to listen to the rest of it, and how to remind your audience at the end of what you said and why it was relevant.

The primacy/recency effect sheds light on the importance of effective speech beginnings and endings. According to this theory, we tend to recall more vividly the beginning and ending, and less so the middle, of an event. When a series of candidates are interviewing for a job, the first and last candidates have an advantage because the interviewer is most likely to recall more about these two than the others. This theory also holds true for speeches; your audience will have greater recall of how you began and ended your speech.

The familiar speaker adage: "Tell them what you are going to say, say it, and then tell them what you said" addresses this truth. Beginning and ending a speech well helps your audience to recall and later, to use, the ideas you present. Let us begin with a closer look at introductions.

❯❯ INTRODUCTIONS

Why pay so much attention to an introduction? If done well, an introduction can help your audience make a smooth transition to the main points of your speech, create a positive first impression, and set an appropriate tone and mood for your talk. If done poorly, your audience may prejudge your topic as unimportant or dull and stop listening.

Consider the following example. As part of a conference for a group of business executives, business consultant Edith Weiner was scheduled to deliver a speech on the unequal distribution of world resources—admittedly, a topic with the potential to put her listeners to sleep. She was experienced enough as a speaker, though, to realize that the last thing her listeners wanted to hear at the beginning was a long list of statistics comparing the bounty of North America to the failures of other parts of the world. Her speech would never recover from such a dull start. The challenge she faced was to capture the audience's attention at the outset.

Arriving at the auditorium early on the morning of her speech, Weiner marked off different size sections of the hall to represent, proportionately, the various continents. She allotted coffee, cake, and chairs according to the availability of food and income in each. Then she assigned audience members to these areas according to actual world population ratios.

What happened was quite memorable. While thirty people in the area representing Africa had to divide three cups of coffee, two pastries, and two chairs, the seventeen people assigned to North America had more coffee and cake than they could eat in a week, surrounded by forty chairs. As participants took their seats (with those in Asia and Africa standing most of the morning), they did so with a new perspective on world hunger and poverty, and with a desire to listen to whatever Weiner had to say.

Edith Weiner's risky introduction grabbed the attention of all audience members in a powerful way.

A good introduction can help you set an appropriate tone for your speech.

▲Functions of Introductions

The emphasis on strong opening comments has long been held as important. In the first century A.D. Roman philosopher Quintillian noted that for a speech to be effective, an introduction must do four things. It must:

- Focus attention on the topic and speaker
- Provide a motive for your audience to care about your speech
- Enhance your credibility as a speaker
- Preview your message and organization

Edith Weiner's introduction was effective because it accomplished each of these objectives, as we shall see.

Focus Attention on Topic and Speaker

Your introduction should first offer a personal greeting, capture and focus attention on your topic, and set an appropriate tone and mood.

Personal Greeting

An introduction should contain a personalized greeting, which is usually your first words and might be considered a preamble to your introduction. A personal greeting at the start of your speech tells your listeners that you see the speech as an opportunity to communicate your point of view. When Martin Luther King Jr. looked out over the sea of faces on the Washington Mall on August 28, 1963, he began by telling his audience, "I am happy to join with you today in what will go down in history as the greatest demonstration for freedom in the history of our nation." Then he delivered his "I Have a Dream" speech—his powerful and memorable civil rights address (King, in Johannesen, Allen, and Linkugel, 1988, 30). Personal greetings make the audience feel welcome and set the stage for the introduction that follows.

Capture and Focus Attention

Every experienced speaker knows that the first few minutes are critical to the success of the entire speech. It is within these minutes that your listeners decide whether they care enough to continue listening. You want your listeners to say to themselves, "Hey, this is interesting," or "I didn't know that," or "I never thought of it in quite that way," or "That was really funny." The common denominator in each of these responses is piqued audience interest. Weiner explains: "I know if I'm successful when I start a speech. I try to establish a rapport with the audience and sail from there. If you wait till the end to deliver the 'Big Bang,' you've already lost most of your audience—and there's no getting them back. I always start with some kind of hook, and from there on, the audience is in the palm of my hand" (Weiner 1989). We do not expect beginning speakers to have the audience "in the palm of their hands," but the importance of capturing attention cannot be understated.

Set the Appropriate Tone and Mood

Imagine observing the following scenario: Angela stood behind the podium beside the closed casket as she delivered the eulogy to tearful faces. Her sentimental message of grief was appropriate in every way except that she delivered it with a smile. The whole speech! The disconnect between her words and facial expressions was a bit unsettling to say the least. When asked about it later, Angela was surprised. She confessed that the smile was her trying to communicate that she was glad to be there and happy to be performing such an important family duty. Unfortunately, Angela did not create an appropriate tone and mood in her introduction.

The mood of a speech refers to the overall feeling you hope to engender in your audience. Tone is the emotional disposition of the speaker as the speech is being delivered. Tone is created verbally by the words and ideas you select and nonverbally by the emotions you communicate. As during most funerals, the mood was of sadness and solidarity. Yet Angela's tone was upbeat and happy. Consider the desired mood and adjust your tone appropriately in the introduction. In this way, you ensure that your tone matches your reason for speaking and that your speech helps to create the desired mood in your audience.

Martin Luther King, Jr. incorporated personal greetings into his introductions to make the audience feel welcome.

Provide a Motive to Listen

An effective speaker will quickly establish a reason for audience members to listen. Edith Weiner's introduction helped build that critical relationship with her public speaking audience. She wanted her listeners to care about her message. She wanted them to decide from the outset that what she was saying had meaning and importance. Although the introduction also helped to make her point with its physical demonstration of world food problems, its primary purpose was to build a psychological bridge that would last throughout the speech. Her well-designed demonstration forced her audience to care about her topic because Weiner had effectively related the topic of her speech to something the audience cared about, their own hunger.

The introduction should seek to establish common ground with the audience. By focusing on something you and your audience can share and announcing it early, you will help people identify with your topic. When people perceive that your message is meant for them and really is relevant to their lives, they will listen attentively.

Enhance Credibility

During your introduction, your listeners make important decisions about you. They decide whether they like you and whether you are credible. Your credibility as a speaker is judged, in large part, on the basis of what you say during your introduction and how you say it.

Edith Weiner became a credible speaker by demonstrating, in a participatory way, that she understood the problems of world food distribution and that she cared enough about her audience—and topic—to come up with a creative way to present her ideas. Credibility also increases as you describe, early on, what qualifies you to speak about a topic. Weiner might have said, "I want to talk to you about world resources because for several years I have studied how your investments overseas can have important impacts on your future economic well-being." In this case, she may not have established her credibility to the extent her actual introduction accomplished.

Audiences may have an initial sense of your credibility even before you speak. Your introduction is an ideal place to enhance that impression. As we will discuss later in the text, you can think of your credibility in terms of your perceived competence, concern for your audience, dynamism, and personal ethics. Put another way, if you know your subject, care about your audience, offer an enthusiastic delivery, and communicate a sense of ethical integrity, your audience's impression of your credibility will likely be positive. The content and delivery of your introduction must maximize these four aspects if you want your audience to listen attentively throughout your speech.

Preview Your Message and Organization

Finally, Weiner used her introduction to tell her audience what she would talk about during the rest of her speech. In a sentence, she previewed her focus. ("I intend to explore several options [for maximizing your role and gain] during the rest of my speech.") This simple statement helped her listeners make the intellectual connections they needed to follow her speech. Instead of wondering, "What will she talk about?" or "What is her point of view?" they were ready for her speech to unfold.

HOW TO INTRODUCE THE SAME SPEECH IN DIFFERENT WAYS

Many topics lend themselves to different types of introductions. A startling statement, a dramatic anecdote, a quotation, or a humorous story may each serve as an effective introduction to the same speech. Here, for example, is the same speech introduced in three different ways:

Startling Statement

Microwave cooking can be hazardous to your child's health. Children have been burned by opening bags of microwave-heated popcorn too close to their faces. Their throats have been scalded by jelly donuts that feel cool to the touch, but are hot enough inside to burn the esophagus. These and other hazards can transform your microwave into an oven of destruction in the hands of a child. What I would like to talk about today is how dangerous microwaves can be to young children and how you can safeguard your family from accidents.

Dramatic Story

Nine-year-old Jenny was one of those kids who managed quite well on her own. Every day she got home from school at 3:30 while her parents were still at work and made herself a snack in the microwave. She had been using the microwave since she was five, and her parents never questioned its safety—that is, not until Jenny had her accident.

It began innocently enough. Jenny heated a bag of microwave popcorn in the oven and opened it inches from her face. The bag was cool to the touch, hiding the danger within. Hot vapors blasted Jenny's face, leaving her with second and third-degree-burns.

What I would like to talk about today is how dangerous microwaves can be to young children and how you can safeguard your family from accidents.

Quotation

Three out of every four American homes have microwave ovens and with them a potential for danger. Louis Slesin, editor of "Microwave News," a health and safety newsletter, explains how this common kitchen appliance can present potential hazards for young children:

"On a rainy day," says Slesin, "a kid could climb up on a stool, put his face to the door and watch something cook for a long time. It's mesmerizing, like watching a fish tank, but his eye will be at the point of maximum microwave leakage. We don't know the threshold for cataract formation—the industry says you need tons of exposure, but some litigation and literature say you don't need much [for damage to occur]. Children younger than 10 or 12 shouldn't use the oven unsupervised. It's not a toy. It's a sophisticated, serious, adult appliance, and it shouldn't be marketed for kids" (Shapiro 1990, 56).

I agree with Slesin, and what I want to talk about today is how dangerous the microwave can be to a young child.

A startling statement (e.g., about the dangers of microwaved food) may serve as an effective introduction for a speech.

As we said in the opening of this chapter, your audience will recall your message more fully if you tell them what you are going to say, say it, and then tell them what you said. Repeating key ideas helps us recall important information. But the first part of that, telling them what you are going to say, also serves to provide a preview of the organization you intend to use. If your audience knows the main points you intend to develop in your speech, they are less likely to be confused and distracted. So, an effective introduction might offer a preview statement similar to "Today it is important that we better understand the nature of world hunger, explore creative solutions to this problem, and finally, see if some of these solutions might also be profitable to your business." In this example, the audience now knows that there will be three main points to the message.

Here is how John E. Jacob, president and chief executive officer of the National Urban League, previewed a speech delivered to the Congressional Clearinghouse of the Future:

> Today I want to begin by briefly sketching what the Urban League is, and going on from there, to discuss the plight of black citizens. Along the way, I'd like to look back at some of the things America has done to deal with its racial problems. And I'd like to look ahead as well, to suggest some of the things we can do to secure the future for black people and for all Americans (1988, 616).

When Jacob finished this statement, his audience had no doubt what his speech would cover. When you preview your message, your audience will listen and understand with increased clarity and will remember more of your message later.

▲Ten Techniques of Introductions

There are many ways to accomplish Quintillian's four functions of an introduction. Following are ten different techniques often used in introductions. You might consider using one or combining several to provide the initial impact you want. This is one area where a little creativity can go a long way. Keep your audience in mind. A few of these techniques may be more appropriate or attention-getting for your specific audience and specific purpose.

1. Startling Facts/Intriguing Statements

Some introductions seem to force listeners to pay attention. They make it difficult to think of other things because of the impact of what is being said. The effectiveness of these introductions in part, comes from the audience's feeling that the speaker's message is directed at them.

2. Dramatic Story/Build Suspense

Closely related to the startling statement is the dramatic story, which involves listeners in a tale from beginning to end. Shortly after returning from a winter vacation break, Shannon delivered a speech to her classmates that began this way:

> My friends and I were driving home from a day at the ski slopes when suddenly, without warning, a pair of headlights appeared directly in front of our car. To avoid a collision, I swerved sharply to the right, forcing our car off the road into a snow-filled ditch.

> It's funny what comes into your mind at moments like this. All I could think of was how New York Yankee manager Billy Martin had died in a ditch a few years ago after his car skidded off an icy road. I thought I was going to die too, just because of another driver's stupidity and carelessness.

> Obviously, I didn't die or even suffer any serious injuries. And my friends are safe too, although my car was totaled. I'm convinced that we are all here today because we were locked into place by our seat belts. Billy Martin might have been here too had he bothered to buckle up.

Everyone in the audience knew what it was like to be driving home with friends—feeling safe and secure—only to be shocked into the realization that they were vulnerable to tragedy. Audience attention was riveted on the speaker as she launched into her speech on seat belt use.

© 2012 Adam Radosavljevic.
Used under license of Shutterstock.

Dramatic stories, which involve listeners in a tale from beginning to end, is a good way to start a speech.

3. Quotation and/or Literature Reference

You can capture audience attention by citing the words of others. If you use an appropriate poem, the words themselves may be compelling enough to engage your listeners. E. Grady Bogue, chancellor of Louisiana State University, opened the commencement address he delivered at Memphis State University with the following quotation:

> They deem me mad because I will not sell my days for gold; And I deem them mad because they think my days have a price (1988, 615).

As Bogue continued, he celebrated the "nobility" of a career in teaching:

> Teaching is a journey of the heart, an opportunity to touch a life forever. It is an unselfish investment in the dignity and potential of one's student. The life of the master teacher honors all that is good and noble in mankind (615).

Introducing a speech with a quote is also appropriate when you cite the words of a well-known individual or a recognized authority whose reputation enhances your topic. Here, for example, is how Tisha Oehmen, a student at Lane Community College, began her speech to capture the attention of her audience. Quoting a knowledgeable public figure, she began:

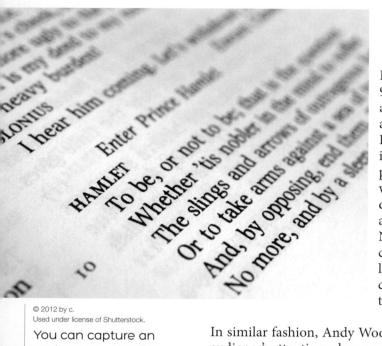

You can capture an audience's attention by quoting the impressive words of others.

Each day the Columbia River dumps in the Pacific Ocean 90 billion gallons of fresh water. That is 3.7 billion gallons an hour, 61 million gallons a minute, and 1 million gallons a second. This is wasteful and sinful.' These are the words of Los Angeles County Supervisor Kenneth Hahn, as quoted in *The Washington Post*, May 20, 1990. This is how Hahn prepared his Board of Supervisors for his proposal to siphon water out of the Columbia River to quench the thirst of his drought-stricken city. If he succeeds in building this aqueduct, the life and the environment in the Pacific Northwest and all who depend on its resources may be changed. The Columbia's diversion would not only scar the landscape, but the proposed diversion would slow shipping, cripple irrigation, harm the fragile salmon runs, and reduce the available electricity (1991, 96).

In similar fashion, Andy Wood, studying at St. Petersburg Junior College, captured his audience's attention when speaking about the nation's trauma centers by stating:

> If a criminal has a right to an attorney, don't you have a right to a doctor?' Democrat Harris Woffard used this slogan last year to win the Pennsylvania senate race. *The Washington Post*, November 24, 1991, reports that Woffard also sent an alarming wakeup call to President Bush and Congress to get serious about health care in America (1992, 8).

4. Humor

At the beginning of a speech, humor helps break down the psychological barriers that exist between speaker and audience. Here is how Karen used humor at the start of a classroom speech on the problem of divorce in America:

> Janet and Lauren had been college roommates, but had not seen each other in the ten years since graduation. They were thrilled when they ran into each other at a college reunion and had a chance to talk.
>
> "Tell me," asked Janet, "has your husband lived up to the promises he made when he was dating you in college?"
>
> "He certainly has!" said Lauren. "He told me then that he wasn't good enough for me and he's proven it ever since."

The class laughed, Karen waited, then:

> I laughed too when I heard that story. But the fact remains that about half the marriages in our country end in divorce and one of the major reasons for these failures is that one partner can't live up to the expectations of the other.

Humor works in this introduction for two reasons. First, the story is genuinely funny;

we chuckle when we hear the punch line. And, second, the humor is tied directly to the subject of the speech; it is appropriate for the topic and the occasion. It also provides an effective transition into the speech body.

5. Rhetorical Question

When you ask your audience, "How many of you ate breakfast this morning?" you expect to see people raise their hands. When you ask a rhetorical question, however, you do not expect an answer. What you hope is that your question will cause your listeners to start thinking about the subject of your speech. This was the plan of Paula Pankow (1991), a student at the Eau Claire campus of the University of Wisconsin, when she began her speech about sleep deprivation:

> Do you ever go through the day feeling like you're missing something? Well, what would you do if I said each one of you probably suffers directly from a deficit every day that you might not even realize? A loss that, according to the May 15, 2006 issue of *The New York Times*, affects 100 million Americans and 200 billion dollars a year in lost creativity and business productivity, industrial and vehicular accidents, and medical costs.

The speaker linked these rhetorical questions and startling statistics firmly to her audience of students by connecting them with the lifestyle familiar to residential college students and to her thesis statement and to a preview of the main points in her speech:

© 2012 Monkey Business Images. Used under license of Shutterstock.

At the beginning of a speech, humor helps break down the psychological barriers that exist between speaker and audience.

> This loss is not our deprivation of national dollars, but a loss concerning deprivation of sleep. Now granted, we're in an academic setting and getting a full night's rest isn't as important to adults as getting our work done. Free from the nagging voices of parents who may order a nine o'clock bedtime, we now enjoy the freedom of going to bed when we want and sometimes where we want, whether it be 10 p.m., 1 a.m., or even 6 a.m. after pulling an all-nighter! Of course, a mild loss of sleep once in awhile won't do that much harm to a person, but most of us would be more good-humored, productive, and satisfied with life in general if we got a full complement of sleep each night. Instead, what we're finding in society today is that sleep deprivation is becoming chronic and extensive, leading to serious consequences. So today I'd like to address the problem of sleep deprivation by explaining its nature and consequences, exploring why we don't get enough sleep and, finally, offering some things we can do to better our chances for a full night's rest (123).

The best rhetorical questions are probing in a personal way. They mean something to every listener and encourage active participation throughout your speech.

6. Illustrations, Examples, and Anecdotes

Speakers often begin with an interesting comment about the immediate surroundings or some recent or historical event. These openings are even more powerful when the speaker carefully plans these comments. Through the skillful use of illustrations ("In the short

© 2012 by iofoto.
Used under license of Shutterstock.

Getting an audience physically involved can boost its members' interest in your speech.

time I will be talking with you, 150 violent crimes will have been committed in our nation…"), examples ("Lisa was a girl from our community who's life was forever altered on January 18th…"), and anecdotes ("Once, while traveling on the subway, I noticed a shifty looking man carefully watching each passenger enter and leave the car…"), speakers gather our attention to them and their message.

7. Physically Involve the Audience

Recall from the opening of this chapter how Edith Weiner began her speech by getting her audience physically involved in her message. Some went hungry while others had too much. Another example of this technique frequently occurs at sales seminars, where the speaker offers a gift, usually money, to the first person in the audience who will simply leave his/her seat and come to the front to get it. Eventually some brave soul approaches, takes the money, and returns to his/her seat. Then everyone else in the audience realizes they could have had the gift themselves if they had only been willing to act instead of sitting passively.

8. Relate Personal Experience

Sharing a story or several examples from your past with your listeners can be an effective start. Be sure your personal experiences will not hurt your credibility and that they relate directly to your topic. Recently, a student giving a speech supporting gun control caught the attention of his audience by retelling an event he had witnessed–an angry driver brandishing a gun at another driver at a stop light. Although the gun was not fired, the story caught the audience's attention and introduced the idea that there is potential harm associated with widespread and unregulated gun ownership. Because he saw the event, we considered the speaker to have more credibility in his speech about gun control.

9. Use a Visual or Media Aid

Before the President of the United States speaks, the broadcast feed from the White House shows the presidential seal. This is no accident; it helps to draw attention to the upcoming speech and also helps reinforce the president's credibility. But you do not have to be the President to use this technique. Beginning your speech with an interesting sound recording, visual, or prop is guaranteed to draw attention to the beginning of your speech, too.

10. Refer to the Situation

Skilled public speakers often begin with a positive comment related to the occasion, the person who spoke before them, the audience, the date, or even the physical location. Each of these may be more appropriate at one time than at another. For example, a commencement speaker at her alma mater might start with, "It's hard for me to believe that twenty-five years ago I sat in those seats listening to the commencement speaker…" Or, if an audience was waiting outside in the rain to hear a Democratic candidate who was late, the candidate might start with, "I bet there isn't a more committed group of voters than those of you here who have been standing in the rain waiting for me..." When you are planning a speech, ask yourself if referencing the event, a prior speaker, the audience or the significance of this date in history would create interest and gather attention.

Each of these ten options is a possible opening for a speech. Keep in mind that your attention-gaining device must relate in some way to your topic or you run the risk of confusing your audience. Your choice should be guided by several other factors. First, consider the mood you are attempting to create. Second, consider your audience's expectations of you and the occasion. Third, consider how much time and resources each approach will require. Finally, consider your strengths and weaknesses—you may not be as strong at joke telling as recalling a powerful story.

▲Five Guidelines and Suggestions for Introductions

As you focus on crafting your introduction for your next speech, consider how you can create a strong and effective message. Remember, as in any recipe, no ingredient stands on its own. Attention to each part of the process leads to an excellent final product. After choosing the most appropriate beginning, consider these general guidelines as you prepare and deliver your introduction.

1. Prepare After Body of Speech

Your introduction will take form more easily after you have created an outline of the body of your speech. When speakers attempt to create the introduction first, they inevitably rewrite it several times as they continue to change the body of their message.

2. Make It Easy to Follow and Be Creative

Whether you are offering a startling statistic or asking a question, be sure to keep things simple. When you offer your thesis and even when you preview your main points for your audience, look for ways to keep things concise and straight-forward. Recently, a student beginning his persuasive speech started with his arms open in a pleading gesture, zealously urging the class, "Please! Please I beg of you—stop washing your hands!" He then briefly noted the dangers of too much cleansing and stated his thesis. His enthusiastic approach and startling plea made for a creative introduction that was simple and easy to understand.

Consider your introduction as an opportunity for you to be creative. The more creative your introduction, the more likely your audience will listen to the entire message.

3. Practice and Communicate High Energy

The most important part of your speech to practice thoroughly is the introduction, followed by the conclusion, and then the body. The first impression created by a well-practiced introduction lays the foundation for your ultimate success. So be sure to rehearse it many times. Your introduction should be enthusiastically delivered. Since introductions are relatively short, put your heart, mind, and energy into it. If you are truly engaged in the introduction, your audience is much more likely also to become involved in your message. It is difficult to communicate high energy if you are dependent on notes. You should be able to speak to the audience for at least fifteen seconds without looking at your notes.

4. Engage Audience Nonverbally Before You Start

Poise counts! Recall that your speech actually begins as you rise to speak. Approach with confidence, once there, pause, catch and hold your audience's eye contact for a moment, and take a deep breath. Each of these measures is critical to beginning your speech effectively. You want your audience to know you are interested in the speech and that you want them to be part of the experience.

5. Consider Time Constraints and Mood

When giving a five-minute speech, telling a protracted, dramatic story would be inappropriate. The same is true of showing a one-minute video clip. Alternately, when delivering a forty-five-minute lecture, such a beginning would be wholly acceptable. The mood you are hoping to create in your audience is related to your tone, and vice versa. The introduction is your best chance to establish your tone and alter the mood of your audience.

▲Ten Common Pitfalls of Introductions

As they say, you never get a second chance at a first impression. Here is a list of problematic approaches to avoid during your introduction.

1. Beginning with an apology

Do not use your introduction to apologize for mistakes you are likely to make, for inadequate visual aids, being ill-prepared or even just plain ill. Apologies set a negative tone that is hard to overcome.

2. Being too brief or too long

Do not jump into the body of the speech or spend too much time setting up the speech. Your introduction should take between ten and twenty percent of your total allotted speaking time. Not adhering to this guideline means violating an audience expectation and potentially annoying them.

3. Giving too much away

While the introduction should provide a road map for your speech, you do not want to give the substance of your speech in your preview. Instead, use general terms to tell your audience what you intend to cover.

4. Reading

We have advised you to rehearse your introduction thoroughly. Do not read your introductory remarks to your audience. Your script becomes a barrier between you and your audience. Worse yet, you will likely sound more like a reader than a public speaker. Avoid reading extensively in the introduction.

5. Relying on shock tactics

Your victory will be short-lived if you capture audience attention by screaming at the top of your lungs, pounding the table, telling a bawdy joke, or using material that has nothing to do with your speech. Your audience will trust you less because of the way you manipulated their attention. Using an innovative approach is effective as long as it is tied directly to the topic of your speech.

6. Promising too much

Some speakers, fearful that their speech says too little, promise more than they can deliver, in the hope that the promise alone will satisfy their listeners. It rarely does. Once you set expectations in the introduction, the body of your speech has to deliver or you will lose credibility.

7. Using unnecessary prefatory remarks

Resist the urge to begin with: "I'm so nervous," "I can't believe I have to do this speech," or "Okay, deep breath, here we go." Even if you feel these things, such verbal adaptors are likely to make you even more nervous and are also likely to hurt your credibility. Instead, begin with your planned opening statement. And avoid having the first word you say be "uh."

8. Using long-winded poems, quotations, and prose

We understand that for full effect, an entire piece of prose or poetry should be read. We also know that editing a poem or piece of prose may not be easy. However, it is possible to find an appropriate nugget embedded within the piece that is perfect for your speech. Consider paraphrasing or moving the longer passage to the body of your speech.

9. Becoming someone else

Because your initial credibility is being established in the introduction, you will want to present a rational view of yourself to your audience. Avoid histrionics and melodrama if you hope to earn the respect of your listeners.

10. Overusing some techniques

Often overused are simple questions, rhetorical questions, and startling, catastrophic stories. This is made worse by relying on trite phrases. Spend some time thinking about how to begin your speech. Think about what might be most effective with your particular audience. Seek to be original and creative.

❯❯ CONCLUSIONS

Think of your conclusion as the pinnacle of your speech—the words you want your listeners to remember as they leave the room. Too often, speakers waste the opportunity with endings like, "That's it," "I guess I'm finished now," or "I'm through. Any questions?" Or they simply stop talking, giving the audience no indication that they have finished their speech. Just as an introduction sets a first impression, a well-delivered conclusion leaves a lasting mark on your audience.

A conclusion should not be viewed as an afterthought. Understand that the conclusion is

© 2012 by Kudryashka.
Used under license of Shutterstock.

Think of your conclusion as the grand finale of your speech—the words you want your listeners to remember as they leave the room.

your last opportunity to have an impact. Just as the introduction should be clear and flow smoothly to the body of the speech, the body should flow smoothly to the conclusion. Following are three functions of conclusions to consider as you think about the transition from the body to the conclusion and determine how to create the greatest effect on your audience.

▲Functions of Conclusions

Strong endings to speeches summarize important information, motivate listeners, and create a sense of closure. After talking about the rebuilding and the reconciliation that took place at the end of World War II, and why the American Rangers risked their lives at Normandy, Peggy Noonan (1990) concluded the Pointe du Hoc speech with these words:

We in America have learned the bitter lessons of two world wars: that it is better to be here and ready to preserve and protect the peace than to take blind shelter in our homes across the sea, rushing to respond only after freedom has been threatened. We have learned that isolationism never was and never will be an acceptable response to tyrannical governments with expansionist intent.

Let our actions say to them the words for which Matthew Ridgway listened: "I will not fail thee nor forsake thee." Strengthened by their courage, heartened by their valor and borne by their memory, let us continue to stand for the ideals for which they lived and died (85–86).

Summarizing Important Information

The transition from the body to the conclusion is pivotal in signaling the impending end of your speech. Your instructor and your own personal preference may help you decide how you want to tell your audience you are ending. Whether you use a formal "In conclusion…" or prefer something less formal, such as "Now, to wrap this up today…" you want your audience to be clear that you are about to finish. Audiences know that when you give them that signal, they are about to get an important recap of your key ideas.

In the process of ending, an effective conclusion also reinforces the main idea of the speech. The conclusion of the Pointe du Hoc speech, for example, reinforced President Reagan's message that the liberties we fought for in World War II are the liberties we are still committed to today.

Depending upon the length and complexity of your speech, your summary may be brief or more extended. Your review can be as simple as this:

I would like to conclude by stating once more that our schools have done a dismal job teaching math and science. As we have seen, the results of standardized tests show that our high school and college students are well behind their counterparts in Japan and Western Europe. And, as we have also seen, the demands of businesses for skilled scientists and mathematicians are growing along with the complexity of technology.

The hard truth is that businesses need many more students trained in math and science than our educational system is now producing. Generally, I don't like to make predictions, but I can say for certain that we face a crisis.

Many speakers believe that the best way to hammer home their point is to tell their audience what they are going to say in their introduction, say it in the body of their speech, and then remind their listeners of what they told them in the conclusion. According to speech communication professor John E. Baird Jr. (1974), "Summaries may be effective when presented at the conclusion of a speech [because] they provide the audience with a general structure under which to subsume the more specific points of the speech" (119–127). Research indicates that in some instances summaries are not essential, but if your audience is unfamiliar with the content of your speech, or if the speech is long or complex, a summary will help reinforce your main points.

Motivating Listeners
Great speakers do more than summarize in their conclusions; they motivate their audiences. Relate your topic to your listeners. Your speech will achieve the greatest success if your listeners feel that you have helped them in some concrete way. Consider making this connection in your conclusion.

Communicate a feeling
Perhaps more importantly, the conclusion sets the psychological mood listeners carry with them from the hall. A student speaking against aspartame noted at the beginning of her speech that she believed aspartame contributed to her previous depression and weight gain. She ended her speech by noting that eliminating aspartame from her diet lifted her depression and led to significant weight loss. Her passion about the topic and the relief she feels were clearly communicated.

Broaden your message
Finally, the conclusion can be used to connect your topic to a broader context. If in your speech you talk about the responsibility of every adult to vote on election day, you can use your conclusion to tie the vote to the continuation of our democratic system. If your speech focuses on caring for aging parents, you can conclude with a plea to value rather than discard the wisdom of the elderly.

Creating Closure
Good conclusions create a sense of closure for the speech. The audience needs to find a sense of completeness as listeners. If you are having dinner with others the dessert often provides a tasty completeness to the dining experience. So, when speaking, it is not enough to simply stop with a comment: "Well, that's it, I guess I can see if anyone has a question." leaving the audience without a sense of closure. An effective conclusion tells

your listeners your speech has ended. There are several techniques speakers use to create a sense of psychological closure.

▲Concluding Techniques

Thanking as Transition

Although saying thank you at the end of the speech indicates that you are finished, it is no substitute for a statement that brings your discussion to a close. You can, however, use the thank you statement as a transition into your concluding remarks. For example:

> And so, in summary, philosophers have provided several compelling arguments for God's existence. Thank you for giving me the honor of being your keynote speaker. Francis Bacon once observed, "A little philosophy inclineth man's mind to atheism, but depth in philosophy bringeth men's minds about to religion." Whatever else this speech does, it illustrates the Bacon's wisdom. Faith in God's existence is not blind. It is, rather, a logically plausible conclusion—one that thinkers, throughout the centuries, have embraced with their minds as well as their hearts.

Call to Action

As you wrap up your speech, you can make a direct appeal to your listeners, urging them to take a specific action or to change their attitudes. In a persuasive speech, the conclusion is where you make your most forcible and most memorable plea to persuade.

Living in an age of mass media, we are bombarded by calls to action every time we turn on the television. Advertisers plead with us to drop everything and buy their products. We see 1-800 numbers flash across the screen, urging us to order knives or DVDs or diet aids. Televangelists urge us to contribute to their mission. The fact that we are all accustomed to these messages makes them a natural conclusion to a speech.

Realizing this, Thomas K. Hearn Jr. (1988), concluded his speech to the College Football Association with these remarks:

> If there are values acquired by a life devoted to a game, even a game as violent as football, then those of you who coach this sport should be examples of the sport's ethical possibilities. Does playing football build ingredients of character? Does it make young men better? Whether team sports are good for people, people at any age, is always a question of coaching leadership. Your game has a noble heritage. All of you are guardians of your sport....

> If football belongs in the university where young minds and character are being formed, and if being called "coach" is a title of honor among all coaches, football can lead the movement of reform, beginning today with all of us (22).

Hearn is challenging his listeners to think and act in a more ethical way. A call to action is an especially appropriate way to conclude a persuasive speech, but it can also be an effective end to an informative speech. Here is how a professor might conclude a lecture:

I have explained my thoughts on the implications of the changes that are now taking place in Eastern Europe. As you review them, keep this in mind: What we are witnessing is nothing less than a change in world politics. In the days ahead, think about this change and about how it will affect each and every one of us in the free and communist worlds.

Use a Dramatic Illustration

Ending your speech with a dramatic story connected to your speech's main theme reinforces the theme in your listeners' minds. It is the last message of your speech the audience will hear and, as a story, it is the most likely to be remembered.

Close with a Quotation

Closing a speech with the words of others is an effective and memorable way to end your presentation.

One of the most famous moments in oratory was the conclusion of President Ronald Reagan's eulogy to the crew of the space shuttle *Challenger*.

> The crew of the space shuttle *Challenger* honored us by the manner in which they lived their lives. We will never forget them, nor the last time we saw them—this morning, as they prepared for their journey, and waved good-bye, and "slipped the surly bonds of earth" to "touch the face of God." (President Ronald Reagan's address to the nation on the *Challenger* disaster from the Oval Office, January 28, 1986.)

As in this example, quotations can be interwoven into the fabric of the speech without telling your listeners that you are speaking the words of others. If you use this technique, it is important that you use the quote exactly and attribute it to the writer.

Conclude with a Metaphor That Broadens the Meaning of Your Speech

You may want to broaden the meaning of your speech through the use of an appropriate metaphor—a symbol that tells your listeners that you are saying more. President Reagan used this technique several times at the conclusion of his State of the Union address by citing the heroism of a select group of individuals who were invited to sit in the balcony of the House of Representatives while the speech was being delivered. Here are Reagan's words:

> Tonight I have spoken of great plans and great dreams. They are dreams we can make come true. Two hundred years of American history should have taught us that nothing is impossible.

One of the most famous moments in oratory was the conclusion of President Ronald Reagan's eulogy to the crew of the space shuttle *Challenger*.

© 2012 by Kzenon.
Used under license of Shutterstock.

Three different techniques can be used to conclude a speech on learning to deal more compassionately with the elderly.

Ten years ago a young girl left Vietnam with her family, part of the exodus that followed the fall of Saigon. They came to the United States with no possessions, and not knowing a word of English. The young girl studied hard, learned English, and finished high school in the top of her class. This May is a big date on her calendar. Just ten years from the time she left Vietnam, she'll graduate from the United States Military Academy at West Point. I thought you might want to meet an American hero named Jean Nguyen.

(The young woman stood and bowed to the applause.)

There's someone else here tonight. Born seventy-nine years ago, she lives in the inner city where she cares for infants born to mothers who are heroin addicts. The children, born in withdrawal, are sometimes even dropped at her doorstep. She heals them with love. Go to her house some night and maybe you'll see her silhouette against the window, as she walks the floor talking softly, soothing a child in her arms. Mother Hale of Harlem—she, too, is an American hero.

(Mrs. Hale stood to acknowledge the applause.)

Your lives tell us that the oldest American saying is new again: Anything is possible in America if we have the faith, the will, and the heart. History is asking us, once again, to be a force for good in the world. Let us begin, in unity, with justice, and love (Noonan 1990, 198–99).

Presidential speechwriter Peggy Noonan explains the symbolic impact of Reagan's conclusion: "The 'heroes in the balcony' was a metaphor for all the everyday heroism that never gets acknowledged. It was for kids, to show them what courage is" (198).

Conclude with Humor

If you leave your listeners with a humorous story, you will leave them laughing and with a reservoir of good feelings about you and your speech. To be effective, of course, the humor must be tied to your core idea.

A Hollywood screenwriter, invited to speak to students in a college writing course about the job of transforming a successful novel into a screenplay, concluded her speech with the following story:

Two goats who often visited the set of a movie company found some discarded film next to where a camera crew was working. One of the goats began munching on the film.

"How's it taste?" asked the other goat, trying to decide whether to start chomping himself.

"Not so great," said the first goat. "I liked the book better."

The audience laughed in appreciation of the humor. When the room settled down, the

HOW TO CONCLUDE THE SAME SPEECH IN DIFFERENT WAYS

Just as many topics lend themselves to different types of introductions, they also lend themselves to various methods of conclusion. Here three different techniques are used to conclude a speech on learning to deal more compassionately with the elderly:

A Quotation That Personalizes Your Message

In 1878, in a poem entitled, "Somebody's Mother," poet Mary Dow Brine wrote these words:

> She's somebody's mother, boys, you know,
> For all she's aged and poor and slow.

Most of us are likely to be somebody's mother—or father—before we die. And further down the road, we're likely to be grandparents, sitting in a rocking chair, hoping that our children have figured out a more humane way to treat us than we have treated our elderly relatives.

A Dramatic Story That Also Serves as a Metaphor

Not too long ago, I had a conversation with a doctor who had recently hospitalized an 82-year-old woman with pneumonia. A widow and the mother of three grown children, the woman had spent the last seven years of her life in a nursing home.

The doctor was called three times a day by these children. At first their calls seemed appropriate. They wanted to be sure their mother was getting the best possible medical care. Then, their tone changed. Their requests became demands; they were pushy and intrusive.

After several days of this, the doctor asked one of the children—a son—when he had last visited his mother before she was admitted to the hospital. He hesitated for a moment and then admitted that he had not seen her for two years.

I'm telling you this story to demonstrate that we can't act like these grown children and throw our elderly away only to feel guilty about them when they are in crisis.

Somehow we have to achieve a balance between our own needs and the needs of our frail and needy parents—one that places reasonable demands on ourselves and on the system that supports the elderly.

Rhetorical Questions

Imagine yourself old and sick, worried that your money will run out and that your family will no longer want you. You feel a pain in your chest. What could it be? You ask yourself whether your daughter will be able to leave work to take you to the hospital—whether your grandchildren will visit you there—whether your medical insurance will cover your bills—whether anyone will care if you live or die.

Imagine asking yourself these questions and then imagine the pain of not knowing the answers. We owe our elderly better than that.

speaker concluded her speech:

> I hope in my case the goat isn't right and that you've enjoyed the films I've written even more than the books on which they were based.

> Thank you for inviting me to speak.

Encourage Thought with a Rhetorical Question

Rhetorical questions encourage thought. At the end of a speech, they leave listeners with a responsibility to think about the questions raised after your speech is over. Your question can be as simple as, "Can our community afford to take the step of hiring fifty new police officers? Perhaps a better question is, can we afford not to?" Rhetorical questions have the power to sway an audience with their emotional impact.

Refer to Your Introduction

In your conclusion, you can refer to an opening story or quotation or answer the rhetorical questions you raised. Here is how Shannon closed her speech on seat belt safety:

> One thing I didn't tell you at the beginning of my speech about my accident was that for years I resisted wearing my belt. I used to fight with my parents. I felt it was such a personal decision. How could they—or the state government, for that matter—dare tell me what to do?

> Thank goodness I had the sense to buckle up that day. And you can be sure that I will never get into a car without wrapping myself securely with my belt of life. I hope that my experience will be enough to convince you to buckle up too.

Like matching bookends, closing your speech with a reference to your introduction provides intellectual and emotional symmetry to your remarks.

▲Ten Common Pitfalls of Conclusions

Knowing what not to do is almost as important as knowing what to do. Here is a list of approaches to avoid during your conclusion.

1. Don't use your conclusion to introduce a new topic.

Develop your main and subordinate points in the body of your speech, not in the conclusion.

2. Don't apologize.

Even if you are unhappy with your performance, do not apologize for your shortcomings when you reach the conclusion. Remarks like, "Well, I guess I didn't have that much to say," or "I'm sorry for taking so much of your time," are unnecessary and usually turn off the audience.

3. Don't end abruptly.

Just because you have made all your points does not mean that your speech is over. Your audience has no way of knowing you are finished unless you provide closure. A one-sentence conclusion is not sufficient closure.

4. Don't change the mood or tone.
If your speech was serious, do not shift moods at the end. A humorous conclusion would be inappropriate and lessen the impact of your speech.

5. Don't use the phrases, "in summary" or "in conclusion," except when you are actually at the end of your speech.
Some speakers use these phrases at various points in their speech, confusing listeners who expect an ending rather than a transition to another point.

Never risk asking, "Any questions?" Think about it, if there are no questions, you will be creating an awkward silence–hardly the climactic conclusion you were hoping for.

6. Don't ask for questions.
Never risk asking, "Any questions?" Think about it, if there are no questions, you will be creating an awkward silence—hardly the climactic conclusion you were hoping for. Also, most speech days in class are designed to have a number of speakers fill the class period. Answering questions or taking comments may interfere with the instructor's schedule.

If there is to be a question and answer session, consider it as a separate event from the speech. Complete your entire conclusion, receive your well-earned applause, and then field any questions.

7. Don't ignore applause.
Graciously accept the praise of your audience by looking around the room and saying thank you.

8. Don't forget to thank your audience and host.
Part of your lasting positive impression will come from a sincere thanks offered to both your audience for their attention and your host for allowing you the opportunity to speak. This is true in many speaking situations, but does not apply to the general public speaking class.

9. Don't run away.
Remember to keep your poise as you confidently make your retreat from the speaking platform. Being in too big a rush to sit down gives the appearance that you are glad it is over. You may be ready to leave, but stifle the urge to flee the podium.

10. Don't read it.
Just as with the introduction, the delivery of the conclusion is very important. Practice it enough that you are not dependent on your speaker's notes. Eye contact with your audience as you wrap up your message will reinforce your perceived credibility as well as your message's importance.

❯SUMMARY

The primacy/recency effect underscores the importance of strong introductions and conclusions. Introductions serve several functions: they focus attention, provide a motive for the audience to listen, build speaker credibility, and preview the topic of your speech.

Several techniques can be used to capture audience attention in the introduction. Among these are startling statements, dramatic stories, quotations, humor, rhetorical questions, illustrations, examples, anecdotes, audience involvement, using personal experiences and visual aids, and making reference to your speaking situation. Your introduction will be successful if you follow established guidelines (such as making it clear and easy to follow), and practicing it as many times as needed, and by avoiding the common pitfalls.

The conclusion of your speech should summarize, motivate, and communicate closure. An effective conclusion reinforces your message, acts as a summary, relates your message to your listeners' lives, and connects your message to a broader context.

Among the techniques you can use to conclude your speech are a call to action, a dramatic story, a closing quotation, a metaphor that broadens meaning, humor, rhetorical questions, and a reference to the introduction.

❯❯ QUESTIONS FOR ANALYSIS

1. What alternatives are available for capturing audience attention in an introduction? What alternatives are available for bringing closure to a speech?

2. What is the relationship between the effectiveness of a speech's introduction and conclusion and speaker credibility?

3. What mistakes do speakers commonly make in preparing the introduction and conclusion of a speech?

4. How do effective introductions and conclusions help meet the psychological needs of the audience?

>> ACTIVITIES

1. Write a thesis statement for a speech, then use different techniques to draft three distinct introductions and conclusions.

2. Examine the transcripts of two speeches in Vital Speeches of the Day, Representative American Speeches, or a similar collection. Analyze and assess the effectiveness of the speeches' introductions and conclusions. Consider the appropriateness of each for the topic, the audience, and the occasion.

3. Prepare a short persuasive speech with two different introductions and conclusions. Then deliver it in both forms to a small group. Ask the group which introduction and conclusion worked best. Find out how the choice influences your speech's specific purpose.

REFERENCES

Baird, Jr., J. E. Summer, 1974. The effects of speech summaries upon audience comprehension of expository speeches of varying quality and complexity. *Central States Speech Journal*, 119–127.

Bogue, E. G. May 7, 1988. A friend of mine: Notes on the gift of teaching, Speech delivered as commencement address, Memphis State University. Reprinted in *Vital speeches of the day*, August 1, 1988, 615.

Hearn, Jr., T. K. June 5, 1988. Sports and ethics: The university response, Speech delivered to the College Football Association, Dallas, TX. Reprinted in *Vital Speeches of the Day*, October 15, 1988, 20.

Jacob, J. E. May 30, 1988. The future of black America: The doomed generation, Speech delivered before the members of Congressional Clearinghouse on the Future. Reprinted in *Vital speeches of the day*, August 1, 1988, 616.

King, Jr., M. L. August 28, 1963, I have a dream, Speech delivered Washington, D.C. Reprinted in Johannesen, R. L., R.R. Allen, and W. A. Linkugel. 1988. *Contemporary American speeches* (6th ed.). Dubuque, IA: Kendall/Hunt Publishing Company.

Noonan, P. 1990. *What I saw at the revolution: A political life in the Reagan era*. New York: Random House.

Oehmen, T. R. 1991. Not a drop to drink, *Winning orations of the interstate oratorical association*. Mankato State University, MN: The Interstate Oratorical Association.

Pankow, P. K. 1991. Hours before I go to sleep, *Winning Orations*, 1991, 123.

Shapiro, L. February 26, 1990. "The Zap Generation," *Newsweek*, 56.

Wood, A. 1992. America's trauma crisis, *Winning orations of the interstate oratorical association*. Mankato State University, MN: The Interstate Oratorical Association.

SHORT ANSWER / SHORT ESSAY

HONOR STATEMENT: I, the undersigned student, hereby declare before God, before the school, and before the professor that I have read Chapter 12 in its entirety, that I have completed the following exercise with help from no other sources, and that I neither have shared nor will share this work with anyone.

Signature: _____   Date: _____

1. An effective introduction should accomplish what four things?

_____

_____

_____

_____

_____

_____

_____

_____

_____

_____

2. When creating an introduction, what guidelines should you follow?

_____

_____

_____

_____

_____

_____

_____

3. When creating a conclusion, what guidelines should you follow?

_____

_____

_____

_____

_____

_____

_____

_____

4. For an informative speech on the topic "one of my favorite places" (identify the place below by name), find a colorful quotation online that would work in an introduction to this topic. Present the quotation verbatim below and be sure, as always, to place it inside quotation marks and to identify who said it and where you got it.

_____

_____

_____

_____

_____

_____

_____

_____

_____

_____

_____

_____

_____

5. For a persuasive speech on a social or cultural problem (identify the problem below by name), come up with an example or illustration that would work well as a captivating introduction to a speech on this topic. Present it below. If you derive the example or illustration from another source, be sure to identify the source.

_____

_____

_____

_____

_____

_____

_____

_____

_____

_____

6. Review the chapter's list of concluding techniques. Then, for a persuasive speech on the same social or cultural problem, choose one of the techniques that you believe would work well in the light of what the chapter says about the purpose of a conclusion section. Present below what you would say in your attempt to practice the technique for this speech.

_____

_____

_____

_____

_____

_____

_____

_____

_____

_____

_____

"Think like a wise man but communicate in the language of the people."
- William Butler Yeatts

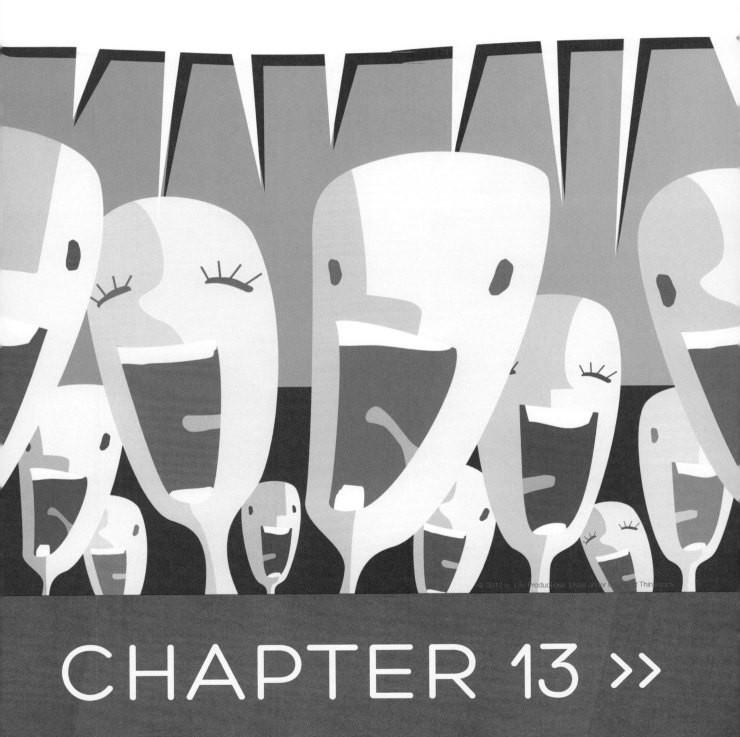

CHAPTER 13 >>

Focus on completing every sentence you start.

13 LANGUAGE, STYLE AND HUMOR

CHARACTERISTICS OF SPOKEN LANGUAGE
- Word Order
- Rhythm
- Signals

GUIDELINES FOR LANGUAGE AND STYLE
- Be Concrete
- Complete Your Thoughts and Sentences
- Use the Active Voice and Follow the Rules of Written English–Most of the Time
- Use Language to Create a Theme
- Use Language That Fits Your Personality and Position
- Vary Language Techniques to Engage Listeners

LANGUAGE PITFALLS
- Long and Unnecessary Words
- Lack of Content, Masking Meaning, or Using Euphemisms
- Jargon, Slang, and Profanity
- Exaggeration and Clichés
- Phrases That Communicate Uncertainty

HUMOR HAS ITS BENEFITS
- Use Humor Only If You Can Be Funny
- Laugh at Yourself, Not at Others
- Understated Anecdotes Can Be Effective
- Find Humor in Your Own Experiences
- Avoid Being NOT Funny

SUMMARY

QUESTIONS FOR ANALYSIS

ACTIVITIES

REFERENCES

How old were you when you realized that your parents were just trying to be helpful when they said, "Sticks and stones may break your bones but words will never hurt you?" We are sure your parents were not intending to mislead you, but we know that while bones mend, words can sting forever. As we write this chapter, Muslims around the world are offended by words the Pope said just recently regarding Islam. Every time a politician speaks, he or she risks losing voters because of word choice. One of your authors still cringes at the memory of her high school principal announcing, "You done good," over the intercom the day after a successful football game. Language matters.

Your language will, in large part, determine the success of your speech. Through words, you create the vivid images that remain in the minds of your audience after your speech is over. Your choice of words and style of language influence your credibility as a speaker. By choosing language that appeals to your audience—by moving your audience intellectually and emotionally through the images of speech—you create a bond that encourages continued listening.

"Ask not what your country can do for you, ask what you can do for your country."

Because speech is slower than silent reading, individual words take on more importance, especially those appearing at the end of the sentence.

In this chapter, we identify characteristics of spoken language and provide guidelines for using spoken language more effectively. We also address pitfalls, aspects of language that a speaker should avoid. Finally, humor is discussed. Although much of the language you use in public speaking will be extemporaneous, it is important to train yourself to think about how words affect your listeners.

❯ CHARACTERISTICS OF SPOKEN LANGUAGE

Having written a paper on a certain topic, using said paper for a speech is expedient. We understand that it certainly saves time and effort. But do not do it. A written report can be used as a speech, but not without major adjustments. The needs of written language and spoken language are different because listeners process information differently from the way readers do. Listen to your instructor speak for a minute. Then imagine what it would be like if that person were reading his remarks from a manuscript; it would be remarkably boring. The spoken and written language differ in many ways, including word order, rhythm, and signals.

▲ Word Order

The first characteristic of spoken language is word order, which relates to the order in which ideas should be arranged in a sentence. In general, the last idea presented is the most powerful. Consider this famous line spoken by John F. Kennedy at his inauguration: "Ask not what your country can do for you, ask what you can do for your country." Inverted, the sentence loses its power: "Ask what you can do for your country, ask not what your country can do for you." Because speech is slower than silent reading, individual words take on more importance, especially those appearing at the end of the sentence.

▲ Rhythm

The second characteristic of spoken language is rhythm. Rhythm in music and poetry distinguishes these genres from others. The rhythm of a piece of music creates different moods. We may want to listen and reflect or dance like a maniac. Rhythm is important in spoken language, also. It is the speech flow or pattern that is created in many ways, including variations in sentence length, the use of parallel structure, and the expression of images in groups of three.

Read aloud Patrick Henry's famous line, "Give me liberty or give me death," to illustrate the importance of rhythm (Tarver 1988):

I know not what course
Others may take.
But as for me,
Give me liberty
Or death.

Now read the original, and notice the greater impact:

I know not what course
Others may take.
But as for me,
Give me liberty
Or give me death.

By taking out one of the repetitive "give me" phrases, the rhythm—and impact—of the sentence changes. As you develop your speech, consider the following ways you can use rhythm to reinforce your ideas and to maintain audience attention.

Vary sentence length. First, create rhythm by varying sentence length. The rhythm of speech is affected by how well you combine sentences of varying lengths. Long sentences can be confusing and short sentences boring, but a combination of long and short sentences adds rhythmic interest. On June 1, 1997, Mary Schmich, columnist for *The Chicago Tribune*, wrote an essay, described as a commencement speech, called, "Wear Sunscreen." Rhythm is a critical element of her speech, as can be seen in the following excerpt:

Wear sunscreen. If I could offer you only one tip for the future, sunscreen would be it…Don't worry about the future.

Schmich continues her speech by discussing all the things in life that are "wasted" on those who are young, and how the things that people typically concern themselves with are never the things that ultimately end up happening. The back-and-forth rhythm of her words holds your attention as you move along with her message.

Schmich's commencement speech is filled with humor and advice, but its impact is due, in part, to the variation in sentence structure. As you probably noticed, the rhythm of this speech was engaging; so much so that two song versions were developed, one by Baz Luhrmann, "Everybody's Free (to Wear Sunscreen)" and one by John Safran, "Not the Sunscreen Song."

" …Give me liberty

Or give me death."

A good introduction can help you set an appropriate tone for your speech.

Use parallel structure. Second, create rhythm by using parallel structure. Parallelism involves the arrangement of a series of words, phrases, or sentences in a similar form. In his inaugural speech, President John F. Kennedy stated, "If a free society cannot help the many who are poor, it cannot save the few who are rich." Also using parallel structure, in his first inaugural speech, President Richard M. Nixon stated, "Where peace is unknown, make it welcome; where peace is fragile, make it strong; where peace is temporary, make it permanent" (Detz 1984, 69). Parallel structure emphasizes the rhythm of speech. When used effectively, it adds harmony and balance to a speech that can verge on the poetic.

© 2012 Pattie Steib / Shutterstock.com. Used under license of Shutterstock.

President Richard M. Nixon used parallel structure in his language to make his inaugural speech memorable.

Use three as a magic number. (Detz 1984, 67–68) Third (yes, we intentionally provided three points!), rhythm can be created by referring to ideas in groups of three. Winston Churchill once said, "If you have an important point to make, don't try to be subtle or clever. Use a pile driver. Hit the point once. Then come back and hit it again. Then hit it a third time—a tremendous whack." Experienced speakers know that saying things three times gets their point across in a way saying it once cannot—not simply because of repetition, but because of the rhythmic effect of the repetition. Many presidents use this device during important speeches. You can hear the emotional impact of Abraham Lincoln's words in his Gettysburg address when he said, "We can not dedicate, we can not consecrate, we can not hallow this ground." Franklin Roosevelt's words created an impact during his second inaugural address when he observed, "I see one-third of a nation, ill-housed, ill-clad, ill-nourished." In his speech "The American Promise" given to Congress in 1965, Lyndon B. Johnson included the following line: "Our mission is at once the oldest and the most basic of this country: to right wrong, to do justice, to serve man" (Detz 1984, 68–69).

Try this device in your classroom speeches. In a speech of tribute, you might say, "I am here to honor, to praise, and to congratulate the members of the campus volunteer fire department."

▲Signals
A third specific characteristic of spoken language involves using signals. You may reread an important passage in a book to appreciate its meaning, but your audience hears your message only once—a fact that may make it necessary to signal critical passages in your speech. The following signals tell your listeners to pay close attention:

- This cannot be overemphasized…
- Let me get to the heart of the matter…
- I want to summarize…
- My five main points are…

Although all speakers hope to capture and hold listeners' attention throughout their speech, you must draw people back to your message at critical points. Signals are more necessary in spoken language than in print.

❯❯ GUIDELINES FOR LANGUAGE AND STYLE

As you strive to be precise, clear, and understandable, keep in mind the difference between denotative and connotative definitions. A dictionary provides the literal, objective, denotative definition of the word. Connotation is the meaning we apply to words as they are framed by our personal experiences. These often lie in the realm of our subjective, emotional responses. For example, the American flag can be described denotatively by its color and design, but connotatively, the meaning varies around the world. Americans, in general, see the flag as a symbol of freedom and democracy, whereas other cultures may view our flag as a symbol of greed and hegemony. Whether the audience favors or disfavors your view, you should ensure that they understand what you mean and what you believe to be the facts that support your ideas. This next section provides six guidelines for effective use of language.

▲ Be Concrete

On a continuum, words range from the most concrete to the most abstract. Concrete language is rooted in real-life experience—things we see, hear, taste, touch, and feel—while abstract language tells us little about what we experience, relying instead on more symbolic references. Compare the following:

Abstract	*Concrete*
Bad weather	Hail the size of golf balls
Nervousness	Trembling hands; knocking knees
An interesting professor	When she started throwing paper airplanes around the room to teach us how air currents affect lift, I knew she was a winner.

Concrete words and phrases create pictures in listeners' minds and can turn a "ho-hum" speech into one that captures listener attention. Winston Churchill understood this premise when he said, during World War II, "We shall fight them on the beaches," instead of "Hostilities will be engaged on the coastal perimeter" (Kleinfeld 1990).Consider the differences between these two paragraphs:

Version 1
On-the-job accidents take thousands of lives a year. Particularly hard hit are agricultural workers who suffer approximately 1,500 deaths and 140,000 disabling injuries a year. One-fifth of all agricultural fatalities are children. These statistics make us wonder how safe farms are.

Version 2
Farmers who want to get their children interested in agriculture often take them on tractors for a ride. About 150 children are killed each year when they fall off tractors and are crushed underneath. These children represent about half the children killed in farm accidents each year—a statistic that tells us that farms can be deadly. About 1,500 people die each year on farms, and an additional 140,000 are injured seriously enough so they can no longer work.

In Version 2 the images and language are more concrete. Instead of wondering "how safe farms are," Version 2 declares that "farms can be deadly." Instead of talking about "disabling injuries," it tells us that workers "are injured seriously enough so they can no longer work." More concrete language produces an emotional response in listeners that is likely to stay with them long after a speech is over.

▲Complete Your Thoughts and Sentences

Focus on completing every sentence you start. This may seem like common sense, but many people do not follow this advice when speaking before groups. Although we accept the fact that many sentences trail off in conversational speech, we lose confidence in a speaker who has this habit. From the mouth of a public speaker, this language is disconcerting:

> In many states, your signature on your driver's license makes you a potential organ donor. If you are killed… . According to the laws in these states, if you are killed in an auto accident, the state has the right… . Your organs can be used to help people in need of organ transplants. There are sick people out there who need the kidneys, corneas, and even the hearts of people killed. Think about it. When you are dead, you can still give the gift of life.

On the other hand, we encourage you to violate this rule by incorporating sentence fragments, where relevant. Keep in mind that carefully chosen sentence fragments can contribute to clear communication. Here is an example:

> Is Christmas too commercial? Well, maybe. It wasn't that long ago when the holiday season began after Thanksgiving. Now the first Christmas catalogs reach shoppers in September. Before summer is over. Before the temperature has dropped below 90 degrees. Even before Labor Day.

Do not confuse sentence fragments with the incomplete thoughts and sentences we discussed earlier. In the case above, the fragments are intentional and are used effectively to enhance meaning.

▲Use the Active Voice and Follow the Rules of Written English—Most of the Time

Rules of grammar and style operate for the spoken language as well as the written language. One rule to follow involves using the active voice. A direct speaking style involves the use of the active rather than passive voice as often as possible. The following example demonstrates the difference between the passive and active voice:

Version 1: Passive voice
Students in an English class at Long Beach Community College were asked by their teacher to stand in line. After a few minutes, the line was broken by a student from Japan who walked a few yards away. The behavior demonstrated by the student shows how cultural differences can affect even the simple act of waiting in line. In this case, the need for greater personal space was felt by the student who considered it impolite to stand so close.

Version 2: Active voice
An English teacher at Long Beach Community College asked the class to stand in line. After a few minutes, a Japanese student broke the line and walked a few yards away. The student's behavior demonstrated how cultural differences affect even the simple act of waiting in line. In this case, the student felt the need for more personal space because the Japanese culture considers it impolite to stand so close.

The same sentences rephrased in the active voice show the subject of the sentence in action. In addition to using fewer words, the active voice is more direct, easier to follow, and more vigorous. We encourage the use of the active voice.

▲Use Language to Create a Theme

A key word or phrase can reappear throughout your speech to reinforce your theme. Each time the image is repeated, it becomes more powerful and is likely to stay with your listeners after your speech is over. The chairman of a real estate investment company developed the "Amber Light Theory of Real Estate Investment" and used this metaphor as the theme of his speeches. His point was that the real estate market rarely gives investors strong signals to proceed or stop. Instead, its signal is always one of caution. By referring to the amber light image several times in his speech, the speaker delivered a message that was effective and memorable (Berg and Gilman 1989).

▲Use Language That Fits Your Personality and Position

If you are delivering a speech on advances in microsurgery, a casual, flippant tone is inappropriate, though it might work for a speech on naming the family dog. Audiences are perceptive. They know very quickly whether you are comfortable with your speaking style or whether you are trying to be something or someone you are not. It is hard to fake an emotional presentation if you are a cool, nonemotional person. If you are naturally restrained, it is difficult to appear daring and impulsive. The language you choose mirrors who you are, so choose carefully to reflect what you want others to know about you.

▲Vary Language Techniques to Engage Listeners

A carpenter uses a saw, a hammer, and nails to construct a building. A speaker uses language to construct a speech. Words are literally the tools of a speaker's trade. When used effectively, they can move an audience to action or to tears. They can change minds or cement opinions. Words can create a bond between you and your listeners or they can destroy a relationship. A speaker has numerous tools to choose from when building a speech.

When constructing your speech, consider using a variety of language techniques to enhance imagery. Imagery involves creating a vivid description through the use of one or more of our five senses. Using imagery can create a great impact and lasting memory. Mental images can be created using many devices, including metaphors, similes, and figures of speech.

Metaphors

Metaphors state that something is something else. Through metaphors we can understand and experience one idea in terms of another. For example, if you ask a friend how a test went, and the friend responded, "I scored a home run," you would know that your friend felt good about the test. In his "Sinews of Peace" speech to Westminster College in Fulton, Missouri, Prime Minister Winston Churchill used the following metaphor on March 5, 1946: "An iron curtain has descended across the continent." During his inaugural address, President Bill Clinton said, "Our democracy must not only be the envy of the world but also the engine of our own renewal."

Similes

Similes also create images as they compare the characteristics of two different things using the words "like" or "as." Here are two examples Ann Beattie uses in her novel, Picturing Will: "Falling snow looked as solid as pearls. Tar could look like satin"; and "Wayne reacted like someone whose cat has proudly brought home a dead mouse." (Beattie 1989) Both metaphors and similes rely on concrete images. Although these can enliven your speech, guard against using images that are trite or too familiar.

Figures of Speech

Figures of speech connect sentences by emphasizing the relationship among ideas and by repeating key sounds to establish a pleasing rhythm. Among the most popular figures of speech are anaphora, epistrophe, alliteration, and antithesis.

Anaphora. Anaphora is the repetition of the same word or phrase at the beginning of successive clauses or sentences. In the following example, Georgie Anne Geyer (1989), foreign correspondent and syndicated columnist, uses this technique as she addresses students at Saint Mary-of-the-Woods College in Indiana.

> There is only one thing that I know to tell you graduates—only one thing—and that is to follow what you love! Follow it intellectually! Follow it sensuously! Follow it with generosity and nobility toward your fellow man! Don't deign to ask what "they" are looking for out there. Ask what you have inside.

Epistrophe. Epistrophe is the repetition of a word or expression at the end of phrases, clauses, or sentences. Lincoln used this device in the phrase, "of the people, by the people, for the people." It is an effective technique for emphasis.

Alliteration. Alliteration is the repetition of the initial consonant or initial sounds in series of words. Tongue twisters such as "Peter Piper picked a peck of pickled peppers" are based on alliteration. With "Peter Piper," the "P" sound is repeated multiple times. Alliteration can be used effectively in speeches, such as in Martin Luther King's 1963 "I have a dream"

Float like a

Sting like a

© 2012 Andrii Muzyka.
© 2012 Dietmar Hoepfl.
Used under license of Shutterstock.

Similes also create images as they compare the characteristics of two different things using the words "like" or "as."

SAMUEL LANGHORNE CLEMENS
From a Late Photograph

© 2012 by iStockphoto
Used under license of Thinkstock.

I never write *metropolis* for seven cents because I can get the same price for *city*. I never write *policeman* because I can get the same price for *cop*.
- Mark Twain

speech when he said, "We have come to our nation's capital to cash a check." Alliteration occurs with the repetition of "C" in "Capital to cash a check."

Antithesis. Antithesis is the use of contrast, within a parallel grammatical structure, to make a rhetorical point. Jesse Jackson told an audience of young African Americans: "We cannot be what we ought to be if we push dope in our veins, rather than hope in our brains." Later, in the same speech, he told his listeners, "You are not a man because you can kill somebody. You are a man because you can heal somebody" (Gustainis 1987, 218.)

❯❯ LANGUAGE PITFALLS

Although your speaking style—the distinctive manner in which you speak to produce the effect you desire—like your style of dress, is personal, it is important to realize that some aspects of styles enhance communication while others detract. You may have a great sense of humor, but some may be put off by your lack of seriousness. You may be very bright and reflective, but your quiet tone may bore your audience. You have read several language guidelines for creating an effective speech. Following are five language pitfalls to avoid.

▲ Long and Unnecessary Words

Using long and unnecessary words violates the first principle of language usage, which is to be simple and concrete. As noted earlier, when you read on your own, you have the opportunity to reread something or to look up a word you do not understand. In a speech, you do not have the rewind option, and if the audience does not understand, they will lose interest.

When Mark Twain wrote popular fiction, he was often paid by the word, a fee schedule that led him to this humorous observation:

> By hard, honest labor, I've dug all the large words out of my vocabulary … I never write metropolis for seven cents because I can get the same price for city. I never write *policeman* because I can get the same price for *cop*.

The best speakers realize that attempting to impress an audience by using four- or five-syllable words usually backfires. When Franklin D. Roosevelt was given this sentence by a speechwriter—"We are endeavoring to construct a more inclusive society"—he simplified it to this: "We are going to make a country in which no one is left out" (Detz 1984, 50–53).

Here are a few multisyllabic words and their simpler alternatives.

Words to Impress	*Words to Communicate*
Periodical	Magazine
Utilize	Use
Reiterate	Repeat
Commence	Begin
Discourse	Talk

Unnecessary words can be as problematic as long words. Spoken language requires some redundancy, but when people are forced to listen to a barrage of unnecessary words, they find it difficult to tell the difference between the important and the trivial. When the listening process becomes too difficult, they stop paying attention. Here is an example of unfocused rambling:

> Let me tell you what I did on my summer vacation. I drove down to Memphis in my car to take part in the dozens of memorial ceremonies marking the anniversary of the death of Elvis Presley. There were about 40,000 or 50,000 other people at the ceremony along with me.

> I took a tour of the mansion Elvis lived in before his death, known as Graceland, and I visited the new museum dedicated solely to his cars. The museum holds twenty different vehicles, including the favorite of Elvis's mother: a pink 1955 Cadillac Fleetwood.

Here is something less verbose:

> During summer vacation, I drove to Memphis to celebrate the anniversary of Elvis Presley's death. With about 40,000 or 50,000 other people, I toured Graceland, Elvis' home, and visited the museum dedicated to his twenty vehicles, including his mother's favorite, a pink 1955 Cadillac Fleetwood.

Not only does the second version eliminate almost half of the words, it also sharpens the message and helps listeners focus on the important points.

▲Lack of Content, Masking Meaning, or Using Euphemisms

As a speaker, you want to be clear and to provide something meaningful for your audience. You want to avoid sentences that lack content, mask meaning, or include euphemisms. Sentences that say nothing or, worse yet, mask meaning or use euphemisms damage a speaker's credibility. Listeners wonder what to believe, and begin to question the speaker's competence. By the time listeners start asking these questions, the speech has almost certainly failed.

Speech tension, lack of preparation, or ill-intentions can cause or contribute to this language pitfall. If you do not know as much as you should about your topic or if you are trying not to reveal your intentions, you may fall into this language trap.

Language that masks or muddies rather than clarifies meaning is the downfall of many speakers. Former Secretary of State Alexander Haig combined the language of the military with the language of diplomacy to create phrases like these:

Franklin D. Roosevelt simplified his language to make his message more accessible.

saddle myself with a statistical fence
caveat my response
epistemologicallywise
careful caution
definitizing an answer (Rackleff 1987, 312)

Although few speakers go as far as Haig in using incomprehensible language, we do find speakers using euphemisms, which are words or phrases substituted for more direct language. Consider, for instance, the number of ways corporate spokespersons refer to firing employees:

Euphemism: We are engaged in downsizing our operation.
Meaning: We are firing 5,000 employees.

Euphemism: We are offering employees over the age of fifty-five early retirement.
Meaning: If these older employees don't accept the deal, we'll fire them.

Euphemism: We are suggesting a career redirection.
Meaning: You no longer have a job here, so we suggest you find another type of work.

Although euphemisms like these serve a purpose (they make it easier for speakers to deal with unpleasant topics), they can make it difficult, sometimes impossible, for listeners to understand what is being said.

▲Jargon, Slang, and Profanity

Jargon is the technical terminology unique to a special activity or group. For example, the jargon of the publishing business includes such terms as "specs," "page proofs," "dummy stage," and ``halftones." Although these terms are not five syllables long, they are difficult to understand if you are unfamiliar with publishing.

A special kind of jargon involves the use of acronyms—the alphabet soup of an organization or profession. Instead of saturating your speech with references to the FDA, PACs, or ACLI on the assumption that everyone knows what the acronyms mean, define these abbreviations the first time they are used. Tell your listeners that the FDA refers to the Food and Drug Administration; PACs, political action committees; and the ACLI, the American Council of Life Insurance.

Jargon can be used effectively when you are sure that everyone in your audience understands the reference. Therefore, if you are the editor-in-chief of a publishing company addressing your editorial and production staffs, publishing jargon requires no definition. However, if you deliver a speech about the publishing business to a group of college seniors, definitions are needed.

SPECS
page proofs
dummy stage
halftones

Jargon can be used effectively when you are sure that everyone in your audience understands the reference.

Listeners almost always expect a degree of decorum in a formal speech, requiring that certain language be avoided. Profanity, of course, is the most obvious offender, but using the vernacular or slang can also be inappropriate. Terms like "ain't," and "you guys" should be used only for specific effect. In public discourse, they can violate an audience's sense of appropriateness—or propriety.

▲Exaggeration and Clichés

Exaggerations are statements made to impress, not aiming for accuracy. Instead of telling your classmates that you "always" exercise an hour a day, tell them that you exercise an hour a day "as often" as you can. Some of your classmates may know you well enough to realize that "always" is a stretching the truth. Instead of saying that you would "never" consider double parking, tell your listeners that you would consider it "only as a last resort in an emergency." Obvious exaggerations diminish your credibility as a speaker.

Clichés, according to communication professors Eugene Ehrlich and Gene R. Hawes (1984), are the "enemies of lively speech." They explain:

> They are deadwood: the shiny suits of your word wardrobe, the torn sandals, the frayed collars, the scuffed shoes, the bobby socks, the fur pieces, the Nehru jackets, the miniskirts—yesterday's chewing gum (48).

Clichés can lull your listeners into a state of boredom as they suggest that both your vocabulary and imagination are limited. Here is a section of a speech filled with slang and clichés, which have been emboldened:

> Two years ago, the real estate market was weak. At that point in time I would guesstimate that there were 400 more houses on the market than there are today. For us, it was time to hustle. We toughed it out and held onto the ball. The game plan we should follow from now on is to convince potential buyers that we have a good thing going in this community—good schools, good libraries, a good transportation system. We should also convince them that we're a community with a heart. We're here to help each other when we're down and out.

Imagine listening to this entire speech. Even if the speaker has something valuable to say, it is virtually impossible to hear it through the clichés. Clichés are unimaginative and add unnecessary words to your speech.

▲Phrases That Communicate Uncertainty

Speakers should avoid phrases that communicate uncertainty. Language can communicate a sense of mastery of your subject, or it can communicate uncertainty. Compare the following paragraphs:

Version 1
It seems to me that too many students choose a career solely on the basis of how much they are likely to earn. In my estimation, they forget that they also have to enjoy what they are going to spend the rest of their work lives doing.

Version 2

Too many students choose a career solely on the basis of how much they are likely to earn. They forget that they also have to enjoy what they are going to spend the rest of their work lives doing.

Version 1 contains weakening phrases: "it seems to me" and "in my estimation," which add nothing but uncertainty to the speaker's message. If you have a position, state it directly without crutch words that signal your timidity to the audience.

❯ HUMOR HAS ITS BENEFITS

Nothing brings you closer to your audience than humor. Humor reveals your human side, it relaxes listeners and makes them respond positively. Through a properly placed anecdote, you let your audience know that you are not taking yourself—or your subject—too seriously. Even in a serious speech, humor can be an effective tool to emphasize an important point.

Research has shown the favorable impact humor can have on an audience. In particular, humor accomplishes two things. First, according to Charles R. Gruner (1985), a communication professor and recognized expert on the use of humor in public speaking, when appropriate humor is used in informative speaking, the humor enhances the speaker's image by improving the audience's perception of the speaker's character. Second, research has also shown that humor can make a speech more memorable over a longer period of time. In one study, two groups of subjects were asked to recall lectures they heard six weeks earlier. The group who heard the lecture presented humorously had higher recall than the group who heard the same lecture delivered without humor (Kaplan and Pascoe 1977).

In another experiment, students who took a statistics course given by an instructor who used humor in class lectures scored fifteen percent higher on objective exams than did students who were taught the same material by an instructor who did not (Ziv 1982).

Humor works only if it is carefully used and only if it is connected to the theme of your speech. Here are five guidelines for the effective use of humor in a speech.

▲ Use Humor Only If You Can Be Funny

Some speakers do not know how to be funny in front of an audience. On a one-on-one basis they may be funny, but in front of a group, their humor vanishes. They stumble over punch lines and their timing is bad. These people should limit themselves to serious speeches or "safe" humor. For example, former Maine senator Ed Muskie made his audience laugh by describing the shortest will in Maine legal history—a will that was only ten words long: "Being of sound mind and memory, I spent it all" (Rackleff 1987, 313).

▲ Laugh at Yourself, Not at Others

Former California governor George Deukmajian sometimes used the following line to break the ice with his audience:

I understand that you have been searching for a speaker who can dazzle you with his charm, wit, and personality. I'm pleased to be filling in while the search continues (Robinson 1989, 68).

Research has shown that speakers who make themselves the object of their own humor often endear themselves to their listeners. In one study, students heard brief speeches from a "psychologist" and an "economist," both of whom explained the benefits of their professions. While half the speeches were read with mildly self-deprecating humor directed at the profession being discussed, the other half were read without humor. Students rated the speakers with the self-deprecating humor higher on a scale of "wittiness" and "sense of humor," and no damage was done to the perceived character or authoritativeness of the speaker (Chang and Gruner 1981).

It can be effective to tell a joke at your own expense, but it is in poor taste to tell a joke at the expense of others. Racial, ethnic, or sexist jokes are rarely acceptable, nor are jokes that poke fun at the personal characteristics of others. Although stand-up comics like Dane Cook, Jeff Foxworthy, and Chris Rock may get away with such humor, public speakers cannot.

▲Understated Anecdotes Can Be Effective

An economist speaking before a group of peers starts with the following anecdote:

I am constantly reminded by those who use our services that we often turn out a ton of material on the subject but we do not always give our clients something of value. A balloonist high above the earth found his balloon leaking and managed to land on the edge of a green pasture. He saw a man in a business suit approaching, and very happily said: "How good it is to see you. Could you tell me where I am?"

The well-dressed man replied: "You are standing in a wicker basket in the middle of a pasture." "Well," said the balloonist, "You must be an economist." The man was startled. "Yes, I am, but how did you know that?"

"That's easy," said the balloonist, "because the information you gave me was very accurate—and absolutely useless"(Valenti 1982, 80–81).

This anecdote is funny in an understated way. It works because it is relevant to the audience. Its humor comes from the recognition that the speaker knows—and shares—the foibles of the audience.

▲Find Humor in Your Own Experiences

The best humor comes from your own experiences. In general, avoid books of jokes and stories from the Internet. Humor is all around you. You might want to start now to record humorous stories for your speeches so that you will have material when the need arises. If you decide to use someone else's material, you have the ethical responsibility to give the source credit. You might start with, "As Jerry Seinfeld would say…"This gives appropriate source citation and makes clear that line or story is meant as a joke. Usually you will get bigger laughs by citing their names than if you tried to convince your audience that the humor was original.

▲Avoid Being NOT Funny

We use the double negative to make a point. When humor works and the audience responds with a spontaneous burst of applause or laughter, there is little that will make you feel better—or more relaxed—as a speaker. Its effect is almost magical. However, when the humor is distasteful to the audience or highly inappropriate, a speaker may find no one is laughing. On April 30, 2006, Stephen Colbert of *The Colbert Report* spoke at the White House Correspondents' Association dinner where the President was in attendance. Although his speech became the number one download on iTunes, he received a very lukewarm reception during his speech because of his critique of the President, which included the following:

> The greatest thing about this man is he's steady. You know where he stands. He believes the same thing Wednesday that he believed on Monday, no matter what happened Tuesday. Events can change, this man's beliefs never will.

It is important to keep in mind that humor is criticism. We laugh at things people do, what they say, how they react, and so on.

Although the few liberals in attendance may have found this humorous, most of those assembled did not. As a result, for the 2007 White House Correspondents Association dinner, Rich Little, a comedian who rose to fame in the 1970s with his Richard Nixon impression, was the after-dinner entertainment. His tamer, less edgy speech was well-received.

It is important to keep in mind that humor is criticism. We laugh at things people do, what they say, how they react, and so on. In fulfilling our ethical responsibilities, however, we need to remember that while someone or some event is being mocked, the speaker needs to do so with taste and appropriateness.

So, to avoid being not funny, audience analysis is vital. As a beginning public speaker, we urge you to err on the side of caution. It is better to avoid humor than to fail at it. While most humor is risky, there are certain things you can be fairly sure your audience will find funny. Stick with those, and try riskier humor as you gain confidence and experience. You might also check with a friend or classmate if you have any question about the humor of a line or story.

❯❯SUMMARY

Spoken language differs from written language in several important ways. In many cases, spoken language requires redundancy; it affects the order of ideas, and requires that the speaker pay attention to rhythm. Spoken language may also require that you signal your audience before you present important material.

The most effective language is simple, clear, and direct. Use short, common words instead of long, unusual ones; avoid euphemisms and jargon; eliminate unnecessary words that pad your speech; be direct and concrete and avoid exaggeration. To improve your speaking style, avoid clichés, complete your thoughts, and use sentence fragments for specific effect. Avoid profanity, slang, and jargon, as well as sentences that say nothing. Because certain phrases communicate uncertainty, avoid using them during your presentation.

Try to engage the imagination of your listeners through the use of metaphors and similes that paint memorable word pictures. Use language to create a theme. Regardless of the choices you make, be certain your language fits your personality, position, and the needs of your audience. The effective use of humor requires that you have confidence in your ability to make people laugh. Do not use humor if you have never been funny. Laugh at yourself, not others. Use understated anecdotes. And remember, humor is everywhere. Find humor in your own experiences. Seriously!

 QUESTIONS FOR ANALYSIS

1. How is spoken language different from written language?

2. How can language contribute to or detract from the effectiveness of your speech?

3. Why must language fit the needs of the speaker, audience, occasion, and message?

4. What do you need to consider when choosing proper language in a speech?

5. What language techniques can you employ when you speak?

6. What are some of the language pitfalls that reduce the effectiveness of your speech?

7. Why is humor important in public speaking?

8. How does humor affect the speaker-audience relationship?

>> ACTIVITIES

1. Read aloud a written report you wrote for another class, then analyze whether the report's language is appropriate as a speech. Analyze the changes necessary to transform the report into an effective oral presentation.

2. Select a speech from Vital Speeches of the Day or from another collection in your library. Study the language of the speech and write an assessment of its effectiveness, strengths, and weaknesses. Because the language was intended to be spoken, you might have to read the speech aloud during your evaluation.

3. Begin collecting humorous ideas, stories, and incidents for your next speech. As you develop your ideas, blend the humor into the speech, remembering to practice your delivery with a tape recorder.

REFERENCES

Beattie, A. 1989. *Picturing will.* New York: Bantam Books.

Berg, K., and A. Gilman. 1989. *Get to the point: How to say what you mean and get what you want.* New York: Random House.

Chang, M. and C. R. Gruner. 1981. Audience reaction to self-disparaging humor. *Southern Speech Communication Journal,* 46: 419–26. Reported in Gruner, Advice to the beginning speaker, 142–47. (Listed below.)

Detz, J. 1984. *How to write and give a speech.* New York: St. Martin's Press.

Ehrlich, E., and G. R. Hawes. 1984. *Speak for success.* New York: Bantam Books.

Geyer, G. A. May 7, 1989. Joy in our times: I am responsible for my own fight. Speech delivered as commencement address at Saint Mary-of-the-Woods College. Reprinted in *Vital Speeches of the Day,* August 15, 1989, 668.

Gruner, C. R. April, 1985. Advice to the beginning speaker on using humor—What the research tells us. *Communication Education* 34:142.

Gustainis, J. J. 1987. Jesse Louis Jackson, in B. K. Duffy and H. R. Ryan, Eds., *American orators of the twentieth century: Critical studies and sources.* New York: Greenwood Press.

Kaplan, R. M., and G. C. Pascoe. 1977. Humorous lectures and humorous examples: Some effects upon comprehension and retentions. *Journal of Educational Psychology,* 69: 61–65.

Kleinfeld, N. R. March 11, 1990. "Teaching the 'Sir Winston' method," *New York Times,* 7.

Rackleff, R. B. September 26, 1987. The art of speech writing: A dramatic event. Speech delivered to the National Association of Bar Executives Section on Communication and Public Relations. Reprinted in *Vital Speeches of the Day,* March 1, 1988.

Robinson, J. W. 1989. *Better speeches in ten simple steps.* Rocklin, CA: Prima Publishing and Communications.

Schmich, M. June 1, 1997. Advice, like youth, probably just wasted on the young. *Chicago Tribune.* Retrieved June 10, 2007 on www.chicagotribune.com.

Tarver, J. March 2, 1988. Words in time: Some reflections on the language of speech. Speech delivered to the Chicago Speech Writer's Forum. Reprinted in *Vital Speeches of the Day*, April 15, 1988, 410–12.

Valenti, J. 1982. *Speak up with confidence*. New York: William Morrow and Company, Inc.

Ziv, A. 1982. Cognitive results of using humor in teaching. Paper presented at the Third International Conference on Humor, Washington, D. C. Cited in Gruner, Advice to the beginning speaker, 144. (Listed above.)

SHORT ANSWER / SHORT ESSAY

HONOR STATEMENT: I, the undersigned student, hereby declare before God, before the school, and before the professor that I have read Chapter 13 in its entirety, that I have completed the following exercise with help from no other sources, and that I neither have shared nor will share this work with anyone.

Signature: _____ Date: _____

1. How is spoken language different from written language?

_____

_____

_____

_____

_____

_____

_____

2. How can language contribute to or detract from the effectiveness of your speech?

_____

_____

_____

_____

_____

_____

_____

3. What is the difference between connotative and denotative meanings? Give an example to illustrate these differences.

_____

_____

_____

_____

_____

_____

_____

4. What are the six guidelines to consider when developing the language of your speech?

_____

_____

_____

_____

_____

_____

_____

_____

_____

_____

_____

_____

_____

_____

5. What is the difference between anaphora and epistrophe?

_____

_____

_____

_____

_____

_____

_____

6. What is the difference between alliteration and antithesis?

_____

_____

_____

_____

_____

_____

_____

7. What are the five pitfalls to avoid when developing the language of your speech?

_____

_____

_____

_____

_____

_____

8. Humor can be used effectively in a speech. What should you keep in mind if you decide to use humor?

_____

_____

_____

_____

_____

_____

_____

_____

_____

_____

_____

_____

_____

_____

Your ability to communicate information, persuade, and entertain is influenced by the manner in which you present yourself to your audience.

CHAPTER 14 >>

14 DELIVERY

Adapted from *Public Speaking: Choices for Effective Results, Fifth Edition* by John Makay et al. Copyright © 2008.
Reprinted with permission of Kendall Hunt Publishing Co.

What do you remember after a speaker is finished? Although you may walk away with the speaker's ideas buzzing through your mind, it is often the quality of the performance that remains with you long after you have forgotten the content of the message. That is to say, the how of public speaking—the speaker's style of delivery—often makes the most lasting impression.

Words alone are not enough to make audiences want to listen to a speech. Many brilliant people—scientists, lawyers, politicians, engineers, environmentalists—never connect with their listeners, not for lack of trying, but for problems with the delivery of their speech. Maybe they are too stiff or appear uninvolved. Worse, they may try to imitate other speakers and be something they are not.

Delivery affects your credibility as a speaker. Your ability to communicate information, persuade, and entertain is influenced by the manner in which you present yourself to your audience. An effective delivery works for you, an ineffective delivery against you—even when the content of your message is strong.

© 2012 by Gelpi.
Used under license of Thinkstock.

While memorization is often unnecessary, there are times when memorizing your speech is preferable.

❯❯METHODS OF DELIVERY

The following section identifies four different methods of delivery. You may find comfort in one style more than the other, but hopefully, you will have an opportunity to explore different methods of delivery during your public speaking course. Each of the four methods is appropriate in certain situations. As a speaker, you need to be aware of your audience and the occasion when choosing the method of delivery that is most appropriate and effective. Performance guidelines accompany each method of delivery. These are aspects to consider as you plan to deliver the speech. Your four choices are to memorize your speech, speak from a manuscript, use carefully prepared notes and speak extemporaneously, or give an impromptu, spur-of-the-moment speech.

▲Memorization

It is every speaker's nightmare: You are in the middle of a ten-minute speech and you cannot remember the next word. Because you memorized the speech (or so you thought), you have no note cards to help you through the crisis. This nightmare becomes reality on a regular basis in public speaking classes. Nervous students who have memorized their speeches find themselves without a clue as to what to say next. Even those who spend hours preparing for the presentation may forget everything when facing an audience. This situation is made worse if you are part of a group presentation because other people depend on you.

While memorization is unnecessary in many situations, there are times when having your speech memorized is preferable. For example, when you know you will be receiving an award or recognition, memorization may be a useful delivery tool. Special occasions, such as toasting the bride and groom or delivering a brief commencement address, are also opportunities for delivering a memorized speech. Memorization enables you to write the exact words you will speak without being forced to read them. It also makes it easier to establish eye contact with your audience and to deliver your speech skillfully. If you find yourself in a situation where memorization is necessary, consider the following four performance guidelines.

Start memorizing the speech as soon as possible. You do not want to delay the process so that you are under a severe time constraint. (Such as the night before!) Make sure you have ample time to work on the memorization aspect of your delivery. Even experienced professional speakers have to work hard to remember their lines.

Memorize small sections of your speech at a time. Do not allow yourself to become overwhelmed with the task. Memorizing small sections of your speech at a time will help minimize the chance that you will forget your speech during the delivery. Remember that some people can memorize speeches more easily than others, so work at your own pace and do not compare yourself to the classmate who memorized her speech in a very short period of time.

Memorize small sections of your speech at a time.

Determine where you need pauses, emphasis, and vocal variety. You want to convey the appropriate tone for your speech—enthusiasm, excitement, anger, bewilderment. You can achieve this by emphasizing certain words, speaking faster or more slowly, and increasing or lowering your volume and/or pitch. More about vocal aspects of delivery will be discussed shortly.

Avoid looking like you are trying to remember the speech. As instructors, sometimes we feel as though we can see the speaker trying to remember the words, as though the speaker has a disk in his/her head, and he/she is trying to access the right file. The speaker might look up, look to the side, or simply look pensive as he/she tries to "retrieve" the information.

Overall, delivering a memorized speech can be very effective, but it is also a gamble. In addition to the actual task of memorization, students need to make sure they work on vocal variety, so they can connect with their audience. For the student in the basic public speaking class, a memorized speech is seldom what an instructor wants to hear.

▲Using a Manuscript

Manuscript reading involves writing your speech out word for word and then reading it. A manuscript speech may be considered in formal occasions when the speech is distributed beforehand or if it is archived. Many presidential speeches are manuscript speeches. The president is expected to follow a teleprompter, which is frequently used. On occasion, scholars give speeches that are then printed in the "proceedings" of a conference. On other occasions, the speaker may be addressing an international conference, and the manuscript is translated into one or more languages. Having a manuscript speech minimizes the temptation to add remarks during the speech.

If an issue or occasion is controversial or sensitive, a speaker may choose to rely on a manuscript. Having a carefully crafted statement may help avoid misstating a position. You may also choose to read from a manuscript when addressing a hostile audience because you know your listeners are ready—and waiting—to attack your statement. You want to be sure your communication is exact.

For those who are not professional speakers, a manuscript may be troublesome. If the font size is too small, it may be difficult to read. Each time you look up and then back down, it is possible to lose your place in the manuscript. Some people tend to sound as though they are reading rather than speaking when working from a manuscript. We encourage students to avoid writing out their speeches verbatim, but recognize that there are occasions when manuscript speaking is appropriate. If you find yourself involved in one of these occasions, we offer four performance guidelines.

Pay special attention to preparing the written text. If you cannot read what you have written, your delivery will falter. Avoid using a handwritten manuscript. Make sure you choose a large enough font to see without squinting, and have the lines spaced well enough that you do not lose your place.

Practice. The key to successful manuscript speaking is practice and more practice. One run through is not sufficient.

Express yourself naturally and communicate your personality. You do not want to look frozen in time. Think about what you want to emphasize and vary the pitch of your voice to avoid being monotone. Pronounce words as you would in normal speech and be conscious of speaking too quickly or too slowly.

Make eye contact with your audience. Glance back and forth between your manuscript and your audience. Take care not to bob your head in the process. When a speech is memorized, this is not an issue. However, when you are dependent on a manuscript, you need to make sure it does not sound like you are reading to the audience. Looking up from the manuscript and making eye contact with members of your audience are important aspects of manuscript delivery.

Looking up from the manuscript and making eye contact with members of your audience are important aspects of manuscript delivery.

A big mistake students make is typing the entire speech on the required number of note cards (even though they have been warned not to do this). A five- to eight-minute speech is typed on three to five note cards. The outcome is not pretty. Students find themselves unable to read the cards—font size is six, and twelve lines of type are on each note card. They cannot read, they lose their place, they stumble as they try to decipher the words, and even worse, because they are concentrating so hard on reading the notes, they forget about the vocal aspects of delivery! The lesson learned? Use a manuscript only when the occasion suggests it.

▲Extemporaneous Speaking

The most appropriate mode of delivery for students of public speaking is extemporaneous speaking, a method of delivery that involves using carefully prepared notes to guide the presentation.

Extemporaneous speaking has many advantages. In particular, speakers can maintain a personal connection with their listeners and can respond to their feedback. The most effective public speaking is often described as the speaker's response to the listener's reaction. This takes shape in the communication transaction. The extemporaneous mode of delivery allows this interaction to occur as you adjust your choice of words and decide what to include—or exclude—in your speech. You can shorten a speech (you may want to follow the advice of the Reverend William Sloane Coffin (1988) who said about the length of an effective sermon, "No souls are saved after twenty minutes") or go into greater detail than you originally planned. This mode of speaking provides flexibility.

Speaking extemporaneously means that your word choice is fresh. Although you know the intent of your message in advance, you choose your words as you are delivering your speech. The result is a spontaneous, conversational tone that puts you and your audience at ease. This is not to say that as you practice your speech, key words or phrases will not remain with you. On the contrary, the more you practice, the more likely you are to commit a particularly fitting word or phrase to memory. Extemporaneous speaking gives you the freedom to gesture as you would in conversational speech. With both hands free, (you can gesture with note cards in one hand) you can move about and emphasize key points with forceful gestures. Consider the following guidelines as you prepare for your extemporaneous speech.

Prepare carefully. In terms of preparation, use the same care you would use when preparing a written report. Choose your purpose, develop your core idea, research your topic, organize your ideas, and select the language and presentation style that is most appropriate for your audience.

Prepare both a full content and key-word speaker's outline. Recently, a student gave his own eulogy as a special occasion speech. He worked from a very brief outline. His speech was too short, and he seemed to have a lapse of memory. Had he used a more fully-developed outline, these problems would have been eliminated.

Develop an outline containing main points and subpoints, then create a key-word outline that can be transferred to index cards of the appropriate size. Cards should be large enough to accommodate information from your key-word outline, yet small enough to be unobtrusive. Cards may be held or placed on a lectern.

Place detailed information on separate note cards. Facts, figures, and quotations may be written on separate note cards for easy reference. Always remember your ethical responsibility not to misrepresent facts or opinions that require careful and precise explanations. Rather than take the chance of misquoting people or facts, it may help to have the information written on separate cards.

Write legibly. Your notes are useless if you cannot read them, so print your words boldly and consider highlighting critical ideas. If typing, use an appropriate font size. Remember, too, that your visual aids can serve as notes to some extent.

Use your notes as a prompter. Notes enable you to keep your ideas in mind without committing every word to memory. Notes also make it possible to maintain eye contact with your listeners. You can glance around the room, looking occasionally at your cards, without giving anyone the impression that you are reading your speech.

▲Impromptu Speaking

Impromptu speaking involves little to no preparation time. This means using no notes or just a few. In your lifetime, there may be many occasions when you are asked to speak briefly without any advanced notice. For example, you may be a principal of a high school attending a local school board meeting, and someone on the school board asks you to comment on the recent basketball victory. Or, at that same meeting, a school board member may decide it is the right moment to recognize the accomplishments of a retiring teacher. During other occasions, you may be asked to "say a few words" about a newlywed couple, the dearly-departed, or a scholarship you just received.

In a public speaking class, many instructors include impromptu speaking opportunities throughout the semester. In particular, it is helpful for students to give a brief impromptu speech at the beginning of the semester just to get on their feet and face the audience. Instructors generally feel that the more opportunities we give students to present, the more comfortable students will feel in the speaking environment. You may have an activity in class where you introduce yourself or someone in the class. You may be called upon to give an impromptu speech on "my proudest moment," or "my favorite vacation spot."

Who knows when you'll be called upon to give a tribute to someone celebrating a special occasion?

Not everyone has the ability of Marcus Garvey, African American nationalist leader, to speak on the spur of the moment. Dorothy L. Pennington, an expert in the rhetoric of African Americans, describes Garvey's oratorical style:

> He often spoke impromptu, gleaning his topic and remarks from something that had occurred during the earlier portion of the program. For example, in speaking before the conference of the Universal Negro Improvement Association in August 1937, Garvey showed how his theme emerged: "I came as usual without a subject, to pick the same from the surroundings, the environment, and I got one from the singing of the hymn 'Faith of our Fathers.' I shall talk to you on that as a theme for my discourse." This type of adaptation allowed Garvey to tap into the main artery of what an audience was thinking and feeling (Duffy and Ryan 1987, 170).

Impromptu speaking forces you to think on your feet. With no opportunity to prepare, you must rely on what you know. Here are several suggestions that will help you organize your ideas:

Focus your remarks on the audience and occasion. Remind your listeners of the occasion, or purpose of the meeting: ("We have assembled to protest the rise in parking fines from $10 to $25.") When unexpectedly called to speak, talk about the people who are present and the accomplishments of the group. You can praise the group leader ("She's done so much to solve the campus parking problem"), the preceding speaker, or the group as a whole. You may want to refer to something a previous speaker said, whether you agree or disagree: ("The suggestion to organize a petition protesting the fine increase is a good one.") The remarks give you a beginning point, and a brief moment to think and organize your comments.

Use examples. Be as concrete as possible. ("I decided to become active in this organization after I heard about a student who was threatened with expulsion from school after accumulating $500 in unpaid parking fines.") Keep in mind that as an impromptu speaker, you are not expected to make a polished, professional speech-- everyone knows you have not prepared. But you are expected to deliver your remarks in a clear, cogent manner.

Do not try to say too much and do not apologize. Instead of jumping from point to point in a vague manner, focus on your specific purpose. When you complete the mission of your speech, turn the platform over to another speaker. Never apologize. Your audience is already aware it is an impromptu moment, apologizing for the informality of your address is unnecessary. You do not need to say anything that will lessen your audience's expectations of your speech.

The informal, careless speech you use when talking with friends is not polished enough for a presentation.

ASPECTS OF VOCAL DELIVERY

The speaker should never forget about the needs of the audience, and this applies to vocal delivery, also. It is always beneficial to speak clearly. A German friend of ours once said, "Americans speak as though they have hot potatoes in their mouths." Indeed, many of us mumble, leave off the endings of our words, and fail to pronounce words correctly. When presenting in public, consider the following aspects of vocal delivery: articulation, pronunciation, volume, rate, pitch, pauses, and emphasis.

▲Articulation

A person who articulates well is someone who speaks clearly and intelligibly. Articulation refers to the production of sound and how precisely we form our words. The more formal the situation, the more precise our articulation needs to be. The more casual the situation, the more likely we are to be relaxed in our speech. Thus, when you are giving a speech in front of an audience, the sloppy or careless pronunciation patterns you use with your friends and family should not find their way into your presentation.

Words should be crisp and clear. The listener should be able to distinguish between sounds and not be confused. The popular phrase, "Da Bears" shows how we mainstream some of our inarticulation. Leaving off the "g" in going, driving, shopping, etc. is common in American culture. Saying "I wanna," "I coulda," and "I hafta" are other examples of sloppy articulation which is perfectly acceptable in informal situations, but not so in a formal context.

Remember to adapt to your audience. In a formal setting, such as a commencement speech or an awards ceremony, you want to be as articulate as possible. In an informal setting, articulation is not as big of an issue, but it is always important to be understood.

Work to eliminate bad habits. Reflect a moment about how you articulate. Do you speak clearly? Do you mumble? Do you have certain words that you mispronounce? Do you leave the endings off of words? You should make a conscious effort to think about articulation. Following are several tongue twisters. You might want to see how well you do.

© 2012 olly.
Used under license of Shutterstock.

How you say something is as important as the words you use to say it.

Betty Botter had some butter,
"But," she said, "this butter's bitter.
If I bake this bitter butter,
it would make my batter bitter.
But a bit of better butter—
that would make my batter better."
So she bought a bit of butter,
better than her bitter butter,
and she baked it in her batter,
and the batter was not bitter.
So 'twas better Betty Botter
bought a bit of better butter.

A big black bug bit a big black bear,
made the big black bear bleed blood.

Toy boat. Toy boat. Toy boat.

▲Pronunciation

In contrast to articulation problems, mispronunciation is not knowing how to say a word and, as a result, saying it incorrectly. Sometimes speakers simply do not know the word and mispronounce it; other times, a word is mispronounced because of dialect differences

© 2012 by Aaron Amat.
Used under license of Shutterstock.

Do not mistake shouting for projection.

among speakers. For example, you may have heard President George W. Bush leave off the "g" in "recognize," so the words sounds like "reconize." Politicians or their detractors sometimes talk about "physical" responsibility, instead of the two-syllable word, "fiscal" responsibility. People also present "satistics" instead of "statistics," and talk about the "I-talians" and the people from "I-raq."

One of your authors lives in Illinois, near a town called Mattoon. Residents of the area can tell when someone is not from the area, because at first, they say, "Ma-toon" instead of "Mat-toon." Are you someone whose name is always mispronounced? If so, you know it can be annoying.

Check pronunciation of unfamiliar words. Part of the ethical responsibility of a speaker is to check his or her pronunciation. The speaker should know how to pronounce all words in his or her speech, including the names of people and places and foreign terms.

Do not comment on your pronunciation. Do not say, "or however you pronounce that" or "I cannot pronounce that." While we are likely to forgive regional differences, our credibility will be reduced if our listeners see we have made little or no effort to determine the correct pronunciation.

Practice the pronunciation of difficult words. You do not want to stumble or draw attention away from the point you are making.

▲Volume

If your audience cannot hear you, your speech serves little purpose. The loudness of your voice is controlled by how forcefully air is expelled through the trachea onto the vocal folds. This exhalation is controlled by the contraction of the abdominal muscles. The more forcefully you use these muscles to exhale, the greater the force of the air, and the louder your voice.

Do not mistake shouting for projection. Shouting involves forcing the voice from the vocal folds, which is irritating to the folds, instead of projecting the sound from the abdominal area. Straining your voice will only make you hoarse. Instead, work on your posture and breathing from the diaphragm.

Use volume to add interest and variety to your speech. Maybe you want to add a bit of humor to your introduction of a speaker. Using a "stage whisper," you could say something like, "And if we all clap very loudly, we can coax him on to the stage…." On his television show, Dr. Phil uses volume effectively by getting loud when he thinks people should be annoyed by what is happening and speaking softly when he is showing amazement or shares a startling fact.

Do not talk to the podium. If you have your notes on the podium and your head is bent, the audience will not be able to hear.

▲Rate

During the first week of teaching at the University of Arkansas at Little Rock, a student said to Dr. Mason, "You are not from around here, are you?" When asked what gave it away, the student replied that it was the rate of speech. In the United States, Southerners generally speak more slowly than Northerners. Overall, the average rate of speech for Americans is between 120 and 160 words per minute.

Nervousness may affect your normal pattern. When practicing alone, you may be relieved when you find that in timing your speech you are just over the minimum time required. However, under the pressure of giving a speech, you may find yourself speeding up ("The faster I talk, the faster I'll finish") or slowing down. Rate is also affected by mode of delivery. If you read a manuscript rather than speak extemporaneously, you may find yourself running a verbal road race.

Choose an appropriate rate. Your rate of speech should be consistent with the ideas being expressed and for the context. For example, it makes sense that a sportscaster announcing a basketball game speaks faster than a sportscaster at a golf match.

Vary your rate of speech. By changing your rate, you can express different thoughts and feelings. You may want to speak slowly to emphasize an important point or to communicate a serious or somber mood. A faster pace is appropriate when you are telling your audience something it already knows (many speeches include background information that sets the scene) or to express surprise, happiness, or fear.

▲Pitch

Pitch refers to your vocal range or key, the highness or lowness of your voice produced by the tightening and loosening of your vocal folds. The range of most people's voices is less than two octaves. Pitch is a problem when your voice is too high-pitched; in men a high-pitched voice may sound immature, and in women it may sound screechy.

Vary your pitch. Variety adds interest to your presentation. Avoid a monotone. When you do not vary the pitch of your voice, you risk putting your listeners to sleep.

Use your voice potential. Take advantage of the fact that our voices have incredible range. To add color, lower the pitch of a word or phrase you want to emphasize. Resist the temptation to raise your voice too much at key points.

▲Pauses

Some speakers talk nonstop until, literally, they run out of breath. Others pause every three or four words in a kind of nervous verbal chop. Still others, particularly those who read their speeches, pause at the wrong times—perhaps in the middle of an important idea—making it difficult for their listeners to follow.

Pausing during a presentation can help listeners process the information you're conveying.

Pauses add color, expression, and feeling to a speech. They should be used deliberately to achieve a desired effect. If used effectively, pauses also can add power and control to your speech. They may get you into trouble when it seems like you have lost your place or forgotten what you were going to say. This may suggest you are unprepared and have not practiced sufficiently.

Pauses serve multiple purposes. First, they communicate self-confidence. Pauses deliver the nonverbal message that you are relaxed enough to stop talking for a moment. Second, they help listeners digest what you are saying and anticipate what you will say next. Third, a significant pause also helps you move from one topic to the next without actually telling your listeners what you are doing. Fourth, a pause signals the audience to pay attention. (This is especially true for long pauses lasting two or three seconds.) According to Don Hewitt, producer of *60 Minutes*, "It's the intonation, the pauses, that tell the story. They are as important to us as commas and periods are to *The New York Times*"(in Fletcher 1990, 15).

In 1993, Nelson Mandela, then President of the African National Congress, received the Nobel Peace Prize. The following is an excerpt from his acceptance speech:

> We speak here of the challenge of the dichotomies of war and peace, violence and non-violence, racism and human dignity, oppression and repression and liberty and human rights, poverty and freedom from want.
>
> We stand here today as nothing more than a representative of the millions of our people who dared to rise up against a social system whose very essence is war, violence, racism, oppression, repression and the impoverishment of an entire people.
>
> I am also here today as a representative of the millions of people across the globe, the anti-apartheid movement, the governments and organizations that joined with us, not to fight against South Africa as a country or any of its peoples, but to oppose an inhuman system and sue for a speedy end to the apartheid crime against humanity.
>
> *Copyright © 1993 by Nelson Mandela Foundation and Nobel Foundation. Reprinted by permission.*

Try reading the excerpt aloud, using pauses where you find commas. Try using pauses of different lengths. While his words are powerful, they gain greater impact as he pauses before or after key words or phrases.

Here are four suggestions for the effective use of pauses:

Pause when you introduce a new idea or term. This gives your listeners time to absorb what you are saying. It helps listeners keep up with you.

Tie your pauses to verbal phrasing. To a speaker, a phrase has a different meaning than it does to a writer. It is a unit you speak in one breath in order to express a single idea. Each pause tells your listeners you are moving from one thought to the next.

Use pauses to change the pace and add verbal variety. Pauses can be an effective tool speakers use to keep attention or to draw attention to a particular thought or emotion. Pause just before you speed up or pause just before you slow down. In both cases, the pause indicates to the audience that something is going to happen.

Extend pauses when displaying a visual. This tactic enables your audience to read the information on the visual without missing your next thought. It is important to pause after the display, not before it. Try pausing for two or three seconds.

▲Emphasis

A speaker uses emphasis to draw attention to a specific word or phrase. It involves stressing certain words or phrases. It can add weight to what you say, and make a particular word or phrase more noticeable or prominent. An emotion can be highlighted through the use of emphasis. Emphasis is a nonverbal way of saying, "Listen to this!" Think about how many ways you can say "Come in." Depending on how they are said and how they are accented by nonverbal behavior, these words can be:

A friendly invitation	(from one friend to another)
A command	(from a supervisor to an employee)
An angry growl	(from a mother with a headache to her teenage son who has already interrupted her five times)
A nondescript response	(to a knock at your office door)

These changes give meaning to a word or phrase. By singling out a few words for special attention, you add color to your speech and avoid monotony. Emphasis can be achieved by using different techniques.

Change your volume and pitch. Whether you choose to speak more loudly or more quietly, you draw attention to your speech through contrast. A quieter approach is often a more effective attention-grabber. When you speak in a monotone, you tell your listeners you have nothing to emphasize. When you vary the pitch of your voice, you let them know that what you are saying is important.

Pause when changing your speaking rate. A change of pace—speeding up or slowing down—draws attention to what will come next: Pausing can do the same.

Use emotion. Emphasis comes naturally when you speak from the heart. When you have deep feelings about a subject—drug abuse, for example, or the need to protect the environment from pollution—you will express your feelings emphatically. Anything other than an impassioned delivery may seem inadequate.

Work with the previous excerpt from Nelson Mandela's acceptance speech. Read it aloud. The first time, do not emphasize anything. Read it in a monotone, just as you would a telephone book. It is hard to get involved, is it not? Now, underscore the words or phrases that, if emphasized, would add meaning to the speech. Then read it a second time, adding the emphasis and emotion you think appropriate. You may find that the words seem to take a life of their own as they demand attention.

▲Non-fluencies

Non-fluencies are meaningless words that interrupt the flow of our speech. We may use them unintentionally, but we need to work consciously to avoid them. Non-fluencies are also known as filled pauses or vocal fillers. While pauses can work for you, non-fluencies distract your listeners. These include: "you know," "uh," "um," "so," and "okay." If your economics professor says "okay" after every concept presented, or your history professor adds "uh" or "um" after every thought, it can cause you to lose focus. A sociology professor told us his students once kept track of his non-fluencies, and reported to him after class that that he said "you know" thirty-two times during the fifty-minute period. Non-fluencies are verbal debris; they add nothing to the content of your speech, and they also annoy an audience. Avoid them.

Throw out other types of speaking debris as well: giggling, throat clearing, lip smacking, and sighing. These interrupt the flow of speech and can also be annoying to the audience. As you give speeches during this term, think about any habits you have that may distract your audience. We do not expect you to be perfect, but striving to improve your speaking ability is a realistic goal.

Be aware of your speech patterns Many people do not realize they use fillers. If you have been videotaped, listen for them as you watch your speech. Or, you can record your own phone conversation on a tape recorder. You can also ask friends to identify them when they hear you use fillers, or ask your teacher or classmates to keep track of non-fluencies.

Train yourself to be silent. Work actively to rid your speech of non-fluencies. Pause for a second or so after completing a phrase or other unit of thought. Because fillers indicate, in part, a discomfort with silence, this approach will help you realize that pauses are an acceptable part of communication.

What are the two central themes throughout this discussion of vocal delivery? To practice and use vocal variety. It is important to practice your speech so it flows smoothly. Practice pronouncing unfamiliar words so they come easily to you when you give your speech. Try varying pitch, rate, and volume to keep the audience's attention. Create interest in your speech, and stress key words, phrases, and thoughts. You have something relevant to share with your audience. You want to make it easy for them to understand you, and you want to keep them interested in what you have to say.

❯❯ASPECTS OF PHYSICAL DELIVERY

Your physical delivery may convey professionalism or lack thereof. It can convey self-confidence or nervousness. Your delivery communicates enthusiasm or lack of interest. The ways you gesture, move, look at people, and dress say a great deal about you. More importantly, these elements leave a lasting impression that affects the speaker-audience connection. Although mastering the art of nonverbal communication will not guarantee your speaking success, it will help you convince your audience to pay attention.

▲Gestures

Gestures involve using your arms and hands to illustrate, emphasize, or provide a visual experience that accompanies your thoughts. Before we discuss the importance of gestures, body movement, and eye contact, we have a story about Katie, a non-traditional student who returned to school after five years of working for the loan department of a bank. She gave a speech adapted specifically to her audience. Her specific purpose was to explain how recent college graduates abuse credit cards and wind up owing thousands of dollars. She began:

© 2012 Comstock.
Used under license of Thinkstock.

When speaking to a large audience, gestures play a key part in reinforcing the ideas in your message.

> When you receive your first credit card, think of it as a loaded gun. If you don't use it properly you may wind up killing your credit for up to ten years.
>
> That means that no one will loan you money to buy a car, a plasma TV, or a house. You may not get the job you want because your credit is bad (prospective employers check applicants' credit ratings). And you'll go through a lot of torment while this is going on.
>
> Take my word for it. I've seen it happen dozens of times to people just like you.

Making a connection between a credit card and a loaded gun is a great attention-getter. Also, college students are usually fairly new to using credit cards, so the message is an important one to the audience. Although Katie's message was effective, her delivery was stiff and uncomfortable. She grasped the lectern for dear life, as if she were afraid to move from her spot. She was a talking statue, and her listeners responded by becoming restless and uncomfortable themselves. During the post-speech criticism, one audience member explained what he was feeling: "You looked so wooden that I had trouble listening to what you were saying, which is amazing since I'm already in credit card trouble."

Katie's problem was a lack of gestures and body movement, which her audience could not ignore despite the inherent interest of her speech. Gestures tell an audience that you are comfortable and self-confident. As an outlet for nervous energy, they actually help you feel more at ease. Gestures encourage an enthusiastic presentation. If you put your body into your speech through movement and gestures, it is difficult to present a stilted speech. Gestures also have a positive effect on breathing, helping you relax the muscles that affect the quality of the voice.

Guidelines for Gesturing

Gestures are especially important when you are speaking to a large audience. People in the back rows may not be able to see the changes in your facial expressions, and gestures may be their only way of seeing your involvement with your speech.

You can tell if your gestures are effective by checking where your listeners are looking. If

© 2012 by UrosK.
Used under license of Shutterstock.

If you hold your hands behind your back, you won't be able to gesture.

they are focusing on the movement of your arms and hands instead of your face, your gestures are a distraction rather than a help. If this situation occurs, reduce the amount of gestures during the rest of your speech. Think about the following three guidelines as your practice using gestures.

Use natural gestures. Your gestures should reinforce both the ideas in the message and your own personality. Stand straight, with your arms bent at the waist and your hands relaxed, so you are ready to gesture. Pay attention to the position of your elbows. If they hang stiffly at your sides, your gestures will look shortened and artificial. To move your hands and forearms freely, make sure there is plenty of room between your elbows and your body.

Gesture purposefully. Gestures should be meaningful and enhance your message. They should not appear random. For example, if you were trying to persuade people to donate blood, you might want to give your audience three reasons for doing so. When you say, "three reasons," you can hold up three fingers. When you say, "First," hold up one finger, and then when you say, "Second," hold up two fingers. You get the picture. These gestures are meaningful because they serve as an organizational guide. They tell your audience where you are in your speech. The same thing is true if you were giving an after-dinner speech in which you were trying to convince your audience to stop complaining. You could put up one or both hands in the "stop" position when you say, "Stop complaining" to your audience. This is meaningful because it emphasizes your assertion.

Gesture appropriately. Gestures should be timely. You do not want to hold three fingers up before or after you say "three reasons," but as you are saying it. You do not want arms flailing around as you speak; they should match what you are saying. Appropriate gestures are timely, and they should make sense within the context of your message. If you are speaking before a large audience, gestures are bigger and, generally, more dramatic. Those same gestures may look awkward and exaggerated in a smaller environment.

Actions That Inhibit Gesturing

The preceding three guidelines are designed to help you gesture effectively. Your authors have over seventy years of combined experience grading student speeches, and we have noticed several actions that reduce the overall effectiveness of a student's speech and/or distract the audience. As you deliver your speech, try to avoid the following:

Clasping your hands together.
It makes gesturing impossible except if you are willing to raise both hands at once.

Hugging your body.
It makes you look as though you are trying to protect yourself from assault.

Clasping your hands in the "fig leaf" stance.
Holding your hands together in front of you is another protective position, and it may be distracting.

Locking your hands behind your back.
That position may encourage you to rock back and forth. This "at ease" military stance is not appropriate for the classroom.

Putting your hands in your pocket.
This restricts movement and may encourage you to play with change in your pocket or something else that will make sound and distract your audience.

Grasping and leaning into the lectern.
Some students do this for support when they are nervous. You can touch the lectern; just do not hold it in a death grip. Free your hands so you can gesture. Release your energy through your movement.

For your next speech, work to make your gestures appear more natural. Ask a friend or colleague to comment on your movement and gestures. Gestures should not draw attention to themselves and away from the ideas.
Corporation.

▲Note Cards and Legal Pads
Many instructors restrict the number and size of the note cards you may use during your speech. Follow their instructions, and consider the following:

- View your note cards as an extension of your arm, gesturing as you would without the note cards.
- Cards should fit into your hand comfortably.
- Generally, 4" x 6" cards are going to be easier to read than 3" x 5" cards.
- Number your note cards so you are able to keep them in order as you write them, transport them, and use them when you deliver your speech.
- Check to see that they are in sequence before speaking.
- Never staple your note cards.

Common Problems Using Note Cards
Using note cards effectively is not as easy as it seems. Sometimes, students wait until the last moment to create their note cards. Just like every other aspect of speaking, students should practice their speech using note cards, and consider the following pitfalls.

Holding note cards with both hands. Holding on to note cards with both hands may be distracting to the audience because cards are relatively small pieces of paper that do not need the support of both hands. Holding on with both hands restricts your movement, also.

Putting too much on the note cards. You only need enough information on your note cards to trigger your thoughts. If you have practiced enough, you do not need many notes. Also, if you have most of your speech on your note cards, you may end up sounding like you are reading to the audience.

Having too many note cards. Teachers sometimes swap stories about how many note cards a particular student used. The assignment may call for three note cards, and a student has a quarter-inch pile of note cards—sometimes as many as twenty for a four- to six-minute speech. This is not necessary if you have practiced your speech!

Writing on both sides of the card. Sometimes students misinterpret the "three cards rule" and use three note cards, but write on both sides. It is easy to lose your place when you have written on both sides, and it can be distracting to the audience ("Hey! She used bright pink ink for her notes!"), and it usually means that you are relying too heavily on your notes. Practice!

Using a Legal Pad

Traditionally, public speaking instructors wince at the notion of allowing students to use something other than note cards. Our professors taught us to use note cards, and we teach our students the same. In reality, not every occasion calls for small note cards. It is certainly not uncommon to see speakers using note pads or legal pads of some kind in the corporate world. Long and detailed presentations may be better served by using a note pad instead.

Your instructor may allow the use of a note pad in your class, or you may be in a situation where having a pad of paper makes sense. Once you have your notes on something larger than your hand, it may be more distracting when you gesture. You do not want a pad of paper waving around in the air. It should not be used as an extension of your arm. Hold the pad in one hand, at a distance from your eyes that allows you to see your notes but not covering your face. Gesture with your free hand.

CAUTION: Holding a piece of paper is different than holding a note card. If you are nervous, the audience is more likely to see a full-sized piece of paper shake than a smaller, sturdier note card.

▲Physical Movement

Remember the second problem related to Katie's delivery? She appeared glued to the lectern. After a while, her listeners got tired of watching her. Katie's mistake is typical. Like many speakers, she failed to realize that an active speaker can encourage an active response from an audience, but an immobile speaker can leave listeners listless. When you move from one place to another while you speak, your listeners are more likely to keep their eyes on you. Movement has an additional advantage of helping to reduce your nervous energy. It can work against you, however, if you look like a moving target or if your movement has no purpose. Think about the following three guidelines as you prepare your speech.

Move naturally. Relax and use movement reasonably. Do not pace back and forth like a caged lion or make small darting movements that return you to the safety of the lectern.

Tie your movements to your use of visual aids. Walk over to the visual as you are presenting it and point to its relevant parts. Walk back to the lectern when you are through. Make sure the movement is fluid.

Be prepared. Your instructor and the speaking environment will influence the opportunities for physical movement. Your instructor may allow or prohibit you from speaking behind a lectern or podium. In informal situations, it may be appropriate to walk through the aisles as you talk. In a small room, you can walk around without a microphone and still be heard. In a large room, you may need the help of a wireless microphone. Be prepared to adapt to your instructor's rules and the speaking environment. Remember that movement is a way to connect with the audience, get them involved, and keep their attention.

▲Eye Contact

No other aspect of nonverbal behavior is as important as eye contact, which is the connection you form with listeners through your gaze. You engage your audience by drawing them in through eye contact. Sustained eye contact can communicate confidence, openness, and honesty. It suggests you are a person of conviction, you care what your listeners are thinking, and you are eager for their feedback. Making eye contact with your audience is a way for you to express nonverbally, "I want you to understand me."

When your eye contact is poor, you may be sending unintentional messages that the audience interprets as nervousness, hostility, being uncomfortable, or lack of interest. The audience may think you have something to hide or that you are not prepared.

In the process of writing this text, one of the authors attended a recognition ceremony where several honorees gave brief speeches. One speaker began by looking at her notes, then made eye contact with the audience, looked back at her notes, and then appeared to look at something on the wall to her right. She repeated these behaviors throughout her speech. Audience members were observed looking up at the same spot. The speaker admitted to being nervous before her speech. Clearly, this nervous tic distracted her audience.

When you don't make eye contact with your audience, it may be interpreted as a lack of interest in your subject.

Sometimes students only look at the instructor during their speech. Do not do this! It makes teachers uncomfortable and you are excluding the rest of the audience. Also, some student speakers ignore half the class by looking at the right side or the left side of the class only.

When you turn on the nightly news, you see the anchor looking straight at you. As a result of television, eye-to-eye contact is what you expect from every speaker; it is the norm. When a speaker looks away, we sense that something is wrong. We offer the following three performance guidelines for reflection.

Distribute your gaze evenly. Work on sustained eye contact with different members in the audience. Avoid darting your eyes around or sweeping the room with your eyes. Instead, try

YOU ARE WHAT YOU WEAR
WHY YOUR VISUAL SELF-PRESENTATION MATTERS

BY CARLA L. SLOAN, M.A. (Instructor of Communication Studies, Liberty University)
& DONALD H. ALBAN JR., PH.D. (Associate Professor of Communication Studies, Liberty University)

You may have heard the old saying, "You are what you eat!" Well, how about this one: "You are what you wear!" This adage, which is the title of no fewer than five different books, may sound odd to you at first, but the point it proposes is valid. Scholarly literature consistently shows that what you wear in the presence of an audience powerfully impacts the way they see you, the way you see yourself, and how well you perform tasks in their presence like delivering a speech. Let's take a minute to review some of this research and then to consider a few relevant thoughts for students, points that derive from my decades of experience as a speech communication instructor. Like it or not, people do form impressions about us based largely on what we wear in their presence. Consider these research findings:

- People in general present themselves more positively when they are well dressed than they do when they are poorly dressed.[1]

- Athletes in uniform are seen as more professional, team-spirited, coordinated, naturally skilled, and stronger than found that when athletes were in uniform than when they were not in uniform.[2]

- Political candidates receive more favorable responses when dressed in formal conservative attire and when dressed in "simple contrasts or white" rather than in dark or patterned outfits." For female candidates, "necklaces and earrings create a more positive political image than no jewelry at all."[3]

- Students perceive educators as most qualified (expert) when the educators are dressed in professional attire and as most dynamic, particularly when the educator is female, when they are dressed in dark, professional attire.[4]

- Female university professors who dress in formal attire and male and female professors who dress in casual attire are seen as more likable than male university professors who dress in formal attire.[5]

- Well dressed individuals are significantly more likely to receive positive responses to their requests for compliance, in survey-taking situations, than poorly dressed individuals.[6]

The clothing we choose to wear when in front of others speaks volumes to them about who we are, who we think we are, how we wish to be perceived, what we believe, what we like or value, where we've been, and who or what we admire, among other points. Putting this point another way, in the form of an acrostic, our attire does the following:

D Defines: Our dress can define how we are perceived by those do not know us.

R Reinforces: Our dress can reinforce how we are perceived by those who do know us.

E Emboldens: Our dress can embolden us to impact other people.

S Sends: Our dress can send a message that we may or may not intend to send.

S Shapes: Our dress can shape our destiny.

Of course, you did not need a textbook to tell you that one's clothing can make a statement to others, but take a minute to think about what this principle as it relates to you right now. Answer the following questions:

• What kind of statement about yourself are you making at this moment through the clothing you wore or are wearing in public today? Why did you choose to wear this style and color combination?

• Conversely, which style and color combinations did you deliberately not wear? Why did you avoid wearing these?

• Do you believe others will interpret your clothing in the same way you do? Why? Where did you learn to associate clothing style and color combinations with the positive or negative meanings that you affix to them?

Bear in mind that personal clothing is but one way in which we visually present ourselves to others. One's hair style, makeup, jewelry, and visual neatness, or the lack thereof, can impact an audience in much the same way. Before you give a speech, analyze your audience and determine, as well as you can, how they likely will respond to clothing colors and styles for a speech of this type, to be given at this particular time and place, at this particular location, under these particular circumstances. Remind yourself of your goal in making this speech and choose the attire that appears most likely to promote your goal in delivering it.

What we wear should never distract your audience from what you are saying. If you want to be taken seriously, be judicious

in your choice of attire. If your speech is a gift, people may judge its quality based on the quality of its wrapping. The research is clear—dressing neatly and professionally can make a positive difference in your audience's response to what you say. In a sense, you truly are what you wear.

[1]Schneider, D. J. "Effects of Dress on Self-Presentation." *Psychological Reports* 35 (1974): 167.

[2]Harris, Mary, Sandra Ramsey, Diana Sims, and Marcia Stevenson. "Effects of Uniforms on Perceptions of Pictures of Athletes." *Perceptual and Motor Skills.* 39.1 (1974): 59-62. Print.

[3]Rosenburg, Shawn W., Shulamit Kahn, and Thuy Tran. "Creating a Political Image: Shaping Appearance and Manipulation the Vote." *Political Behavior.* 13.4 (1991): 345-367. Print.

[4]Roberts, Anna Duggins. "Selected Clothing Characteristics and Educator Credibility." The University of North Carolina at Greensboro, 1990. United States -- North Carolina: *ProQuest.* Web. 26 May 2013.

[5]Lightstone, Karen, Rob Francis, and Lucie Kocum. "University Faculty Style of Dress and Students' Perception of Instructor Credibility." *International Journal of Business and Social Science* 2.15 (2011): n/a. ProQuest. Web. 26 May 2013.

[6]Walker, Michael, Susan Harriman, and Stuart Costello. "The Influence Of Appearance On Compliance With A Request." *Journal Of Social Psychology* 112.1 (1980): 159. *SPORTDiscus with Full Text.* Web. 26 May 2013.

© 2012 by Hasloo Group Production Studio. Used under license of Shutterstock.

Your appearance should be in harmony with your message.

maintaining eye contact with a single person for a single thought. This may be measured in a phrase or a sentence. It may help to think of your audience as divided into several physical sectors. Focus on a different person in each sector, rotating your gaze among the people and the sectors as you speak.

Glance only briefly and occasionally at your notes. Do not keep your eyes glued to your notes. You may know your speech well, but when you are nervous, it may feel safer to keep looking at your notes. However, this is counterproductive.

Do not look just above the heads of your listeners. Although this advice is often given to speakers who are nervous, it will be obvious to everyone that you are gazing into the air.

▲Appearance

Standards for appearance are influenced by culture and context. Americans visiting the Vatican will find that shoulders and knees should be covered in order to gain entry. It is okay for students to wear baseball caps outside, but some in some contexts, it may be offensive to keep one on inside. In high school, you may have violated the student conduct code by wearing something that was deemed inappropriate. Most school districts have clearly-stated standards related to appearance. However, these standards differ from one district to another.

An effective speaker is aware of the norms and expectations for appearance as he or she moves from one culture to another. In a 1989 summit between Soviet President Mikhail Gorbachev and Chinese leader Deng Xiaoping, Gorbachev made a nearly fatal blunder: He wore a pair of beige loafers with his formal suit, a choice that offended the Chinese who believed that "holiday shoes" should not be worn on such a special occasion. Gorbachev's advisors failed to provide him with such relevant information.

We do not have to move from one country to another to experience differences in perspectives on appearance. Some businesses allow more casual attire; others expect trendy, tailored clothing. As rhetorical theorist Kenneth Burke (1969, 119) reminds us, your clothes make a rhetorical statement of their own by contributing to your spoken message.

Your choice of shoes, suits, dresses, jewelry, tattoos, hair style, and body piercings should not isolate you from your listeners. If that occurs, the intent of your speech is lost. We offer the following guidelines for appearance, but the bottom line is, do nothing to distract from the message.

Your appearance should be in harmony with your message. Communication professor Leon Fletcher (1990) describes a city council meeting addressed by college students pleading for a clean-up of the local beaches. Although the speeches were clearly organized, well-supported, and effectively presented, the unkempt physical appearance of the speakers conflicted with their message. They wore torn jeans, T-shirts and sloppy sandals. Their hair looked ungroomed. The city council decided to take no action. Several months later, the same issue was brought before the council by a second group of students, all of whom wore ties and sport jackets—symbols of the neatness they wanted for the beaches. This time the proposal was accepted (14).

Although no one would tell you that wearing a certain suit or dress will make your listeners agree with your point of view, the image you create is undoubtedly important. Research on employment interviews suggests that "physical appearance and grooming habits are factors in the hiring process" (Shannon and Stark 2003, 613).

Be clean and appropriately dressed and groomed. In your public speaking class, your shoe choice is not likely to create a stir. However, your audience expects that you will be clean and appropriately groomed. Your instructor may provide you with specific guidelines regarding your appearance on the day you speak. A general guideline is to be modest and slightly more formal than your audience.

Avoid clothing that detracts from your message. If the audience focuses on your appearance, your speech loses effectiveness. Wearing a cap is usually frowned upon. The audience wants to see your eyes, and you should not ignore the possibility that your instructor views caps as outdoor, not indoor, wear.

Avoid shirts that have writing on them. It is probably not wise to give a persuasive speech on the day you wear a t-shirt with "I make stuff up" on it. One of our female students held her poster in front of her, with lettering showing on her t-shirt, just above the visual aid. Whether what is written on your t-shirt is witty or offensive, it takes focus off the message.

Some students may need the following gentle reminder: Your instructors, and probably many of your classmates, are not interested in seeing your belly or any type of cleavage. And a note to the females—if you wear a tight shirt or a short skirt, and you tug or pull on it, you draw attention to yourself, not to what you are trying to say.

❯SUMMARY

The four methods of speech delivery are memorization, manuscript speaking, extemporaneous speaking, and impromtu speaking. Each method is appropriate in varying circumstances. Following the guidelines for the method you choose will enhance the effectiveness of your speech. In this chapter we focus on extemporaneous speaking, a method in which you prepare the content of your speech in advance, but speak from a key-word outline. Impromptu speaking involves speaking without preparation.

Nonverbal communication is an important part of delivery. Your vocal and physical delivery affect your presentation. Aspects of vocal delivery include articulation, pronunciation, volume, rate, pitch, pauses, and emphasis. Guidelines for effective vocal delivery are provided. In addition, an effective speaker has relatively few non-fluencies. Aspects of physical delivery include gestures, physical movement, eye contact, and appearance. A good speaker will use nonverbal delivery to capture and maintain the attention of the listeners.

MANAGING SPEECH ANXIETY

Most public speakers become nervous when they anticipate the challenge of giving a formal presentation before a group of people. "Speech anxiety" is the formal term for this unsettled feeling. In the articles that follow, several experienced speech professors share their insights into this phenomenon and offer advice for handling it in a way that can actually help you achieve your goals in the speech presentation.

TAMING THE INNER TIGER

By FAITH E. MULLEN, PH.D.
& WILLIAM L. MULLEN, PH.D.

Believe it or not, researchers have shown that many people are more afraid of giving a speech to a group of people than they are of dying. Because of this, someone has joked that perhaps it's better to be the person in the casket at the funeral than the speaker who is asked to deliver the eulogy. Speech anxiety can be a very real challenge for novice speakers. However, fear of public speaking can be managed. We believe that there are three things to keep in mind if you are trying to reduce anxiety when you speak.

First, control what you can control and forget the rest.

The words of the serenity prayer are appropriate here! "God, grant me the serenity to accept the things I cannot change: courage to change the things I can: and wisdom to know the difference." You cannot control the whole situation when you speak, but there are many things you can control. Only you can control how much effort you put into preparation for the speech. Preparation includes researching your topic, organizing your ideas, and practicing your speech. We suggest that you devote six to ten hours for each hour you plan to speak. Careful, thorough preparation is the single, best way to reduce the stage fright that otherwise can paralyze you during your speech presentation. Remember, only you can control how much you prepare for a presentation, so control what you can control and put the uncontrollable issues out of your mind.

Second, remember that adrenaline is your friend.

A physiological response to stress is the release of adrenaline into your body. Although adrenaline may make you feel sweaty and make your heart race, it can also benefit you in multiple ways. Adrenaline will make you feel awake and excited. Adrenaline can help you think more clearly and help you appear to be more enthusiastic and full of life. So, instead of fearing your physiological response to stress,

embrace the adrenaline as a friend and use it to your advantage.

Finally, realize that practice will help minimize your fear of public speaking.

The more you speak in front of others, the easier it will become. Although you may still struggle with public presentations, the experience of having spoken publicly multiple times will help eliminate your fear of the unknown and will tend to have a calming effect on you. Thus, we encourage you to welcome every opportunity you have to give a speech to a group. By seizing these opportunities today, you can develop your ability to become a greater speaker tomorrow.

Drs. Faith Mullen and William Mullen are Professors of Communication Studies at Liberty University, in Lynchburg, Virginia.

HARNESSING THE RACE HORSE

BY JOSEPH BAILEY, PH.D.

In an excellent book about surviving and survivors, Laurence Gonzales uses a horse-racing metaphor to describe the power of human emotions. In it he writes that in any stressful situation, "the system we call emotion works powerfully and quickly to motivate behavior" (Gonzales, 2003). Gonzales likens the logical senses to a jockey and the powerful emotions to a thoroughbred. In the speechmaking process, the emotions (the thoroughbred) can run rampant over the logical faculties (the jockey) in a phenomenon that we call "speech anxiety."

Speech anxiety is the powerful, sometimes overwhelming fear we experience when we realize we're going to deliver a presentation to a group of people. Although it's difficult to rid ourselves of this fear altogether, it is possible to manage it in a way that creates a pleasant, effective speech-delivery experience. Among the proven techniques that can help you manage your speech anxiety are the following.

Realize that every speaker gets nervous.

If you're nervous before a speech, you're in good company. Studies indicate that as many as 75 percent of public speakers deal with feelings of nervousness about making a public presentation to a group. The anxiety can affect us in lots of ways—an increased heartbeat, shorter breaths, sweating, fidgeting, and so on. A prominent pastor, who regularly preaches to more than 9,000 church members, recently admitted in a sermon that he once threw up before a big Easter service because his speaking anxiety became so intense. Although your speech anxiety is not likely to be this extreme, you are likely to experience some feelings of nervousness before you address an audience. Just realizing that this anxiety is a normal human response should help you feel better about it. Knowing this is the first vital step you must take to be sure this thoroughbred does not control you when you speak.

Choose the right topic.

Another important step you can take to offset the negative effects of speech anxiety is choosing a familiar topic to address when you speak. If you choose a topic about which you are knowledgeable and passionate, you probably will feel more confident when you address that topic in the presence of an audience. When you begin to brainstorm ideas for your speech, contemplate which topics excite you. If you are asked to speak informatively about a job-field's potential as a platform for advancing what God values, why not choose a job field with which you are familiar or that interests you? If you are asked to speak persuasively about a redemptive solution to a social problem, why not choose a social problem that you understand or about which you have strong feelings? Choosing a topic that you can address intelligently and passionately before your audience can help tame your speech anxiety.

Talk through your topic.

Another important step in handling speech anxiety is being sure you have carefully thought through your topic before you attempt to address it in the presence of your audience. What is your speech's thesis or main point? Which specific main points will you need to establish in the speech in order to successfully support the thesis? After you determine this, do the research you must complete in order to put together a thorough, logical presentation in support of your thesis. Find a friend or roommate and spend some time discussing the topic and your presentation of it with them. Interacting with others, which is called "dialectic," can help you determine whether the topic

you have chosen is a strong one. In the end, you are better equipped to speak if you enter the speech-delivery process knowing that you have a tested, workable topic.

Focus on the introduction.

In an article in *Psychology Today,* Dr. Michael T. Motley claims that speakers struggle with speech anxiety mostly in the first 30 seconds of the speech. He says speech anxiety starts to diminish within half a minute. This is good news for the speakers who struggle with high levels of speech anxiety. Generally, a speech introduction will last 30 seconds to one minute. What this means in practice is that your feelings of speech anxiety will likely subside considerably after the introduction. Focus, then, on getting the race horse pointed in the right direction. If you do, keeping it going in that direction will likely be less challenging for you.

Rehearse out loud.

Practice delivering your speech several days before your speech is due. Record yourself and review the recording to determine whether your thoughts and words are sensible and whether your presentation of them is compelling. Be especially attentive to any difficult-to-explain words or concepts that leave you tongue-tied or that threaten to confuse your audience. Either reword or revise these statements until you can deliver them out loud in an effective way.

Visualize yourself giving a great speech.

Public speaking is not a talent that you either have or don't have. Rather, it is a skill that one acquires with diligence and practice. If you were asked to run five miles right now, you might shutter at the thought. You might think "There's no way I can do that right now!" and perhaps you would be right. However, given the proper preparation techniques, training, and time, you could someday run five miles with only moderate exertion. So it is with public speaking. Consider this course and its speech requirements a training ground that will help you become the great speaker that you can be. Believe in your heart that you are capable of giving an excellent speech, and do all you can to do so. Your diligence will pay off in the end.

Dr. Joseph Bailey is an Associate Professor of Communication at Hardin-Simmons University, in Abilene, Texas.

QUESTIONS FOR ANALYSIS

1. Why is extemporaneous speaking generally the most appropriate form of delivery? Under what circumstances is manuscript reading, memorization, and impromptu speaking appropriate?

2. How do your movements, gestures, eye contact, and clothing influence your relationship with your audience and the communication of your message?

3. What do you need to remember about using note cards during your speech?

ACTIVITIES

1. Select a CD/DVD/Video that contains a complete speech. With your classmates, study the speaker's delivery style, examining strengths and weaknesses.

2. Prepare a two- to three-page report on a public speaker's delivery style. Assess how the speaker's delivery contributes to or diminishes his or her power as a speaker.

3. Record your own speech and make a written inventory of your strengths and weaknesses. Then describe what you must do to improve your delivery.

4. Write twenty to thirty different speech topics, each on a different piece of paper. Fold the papers and place them in a bowl. In small groups of three or four, each person then pulls a topic from the bowl and delivers an impromptu speech lasting one and a half to two minutes. Try to make your presentation as clear, organized, and fluent as possible.

5. Try a group speech. Five classmates stand in front of the class, and decide on a topic. The first person starts, and as soon as that person uses a non-fluency, the next person takes over. See how long each person can speak without using vocal fillers.

REFERENCES

Burke, K. 1969. *A rhetoric of motives*. Berkeley, CA: University of California Press.

Duffy, B., and H. Ryan, eds. 1987. *American Orators of the Twentieth Century: Critical Studies and Sources*. New York: Greenwood Press.

Fletcher, L. 1990. Polishing your silent languages. *The Toastmaster* (March), 14.

Shannon, M.L. and Stark, C.P. 2003. The influence of physical appearance on personnel selection. *Social Behavior and Personality*, 31(6), 613–124.

Sloane Coffin, W. 1988. How to wow 'em when you speak. *Changing Times*, August, 30.

SHORT ANSWER / SHORT ESSAY

HONOR STATEMENT: I, the undersigned student, hereby declare before God, before the school, and before the professor that I have read Chapter 14 in its entirety, that I have completed the following exercise with help from no other sources, and that I neither have shared nor will share this work with anyone.

Signature: _____   Date: _____

1. What are the four methods of delivery? Provide a specific example of a context/circumstance when each would be the best method of delivery.

_____

_____

_____

_____

_____

_____

_____

2. List and define each of the seven aspects of verbal delivery.

_____

_____

_____

_____

_____

_____

_____

_____

3. List and provide suggestions for each of the four aspects of physical delivery discussed in the chapter.

_____

_____

_____

_____

_____

_____

_____

_____

_____

_____

4. What do you need to remember about using note cards during your speech?

_____

_____

_____

_____

_____

_____

_____

_____

_____

5. Why is extemporaneous speaking generally the most appropriate form of delivery?

_____

_____

_____

_____

_____

_____

_____

_____

_____

_____

_____

_____

_____

6. Drawing from the chapter, list and explain at least six specific steps you will take in an attempt to improve vocal and physical aspects of your speech delivery? Be sure to explain each of these and why you listed it.

_____

_____

_____

_____

_____

_____

_____

_____

_____

_____

_____

_____

_____

_____

7. Drawing from the "Managing Speech Anxiety" sidebar toward the end of this chapter, define speech anxiety and state, in your own words, the specific steps the authors recommend for handling it as you prepare to give a speech.

_____

_____

_____

_____

_____

_____

_____

_____

_____

_____

_____

_____

_____

_____

_____

When you deliver
an informative speech,
your intent is to enlighten
your audience–to increase
understanding or awareness
and, perhaps, to create
a new perspective.

© 2012 by iStockphoto. Used under license of Thinkstock.

CHAPTER 15 >>

15 SPEAKING TO INFORM

Adapted from *Public Speaking: Choices for Effective Results, Fifth Edition* by John Makay et al. Copyright © 2008.
Reprinted with permission of Kendall Hunt Publishing Co.

❯ INFORMATIVE SPEAKING

When you deliver an informative speech, your goal is to communicate information and ideas in a way that your audience will understand and remember. Whether you are a nurse conducting CPR training for new parents at the local community center, a museum curator delivering a speech on impressionist art, or an auto repair shop manager lecturing to workers about the implications of a recent manufacturer's recall notice, you want your audience to gain understanding of your topic. An important caveat for students of public speaking to remember is that the audience should hear new knowledge, not facts they already know. For example, the nurse conducting CPR training for new parents would approach the topic differently than if the audience was comprised of individuals from various fields working on their yearly recertification. New parents may have never had CPR training, whereas the others receive training at least once a year.

© 2012 by Joseph August / Shutterstock.com. Used under license of Shutterstock.

If a doctor is outlining the latest advances in neurosurgery, he is giving an informational speech.

In this chapter, we first distinguish an informative speech from a persuasive one. The different types of informative speeches are identified, and goals and strategies for informative speaking are presented.

❯ INFORMATIVE VERSUS PERSUASIVE INTENT

When you deliver an informative speech, your intent is to enlighten your audience—to increase understanding or awareness and, perhaps, to create a new perspective. In contrast, when you deliver a persuasive speech, your intent is to influence your audience to agree with your point of view—to change attitudes or beliefs or to bring about a specific, desired action. In theory, these two forms are distinctly different. In practice, as we noted earlier, this may not be the case.

For example, if during an informative speech on the ramifications of calling off a marriage you suggest to the engaged couples in your audience that safeguards may have to be taken to prevent emotional or financial damage, you are being persuasive implicitly. If you suggest to the men in your audience that they obtain a written statement from their fiancées pledging the return of the engagement ring if the relationship ends, you are asking for explicit action, and you have blurred the line between information and persuasion.

The key to informative speaking is intent. If your goal is to expand understanding, your speech is informational. If, in the process, you also want your audience to share or agree with your point of view, you may also be persuasive. In describing the different kinds of assault rifles available to criminals, you may persuade your audience to support measures for stricter gun control. Some of your listeners may write to Congress while others may send contributions to lobbying organizations that promote the passage of stricter gun control legislation. Although your speech brought about these actions, it is still informational because your intent was educational.

To make sure your speech is informational rather than persuasive, start with a clear specific purpose signifying your intent. Compare the following two specific purpose statements:

Specific purpose statement #1 (SPS#1) To inform my listeners about the significance of the bankruptcy of the leading American energy company, Enron Corporation

Specific purpose statement #2 (SPS#2) To inform my listeners why the investment firm Drexel Burnham Lambert was a symbol of Wall Street greed, power, and the corruption that marked the decade of the 1980s

While the intent of the first statement is informational, the intent of the second is persuasive. The speaker in SPS#1 is likely to discuss the fallout of Enron's bankruptcy, such as decrease in consumer confidence, changes in federal securities laws, and how employees were affected. The speaker in SPS#2 uses subjective words such as "greed, power, and corruption." Most likely this speech would focus more on the unethical practices that resulted in employees and investors losing their life savings, children's college funds, and pensions when Enron collapsed.

❯TYPES OF INFORMATIVE SPEAKING

Although all informative speeches seek to help audiences understand, there are three distinct types of informative speeches. A speech of description helps an audience understand what something is. When the speaker wants to help us understand why something is so, he or she is offering a speech of explanation. Finally, when the focus is on how something is done, it is a speech of demonstration. Each of these will be discussed in more detail.

© 2012 by Peeradach Rattanakoses / Shutterstock.com.
Used under license of Shutterstock.

When the speaker wants to help us understand why something is so, he or she is offering a speech of explanation.

▲Speeches of Description

Describing the circus to a group of youngsters, describing the effects of an earthquake, and describing the buying habits of teenagers are all examples of informative speeches of description. These speeches paint a clear picture of an event, person, object, place, situation, or concept. The goal is to create images in the minds of listeners about your topic or to describe a concept in concrete detail. Here, for example, is a section of a speech describing a reenactment of the 1965 civil rights march in Selma, Alabama. We begin with the specific purpose and thesis statement:

Specific purpose. To have my audience learn of the important connections between the civil rights marches in Selma, Alabama in 1965 and 2005.

Thesis statement. Civil rights marchers returned to Selma, Alabama, in 2005 to commemorate the violence-marred march forty years earlier.

Thousands of civil rights marchers came together in Selma, Alabama, to walk slowly across the Edmund Pettus Bridge. The year was 2005 and the reason for the march was to commemorate the brutal and violent march that took place in Selma forty years earlier. The first march awakened the country to the need to protect the civil liberties of African Americans, but this one was a time of celebration and rededication to the cause of civil rights.

The 2005 march was peaceful. Only sound effects reminded participants of the billy club-wielding state troopers, of the screams and clomping horse hoofs, of the beatings and the inhumanity (Smothers, 1990).

In this excerpt, the speaker is making a contrast between two similar events that occurred forty years apart. Audience members are provided with images of what was named "Bloody Sunday," in 1965, and they can picture the peaceful, even celebratory, mood of the similar event forty years later. Specific, concrete language conveys the information through vivid word pictures.

Describing the circus to a group of youngsters, describing the effects of an earthquake, and describing the buying habits of teenagers are all examples of informative speeches of description.

▲Speeches of Explanation

Speeches of explanation deal with more abstract topics (ideas, theories, principles, and beliefs) than speeches of description or demonstration. They also involve attempts to simplify complex topics. The goal of these speeches is audience understanding. A psychologist addressing parents about the moral development of children or a cabinet official explaining U.S. farm policy are examples of speeches of explanation.

To be effective, speeches of explanation must be designed specifically to achieve audience understanding of the theory or principle. Avoid abstractions, too much jargon, or technical terms by using verbal pictures that define and explain. Here, for example, a speaker explains the concept of depression by telling listeners how patients describe it. Serious depression, a patient once said, is "like being in quicksand surrounded by a sense of doom, of sadness." Author William Styron described his own depression as "a veritable howling tempest in the brain" that took him down a hole so deep that he nearly committed suicide.

Veteran and senior CBS correspondent Mike Wallace reached a point in his life where he found himself unable to sleep, losing weight, and experiencing phantom pains in his arms and legs. "Depression is palpable," explained Wallace. "You begin to feel like a fake and a fraud. You second guess yourself about everything" (1990, 48–55).

Compare this vivid description with the following, more abstract version:

Severe depression involves dramatic psychological changes that can be triggered by heredity or environmental stress. Depression is intense and long lasting and may result in hospitalization. The disease may manifest itself in agitation or lethargy.

If the second is presented alone, listeners are limited in their ability to anchor the concept to something they understand. The second explanation is much more effective when combined with the first.

Speeches of explanation may involve policies: statements of intent or purpose that guide or drive future decisions. The president may announce a new arms control policy. A school superintendent may implement a new inclusion policy. The director of human resources of a major corporation may discuss the firm's new flextime policy.

A speech that explains a policy should focus on the questions that are likely to arise from an audience. For example, prior to a speech to teachers and parents before school starts, the superintendent of a school district implementing a new inclusion policy needs to anticipate what the listeners will probably want to know—when the policy change will be implemented, to what extent it will be implemented, when it will be evaluated, and how problems will be monitored, among other issues. When organized logically, these and other questions form the basis of the presentation. As in all informative speeches, your purpose is not to persuade your listeners to support the policy, but to inform them about the policy.

▲Speeches of Demonstration

Speeches of demonstration focus on a process by describing the gradual changes that lead to a particular result. These speeches often involve two different approaches, one is "how," and the other is a "how to" approach. Here are four examples of specific purposes for speeches of demonstration:

- To inform my audience how college admissions committees choose the most qualified applicants
- To inform my audience how diabetes threatens health
- To inform my audience how to sell an item on Ebay
- To inform my audience how to play the Internet game Bespelled

Speeches that take a "how" approach have audience understanding as their goal. They create understanding by explaining how a process functions without teaching the specific skills needed to complete a task. After listening to a speech on college admissions, for example, you may understand the process but may not be prepared to take a seat on an admissions committee.

In contrast, "how to" speeches try to communicate specific skills, such as selling an item on Ebay, changing a tire, or making a lemon shake-up. Compare the previous "how" example discussing network television show selection with the following "how to" presentation on "how to" make a lemon shake-up.

In front of me are all the ingredients for a lemon shake-up: lemons, water, sugar, a knife, and two cups. First, cut the lemons into quarters. If you love the tart taste of lemons...

At the end of this speech of demonstration, the listener should know the ingredients and how to make a lemon shake-up.

One clear difference between the speech of demonstration and the speeches of presentation and explanation is that the speech of demonstration benefits from presentational aids. When your goal is to demonstrate a process, you may choose to complete the entire process—or a part of it—in front of your audience. The nature of your demonstration and the constraints of time determine your choice. If you are giving CPR training, a partial demonstration will not give your listeners the information they need to save a life. If you are demonstrating how to cook a stew, however, your audience does not need to watch you chop onions; prepare in advance to maintain audience interest and save time.

❯❯GOALS AND STRATEGIES OF INFORMATIVE SPEAKING

Although the overarching goal of an informative speech is to communicate information and ideas in a way that the audience will understand, there are other goals that will help you create the most effective informative speech. Whether you are giving a speech to explain, describe, or demonstrate, the following five goals are relevant: be accurate, objective, clear, meaningful, and memorable. After each goal, two specific strategies for achieving that goal are presented.

© 2012 by Bevan Goldswain. Used under license of Shutterstock.

After a speech about how to play a digital game, the audience should know the game's objective and how to play it.

1. Be Accurate

Facts must be correct and current. Research is crucial to attaining this goal. Do not rely solely on your own opinion; find support from other sources. Information that is not current may be inaccurate or misleading. Informative speakers strive to present the truth. They understand the importance of careful research for verifying information they present. Offering an incorrect fact or taking a faulty position may hurt speaker credibility and cause people to stop listening. The following two strategies will help speakers present accurate information.

Question the source of information. Is the source a nationally recognized magazine or reputable newspaper, or is it from someone's post on a random blog? Source verification is important. Virtually anyone can post to the Internet. Check to see if your source has appropriate credentials, which may include education, work experience, or verifiable personal experience.

Consider the timeliness of the information. Information can become dated. There is no hard and fast rule about when something violates timeliness, but you can apply some common sense to avoid problems. Your instructor may take this decision-making out of your hands by requiring sources from the last several years or so. If not, the issue of timeliness relates directly to the topic. If you wanted to inform the class about the heart transplant process, relying on sources more than a few years old would be misleading because scientific developments occur continuously.

2. Be Objective

Present information that is fair and is unbiased. Purposely leaving out critical information or "stacking the facts" to create a misleading picture violates the rule of objectivity. The following two strategies should help you maintain objectivity.

Take into account all perspectives. Combining perspectives creates a more complete picture. Avoiding other perspectives creates bias, and may turn an informative speech into a persuasive one. The chief negotiator for a union may have a completely different perspective than the administration's chief negotiator on how current contract negotiations are proceeding. They may be using the same facts and statistics, but interpreting them differently. An impartial third party trying to determine how the process is progressing needs to listen to both sides and attempt to remove obvious bias.

Show trends. Trends put individual facts in perspective as they clarify ideas within a larger context. The whole—the connection among ideas—gives each detail greater meaning. If a speaker tries to explain how the stock market works, it makes sense to talk about the stock market in relation to what it was a year ago, five years ago, ten years ago, or even longer, rather than focus on today or last week. Trends also suggest what the future will look like.

3. Be Clear

To be successful, your informative speech must communicate your ideas without confusion. When a message is not organized clearly, audiences can become frustrated and confused and, ultimately, they will miss your ideas. Conducting careful audience analysis helps you understand what your audience already knows about your topic and allows you to offer a clear, targeted message at their level of understanding. The following strategies are designed to increase the clarity of your speech.

Carefully organize your message. Find an organizational pattern that makes the most sense for your specific purpose. Descriptive speeches, speeches of demonstration, and speeches of explanation have different goals. Therefore, you must consider the most effective way to organize your message. Descriptive speeches are often arranged in spatial, topical, and chronological patterns. Speeches of demonstration often use spatial, chronological, and cause-and-effect or problem-solution patterns. Speeches of explanation are frequently arranged chronologically, or topically, or according to cause-and-effect or problem-solution.

© 2012 by Robert Kneschke.
Used under license of Shutterstock.

Research is crucial to attain correct information to present in your speech.

Define unfamiliar words and concepts. Unfamiliar words, especially technical jargon, can defeat your purpose of informing your audience. When introducing a new word, define it in a way your listeners can understand. Because you are so close to your material, knowing what to define can be your hardest task. The best advice is to put yourself in the position of a listener who knows less about your topic than you do or ask a friend or colleague's opinion. In addition to explaining the dictionary definition of a concept or term, a speaker may rely on two common forms of definitions: operational and through example.

Operational definitions specify procedures for observing and measuring concepts. We use operational definitions to tell us who is "smart," based on a person's score on IQ test.

The government tells us who is "poor" based on a specified income level, and communication researchers can determine if a person has high communication apprehension based on his or her score on McCroskey's Personal Report of Communication Apprehension.

Definition through example helps the audience understand a complex concept by giving the audience a "for instance." In an effort to explain what is meant by the term, "white-collar criminal," a speaker could provide several examples, such as Jeff Skilling, (former Enron executive convicted on federal felony charges relating to the company's financial collapse), George Ryan (former Illinois governor indicted on federal racketeering, fraud, and conspiracy charges), and Duke Cunningham (former congressional representative from California, convicted of various bribery and fraud charges).

4. Be Meaningful

A meaningful, informative message focuses on what matters to the audience as well as to the speaker. Relate your material to the interests, needs, and concerns of your audience. A speech explaining the differences between public and private schools delivered to the parents of students in elementary and secondary school would not be as meaningful in a small town where no choice exists as it would be in a large city where numerous options are available. Here are two strategies to help you develop a meaningful speech:

Consider the setting. The setting may tell you about audience goals. Informative speeches are given in many places, including classrooms, community seminars, and business forums. Audiences may attend these speeches because of an interest in the topic or because attendance is required. Settings tell you the specific reasons your audience has gathered. A group of middle-aged women attending a lifesaving lecture at a local YMCA may be concerned about saving their husbands' lives in the event of a heart attack, while a group of nursing students listening to the same lecture in a college classroom may be doing so to fulfill a graduation requirement.

Avoid information overload. When you are excited about your subject and you want your audience to know about it, you can find yourself trying to say too much in too short a time. You throw fact after fact at your listeners until you literally force them to stop listening. Saying too much is like touring London in a day—it cannot be done if you expect to remember anything.

Information overload can be frustrating and annoying because the listener experiences difficulty in processing so much information. Your job as an informative speaker is to know how much to say and, just as importantly, what to say. Long lists of statistics are mind-numbing. Be conscious of the relationship among time, purpose, and your audience's ability to absorb information. Tie key points to anecdotes and humor. Your goal is not to "get it all in" but to communicate your message as effectively as possible.

5. Be Memorable

Speakers who are enthusiastic, genuine, and creative and who can communicate their excitement to their listeners deliver memorable speeches. Engaging examples, dramatic stories, and tasteful humor applied to your key ideas in a genuine manner will make a long-lasting impact.

Use examples and humor. Nothing elicits interest more than a good example, and humorous stories are effective in helping the audience remember the material. A speech on the negative effects of legalized abortion in American culture might be more powerful if it includes stories of individuals who exemplify this very point. The speaker might include specific examples of women who have been psychologically traumatized by their abortion experiences or of persons like Gianna Jessen who survived a botched abortion attempt with life-altering injuries. Never underestimate the power of good supportive examples. As Albert Schweitzer reportedly once put it, "Example is not the main thing in influencing others, it's the only thing."

Physically involve your audience. Ask for audience response to a question: "Raise your hand if you have…" Seek help with your demonstration. Ask some audience members to take part in an experiment that you conduct to prove a point. For example, hand out several headsets to volunteers and ask them to set the volume level where they usually listen to music. Then show how volume can affect hearing.

❯❯GUIDELINES FOR EFFECTIVE INFORMATIVE SPEECHES

Regardless of the type of informative speech you plan to give, there are characteristics of effective informative speeches that cross all categories. As you research, develop, and present your speech, keep the following nine characteristics in mind.

▲Consider Your Audience's Needs and Goals

Considering your audience is the theme of the book, but it is always worth repeating. The best informative speakers know what their listeners want to learn from their speech. A group of Weight Watchers members may be motivated to attend a lecture on dieting to learn how to lose weight, while nutritionists drawn to the same speech may need the information to help clients. Audience goals are also linked to knowledge. Those who lack knowledge about a topic may be more motivated to listen and learn than those who feel they already know the topic. However, it is possible that technology has changed, new information has surfaced, or new ways to think about or do something have emerged. The speaker needs to find a way to engage those who are less motivated.

Make connections between your subject and your audience's daily needs, desires, and interests. For example, some audience members might have no interest in a speech on the effectiveness of half-way houses until you tell them how much money is being spent on prisons locally, or better yet, how much each listener is spending per year. Now the topic is more relevant. People care about money, safety, prestige, family and friends, community, and their own growth and progress, among other things. Show how your topic influences one or more of these and you will have an audience motivated to listen.

▲Consider Your Audience's Knowledge Level

If you wanted to describe how to use eSnipe when participating in Ebay auctions, you may be speaking to students who have never heard of it. To be safe, however, you might develop a brief pre-speech questionnaire to pass out to your class. Or you can select several individuals at random and ask what they know. You do not want to bore the class with mundane minutia, but you do not want to confuse them with information that is too advanced for their knowledge level. Consider this example:

> As the golf champion of your district, you decide to give your informative speech on the game. You begin by holding up a golf club and saying, "This is a golf club. They come in many sizes and styles." Then you hold up a golf ball. "This is a golf ball. Golf balls are all the same size, but they come in many colors. Most golf balls are white. When you first start playing golf, you need a lot of golf balls. So, you need a golf club and a golf ball to play golf."

Expect your listeners to yawn in this situation. They do not want to hear what they already know. Although your presentation may be effective for an audience of children who have never seen a golf club or ball, your presentation has started out too simplistic even for people who have some knowledge of the game.

▲Capture Attention and Interest Immediately

As an informative speaker, your goal is to communicate information about a specific topic in a way that is understandable to your listeners. In your introduction, you must first convince your audience that your topic is interesting and relevant. For example, if you are delivering a speech on white-collar crime, you might begin like this:

> Imagine taking part of your paycheck and handing it to a criminal. In an indirect way, that's what we all do to pay for white-collar crime. Part of the tax dollars you give the federal government goes into the hands of unscrupulous business executives who pad their expenses and over-charge the government by millions of dollars. For example, General Dynamics, the third-largest military supplier, tacked on at least $75 million to the government's bill for such "overhead" expenses as country-club fees and personal travel for corporate executives...

This approach is more likely to capture audience attention than a list of white-collar crimes or criminals.

▲Sustain Audience Attention and Interest by Being Creative, Vivid, and Enthusiastic

Try something different. Change your pace to bring attention or emphasis to a point. Say the following phrase at a regular rate, and then slow down and emphasize each word: "We must work together!" Slowing down to emphasize each word gives the sentence much greater impact. Varying rate of speech can be an effective way to sustain audience attention.

Also, show some excitement! Talking about accounting principles, water filters, or changes in planet designations with spirit and energy will keep people listening. Delivery can make a difference. Enthusiasm is infectious, even to those who have no particular interest in

© 2012 by Comstock Images.
Used under license of Thinkstock.

Show some excitement regardless of your topic!

your subject. It is no accident that advertising campaigns are built around slogans, jingles, and other memorable language that people are likely to remember after a commercial is over. We are more likely to remember vivid language than dull language.

▲Cite Your Sources Orally and Accurately

Anytime you offer facts, statistics, opinions, and ideas that you found in research, you should provide your audience with the source. In doing this, you enhance your own credibility. Your audience appreciates your depth of research on the topic, and you avoid accusations of plagiarism. However, your audience needs enough information in order to judge the credibility of your sources. If you are describing how a specific TV show became an acclaimed yet controversial drama, it is not sufficient to say, "Ashley Smith states…" because Ashley Smith's qualification to comment on this show may be based on the fact that she watches television regularly. If the speaker said, "Ashley Smith, television critic for *The Chicago Tribune*, states…" then we know she has some expertise in the area.

▲Signpost Main Ideas

Your audience may need help keeping track of the information in your speech. Separating one idea from another may be difficult for listeners when trying to learn all the information at once. You can help your audience understand the structure of your speech by creating oral lists. Simple "First, second, third, fourth…" or "one, two, three, four…" help the audience focus on your sequence of points. Here is an example of signposting:

> Having a motorized scooter in college instead of a car is preferred for two reasons. The first reason is a financial one. A scooter gets at least 80 miles per gallon. Over a period of four years, significant savings could occur. The second reason a scooter is preferred in college is convenience. Parking problems are virtually eliminated. No longer do you have to worry about being late to class, because you can park in the motorcycle parking area. They're all around us…

Signposting at the beginning of a speech tells the audience how many points you have or how many ideas you intend to support. Signposting during the speech keeps the audience informed as to where you are in the speech.

▲Relate the New with the Familiar

Informative speeches should introduce new information in terms of what the audience already knows. Analogies can be useful. Here is an example:

> A cooling-off period in labor management negotiations is like a parentally-imposed time-out. When we were children, our parents would send us to our rooms to think over what we had done. We were forbidden to come out for at least an hour in the hope that by the time we were released our tempers had cooled. Similarly, by law, the President can impose an 80-day cooling-off period if a strike threatens to imperil the nation's health or safety.

Most of us can relate to the "time out" concept referred to in this example, so providing the analogy helps us understand the cooling-off period if a strike is possible. References to the familiar help listeners assimilate new information.

▲Use Repetition

Repetition is important when presenting new facts and ideas. You help your listeners by reinforcing your main points through summaries and paraphrasing. For example, if you were trying to persuade your classmates to purchase a scooter instead of a car, you might have three points: (1) A scooter is cheaper than a car; (2) A scooter gets better gas mileage than a car; and (3) You can always find a nearby parking spot for your scooter. For your first point, you mention purchase price, insurance, and maintenance cost. As you finish your first point, you could say, "So a scooter is cheaper than a car in at least three ways, purchase price, insurance, and maintenance." You have already mentioned these three sub-points, but noting them as an internal summary before your second main point will help reinforce the idea that scooters are cheaper than cars.

▲Offer Interesting Visuals

Using pictures, charts, models, PowerPoint slides, and other presentational aids helps maintain audience interest. Jo Sprague and Douglas Stuart, (1988) explain:

> Your message will be clearer if you send it through several channels. As you describe a process with words, also use your hands, a visual aid, a chart, a recording. Appeal to as many senses as possible to reinforce the message…If a point is very important or very difficult, always use one other channel besides the spoken word to get it across (299).

Use humorous visuals to display statistics, if appropriate. Demonstrate the physics of air travel by throwing paper airplanes across the room. With ever-increasing computer accessibility and WiFi in the classroom, using computer-generated graphics to enhance and underscore your main points and illustrations is a convenient and valuable way to help you inform your audience effectively.

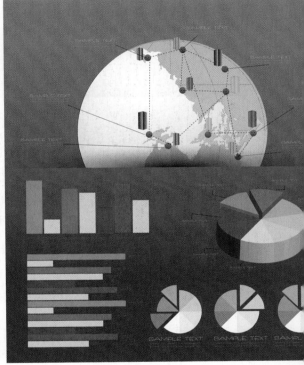

Using pictures, charts, models, PowerPoint slides, and other presentational aids helps maintain audience interest.

❯ETHICS OF INFORMATIVE SPEAKING

Think about the advertising you see on television and the warning labels on certain products you purchase. Listening to a commercial about a new weight-loss tablet, you think you have just found a solution to get rid of those extra twenty pounds you carry with you. Several happy people testify about how wonderful the drug is, and how it worked miracles for them. At the end of the commercial, you hear a speaker say, "This drug is not for children under 16. It may cause diarrhea, restlessness, sleeplessness, nausea, and stomach cramps. It can lead to heat strokes and heart attacks. Those with high blood pressure, epilepsy, diabetes, or heart disease should not take this medicine…" After

© 2012 by George Doyle.
Used under license of Thinkstock.

People in all vocations are ethically obligated to tell the truth and to not withhold information to serve personal gain.

listening to the warnings, the drug may not sound so miraculous. We have government regulations to make sure consumers make informed choices.

As an individual speaker, you need to regulate yourself. A speaker has ethical responsibilities, no matter what type of speech he or she prepares and delivers. The informative speeches you deliver in class and those you listen to on campus are not nearly as likely to affect the course of history as those delivered by high-ranking public officials in a time of war or national political campaigns. Even so, the principles of ethical responsibility are similar for every speaker.

The President of the United States, the president of your school, and the president of any organization to which you belong all have an obligation to inform their constituencies (audiences) in non-manipulative ways and to provide them with information they need and have a right to know. Professors, doctors, police officers, and others engaged in informative speaking ought to tell the truth as they know it, and not withhold information to serve personal gain. You, like others, should always rely on credible sources and avoid what political scientists label as "calculated ambiguity." Calculated ambiguity is a speaker's planned effort to be vague, sketchy, and considerably abstract.

You have many choices to make as you prepare for an informative speech. Applying God-honoring ethical standards will help with your decision-making. An informative speech requires you to assemble accurate, sound, and pertinent information that will enable you to tell your audience what you know to be the truth. Relying on outdated information, not giving the audience enough information about your sources, omitting relevant information, being vague intentionally, and taking information out of context are all violations of ethical principles.

❯SUMMARY

Informative speeches fall into three categories. Speeches of description paint a picture of an event, person, object, place, situation, or concept; speeches of explanation deal with such abstractions as ideas, theories, principles, and beliefs; and speeches of demonstration focus on a process, describing the gradual changes that lead to a particular result.

A somewhat blurry line exists between informative and persuasive speaking. Remember that in an informative speech your goal is to communicate information and ideas in a way that your audience will understand and remember. The key determinant in whether a speech is informative is speaker intent.

As an informative speaker, you should strive to be accurate, objective, clear, meaningful, and memorable. Preparing and delivering an effective informative speech involves applying the strategies identified in this chapter. In order to increase accuracy, make sure

HANDLING QUESTIONS & INTERRUPTIONS

In an informative speech, you are likely to encounter questions, comments, and interruptions while you speak. Here are some tips to cope with these unpredictable events.

Decide whether you want questions during your presentation or at the end. If you prefer they wait, tell your audience early in your speech or at the first hand raised something like, "I ask that you hold all questions to the end of this presentation, where I have built in some time for them."

When fielding questions, develop the habit of doing four things in this order: thank the questioner, paraphrase the question in your own words (for the people who may not have heard the question), answer the question briefly, and then ask the questioner if you answered their question.

Note that the second step in answering questions is to paraphrase the question in your own words. This provides you with the opportunity to point questions in desirable directions or away from areas you are not willing to go. Paraphrasing allows the speaker to stay in control of the situation.

For any question, you have five options: (1) answer it, and remember "I do not know" is an answer; (2) bounce it back to the questioner, "Well, that is very interesting. How might you answer that question?"; (3) Bounce it to the audience, "I see, does anyone have any helpful thoughts about this?"; (4) Defer the question until later, "Now you and I would find this interesting, but it is outside the scope of my message today. I'd love to chat with you individually about this in a moment"; (5) Promise more answer later, "I would really like to look further into that. May I get back to you later?" Effective speakers know and use all five as strategies to keep their question-and-answer period productive and on track.

When random interruptions occur, do not ignore them. Call attention to the distraction. This allows your audience to get it out and then return their attention to you. One speaker was interrupted when a window washer suspended outside the building dropped into view, ropes and all. The speaker paused, looked at the dangling distraction and announced, "Spiderman!" Everyone laughed, and he then returned to his speech. At a banquet, a speaker was interrupted by the crash of shattering dishes from the direction of the kitchen. She quipped, "Sounds like someone lost a contact lens." Whether humorous or not, calling attention to distractions is key to maintaining control.

The heckler is a special kind of distraction that requires prompt attention. If you notice a man in the audience making comments for others to hear that undercut your message, first, assume he is trying to be helpful. Ask him to share his comments for all to hear. This will usually stop the heckler. If it does not, ask him his name, and use it as often as you can in your message. This usually works because oftentimes the heckler simply wants more attention. When all else fails, enlist the assistance of your audience. Ask if anyone wants to hear what you have to say more than what the heckler is saying. (Your audience will indicate they do.) Then ask if there is a volunteer, preferably a big one, who can help us all out. The combination of humiliation and the implied threat should do the trick.

you question the source of information, consider the timeliness, and accurately cite your sources orally. Being objective includes taking into account all perspectives and showing trends. Crucial to any speech is clarity. To aid your audience, carefully organize your message, define unfamiliar words and concepts, signpost main ideas, relate the new with the familiar, and use repetition.

Audience members have gathered for different reasons. No matter what the reason, you want your speech to be meaningful to all listeners. In doing so, consider the setting, your audience's needs and goals and knowledge level, and try to avoid information overload. An informative speaker also wants people to remember his or her speech. In order to meet that goal, try to capture attention and interest immediately, sustain audience attention and interest by being creative, vivid, and enthusiastic, use examples and humor, offer interesting visuals, and physically involve your audience.

As you prepare your informative speech, make sure the choices you make are based on a God-honoring ethical standard. You have an obligation to be truthful, and we presented many ways to accomplish this as you prepare your speech as well as when you deliver it.

QUESTIONS FOR ANALYSIS

1. How does speaker intent differentiate informative from persuasive speaking?

2. How do the three types of informative speeches differ?

3. What are the characteristics of an effective informative speech?

4. What is the purpose of providing five goals for informative speeches?

5. How can effective visuals enhance an informative speech?

6. What role do ethics play in informative speaking?

 ACTIVITIES

1. Attend an informative lecture on campus (not a class lecture). Assess whether the lecture was strictly informative or whether it was also persuasive. Describe and explain your findings in a written report.

2. Prepare a five-to-six minute informative speech that is primarily a description, an explanation, or a demonstration. Develop a planning and key-word outline, and practice the speech aloud.

3. Attend another informative lecture in your community. Take notes on the effectiveness of the speaker's message. Describe the techniques the speaker used to improve communication. Evaluate the speech on the message and the presentation.

REFERENCES

Beating depression. 1990. *U.S. News & World Report*, March 5, 48–55.

Carter, B. 1992. Right of spring in assessing the next season's hopefuls. *New York Times*, May 11, C6.

Crime in the suites. 1985. Time, June 10, 56–7; Stealing $200 billion 'the respectable' way. 1985. *U.S. News & World Report*, May 20, 83–85; Making punishment fit white-collar crime.1987. *Business Week*, June 15, 84–85.

Smothers, R. 1990. A Selma march relives those first steps of '65, *New York Times*, March 5, B6.

Sprague, J., and D. Stuart. 1988. *The speaker's handbook (2nd ed.)*. San Diego, CA: Harcourt Brace Jovanovich.

SHORT ANSWER / SHORT ESSAY

HONOR STATEMENT: I, the undersigned student, hereby declare before God, before the school, and before the professor that I have read Chapter 15 in its entirety, that I have completed the following exercise with help from no other sources, and that I neither have shared nor will share this work with anyone.

Signature: _____   Date: _____

1. How does speaker intent differentiate informative from persuasive speaking?

_____

_____

_____

_____

_____

_____

_____

2. How can you avoid having an informative speech that ends up actually being a persuasive speech?

_____

_____

_____

_____

_____

_____

_____

_____

_____

_____

3. What are the three types of informative speeches? Describe how they differ from each other.

_____

_____

_____

_____

_____

_____

_____

_____

_____

_____

_____

4. Review the nine guidelines for effective informative speeches. Which three of these do you believe to be the most important? Identify these and explain why you chose them.

_____

_____

_____

_____

_____

_____

_____

_____

_____

5. Why is extemporaneous speaking generally the most appropriate form of delivery?

_____

_____

_____

_____

_____

_____

_____

_____

_____

_____

_____

6. Review chapter 5's list of things God values according to Scripture. Identify three items on this list that relate directly to a public speaker's duty to be ethical in the speech preparation and delivery process. Explain your answers.

_____

_____

_____

_____

_____

_____

_____

_____

_____

Persuasion is intended to influence choice through appeals to the audience's sense of ethics, reasoning, and emotion.

CHAPTER 16 »

© 2012 by iStockphoto.
Used under license of Thinkstock.

16 SPEAKING TO PERSUADE

Adapted from *Public Speaking: Choices for Effective Results, Fifth Edition* by John Makay et al. Copyright © 2008.
Reprinted with permission of Kendall Hunt Publishing Co.

Individuals engage in persuasive speaking at all levels of communication. Interpersonally, we try to convince people to share our opinions or attitudes about very small things ("Burger King fries are better than McDonald's fries") and very significant things ("We shouldn't have children until we've been married for ten years"). We also engage in persuasive discourse at a societal level ("God loathes homosexual behavior"). The ability to express one's self is a cornerstone of our democracy. The power of free speech is most clearly realized in speeches to persuade.

© 2012 by Regina Jershova.
Used under license of Shutterstock.

Sharing your opinion on something even as simple as where you will go to eat lunch involves persuasion skills.

ELEMENTS OF PERSUASION

Persuasion is intended to influence choice through appeals to the audience's sense of ethics, reasoning, and emotion. Aristotle's views on the use of what he termed ethos, pathos, and logos provide the underpinnings of our modern study of persuasion.

Ethos and the Power of the Speaker's Credibility

Aristotle believed that ethos, which refers to speaker credibility, makes speakers worthy of belief. Audiences trust speakers they perceive as honest, especially "on points outside the realm of exact knowledge, where opinion is divided." In this regard, he believed, "we trust [credible speakers] absolutely. . . ."(Cooper 1960, 8). Politicians often appeal to their title (president, chairperson, senator, etc) when attempting to be persuasive because they assume the title will help them appear to be more trustworthy or believable in the eyes of the audience.

Dimensions of Speaker Credibility

What your audience knows about you before you speak and what they learn about your position during your speech may influence your ability to persuade them. Credibility can be measured according to four dimensions: perceived competence, concern for the audience, dynamism, and ethics.

Perceived competence. In many cases, your audience will decide your message's value based on perceived speaker competence. Your listeners will first ask themselves whether you have the background to speak. If the topic is crime, an audience is more likely to be persuaded by the Atlanta chief of police than by a postal worker delivering his personal opinions. Second, your audience will consider whether the content of your speech has firm support. When it is clear that speakers have not researched their topic, their ability to persuade diminishes. Finally, audiences will determine whether you communicate confidence and control of your subject matter through your delivery.

Concern for audience. Persuasion is also influenced by concern for your audience. Communication Professor Richard L. Johannesen (1974) differentiates between speakers who engage in "dialogue" and those who engage in "monologue." A dialogue considers the welfare of the audience; a monologue focuses only on the speaker's self-interest (95).

Audiences sense a speaker's concern by first analyzing the actions a speaker has taken before the speech. If the group has formed to protest the location of a highway through a residential community, the audience will consider what the speaker has already done to convince highway officials to change their minds. Second, audiences listen carefully to the strength and conviction of the speaker's message. For instance, does the speaker promise to fly to Washington, D.C., if necessary, to convince federal officials to withhold funds until a new site is chosen? Persuasive speakers are able to convince their audiences that they are on their side.

Dynamism. Your credibility and, therefore, your ability to persuade are also influenced by the audience's perception of you as a dynamic spokesperson. A person who is dynamic is lively, active, vigorous, and vibrant. Your listeners will ask themselves whether you have the reputation for being someone who gets the job done. They will listen for an energetic style that communicates commitment to your point of view, and for ideas that build upon one another in a convincing, logical way.

Ethics. Finally, your ability to persuade is influenced by the audience's perception of your ethical standards. If you come to the lectern with a reputation for dishonesty, few people will be persuaded to trust what you say. If your message is biased and you make little attempt to be fair or to concede the strength of your opponent's point of view, your listeners may question your integrity. They may have the same questions if you appear manipulative (Sprague and Stuart 1988, 208–10).

Does credibility make a difference in your ability to persuade? Researchers have found that, in many cases, the most credible speakers are also the most persuasive (Aronson, Turner, and Carlsmith 1963). One powerful way speakers enhance their credibility is by creating a strong sense of identification in their audiences.

The Strategy of Identification: Seeking Common Ground

Your credibility and your ability to persuade may increase if you convince your audience that you share "common ground." In his classic work, *Public Speaking*, published in 1915, James A. Winans introduced the concept of "common ground." "To convince or persuade a man," he writes, "is largely a matter of identifying the opinion or course of action which you wish him to adopt with one or more of his fixed opinions or customary courses of action. When his mind is satisfied of the identity, then doubts vanish" (Day 1959).

Left-wing labor leader Cesar Chavez forged a common bond with his audience after a twenty-day fast in 1968 to call attention to the plight of California farm workers by proclaiming that the end of his fast was not the true reason for the gathering. Rather, people had come to observe that, "we are a family bound together in a common struggle for justice. We are a Union family celebrating our unity and the nonviolent nature of our movement." Chavez explained why he had fasted: "My heart was filled with grief and pain for the suffering of farm workers. The Fast was first for me and then for all of us in this Union. It was a Fast for nonviolence and a call to sacrifice." Chavez concluded with, "We have something the rich do not own. We have our own bodies and spirits and the justice of our cause as our weapons. It is how we use our lives that determines what kind of men we are. . . . I am convinced that the truest act of courage, the strongest act of manliness is to sacrifice ourselves for others in a totally non-violent struggle for justice. To be a man is to suffer for others. God help us to be men" (Hammerback and Jensen 1987, 57).

In this instance, Chavez establishes a common ground through identifying with his audience and provoking them to identify with him. Moreover, Chavez also makes effective use of emotional arguments, which Aristotle referred to as pathos.

▲Pathos and the Power of Emotion

Aristotle believed in the power of speakers to persuade through emotional appeals. He explained, "Persuasion is effected through the audience, when they are brought by the speech into a state of emotion; for we give very different decisions under the sway of pain or joy, and liking or hatred. . . ."(Cooper 1960, 9).

© 2012 Paul Horvath.
Used under license of Shutterstock.

Aristotle believed that ethos, which refers to speaker credibility, makes speakers worthy of belief.

Appeal to Audience Emotion

Emotional appeals have the power to elicit happiness, joy, pride, patriotism, fear, hate, anger, guilt, despair, hope, hopelessness, bitterness, and other feelings. George Kennedy (1991), a scholar of classical rhetoric, tells us, "Emotions in Aristotle's sense are moods, temporary states of mind (123–4). But according to persuasion theorists Martha Cooper and William Nothstine (1992), "modern research into motivation and the passions moved beyond Aristotle's emphasis on the emotions themselves and moved extensively into broader theories of human psychology" (74). The persuader, they advise us, can influence his or her audience by using appeals to create an emotional, as well as a cognitive, state of imbalance in listeners, which arouses feelings that something is wrong and something must be done. By taking the essential needs of an audience into consideration, the persuader can develop lines of reasoning that respond to pertinent needs. Yes, human needs can be described in terms of logic or what makes sense to a listener, but needs are immersed in emotions of the individual as well.

Maslow's Hierarchy of Needs

Psychologist Abraham Maslow classified human needs according to the hierarchy pictured in figure 16.1 (page 450). An analysis of these needs will help you understand audience motivation as you attempt to persuade. Maslow believed that our most basic needs—those at the bottom of the hierarchy—must be satisfied before we can consider those on the next levels. In effect, these higher level needs are put on "hold" and have little effect on our actions until the lower level needs are met.

Physiological needs. At the bottom of the hierarchy are our biological needs for food, water, oxygen, rest, and release from stress. If you were delivering a speech in favor of a proposed new reservoir to a community experiencing problems with its water supply, it would be appropriate to appeal to the need for safe and abundant water.

Safety needs. Safety needs in-clude the need for security, freedom from fear and attack, a home that offers tranquility and comfort, and a means of earning a living. If you are delivering the same speech to a group of unemployed construction workers, you might link the reservoir project to jobs and a steady family income.

Belongingness and love needs. These needs refer to our needs for affiliation, friendship, and love. When appealing to the need for social belonging, you may choose to emphasize the camaraderie that will emerge from the community effort to bring the reservoir from the planning stage to completion.

Esteem needs. Esteem needs include the need to be seen as worthy and competent and to have the respect of others. In this case, an effective approach would be to praise community members for their initiative in helping to make the reservoir project a reality.

© 2012 by Robert Kneschke.
Used under license of Shutterstock.

FIGURE 16.1
Maslow's Hierarchy
of Needs

Self-actualization needs. People who reach the top of the hierarchy seek to fulfill their highest potential through personal growth, creativity, self-awareness and knowledge, social responsibility, and responsiveness to challenge. Addressing this audience, you might emphasize the long-range environmental and ecological implications of the reservoir. Your appeal may include the need to safeguard the water supply for future generations.

Maslow's Hierarchy of Needs can guide you in preparing a persuasive speech when you think about the feelings of your audience and how you can reach them in combination with the factors of credibility and sound argument. Understanding the basis for Maslow's hierarchy is critical to your success as a persuasive speaker, for if you approach your listeners at an inappropriate level of need, you will find them unable or unwilling to respond.

Our emotions are powerful ingredients in our human composition. You accept an ethical responsibility when you use emotional appeals. The ethically responsible speaker does not distort, delete, or exaggerate information for the sole purpose of emotionally charging an audience in order to manipulate their feelings for self-centered ends.

Yet, emotional appeals are often the most persuasive type of appeal because they provide the motivation listeners need to change their minds or take action. Instead of simply listing the reasons high fat foods are unhealthy, a more effective approach is to tie these foods to frightening consequences:

Jim thought nothing could ever happen to him. He was healthy as an ox—or so he thought. His world fell apart one sunny May morning when he suffered a massive heart attack. He survived, but his doctors told him that his coronary arteries were blocked and that he needed bypass surgery. "Why me?" he asked. "I'm only 42 years old." The answer, he was told, had a lot to do with the high fat diet he had eaten since childhood.

Some subjects are more emotionally powerful than others and lend themselves to emotional appeals. Stories such as personal health crises, children in need, or experiences with crime and deprivation engage the emotions of listeners. Delivery also has an impact. Your audience can tell if you are speaking from the heart or just mouthing words. They respond to the loudness of your voice, the pace and rhythm of your speech, and to your verbal cues. Finally, the placement of the appeal is important. Corporate speech consultant James Humes suggests using an emotional ending to motivate an audience to action. In his view, the same emotions that stir people in their private lives motivate audiences. He explains, "CEOs tell me, 'Listen, Jim, I'm not trying to save England, I'm just trying to get a message across to the company.' Well, you still want to ask the employees to join you in something. End on an emotional pitch. Work that audience up" (Kleinfeld 1990).

Because of their power, emotional appeals can be tools of manipulation in the hands of unscrupulous speakers who attempt to arouse audiences through emotion rather than logic. These speakers realize that fear and other negative emotions can be more powerful persuaders than reason when the audience is receptive to their emotional message.

Your credibility and your ability to persuade may increase if you convince your audience that you share common ground with them.

▲Logos and the Power of Logical Appeals and Arguments

In addition to ethical (ethos) and emotional (pathos) appeals and arguments, logos or logical appeals and arguments are critical to the persuasive process. A logical appeal is rational and reasonable based on evidence provided. For example, if a friend tried to convince you not to buy a new car by pointing out that you are in college, have no savings account, and are currently unemployed, that friend would be making a logical argument. Aristotle saw the power of persuasion relying on logical arguments and sound reasoning.

Reasoning refers to the sequence of interlinking claims and arguments that, together, establish the content and force of your position. Although we believe the treatment of public speaking throughout this book promotes being reasonable, no aspect of our book is more instrumental in guiding you to improve your critical thinking than reasoning as logical appeal. Logical thought as critical thinking is intended to increase your ability to assess, analyze, and advocate ideas. As a persuasive speaker you will reason logically either through induction or deduction. Your responsibility is to reason by offering your audience factual or judgmental statements based on sound inferences drawn from unambiguous statements of knowledge or belief (Freeley 1993, 2).

To construct a sound, reasonable statement as a logical appeal for your audience you need to distill the essential parts of an argument:

1. The evidence in support of an idea you advocate;
2. A statement or contention the audience is urged to accept; and,
3. The inference linking the evidence with the statement.

Of the three parts to an argument, the most difficult part to understand is often the inference. It may be an assumption that justifies using evidence as a basis for making a claim or drawing a conclusion. For example, suppose you take a big bite out of food you have taken for dinner in your cafeteria or apartment and claim, "This is the worst piece of meat I have ever put in my mouth." With this claim you are making a statement that you infer from tasting the meat.

What is the evidence? The meat before you. The statement or contention is, "The meat is awful." The relation of the evidence to the claim is made by an inference, which may be an unstated belief that spoiled, old, or poorly prepared meat will taste bad. Stephen Toulmin, the British philosopher acknowledged as an expert on argument, speaks of the inferential link between evidence and claim as the warrant. Toulmin points out that a warrant is the part of the argument that states or implies an inference (Vancil 1993, 120–24).

When you reason with your audience by trying to persuade the listeners with an argument you want them to accept and act upon, you must use evidence, inferences, and statements as contentions the audience can understand and accept. Sound reasoning is especially important when your audience is skeptical. Faced with the task of trying to convince people to change their minds or do something they might not otherwise be inclined to do, your arguments must be impressive.

Sound reasoning is especially important when your audience is hostile.

Supporters in an audience may require arguments in the form of reinforcement. You may have to remind a sympathetic crowd of the reasons your shared point of view is correct. This reminder is especially important if your goal is audience action. If you want a group of sympathetic parents to attend a board of trustees meeting to protest tuition increases, you must persuade them that a large turnout is necessary. It is up to you, through the presentation of an effective argument, to make action the most attractive course.

In persuasion, ethical and emotional appeals may be powerful factors, but reasoning or logical appeal can be your most effective tool. Well-developed reasons stated without exaggeration tell your listeners that you trust them to evaluate the facts on their merit rather than emotional appeal. Through the framework of a logical appeal, we piece together important elements to persuade listeners to accept our position and respond to a call to action. The framework for logical appeal is based on inductive and deductive modes of reasoning, in particular reasoning by analogy, reasoning from cause, and reasoning from sign.

To persuade your audience that a claim or conclusion is highly probable, you must have strong evidence and show that you have carefully reasoned the support of your points. Only when strong probability is established can you ask your listeners to make the inductive leap from specific cases to a general conclusion, or to take the deductive move from statements as premises to a conclusion you want them to accept. We will look more closely now at inductive and deductive reasoning.

Inductive Reasoning

Aristotle spoke of inductive reasoning in his *Rhetoric* (Cooper 1960, 10). Through inductive reasoning, we generalize from specific examples and draw conclusions from what we observe. Inductive reasoning moves us from the specific to the general in an orderly, logical fashion.

When you argue on the basis of example, the inference step in the argument holds that what is true of specific cases can be generalized to other cases of the same class, or of the class as a whole. Suppose you are trying to persuade your audience that the disappearance of downtown merchants in your town is a problem that can be solved with an effective plan you are about to present. You may infer that what has worked to solve a similar problem in a number of highly similar towns is likely to work in the town that is the subject of your speech.

One problem associated with inductive reasoning is that individual cases do not always add up to a correct conclusion. Sometimes a speaker's list of examples is too small, leading his/her audience to an incorrect conclusion based on limited information. Here, as in all other cases of inductive reasoning, you can never be sure that your conclusions are absolutely accurate. Because you are only looking at a sample, you must persuade your audience to accept a conclusion that is probable, or maybe even just possible.

a. Reasoning by Analogy

Analogies establish common links between similar and not-so-similar concepts. They are effective tools of persuasion when you can convince your audience that the characteristics of one case are similar enough to the characteristics of the second case that your argument about the first also applies to the second.

As noted in Chapter Six, a figurative analogy draws a comparison between things that are distinctly different, such as "Eating fresh marshmallows is like floating on a cloud." Figurative analogies can be used to persuade, but they must be supported with relevant facts, statistics, and testimony that link the dissimilar concepts you are comparing.

Although figurative analogies can provide valuable illustrations, they will not prove your point. For example, before the United States entered World War II, President Franklin D. Roosevelt used the analogy of a "garden hose" to support his position that the United States should help England, France, and other European countries already involved in the war. In urging the passage of the Lend-Lease Bill, he compared U.S. aid to the act of lending a garden hose to a neighbor whose house was on fire. Although this analogy supplied ethical and emotional proof, it did not prove the point on logical grounds. It is vastly different to lend a garden hose to a neighbor than it is to lend billions of dollars in foreign aid to nations at war (Freeley 1993, 119).

Whereas a figurative analogy compares things that are distinctly different and supply useful illustrations, a literal analogy compares things with similar characteristics and, therefore, requires less explanatory support. One speaker in our class compared the addictive power of tobacco products, especially cigarettes, with the power of alcoholic beverages consumed on a regular basis. His line of reasoning was that both are consumed

© 2012 by Feng Yu.
Used under license of Shutterstock.

You must have strong evidence and show that you've carefully supported your points to convince your audience that your claim has merit.

for pleasure, relaxation, and often as relief for stress. While his use of logical argument was obvious, the listener ultimately assesses whether or not these two things—alcohol and tobacco are sufficiently similar. It may be that their differences diminish the strength of the speaker's argument. The distinction between literal and figurative analogies is important because only literal analogies are sufficient to establish a logical proof. The degree to which an analogy works depends on the answers to the following questions:

1. *Are the cases being compared similar?* Only if you convince your listeners of significant points of similarity will the analogy be persuasive.

2. *Are the similarities critical to the success of the comparison?* The fact that similarities exist may not be enough to prove your point. Persuasion occurs when the similarities are tied to critical points of the comparison.

3. *Are the differences relatively small?* In an analogy, you compare similar, not identical, cases. Differences can always be found between the items you are comparing. It is up to you as an advocate for your position to decide how critical the differences are.

4. *Can you point to other similar cases?* You have a better chance of convincing people if you can point to other successful cases. If you can show that the similarities between your position and these additional cases are legitimate, you will help sway audience opinion (Freely 1993, 119–20).

b. Reasoning from Cause

When you are reasoning from cause the inference step is that an event of one kind contributes to or brings about an event of another kind. The presence of a cat in a room when you are allergic to cats is likely to bring about a series of sneezes until the cat is removed. As the preceding example demonstrated, causal reasoning focuses on the cause-and-effect relationship between ideas.

> *Cause:* inaccurate count of the homeless for the 2000 census
> *Effect:* less money will be spent aiding the homeless

An advocate for the homeless delivered the following message to a group of supporters: We all know that money is allocated by the federal government, in part, according to the numbers of people in need. The census, conducted every ten years, is supposed to tell us how many farmers we have, how many blacks and Hispanics, how many homeless.

Unfortunately, in the 2000 census, many of the homeless were not counted. The government told us census takers would go into the streets, into bus and train station waiting rooms, and into the shelters to count every homeless person. As advocates for the homeless, people in my organization know this was not done. Shelters were never visited. Hundreds and maybe thousands of homeless were ignored in this city alone. A serious undercount is inevitable. This undercount will cause fewer federal dollars to be spent aiding those who need our help the most.

When used correctly, causal reasoning can be an effective persuasive tool. You must be sure that the cause-and-effect relationship is sound enough to stand up to scrutiny and criticism. To test the validity of your reasoning, ask yourself the following questions:

1. *Do the cause and effect you describe have anything to do with one another?* Some statements establish a cause-and-effect relationship between ideas when the relationship is, at best, questionable. Ask yourself whether other factors contributed to the change. You may be attributing cause and effect where there is only coincidence.

2. *Is the cause acting alone or is it one of many producing the effect?* Even if the connection you draw is valid, it may be only one of several contributing factors that bring about an effect. To isolate it as solely responsible for an effect is to leave listeners with the wrong impression.

3. *Is the effect really the effect of another cause?* To use a medical example, although fatigue and depression often occur simultaneously, it may be a mistake to conclude that depression causes fatigue when other factors may also be involved. Both conditions may be symptoms of other illnesses such as mononucleosis, or the result of stress.

4. *Are you describing a continuum of causes and effects?* When you are dealing with an interrelated chain of causes and effects, it is wise to point out that you are looking at only one part of a broader picture.

5. *Are the cause and effect related but inconsequential?* Ask yourself whether the cause you are presenting is sufficient to bring about the effect you claim.

6. *Is your claim and evidence accurate?* To be an effective persuasive tool, causal reasoning must convince listeners that the link you claim is accurate. Your listeners should be able to judge probability based on your supporting evidence. They will ask themselves if your examples prove the point and if you explain or minimize conflicting claims (Sprague and Stuart 1988, 165–66).

To be effective, causal reasoning should never overstate. By using phrases like, "This is one of several causes," or "The evidence suggests there is a cause-and-effect link," you are giving your audience a reasonable picture of a complex situation. Public speakers could learn from medical researchers who are reluctant to say flatly that one thing causes another. More often than not, researchers indicate that cause-and-effect relationships are not always clear and that links may not be as simple as they seem.

A figurative analogy draws a comparison between things that are distinctly different, such as "Eating fresh marshmallows is like floating on a cloud."

c. Reasoning from Sign

In the argument from sign, the inference step is that the presence of an attribute can be taken as the presence of some larger condition or situation of which the attribute is a part. As you step outside in the early morning to begin jogging, the gray clouds and moist air can be interpreted as signs that the weather conditions are likely to result in a rainy day. Argumentation Professor David Vancil (1993) tells us that, "arguments from sign are based on our understanding of the way things are associated or related to each other in the world with them, [so] we conclude that the thing is present if its signs are present. The claim of a sign argument is invariably a statement that something is or is not the case" (149).

The public speaker who reasons from sign must do so with caution. Certainly, there are signs all around us to interpret in making sense of the world, but signs are easy to misinterpret. Therefore, the responsible speaker must carefully test any argument before using it to persuade an audience.

Deductive Reasoning

Aristotle also spoke of deduction as a form of reasoning in persuasive argument. Through deductive reasoning, we draw conclusions based on the connections between statements that serve as premises. Rather than introducing new facts, deductions enable us to rearrange the facts we already know, putting them in a form that will make our point. Deductive reasoning is the basis of police work and scientific research, enabling investigators to draw relationships between seemingly unrelated pieces of information. At the heart of deductive reasoning is the syllogism, a pattern of reasoning involving a major and a minor premise and a conclusion. Syllogisms take this form:

$$a = b$$
$$b = c$$
$$c = a$$

Here is an example:

1. All basketball players can dribble the ball.
2. Anthony is a basketball player.
3. Anthony can dribble the ball.

Using this pattern of logic, the conclusion that Anthony can dribble the ball is inescapable. If your listeners accept your premise, they are likely to accept your conclusion. The major premise in this case is the statement (1) "All basketball players can dribble the ball," while the minor premise is statement (2) "Anthony is a basketball player." Whether the deductive reasoning is stated in part or not, it leads us down an inescapable logical path. By knowing how two concepts relate to a third concept, we can say how they relate to each other.

Recognizing that people do not usually state every aspect of a syllogism as they reason deductively, Aristotle identified the enthymeme as the deductive reasoning used in persuasion. Because speakers and listeners often share similar assumptions, the entire argument may not be explicitly stated, even when the elements of a syllogism are all present. This truncated, or shortened, form of deductive reasoning is the enthymeme. The inference step in reasoning with an enthymeme is that the audience, out of its judgment and values, must supply and accept the missing premises or conclusions. If a classmate in a persuasive speech makes the claim that a newly elected congressional representative will probably take unnecessary trips costly to the taxpayers, your classmate's claim is drawn from the major premise (unspoken) that most, if not all, congressional representatives engage in unnecessary and costly travel.

The interrelationships in a syllogism can be established in a series of deductive steps:

1. Step One: Define the relationship between two terms.

   Major premise: Plagiarism is a form of ethical abuse.

2. Step Two: Define a condition or special characteristic of one of the terms.

   Minor premise: Plagiarism involves using the words of another author without quotations or footnotes as well as improper footnoting.

3. Step Three: Show how a conclusion about the other term necessarily follows (Sprague and Stuart 1988, 160).

   Conclusion: Students who use the words of another, but fail to use quotations or footnotes to indicate this, or who intentionally use incorrect footnotes, are guilty of an ethical abuse.

Your ability to convince your listeners depends on their acceptance of your original premise and the conclusion you draw from it. The burden of proof rests with your evidence. Your goal is to convince your listeners through the strength of your supporting material to grant your premises and, by extension, your conclusion. Considering persuasion from the vantage point of such outcomes will be considered next.

Causal reasoning is effective if your argument can withstand scrutiny.

▲Persuasive Goals, Aims, and Claims

Since Aristotle, scholars have focused on the elements of ethos, pathos, and logos as the primary aspects of persuasion. Some researchers have added to these principles an emphasis on outcomes. Gary Woodward and Robert Denton, Jr. (1992), explain: "Persuasion is the process of preparing and delivering messages through verbal and nonverbal symbols to individuals or groups in order to alter, strengthen, or maintain attitudes, beliefs, values, or behaviors" (18–19). Careful consideration of the goals of persuasion, the aims of your speech, and the type of claim you are making will help your message achieve the influence that will allow you to advance your agenda.

1. Goals of Persuasion

Critical to the success of any persuasive effort is a clear sense of what you are trying to accomplish. As a speaker, you must define for yourself your overall persuasive goals and the narrower persuasive aims. The two overall goals of persuasion are to address attitudes and to move an audience to action.

Speeches that focus on attitudes. In this type of speech, your goal is to convince an audience to share your views on a topic (e.g., "The tuition at this college is too high" or "too few Americans bother to vote"). The way you approach your goal depends on the nature of your audience.

When dealing with a negative audience, you face the challenge of trying to change your listeners' opinions. The more change you hope to achieve the harder your persuasive task. In other words, asking listeners to agree that U.S. automakers need the support of U.S. consumers to survive in the world market is easier than asking the same audience to agree that every American who buys a foreign car should be penalized through a special tax. By contrast, when you address an audience that shares your point of view, your job is to reinforce existing attitudes (e.g., "U.S. automakers deserve our support"). When your audience has not yet formed an opinion, your message must be geared to presenting persuasive evidence. You may want to explain to your audience, for example, the economic necessity of buying U.S. products.

Speeches that require action. Here your goal is to bring about actual change. You ask your listeners to make a purchase, sign a petition, attend a rally, write to Congress, attend a lecture, and so on. The effectiveness of your message is defined by the actions your audience takes.

Motivating your listeners to act is perhaps the hardest goal you face as a speaker, since it requires attention to the connection between attitudes and behavior. Studies have shown that what people feel is not necessarily what they do. That is, little consistency exists between attitudes and actions (Wicker 1969, 41–70). Even if you convince your audience that you are the best candidate for student body president, they may not bother to vote. Similarly, even if you persuade them of the dangers of smoking, confirmed smokers will probably continue to smoke. Researchers have found several explanations for this behavior.

First, people say one thing and do another because of situational forces. If support for your position is strong immediately after your speech, it may dissipate or even disappear in the context in which the behavior takes place. For example, even if you convince listeners to work for your political campaign, if their friends ridicule that choice, they are unlikely to show up at campaign headquarters.

Researchers have found that an attitude is likely to predict behavior when the attitude involves a specific intention to change behavior, when specific attitudes and behaviors are involved, and when the listener's attitude is influenced by firsthand experience (Zimbardo 1988, 618–19). Firsthand experience is a powerful motivator. If you know a sun worshipper dying from melanoma, you are more likely to heed the speaker's advice to wear sun block than if you have no such acquaintance. An experiment by D. T. Regan and R. Fazio (1977) proves the point:

> A field study on the Cornell University campus was conducted after a housing shortage had forced some of the incoming freshmen to sleep on cots in the dorm lounges. All freshmen were asked about their attitudes toward the housing crisis and were then given an opportunity to take some related actions (such as signing a petition or joining a committee of dorm residents). While all of the respondents expressed the same attitude about the crisis, those who had had more direct experience with it (were actually sleeping in a lounge) showed a greater consistency between their expressed attitudes and their subsequent behavioral attempts to alleviate the problem (28–45).

Therefore, if you were a leader on this campus trying to persuade freshmen to sign a petition or join a protest march, you would have had greater persuasive success with listeners who had been forced to sleep in the dorm lounges. Once you establish your overall persuasive goals, you must then decide on your persuasive aims.

2. Persuasive Aims

The aims of persuasion, or the type and direction of the change you seek, is the important next consideration. You must define the narrower aims of your speech. Four persuasive aims define the nature of your overall persuasive goal.

Adoption. When you want your audience to start doing something, your persuasive goal is to urge the audience to adopt a particular idea or plan. As a spokesperson for the American Cancer Society, you may deliver the following message: "I urge every woman over the age of forty to get a regular mammogram."

Continuance. Sometimes your listeners are already doing the thing you want them to do. In this case, your goal is to urge continuance. For example, the same spokesperson might say:

> I am delighted to be speaking to this organization because of the commitment of every member to stop smoking. I urge all of you to maintain your commitment to be smoke free for the rest of your life.

Speeches which urge continuance are necessary when the group is under pressure to change. In this case, the spokesperson realized that many reformed smokers constantly fight the urge to begin smoking again.

Discontinuance. You attempt to persuade your listeners to stop doing something:
> I can tell by looking around that many people in this room spend hours sitting in the sun. I want to share with you a grim fact. The evidence is unmistakable that there is a direct connection between exposure to the sun and the deadliest of all skin cancers—malignant melanoma.

Deterrence. In this case, your goal is avoidance. You want to convince your listeners not to start something, as in the following example:

> We have found that exposure to asbestos can cause cancer twenty or thirty years later. If you have flaking asbestos insulation in your home, don't remove it yourself. Call in experts who have the knowledge and equipment to remove the insulation, protecting themselves as well as you and your family. Be sure you are not going to deal with an unscrupulous contractor who is likely to send in unqualified and unprotected workers likely to do a shoddy job.

Speeches that focus on deterrence are responses to problems that can be avoided. These messages are delivered when a persuasive speaker determines that an audience possesses something which the speaker sees as highly threatening or likely to result in disaster. The speaker may try to bring about some sort of effective block or barrier to minimize, if not eliminate, the threat or danger. New homeowners, for example, may find themselves listening to persuasive presentations about the purchase of a home security system. The thrust of such a persuasive speech is the need to prevent burglary through use of an effective and economical security system.

3. Types of Persuasive Claims

Within the context of these persuasive goals and aims, you must decide the type of persuasive message you want to deliver. Are you dealing with a question of fact, value, or policy? To decide, look at your thesis statement which expresses your judgment or point of view. In persuasive speeches, the thesis statement is phrased as a proposition that must be proved.

For example, if your thesis statement was, "All college students should be required to take a one-credit Physical Education course each year," you would be working with a proposition of policy. If instead, your thesis statement was, "Taking a Physical Education course each year will benefit all college students," this would be a proposition of value. Propositions are necessary because persuasion always involves more than one point of view. If yours were the only way of thinking, persuasion would be unnecessary. Because your audience is faced with differing opinions, your goal is to present your opinion in the most effective way. The three major types of propositions are those of fact, value, and policy.

Proposition of fact. Because facts, like beauty, are often in the eye of the beholder, you may have to persuade your listeners that your interpretation of a situation, event, or concept is accurate. Like a lawyer in a courtroom, you have to convince people to accept the facts as you understand them. Here are two examples of facts which would require proof:

1. Water fluoridation can lead to health problems.
2. American corporations are losing their hold on many world markets.

When dealing with propositions of fact, you must convince your audience that your evaluation is based on widely accepted standards. For example, if you are trying to prove that water fluoridation can lead to health problems, you might point to a research article that cites the Environmental Protection Agency (EPA) warning that long-term exposure to excessive fluoridation can lead to joint stiffness and pain and weak bones. You may also support your proposition by citing another research study that reports that children who are exposed to too much fluoridation may end up having teeth that are pitted and/or permanently stained.

Informative speakers become persuasive speakers when they cross the line from presenting facts to presenting facts within the context of a point of view. The informative speaker lets listeners decide on a position based on their own analysis of the facts. By contrast, the persuasive speaker draws the conclusion for them.

© 2012 by AISPIX by Image Source. Used under license of Shutterstock.

Even if you convince a group that you are the best candidate, they may not bother to vote in the election.

Proposition of value. Values are deep-seated beliefs that determine what we consider good or bad, moral or immoral, satisfying or unsatisfying, proper or improper, wise or foolish, valuable or invaluable, and so on. Persuasive speeches that deal with propositions of value are assertions based on these beliefs. The speaker's goal is to prove the worth of an evaluative statement, as in the following examples:

1. It is *wrong* for men to leave all the housework and childcare to their working wives.
2. Plagiarism is terribly *dishonest* for anyone who engages in it to complete an assignment.

When you use words that can be considered judgments or evaluations, such as those italicized above, you are making a proposition of value.

Proposition of policy. Propositions of policy are easily recognizable by their use of the word "should":

1. Campus safety should be the number one priority of the college.
2. Student-athletes should adhere to the same academic standards as other students.

In a policy speech, speakers convince listeners of both the need for change and what that change should be. They also give people reasons to continue listening and, in the end, to agree with their position and to take action.

A speaker's persuasive appeal, in summary, derives from the audience's sense of the speaker's credibility as well as from appeals to an audience's emotion and logic. At times, one persuasive element may be more important than others may. Many speakers try to convince audiences based primarily on logical appeal, some use mainly emotional appeals, and others rely on their image and credibility as a speaker. The most effective speakers consider their intended outcomes and appropriately combine all persuasive elements to meet a variety of audience needs and achieve their ultimate persuasive ends. Now we will wturn our attention to a powerfully influential sequence of steps often used to organize persuasive messages.

❯❯MONROE'S MOTIVATED SEQUENCE

As emphasized throughout this text, communication is a process connecting both speaker and audience. This awareness is particularly important in speeches to persuade, for without taking into account the mental stages your audience passes through, your persuasion may not succeed. The motivated sequence, a widely used method for organizing persuasive speeches developed by the late communication professor Alan H. Monroe (1965), is rooted in traditional rhetoric and shaped by modern psychology.

The method focuses on five steps to motivate your audience to act, and as Monroe would tell his students, they follow the normal pattern of human thought from attention to action. The motivated sequence clearly serves the goal of action if all five steps are followed. When the goal is to move your audience to act, each of the following five steps would be needed.

If someone wants only to persuade the audience there is a problem, then only the first two steps are necessary. If the audience is keenly aware of a problem, then a speaker may focus only on a solution.

Attention. Persuasion is impossible without attention. Your first step is to capture your listeners' attention in your introduction and convince them that you have something to say that is of genuine importance to them. You have several possibilities, including making a startling statement, using an anecdote, and asking a rhetorical question. For example, in addressing the problem of injuries and deaths in youth baseball, Cherie Spurling (1992) began her speech by saying:

> Take me out to the ball game. Take me out to the crowd. Buy me some peanuts and Cracker Jack. I don't care if I ever get back …" Have you ever thought you might go to a ball game and never get back? Neither did nine-year-old Ryan Wojic. As his mother drove him to the ball field one day Ryan announced, "I am going to steal two bases, Mom …" His mother replied: "Ryan, you don't have to steal two bases; just do the best you can." We'll never know whether Ryan would have stolen two bases or done the best he could, because his first time up to bat was his last time up to bat. He sustained a lethal injury, and Ryan Wojic never got back.

Need. In the need step, you describe the problem you will address in your speech. You hint or suggest at a need in your introduction, then state it in a way that accurately reflects your specific purpose. Your aim in the need step is to motivate your listeners to care about the problem by making it clear the problem affects them. You can illustrate the need by using examples, intensifying it through the use of carefully selected additional supporting material, and linking it directly to the audience. Too often the inexperienced speaker who uses the motivated sequence will pass through the need step too quickly in haste to get to the third step, the satisfaction step. Let us look at how Ms. Spurling described part of the need to recognize and eliminate a serious problem she asked her audience to face.

> Ryan Wojic was killed when one of these speeding balls struck his chest. His heart went into immediate cardiac arrhythmia and paramedics could not revive him. And Ryan is not alone, as I mentioned previously. A Consumer Product Safety

Commission Report stated that in a single ten-year period 51 children have died from baseball injuries. Of these, 23 were caused by the impact of the ball to the chest. The players at greatest risk are the pitchers and batters, and every kid bats at some point.

The same holds true for the risk of head and facial injuries. Take the case of Daniel Schwartz for instance, as reported by ABC's Stone Phillips. Thirteen-year-old Daniel went up to bat. The first ball was pitched low; the second to the inside. The third nailed Daniel in the face, shattering his cheekbone and nearly destroying his left eye. According to the April 1988 issue of *American Health*, each year baseball produces thousands of stories like Daniel's.

Satisfaction. The satisfaction step presents a solution to the problem you have just described. You offer a proposal in the form of an attitude, belief, or action you want your audience to adopt and act upon. Explanations in the form of statistics, testimony, examples, and other types of support ensure that your audience understands exactly what you mean. You clearly state what you want your audience to adopt and then explain your proposal. You have to show your audience how your proposal meets the need you presented. To be sure everyone understands what you mean, you may wish to use several different forms of support accompanied by visuals or audiovisual aids. An audience is usually impressed if you can show where and how a similar proposal has worked elsewhere. Before you move to the fourth step, you need to meet objections that you predict some listeners may hold. We are all familiar with the persuader who attempts to sell us a product or service and wants us to believe it is well worth the price and within our budget. In fact, a considerable amount of sales appeal today aims at selling us a payment we can afford as a means to purchasing the product, whether it is an automobile, a vacation, or some other attractive item. If we can afford the monthly payment, a major objection has been met. Here is how Ms. Spurling wanted to solve the problem she addressed:

> Well, "some sort" of protection has been developed. *American Health* reports that Home Safe, Inc. has found an all-star solution. Teams like the Atlee Little Leaguers in Mechanicsville, Virginia, have solved many of their safety problems by wearing face shields like this one [shown]. This molded plastic shield snaps onto the earflaps of the standard batter's helmet, which incidentally, was invented in 1959 by none other than Creighton Hale. Most youth teams require the use of a batter's helmet, but with this shield they could add complete facial protection, including the eyes, for a cost of under $15 per shield. Daniel Schwartz's injuries have cost $23,000 so far.

> Players could also be protected from chest impact death by wearing one of these padded vests [shown]. The vest may be a bit of a hindrance, that's true, but had Ryan Wojic been wearing one he would probably be stealing bases today.

Visualization. The visualization step encourages listeners to picture themselves benefiting from the adoption of your proposal. It focuses on a vision of the future if your proposal is adopted and, just as important, if it is rejected. It may also contrast these two visions, strengthening the attractiveness of your proposal by showing what will happen if no action is taken.

Positive visualization is specific and concrete. Your goal is to help listeners see themselves under the conditions you describe. You want them to experience enjoyment and satisfaction. In contrast, negative visualization focuses on what will happen without your plan. Here you encourage discomfort with conditions that would exist. Whichever method you choose, make your listeners feel part of the future. Ms. Spurling's speech did not include the visualization step but rather moved from satisfying the need to calling for action. Before moving to her strong call for audience action she could have added persuasive appeal to this important message. She might have said:

© 2012 by wavebreakmedia ltd.
Used under license of Shutterstock.

How can you capture an audience's attention in your introduction to keep them listening?

Imagine yourself on a quiet and lazy summer afternoon watching your own child, a niece, a nephew, a cousin or a neighborhood friend up to bat in an exciting youth-league baseball game. Think about the comfort you will experience when you see that she or he has the proper safety equipment on so that there is no possibility that a speeding baseball will take his or her life, or result in any permanent disability. See for a moment the face and the form of a child enthusiastically awaiting the pitch and see as well this child effectively shielded from impact that could come from a missed pitch.

Action. The action step acts as the conclusion of your speech. Here you tell your listeners what you want them to do or, if action is not necessary, the point of view you want them to share. You may have to explain the specific actions you want and the timing for these actions. This step is most effective when immediate action is sought.

Many students find the call to action a difficult part of the persuasive speech. They are reluctant to make an explicit request for action. Can you imagine a politician failing to ask people for their vote? Such a candidate would surely lose an election. When sales representatives have difficulty in closing a deal because they are unable to ask consumers to buy their products, they do not last long in sales. Persuasion is more likely to result when direction is clear and action is the goal. Ms. Spurling concluded her speech by asking her audience:

We must realize, however, that it may be awhile before this equipment scores a home run, so now it is your turn up to bat. If you are personally interested in protecting these young ball players, spread the word about these injuries, especially to businesses that sponsor youth teams. Encourage them to purchase safety equipment for the teams and then to sponsor them only on the condition that the equipment be used.

You can also write to Little League of America or any other youth league, requesting that they take their members' safety more seriously. And yes, do write to your congressional representative, because he or she may have a child or grandchild who plays on a youth team. Finally, if you happen to have a few extra dollars in your pocket, you could purchase some of this equipment and donate it to a local team as I'll do with this [equipment shown].

Ms. Spurling provided effective closure to her persuasive speech and call for action when she told her audience:

Now that we have discovered how children are being seriously injured and even killed while playing baseball, I know that you agree that given the children's lack of skill, we need to mandate the use of face shields, padded vests, and safer balls. So take them out to the ball game, but make it one that children can play safely, because children may be dying to play baseball, but they should never die because of it.

In review, remember the five-step pattern if you want to lead your audience from attention to action. The motivated sequence is effective, and like all tools of persuasion, can be misused. The line between use and abuse of persuasive tools warrants further examination.

❯ETHICS AND PERSUASIVE SPEAKING

Do you want to be lied to—by anyone? Even when the truth hurts, we prefer it to deception. Telling the truth is the paramount ethical standard for the persuasive speaker. The importance of ethics in public speaking is stressed both implicitly and explicitly throughout this book. Ethics provide standards for conduct that guides us. Persuasive speaking requires asking others to accept and act on ideas we believe to be accurate and true. The ethics of persuasion merit particular consideration in our plans for persuasion.

Think for a few moments about rhetoric as persuasive speaking. Rhetoric is framed and expressed in language and presents ideas within a range of choice. As a speaker, when you make choices, some degree of value is involved in your choosing, whether you speak about the quality of the environment or television programs to select. When choice is involved, ethics are involved. Rhetoric and ethics are bound together.

As a speaker, you must decide not only what to tell your audience, but also what you should avoid saying. In a persuasive speech, you are asking listeners to think or act in ways needed to achieve your specific purpose, a desired response. Emotional appeals entail ethical responsibility, and this responsibility extends to other appeals as well. In your attempt to be ethical in persuasive speaking, consider four principles, or habits, that must be considered:

1. The habit of search, in which we look for information to confirm or contradict a point of view, demands that we express genuine knowledge of our subject and an awareness of its issues and implications. As a persuasive speaker, you know that controversy exists in matters requiring persuasion. Your task, within the time

constraints you face and resources you utilize, is to develop sound and good reasons for the response you desire from an audience. This task is centered in a careful search for the truth.

2. The habit of justice asks that you be fair in your search, selection, and presentation of facts for the audience to consider and accept. You should not distort ideas or hide information that an audience needs to properly evaluate your speech, neither should you use loaded language or guilt-by-association tactics.

3. The habit of preferring public to private motivation stems from the fact that when you are involved in public speaking, you act as public persons. As such, you have a responsibility to disclose any special bias, prejudice, and private motivations in your sources and in your own motives. There are times in our society when political, religious, or economic spokespersons will articulate a public position that clearly indicates motives in the public interest when, in fact, their persuasive message is actually rooted in a private agenda that is self-serving.

4. The habit of respect for dissent requires that, as a persuasive speaker, you must recognize the legitimate diversity of positions that differ from yours. As a persuader, you are not compelled to sacrifice principle but, as Karl Wallace (1955) puts it, you should "prefer facing conflict to accepting appeasement" (9). Leaders who serve as spokespersons, from local community centers to the centers of power in Washington, DC, are constantly being challenged about their opinions, policies, and actions. As a persuasive speaker, you can ask with respect for dissent:

"May I freely admit the force of opposing evidence and argument and still advocate a position that represents my convictions?"

The ethics of persuasion call for honesty, care, thoroughness, openness, and a concern for the audience without manipulative intent. The end does not justify the means at all costs. In a society as complex as ours, one marked in part by unethical as well as ethical persuaders, the moral imperative is to speak ethically.

❯❯ SUMMARY

Your credibility as a speaker is determined by the way the audience perceives you. Credibility is measured in terms of perceived competence, concern for the audience, dynamism, and ethics. According to rhetorical theorist Kenneth Burke, you can increase your credibility and ability to persuade if you convince your audience that you share "common ground" by identifying with your listeners.

Emotional appeals (pathos) can be powerful because they provide the motivation for action and attitude change. Through emotional appeals you can elicit the full range of human feelings in your listeners. To strengthen your appeal, use concrete detail and emotional language, and concentrate on delivering your speech effectively. Persuasive speaking also invites ethical responsibility (ethos). As a persuasive speaker, you should be conscious of ethical standards and what the implications are of the choice you are asking your audience to make. The audience needs to be treated to the truth, without manipulative intent.

Understanding Abraham Maslow's hierarchy of human needs is helpful to persuasive speakers. The five levels of Maslow's hierarchy form a pyramid, with the basic levels forming the base. From bottom to top, these needs are physiological, safety, belongingness and love, esteem, and self-actualization. If you approach your listeners at an appropriate level of need, you will find them more able or willing to respond.

When making logical arguments (logos), one can take an inductive or deductive approach. Inductive reasoning enables you to generalize from specific instances and draw a conclusion from your observations. Deductive reasoning draws a conclusion based on the connections between statements. Depending on your purpose for persuasion, you may choose to reason from examples, analogies, causal relations, or with enthymemes. Choosing the right amount of support, the most persuasive kind of evidence, and then reasoning carefully are essential for successful persuasion.

The two overall persuasive goals are to address audience attitudes and to move an audience to action. Four specific persuasive aims define the focus of your speech. These aims include adoption, continuance, discontinuance, and deterrence. Your point of view, or thesis statement, is expressed in the form of a proposition that must be proved. Propositions take three basic forms: fact, value, and policy.

An effective method for organizing a persuasive speech is Monroe's Motivated Sequence that includes five steps designed to motivate the audience to action: attention, need, satisfaction, visualization, and action. The motivated sequence is a widely used method for organizing persuasive speeches which follows the normal pattern of human thought from attention to action.

Honesty is an essential quality in public speaking.

QUESTIONS FOR ANALYSIS

1. What are the dimensions of credibility, and how important is credibility to the overall effectiveness of a persuasive speech?

2. How would you define persuasion, persuasive goals, and persuasive aims? Illustrate your definitions with specific examples.

3. Why is the motivated sequence audience-centered? How does the motivated sequence relate to Maslow's hierarchy of needs?

4. What are ethical, logical, and emotional appeals? How are these appeals distinct, yet interrelated?

5. After choosing a specific purpose for a persuasive speech, decide on the kind of reasoning that will provide the strongest arguments. Why did you choose this reasoning form?

6. How important is evidence in a persuasive speech? How important are ethics in persuasive speaking? Does the importance depend on the audience and its shared needs and expectations? Is there a relationship among evidence, emotions, and credibility, or is evidence simply a matter a presenting the facts?

ACTIVITIES

1. List three people you recognize as spokespersons on important public issues. In a written analysis, describe the ethos of each speaker.

2. Select a persuasive political speech and analyze the reasoning used in the speech. Present an oral analysis to the class.

3. Find transcripts, excerpts, or detailed news accounts of a well-known courtroom trial. Write a 500- to 750-word essay on the role of persuasive appeals in the attorneys' opening and closing arguments. Your focus should be on the strengths and weaknesses of the attorneys' persuasive appeals.

4. Prepare a five- to six-minute persuasive speech, organizing it according to the motivated sequence. Prepare a written analysis of why the speech fits the requirements of the sequence. Then deliver the speech to your class.

5. Look through an anthology of speeches, such as Vital Speeches of the Day, or a video collection, to find an effective persuasive speech. Evaluate the persuasion used in the speech according to what you learned in this chapter.

REFERENCES

Aronson, E., J. A. Turner, and J. M. Carlsmith. 1963. Communicator credibility and communication discrepancy as determinants of opinion change. *Journal of Abnormal and Social Psychology*, 67: 31–36.

Cooper, L. 1960. *The rhetoric of Aristotle*. New York: Appleton-Century-Crofts.

Cooper, M. D., and W. L. Nothstine. 1992. *Power persuasion moving from an ancient art into the media age.* Greenwood, IN: The Educational Video Group.

Day, G. D. 1959. *Persuasion and the concept of identification.* Paper delivered at the SAA Convention, Washington, DC.

Freeley, A. J. 1993. *Argumentation and debate: Critical thinking for reasonable decision-making (8th ed.).* Belmont, CA: Wadsworth Publishing.

Hammerback, J. C., and R. J. Jensen. 1987. Cesar Estrada Chavez, in B.K. Duffy and H. R. Ryan (Eds.), *American orators of the twentieth century: Critical studies and sources* New York: Greenwood Press.

Johannesen, R. L. Summer 1974. Attitude of speaker toward audience: A significant concept for contemporary rhetorical theory and criticism. *Central States Speech Journal*, 95.

Kennedy, G. A. (Trans.). 1991. *Aristotle's on rhetoric—A theory of civic discourse.* New York: Oxford Press.

Kleinfield, N. R. March 11, 1990. "Teaching the 'Sir Winston' method," *New York Times*, Section 3, 7.

Monroe, A. H. 1965. Monroe first explained the motivated sequence to the author in a 1965 seminar on "The Psychology of Speech" at Purdue University. See also Gronbeck, B. E.,

German, K., Ehninger, D. and Monroe, A. H. *Principles of speech communication (11th brief ed.)* New York: Harper Collins, 263–272.

Regan, D. T., and R. Fazio. 1977. On the consistency between attitudes and behavior: Look to the method of attitude formation. *Journal of Experimental Social Psychology*, 13: 28–45. Cited in Zimbardo, 618. (Listed below.)

Sprague, J., and D. Stuart. 1988. *Speaker's handbook (2nd ed.).* San Diego, CA: Harcourt Brace Jovanovich.

Spurling, C. 1992. Batter up—Batter down. *Winning orations of the interstate oratorical association.* Mankato State University: The Interstate Oratorical Association.

Vancil, D. L. 1993. *Rhetoric and argumentation.* Boston: Allyn and Bacon.

Wicker, A. W. 1969. Attitudes versus actions. The relationship of verbal and overt behavioral responses to attitude objects. *Journal of Social Sciences* 25, no. 4, 41–78.

Wallace, K. R. January 1955. An ethical basis of communication. *The Speech Teacher*: 9.

Woodward, G., and R. Denton, Jr. 1992. *Persuasion and influence in American life (2nd ed.),* Prospect Heights, IL: Waveland Press.

Zimbardo, P. G. 1988. *Psychology and life (12th ed.).* Glenview, IL: Scott, Foresman and Company.

SHORT ANSWER / SHORT ESSAY

1. What are the three critical elements of persuasion according to Aristotle?

_____

_____

_____

_____

_____

_____

_____

_____

2. Explain the four dimensions that make up a speaker's credibility.

_____

_____

_____

_____

_____

_____

_____

_____

_____

3. Explain what is meant by term "common ground" and why is it important for the speaker to establish this with the audience.

_____

_____

_____

_____

_____

_____

_____

_____

_____

4. Explain the three parts of a logical argument.

_____

_____

_____

_____

_____

_____

_____

_____

_____

5. What is the difference between a syllogism and an enthymeme? Why are these considered deductive forms of reasoning?

_____

_____

_____

_____

_____

_____

_____

_____

_____

6. Explain each of the steps in Monroe's Motivated Sequence.

_____

_____

_____

_____

_____

_____

_____

_____

_____

_____

_____

_____

_____

Individual commitment
to a group effort –
that is what makes
a team work, a company
work, a society work,
a civilization work."
- Vince Lombardi

CHAPTER 17 >>

17 SMALL GROUP PRESENTATIONS

Adapted from *Public Speaking: Choices for Effective Results, Fifth Edition* by John Makay et al. Copyright © 2008.
Reprinted with permission of Kendall Hunt Publishing Co.

◆SMALL GROUPS IN LIFE

Small groups are a part of life. If you are on the editorial board of your school newspaper or are an organizer of the community blood drive, you are a member of a small group. If you are a member of a church, a musical, athletic, or academic group, you are a member of a small group. Think about how many groups you have participated in, and realize your membership in small groups may increase after you leave college. In business, academic life, government, and civic affairs, tasks are defined and completed through small-group communication. Many of the major decisions affecting your life are made by small groups. College admissions departments, school boards, and zoning boards are a few groups whose policies directly influence behavior.

Small groups are a part of life and you may have opportunities to speak before your city council, school board, or other community groups.

As a homeowner, you may have an opportunity to present before a governing board. Perhaps you are a budding environmentalist who has noticed that the city has been pruning trees excessively or is making plans to eliminate landmark trees in order to widen streets. You take an opportunity to encourage the city council to approach city growth in a more "green" fashion. As a parent, you speak before the school board to convince them to eliminate vending machine drinks that contain sugar and/or caffeine. You argue that these are not healthy choices for young school children. In these situations, you have asked to speak before some group. As a professional, however, you receive requests to speak before a group because of your expertise. A state senator might talk to the local League of Women Voters about proposed state legislation. An insurance agent presents a bid before the city council or school board. As the chair of a university-funded organization, you present a budget request before the school's Apportionment Board, the group that allocates funds to college organizations.

▲Participating in a Small Group

The most common way to be involved in groups is to participate in a small group. Groups meet for a variety of purposes. Sometimes the purpose of a small group meeting is to discuss a current problem. For example, if your organization is low on funds. You must find a way to raise money. A group of individuals wanting to become a recognized group on campus, needs to think of a strategy for presenting your case to the appropriate governing body. Everyone contributes to the discussion, and usually a designated leader facilitates the discussion. In college, study groups, sororities and fraternities, residence halls, honorary societies, academic groups, athletic groups, and church groups are just some of the possible ways you connect with others through small group communication.

▲Speaking as an Individual Before a Group

A second way to be involved with a small group is by speaking before one. This is considered public speaking and is the focus of this part of the text book. Unlike regular public speaking, however, you may have two audiences, not one. The primary audience is the small group, such as a seven-member school board, a five-member city council, or a ten-member Apportionment Board. Your purpose is to provide information, to express a concern, or attempt to persuade. Also in attendance, however, may be a secondary audience. This is a collection of individuals who attend the open meeting for any number of reasons, including simply observing its proceedings. It's possible these individuals may have no knowledge or interest in your specific topic, and did not know you were planning to speak.

In a situation involving both primary and secondary audiences, do you construct a message for the primary audience, accepting the fact that the secondary audience may not understand the context, concern or content? Or do you construct a message that takes into account both audiences, knowing that for members of the primary audience, some of the information will be unnecessary or redundant? Complexity of the issue, size of the secondary audience, and time constraint are a few of the factors to consider before developing your message.

When presenting in small groups, members need to consider which format is most appropriate for the occasion.

▲Speaking as a Member of a Group Before a Group

Alternatively, you may find yourself in a third speaking situation where you are a member of a small group presenting before another group. This may occur in your business class when you are part of a group presenting a case study, in a psychology class when your group presents results of its research project, or in a public relations class when you are asked, as a group, to present your public relations campaign. There are many instances in college when you work as a group to accomplish a task and report the results to your classmates. In your community, as a health care professional, you may be asked to join a panel with several other health care professionals to discuss the health care crisis before a group of senior citizens. The focus is not just on you, but on your group.

Many contexts are possible with the small group presentation, including being the only person who speaks before a small group or being one of many individuals who speak before a group. In some instances you will find yourself on a panel with individuals you have never met and in others you will participate in significant small group interaction before your group presents. Given our interest in helping you become the most effective speaker possible regardless of context, this chapter will focus on (1) working in small groups, and (2) presenting in small groups. In order to work in a small group, it is helpful to know the characteristics of small groups, including purpose, goals, and size. When presenting in small groups, each person should understand his or her role responsibilities, and the members should consider which group format is most appropriate for the purpose and audience. Included in this chapter are suggestions for working in a small group and small group performance guidelines.

❯WORKING IN SMALL GROUPS

In a college classroom, whether or not you were able to choose your "groupmates," the members of your group, these are the individuals with whom you must interact and cooperate. Each person brings to the group his or her own predispositions, attitudes, work ethic, personality, knowledge, and ability. You may find your groupmates friendly, fascinating, frustrating, or infuriating. Likewise, they will have their own perceptions of you and of each other. Regardless, in all but the most dire circumstances, you will traverse the hills and valleys of group work with these people.

© 2012 Rido.
Used under license of Shutterstock.

Chances are you've been involved in various small groups, such as a study group, during college.

▲Characteristics of Small Groups

We should acknowledge that many academic institutions have semester-long courses devoted to the topic of small group communication, and we could discuss small group characteristics indefinitely. However, for our purposes, three characteristics seem to be most relevant to the public speaking classroom.

Shared purpose. One characteristic of a small group is that group members share a purpose for communication, unlike a collection of individuals who share the same physical space. Seven people waiting in line for tickets to see the Los Angeles Lakers are not considered members of a small group. Neither are five people sharing a taxi from the Dallas-Fort Worth airport or eight people sitting in a dentist's waiting room. They lack a communication purpose. But if the individuals waiting in line for tickets interact with each other to form a cooperative so that only one of the seven individuals will wait in line for tickets at subsequent games, they would then have a shared purpose that would guide communication in all future meetings.

Group-oriented and self-oriented goals. A second characteristic of small groups is that members usually have both group-oriented and self-oriented goals. Group-oriented goals center around specific tasks to be performed, whereas self-oriented goals relate to the individual's personal needs and ambitions. Say you are a member of a small group charged with the responsibility of determining policies of a new campus radio station. Some of the tasks you face are developing station operating policies, purchasing equipment, and attracting advertisers. As an individual, however, a self-oriented goal may be to emerge as leader of the group in order to demonstrate leadership potential. Self-oriented goals may complement group-oriented goals, or they may provide distracting roadblocks.

Size. A third characteristic of small groups is group size. Scholars agree that a group must have a minimum of three members to be considered a small group. Communication professor Vincent DiSalvo notes that the ideal group size is from five to seven members (DiSalvo 1973, 111–112). According to Philip E. Slater, "These groups are large enough for individuals to express their feelings freely and small enough for members to care about the feelings and needs of other group members" (Slater 1958). However, a three-person group may lose effectiveness if one member is left out or if one member withdraws or chooses not to contribute. Also, groups with even numbers need to have some mechanism in place for solving the problem of a potential tie. As groups grow in numbers, the need for coordination and structure increases.

▲Role Responsibilities

When you become a group member, how you communicate is shaped, in large part, by your role in the group. If you have been appointed leader or have a special expertise that sets you apart from the other members, you may be given more responsibility than the other members.

Roles quickly emerge in small groups. While one group member emerges as the leader, taking the initiative in setting the group's agenda, another is uncommunicative and plays a minor role in group discussions. Still other members of the group may try to dominate the discussion, oppose almost every point raised, and close their minds before the discussion begins (Bales 1953, 111–61).

The role you assume determines how you will communicate in the group and how effective the group will be. Although there are many types of roles, we focus on two broad categories: your role as a group leader and your role as a group member.

Leader Responsibilities

You may be elected or appointed as leader of a group, or you may emerge as leader over time. As leader, you need to be aware of the group's process and the relationships among group members. Behaviors that relate to process are designed to help the group complete the task. These include providing direction and purpose, keeping the group on track, and providing clarifying summaries.

Provide direction and purpose. As part of your responsibility to provide direction and purpose, you may choose to open the meeting with action-directed comments ("We are here to establish whether or not it is feasible to add another organization to our college") or to examine items on an agenda. Once the discussion begins, others will contribute, but it is the leader's role to focus the meeting at the start.

Keeping the group on track. Keeping the group on track simply means making sure the group does not drift too far from the task at hand. If you are talking about offering healthy alternatives in the cafeteria line, it is easy to start talking about favorite foods or incidents that occurred in the cafeteria or people who work or who eat in the cafeteria. While some extraneous conversation help build relationships among group members, the leader is responsible for making sure time is not wasted and the group does not get side-tracked on irrelevant issues.

Provide a clarifying summary. Groups, like the individuals who comprise them, can be confused by the information they hear. Warning signs include questions for clarification, puzzled looks, and drifting attention. When you sense confusion, one of the best ways to move forward is to provide a clarifying summary, which recaps what has just occurred. For example, after hearing evidence and testimony at a student disciplinary hearing, the board voted that a student (Martin) was guilty of vandalism. After some time, the group was getting nowhere in terms of determining a punishment. As a leader, you say,

> We've agreed that Martin is guilty of vandalism, and that his actions are worthy of punishment, but we seem to be stuck on the concept of expulsion. We agree that

suspension is too lenient, and expulsion is more warranted. The confusion seems to rest on how we are interpreting 'expulsion,' with some thinking the student may never return to our school and others thinking the student may return after a specified period of time, provided certain conditions are met.

With this type of clarifying summary, you have eliminated suspension from further discussion and identified the source of confusion. Clarifying summaries help bring focus back to the meeting.

In addition to facilitating the group's process, an effective group leader is concerned with relationship aspects, which facilitate communication. An effective leader will draw information from participants, keep group communication from being one-sided, and try to maintain the cohesiveness of the group. Ultimately, the relationship aspects allow the group to accomplish its task.

© 2012 by Mopic.
Used under license of Shutterstock.

Group roles evolve quickly and if you are the appointed leader, you will likely have more responsibility than other members.

Draw information from participants. Each person has something to contribute to the group, whether it is in the form of offering specific information, analyzing the issue, or being creative. However, some people are hesitant to speak even when they have something valuable to contribute. Their reasons may range from communication anxiety to uncertainty about their role in the group. As a leader, draw information from participants by directing questions to those who remain silent, asking each group member to speak, and being supportive when a normally quiet member makes a comment in the hope of encouraging additional responses at a later time. Getting everyone to contribute is particularly important when one or more members of the group seem to dominate the discussion. It is up to the group leader to make sure the group benefits from the combined wisdom of all its members.

Try to keep group communication from being one-sided. A leader should try to keep group communication from being one-sided. We often have preconceived ideas of how something should be done. While dissent is healthy, these ideas may be obstacles to group communication if the leader allows the discussion to become one-sided. The leader needs to recognize when one point of view is dominating the discussion. Inviting others into the discussion or providing a varying opinion yourself may open up the discussion for multiple perspectives.

Try to maintain the cohesiveness of the group. As a leader, you should try to maintain the cohesiveness of the group. You want the group to see themselves as a group and function as a group, not as a collection of individuals. Everyone needs to work toward the group goal, while not ignoring his or her personal goals. Nothing is inherently wrong with a heated discussion, especially when the issue is controversial. But when the discussion turns into a shouting match, it is no longer productive. In a conflict situation, the leader

Group members must feel that their contributions are valued and important.

should acknowledge the person's point of view but suggest that the problem be analyzed from other perspectives as well. Conflict is healthy, but unproductive conflict is a major obstacle to task completion. Keeping communication flowing effectively and making sure members feel their contributions are valued are important to the overall cohesiveness of the group.

Member Responsibilities

Being an active participant is the most important responsibility of each group member. An active participant contributes to the discussion, shares responsibility for task completion, and works effectively with other group members. Some group members believe that their participation is unnecessary because others will pick up their slack. Others view the experience as less important than other college work or activities. Complaining about group members is nothing new. Here are common complaints about other group members:

- Doesn't work or prepare enough
- Others have to nag group members to get work done
- Procrastinates
- Doesn't keep group members informed of content of presentation
- Information in presentation overlaps too much
- Information is excessive or too brief
- Too controlling
- Too apathetic
- Doesn't return calls or email
- Difficult to contact
- Doesn't stay after class to check with group
- Doesn't come to class on group work days
- Doesn't proofread PowerPoint

The preceding is only a partial list of complaints we hear about group members. We understand that students take several academic courses. They have a social and/or work life, and priorities differ among students. But once you are part of a group, your actions have an impact on the other people in that group. In a classroom setting, you may not be thrilled with the topic, the assignment, or the other group members. But you do need to work with your group in order to complete the required assignment. Actively working to complete your individual tasks and being available and cooperative will make the situation better for all involved. Fulfill a commitment to the group.

▲Suggestions for Group Members

The following seven suggestions are designed to create the most effective small group experience within the context of your classroom. Many of these translate easily to experiences outside the college classroom. The suggestions are derived partially from *Speak from Success* by Eugene Ehrlich and Gene R. Hawes (1984, 133).

Know the constraints of the assignment. Read the syllabus or any other material given to you related to the assignment. Make sure everyone agrees as to the constraints of the assignment. The following are some questions that may guide your group:

- When does the group present?
- How much time does the group have to present?
- Does each speaker have the same amount of time?
- What information needs to be included in the presentation?
- Are presentational aids required?
- Does each speaker use a set of note cards? Is there a restriction?
- Is there audience involvement at some point during the group presentation?
- Can group members interrupt each other to comment or add insight?
- Is there a paper required? Or an outline?
- How many and what type of sources are required, and should they be cited during the presentation?
- Does the group choose its format, or is there a particular format that is required?
- Are students being graded individually, as a group, or both?
- Will there be any peer evaluations?

Work to achieve group goals. Instructors understand that each individual is concerned about his or her own grade. However, the purpose of a group assignment is to work collectively and collaboratively. Make group goals your top priority. Making a commitment to the group means making a commitment to achieve group goals at each meeting. When you feel strongly about your position, it is legitimate to try to convince the group you are correct. But if others disagree, it is important that you listen to their objections and try to find merit in them. You need an objective detachment from your own proposals to enable you to place the group's goals above your own. A group needs a shared image of the group, in which individual aspirations are subsumed under the group umbrella that strives for the common good.

Be responsible for completing your part of the assignment. Group membership brings with it a set of roles and responsibilities. It may not have been your choice to work in a group or to work with that specific group of individuals. The fact is, the assignment is mandatory. Everyone has a life. Everyone has distractions in their lives. You may be very busy, or you may be uninterested, but your group needs your help. If a group member volunteers to make the PowerPoint presentation consistent from speaker to speaker, you need to make sure that person has your slides when they are requested. If you are supposed to make contact with city officials or individuals who may help with a fundraising idea, you need to come to the group with that information. Do not be responsible for the group's progress being delayed, or the task not completed. If you cannot attend a meeting, make sure someone knows. Send your work with someone else. If you do get behind, make sure group members know so they have an opportunity to respond in some way.

Research sufficiently. Most group work involves research of some type. When you are finished researching, you should feel confident that you have ample support or that the topic or issue has been covered in enough depth. Depending on the group's purpose or goal, research may involve surfing the Internet, conducting a library search, looking through the local Yellow Pages, calling different social service agencies in town, or

© 2012 by Andresr.
Used under license of Shutterstock.

Most group work involves some research so you feel confident that the topic has been covered in enough depth.

interviewing members of the local city council. If your group sought to determine what Americans consider the most important political issues for a presidential campaign, locating one website or one magazine article is not sufficient. If your group wanted to determine which pizza place in town served the best pizza, selecting two from the Yellow Pages is not sufficient, particularly in a city that has ten or more places that sell pizza. If you have been assigned to interview city council members, talking to one person for five minutes is not sufficient.

Communicate effectively and efficiently. Different people bring to a group a wide range of knowledge and views that help complete the task. Group discussion often produces creative approaches that no one would have thought of alone. Group involvement through communication increases the likelihood that the group's decision will be accepted and supported by all group members and by the broader community. Do not waste time and do not monopolize the group discussions or the presentation.

Avoid personal attacks. Comments like, "You have to be an idiot to believe that will work," or "My six-year-old cousin has better ideas than that," accomplish nothing. On the contrary, these comments are so antagonistic that they make it virtually impossible for people to work together. If you do not like an idea, say so directly by focusing on the idea, not the person, such as "It may be difficult to get funds for that project," or "I don't think parents will want to volunteer their time for that." Try not to make your disagreement too negative. Find areas of agreement, where possible.

Leave personal problems at home. Group conflicts are often the result of personal problems brought to the group meeting. A fight with a family member, a poor test grade, an alarm clock that failed to ring, a near-accident on the highway, or school or work pressure can put you in a bad mood for the meeting and lessen your tolerance for other group members. Although an outburst of anger may make you feel better for the moment, it can destroy the relationships you have with other members of the group.

▲Problem Solving: Reflective Thinking Process

You may be called upon in a college course or in an organization to work with others on a problem-solving task. On campus for example, the Student Senate needs to find ways to get more students involved in campus events , while off campus the local Chamber of Commerce is trying to find ways to entice new businesses to join their organization. Groups are faced with small and large problems on a regular basis. Almost 100 years ago, John Dewey developed a theory of reflective thinking that is now applied to group communication (1910). If you are working on a problem-solving task, consider following the following seven steps:

1. Identify and Define the Problem

The first step of this process is to make sure group members understand and agree on what the problem is. Otherwise, the discussion may scatter into many different directions and time will be misused. For example, a newly elected Student Senate member wants to work with a group to deal with student complaints about residence hall assignments. One problem is that students are not given enough options about where they may live or with whom. A second problem is that the administration does not process complaints effectively. Third, students are unhappy about meal plan options and residence hall rules and contracts. Does the group want to take on all of these problems, or to focus on the complaint process? The first thing the group needs to do is identify the problem.

2. Analyze the Problem

In the process of analyzing the problem, group members need to identify what they know about the problem, what they do not know, and what resources are available to help them acquire more information. In this step, group members should find out what caused the problem, how long the problem has been an issue, and the extent of the problem. If only one student has complained about her residence hall assignment, there is not much of a problem. But if significant staff time is devoted to addressing students' complaints, then the problem is significant. Perhaps the problem started when a new administrator took office. Perhaps the problem is ongoing. This is the information-gathering, sorting, and evaluation stage of the reflective thinking process.

3. Determine Criteria for an Acceptable Solution

Many groups skip this step, whether they are newly formed groups in a college classroom or well-established policy groups in a community. However, it is a mistake to come into the problem-solving process with a firm idea of what you think is the best solution. Whatever solution your group suggests must meet agreed-upon criteria or standards. Criteria will differ vastly from situation to situation. For example, if four students turned in a group paper that was clearly plagiarized, before determining the punishment, an instructor might consider the following criteria:

In order to present a solution, a group needs sufficient information gathering and sorting and a sufficient evaluation of the problem.

- Is (the punishment) it fair (to the four students and the rest of the class)?
- Is it appropriate (given the nature of the misconduct)?
- Will it deter future misconduct (on the part of the students who cheated as well as other students who might be contemplating misconduct)?

Criteria related to the residence hall complaints issue might include the following:

- Does the solution consider both the needs of students and college administrators?
- Does the solution apply to all students living in residence halls, not just incoming freshmen?
- Does the solution allow students to change residence halls?
- Does the solution recognize that freshmen do not have cars?

Establishing criteria keeps group members from simply proposing their solution. Any solution presented needs to meet the criteria established by group members.

4. Generate Possible Solutions

According to Dewey, suspended judgment is critical at this point in the decision-making process (Ross and Ross 1989, 77). Group members need to identify available options without stifling the process by providing immediate evaluation. Brainstorming, which involves generating as many solutions as possible without critical evaluation, may be useful during this step of the reflective thinking process. Be creative. Encourage group members to think "outside the box." Avoid the temptation to say, "that won't work," "that's not possible," or worse, "that's a dumb idea." Instead, generate ideas until you agree you have exhausted the possibilities. If possible, give yourselves time to think about these solutions before evaluating or moving on to the next step. For the teacher who caught the group of students plagiarizing, some of the punishment options include ignoring it, talking to the students, requiring them to give a group presentation on the evils of plagiarism, requiring them to write another paper, lowering their grade on the paper, failing them for the assignment, failing them for the semester, and reporting the students to the Office of Judicial Affairs.

Regarding the problem of residence hall complaints, the group may develop several options, including changing the forms students fill out, suggesting a policy change, providing clearer, more specific information to students, and establishing a committee to hear complaints not resolved between students and administration. The important thing is to have alternatives, and not be single-minded in your approach.

5. Choose the Solution That Best Fits the Criteria

Each solution identified in Step Four needs to be evaluated based on the criteria established in Step Three. Ideally, the best solution is one that meets all the established criteria. If that does not happen, the group may need to revisit the possible solutions, and determine if amending one of the solutions might result in it meeting all of the established criteria. The instructor who caught students plagiarizing needs to evaluate her possible options by the criteria she has set. For example, if she ignores the misconduct, is that fair to those in the class who did not plagiarize? Is failing the students for the course an appropriate punishment for the students' misconduct?

In terms of the residence hall complaints, does changing the form students fill out meet both the needs of students and administrators? Will the form address the issue of changing residence hall assignments? Will a committee be formed to hear complaints from all students in residence halls? An option might not meet each of the criteria perfectly, but the point of this step is to choose the solution that best meets the criteria. If multiple options are acceptable, the group needs to determine how it will decide on which solution to implement.

6. Implement the Solution

Implementing the solution means putting it into effect. It is one thing to decide that a car wash will raise the most money; it is another thing to advertise, staff, supply, and conduct the fundraiser. The work involved in implementing the solution will vary according to the problem. For example, an instructor dealing with plagiarism can determine the best solution and then communicate that decision to the students and/or administration. If the group dealing with residence hall complaints decides to form a committee to hear complaints, then implementing the solution entails setting up committee structure, policies and procedures, soliciting membership, and informing students about the committee.

In a public speaking class, your group may be involved in determining a solution and suggesting how it could be implemented, but it is possible the group will not be involved with the actual implementation. For example, your group may be given the task of determining how to get students more involved in their department's activities. Your group could work through Step Five and decide that the best solution is to advertise activities earlier so that students can work them into their schedules. As a group, you may present Steps One through Five to a faculty committee, but Step Six might ultimately be the committee's responsibility.

7. Reassess

Reassessing at some point prevents the group from saying "we're done" after implementing the solution. It is an important part of the process because you evaluate your group's success or lack thereof. Fundraisers are carefully planned and executed, but still may fail. New policies are developed with the best intentions, but may still be ineffective. Do you try the same fundraiser again? Do you keep the new policy? Before you answer "yes" or "no" to these questions, the group needs to answer some other questions. Did the fundraiser fail because it was held at a bad time? Was it advertised sufficiently? Did it ask too much of the people working it or attending the fundraiser? In other words, the group needs to decide what contributed to the lack of success. Similarly, with the ineffective policy, did administration evaluate its effectiveness too soon? Were students inadequately informed? Was administration insufficiently trained? Those engaged in reassessment need to discuss what factors influenced the lack of success. In a sense, this final step can be the beginning step of a new process, if the solution has not been effective.

Effective group presentations require much advance interaction and planning.

The seven-step reflective thinking process is one way to help groups move through the problem-solving process. It is certainly not the only way. However, regardless of the approach groups take, it is important that a clear process be established that allows for rational, deliberative discussion of all relevant aspects of the problem. A leader should help the group through this process, and group members should contribute productively throughout the process.

❯❯PRESENTING IN SMALL GROUPS

Just because you are part of a small group discussion does not mean that you will report your results through some type of oral presentation. Some groups prepare written reports that some administrator, council, or committee will evaluate. Sometimes the results of your deliberation are presented before a group, and in many instances a group presents before another group for other reasons. For example, a group of teachers who attended a workshop on working with gifted students present their observations of the workshop to the group of teachers who were unable to attend. Members of the League of Women Voters who attended the national convention present a summary of their experiences to the rest of the membership. Also, many careers have national conferences where people with similar interests have the opportunity to attend or present seminars and panel presentations.

Whether presenting as a group or as an individual to a group successful public speaking strategies are necessary. So all information presented in this textbook is relevant to this context. Audience analysis is essential. Any presentation you prepare should have a clear introduction, body, and conclusion. Your presentation should be well-research, sufficiently supported, and organized effectively. Your delivery should be engaging and extemporaneous. Be sure you are not too dependent on notes.

Speaking as a member of a group, however, involves additional reflection. First, it is important to find a small group format that best suits your purpose. Second, it is important that the speeches all group members give flow as though they were one coherent speech. The last section of this chapter describes a variety of small group formats concerns that need to be addressed before the group speaks, and makes suggestions for the presentation.

▲Small Group Formats

Most of your group work in class occurs before the day you present. You spend time defining your purpose, setting goals, distributing the work load, researching your topic/issues, and organizing your research into something meaningful. If in business or civic life, you are already an expert on the topic, your task is to determine what you need to bring to this particular presentation. It is possible that you never meet the other group members until moments before the presentation.

In a public speaking class, your instructor may suggest a particular small group format. In business or civic life, a moderator or facilitator decides how the group should present. It is also possible that you determine your format. Regardless, there are three main small group formats: panel discussion, symposium, and forum.

1. Panel Discussion

In a panel discussion, group members have an informal interchange on the issues in front of an audience. The positive and negative features of issues are debated, just as they were in the closed group meeting, but this time in front of an audience. When you are part of a panel discussion, it is important to keep in mind that you are talking for the benefit of the audience rather than for other group members. Although your responses are spontaneous, they should be thought out in advance, just as in any other public speaking presentation.

Panel discussions are directed by a moderator who attempts to elicit a balanced view of the issues and to involve all group members. The role of the moderator is to encourage the discussion—he or she does not take part in the debate. Moderators coordinate and organize the discussion, ask pertinent questions, summarize conclusions, and keep the discussion moving. Once the discussion is over, the moderator often opens the discussion to audience questions.

As you can tell from the previous description, the critical elements of a panel discussion are: (1) it is an informal discussion moderated or facilitated by someone who is not an active participant, (2) interaction should be distributed equitably among group members with no pre-determined time limit for each group member, and (3) generally, there are no prepared remarks.

2. Symposium

A symposium is more formal and predictable than a panel discussion. Instead of focusing on the interaction among group members, it centers on prepared speeches on a specified subject given by group members who have expertise on the subject. The topic and speakers are introduced by a moderator. A symposium is structured, and speakers are generally given a time frame for their comments. After the formal presentation, a panel discussion or forum may follow. This allows for interaction among group members, and for the audience to ask questions of individual speakers.

3. Forum

In a forum, group members respond to audience questions. Someone may provide a prepared statement, but it is also possible to introduce group members and their credentials, and then ask for audience questions. Unlike a panel discussion or the second half of a symposium, a forum does not include interactions among group members. The forum is very audience-centered.

The success of the forum depends on how carefully the audience has thought about the topic (the topic is announced in advance) and the nature of their questions. For example, school boards hold public hearings about their annual budget. In addition to the school board, the superintendent and district financial officer will be present. Generally, there is a presentation by the financial officer, and then anyone present at the meeting may ask questions. Questions could be asked about transportation, food service, athletics, computer equipment, and so on. If several concerned citizens show up with questions in mind, the meeting could last for hours. If no one in the community attends the meeting, then it will be very short.

A forum also needs a moderator. When the League of Women Voters holds a candidates' forum, selected League members collect questions from the audience and give them to the moderator who then addresses questions to the appropriate panelists. A forum is not just a collection of individuals, but a group of people who have been chosen for their interest in the topic/issue or because of their expertise.

▲Preparing to Present as a Group

When you prepare a speech for class, you are responsible for all aspects of the speech. As an individual, you need to prepare, practice, and present. Once you join a group, however, you need to be prepared, but you also need to be aware of how your speech fits into the other speeches, and the group needs to make sure everyone is viewing the presentation from a similar perspective. With this interest in mind, we present the following aspects of the presentation to consider before the group speaks. All group members should know and be in agreement with the following:

1. **Speaker order**

2. **Formality of the presentation**
   - Can group members interrupt each other?
   - Can group members wander from their prepared remarks?

3. **Determine where will the group sit/stand?**
   - Group members need to realize that if they are all in front of the class, whether standing or speaking, audience members will be aware of them, even when they are not speaking.
   - Will all sit and then stand up to speak or will all stand throughout the entire presentation?
   - Should the group sit to the side and have the speaker stand in the middle of the front of the class?

4. **Delivery**
   - Use note cards? Legal pad? PowerPoint slides?
   - Prepare individually—think about eye contact (speak to the group, not the instructor), gestures, and vocal aspects

5. **Time constraints for each speech**

6. **Determine how to signal if someone is speaking too long or if the group is going too long**

7. **Introduction, body, conclusion**
   - Who will deliver the group's introduction and conclusion?
   - How will each person's introduction and conclusion relate to the group?
   - How do you make transitions between speeches so all presentations are connected?

8. **Presentational aids**
   - What is available in the classroom?
   - Will they benefit the presentation?
   - Who will be responsible for making them and setting them up?

If group members wait until they approach the front of the room to address these concerns, they will appear unprepared. Deciding where to stand, how to signal each other, and what the speaking order is will reduce awkwardness and uncertainty, and should give a more professional, polished look to the presentation.

▲General Suggestions for Presenting in a Small Group

The following guidelines will help you be a successful participant in a panel discussion, symposium, or forum. Many of the guidelines apply to all three group formats, but others apply just to one.

Limit the number of points you make. Since you will be given some time constraints, limit the number of points you make. Remember that each person has information to present. Your audience cannot process an overload of material. Be brief. Make your point as briefly and clearly as possible and do not confuse your listeners with too many details.

Because the question-and-answer period is often the most important part of the program, spend as much time preparing for the questions as you did for your formal remarks.

Avoid repetition. Avoid repetition by learning in advance what the other panelists will cover in their speeches. The job of assigning topics should be the responsibility of the presentation organizer. If the organizer is negligent, you may want to get in touch with the other panelists yourself. Keep communication channels open with your group members so you do not find yourself giving the same presentation as the person who spoke before you.

Try to meet in advance. Try to meet your fellow panelists in advance. When group members meet for the first time on stage, there is often an awkwardness in their interchange that comes from not knowing one another. This discomfort may be communicated to the audience.

Restrict your speech to the allotted time. If speakers exceed the time limit, the audience will find it difficult to sit through the entire program, and little opportunity will remain for a panel interchange or a question-and-answer period. In addition, by violating the time constraints, you may cause another speaker to modify his or her speech significantly. Staying within the allotted time frame is a necessary courtesy to the other group members.

Prepare for audience questions. Because the question-and-answer period is often the most important part of the program, spend as much time preparing for the questions as you did for your formal remarks. Anticipate the questions you are likely to be asked and frame your answers. During the question-and-answer period, be willing to speak up and add to someone else's response if none of the questions are being directed to you. When a fellow panel member finishes a response, simply say, "I'd like to make one more point that …" If, on the other hand, a question is directed to you that you think would be better handled by another panel member, say, "I think that considering her background, Therese is better able to answer that question."

Consider enhancing your presentation with visual aids. Simple visual aids are as appropriate in group presentations as they are in single-person public speaking. Coordinate the use of visual aids so information is not repeated by multiple speakers. Be consistent and professional. It is inconsistent to allow one group member to use the blackboard when the rest of the group has PowerPoint slides.

❯SUMMARY

We are all involved in small group activities whether they occur within or outside of the classroom. Opportunities exist for interacting within a group or speaking before a group. As a speaker, consider both primary and secondary audiences. As group members, we share a purpose for communication. Also, group members usually have both group-oriented and self-oriented goals, and group size influences the need for structure and how we communicate.

Each individual has responsibilities within the group setting regardless of the person's role. As leader, you can contribute to the group's process by providing direction and purpose, especially at the beginning of the meeting, keeping the group on track throughout the meeting, and providing a clarifying summary when appropriate. In terms of helping the group communicate effectively, the leader should draw information from participants, try to keep group communication from being one-sided, and try to maintain the cohesiveness of the group.

As a group member, you have several responsibilities, including knowing the constraints of the assignment, working to achieve group goals, being responsible for completing your part of the assignment, researching sufficiently, communicating effectively and efficiently, avoiding personal attacks, and leaving your personal problems at home. Following the seven-step reflective process helps to keep the group organized and focused and helps to make sure that members do not jump to quick solutions without sufficient analysis and deliberation.

When the occasion arises for you to present as a group member before an audience, it is important to determine whether a panel discussion, symposium, or forum best suits your needs and the needs of your audience. Your knowledge of public speaking and your individual skills come into play as you present before the group. However, it is important to meet as a group beforehand to determine such things as speaker order, amount of speaking time allotted for each individual, whether or not presentational aids will be useful, and who will be responsible for preparing such aids. Each person's presentation should cover only a few points. The presentations should not overlap, and group members should be prepared for audience questions. An effective presentation involves preparation on the part of all group members as well as attention to detail regarding content connection, transitions from speaker to speaker, and overall professional performance.

QUESTIONS FOR ANALYSIS

1. What is the difference between being a member of a small group that works together and then presents before another group and being a member of a panel that never meets before it presents before another group?

2. How would your presentation differ if you had a primary audience only or you had both a primary and a secondary audience?

3. When you work with others to accomplish tasks in college, can you usually identify who the leader is? How? What seems to be the most difficult aspect of being a leader in a college classroom project?

4. Can you think of a situation when your fellow group members did not fulfill their group responsibilities? If so, how did you react? How did other group members react?

5. Under what circumstances would it make sense to present as a member of a panel? Of a symposium? When is a forum appropriate?

6. If you were giving advice to a friend who had not participated in a small group presentation, what would you tell your friend about speaking as a member of a group before another group?

# ACTIVITIES

1. Select an actual small group on campus or in your community and obtain permission to observe several meetings. Take notes on what you observe, and write a 500- to 750-word paper connecting your observations to concepts discussed in this chapter. Pay particular attention to how the group approaches problem-solving.

2. Join with three or four other class members to work on a common problem. Use a panel or symposium to present your analysis and recommendations. The group should move through all steps of the reflective thinking process. Present the process and your solution to the class.

REFERENCES

Bales, R. F. 1953. "The equilibrium problems in small groups" in T. Parson, R. F. Bales and E. A. Shils (Eds.), *Working papers in the theory of action*. Glencoe, IL: Free Press.

Dewey, J. 1910. *How we think*. Boston, MA: D. C. Heath.

DiSalvo, V. 1973. "Small group behavior," in *Explorations in speech communications*, J. J. Makay (Ed.), (111–112). Colombus, OH: Charles E. Merrill Publishing Co.

Ehrlich, E. and Hawes, G. R. 1984. *Speak for success*. New York: Bantam Books.

Ross, R. S. and Ross, J. R. *Small groups in organizational settings*. (Englewood Cliffs, NJ: Prentice-Hall.

Slater, P. E. 1958. "Contrasting correlates of group size," *Sociometry* 21, 129–39.

SHORT ANSWER / SHORT ESSAY

HONOR STATEMENT: I, the undersigned student, hereby declare before God, before the school, and before the professor that I have read Chapter 17 in its entirety, that I have completed the following exercise with help from no other sources, and that I neither have shared nor will share this work with anyone.

Signature: _____   Date: _____

1. List the three characteristics of small groups are most relevant to the public speaking classroom.

_____

_____

_____

_____

_____

_____

_____

2. What are some suggestions for getting the most out of the group experience in the classroom?

_____

_____

_____

_____

_____

_____

_____

_____

_____

_____

3. List and describe, in proper order, each of the seven steps of the Reflective Thinking Process.

_____

_____

_____

_____

_____

_____

_____

_____

_____

_____

_____

_____

_____

_____

_____

_____

_____

4. When making a group presentation, what aspects of public speaking should each speaker keep in mind?

_____

_____

_____

_____

_____

_____

_____

_____

_____

_____

_____

_____

_____

5. Under what circumstances would it make sense to present as a member of a panel? Of a symposium? When is a forum appropriate?

_____

_____

_____

_____

_____

_____

_____

_____

_____

_____

_____

_____

_____

6. If you were giving advice to a friend who had not participated in a small group presentation, what would you tell your friend about speaking as a member of a group before another group?

_____

_____

_____

_____

_____

_____

_____

_____

_____

PART 3

························

COMMUNICATION VOCATIONS:

PUBLIC PLATFORMS FOR REDEMPTIVE COMMUNICATORS

Each generation of the church in each setting
has the responsibility of communicating the
gospel in understandable terms, considering
the language and thought-forms of that setting.

–Francis A. Schaeffer (1912-1984)

[NOTE]: The job descriptions that follow are adapted from the Bureau of Labor Statistics, U.S. Department of Labor, Occupational Outlook Handbook, 2010-11 Edition. This resource is available on the Internet at http://www.bls.gov/oco. Public domain.

COMMUNICATION VOCATIONS

Public Platforms for Redemptive Communicators

By Donald H. Alban Jr, PhD

We began this textbook, in Part 1, by defining communication, evaluating why it happens or fails to happen, and considering what makes our communications significant or valuable. Developing strong communication skills is important because this can help you reach your personal goals and become a more productive member of society. More than this, these skills, if developed, can help you realize your God-given overarching purpose in life–to express authentic love for Him by interacting with others in a way that promotes what He values in this world according to Scripture.

With this as our guiding rationale for becoming more skillful communicators, we proceeded in Part 2 to review an eight-step process that can help you become a more effective public communicator. Although this section of the book emphasized public speaking as the mode for presenting your information to an audience, most of the eight steps are applicable to communication in general, regardless of which mode you utilize to express your information. Writers, no less than public speakers, must analyze their audiences, formulate purpose and thesis statements, research credible sources, extract supportive information, organize and bring unity to the extracted information, and use audience-appropriate message forms to present the information to a public audience in a rhetorically effective way.

In this section of the textbook, we invite you to consider several job fields through which you, as a communications professional, can put your information presentation skills into practice, whether you are speaking-oriented, writing-oriented, media-oriented, or some combination of these. Some of these vocations emphasize the accurate presentation of factual information to specific audiences for informational or persuasive purposes. Others emphasize the creative presentation of information to audiences for aesthetic or

If you want to make a **redemptive difference** in the world, above all else, a communications career might be the very platform for engaging the world to which you are called.

entertainment purposes. Still others have more generalized goals that emphasize a combination of these emphases. Many of these occupations, particularly the media job fields, require practitioners to go through more specialized information research and presentation processes very much like the general one that Part 2 presented. If your college or university offers majors in these job fields, they almost certainly involve course-work that can help you develop these more specialized communication skills.

As you read through these timely occupational descriptions, consider the rich opportunities each affords you not only for earning an income but for interacting with large audiences through your job in a way that promotes something God values in this world according to Scripture. In all likelihood, your way of thinking, talking, and acting was impacted by people who work in these job fields, whether they are advertisers, novelists, movie makers, game designers, website designers, TV or radio programmers, newscasters, print journalists, performing artists, photographers, videographers, or graphic illustrators. What is your favorite movie? What is your favorite TV or radio show? Do you have a favorite website? How about a favorite book, magazine, or print publication? Communications professionals created these, and the obviously impacted you. If the future belongs to those who tell the best stories, as someone once told me, communications professionals are the storytellers whose potential impact is the most widespread. If you want to make a redemptive difference in the world, above all else, a communications career might be the very platform for engaging the world to which you are called.

The job field descriptions that follow are adapted from the Occupational Outlook Index. Each job listing provides an overview of the job field, emphasizing the nature of its work, any qualifications or credentials required for one to practice it, the job field's current employment situation and its outlook for the future, and the earnings currently earned by practitioners in this field.

As the final section of this book will explain with real-life examples, you can impact the world in a redemptive way in many job fields. As an accountant, you can promote such God-valued qualities as truth, organization, and personal property rights. As a zoologist, you can promote such God-valued qualities as animal life, the earth, and human care of the earth. For now, though, consider communications and the unique opportunities this field presents for making a redemptive difference in the world.

MEDIA >>

>> ANNOUNCERS
(TV & RADIO)

SIGNIFICANT POINTS

- Competition for announcer jobs will continue to be keen.

- Jobs at small stations usually have low pay, but offer the best opportunities for inexperienced announcers.

- Applicants who have completed internships or have related work experience, and those with more advanced computer skills, may have an advantage in the job market.

- Employment is projected to decline slowly.

❯NATURE OF THE WORK

Radio and television announcers perform a variety of tasks on and off the air. They announce station program information, such as program schedules and station breaks for commercials, or public-service information, and they introduce and close programs. Announcers read prepared scripts or make ad-lib commentary on the air as they present news, sports, the weather, the time, and commercials. If a written script is required, they may do the research and writing. Announcers also interview guests and moderate panels or discussions. Some provide commentary for the audience during sporting events, at parades, and on other occasions. Announcers often are well known to radio and television audiences and may make promotional appearances and do remote broadcasts for their stations.

Announcers at smaller stations may have more off-air duties as well. They may operate the control board, monitor the transmitter, sell commercial time to advertisers, keep a log of the station's daily programming, and produce advertisements and other recorded material. At many radio stations, announcers do much of the work previously performed by editors and broadcast technicians, such as operating the control board, which is used to broadcast programming, commercials, and public-service announcements according to the station's schedule. Radio and television announcers also are involved in station fundraising efforts.

Announcers frequently participate in community activities. Sports announcers, for example, may serve as masters of ceremony at sports club banquets or may greet customers at openings of sporting-goods stores.

Radio announcers who broadcast music often are called disc jockeys (DJs). Some DJs specialize in one kind of music, announcing selections as they air them. Most DJs do not select much of the music they play (although they often did so in the past); instead, they follow schedules of commercials, talk, and music provided to them by management. While on the air, DJs comment on the music, weather, and traffic. They may take requests from listeners, interview guests, and manage listener contests. Many radio stations now require DJs to update their station website.

Some DJs announce and play music at clubs, dances, restaurants, and weddings. They often have their own equipment with which to play the music. Many are self-employed and rent their services out on a job-by-job basis.

Show hosts may specialize in a certain area of interest, such as politics, personal finance, sports, or health. They contribute to the preparation of the program's content, interview guests, and discuss issues with viewers, listeners, or the studio audience.

Public-address-system announcers provide information to the audience at sporting, performing arts, and other events.

▲Work environment

Announcers usually work in well-lighted, air-conditioned, soundproof studios. Announcers often work within tight schedules, which can be physically and mentally stressful. For many announcers, the intangible rewards—creative work, many personal contacts, and the satisfaction of becoming widely known—far outweigh the disadvantages of irregular and often unpredictable hours, work pressures, and disrupted personal lives.

The broadcast day is long for radio and TV stations—many are on the air 24 hours a day—so announcers can expect to work unusual hours. Many present early-morning shows, when most people are getting ready for work or commuting, while others do late-night programs. The shifts, however, are not as varied as in the past, because new technology has allowed stations to eliminate most of the overnight hours. Many announcers work part time.

❯❯TRAINING, OTHER QUALIFICATIONS, AND ADVANCEMENT

Entry into this occupation is highly competitive, and postsecondary education or long-term on-the-job training is common. Trainees usually must have several years of experience in the industry before receiving an opportunity to work on the air. An applicant's delivery and—in television—appearance and style are important.

▲Education and training

Formal training in broadcasting from college or a technical school is valuable. These programs prepare students to work with the computer equipment and software to which they might otherwise not have access. In radio, many announcers will also need website-editing skills. It is common for announcers to have a bachelor's degree in a subject such as communications, broadcasting, or journalism. High school and college courses in English, public speaking, drama, foreign languages, and computer science are valuable, and hobbies such as sports and music are additional assets.

There are many broadcast programs available and they have varying reputations. Individuals considering enrolling in a broadcasting school should contact personnel managers of radio and television stations, as well as broadcasting trade organizations, to determine the school's reputation for producing suitably trained candidates.

Announcers are often required to complete long-term on-the-job training. This can be accomplished at campus radio or TV facilities and at commercial stations while students serve as interns. Work experience at college or high school radio or TV stations is very valuable. Oftentimes, even for entry-level positions, employees need to have experience, which students can acquire at these stations. Paid or unpaid internships also provide students with hands-on training and the chance to establish contacts in the industry. Unpaid interns frequently receive college credit and are allowed to observe and assist station employees. This experience sometimes leads to paid internships which are valuable because interns may do work ordinarily performed by regular employees.

Once hired by a television station, an employee usually starts out as a production assistant, researcher, or reporter and is given a chance to move into announcing if he or she shows an aptitude for "on-air" work. A beginner's chance of landing an on-air job is remote. The best chances for an on-air job for inexperienced announcers may be as a substitute for a familiar announcer at a small radio station. In radio, newcomers usually start out taping interviews and operating equipment.

▲Other qualifications

Announcers must have a pleasant and well-controlled voice, good timing, excellent pronunciation, and correct grammar. College broadcasting programs offer courses, such as voice and diction, to help students improve their vocal qualities. Television announcers need a neat, pleasing appearance as well. Knowledge of theater, sports, music, business, politics, and other subjects likely to be covered in broadcasts improves one's chances for success. Announcers, especially those seeking radio careers, should have good information-technology skills and be capable of using computers, editing equipment, and other broadcast-related devices because new advances in technology have made these abilities important. Announcers also need strong writing skills, because they normally write their own material. In addition, they should be able to ad lib all or part of a show and to work under tight deadlines. The most successful announcers attract a large audience by combining a pleasing personality and voice with an appealing style.

▲Advancement

Announcers usually begin at a station in a small community and, if they are qualified, may move to a better-paying job in a large city. They also may advance by hosting a regular program as a disc jockey, sportscaster, or other specialist. Competition for employment by networks is particularly intense, and employees will need a college degree with at least several years of successful announcing experience if they wish to advance.

▲Employment

Announcers held about 67,400 jobs in 2008. About 51 percent were employed in radio and television broadcasting. Many other announcers were self-employed freelance announcers, who sold their services to networks and stations, advertising agencies, other independent producers, or to sponsors of local events.

▲Job Outlook

Competition for jobs as announcers will be keen because the broadcasting field attracts many more jobseekers than there are jobs. Furthermore, employment of announcers is projected to decline slowly. In some cases, announcers leave the field because they cannot advance to better-paying jobs. Changes in station ownership, format, and ratings frequently cause periods of unemployment for many announcers.

▲Employment change

Employment of announcers is expected to decline by 4 percent from 2008 to 2018. Improving technology continues to increase the productivity of announcers, reducing the time required to edit material or perform other off-air technical and production work. The ability of radio announcers to broadcast a program live and record a show for another time has eliminated most late-night shifts and allowed multiple stations to use material from the same announcer. Increasing consolidation among broadcasting companies also may contribute to the increased use of syndicated programming and programs originating outside a station's viewing or listening area. The growth of alternative media sources, such as satellite radio, may contribute to the expected decline.

A possible positive area for radio announcers is hybrid digital (HD) radio, which broadcasters hope will increase in the coming years. HD radio offers more channels and could result in higher demand for on-air personalities. There will always be some demand for this occupation, because the public continues to desire local radio and television broadcasting and announcers play a necessary role in bringing it to them.

▲Job prospects

Some job openings will arise from the need to replace those who transfer to other kinds of work or leave the labor force. Nevertheless, competition for jobs as announcers will be keen because the broadcasting field attracts many more jobseekers than there are jobs. Small radio stations are more inclined to hire beginners, but the pay is low. Applicants who have completed internships and those with related work experience usually receive preference for available positions. Jobseekers with good computer and technical skills also will have an advantage. Large stations will seek announcers who have proven that they can attract and retain a sizable audience, because competition for ratings is so intense in major metropolitan areas. Announcers who are knowledgeable about business, consumer, and health news also may have an advantage over others. Although subject-matter specialization is more common at large stations and the networks, many small stations also encourage it. There will be some opportunities for self-employed DJs who provide music at clubs and special events, but most of these jobs will be part time.

▲Earnings

Salaries in broadcasting vary widely, but generally are relatively low, except for announcers who work for large stations in major markets or for networks. Earnings are higher in television than in radio and higher in commercial broadcasting than in public broadcasting.

Median hourly wages of radio and television announcers in May 2008 were $12.95. The middle 50 percent earned between $9.05 and $20.31. The lowest 10 percent earned less than $7.45, and the highest 10 percent earned more than $36.42. Median hourly wages of announcers in the radio and television broadcasting industry were $12.61.

Median hourly wages of public address and other system announcers in May 2008 were $13.18. The middle 50 percent earned between $8.82 and $21.04. The lowest 10 percent earned less than $7.51 and the highest 10 percent earned more than $33.58.

>> AUTHORS, WRITERS & EDITORS

SIGNIFICANT POINTS

- Most jobs require a college degree, preferably in communications, journalism, or English.

- Keen competition is expected for writing and editing jobs as many people are attracted to this occupation.

- Online publications and services are growing in number and sophistication, spurring the demand for writers and editors with Web or multimedia experience.

❯ NATURE OF THE WORK

Authors, writers and editors produce a wide variety of written materials in an increasing number of ways. They develop content using any number of multimedia formats that can be read, listened to, or viewed onscreen. Although many people write as part of their primary job, or on online chats or blogs, only writers and editors who are paid to primarily write or edit are included in this occupation.

Writers and authors develop original-written materials for books, magazines, trade journals, online publications, company newsletters, and advertisements. Their works are classified broadly as either fiction or nonfiction and writers often are identified by the type of writing they do—for example, novelists, playwrights, biographers, and textbook writers. Writers such as songwriters, screenwriters, or scriptwriters produce content for radio and television broadcasts, motion pictures, and other types of performance. An increasing number of writers are producing scripted material directly for the Web and other communication devices.

Copy writers prepare advertising copy for use in publications or for broadcasting and they write other materials to promote the sale of a good or service. They often must work with the client to produce advertising themes or slogans and may be involved in the marketing of the product or service.

All writers conduct research on their topics, which they gather through personal observation, library and Internet research, and interviews. Some staff writers who work in the newspaper or magazine-publishing industry are news analysts, reporters, and correspondents and, like most writers, are typically assigned articles to write by editors and publishers, and may propose their own story ideas. Writers, especially of nonfiction, are expected to establish their credibility with editors and readers through strong research and the use of appropriate sources and citations. Writers and authors then select the material they want to use, organize it, and use the written word to express story lines, ideas, or to convey information. With help from editors, they may revise or rewrite sections, searching for the best organization or the right phrasing.

Most writers and editors use desktop or electronic publishing software, scanners, and other electronic communications equipment in the production of their material. In addition, because many writers today prepare material directly for the Internet, such as online newspapers and text for video games, they should be knowledgeable about graphic design, page layout, and multimedia software. In addition, they should be familiar with interactive technologies of the Web so that they can blend text, graphics, and sound together. Some writers maintain blogs or issue text messages as a way of keeping in touch with readers or providing information to them quickly, but only those who are paid to write their blogs or send text messages may be considered writers.

An increasing number of writers today are freelance writers—that is, they are self-employed and make their living by selling their written content to book and magazine publishers, news organizations, advertising agencies, or movie, theater, or television producers or by working under contract with an organization. Some writers may be commissioned by a sponsor to write a script; others to write a book on the basis of a proposal in the form of a draft or an outline. Many freelance writers are hired to complete specific, short-term or recurring assignments, such as contributing a column or a series of articles on a specific topic to a news agency or for an organization's newsletter.

Editors review, rewrite, and edit the work of writers. They also may do original writing. An editor's responsibilities vary with the employer and type and level of editorial position held. Editorial duties may include planning the content of books, journals, magazines, and other general-interest publications. Editors also review story ideas proposed by staff and freelance writers, then decide what material will appeal to readers. They review and edit drafts of books and articles, offer comments to improve the work, and suggest possible titles. In addition, they may oversee the production of publications. In the book-publishing industry, an editor's primary responsibility is to review proposals for books and decide whether to buy the publication rights from the author.

Most editors begin work as writers. Those who are particularly adept at identifying stories, recognizing writing talent, and interacting with writers, may be interested in editing jobs. Major newspapers and newsmagazines usually employ several types of editors. The executive editor oversees assistant editors, and generally has the final say about what stories are published and how they are covered. Assistant editors have responsibility for particular subjects, such as local news, international news, feature stories, or sports. The managing editor usually is responsible for the daily operation of the news department. Assignment editors determine which reporters will cover a given story.

In smaller organizations—such as small daily or weekly newspapers—a single editor may do everything or share responsibility with only a few other people. Executive and managing editors typically hire writers, reporters, and other employees. They also plan budgets and negotiate contracts with freelance writers, sometimes called "stringers" in the news industry. Copy editors review copy for errors in grammar, punctuation, and spelling and check the copy for readability, style, and agreement with editorial policy. They suggest revisions, such as changing words and rearranging sentences and paragraphs, to improve clarity or accuracy. They may also carry out research and confirm sources for writers and verify facts, dates, and statistics. In addition, they may arrange page layouts of articles, photographs, and advertising; compose headlines; and prepare copy for printing.

Editors often employ others, such as interns, fact checkers, or editorial assistants, for some entry-level positions. While gaining practical experience in a newsroom, they may carry out research and verify facts, dates, and statistics for other writers. In addition, they may arrange page layouts of articles, photographs, and advertising; compose headlines; and prepare copy for printing. Publication assistants who work for book-publishing houses may read and evaluate manuscripts submitted by freelance writers, proofread printers' galleys, and answer inquiries about published material. Assistants on small newspapers or in smaller media markets may compile articles available from wire services or the Internet, answer phones, and proofread articles.

▲Work environment

Advances in electronic communications have changed the work environment for many writers. Laptop computers and wireless communications technologies allow growing numbers of writers and authors to work from home and on the road. The ability to send e-mail or text messages, transmit and download stories, perform research, or review materials using the Internet allows writers and editors greater flexibility in where and how they complete assignments. Still, some writers and authors work in offices and many travel to conduct on-site research on their topic.

Some writers keep regular office hours, either to maintain contact with sources and editors or to establish a writing routine, but most writers set their own hours. Many writers—especially freelance writers—are paid per assignment; therefore, they work any number of hours necessary to meet a deadline. As a result, writers must be willing to work evenings, nights, or weekends to produce a piece acceptable to an editor or client by the deadline.

While many freelance writers enjoy running their own businesses and the advantages of working flexible hours, most routinely face the pressures of juggling multiple projects with competing demands and the continual need to find new work. Deadline pressures and long, erratic work hours—often part of the daily routine in these jobs—may cause stress, fatigue, or burnout. In addition, the use of computers for extended periods may cause some individuals to experience back pain, eyestrain, or fatigue.

Editors' schedules generally are determined by the production schedule and the type of editorial position. Most salaried editors work in busy offices much of the time and have to deal with production deadline pressures and the stresses of ensuring that the information they publish is accurate. As a result, editors often work long hours, especially at those times leading up to a publication deadline, which can be daily or even more frequently when editing material for the Internet or for a live broadcast. Overseeing and coordinating multiple writing projects simultaneously is common in these jobs, which may lead to stress, fatigue, or other chronic problems. Freelance editors face the added pressures of finding work on an ongoing basis and continually adjusting to new work environments.

❯❯TRAINING, OTHER QUALIFICATIONS, AND ADVANCEMENT

A college degree generally is required for a position as an author, writer, or editor. Good facility with computers and communications equipment is necessary in order to stay in touch with sources, editors, and other writers while working on assignments, whether from home, an office, or while traveling.

▲Education and training

A bachelor's degree or higher is typically needed for a job as an author, writer, or editor. Because writing skills are essential in this occupation, many employers like to hire people with degrees in communications, journalism, or English, but those with other backgrounds and who can demonstrate good writing skills may also find jobs as writers. Writers who want to focus on writing about a particular topic may need formal training or experience related to that topic. For example, textbook writers and fashion editors may need expertise in their subject areas that they acquired either through formal academic training or work experience. The Internet and other media allow some people to gain writing experience through blog posts, text messages, or self-publishing software. Some of this writing may lead to paid assignments based upon the quality of the writing, unique perspective, or the size of the potential audience, without regard to the absence of a degree.

Training and experience for author, writer, and editor jobs can be obtained by working on high school and college newspapers, community newspapers, and radio and television stations and submissions to literary magazines. College theater and music programs offer playwrights and songwriters an opportunity for them to have their work performed. Many magazines, newspapers, and broadcast stations also have internships for students. Interns may write stories, conduct research and interviews, and learn about the publishing or broadcasting business.

▲Other qualifications

Authors, writers and editors must be able to express ideas clearly and logically and should enjoy writing. Creativity, curiosity, a broad range of knowledge, self-motivation, and perseverance are also valuable. Authors, writers, and editors must demonstrate good judgment and a strong sense of ethics in deciding what material to publish. In addition, the ability to concentrate and to work under pressure is essential. Editors also need tact and the ability to guide and encourage others in their work.

Familiarity with electronic publishing, graphics, Web design, and multimedia production increasingly is needed. Use of electronic and wireless communications equipment to send e-mail, transmit work, and review copy often is necessary. Online publications require knowledge of computer software and editing tools used to combine text with graphics, audio, video, and animation.

▲Advancement

Writers and authors generally advance by building a reputation, taking on more complex writing assignments, and getting published in more prestigious markets and publications. Examples of previously published work form the best route to advancement. Establishing a track record for meeting deadlines also makes it easier to get future assignments. Writing for smaller businesses, local newspapers, advertising agencies, or not-for-profit organizations either as a staff writer or on a freelance basis, allows beginning writers and authors to begin writing right away and take credit for their work. Opportunities for advancement within these organizations may be limited, because they either do not have enough regular work or do not need more advanced writing.

In larger businesses, jobs and promotions usually are more formally structured. Beginners often read submissions, do research, fact-check articles, or copyedit drafts, and advance to writing and editing more substantive stories and articles.

Most editors begin work as writers. Those who are particularly adept at identifying stories, recognizing writing talent, and interacting with writers, may be interested in editing jobs. Except for copy editors, most editors hold management positions and must also enjoy making decisions related to running a business. For them, advancement generally means moving up the corporate ladder or to publications with larger circulation or greater prestige. Copy editors may move into original writing or substantive editing positions or become freelancers.

▲Employment

Authors, writers, and editors held about 281,300 jobs in 2008. Writers and authors held about 151,700 jobs and editors held about 129,600 jobs. About 70 percent of writers and authors were self-employed, while 12 percent of editors were self-employed.

Among the 30 percent of salaried writers and authors, about half work in the professional, scientific, and technical services and in publishing (except Internet) industries. These industries include advertising, public relations and related services, and newspaper, periodical, book, and directory publishers, respectively. Other salaried writers and authors work in broadcasting, professional and social organizations, and the motion picture and video industries.

While 51 percent of salaried editors worked in the publishing (except Internet) industry (half of those for newspapers), a large number of editors were also employed in other industries. Business, professional and social organizations, information services, and educational institutions employed editors to work on their publications or Web content.

Jobs are somewhat concentrated in major media and entertainment markets—Boston, Chicago, Los Angeles, New York, and Washington, DC—but improved communications and Internet capabilities allow writers to work from almost anywhere. Many prefer to work outside these cities and travel regularly to meet with publishers and clients and to do research or conduct interviews in person. As a result, job location is less of a requirement for many writing or editing positions than it once was.

▲Job Outlook

Employment is expected to grow about as fast as average. Keen competition is expected for writing and editing jobs as many people are attracted to this occupation. At the same time, many employers are downsizing.

▲Employment change

Employment of authors, writers, and editors is expected to grow 8 percent, about as fast as the average for all occupations, from 2008 to 2018. Employment in salaried writing and editing positions is expected to increase slightly as jobs become more prevalent throughout the economy. Companies in a wide array of industries are using newer multimedia technologies and online media to reach a more technology-friendly consumer and meet the growing demand for Web-based information. Online publications and services are growing in number and sophistication, spurring the demand for authors, writers, and editors, especially those with Web or multimedia experience. Businesses and organizations are adding text-messaging services to expanded newsletters and websites as a way of attracting new customers. They may hire writers or editors on either a salaried or freelance basis to contribute additional content. Some publishing companies, however, especially those that rely on advertising revenues and sales receipts to support large staffs of writers, will employ fewer writers and editors. But many experienced writers and editors will find work with nonprofit organizations and associations in their public relations offices, or in the public affairs departments of large companies or agencies. Others will find freelance work for newspaper, magazine, or journal publishers; some will write books.

▲Job prospects

Competition is expected for writing and editing jobs as many people are attracted to this occupation. Competition for jobs with established newspapers and magazines will be particularly keen as many organizations move their publication focus from a print to an online presence and as the publishing industry continues to contract. Writers and editors who have adapted to the new media and are comfortable writing for and working with a variety of electronic and digital tools will have an advantage in finding new work. The declining costs of self-publishing and the growing popularity of electronic books and book readers will allow many freelancers to get their work published. Some job openings will arise as experienced workers retire, transfer to other occupations, or leave the labor force.

>> BROADCAST/SOUND ENGINEERING
(TECHNICIANS & OPERATORS)

SIGNIFICANT POINTS

- Job applicants will face keen competition for jobs in major metropolitan areas, where pay generally is higher; prospects are expected to be better in small cities and towns.

- Technical school, community college, or college training in broadcast technology, electronics, or computer networking provides the best preparation.

- About 29 percent of these workers are in broadcasting, mainly in radio and television stations, and 15 percent work in the motion picture, video, and sound-recording industries.

- Evening, weekend, and holiday work is common.

❯ NATURE OF THE WORK

Broadcast and sound-engineering technicians and radio operators perform a wide variety of tasks. Their duties include setting up and maintaining the electrical equipment used in nearly all radio and television broadcasts, concerts, plays, sound recordings, and movies. There are many specialized occupations in this field.

Audio and video equipment technicians set up and operate audio and video equipment, including microphones, speakers, video screens, projectors, video monitors, and recording equipment. They also connect wires and cables and set up and operate sound and mixing boards and related electronic equipment for concerts, sports events, meetings and conventions, presentations, and news conferences. They may set up and operate associated spotlights and other custom-lighting systems. They also are needed to install and maintain equipment in many large businesses and universities that are upgrading their facilities with audio and video equipment.

Broadcast technicians set up, operate, and maintain equipment that regulates the signal strength, the clarity, and the ranges of sounds and colors of radio or television broadcasts. These technicians also operate control panels to select the source of the material. Technicians may switch from one camera or studio to another, from film to live programming, or from network to local programming.

Sound engineering technicians operate machines and equipment to record, synchronize, mix, or reproduce music, voices, or sound effects in recording studios, sporting arenas, theater productions, or movie and video productions.

Broadcast and sound engineering technicians and radio operators perform a variety of duties at small stations. At large stations and at the networks, technicians are more specialized, although job assignments may change from day to day. The terms "operator," "engineer," and "technician" often are used interchangeably to describe these workers. They may monitor and log outgoing signals and operate transmitters; set up, adjust, service, and repair electronic broadcasting equipment; and regulate fidelity, brightness, contrast, volume, and sound quality of television broadcasts.

Technicians also work in program production. Recording engineers operate and maintain video and sound recording equipment. They may operate equipment designed to produce special effects, such as the illusion of a bolt of lightning or a police siren. Sound mixers or re-recording mixers produce soundtracks for movies or television programs. After filming or recording is complete, these workers may use a process called "dubbing" to insert sounds. Field technicians set up and operate portable transmission equipment outside the studio. Because television news coverage requires so much electronic equipment and the technology is changing so rapidly, many stations assign technicians exclusively to news. Chief engineers, transmission engineers, and broadcast field supervisors oversee other technicians and maintain broadcasting equipment.

Radio operators mainly receive and transmit communications using a variety of tools. These workers also repair equipment, using such devices as electronic testing equipment, hand tools, and power tools. One of their major duties is to help ensure communication systems remain in good condition.

Work environment. Broadcast and sound-engineering technicians and radio operators generally work indoors in pleasant surroundings. However, those who broadcast news and other programs from locations outside the studio may work outdoors in all types of weather or in other dangerous conditions. Technicians doing maintenance may climb poles or antenna towers, and those setting up equipment do heavy lifting.

Technicians at large stations and the networks usually work a 40-hour week under great pressure to meet broadcast deadlines, and may occasionally work overtime. Technicians at small stations routinely work more than 40 hours a week. Evening, weekend, and holiday work is usual because most stations are on the air 18 to 24 hours a day, seven days a week. Some technicians need to be available on call whenever the station is broadcasting; technicians must handle any problems that occur during this time.

Technicians who work on motion pictures may be on a tight schedule and may work long hours to meet contractual deadlines.

❯❯TRAINING, OTHER QUALIFICATIONS, AND ADVANCEMENT

Broadcast and sound-engineering technicians, as well as audio- and video-equipment technicians, should have some kind of formal training related to their field. Radio operators do not need an education beyond high school and can usually learn their jobs through several months of on-the-job training.

▲Education and training

Audio- and video-equipment technicians should complete a technical-training program related to the field, which may take several months to a year to complete. Many recent entrants to the field have also received an associate degree or bachelor's degree, although it is generally not required for entry-level positions. In addition to coursework, experience in high school or college audiovisual clubs can provide a student with good training for this occupation. Working as an assistant is a useful way to gain experience and knowledge for an entry-level employee.

For broadcast technicians an associate degree in broadcast technology, electronics, computer networking, or a related field is generally recommended. Because of the competitiveness of the broadcast industry, many jobs require a bachelor's degree. A four-year degree also gives employees much better prospects for advancement in the field.

Most entry-level employees find jobs in small markets or with small stations in big markets and can transfer to larger, better-paying stations after gaining experience and learning the necessary skills. Small stations usually value more general skills since they have fewer employees doing less specialized work. Large stations almost never hire someone without previous experience, and they value more specialized skills. Working at a college radio or television station can be very advantageous for prospective employees. Sound-engineering technicians usually complete a vocational program, which can take about a year, although there are shorter programs. Prospective technicians should take high school courses in math, physics, and electronics. Technicians need to have excellent computer training to be successful in this field.

Radio operators are not usually required to complete any formal training. This is an entry-level position that generally requires on-the-job training.

In the motion picture industry, people are hired as apprentice editorial assistants and work their way up to jobs requiring higher-level skills. Employers in the motion picture industry usually hire experienced freelance technicians on a picture-by-picture basis. Reputation and perseverance are important in getting jobs.

Continuing education to become familiar with emerging technologies is recommended for all broadcast and sound-engineering technicians and radio operators.

▲Other qualifications

Broadcast and sound-engineering technicians and radio operators need skills in information technology and electronics since most recording, editing, and broadcasting are done on computers. Prospective technicians must have manual dexterity and an aptitude for working with electrical, electronic, and mechanical systems and equipment.

▲Certification and advancement

Licensing is not required for broadcast technicians. However, certification by the Society of Broadcast Engineers is issued to experienced technicians who pass an examination, and the certification may help with advancement.

Experienced technicians can become supervisory technicians or chief engineers. A college degree in engineering is needed to become chief engineer at large television stations.

▲Employment

Broadcast and sound-engineering technicians and radio operators held about 114,600 jobs in 2008.

About 29 percent of broadcast and sound-engineering technicians and radio operators worked in broadcasting (except Internet broadcasting), and 15 percent worked in the motion picture, video, and sound-recording industries. About 13 percent were self-employed. Television stations employ, on average, many more technicians than radio stations. Some technicians are employed in other industries, producing employee communications, sales, and training programs. Technician jobs in television and radio are located in virtually all U.S. cities; jobs in radio also are found in many small towns. The highest-paying and most specialized jobs are concentrated in New York City, Los Angeles, Chicago, and Washington, DC—the headquarters of most network and news programs. Motion picture production jobs are concentrated in Los Angeles and New York City.

▲Job Outlook

Employment is expected to grow about as fast as the average through 2018. But people seeking entry-level jobs as technicians in broadcasting are expected to face keen competition in major metropolitan areas. Prospects are expected to be better in small cities and towns.

▲Employment change

Overall employment of broadcast and sound-engineering technicians and radio operators is expected to grow by 8 percent over the 2008–18 decade, which is about as fast as the average of all occupations. Projected job growth varies among detailed occupations in this field. Employment of audio- and video-equipment technicians is expected to grow 13 percent, about as fast as average. Audio and video equipment is in heavy demand in many new buildings, especially new schools, and in existing schools as well. Many new technicians will be needed, not only to install, but to maintain and repair the equipment as well. A growing number of companies will plan permanent departments employing audio and video technicians. An increase in the use of digital signage will also lead to higher demand for audio- and video-equipment technicians. In the motion picture industry, employment for these workers will grow because they are needed to install digital movie screens.

Employment of broadcast technicians is expected to grow by 2 percent, signifying little or no change, and employment of sound-engineering technicians is expected to grow by 6 percent, which is slower than average. Advancements in technology will enhance the capabilities of technicians to produce higher quality radio and television programming; however, this improved technology will also increase the productivity of technicians, which may hold down employment growth. Jobs in radio and television broadcasting will also be limited by further consolidation of stations and by labor-saving advances, such as computer-controlled programming. In the cable and pay portion of the broadcasting industry, employment is expected to grow as the range of products and services expands, including cable Internet access and video-on-demand. An area in which technicians will be in increasing demand over the next several years is mobile broadcasting.

▲Job prospects

People seeking entry-level jobs as broadcast technicians are expected to face keen competition because of the large number of people attracted by the glamour of working in television or radio. Competition will be stronger in large metropolitan areas where pay is generally higher and the number of job seekers usually exceeds the number of openings. Prospects for entry-level positions are expected to be better in small cities and towns, provided that the jobseeker has appropriate training.

▲Earnings

Television stations usually pay higher salaries than radio stations; commercial broadcasting usually pays more than noncommercial broadcasting; and stations in large markets pay more than those in small markets.

Median annual wages of audio- and video-equipment technicians in May 2008 were $38,050. The middle 50 percent earned between $28,130 and $51,780. The lowest 10 percent earned less than $21,500, and the highest 10 percent earned more than $66,030. Median annual wages in motion picture and video industries, which employed the largest number of audio- and video-equipment technicians, were $39,410.

Median annual wages of broadcast technicians in May 2008 were $32,900. The middle 50 percent earned between $22,900 and $49,340. The lowest 10 percent earned less than $17,510, and the highest 10 percent earned more than $66,550. Median annual wages in radio and television broadcasting, which employed the largest number of broadcast technicians, were $29,220.

Median annual wages of sound-engineering technicians in May 2008 were $47,490. The middle 50 percent earned between $32,770 and $69,700. The lowest 10 percent earned less than $23,790, and the highest 10 percent earned more than $92,700.

Median annual wages of radio operators in May 2008 were $37,120. The middle 50 percent earned between $27,890 and $48,200. The lowest 10 percent earned less than $19,240, and the highest 10 percent earned more than $61,290.

NEWS ANALYSTS, REPORTERS, AND CORRESPONDENTS

SIGNIFICANT POINTS

- Competition will be keen for jobs at large metropolitan and national newspapers, broadcast stations, and magazines; small publications and broadcast stations and online newspapers and magazines should provide the best opportunities.

- Most employers prefer individuals with a bachelor's degree in journalism or mass communications and experience gained at school newspapers or broadcasting stations or through internships with news organizations.

- Jobs often involve long, irregular hours and pressure to meet deadlines.

❯ NATURE OF THE WORK

News analysts, reporters, and correspondents gather information, prepare stories, and make broadcasts that inform the public about local, state, national, and international events; they present points of view on current issues; and they report on the actions of public officials, corporate executives, interest groups, and others who exercise power.

News analysts—also called newscasters or news anchors—examine, interpret, and broadcast news received from various sources. News anchors present news stories and introduce videotaped news or live transmissions from on-the-scene reporters. News correspondents report on news occurring in the large U.S. and foreign cities where they are stationed.

In covering a story, reporters, sometimes referred to as journalists, investigate leads and news tips, look at documents, observe events at the scene, and interview people. Reporters take notes and also may take photographs or shoot videos. At their office, they organize the material, determine the focus or emphasis, write their stories, and edit accompanying video material. Many reporters enter information or write stories on laptop computers and electronically submit the material to their offices from remote locations. Increasingly, reporters are asked to maintain and produce material for a newspaper's website. In some cases, newswriters write a story from information collected and submitted by reporters. Radio and television reporters often compose stories and report "live" from the scene. At times, they later tape an introduction to or commentary on their story in the studio. Some journalists also interpret the news or offer opinions to readers, viewers, or listeners. In this role, they are called commentators or columnists.

Newscasters at large stations and networks usually specialize in a particular type of news, such as sports or weather. Weathercasters, also called weather reporters, report current and forecasted weather conditions. They gather information from national satellite weather services, wire services, and local and regional weather bureaus. Some weathercasters are trained meteorologists and can develop their own weather forecasts. Sportscasters select, write, and deliver sports news, which may include interviews with sports personalities and coverage of games and other sporting events.

General-assignment reporters write about newsworthy occurrences—such as accidents, political rallies, visits of celebrities, or business closings—as assigned. Large newspapers and radio and television stations assign reporters to gather news about specific topics—for example, crime or education. Some reporters specialize in fields such as health, politics, foreign affairs, sports, theater, consumer affairs, social events, science, business, or religion. Investigative reporters cover stories that may take many days or weeks of information gathering.

Some publications use teams of reporters instead of assigning each reporter one specific topic. As a member of a team, a reporter can cover a greater variety of stories. News teams may include reporters, editors, graphic artists, and photographers working together to complete a story.

Reporters on small publications cover all aspects of the news. They take photographs, write headlines, lay out pages, edit wire-service stories, and write editorials. Some also solicit advertisements, sell subscriptions, and perform general office work.

Work environment. The work of news analysts, reporters, and correspondents is usually hectic. They are under great pressure to meet deadlines. Broadcasts sometimes are aired with little or no time for preparation. Some news analysts, reporters, and correspondents work in comfortable, private offices; others work in large rooms filled with the sound of keyboards and computer printers, as well as the voices of other reporters. Curious onlookers, police, or other emergency workers can distract those reporting from the scene for radio and television. Covering wars, political uprisings, fires, floods, and similar events can be dangerous; however, the rate of injuries for reporters and correspondents is relatively low.

Work hours vary. Reporters on morning papers often work from late afternoon until midnight. Radio and television reporters usually are assigned to a day or evening shift. Magazine reporters usually work during the day.

Reporters sometimes have to change their work hours to meet a deadline or to follow late-breaking developments. Their work may require long hours, irregular schedules, and some travel. Because many stations and networks are on the air 24 hours a day, newscasters can expect to work unusual hours.

❯❯ TRAINING, OTHER QUALIFICATIONS, AND ADVANCEMENT

Most employers prefer individuals with a bachelor's degree in journalism or mass communications, but some hire graduates with other majors. They look for experience at school newspapers or broadcasting stations, and internships with news organizations. Large-city newspapers and stations also may prefer candidates with a degree in a subject-matter specialty such as economics, political science, or business. Some large newspapers and broadcasters may hire only experienced reporters.

▲ Education and training

More than 1,500 institutions offer programs in communications, journalism, and related programs. In 2008, more than 100 of these were accredited by the Accrediting Council on Education in Journalism and Mass Communications. Most of the courses in a typical curriculum are in liberal arts; the remaining courses are in journalism. The most important skills for journalism students to learn are writing and communication. Students planning a career in broadcasting take courses in radio and television news and production. Those planning newspaper or magazine careers usually specialize in more specific forms of writing. To create stories for online media, they need to learn to use computer software to combine online story text with audio and video elements and graphics.

Some schools also offer a master's or doctoral degree in journalism. Some graduate programs are intended primarily as preparation for news careers, while others prepare journalism teachers, researchers and theorists, and advertising and public relations workers.

High school courses in English, journalism, and social studies provide a good foundation for college programs. Useful college liberal arts courses include English, with an emphasis on writing; sociology; political science; economics; history; and psychology. Courses in computer science, business, and speech are useful as well. Fluency in a foreign language is necessary in some jobs.

Employers report that practical experience is the most important part of education and training. Upon graduation, many students already have gained much practical experience through part-time or summer jobs or through internships with news organizations. Most newspapers, magazines, and broadcast news organizations offer reporting and editing internships. Work on high school and college newspapers, at broadcasting stations, or on community papers also provides practical training. In addition, journalism scholarships, fellowships, and assistantships awarded to college journalism students by universities, newspapers, foundations, and professional organizations are helpful. Experience as a freelancer or stringer—a part-time reporter who is paid only for stories printed—is advantageous.

▲Other qualifications

Reporters typically need more than good word-processing skills. Computer graphics and desktop-publishing skills are essential as well. Students should be completely proficient in all forms of multimedia. Computer-assisted reporting involves the use of computers to analyze data in search of a story. This technique and the interpretation of the results require computer skills and familiarity with databases. Knowledge of news photography also is valuable for entry-level positions, which sometimes combine the responsibilities of a reporter with those of a camera operator or photographer.

Reporters should be dedicated to providing accurate and impartial news. Accuracy is important both to serve the public and because untrue or libelous statements can lead to lawsuits. A nose for news, persistence, initiative, poise, resourcefulness, a good memory, and physical stamina are important, as is the emotional stability to deal with pressing deadlines, irregular hours, and dangerous assignments. Broadcast reporters and news analysts must be comfortable on camera. All reporters must be at ease in unfamiliar places and with a variety of people. Positions involving on-air work require a pleasant voice and appearance.

▲Advancement

Most reporters start at small publications or broadcast stations as general-assignment reporters or copy editors. They are usually assigned to cover court proceedings and civic and club meetings, summarize speeches, and write obituaries. With experience, they report more difficult assignments or specialize in a particular field. Large publications and stations generally require new reporters to have several years of experience.

Some news analysts and reporters can advance by moving to larger newspapers or stations. A few experienced reporters become columnists, correspondents, writers, announcers, or public relations specialists. Others become editors in print journalism or program managers in broadcast journalism, supervising reporters. Some eventually become broadcasting or publishing-industry managers.

▲Employment

News analysts, reporters, and correspondents held about 69,300 jobs in 2008. About 53 percent worked for newspaper, periodical, book, and directory publishers. Another 21 percent worked in radio and television broadcasting. About 19 percent of news analysts, reporters, and correspondents were self-employed (freelancers or stringers).

▲Job Outlook

Employment is expected to decline moderately through 2018. Competition will continue to be keen for jobs on large metropolitan and national newspapers, broadcast stations and networks, and magazines. Small broadcast stations and publications and online newspapers and magazines should provide the best opportunities. Talented writers who can handle highly specialized scientific or technical subjects will have an advantage.

▲Employment change

Employment of news analysts, reporters, and correspondents is expected to decline 6 percent between 2008 and 2018. Many factors will contribute to the decline in this occupation. Consolidation and convergence should continue in the publishing and broadcasting industries. As a result, companies will be better able to allocate their news analysts, reporters, and correspondents to cover news stories. Since broadcasting and newspapers—the two industries employing most of these workers—are dependent on advertising revenue, employment growth will suffer during an economic downturn. Improving technology may eventually lead to more employment growth in this occupation by opening up new areas of work, such as online or mobile news divisions. The continued demand for news will create some job opportunities. Job openings also will result from the need to replace workers who leave their occupations permanently; some news analysts, reporters, and correspondents find the work too stressful and hectic or do not like the lifestyle, and transfer to other occupations.

▲Job prospects

Competition will continue to be keen for jobs at large metropolitan and national newspapers, broadcast stations and networks, and magazines. Job opportunities will be best for applicants in the expanding world of new media, such as online newspapers or magazines. Small local papers and news stations also will provide greater job prospects for potential reporters and news analysts. For beginning newspaper reporters, freelancing will supply more opportunities for employment as well. Students with a background in journalism as well as another subject, such as politics, economics, or biology, will have an advantage over those without additional background knowledge in moving beyond an entry-level position.

▲Earnings

Salaries for news analysts, reporters, and correspondents vary widely. Median annual wages of reporters and correspondents were $34,850 in May 2008. The middle 50 percent earned between $25,760 and $52,160. The lowest 10 percent earned less than $20,180, and the highest 10 percent earned more than $77,480. Median annual wages of reporters and correspondents were $33,430 in newspaper, periodical, book, and directory publishing, and $37,710 in radio and television broadcasting.

Median annual wages of broadcast news analysts were $51,260 in May 2008. The middle 50 percent earned between $32,000 and $88,630. The lowest 10 percent earned less than $23,470, and the highest 10 percent earned more than $156,200. Median annual wages of broadcast news analysts were $51,890 in radio and television broadcasting.

>> PUBLIC RELATIONS SPECIALISTS

SIGNIFICANT POINTS

- Although employment is projected to grow much faster than average, keen competition is expected for entry-level jobs.

- Opportunities should be best for college graduates who combine a degree in public relations, journalism, or another communications-related field with a public relations internship or other related work experience.

- Strong communication skills are essential.

❯❯NATURE OF THE WORK

An organization's reputation, profitability, and its continued existence can depend on the degree to which its targeted public supports its goals and policies. Public relations specialists—also referred to as communications specialists and media specialists, among other titles—serve as advocates for clients seeking to build and maintain positive relationships with the public. Their clients include businesses, nonprofit associations, universities, hospitals, and other organizations. As managers recognize the link between good public relations and the success of their organizations, they increasingly rely on public relations specialists for advice on the strategy and policy of their communications.

Public relations specialists handle organizational functions, such as media, community, consumer, industry, and governmental relations; political campaigns; interest-group representation; conflict mediation; and employee and investor relations. Public relations specialists must understand the attitudes and concerns of community, consumer, employee, and public interest groups to establish and maintain cooperative relationships between them and representatives from print and broadcast journalism.

Public relations specialists draft press releases and contact people in the media who might print or broadcast their material. Many radio or television special reports, newspaper stories, and magazine articles start at the desks of public relations specialists. Sometimes, the subject of a press release is an organization and its policies toward employees or its role in the community. For example, a press release might describe a public issue, such as health, energy, or the environment, and what an organization does to advance that issue.

Public relations specialists also arrange and conduct programs to maintain contact between organization representatives and the public. For example, public relations specialists set up speaking engagements and prepare speeches for officials. These media specialists represent employers at community projects; make film, slide, and other visual presentations for meetings and school assemblies; and plan conventions.

In government, public relations specialists may be called press secretaries. They keep the public informed about the activities of agencies and officials. For example, public affairs specialists in the U.S. Department of State alert the public of travel advisories and of U.S. positions on foreign issues. A press secretary for a member of Congress informs constituents of the representative's accomplishments.

In large organizations, the key public relations executive, who often is a vice president, may develop overall plans and policies with other executives. In addition, public relations departments employ public relations specialists to write, research, prepare materials, maintain contacts, and respond to inquiries.

People who handle publicity for an individual or who direct public relations for a small organization may deal with all aspects of the job. These public relations specialists contact people, plan and research, and prepare materials for distribution. They also may handle advertising or sales-promotion work to support marketing efforts.

▲Work environment

Public relations specialists work in busy offices. The pressures of deadlines and tight work schedules can be stressful.

Some public relations specialists work a standard 35- to 40-hour week, but overtime is common, and work schedules can be irregular and are frequently interrupted. Occasionally, they must be at the job or on call around the clock, especially if there is an emergency or crisis. Schedules often have to be rearranged so workers can meet deadlines, deliver speeches, attend meetings and community activities, and travel.

❯❯TRAINING, OTHER QUALIFICATIONS, AND ADVANCEMENT

A bachelor's degree in a communications-related field combined with public relations experience is excellent preparation for a person interested in public relations work.

▲Education and training

Many entry-level public relations specialists have a college degree in public relations, journalism, marketing, or communications. Some firms seek college graduates who have worked in electronic or print journalism. Other employers seek applicants with demonstrated communication skills and training or experience in a field related to the firm's business—information technology, health care, science, engineering, sales, or finance, for example.

Many colleges and universities offer bachelor's and postsecondary programs leading to a degree in public relations, usually in a journalism or communications department. In addition, many other colleges offer courses in this field. Courses in advertising, business administration, finance, political science, psychology, sociology, and creative writing also are helpful. Specialties may be offered in public relations for business, government, and nonprofit organizations.

Internships in public relations provide students with valuable experience and training and are the best route to finding entry-level employment. Membership in local chapters of the Public Relations Student Society of America (affiliated with the Public Relations Society of America) or in student chapters of the International Association of Business Communicators provides an opportunity for students to exchange views with public relations specialists and to make professional contacts that may help them to find a full-time job after graduation.

Some organizations, particularly those with large public relations staffs, have formal training programs for new employees. In smaller organizations, new employees work under the guidance of experienced staff members. Entry-level workers often maintain files of material about company activities, skim newspapers and magazines for appropriate articles to clip, and assemble information for speeches and pamphlets. New workers also may answer calls from the press and the public, prepare invitation lists and details for press conferences, or escort visitors and clients. After gaining experience, they write news releases, speeches, and articles for publication or plan and carry out public relations programs. Public relations specialists in smaller firms usually get well-rounded experience, whereas those in larger firms become more specialized.

▲Other qualifications

In addition to the ability to communicate thoughts clearly and simply, public relations specialists must show creativity, initiative, and good judgment. Decision-making, problem-solving, and research skills also are important. People who choose public relations as a career should have an outgoing personality, self-confidence, an understanding of human psychology, and an enthusiasm for motivating people. They should be assertive but able to participate as part of a team and be open to new ideas.

▲Certification and advancement

The Universal Accreditation Board accredits public relations specialists who are members of the Public Relations Society of America and who participate in the Examination for Accreditation in Public Relations process. This process includes both a readiness review and an examination, which are designed for candidates who have at least five years of full-time work or teaching experience in public relations and who have earned a bachelor's degree in a communications-related field. The readiness review includes a written submission by each candidate, a portfolio review, and dialogue between the candidate and a three-member panel. Candidates who successfully advance through readiness review and pass the computer-based examination earn the Accredited in Public Relations (APR) designation.

The International Association of Business Communicators (IABC) also has an accreditation program for professionals in the communications field, including public relations specialists. Those who meet all the requirements of the program earn the Accredited Business Communicator (ABC) designation. Candidates must have at least five years of experience and a bachelor's degree in a communications field and must pass written and oral examinations. They also must submit a portfolio of work samples that demonstrate involvement in a range of communications projects and a thorough understanding of communications planning.

Employers may consider professional recognition through accreditation as a sign of competence in this field, and such designations could be especially helpful in a competitive job market.

Public relations specialists who show that they can handle more demanding assignments are more likely to be promoted to supervisory jobs than those who are unable to do so. In public relations firms, an entry-level worker might be hired as a junior account executive and be promoted over the course of a career to account executive, senior account executive, account manager, and, eventually, vice president. Specialists in corporate public relations follow a similar career path, although the job titles may differ.

Some experienced public relations specialists start their own consulting firms.

▲Employment

Public relations specialists held about 275,200 jobs in 2008. They are concentrated in service-providing industries, such as advertising and related services; health care and social assistance; educational services; and government. Others work for communications firms, financial institutions, and government agencies.

Public relations specialists are concentrated in large cities, where press services and other communications facilities are readily available and where many businesses and trade associations have their headquarters. Many public relations consulting firms, for example, are in New York, Los Angeles, San Francisco, Chicago, and Washington, DC. There is a trend, however, toward public relations jobs to be dispersed throughout the nation, closer to clients.

▲Job Outlook
Employment is projected to grow much faster than average; however, keen competition is expected for entry-level jobs.

▲Employment change
Employment of public relations specialists is expected to grow 24 percent from 2008 to 2018, much faster than the average for all occupations. The need for good public relations in an increasingly competitive and global business environment should spur demand for these workers, especially those with specialized knowledge or international experience. Employees who possess additional language capabilities also are in great demand.
The recent emergence of social media in public relations is expected to increase job growth as well. Many public relations firms are expanding their use of these tools, and specialists with skills in them will be needed.

Employment in public relations firms is expected to grow as firms hire contractors to provide public relations services, rather than support more full-time staff when additional work is needed.

Among detailed industries, the largest job growth will continue to be in advertising and related services.

▲Job prospects
Keen competition likely will continue for entry-level public relations jobs, as the number of qualified applicants is expected to exceed the number of job openings. Many people are attracted to this profession because of the high-profile nature of the work. Opportunities should be best for college graduates who combine a degree in journalism, public relations, or another communications-related field with a public relations internship or other related work experience. Applicants who do not have the appropriate educational background or work experience will face the toughest obstacles.

Additional job opportunities should result from the need to replace public relations specialists who retire or leave the occupation for other reasons.

▲Earnings
Median annual wages for salaried public relations specialists were $51,280 in May 2008. The middle 50 percent earned between $38,400 and $71,670; the lowest 10 percent earned less than $30,140, and the top 10 percent earned more than $97,910.

>> TECHNICAL WRITERS

SIGNIFICANT POINTS

- Most jobs in this occupation require a college degree–preferably in communications, journalism, or English–but a degree in a technical subject may be useful.

- Job prospects for most technical writing jobs are expected to be good, particularly for those with Web or multimedia experience.

- Excellent communications skills, curiosity, and attention to detail are highly desired traits.

❯ NATURE OF THE WORK

Technical writers, also called technical communicators, put technical information into easily understandable language. They work primarily in information-technology-related industries, coordinating the development and dissemination of technical content for a variety of users; however, a growing number of technical communicators are using technical content to resolve business communications problems in a diversifying number of industries. Included in their products are operating instructions, how-to manuals, assembly instructions, and other documentation needed for online help and by technical-support staff, consumers, and other users within the company or industry. Technical writers also develop documentation for computer programs and set up communications systems with consumers to assess customer satisfaction and quality-control matters. In addition, they commonly work in engineering, scientific, health care, and other areas in which highly specialized material needs to be explained to a diverse audience, often of laypersons.

Technical writers often work with engineers, scientists, computer specialists, and software developers to manage the flow of information among project workgroups during development and testing. They also may work with product liability specialists and customer service or call center managers to improve the quality of product support and end-user assistance. Technical writers also oversee the preparation of illustrations, photographs, diagrams, and charts. Technical writers increasingly are using a variety of multimedia formats to convey information in such a way that complex concepts can be understood easily by users of the information.

Applying their knowledge of the user of the product, technical writers may serve as part of a team conducting usability studies to help improve the design of a product that is in the prototype stage. Technical writers may conduct research on their topics through personal observation, library and Internet research, and discussions with technical specialists. They also are expected to demonstrate their understanding of the subject matter and establish their credibility with their colleagues.

Technical writers use computers and other electronic communications equipment extensively in performing their work. They also work regularly with desktop and other electronic publishing software and prepare material directly for the Internet. Technical writers may work with graphic design, page layout, and multimedia software; increasingly, they are preparing documents by using the interactive technologies of the Web to blend text, graphics, multidimensional images, and sound.

Some technical writers work on a freelance or contract basis. They either are self-employed or work for a technical consulting firm and may be hired to complete specific short-term or recurring assignments, such as writing about a new product or coordinating the work and communications of different units to keep a project on track. Whether a project is to be coordinated among an organization's departments or among autonomous companies, technical writers ensure that the different entities share information and mediate differences in favor of the end user in order to bring a product to market sooner.

Work environment. Advances in computer and communications technologies make it possible for technical writers to work from almost anywhere. Laptop computers and wireless communications permit technical writers to work from home, an office, or on the road. The ability to use the Internet to e-mail, transmit, and download information and assignments, conduct research, or review materials allows them greater flexibility in where and how they complete assignments.

Many technical writers work with people located around the world and with specialists in highly technical fields, such as science and engineering. As a result, they must be able to assimilate complex information quickly and be comfortable working with people from diverse professional and cultural backgrounds. Although most technical writers are employed directly by the companies that use their services, many freelance writers are paid on a project basis and routinely face the pressures of juggling multiple projects and the continual need to find new work. Technical writers may be expected to work evenings, nights, or weekends to coordinate with those in other time zones, meet deadlines, or produce information that complies with project requirements and is acceptable to the client.

❯❯TRAINING, OTHER QUALIFICATIONS, AND ADVANCEMENT

A college degree is required for a position as a technical writer. In addition, knowledge in a technical subject, as well as experience in Web design and computer graphics, is important.

▲Education and training

Employers look for candidates with a bachelor's degree, often preferring those with a major in communications, journalism, or English. Some technical-writing jobs may require both experience and either a degree or knowledge in a specialized field—for example, engineering, medicine, or one of the sciences; others have broader requirements, such as a background in liberal arts. Knowledge of a second language is helpful for some positions. Experience in Web design and computer graphics also is helpful, because of the growing use of online technical documentation.

▲Other qualifications

Technical writers must have excellent writing and communication skills and be able to express ideas clearly and logically in a variety of media. Increasingly, technical writers need familiarity with electronic publishing, graphics, and sound and video production. Also needed is knowledge of computer software for combining online text with graphics, audio, video, and animation, as well as the ability to manage large, complex, and interconnected files.

Technical writers must be detail oriented, curious, persistent in solving problems, self-motivated, and able to understand complex material and explain it clearly. Technical writers also must demonstrate good working relationships and sensitivity toward others, especially those from different backgrounds. In addition, the ability to work under pressure and in a variety of work settings is essential.

▲Advancement
Some technical writers begin their careers not as writers, but as specialists in a technical field or as research assistants or trainees in a technical-information department. By transferring or developing technical-communication skills, they eventually assume primary responsibilities for technical writing. In small firms, beginning technical writers may work on projects right away; in larger companies with more standard procedures, beginners may observe experienced technical writers and interact with specialists before being assigned projects. Prospects for advancement generally include working on more complex projects, leading or training junior staff, and getting enough work to make it as a freelancer.

Many firms and freelancers provide technical-writing services on a contract basis, often to small or not-for-profit organizations that do not have enough regular work to employ technical writers full time. Building a reputation and establishing a record for meeting deadlines also makes it easier to get future assignments. An experienced, credible, and reliable freelance technical writer or editor often is able to establish long-term dealings with the same companies.

▲Employment
Technical writers held about 48,900 jobs in 2008. There are technical writers in almost every industry, but they are concentrated in industries related to computer systems and software, publishing (except Internet), science, and engineering. The industry that employed the most technical writers in 2008 was the computer systems-design industry, which had 18 percent of these workers. The second-largest employer was the computer- and electronic-manufacturing industry, with 8 percent of workers. Software publishers; architectural, engineering, and related services; management, scientific, and technical consulting services; and scientific research and development services industries also employed a sizeable number of technical writers. Two percent of technical writers were self-employed in 2008.

Jobs usually are concentrated in areas with high-information technology or scientific- and technical-research industry employment, such as San Francisco and San Jose, California; Boston, Massachusetts; and Washington, DC. However, technology permits technical writers to work in one location while communicating with clients and colleagues in another. As a result, geographic concentration is less of a requirement than it once was.

▲Job Outlook
Employment of technical writers is expected to grow faster than the average for all occupations as the need to explain a growing number of electronic and scientific products increases. Job prospects are expected to be good for those with solid writing and communications skills and a technical background.

▲Employment change
Employment of technical writers is expected to grow 18 percent, or faster than the average for all occupations, from 2008 to 2018. Demand over this decade is expected to increase

because of the continuing expansion of scientific and technical information and the growing presence of customer service and Web-based product support networks. Legal, scientific, and technological developments and discoveries will generate demand for people who can interpret technical information for a general audience. Rapid growth and change in the high-technology and electronics industries will result in a greater need for people who can write users' guides, instruction manuals, and training materials in a variety of formats and communicate information clearly to others. This occupation requires workers who are both skilled writers and effective communicators and familiar with a specialized subject area.

Increasing acceptance of interactive media to provide nearly real-time information will create employment opportunities for technical writers because of the need to revise online information. Businesses and organizations are making more material available online often in formats that permit greater scrutiny and comparison of detailed information. The growing amount and complexity of information available on the Web will spur demand for technical writers. Professional, scientific, and technical services firms will continue to grow and should be a good source of new jobs even as the occupation finds acceptance in a broader range of industries, including data processing, hosting, and related services and educational services.

▲Job prospects

Job prospects, especially for applicants with solid communication and technical skills, are expected to be good. The growing reliance on technologically sophisticated products in the home and the workplace and the increasing complexity of medical or scientific information needed for daily living will create many new job opportunities for technical writers. However, competition will exist for technical-writing positions with more desirable companies and for workers who are new to the occupation.

In addition to job openings created by employment growth, some openings will arise as experienced workers retire, transfer to other occupations, or leave the labor force. Also, many freelancers may not earn enough money by freelancing to remain in the occupation, thus generating additional job openings.

▲Earnings

Median annual wages for salaried technical writers were $61,620 in May 2008. The middle 50 percent earned between $47,100 and $78,910. The lowest 10 percent earned less than $36,500, and the highest 10 percent earned more than $97,460.

MUSICAL &
PERFORMING ARTS >>

MUSICIANS, SINGERS, AND RELATED WORKERS

SIGNIFICANT POINTS

- Part-time schedules–typically at night and on weekends–intermittent unemployment, and rejection when auditioning for work are common; many musicians and singers supplement their income with earnings from other sources.

- Aspiring musicians and singers begin studying an instrument or training their voice at an early age.

- Competition for jobs, especially full-time jobs, is keen; talented individuals who can play several instruments and perform a wide range of musical styles should enjoy the best job prospects.

❯NATURE OF THE WORK

Musicians, singers, and related workers play musical instruments, sing, compose or arrange music, or conduct groups in instrumental or vocal performances. They perform solo or as part of a group, mostly in front of live audiences in nightclubs, concert halls, and theaters. They also perform in recording or production studios for radio, TV, film, or video games. Regardless of the setting, they spend considerable time practicing alone and with their bands, orchestras, or other musical ensembles.

Musicians play one or more musical instruments. Many musicians learn to play several related instruments and can perform equally well in several musical styles. Instrumental musicians, for example, may play in a symphony orchestra, rock group, or jazz combo one night, appear in another ensemble the next, and work in a studio band the following day. Some play a variety of string, brass, woodwind, or percussion instruments or electronic synthesizers.

Singers use their knowledge of voice production, melody, and harmony to interpret music and text. They sing character parts or perform in their own individual styles. Singers often are classified according to their voice range—soprano, contralto, tenor, baritone, or bass—or by the type of music they sing, such as rock, pop, folk, opera, rap, or country.

Music directors and conductors conduct, direct, plan, and lead instrumental or vocal performances by musical groups such as orchestras, choirs, and glee clubs. These leaders audition and select musicians, choose the music most appropriate for their talents and abilities, and direct rehearsals and performances. Choral directors lead choirs and glee clubs, sometimes working with a band or an orchestra conductor. Directors audition and select singers and lead them at rehearsals and performances to achieve harmony, rhythm, tempo, shading, and other desired musical effects.

Composers create original music such as symphonies, operas, sonatas, radio and television jingles, film scores, and popular songs. They transcribe ideas into musical notation, using harmony, rhythm, melody, and tonal structure. Although most composers and songwriters practice their craft on instruments and transcribe the notes with pen and paper, some use computer software to compose and edit their music.

Arrangers transcribe and adapt musical compositions to a particular style for orchestras, bands, choral groups, or individuals. Components of music—including tempo, volume, and the mix of instruments needed—are arranged to express the composer's message. Although some arrangers write directly into a musical composition, others use computer software to make changes.

▲Work environment

Musicians typically perform at night and on weekends. They spend much additional time practicing or in rehearsal. Full-time musicians with long-term employment contracts, such as those with symphony orchestras or television and film production companies, enjoy steady work and less travel. Nightclub, solo, or recital musicians frequently travel to perform in a variety of local settings and may tour nationally or internationally. Because many musicians find only part-time or intermittent work and experience unemployment between engagements, they often supplement their income with other types of jobs. The stress of constantly looking for work leads many musicians to accept permanent full-time jobs in other occupations while working part time as musicians.

Most instrumental musicians work closely with a variety of other people, including colleagues, agents, employers, sponsors, and audiences. Although they usually work indoors, some perform outdoors for parades, concerts, and festivals. In some nightclubs and restaurants, smoke and odors may be present and lighting and ventilation may be poor.

❯❯TRAINING, OTHER QUALIFICATIONS, AND ADVANCEMENT

Long-term on-the-job training is the most common way people learn to become musicians or singers. Aspiring musicians begin studying an instrument at an early age. They may gain valuable experience playing in a school or community band or orchestra or with a group of friends. Singers usually start training when their voices mature. Participation in school musicals or choirs often provides good early training and experience. Composers and music directors usually require a bachelor's degree in a related field.

▲Education and training

Musicians need extensive and prolonged training and practice to acquire the skills and knowledge necessary to interpret music at a professional level. Like other artists, musicians and singers continually strive to improve their abilities. Formal training may be obtained through private study with an accomplished musician, in a college or university music program, or in a music conservatory. An audition generally is necessary to qualify for university or conservatory study. The National Association of Schools of Music is made up of 615 accredited college-level programs in music. Courses typically include music theory, music interpretation, composition, conducting, and performance, either with a particular instrument or a voice performance. Music directors, composers, conductors, and arrangers need considerable related work experience or advanced training in these subjects.

A master's or doctoral degree usually is required to teach advanced music courses in colleges and universities; a bachelor's degree may be sufficient to teach basic courses. A degree in music education qualifies graduates for a state certificate to teach music in public elementary or secondary schools. Musicians who do not meet public school music education requirements may teach in private schools and recreation associations or instruct individual students in private sessions.

▲Other qualifications

Musicians must be knowledgeable about a broad range of musical styles. Having a broader range of interest, knowledge, and training can help expand employment opportunities and musical abilities. Voice training and private instrumental lessons, especially when taken at a young age, also help develop technique and enhance one's performance.

Young persons considering careers in music should have musical talent, versatility, creativity, poise, and good stage presence. Self-discipline is vital because producing a quality performance on a consistent basis requires constant study and practice. Musicians who play in concerts or in nightclubs and those who tour must have physical stamina to endure frequent travel and an irregular performance schedule. Musicians and singers also must be prepared to face the anxiety of intermittent employment and of rejection when auditioning for work.

▲Advancement

Advancement for musicians usually means becoming better known, finding work more easily, and performing for higher earnings. Successful musicians often rely on agents or managers to find them performing engagements, negotiate contracts, and develop their careers.

▲Employment

Musicians, singers, and related workers held about 240,000 jobs in 2008, of which 186,400 were held by musicians and singers; 53,600 were music directors and composers. Around 43 percent worked part time; 50 percent were self-employed. Many found jobs in cities in which entertainment and recording activities are concentrated, such as New York, Los Angeles, Las Vegas, Chicago, and Nashville.

Musicians, singers, and related workers are employed in a variety of settings. Of those who earn a wage or salary, 33 percent were employed by religious, grant-making, civic, professional, and similar organizations and 12 percent by performing arts companies, such as professional orchestras, small chamber music groups, opera companies, musical theater companies, and ballet troupes. Musicians and singers also perform in nightclubs and restaurants and for weddings and other events. Well-known musicians and groups may perform in concerts, appear on radio and television broadcasts, and make recordings and music videos. The U.S. Armed Forces also offer careers in their bands and smaller musical groups.

▲Job Outlook

Employment is expected to grow as fast as average. Keen competition for jobs, especially full-time jobs, is expected to continue. Talented individuals who are skilled in multiple instruments and musical styles will have the best job prospects.

▲Employment change

Employment of musicians, singers, and related workers is expected to grow 8 percent during the 2008–18 decade, as fast as the average for all occupations. Most new wage-and-salary jobs for musicians will arise in religious organizations. Slower than average employment growth is expected for self-employed musicians, who generally perform in nightclubs, concert tours, and other venues. The Internet and other new forms of media may provide independent musicians and singers alternative methods for distributing music.

▲Job prospects

Growth in demand for musicians will generate a number of job opportunities, and many openings also will arise from the need to replace those who leave the field each year because they are unable to make a living solely as musicians or singers, as well as those who leave for other reasons.

Competition for jobs as musicians, singers, and related workers—especially full-time jobs—is expected to be keen. The vast number of people with the desire to perform will continue to greatly exceed the number of openings. New musicians or singers will have their best chance of landing a job with smaller, community-based performing arts groups or as freelance artists. Instrumentalists should have better opportunities than singers because of a larger pool of work. Talented individuals who are skilled in multiple instruments or musical styles will have the best job prospects. However, talent alone is no guarantee of success: many people start out to become musicians or singers but leave the profession because they find the work difficult, the discipline demanding, and the long periods of intermittent unemployment a hardship.

▲Earnings

Median hourly wages of wage-and-salary musicians and singers were $21.24 in May 2008. The middle 50 percent earned between $11.49 and $36.36. The lowest 10 percent earned less than $7.64, and the highest 10 percent earned more than $59.92. Median hourly wages were $23.68 in performing arts companies and $12.50 in religious organizations. Annual wage data for musicians and singers were not available because of the wide variation in the number of hours worked by musicians and singers and the short-term nature of many jobs. It is rare for musicians and singers to have guaranteed employment that exceeds three to six months.

Median annual wages of salaried music directors and composers were $41,270 in May 2008. The middle 50 percent earned between $26,480 and $63,200. The lowest 10 percent earned less than $16,750, and the highest 10 percent earned more than $107,280.

For self-employed musicians and singers, earnings typically reflect the number of jobs a freelance musician or singer played or the number of hours and weeks of contract work, in addition to a performer's professional reputation and setting. Performers who can fill large concert halls, arenas, or outdoor stadiums generally command higher pay than those who perform in local clubs. Soloists or headliners usually receive higher earnings than band members or opening acts. The most successful musicians earn performance or recording fees that far exceed the median earnings.

The American Federation of Musicians negotiates minimum contracts for major orchestras during the performing season. Each orchestra works out a separate contract with its local union, but individual musicians may negotiate higher salaries. In regional orchestras, minimum salaries often are less because fewer performances are scheduled. Regional orchestra musicians frequently are paid for their services without any guarantee of future employment. Community orchestras often have limited funding and offer salaries that are much lower for seasons of shorter duration.

Although musicians employed by some symphony orchestras work under master wage agreements, which guarantee a season's work up to 52 weeks, many other musicians face relatively long periods of unemployment between jobs. Even when employed, many musicians and singers work part time in unrelated occupations. Thus, their earnings for music usually are lower than earnings in many other occupations. Moreover, because they may not work steadily for one employer, some performers cannot qualify for unemployment compensation and few have typical benefits such as sick leave or paid vacations. For these reasons, many musicians give private lessons or take jobs unrelated to music to supplement their earnings as performers.

Many musicians belong to a local of the American Federation of Musicians. Professional singers who perform live often belong to a branch of the American Guild of Musical Artists; those who record for the broadcast industries may belong to the American Federation of Television and Radio Artists.

>> ACTORS, PRODUCERS, AND DIRECTORS

SIGNIFICANT POINTS

- Actors endure long periods of unemployment, intense competition for roles, and frequent rejections in auditions.

- Formal training through a university or acting conservatory is typical; however, many actors, producers, and directors find work on the basis of their experience and talent alone.

- Because earnings may be erratic, many actors, producers, and directors supplement their incomes by holding jobs in other fields.

❯❯ NATURE OF THE WORK

Actors, producers, and directors express ideas and create images in theater, film, radio, television, and other performing arts media. They interpret a writer's script to entertain, inform, or instruct an audience. Although many actors, producers, and directors work in New York or Los Angeles, far more work in other places. They perform, direct, and produce in local or regional television studios, theaters, or film production companies, often creating advertising or training films or small-scale independent movies.

Actors perform in stage, radio, television, video, or motion picture productions. They also work in cabarets, nightclubs, and theme parks. Actors portray characters, and, for more complex roles, they research their character's traits and circumstances so that they can better understand a script.

Most actors struggle to find steady work and only a few achieve recognition as stars. Others work as "extras," with no lines to deliver. Some actors do voiceover and narration work for advertisements, animated features, books on tape, and other electronic media. They also teach in high school or university drama departments, acting conservatories, or public programs.

Producers are entrepreneurs who make the business and financial decisions involving a motion picture, television show, or stage production. They select scripts, approve the development of ideas, arrange financing, and determine the size and cost of the endeavor. Producers hire or approve directors, principal cast members, and key production staff members.

Large productions often have associate, assistant, or line producers who share responsibilities. The number of producers and their specific job duties vary with the size and budget of each production; however, all work is done under the overall direction of an executive producer. Together the producers coordinate the activities of writers, directors, managers, and agents to ensure that each project stays on schedule and within budget.

Directors are responsible for the overall creative decisions of a production. They interpret scripts, audition and select cast members, conduct rehearsals, and direct the work of cast and crew. They approve the design elements of a production, including the sets, costumes, choreography, and music. As with producers, large productions often have many levels of directors working on them. Assistant directors cue the performers and technicians, telling them when to make entrances or light, sound, or set changes. All directors must ultimately answer to the executive producer, who has the final say on all factors related to the production.

▲ Work environment

Actors, producers, and directors work under constant pressure. Many face stress from the continual need to find their next job. To succeed, actors, producers, and directors need patience and commitment to their craft. Actors strive to deliver flawless performances, often while working under undesirable and unpleasant conditions. Producers and directors organize rehearsals and meet with writers, designers, financial backers, and production technicians. They experience stress not only from these activities, but also from the need to adhere to budgets, union work rules, and production schedules.

Work assignments typically are short term—ranging from one day to a few months—which means that workers frequently experience long periods of unemployment between jobs. The uncertain nature of the work results in unpredictable earnings and intense competition for jobs. Often, actors, producers, and directors must hold other jobs in order to sustain a living.

Work hours are often long and irregular—evening and weekend work is a regular part of life in the performing arts. Actors, producers, and directors who work in theater may travel with a touring show across the country, whereas those who work in film may work on location, sometimes under adverse weather conditions. Actors who perform in a television series often appear on camera with little preparation time, because scripts tend to be revised frequently or even written moments before taping. Those who appear live or before a studio audience must be able to handle impromptu situations and calmly ad lib, or substitute, lines when necessary.

Actors should be in good physical condition and have the necessary stamina and coordination to move about theater stages and large movie and television studio lots. They also need to maneuver about complex technical sets while staying in character and projecting their voices audibly. Actors must be fit to endure heat from stage or studio lights and the weight of heavy costumes. Producers and directors ensure the safety of actors by conducting extra rehearsals on the set so that the actors can learn the layout of set pieces and props, by allowing time for warm-ups and stretching exercises to guard against physical and vocal injuries, and by providing an adequate number of breaks to prevent heat exhaustion and dehydration.

❯❯TRAINING, OTHER QUALIFICATIONS, AND ADVANCEMENT

People who become actors, producers, and directors follow many paths to employment. The most important qualities employers look for are creative instincts, innate talent, and the intellectual capacity to perform. The best way to prepare for a career as an actor, especially in the theater, is through formal dramatic training, preferably obtained as part of a bachelor's degree program. Producers and especially directors need experience in the field, either as actors or in other related jobs.

▲Education and training

Formal dramatic training, either through an acting conservatory or a university program, generally is necessary for these jobs, but some people successfully enter the field without it. Most people studying for a bachelor's degree take courses in radio and television broadcasting, communications, film, theater, drama, or dramatic literature. Many stage actors continue their academic training and receive a master of fine arts (MFA) degree. Advanced curricula may include courses in stage speech and movement, directing, playwriting, and design, as well as intensive acting workshops. The National Association of Schools of Theatre accredits over 150 programs in theater arts.

Most aspiring actors participate in high school and college plays, work at college radio or television stations, or perform with local community theater groups. Local and regional theater experience may also help many young actors hone their skills. In television and film, actors and directors typically start in smaller roles or independent movie production companies and then work their way up to larger productions. Actors, regardless of their level of experience, may pursue workshop training through acting conservatories or mentoring by a drama coach.

There are no specific training requirements for producers. They come from many different backgrounds. Actors, writers, film editors, and business managers commonly enter the field. Producers often start in a theatrical management office, working for a press agent, managing director, or business manager. Some start in a performing arts union or service organization. Others work behind the scenes with successful directors, serve on the boards of art companies, or promote their own projects. Although there are no formal training programs for producers, a number of colleges and universities offer degree programs in arts management and in managing nonprofit organizations.

Some directors have experience as actors or writers, while others gain experience in the field by assisting established directors. Many also have formal training in directing.

▲Other qualifications

Actors need talent and creativity that will enable them to portray different characters. Because competition for parts is fierce, versatility and a wide range of related performance skills, such as singing, dancing, skating, juggling, acrobatics, or miming are especially useful. Actors must have poise, stage presence, the ability to affect an audience, and the ability to follow direction. Modeling experience also may be helpful. Physical appearance, such as having certain features and being the specified size and weight, often is a deciding factor in who gets a particular role.

Some actors begin as movie extras. To become an extra, one usually must be listed by casting agencies that supply extras to the major movie studios in Hollywood. Applicants are accepted only when the number of people of a particular type on the list—for example, athletic young women, old men, or small children—falls below what is needed. In recent years, only a very small proportion of applicants have succeeded in being listed.

Like actors, directors and producers need talent and creativity. Directors need management ability because they are often in charge of a large number of people in a production. Producers need business acumen.

▲Advancement

As the reputations and box-office draw of actors, producers, and directors grow, some of them work on bigger budget productions, on network or syndicated broadcasts, in more prestigious theaters, or in larger markets. Actors may advance to lead roles and receive star billing. A few actors move into acting-related jobs, becoming drama coaches, directors, or producers. Some actors teach drama privately or in colleges and universities.

▲Employment

In May 2008, actors, producers, and directors held about 155,100 jobs, primarily in the motion picture and video, performing arts, and broadcast industries. This statistic does not capture large number of actors, producers, and directors who were available for work but were between jobs during the month in which data were collected. About 21 percent of actors, producers, and directors were self-employed.

Employment in motion pictures and in films for television is centered in New York and Los Angeles. However, small studios exist throughout the country. Many films are shot on location and may employ local professional and nonprofessional actors. In television, opportunities are concentrated in the network centers of New York and Los Angeles, but cable television services and local television stations around the country also employ many actors, producers, and directors.

Employment in the theater, and in other performing arts companies, is cyclical—higher in the fall and spring seasons—and concentrated in New York and other major cities with large commercial houses for musicals and touring productions. Also, many cities support established professional regional theaters that operate on a seasonal or year-round basis.

Actors, producers, and directors may find work in summer festivals, on cruise lines, and in theme parks. Many smaller, nonprofit professional companies, such as repertory companies, dinner theaters, and theaters affiliated with drama schools, acting conservatories, and universities, provide employment opportunities for local amateur talent and professional entertainers. Auditions typically are held in New York for many productions across the country and for shows that go on the road.

▲Job Outlook

Employment is expected to grow as fast as the average for all occupations. Competition for jobs will be keen. Although a growing number of people aspire to enter these professions, many will leave the field early because the work—when it is available—is hard, the hours are long, and the pay is often low.

▲Employment change

Employment in these occupations is expected to grow 11 percent during the 2008–18 decade, about as fast as the average for all occupations. Expanding cable and satellite television operations and increasing box-office receipts of major studio and independent films will increase the need for workers. Additionally, a rising demand for U.S. films in other countries should create more employment opportunities for actors, producers, and directors. Also fueling job growth is the continued development of interactive media, online movies, and mobile content produced for cell phones or other portable electronic devices. Attendance at live theater performances should continue to be steady, and drive employment of stage actors, producers and directors. However, station consolidation may restrict employment opportunities in the broadcasting industry for producers and directors.

▲Job prospects

Competition for acting jobs is intense, as the number of actors auditioning for roles greatly exceeds the number of parts that become available. Only performers with the most stamina and talent will find regular employment.

Venues for live entertainment, such as theaters, touring productions, and repertory theaters in many major metropolitan areas, as well as theme parks and resorts, are expected to offer many job opportunities. However, prospects in these venues are variable because they fluctuate with economic conditions.

▲Earnings

Many of the most successful actors, producers, and directors have extraordinarily high earnings, but many more of these professionals, faced with erratic earnings, supplement their income by holding jobs in other fields.

Median hourly wages of actors were $16.59 in May 2008. The middle 50 percent earned between $9.81 and $29.57. Median hourly wages were $14.48 in performing arts companies and $28.72 in the motion picture and video industry. Annual wage data for actors were not available because of the wide variation in the number of hours worked by actors and the short-term nature of many jobs, which may last for one day or one week; it is extremely rare for actors to have guaranteed employment that exceeds three to six months.

Median annual wages of producers and directors were $64,430 in 2008. The middle 50 percent earned between $41,890 and $105,070. Median annual wages were $85,940 in the motion picture and video industry and $55,380 in radio and television broadcasting.

Minimum salaries, hours of work, and other conditions of employment are often covered in collective-bargaining agreements between the producers and the unions representing workers. While these unions generally determine minimum salaries, any actor or director may negotiate for a salary higher than the minimum.

A joint agreement between the Screen Actors Guild (SAG) and the American Federation of Television and Radio Artists (AFTRA) guarantees all unionized motion picture and television actors with speaking parts a minimum daily rate of $782, or $2,713 for a five-day week, as of June 2009. Actors also receive contributions to their health and pension plans and additional compensation for reruns and foreign telecasts of the productions in which they appear.

Some well-known actors earn well above the minimum; their salaries are many times the figures cited here, creating the false impression that all actors are highly paid. For example, of the nearly 100,000 SAG members, only about 50 might fall into this category. The average income that SAG members earn from acting is low because employment is sporadic and most actors must supplement their incomes by holding jobs in other occupations.

Actors Equity Association (AEA), which represents stage actors, has negotiated minimum weekly salary requirements for their members. Salaries vary depending on the theater or venue the actor is employed in. Many stage directors belong to the Society of Stage Directors and Choreographers (SSDC), and most film and television directors belong to the Directors Guild of America. Earnings of stage directors vary greatly. The SSDC usually negotiates salary contracts which include royalties (additional income based on the number of performances) with smaller theaters. Regional theaters may hire directors for longer periods, increasing compensation accordingly. The highest-paid directors work on Broadway; in addition to their contract fee, they also receive payment in the form of royalties—a negotiated percentage of gross box-office receipts—that can exceed the contract fee for long-running box-office successes.

Stage producers seldom receive a set fee; instead, they get a percentage of a show's earnings or ticket sales.

>> DANCERS AND CHOREOGRAPHERS

SIGNIFICANT POINTS

- Many dancers stop performing by their late 30s, but some remain in the field as choreographers, dance teachers, or artistic directors.

- Most dancers begin formal training at an early age–between 5 and 15–and many have their first professional audition by age 17 or 18; becoming a choreographer usually requires years of experience.

- Dancers and choreographers face intense competition; only the most talented find regular work.

- Earnings from dancing are usually low because employment is irregular; dancers often supplement their income.

❯❯NATURE OF THE WORK

Complex movements and dances on stage and screen do not happen without a lot of hard work. Dancers spend years learning dances and honing skills, as do most choreographers. Together, they then translate those skills into movement that expresses ideas and stories. Dancers perform in a variety of settings, including opera, musical theater, and other musical productions, and may present folk, ethnic, tap, jazz, or other popular kinds of dance. They also perform in television, movies, music videos, and commercials, in which they may sing and act. Dancers most often perform as part of a group, although a few top artists perform solo.

Choreographers create original dances and develop new interpretations of existing dances. They work in theaters, dance schools, dance and movie studios, and at fashion shows, and are involved in auditioning performers for dance parts. Because few dance routines are written down, choreographers instruct performers at rehearsals to achieve the desired effect, often by demonstrating the exact technique. Choreographers also work with performers other than dancers. For example, the complex martial arts scenes in movies are arranged by choreographers who specialize in the martial arts. Choreographers also may help coordinate costume design and lighting, as well as choose the music and sound effects that convey the intended message.

▲Work environment

Dance is strenuous. In fact, dancers have one of the highest rates of nonfatal on-the-job injury. Many dancers, as a result, stop performing by their late 30s because of the physical demands on the body. Nonetheless, some continue to work in the field as choreographers, artistic directors, and dance teachers and coaches, while a small number may move into administrative positions, such as company managers. A few celebrated dancers, however, continue performing most of their lives.

Many dance companies tour for part of the year to supplement a limited performance schedule at home. Dancers who perform in musical productions and other family entertainment spend much of their time on the road; others work in nightclubs or on cruise ships. Most dance performances are in the evening, whereas rehearsals and practice usually take place during the day. As a result, dancers often work very long and late hours. Generally, dancers and choreographers work in modern and temperature-controlled facilities; however, some studios may be older and less comfortable.

❯❯TRAINING, OTHER QUALIFICATIONS, AND ADVANCEMENT

Dancers generally need long-term on-the-job training to be successful. Most dancers begin formal training at an early age—between 5 and 15—and many have their first professional audition by age 17 or 18. Some earn a bachelor's degree or attend dance school, although neither is required. Becoming a choreographer usually requires years of experience.

▲Education and training

Training varies with the type of dance and is a continuous part of all dancers' careers. Many believe that dancers should start with a good foundation in classical technique before selecting a particular style. Ballet training for girls usually begins between the ages of 5 to 8 with a private teacher or through an independent ballet school, with more serious training beginning between the ages of 10 and 12. Boys often begin their ballet training between the ages of 10 and 15. Students who demonstrate potential in their early teens may seek out more intensive and advanced professional training. At about this time, students should begin to focus their training on a particular style and decide whether to pursue additional training through a dance company's school or a college dance program. Leading dance school companies often have summer training programs from which they select candidates for admission to their regular full-time training programs. Formal training for modern and culturally specific dances often begins later than training in ballet; however, many folk dance forms are taught to very young children. As a result, a good number of dancers have their first professional auditions by age 17 or 18.

Training is an important component of professional dancers' careers. Dancers normally spend eight hours a day in class and rehearsal, keeping their bodies in shape and preparing for performances. Their daily training period usually includes time to warm up and cool down before and after classes and rehearsals.

Because of the strenuous and time-consuming training required, some dancers view formal education as secondary. However, a broad, general education including music, literature, history, and the visual arts is helpful in the interpretation of dramatic episodes, ideas, and feelings. Dancers sometimes conduct research to learn more about the part they are playing.

Many colleges and universities award a bachelor's or master's degree in dance, typically through departments of dance, theater, or fine arts. The National Association of Schools of Dance is made up of 74 accredited dance programs. Many programs concentrate on modern dance, but some also offer courses in jazz, culturally specific dance, ballet, or classical techniques. Courses in dance composition, history and criticism, and movement analysis are also available.

A college education is not essential for employment as a professional dancer; however, many dancers obtain degrees in unrelated fields to prepare themselves for careers after dance. The completion of a college program in dance and education is usually essential to qualify to teach dance in college, high school, or elementary school. Colleges and conservatories sometimes require graduate degrees but may accept performance experience. A college background is not necessary for teaching dance or choreography in local recreational programs. Studio schools prefer teachers to have experience as performers.

Choreographers should have a thorough understanding of the dance style that they arrange. This often is gained through years of performing and practicing. Some dance conservatories offer choreography courses.

▲Other qualifications

Because of the rigorous practice schedules of most dancers and choreographers, self-discipline, patience, perseverance, and a devotion to dance are essential for success in the field. Dancers and choreographers also must possess good problem-solving skills and an ability to work with people. Dancers, above all, must have good health and physical stamina, along with flexibility, agility, coordination, and grace, a sense of rhythm, a feeling for music, and a creative ability to express themselves through movement. Choreographers should possess many of the same attributes while also being able to plan and coordinate activities.

Because dancers and choreographers are typically members of an ensemble made up of other dancers, musicians, and directors or choreographers, they must be able to function as part of a team. They also should be highly motivated and prepared to face the anxiety of intermittent employment and rejections when looking for work.

▲Advancement

For dancers, advancement takes the form of a growing reputation, more frequent work, bigger and better roles, and higher pay. Some dancers may take on added responsibilities, such as by becoming a dance captain in musical theater, or ballet master/ballet mistress in concert-dance companies, by leading rehearsals, or by working with less experienced dancers in the absence of a choreographer.

Choreographers typically are experienced dancers with years of practice working in the theater. Through their performance as dancers, they develop reputations that often lead to opportunities to choreograph productions.

▲Employment

Professional dancers and choreographers held about 29,200 jobs in 2008. Many others were between engagements; as a result, the total number of people available for work as dancers over the course of the year was greater. Dancers and choreographers worked in a variety of industries, such as public and private educational services, which includes dance studios and schools, as well as colleges and universities; food services and drinking establishments; performing arts companies, which include dance, theater, and opera companies; and amusement and recreation venues, such as casinos and theme parks. About 14 percent of dancers and choreographers were self-employed.
Most major cities serve as home to major dance companies; however, many smaller communities across the nation also support home-grown, full-time professional dance companies.

▲Job Outlook

Employment is expected to grow more slowly than the average. Dancers and choreographers face keen competition for jobs. Only the most talented find regular employment.

▲Employment change

Employment of dancers and choreographers is expected to grow 6 percent during the 2008–18 decade, more slowly than the average for all occupations. The public's interest in dance will sustain large and mid-size dance companies, but limited funding from public and private organizations is not expected to allow for additional dance companies. For many small organizations, the result will be fewer performances and more limited employment opportunities.

▲Job prospects

Because many people enjoy dance and would like to make their careers in dance, dancers and choreographers face intense competition for jobs. Only the most talented find regular employment.

Although job openings will arise each year because dancers and choreographers retire or leave the occupation for other reasons, the number of applicants will continue to vastly exceed the number of job openings.

National dance companies likely will continue to provide jobs in this field. Opera companies and dance groups affiliated with television and motion pictures also will offer some opportunities. Moreover, the growing popularity of dance for recreational and fitness purposes has resulted in increased opportunities to teach dance, especially for older dancers who may be transitioning to another field. Musicians will provide a small number of openings for both dancers and choreographers, and candidates are expected to face keen competition. Amusement parks and cruise ships should also provide some opportunities for dancers and choreographers.

▲Earnings

Median hourly wages of dancers were $12.22 in May 2008. The middle 50 percent earned between $8.03 and $18.82. The lowest 10 percent earned less than $7.28, and the highest 10 percent earned more than $27.26. Annual wage data for dancers were not available, because the wide variation in the number of hours worked by dancers and the short-term nature of many jobs—which may last for one day or one week—make it rare for dancers to have guaranteed employment that exceeds a few months.

Median annual wages of salaried choreographers were $38,520 in May 2008. The middle 50 percent earned between $25,320 and $55,360. The lowest 10 percent earned less than $17,880, and the highest 10 percent earned more than $67,160. Median annual wages were $37,570 in "other schools and instruction," the North American Industry Classification System category that includes dance studios and schools.

Dancers who were on tour usually received an additional allowance for room and board, as well as extra compensation for overtime. Earnings from dancing are usually low because employment is irregular. Dancers often supplement their income by working as guest artists with other dance companies, teaching dance, or taking jobs unrelated to the field.

Earnings of dancers at some of the largest companies and in commercial settings are governed by union contracts. Some dancers in major opera ballet, classical ballet, and modern dance corps belong to the American Guild of Musical Artists, Inc. of the AFL-CIO; those who appear on live or videotaped television programs belong to the American Federation of Television and Radio Artists; those who perform in films and on television belong to the Screen Actors Guild; and those in musical theater are members of the Actors' Equity Association. The unions and producers sign basic agreements specifying minimum salary rates, hours of work, benefits, and other conditions of employment. However, the contract each dancer signs with the producer of the show may be more favorable than the basic agreement.

Most salaried dancers and choreographers covered by union contracts receive some paid sick leave and various health and pension benefits, including extended sick pay and family-leave benefits provided by their unions. Employers contribute toward these benefits. Dancers and choreographers not covered by union contracts usually do not enjoy such benefits.

VISUAL ARTS »

>> GRAPHIC DESIGNERS

SIGNIFICANT POINTS

- Employment is expected to grow about as fast as the average, with many new jobs associated with interactive media.

- A bachelor's degree in graphic design is usually required.

- Jobseekers are expected to face keen competition; individuals with website-design and animation experience will have the best opportunities.

❯NATURE OF THE WORK

Graphic designers—or graphic artists—plan, analyze, and create visual solutions to communications problems. They find the most effective way to get messages across in print and electronic media using color, type, illustration, photography, animation, and various print and layout techniques. Graphic designers develop the overall layout and production design of magazines, newspapers, journals, corporate reports, and other publications. They also produce promotional displays, packaging, and marketing brochures for products and services, design distinctive logos for products and businesses, and develop signs and signage systems—called "environmental graphics"—for business and government. An increasing number of graphic designers also develop material for Internet Web pages, interactive media, and multimedia projects. Graphic designers also may produce the credits that appear before and after television programs and movies.

The first step in developing a new design is to determine the needs of the client, the message the design should portray, and its appeal to customers or users. Graphic designers consider cognitive, cultural, physical, and social factors in planning and executing designs for the target audience. Designers gather relevant information by meeting with clients, creative or art directors, and by performing their own research. Identifying the needs of consumers is becoming increasingly important for graphic designers as they continue to develop corporate communication strategies in addition to creating designs and layouts.

Graphic designers prepare sketches or layouts—by hand or with the aid of a computer—to illustrate their vision for the design. They select colors, sound, artwork, photography, animation, style of type, and other visual elements for the design. Designers also select the size and arrangement of the different elements on the page or screen. They may create graphs and charts from data for use in publications, and they often consult with copywriters on any text that accompanies the design. Designers then present the completed design to their clients or art or creative director for approval. In printing and publishing firms, graphic designers also may assist the printers by selecting the type of paper and ink for the publication and reviewing the mock-up design for errors before final publication.

Graphic designers use specialized computer software packages to help them create layouts and design elements and to program animated graphics.

Graphic designers sometimes supervise assistants who follow instructions to complete parts of the design process. Designers who run their own businesses also may devote a considerable time to developing new business contacts, choosing equipment, and performing administrative tasks, such as reviewing catalogues and ordering samples. The need for up-to-date computer and communications equipment is an ongoing consideration for graphic designers.

▲Work environment

Working conditions and places of employment vary. Graphic designers employed by large advertising, publishing, or design firms generally work regular hours in well-lighted and comfortable settings. Designers in smaller design-consulting firms and those who freelance generally work on a contract, or job, basis. They frequently adjust their workday to suit their clients' schedules and deadlines. Consultants and self-employed designers tend to work longer hours and in smaller, more congested, environments.

Designers may work in their own offices or studios or in clients' offices. Designers who are paid by the assignment are under pressure to please existing clients and to find new ones to maintain a steady income. All designers sometimes face frustration when their designs are rejected or when their work is not as creative as they wish. Graphic designers may work evenings or weekends to meet production schedules, especially in the printing and publishing industries where deadlines are shorter and more frequent.

❯❯TRAINING, OTHER QUALIFICATIONS, AND ADVANCEMENT

A bachelor's degree in graphic design is usually required. Creativity, communication, and problem-solving skills are important, as is a familiarity with computer graphics and design software.

▲Education and training

A bachelor's degree in graphic design is usually required for most entry-level and advanced graphic-design positions. Bachelor's degree programs in fine arts or graphic design are offered at many colleges, universities, and private design schools. Most curriculums include studio art, principles of design, computerized design, commercial graphics production, printing techniques, and website design. In addition to design courses, a liberal arts education that includes courses in art history, writing, psychology, sociology, foreign languages and cultural studies, marketing, and business are useful in helping designers work effectively.

Associate degrees and certificates in graphic design also are available from two-year and three-year professional schools, and graduates of these programs normally qualify as assistants to graphic designers or for positions requiring technical skills only. Creative individuals who wish to pursue a career in graphic design—and who already possess a bachelor's degree in another field—can complete a two-year or three-year program in graphic design to learn the technical requirements.

The National Association of Schools of Art and Design accredits about 300 postsecondary institutions with programs in art and design. Most of these schools award a degree in graphic design. Many schools do not allow formal entry into a bachelor's degree program until a student has successfully finished a year of basic art and design courses, which can be completed in high school. Applicants may be required to submit sketches and other examples of their artistic ability.

Graphic designers must keep up with new and updated computer graphics and design software, either on their own or through formal software-training programs.

▲Other qualifications

In addition to postsecondary training in graphic design, creativity, communication, and problem-solving skills are crucial. Graphic designers must be creative and able to communicate their ideas visually, verbally, and in writing. They also must have an eye for details. Designers show employers these traits by putting together a portfolio—a collection of examples of a person's best work. A good portfolio often is the deciding factor in getting a job.

Because consumer tastes can change fairly quickly, designers also need to be well read, open to new ideas and influences, and quick to react to changing trends. The abilities to work independently and under pressure are equally important traits. People in this field need self-discipline to start projects on their own, to budget their time, and to meet deadlines and production schedules. Good business sense and sales ability also are important, especially for those who freelance or run their own firms.

▲Advancement

Beginning graphic designers usually need one to three years of working experience before they can advance to higher positions. Experienced graphic designers in large firms may advance to chief designer, art or creative director, or other supervisory positions. Some designers leave the occupation to become teachers in design schools or in colleges and universities. Many faculty members continue to consult privately or operate small design studios to complement their classroom activities. Some experienced designers open their own firms or choose to specialize in one area of graphic design.

▲Employment

Graphic designers held about 286,100 jobs in 2008. Most graphic designers worked in specialized design services; advertising and related services; printing and related support activities; or newspaper, periodical, book, and directory publishers. A small number of designers produced computer graphics for computer-systems-design firms.

Some designers do freelance work—full time or part time—in addition to holding a salaried job in design or in another occupation.

▲Job Outlook

Employment is expected to grow about as fast as average. Keen competition for jobs is expected; individuals with website-design and animation experience will have the best opportunities.

▲Employment change

Employment of graphic designers is expected to grow 13 percent, as fast as the average for all occupations from 2008 to 2018, as demand for graphic design continues to increase from advertisers and computer-design firms.

Moreover, graphic designers with website-design and animation experience will especially be needed as demand increases for design projects for interactive media—websites, mobile phones, and other technology. Demand for graphic designers also will increase as advertising firms create print and Web-marketing and promotional materials for a growing number of products and services. Growth in Internet advertising, in particular, is expected to increase the number of designers. However, growth may be tempered by reduced demand in print publishing, where many graphic designers are employed.

▲Job prospects

Graphic designers are expected to face keen competition for available positions. Many talented individuals are attracted to careers as graphic designers. Individuals with website-design and animation experience will have the best opportunities.

Graphic designers with a broad liberal arts education and experience in marketing and business management will be best suited for positions developing communication strategies.

▲Earnings

Median annual wages for graphic designers were $42,400 in May 2008. The middle 50 percent earned between $32,600 and $56,620. The lowest 10 percent earned less than $26,110, and the highest 10 percent earned more than $74,660.

According to the American Institute of Graphic Arts, median annual cash compensation for entry-level designers was $35,000 in 2008. Staff-level graphic designers earned a median of $45,000. Senior designers, who may supervise junior staff or have some decision-making authority that reflects their knowledge of graphic design, earned a median of $60,000. Solo designers who freelanced or worked under contract to another company reported median earnings of $57,000. Design directors, the creative heads of design firms or in-house corporate design departments, earned $95,000. Graphic designers with ownership or partnership interests in a firm or who were principals of the firm in some other capacity earned $95,000.

>> ARTISTS AND RELATED WORKERS

SIGNIFICANT POINTS

- About 60 percent of artists and related workers are self-employed.

- Keen competition is expected for both salaried jobs and freelance work because the arts attract many talented people with creative ability.

- Artists usually develop their skills through a bachelor's degree program or other postsecondary training in art or design.

- Earnings for self-employed artists vary widely; some well-established artists earn more than salaried artists, while others find it difficult to rely solely on income earned from selling art.

❱❱ NATURE OF THE WORK

Artists create art to communicate ideas, thoughts, or feelings. They use a variety of methods—painting, sculpting, or illustration—and an assortment of materials, including oils, watercolors, acrylics, pastels, pencils, pen and ink, plaster, clay, and computers. Artists' works may be realistic, stylized, or abstract and may depict objects, people, nature, or events.

Artists generally fall into one of four categories. Art directors formulate design concepts and presentation approaches for visual communications. Craft artists create or reproduce handmade objects for sale or exhibition. Fine artists, including painters, sculptors, and illustrators, create original artwork, using a variety of media and techniques. Multimedia artists and animators create special effects, animation, or other visual images on film, on video, or with computers or other electronic media.

Art directors develop design concepts and review material that is to appear in periodicals, newspapers, and other printed or digital media. They control the overall visual direction of a project in fields such as advertising and publishing. They decide how best to present a concept visually, so that it is organized, eye catching, and appealing. Art directors decide which photographs or artwork to use and oversee the design, layout, and production of material to be produced. They may direct workers engaged in artwork, design, layout, and copywriting.

Craft artists make a wide variety of objects, mostly by hand, that are sold in their own studios, in retail outlets, or at arts-and-crafts shows. Some craft artists display their works in galleries and museums. Craft artists work with many different materials, including ceramics, glass, textiles, wood, metal, and paper, to create unique pieces of art such as pottery, stained glass, quilts, tapestries, lace, candles, and clothing. Many craft artists also use fine-art techniques—for example, painting, sketching, and printing—to add finishing touches to their art.

Fine artists typically display their work in museums, commercial art galleries, corporate collections, and private homes. Some of their artwork may be commissioned (done on request from clients), but most is sold by the artist or through private art galleries or dealers. The gallery and the artist predetermine how much each will earn from the sale. Only the most successful fine artists are able to support themselves solely through the sale of their works. Most fine artists have at least one other job to support their art careers. Some work in museums or art galleries as fine-arts directors or as curators, planning and setting up art exhibits. A few artists work as art critics for newspapers or magazines or as consultants to foundations or institutional collectors. Other artists teach art classes or conduct workshops in schools or in their own studios. Some artists also hold full-time or part-time jobs unrelated to art and pursue fine art as a hobby or second career.

Usually, fine artists specialize in one or two art forms, such as painting, illustrating, sketching, sculpting, printmaking, and restoring. Painters, illustrators, cartoonists, and sketch artists work with two-dimensional art forms, using shading, perspective, and color to produce realistic scenes or abstractions.

Illustrators usually create pictures for books, magazines, and other publications and for commercial products such as textiles, wrapping paper, stationery, greeting cards, and calendars. Increasingly, illustrators are working in digital format—for example, creating scenery or objects for a video game. This has created new opportunities for illustrators to work with animators and in broadcast media.

Medical and scientific illustrators combine drawing skills with knowledge of biology or other sciences. Medical illustrators work digitally or traditionally to create images of human anatomy and surgical procedures as well as three-dimensional models and animations. Scientific illustrators draw animal and plant life, atomic and molecular structures, and geologic and planetary formations. These illustrations are used in medical and scientific publications and in audiovisual presentations for teaching purposes. Illustrators also work for lawyers, producing exhibits for court cases.

Cartoonists draw political, advertising, social, and sports cartoons. Some cartoonists work with others who create the idea or story and write captions. Some cartoonists write captions themselves. Most cartoonists have comic, critical, or dramatic talents in addition to drawing skills.

Sketch artists create likenesses of subjects with pencil, charcoal, or pastels. Sketches are used by law enforcement agencies to assist in identifying suspects, by the news media to depict courtroom scenes, and by individual patrons for their own enjoyment.

Sculptors design three-dimensional artworks, either by molding and joining materials such as clay, glass, wire, plastic, fabric, or metal, or by cutting and carving forms from a block of plaster, wood, or stone. Some sculptors combine various materials to create mixed-media installations. Some incorporate light, sound, and motion into their works. Printmakers create printed images from designs cut or etched into wood, stone, or metal. After creating the design, the artist uses a printing press to roll the image onto paper or fabric. Some make prints by pressing the inked surface onto paper by hand or by graphically encoding and processing data, using a computer. The digitized images can then be printed onto paper.

Painting restorers preserve and restore damaged and faded paintings. They apply solvents and cleaning agents to clean the surfaces of the paintings, they reconstruct or retouch damaged areas, and they apply preservatives to protect the paintings. Restoration is highly detailed work and usually is reserved for experts in the field.

Multimedia artists and animators work primarily in motion picture and video industries, advertising, and computer-systems-design services. They draw by hand and use computers to create the series of pictures that form the animated images or special effects seen in movies, television programs, and computer games. Some draw storyboards for television commercials, movies, and animated features. Storyboards present television commercials in a series of scenes similar to a comic strip and allow an advertising agency to evaluate commercials proposed by advertising companies. Storyboards also serve as guides to placing actors and cameras on the television or motion picture set and to other production details. Many multimedia artists model objects in three dimensions by computer and work with programmers to make the images move.

▲Work environment

Many artists work in fine art or commercial art studios located in office buildings, warehouses, or lofts. Others work in private studios in their homes. Some fine artists share studio space, where they also may exhibit their work. Studio surroundings usually are well lighted and ventilated; however, fine artists may be exposed to fumes from glue, paint, ink, and other materials and to dust or other residue from filings, splattered paint, or spilled cleaners and other fluids. Artists who sit at drafting tables or who use computers for extended periods may experience back pain, eyestrain, or fatigue.

Artists employed by publishing companies, advertising agencies, and design firms generally work a standard workweek. During busy periods, they may work overtime to meet deadlines. Self-employed artists can set their own hours. They may spend much time and effort selling their artwork to potential customers or clients and building a reputation.

❯❯TRAINING, OTHER QUALIFICATIONS, AND ADVANCEMENT

Art directors usually have years of work experience and generally have at least a bachelor's degree. Because of the level of technical expertise demanded, multimedia artists and animators also need a bachelor's degree. Although formal schooling is not strictly required for craft and fine artists, it is very difficult to become skilled enough to make a living without some training.

▲Education and training

Many colleges and universities offer programs leading to a bachelor's or master's degree in fine arts. Courses usually include core subjects such as English, social science, and natural science, in addition to art history and studio art. Independent schools of art and design also offer postsecondary studio training in the craft, fine, and multimedia arts leading to certificates in the specialties or to an associate or bachelor's degree in fine arts. Typically, these programs focus more intensively on studio work than do the academic programs in a university setting. In 2009 the National Association of Schools of Art and Design accredited approximately 300 postsecondary institutions with programs in art and design; most of these schools award a degree in art.

Art directors usually begin as entry-level artists or designers in advertising, publishing, design, or motion picture production firms. An artist is promoted to art director after having demonstrated artistic and leadership abilities. Depending on the scope of their responsibilities, some art directors may pursue a degree in art administration or management, which teaches business skills such as project management and finance.
Many educational programs in art also provide training in computer techniques. Computers are used widely in the visual arts, and knowledge and training in computer graphics and other visual display software are critical elements of many jobs in these fields.

Medical illustrators must have both a demonstrated artistic ability and a detailed knowledge of living organisms, surgical and medical procedures, and human and animal anatomy. A bachelor's degree combining art and premedical courses usually is required. However, most medical illustrators also choose to pursue a master's degree in medical illustration. This degree is offered in four accredited schools in the United States.

Those who want to teach fine arts at public elementary or secondary schools usually must have a teaching certificate in addition to a bachelor's degree. An advanced degree in fine arts or arts administration is usually necessary for management or administrative positions in government or in foundations or for teaching in colleges and universities.

▲Other qualifications
Evidence of appropriate talent and skill, displayed in an artist's portfolio, is an important factor used by art directors, clients, and others in deciding whether to hire an individual or contract for his or her work. A portfolio is a collection of samples of the artist's best work. Assembling a successful portfolio requires skills usually developed through postsecondary training in art or visual communications. Internships also provide excellent opportunities for artists to develop and enhance their portfolios.

▲Advancement
Artists hired by firms often start with relatively routine work. While doing this work, however, they may observe other artists and practice their own skills.

Craft and fine artists advance professionally as their work circulates and as they establish a reputation for a particular style. Many of the most successful artists continually develop new ideas, and their work often evolves over time.

Many artists do freelance work while continuing to hold a full-time job until they are established. Others freelance part time while still in school to develop experience and to build a portfolio of published work.

Freelance artists try to develop a set of clients who regularly contract for work. Some freelance artists are widely recognized for their skill in specialties such as cartooning or children's book illustration. These artists may earn high incomes and can choose the type of work they do.

▲Employment
Artists held about 221,900 jobs in 2008. About 60 percent were self-employed.

Of the artists who were not self-employed, many worked for advertising and related services; newspaper, periodical, book, and software publishers; motion picture and video industries; specialized design services; and computer systems design and related services. Some self-employed artists offered their services to advertising agencies, design firms, publishing houses, and other businesses.

▲Job Outlook

Employment is projected to grow about as fast as the average. Competition for jobs is expected to be keen for both salaried and freelance jobs in all specialties because the number of people with creative ability and an interest in this career is expected to continue to exceed the number of available openings. Despite the competition, employers and individual clients are always on the lookout for talented and creative artists.

▲Employment change

Employment of artists and related workers is expected to grow 12 percent through 2018, about as fast as the average for all occupations. An increasing reliance on artists to create digital or multimedia artwork will drive growth.

Art directors will see an increase in jobs in advertising due to demand for the overall vision they bring to a project. However, declining opportunities in publishing will hold down job growth. With many magazines moving to an online-only format, art directors are used less in this field.

Demand for illustrators who work on a computer will increase as media companies use more detailed images and backgrounds in their designs. However, illustrators and cartoonists who work in publishing may see job opportunities decline as newspapers continue to cut staffs. Many are instead opting to post their work on political websites and online publications. The small number of medical illustrators will also be in greater demand as medical research continues to grow.

Demand for multimedia artists and animators will increase as consumers continue to demand more realistic video games, movie and television special effects, and 3D-animated movies. Additional job openings will arise from an increasing need for computer graphics in the growing number of mobile technologies. The demand for animators is also increasing in alternative areas such as scientific research and design services. Some lower priority animation has been offshored, negatively affecting employment of animators.

▲Job prospects

Competition for jobs as artists and related workers will be keen because there are more qualified candidates than available jobs. Employers in all industries should be able to choose from among the most qualified candidates.

Despite the competition, studios, galleries, and individual clients are always on the lookout for artists who display outstanding talent, creativity, and style. Among craft and fine artists, talented individuals who have developed a mastery of artistic techniques and skills will have the best job prospects. Multimedia artists and animators should have better job opportunities than other artists but still will experience competition. Despite an expanding number of opportunities, art directors should experience keen competition for the available openings. Craft and fine artists work mostly on a freelance or commission basis and may find it difficult to earn a living solely by selling their artwork. Only the most successful craft and fine artists receive major commissions for their work.

Competition among artists for the privilege of being shown in galleries is expected to remain intense, as will competition for grants from sponsors such as private foundations, state and local arts councils, and the National Endowment for the Arts. Because of their reliance on grants, and because the demand for artwork is dependent on consumers having disposable income, many of these artists will find that their income fluctuates with the overall economy.

▲Earnings

Median annual wages of salaried art directors were $76,980 in May 2008. The middle 50 percent earned between $54,490 and $108,090. The lowest 10 percent earned less than $40,730, and the highest 10 percent earned more than $154,840. Median annual wages were $80,170 in advertising, public relations and related services.

Median annual wages of salaried craft artists were $29,080. The middle 50 percent earned between $20,730 and $39,120. The lowest 10 percent earned less than $16,290, and the highest 10 percent earned more than $54,550.

Median annual wages of salaried fine artists, including painters, sculptors, and illustrators, were $42,650. The middle 50 percent earned between $29,230 and $60,650. The lowest 10 percent earned less than $20,780, and the highest 10 percent earned more than $83,410. Median annual wages of salaried multimedia artists and animators were $56,330. The middle 50 percent earned between $41,710 and $77,010. The lowest 10 percent earned less than $31,570, and the highest 10 percent earned more than $100,390. Median annual wages were $65,600 in motion picture and video industries, and $52,530 in advertising and related services.

Earnings for self-employed artists vary widely. Some charge only a nominal fee while they gain experience and build a reputation for their work. Others, such as well-established freelance fine artists and illustrators, can earn more than salaried artists. Many, however, find it difficult to rely solely on income earned from selling paintings or other works of art. Like other self-employed workers, freelance artists must provide their own benefits.

>> FASHION DESIGNERS

SIGNIFICANT POINTS

- The greatest numbers of fashion designers were employed in New York and California.

- Employers usually seek designers with a two-year or four-year degree who are knowledgeable about textiles, fabrics, ornamentation, and fashion trends.

- Keen competition for jobs is expected as many applicants are attracted to the creativity and glamour associated with the occupation.

❯ NATURE OF THE WORK

Fashion designers help create the billions of dresses, suits, shoes, and other clothing and accessories purchased every year by consumers. Designers study fashion trends, sketch designs of clothing and accessories, select colors and fabrics, and oversee the final production of their designs. Clothing designers create and help produce men's, women's, and children's apparel, including casual wear, suits, sportswear, formalwear, outerwear, maternity, and intimate apparel. Footwear designers help create and produce different styles of shoes and boots. Accessory designers help create and produce items such as handbags, belts, scarves, hats, hosiery, and eyewear, which add the finishing touches to an outfit. Some fashion designers specialize in clothing, footwear, or accessory design, but others create designs in all three fashion categories.

The design process from initial design concept to final production takes between 18 and 24 months. The first step in creating a design is researching current fashion and making predictions of future trends. Some designers conduct their own research, while others rely on trend reports published by fashion industry trade groups. Trend reports indicate what styles, colors, and fabrics will be popular for a particular season in the future. Textile manufacturers use these trend reports to begin designing fabrics and patterns while fashion designers begin to sketch preliminary designs. Designers then visit manufacturers or trade shows to procure samples of fabrics and decide which fabrics to use with which designs.

Once designs and fabrics are chosen, a prototype of the article using cheaper materials is created and then tried on a model to see what adjustments to the design need to be made. This also helps designers to narrow their choices of designs to offer for sale. After the final adjustments and selections have been made, samples of the article using the actual materials are sewn and then marketed to clothing retailers. Many designs are shown at fashion and trade shows a few times a year. Retailers at the shows place orders for certain items, which are then manufactured and distributed to stores.

Computer-aided design (CAD) is increasingly being used in the fashion design industry. Although most designers initially sketch designs by hand, a growing number also translate these hand sketches to the computer. CAD allows designers to view designs of clothing on virtual models and in various colors and shapes, thus saving time by requiring fewer adjustments of prototypes and samples later.

Depending on the size of their design firm and their experience, fashion designers may have varying levels of involvement in different aspects of design and production. In large design firms, fashion designers often are the lead designers who are responsible for creating the designs, choosing the colors and fabrics, and overseeing technical designers who turn the designs into a final product. They are responsible for creating the prototypes and patterns and work with the manufacturers and suppliers during the production stages. Large design houses also employ their own patternmakers, tailors, and sewers who create the master patterns for the design and sew the prototypes and samples. Designers working in small firms, or those new to the job, usually perform most of the technical, patternmaking, and sewing tasks, in addition to designing the clothing.

Fashion designers working for apparel wholesalers or manufacturers create designs for the mass market. These designs are manufactured in various sizes and colors. A small number of high-fashion (haute couture) designers are self-employed and create custom designs for individual clients, usually at very high prices. Other high-fashion designers sell their designs in their own retail stores or cater to specialty stores or high-fashion department stores. These designers create a mixture of original garments and those that follow established fashion trends.

Some fashion designers specialize in costume design for performing arts, motion picture, and television productions. The work of costume designers is similar to other fashion designers. Costume designers, however, perform extensive research on the styles worn during the period in which the performance takes place, or they work with directors to select and create appropriate attire. They make sketches of designs, select fabric and other materials, and oversee the production of the costumes. They also must stay within the costume budget for the particular production item.

▲Work environment

Fashion designers employed by manufacturing establishments, wholesalers, or design firms generally work regular hours in well-lighted and comfortable settings. Designers who freelance generally work on a contract, or by the job. They frequently adjust their workday to suit their clients' schedules and deadlines, meeting with the clients during evenings or weekends when necessary. Freelance designers tend to work longer hours and in smaller, more congested, environments, and are under pressure to please clients and to find new ones in order to maintain a steady income. Regardless of their work setting, all fashion designers occasionally work long hours to meet production deadlines or prepare for fashion shows.

The global nature of the fashion business requires constant communication with suppliers, manufacturers, and customers all over the United States and the world. Most fashion designers travel several times a year to trade and fashion shows to learn about the latest fashion trends. Designers also may travel frequently to meet with fabric and materials suppliers and with manufacturers who produce the final apparel products.

❯❯TRAINING, OTHER QUALIFICATIONS, AND ADVANCEMENT

In fashion design, employers usually seek individuals with a two-year or four-year degree who are knowledgeable about textiles, fabrics, ornamentation, and fashion trends.

▲Education and training

Fashion designers typically need an associate or a bachelor's degree in fashion design. Some fashion designers also combine a fashion-design degree with a business, marketing, or fashion-merchandising degree, especially those who want to run their own business or retail store. Basic coursework includes color, textiles, sewing and tailoring, pattern making, fashion history, computer-aided design (CAD), and design of different types of clothing such as menswear or footwear. Coursework in human anatomy, mathematics, and psychology also is useful.

The National Association of Schools of Art and Design accredits approximately 300 postsecondary institutions with programs in art and design. Most of these schools award degrees in fashion design. Many schools do not allow formal entry into a program until a student has successfully completed basic art and design courses. Applicants usually have to submit sketches and other examples of their artistic ability.

Aspiring fashion designers can learn these necessary skills through internships with design or manufacturing firms. Some designers also gain valuable experience working in retail stores, as personal stylists, or as custom tailors. Such experience can help designers gain sales and marketing skills while learning what styles and fabrics look good on different people.

Designers also can gain exposure to potential employers by entering their designs in student or amateur contests. Because of the global nature of the fashion industry, experience in one of the international fashion centers, such as Milan or Paris, can be useful.

▲Other qualifications

Designers must have a strong sense of the aesthetic—an eye for color and detail, a sense of balance and proportion, and an appreciation for beauty. Fashion designers also need excellent communication and problem-solving skills. Despite the advancement of computer-aided design, sketching ability remains an important advantage in fashion design. A good portfolio—a collection of a person's best work—often is the deciding factor in getting a job.

In addition to creativity, fashion designers also need to have sewing and patternmaking skills, even if they do not perform these tasks themselves. Designers need to be able to understand these skills so they can give proper instruction in how the garment should be constructed. Fashion designers also need strong sales and presentation skills to persuade clients to purchase their designs. Good teamwork and communication skills also are necessary because increasingly the business requires constant contact with suppliers, manufacturers, and buyers around the world.

▲Advancement

Beginning fashion designers usually start out as pattern makers or sketching assistants for more experienced designers before advancing to higher level positions. Experienced designers may advance to chief designer, design department head, or another supervisory position. Some designers may start their own design company, or sell their designs in their own retail stores. A few of the most successful designers can work for high-fashion design houses that offer personalized design services to wealthy clients.

▲Employment

Fashion designers held about 22,700 jobs in 2008. About 31 percent of fashion designers worked for apparel, piece goods, and notions merchant wholesalers; and 13 percent worked for apparel manufacturers. Many others were self-employed.

Employment of fashion designers tends to be concentrated in regional fashion centers. In 2008, the highest numbers of fashion designers were employed in New York and California.

▲Job Outlook

Little or no change in employment is projected. Competition for jobs is expected to be keen as many applicants are attracted to the creativity and glamour associated with the occupation.

▲Employment change

Employment of fashion designers is projected to grow by 1 percent between 2008 and 2018. Some new jobs will arise from an increasing population demanding more clothing, footwear, and accessories. Demand is increasing for stylish clothing that is affordable, especially among middle-income consumers which will increase the need for fashion designers among apparel wholesalers. However, job opportunities in cut-and-sew manufacturing will continue to decline as apparel is increasingly manufactured overseas. Employment of fashion designers in this industry will not decline as fast as other occupations because firms are more likely to keep design work in house.

▲Job prospects

Job competition is expected to be keen as many applicants are attracted to the creativity and glamour associated with the occupation. The best job opportunities will be in design firms that design mass-market clothing sold in department stores and retail chain stores, such as apparel wholesale firms. Few employment opportunities are expected in design firms that cater to high-end department stores and specialty boutiques as demand for expensive, high-fashion design declines relative to other luxury goods and services.

▲Earnings

Median annual wages for salaried fashion designers were $61,160 in May 2008. The middle 50 percent earned between $42,150 and $87,120. The lowest 10 percent earned less than $32,150, and the highest 10 percent earned more than $124,780.

Earnings in fashion design can vary widely based on the employer and years of experience. Starting salaries in fashion design tend to be very low until designers are established in this occupation. Salaried fashion designers usually earn higher and more stable incomes than self-employed or freelance designers. However, a few of the most successful self-employed fashion designers may earn many times the salary of the highest-paid salaried designers. Self-employed fashion designers must provide their own benefits and retirement.

PART 4

·········

REDEMPTIVE COMMUNICATORS:

PROFILES FROM ACROSS THE JOB FIELDS

The fellowship of being near unto God must become reality, in the full and vigorous prosecution of our life. It must permeate and give color to our feeling, our perception, our sensations, our thinking, our imagining, our willing, our acting, our speaking. It must not stand as a foreign factor in our life, but it must be the passion that breathes throughout our whole existence.

–Abraham Kuyper (1837-1920)

YOUR VOCATION AS A REDEMPTIVE PLATFORM

By Donald H. Alban Jr, PhD

LET'S FACE IT. There are only so many communications jobs available in today's economy, and not everyone has the specific interests, skills and capabilities that working as a communications professional requires. Still, because interacting with others is a part of life for people in virtually all occupations, developing effective communication skills through studies like this one is vitally essential. As noted earlier in this text, your communication aptitude (your skillfulness or lack of skillfulness as a communicator) will affect your ability to achieve your personal goals and to make a difference in the world.

As Part 1 of this textbook established in greater detail, Christian college students must bear in mind, regardless of which vocational path they follow, that they are called, above all, to be redemptive communicators. A redemptive communicator, you may remember, is someone who sees the world as God intended it to be and who interacts with others in a way that promotes His redemptive purpose in their lives. Although not everyone can do this as a communications professional, any Christ follower can be a redemptive communicator within the context of his or her occupation. Indeed, many occupations can function as platforms for interacting with other people in a way that manifests authen-tic love for God and that promotes something He cherishes according to Scripture.

The final section of this textbook profiles real people from a variety of job fields who have used or are using their vocations in this redemptive way. Although far from exhaus-tive, the job fields that these profilees represent are diverse— religion, education, media, law and government, business and finance, musical arts, performing arts, visual arts, medicine, math and science, engineering, and the military. Whether you are artistically inclined or analytically gifted, you likely will find in these stories a profilee from job field that either is

Your communication aptitude will affect your ability to achieve your personal goals and to make a difference in the world.

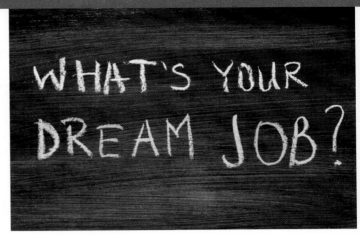

or else resembles the one or ones to which you are drawn.

These profiles are designed to challenge your thinking about what it means to be a redemptive communicator in today's world. Before you read through each occupationally arranged set of profiles, you should revisit and closely study the fifth chapter's listing of things God values according to Scripture. Because this listing is not exhaustive, you should consider searching Scripture itself for other God-valued things that could be added to the list and that are relevant to the highlighted vocations, along with any biblical passages that clearly affirm this. To enrich your evaluation of the stories in this section, we have included at the end of each chapter an evaluation guide that can help you discern and exposit the variety of ways in which one's occupation can function as a platform for redemptive interaction with other people.

We would be remiss at this point to dismiss the fact that many college students, at this stage of their academic journeys, remain uncertain about which vocational path they should follow. Such a student might suppose that a reading of these profiles, therefore, is potentially less personally rewarding than it otherwise might be. This assumption is false. Admittedly, with so many career options to consider in the modern economy—the 2012 Occupational Outlook Index lists 4,999

distinct job titles—making a career choice is perhaps more complicated than ever. Still, the college years are a time for investigating career options and for making informed decisions about the vocational direction one should follow. For the undecided student, a reading of the profiles in this section of the text can be a useful step in the investigation process. Unlike other career planning resources, which narrowly emphasize the linking of interests and abilities to specific job fields, these readings can enrich the search by showing how various options can enable the Christian college student to make the enduringly significant difference in the world that so many hope to make.

As you read through these profiles, we encourage you to take several additional steps as you consider your career options. First, consult the U.S. Bureau of Labor Statistics' Occupational Outlook Index, which you can access online. This resource describes thousands of job fields in terms of the work each involves, the academic or professional credentials each requires, the range of compensation each pays, and the employment rate each likely faces in the future. Second, consult your college or university's career center for vocational planning resources and for counsel. The center's available aptitude tests, like the Multiple Intelligence Test, the Myers-Briggs Type Indicator, the Strong Interest Inventory, the

"If you aim at nothing, you'll hit it every time."

CareerLeader Career Assessment, and the Focus-2 Career Assessment, can be very helpful for the student who needs to know which career options best match his or her personality, interests, capabilities, and skills. Third, ask your family and friends for their thoughts about your strengths and about careers that they believe would be a good match for you. Give them permission to be honest with you, and be open-minded to what they say. Our closest acquaintances often know us better than we know ourselves and impart wisdom to us that helps us avoid making avoidable mistakes. As Proverbs 11:14 states, "there is safety in having many advisors."

Finally, based on what you derive from the first three steps, make an informed decision about the best career option for you and about the academic major, if any, that most likely will prepare you for it. Commit to the major and pursue the degree. If instead you merely continue to mull your options

and to remain uncommitted, you could end up wasting invaluable time and money on coursework that you ultimately will never need as you step into the professional world. As someone has said, "If you aim at nothing, you'll hit it every time."

If you do not know at this stage which vocation you will pursue, we encourage you to retain this book for future reference. When your direction becomes clearer and you commit to a specific career path, consider once again how you might be able to use that vocation as a platform for interacting with others in a way that promotes what God values. Your analysis of the profiles in this section can prepare you to do this when that decisive, directive moment comes.

© 2012 by 2happy Used under license of Shutterstock, Inc.

RELIGION »

RELIGION

DON RICHARDSON

A famed missionary-author devises a strategy for evangelizing everyone.

The term *redemptive analogies* may be foreign to many, but not to Canadian-born Don Richardson. Best-selling author of four books including *Peace Child* and *Lords of the Earth*, and popular speaker at missions conferences across North America, he states the definition in simple terms: "Redemptive analogies are eye-openers that become heart-openers. They're cultural compasses that point mankind to Jesus."

Richardson, now in his seventies, discovered these redemptive analogies through personal experience. In 1962, he and his late wife Carol Joy embarked on a missionary career in Irian Jaya. They settled among the Sawi, a Stone-age tribe of cannibalistic headhunters. The couple's lifestyle fascinated the tribesmen, who regarded them as beings from another planet. Their modern technology—steel axes, machetes, nylon fish line, metal fish hooks, and medicine—amazed them.

© 2012 by Uryadnikov Sergey / Shutterstock.com
Used under license of Shutterstock, Inc.

As Richardson tried to share the Gospel with the Sawi, he discovered that they regarded treachery as a virtue. In fact, they applauded Judas as the hero in the story of Jesus's death. With such high value placed on deceit, how then could they possibly trust each other for a peace settlement?

Before long, however, a conflict arose. The two tribes living nearest to the Richardsons had been at war before the missionaries arrived. Now their competitive desire to live near the foreigners fueled their hatred for each other, and fighting escalated.

Don begged the tribesmen to end the killings and make peace. "You talk about making peace as though it's an easy thing to do," they said. "But the Sawi shed each other's blood, sever heads, save skulls as trophies, and eat each other's flesh. Once these things happen, making peace is not easy."

As Richardson tried to share the Gospel with the Sawi, he discovered that they regarded treachery as a virtue. In fact, they applauded Judas as the hero in the story of Jesus's death. With such high value placed on deceit, how then could they possibly trust each other for a peace settlement? He concluded that this culture was void of any mechanism for making peace and considered moving his family to a different location, hoping this would end the bloodshed. That's when Kaiyo intervened.

Kaiyo lived in Kamur, one of the two warring villages. "The two foreigners chose to live among us and help us," he reasoned. "They're learning our language. Perhaps when they learn it more completely, they will help us in ways beyond our comprehension. I cannot let the senseless violence of my people drive this man and woman away from us. I must make peace."

According to Sawi culture, there was only one means for warring tribes to do so: A man must give his son to be raised by a father in the enemy village. The Sawi believed no insincere person could do such a thing, therefore this sacrifice was a basis for mutual trust. As long as that child remained alive, the enemy village would be bound to the commitment of peace.

Kaiyo and his wife had one child. He picked up his infant Biakadon, hugged him, and then ran from Kamur towards the neighboring village holding the boy in his arms. Neighbors shouted encouragement, but his wife screamed in anguish when she realized what was happening. "Please—no! Change your mind! Bring my baby back to me!" she cried. In times past when a peace child was offered, he had always been the son of a man with several children. It never occurred to her that her husband, the father of one child, might make that sacrifice.

It was too late. Kaiyo had already scanned the men's faces in the enemy village and chosen Mahor. He placed the baby in Mahor's arms and said, "I give you my only son as a peace child. Do you promise to be an advocate for peace so long as this child remains alive in your house?"

© 2012 by Tyler Olson
Used under license of Richardson's, Inc.

Hato's four wives and their children committed their lives to Christ the same day. He later became Richardson's travel companion, telling about Jesus in villages throughout the region. Before long, every village had believers and all warfare ceased.

Honored to be chosen as the adoptive father, Mahor said, "Kaiyo, you've made the greatest possible sacrifice by giving your only son. Yes, I will guard the peace between your village and mine so long as this child remains alive in my house." He turned and called to his villagers, "Come, lay your hands on this peace child, Kaiyo's only son." Men, women, and children responded saying, "I receive this child as a basis for peace." Then another father, deeply moved by Kaiyo's sacrifice, placed his infant son in Kaiyo's arms as a peace child for Kamur village.

Richardson watched the scene thinking, *Why is there something familiar about this?* And then the answer came: The Sawi's custom of giving a child to achieve reconciliation depicted God's sacrifice made to establish peace between Himself and man!

This was the breakthrough Richardson needed to effectively share the Gospel with the Sawi people. The day came when Hato, a one-eyed chief, said, "I'm ready to lay my hand on Jesus. How do I do that?" Don led Hato in prayer, inviting the Spirit of God's holy peace child to dwell within him and to keep him in the way of peace with God and man. Hato's four wives and their children committed their lives to Christ the same day. He later became Richardson's travel companion, telling about Jesus in villages throughout the region. Before long, every village had believers and all warfare ceased.

Inspired by the Biblical example of Paul, who used a redemptive analogy when presenting the Gospel to pagan Athenians (see Acts 17:22–34) and by his experience with the Sawi, Richardson began to study other cultures for other such connecting points for presenting the Gospel. He found that once a year, the Dyak tribe in Kalimantan brings two chickens—without spot or blemish—to the riverside near a village. They kill one bird and sprinkle its blood on the shore. They tether the live bird at the end of a dugout canoe and place a burning kerosene lantern at the opposite end. At sunset, as the chicken pecks at rice grains, every villager places something invisible, symbolic of their sin, in the canoe. Then two elders push the craft into the river's current.

The people watch and wait. If the canoe drifts back to shore or overturns in the water within sight of the village, they live in apprehension for another year. If it disappears around the river's bend, they raise their hands and exclaim, "We're safe! We're safe!" The ceremony must be repeated every year to remove their sins.

"This analogy reminds us of two goats in the Old Testament," explains Richardson. "One was sacrificed after the Jewish high priest laid his hands on its head, symbolically depositing his sins and the sins of the Israelites there. The second goat was led into the wilderness and released. The Jews had their scapegoat; the Dyaks have a scapeboat."

Richardson also discovered redemptive analogies in the Chinese writing system. For instance, the word for "righteous" is written with two small pictures, one above and one below. The upper picture symbolizes a lamb. The lower represents the first person singular pronoun. "When the Chinese write the word for 'righteous,' they're actually writing 'the lamb over me,'" explains Richardson. "The Chinese language contains 120 such words that have spiritually significant encoded messages."

More recently, Richardson has searched Islam for redemptive analogies to help believers effectively reach this culture with the Gospel. "Islam has historically been the most resistant force on earth," he says. "It's as though there's a firewall, to borrow computer terminology, separating the minds and hearts of Muslims from our Christian appeal."
After studying the Koran, he concludes, "Cultures worldwide contain redemptive analogies to point to Jesus—the sacrifice made to atone for our sin. But Islam is different because Mohammed said Jesus didn't die. If he was correct, there's no atonement. Redemptive analogies would have to point to something Mohammed denied; therefore, there are no such analogies in Islam."

So how can a believer introduce a Muslim to faith in Christ without a cultural compass to point him to the Savior? In his latest book, *Secrets of the Koran*, Richardson suggests asking strategic questions whose answers show how Mohammed discredited himself as a prophet. He says, "Ask why Mohammed told the story of the Exodus 27 times in the first 89 chapters of the Koran, and why he repeated the story of Noah and the flood 28 times in the first 57 chapters.

"By doing word searches, I learned that the Koran's length could be reduced by 45 per cent if each story repeated dozens of times was told only once. Since Muslims love to memorize the Koran, elimination would make it much easier for them. Most have never thought about this, and it surprises them. These eye-openers become heart-openers for Muslims as they search the Koran and the Hadith for the answers."

Richardson says millions of Muslims nowadays are telling of seeing Jesus in their dreams. This phenomenon provides a natural bridge for believers to speak with them about Christ. The subject can be approached by saying, "I've heard about people seeing a kind-faced man dressed in shining garments appear to them. I'd like to meet someone who's had that experience." The hearts of those seeing this dream are ready to hear the Gospel.

"Gentile culture is filled with things that relate to an aspect of God and His law," says Richardson. "Who arranges these? They don't happen by accident, nor do they come from the evil one. God, in His mercy, has given these things to people as a sign that echoes in their hearts saying 'Jesus is our Savior. He's for us.'"

>> TRESHA MCKNIGHT

Bringing hope to Romania's youngest AIDS patients

Four-year-old Costel looked like any other Romanian boy his age, but there was one difference—a silent killer, the HIV virus, lurked within his body. When his parents learned of their boy's illness, they dumped him into a garbage can and left him there to die.

Costel represents an estimated 30,000 other Romanian children and teens stricken with HIV/ AIDS today. Many were infected because their mothers received contaminated blood transfusions for anemia while pregnant. Scores were infected when medical personnel vaccinated them against childhood diseases using the same contaminated needle. Some were infected when they visited health clinics where HIV-infected patients were treated. There, as in the schools, professionals used one needle in treating multiple patients.

Shunned by society as modern-day lepers due to fear and ignorance about HIV and AIDS, these youngsters are banned from school and the workplace. Sometimes their parents force them to leave home because they're afraid the disease will spread to other family members or because they cannot afford costly medications. Many eventually die alone and are buried as paupers in unmarked graves—unless The Joshua Project intervenes. Tresha McKnight is one of four career staff with The Joshua Project. "Society's attitude is, 'These kids are dying, so why bother with them?' But we regard them as kids who are living with, not dying from AIDS," she says. "It's our goal to care for them in practical ways and to do whatever's necessary to ensure they understand that Christ loves them and died for them."

The Joshua Project was founded in 1999 after two Christian women met at a tram stop in Romania. One of these women was McKnight, a 21-year-old home health care nurse from Texas. Three years prior, her aspirations to pursue a career in opera had ended when she suffered a grand mal seizure on stage during her largest concert. Several seizures followed within three months. Doctors suspected a brain tumor and said one more seizure would kill her.

McKnight sank into depression. In desperation, she cried to God, "Do something with my miserable life!" He answered by healing her body and directing her to pursue nurses' training rather than a career in opera.

© 2012 by thefinalmiracle.
Used under license of Shutterstock, Inc.

As McKnight and the other woman—Claudia Udrea, a Romanian psychologist and social worker—conversed at the tram stop, they discovered a shared passion for helping the defenseless. Udrea was familiar with the plight of HIV-infected children in the local infectious disease hospital, so she invited McKnight to see it firsthand.

"That hospital required official nametags for entry, and a gatekeeper stood guard to keep everyone else out," McKnight recalls. "We waited until he wasn't looking, and then we slipped in unnoticed."

The children's desperate state gripped the women's hearts. The two visited the hospital regularly for more than three years. They brought homemade soup, French fries, ham, and fried eggs to supplement the youngsters' meager diet. They earned the nurses' trust and were allowed to take the kids home where they bathed, clothed, fed them, and took them to church on Sundays.

The ministry grew. Tresha married Andy McKnight, a building contractor from Northern Ireland, and Claudia married Tony Udrea, a former Romanian police officer. Both men shared their wives' passion to help the less fortunate. They eagerly pitched in when God supplied funds to purchase and remodel a dilapidated orphanage.

The building had dirt walls, a floor made of wooden slats covered in coal dust, no heat, and no hot water. Within weeks they'd transformed it into a warm and welcoming day center with bright walls and big windows. The main room houses up to 20 teens who gather for art therapy, ping-pong, snacks, Bible studies and worship, the chance to joke and wrestle with their friends, and to feel valued. There's also a counseling room and state-of-the-art dental office. The debt-free facility nestles on a residential street in a small city. To respect the patrons' privacy, it bears no sign to identify its presence.

Some of the center's visitors have been raised in group homes because their parents abandoned them. Most come from abusive family situations. One girl, 13-year-old

The Joshua Project staff have ongoing contact with more than 400 children and teens at any given time.

Daniella, was set ablaze by her uncle when he discovered her illness. Nine-year-old Marinella was referred to the center for counseling after her neighbors burned down her family's home upon learning she had HIV/AIDS. Four-year-old Costel, the little boy left to die in a garbage can, was found by a stranger and taken to a hospital where he lived for nearly seven years until McKnight claimed him as her foster son.

"These stories are sad, but they're just the small stuff compared to the abuses these kids experience day-to-day," says McKnight. "The saddest part is that they never did anything to warrant getting HIV/AIDS. We try to help them understand that it's not their fault, even though society tries to blame them."

The Joshua Project staff have ongoing contact with more than 400 children and teens at any given time. Besides offering the day-center services, they distribute clothing to needy families, do home and hospital visitations, and provide grief counseling for families whose children have died. They host a worship service at the day center once each month, and they hold in-depth Bible studies twice weekly to study how God's Word applies to life.

The topic of suicide has generated the most response, says McKnight. She explains that many of the kids suffer from manic depression and will attempt suicide by refusing to eat or drink, or by stopping their medications. "When they refuse to eat or drink, they slip into a coma and never come back," she says. "If they stop their medications, the disease multiplies, the organs shut down, and they die within weeks.

"When we discuss suicide, they're amazed and humbled to learn that their lives are not their own. They were bought with a price. On one occasion, the kids stayed after the study and cried when they realized how much God loves them and how suicide hurts His heart." Since The Joshua Project began, it has touched the lives of several thousand teenagers. Many of those have already died, but not without hope. "To our knowledge, only five have passed into eternity without Christ," says Tresha.

"These kids know what it's like to hunger for something more in life," adds Andy McKnight. "They only need someone to tell them about Jesus. That's what we do through words and actions."

Holding week-long evangelistic camps has proven to be an effective method for communicating the Gospel to the teens. Volunteers from North America serve as counselors, teaching three short Bible studies every day and leading discussion groups afterwards. Days are filled with crafts and physical activities. "We have great fun," says McKnight. "These kids soon learn that Christians are not blah and boring."

Because the majority of the youth with whom they have contact are now Christians, The

Joshua Project launched week-long discipleship camps in 2008. A team of North American believers leads intensive Bible studies that address issues such as bitterness, anger, and forgiveness. The discipleship curriculum also includes teaching about Biblical servanthood and the responsibility to share Christ with others—even their families who may have abandoned them.

"One of the deepest questions asked was, 'How can I love someone who hates me?' That was really tough—I can't imagine the kind of hatred these kids have experienced. It takes a great deal of maturity to love someone who despises them," says McKnight. "The leaders learned that these kids hunger to be different. They want to love in spite of the hatred shown them. Only Christ can heal someone's heart that much."

These camps, which rely on the participation of volunteer short-term missionaries from North America, face an ongoing obstacle—lack of adequate accommodation. Most facilities will not permit a group of AIDS-infected youth on their premises. The Joshua Project has found only one suitable hotel that will allow them to stay, but it can host only 25 guests. And so, the project has a vision of someday building a facility that includes a big red barn in the countryside—a place where they can host two camps every month all year long.

"It's at these camps where our kids experience their biggest 'God moments,'" says McKnight. "Besides learning more about His Word, these kids are reassured of His love by knowing that North Americans have traveled several thousand miles to be with them, the modern-day lepers."

The two couples testify to the intensity of this ministry. Building relationships with youngsters destined for early death can wreak havoc on one's emotions. But they consider this a calling from God, a lifestyle that demands their availability especially when "their kids" are hospitalized and need advocates to ensure adequate treatment or to hold their hands as death approaches.

"These kids are an unreached people group," says McKnight. "Looking into their eyes and seeing the light of life when they pray to accept Jesus makes it all worthwhile. I wouldn't trade that for anything in the world."

>> TAYLOR FIELD

An Oklahoman reaches the destitute of inner city Manhattan.

Taylor Field sounds like the name of a high-end department store. But it actually is the name of a storefront minister. But given the fact that this inner-city man of the cloth takes his cues for ministry from the One who clothes the lilies of the field, Taylor's name is most appropriate. Like the Heavenly Father whose unconditional love of His creation translates into tailoring nature's garments and feeding the anxious-free sparrows, Taylor has a passion for people.

"Early on the Lord opened my eyes to the value in all people, but especially those in the city," the pastor of New York's East 7th Street Baptist Church says without hesitation. "I love the way Francis Schaeffer put it. He said people are precious to God, so cities must be his treasure."

While attending Wake Forest College, Taylor was following in his lawyer-father's footsteps. That included majoring in prelaw and spending a year as an exchange student in Europe. He chose Berlin. In addition to studying German, Taylor learned the emotional pain of loneliness in a depersonalized city firsthand. Not only did he discover what it feels like to be overlooked by society, he began to realize his need of a personal Savior.

"I grew up in a Christian home in the Bible Belt of Oklahoma, but I never saw the importance of embracing my parents' faith," Taylor recalls. "When I left for Berlin, I reluctantly packed a pocket-size New Testament my mom had given me. When I got lonely, I'd pick it up. But since I didn't want my roommates to see, I read it in secret and hid it under my bed as if it were a pornographic magazine."

Taylor found more than familiar English words in that little Bible. He found a Father calling him to Himself. Shortly after returning home for his senior year of college, he invited Jesus into his heart. Taylor soon knew he wanted to spend his life finding ways to show the Savior's love in practical ways.

While studying at a seminary in New Jersey, Taylor first visited the storefront outreach center in the Lower East Side of Manhattan that one day would call him as pastor. Although the brick exterior was covered with graffiti, Taylor saw more than spray-painted slogans, pictures, and designs. He saw the hand of God.

"I was intrigued by these inner-city missionaries who were willing to do whatever it took to reach kids in their own subculture," Taylor admits. "Here was a group who initially tried to paint over gang graffiti on the front of the building. When the designs and slogans appeared the next day, these Spirit-led Christians chose to put down their paint brushes and pick up a spray can. They created their own graffiti with Christian-oriented symbols and words."

With so many hours of hands-on ministry credits to fulfill, Taylor volunteered at Graffiti Outreach Center working with children and youth in literacy programs in a neighborhood comprising abandoned buildings, drug traffic, and prostitution. As he walked the streets several worlds removed from his native Enid, Oklahoma, Taylor had no idea this run-down section of the Big Apple one day would become home.

Twelve years later while completing his doctorate at a seminary in California, Taylor contemplated what kind of ministry he should commit to. Although encouraged to take a traditional pastorate in suburbia, Taylor bristled at the idea. His heart still beat for broken people few ministries were reaching. A speaker in chapel challenged the students to have the courage to set out to do the thing that makes their hearts sing.

"That was such a freeing thought," Taylor recalls. "I knew what made my heart sing. It was expressing God's love in physical and tangible ways. I couldn't get the unique ministry at Graffiti out of my head. In a very real way the handwriting was on the wall. I knew that's where God wanted me."

Taylor arrived in Manhattan's "Alphabet City" in 1986 with his wife and two sons (a two-year-old and two-month-old). The 32-year-old was committed to serve the needs of those in his neighborhood before attempting to spell out the claims of Christ. For many, that meant teaching the alphabet and helping adults as well as children learn how to read. It also meant staking a claim in a neighborhood that literally was controlled by drug dealers.

"Initially I was concerned for my family's safety," Taylor confesses. "I remember watching my little boy pick up a hypodermic needle some addict had discarded. Another time I took my sons to the park. As they ran up to chase a squirrel, I realized it was a big rat."

Taylor learned he had to trust God for his own safety as well. His arrival as director of Graffiti Outreach Center was not appreciated by everyone on the Lower East Side. The drug lord was not pleased that those he'd controlled now had other options for income or protection. Someone tried to strangle him while someone else pulled a knife on him. A homeless woman even tried to attack him with a nail-pierced board.

Although the brick exterior was covered with graffiti, Taylor saw more than spray-painted slogans, pictures, and designs. He saw the hand of God.

Since Taylor and his family moved to New York City in 1986, the Graffiti Outreach Center became a full-fledged church. But East 7th Street Baptist Church is anything but your typical congregation. It worships in an abandoned Jewish synagogue it purchased and recently refurbished. Between Sundays, it is involved in 26 hands-on ministries that include literacy training, after-school tutoring, soup kitchens, Bibles studies, drug rehab, and legal advocacy.

"Although we've been at Graffiti for 20 years, the last five or so years have been the most difficult and the most fulfilling." Taylor muses. "Since our church is located only 5,000 feet from Ground Zero, September 11th opened up opportunities for ministry to our community exponentially. We have been deeply involved in the emotional and spiritual rebuilding of lives. The shadows of that terrible Tuesday continue to linger."

Stories of how Taylor and his team of 20-plus associates are being used by God to reach lost people as well as literally to redeem a community are told in *Mercy Streets*, a book published by Broadman and Holman. In addition to Taylor's candid reflections on how experiencing the trauma of September 11th impacted his young family, the book offers testimonies that validate the ministry to which Taylor has invested his life.

Asked if the ministry of Graffiti church is still causing his heart to sing, Taylor is quick to answer. "You better believe it! I'll be here as long as the Lord lets me."

NAME: _____   DATE: _____

RELIGION

· ·

REDEMPTIVE FIELD ANALYSIS 1

HONOR STATEMENT: I, the undersigned student, hereby declare before God, before the school, and before the professor that I have read this chapter in its entirety, that I have completed the following exercise with help from no other sources, except as required by the questions, and that I neither have shared nor will share this work with anyone.

Signature: _____   Date: _____

Analysis 1

1. Using words from the fifth chapter, define the term redemptive communicator.

_____

_____

_____

_____

_____

_____

2. Summarize one of this chapter's profiles in the space below. Include the most important details. Omit unnecessary details.

_____

_____

_____

_____

_____

_____

_____

_____

_____

_____

_____

3. If you were asked to use this story or a specific part of this story to support an idea, one that you could present as its main point to an audience, which idea would you present? State this idea as a single declarative sentence in the space that follows:

_____

_____

_____

_____

_____

_____

4. The fifth chapter states that a redemptive communicator interacts with other people in a way that promotes what God values in this world according to Scripture. Review the chapter's list of things that God values. Then, in the space below, identify the specific God-valued thing that this profilee promotes according to the profile. Be sure to explain both how the profilee promotes this specific thing and why you believe this thing is something God values according to Scripture.

_____

_____

_____

_____

_____

_____

_____

_____

_____

_____

_____

_____

_____

_____

_____

_____

_____

5. Which other God-valued things does this profilee promote? Identify these and explain how he or she promotes them.

_____

_____

_____

_____

_____

_____

_____

_____

_____

_____

_____

_____

RELIGION

· ·

REDEMPTIVE FIELD ANALYSIS 2

HONOR STATEMENT: I, the undersigned student, hereby declare before God, before the school, and before the professor that I have read this chapter in its entirety, that I have completed the following exercise with help from no other sources, except as required by the questions, and that I neither have shared nor will share this work with anyone.

Signature: _____   Date: _____

Analysis 2

1. Using words from the fifth chapter, define the term redemptive communicator.

_____

_____

_____

_____

_____

_____

_____

2. Summarize another of this chapter's profiles in the space below. Include the most important details. Omit unnecessary details.

_____

_____

_____

_____

_____

_____

_____

_____

_____

_____

_____

_____

_____

3. If you were asked to use this story or a specific part of this story to support an idea, one that you could present as its main point to an audience, which idea would you present? State this idea as a single declarative sentence in the space that follows:

_____

_____

_____

_____

_____

_____

_____

_____

_____

_____

4. The fifth chapter states that a redemptive communicator interacts with other people in a way that promotes what God values in this world according to Scripture. Review the chapter's list of things that God values. Then, in the space below, identify the specific God-valued thing that this profilee promotes according to the profile. Be sure to explain both how the profilee promotes this specific thing and why you believe this thing is something God values according to Scripture.

_____

_____

_____

_____

_____

_____

_____

_____

_____

_____

_____

_____

_____

_____

_____

5. Which other God-valued things does this profilee promote? Identify these and explain how he or she promotes them.

_____

_____

_____

_____

_____

_____

RELIGION

· · · · · · · · · · · · · · · · · · · ·

REDEMPTIVE FIELD ANALYSIS 3

HONOR STATEMENT: I, the undersigned student, hereby declare before God, before the school, and before the professor that I have read this chapter in its entirety, that I have completed the following exercise with help from no other sources, except as required by the questions, and that I neither have shared nor will share this work with anyone.

Signature: _____   Date: _____

Analysis 3

1. Using words from the fifth chapter, define the term redemptive communicator.

_____

_____

_____

_____

_____

_____

_____

_____

2. Summarize another of this chapter's profiles in the space below. Include the most important details. Omit unnecessary details.

_____

_____

_____

_____

_____

_____

_____

_____

_____

_____

_____

_____

_____

3. If you were asked to use this story or a specific part of this story to support an idea, one that you could present as its main point to an audience, which idea would you present? State this idea as a single declarative sentence in the space that follows:

_____

_____

_____

_____

_____

_____

_____

_____

_____

_____

4. The fifth chapter states that a redemptive communicator interacts with other people in a way that promotes what God values in this world according to Scripture. Review the chapter's list of things that God values. Then, in the space below, identify the specific God-valued thing that this profilee promotes according to the profile. Be sure to explain both how the profilee promotes this specific thing and why you believe this thing is something God values according to Scripture.

_____

_____

_____

_____

_____

_____

_____

_____

_____

_____

_____

_____

_____

_____

_____

_____

5. Which other God-valued things does this profilee promote? Identify these and explain how he or she promotes them.

_____

_____

_____

_____

_____

EDUCATION >>

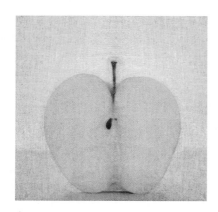

EDUCATION

>> KENNETH ELZINGA

A distinguished economics professor uses Jesus as a model for teaching.

Kenneth G. Elzinga had a mother deeply committed to the Christian faith and a father whose hostility toward religion exhibited itself by moodiness on Sundays. Elzinga's mother's influence won out, and he attended church with her every Sunday while growing up.

As he continued the weekly practice of Sunday worship in graduate school, though, Elzinga discovered a different type of Christian: those who talked about a personal relationship with Jesus Christ as a defining element of their lives. Their example provoked Elzinga to ponder the difference between believing facts about God, which he did, and trusting in God, as his new church contacts did.

"If Jesus was Who He said He was—and I had believed this for some time—His claim on my life needed to involve far more than regular church attendance," Elzinga says. Soon after, at a church missions conference, he surrendered his life to Christ. Ever since, Elzinga has sought to follow Jesus's example in all parts of his life.

© 2012 by Robert Kneschke
Used under license of Shutterstock, Inc.

Over the years, Elzinga has developed a philosophy that his authority as a teacher goes only as far as his willingness to serve his students.

Elzinga's main sphere of influence is as a University of Virginia professor of economics and researcher in Charlottesville. Right after he earned his doctorate at Michigan State University in 1967, Elzinga joined the faculty at the University of Virginia, where he has instructed 30,000 students.

Along the way, he has earned a reputation as a leading analyst of market structures and antitrust policy. His many honors include winning a Phi Beta Kappa award for a text he coauthored on antitrust penalties, a Phi Eta Sigma teacher-of-the-year award, a Commonwealth of Virginia outstanding-faculty award, and being honored with the first distinguished chair for teaching-excellence in the history of the University of Virginia. "I am firmly convinced that if I were not a follower of Jesus, I would not have received one of them," Elzinga says. "I recognize them all as God's grace to me, for taking someone who has no business, in terms of natural talents, receiving these honors."

Over the years, Elzinga has developed a philosophy that his authority as a teacher goes only as far as his willingness to serve his students. In addition, he believes that teaching is not confined to the classroom. It can take place in a professor's office, during lunch, or even in the teacher's residence.

"A good teacher must know his material cold," Elzinga says. He doesn't allow lecturing about economics to become routine because he believes every year students deserve to have him teaching at his best. He doesn't schedule any substantive activities before classes because he wants to use the time to prepare material. Elzinga doesn't rely on notes he scribbled 35 years ago. He looks at newspapers and scholarly journals to ensure that his lectures are relevant to today's society. Stories about OPEC come and go depending on the cartel's influence. He also keeps pace with technology. In addition to overhead transparencies and the chalkboard, he teaches with videos. He occasionally uses Bible stories to illustrate an economic principle.

"I'm reminded of the admonition, 'whatsoever you do, in word and deed, do it as unto the Lord,'" Elzinga says, referencing Colossians 3:17. "It would be an affront to the Lord if I did not try to teach economics excellently."

In smaller, upper-level courses, Elzinga teaches by the Socratic dialogue method in which students must be prepared to answer aloud questions about the day's assigned reading material. There is a give and take, a matching of wits.

By the semester's end, many shy students have been transformed into students who can confidently and clearly defend a line of reasoning.

"When this occurs, I experience the joy of teaching, and not simply the satisfaction of the task," says Elzinga, who prays in his office to the Lord before classes. "I sense a great dependence upon the Lord in teaching, especially the large classes," he says. "I do not have natural gifts to do this."

Beyond teaching excellence, Elzinga believes part of Jesus's example as a servant teacher means that he must likewise be available.

"A Christian professor can have a spiritual impact on a secular campus by exercising whatever gifts the Holy Spirit has given to that faculty member," Elzinga says. "For some, it is the gift of evangelism; for some, prayer; for some, hospitality."

Elzinga seems to have all three gifts. He stays after a lecture as long as there are students with questions. The commitment to students doesn't end in the classroom. On the days when Elzinga holds office hours, students visit nonstop from 2:30 to 6:00 p.m., longer if needed. He sees this as an exciting time to serve, dispensing not only lessons in economics but lessons in life. He gives Biblical counsel to students, some of whom aren't even in his classes but are seeking spiritual direction.

By the semester's end, many shy students have been transformed into students who can confidently and clearly defend a line of reasoning.

"Their underlying problem is with broken relationships or broken lives," Elzinga says. "Their problem is not with economic analysis; it is with the fall of Adam." Not all problems are within his realm of understanding. At such times he asks students if they would mind if he prayed.

In part because his introductory economics course has a thousand students, the institution's largest class, Elzinga encourages students to phone him at home, much like a doctor on call. Elzinga and his wife, Terry, also open their home, located on the campus grounds, to a diverse lot of students, from rehearsals by a Jewish a capella group to a student who uses the kitchen to make baked Alaska for friends.

Sometimes they have students over for a late-night brownies and milk break. Foreign students may be treated to a Thanksgiving dinner. Elzinga says he learned hospitality from his first wife, Barbara, whom he married just out of graduate school. Barbara died after 12 years of marriage, of cancer, at age 33. She taught her husband about faith. "As the cancer advanced, her love for and trust in the Lord also grew," he recalls.

Terry, an architect, has continued the hospitality tradition. Elzinga says students at school crave a home in which they feel comfortable, either because they miss their own family or because they never had such a homey environment.

"We think opening our home is pretty important," Elzinga says. "It is a way of keeping our own selfishness in check. And it demonstrates to others that if they have a home, someday they need not hold a tight rein on it, but they can share it with others."

With all the kindness and generosity, Elzinga doesn't allow himself to become a doormat. For instance, he does not think it's his place to help a student who is transferring to another school pick courses, or to guide a student through the completion of income tax forms.

Elzinga has never been accused of showing favoritism to Christian students. He has had to flunk a number of Christian students because of their lack of effort.

It is no secret on campus that Elzinga is a Christian. Annually he addresses groups ranging from Law Christian Fellowship to Chinese Christian Fellowship.

Elzinga suggests that Christian faculty members at public institutions have a website that identifies them as followers of Jesus, as he has done. "If you are a teacher, or have some other position of leadership, you shouldn't hide your light under a bushel by concealing from others the very focus of your life."

He also has advice for Christians working in any secular environment: "Be excellent in your work, so your colleagues cannot dismiss you as a shirker or someone who is no earthly good," he says. "Be loving, courteous, helpful, thoughtful, cheerful. Christians who do not work hard bug me. And they give an excuse to their colleagues to ignore the Gospel. Be particularly kind to colleagues who are suffering. Kindness can be the best apologetic in some circumstances."

Part of the reason Elzinga is at the University of Virginia is because he understands that secular institutions are powerful shapers of American culture because they train the majority of minds. "It would be a shame if Christians abandoned the very setting where so many young people are being educated," he says.

As a sideline, Elzinga has coauthored, with fellow economist William Breit, three mystery novels. The hero in *The Fatal Equilibrium*—now in its twentieth printing and used at more than 400 colleges and universities as a text—is an economist who solves the crime using economic theory.

Elzinga has had multiple offers to teach, do research, or be an administrator elsewhere.

And although many contemporaries have opted for early retirement, Elzinga has no such plans. His calling remains on the secular campus. "I have one of the greatest jobs in the world," Elzinga says. "I get to work with young people, I live in a beautiful part of the country, I have a lot of freedom to pick what I choose to research and write on, and I have a good church home."

Even after more than four decades, Elzinga is having fun. "When one might expect boredom to set in, or at least the law of diminishing marginal utility to take its toll, teaching continues to be fresh, challenging, scary and rewarding."

MARVIN OLASKY

A former Marxist professor now promotes Biblical compassion.

Only now does Marvin Olasky understand God's grace, after his lengthy journey from Judaism to atheism to born-again Christianity. Along the way, Olasky, now in his sixties, has become a leading proponent in public life of espousing Biblical solutions to societal problems.

His grandparents emigrated from Russia to Massachusetts. In Olasky's early years, the family kept religious customs and rituals as Orthodox Jews, including sending him to Hebrew school for seven years and his bar mitzvah at age 13. Yet, as his parents became increasingly secularized during his childhood, he became increasingly skeptical about God. By 14 he considered himself an atheist.

The godless, materialistic books he read, including *History of the World* by H. G. Wells and *Future of an Illusion* by H. G. Wells, contributed to his ideology.

"My own pride and arrogance fueled my heading toward atheism, too," Olasky says. He came to believe that only silly and pathetic people needed God. Olasky instead looked to human gods to right the ills of society.

A scholarship to Yale University cemented his confidence in atheism. Liberals and radicals dominated the late 1960s campus scene, and Olasky kept moving further left, both theologically and politically. After serving a brief stint with the *Bend Bulletin*, a newspaper in Oregon, Olasky joined America's Communist party. He rode a Soviet freighter across the Pacific Ocean and the Trans-Siberian Railroad across Russia in order to better relate to those living under Marxist-Leninist dogma.

He returned to the United States and fit right in at *The Boston Globe*. But becoming a professor became his real craving, and he headed to the University of Michigan at Ann Arbor to obtain his MA and PhD degrees in an effort to be part of "the tenured left."

"That's where God surprised me," Olasky remembers. In November 1973, as he became disillusioned with communism and atheism, Olasky came to realize God does exist. A Russian New Testament he had read to brush up on his Russian had played a role in changing his mind. So did teaching a course in early American literature, which included Puritan sermons preaching to him from the grave.

"God changed my worldview, not through thunder or a whirlwind, but by means of a small whisper that became a repeated, resounding question in my brain: 'What if Lenin is wrong? What if there is a God?'" Olasky says.

He went on to read the writings of C. S. Lewis and Francis Schaeffer, which laid the groundwork for his conversion. In 1976, just before moving to San Diego to teach, Olasky married his wife, Susan. They selected a Baptist church from the Yellow Pages, heard sermons about being born again, and received Christ as Savior.

In 1978, Olasky began a five-year job as an executive speech writer for the DuPont Company in Wilmington, Delaware. In 1983 he moved to the University of Texas at Austin, where he has been ever since. He teaches only two journalism courses per term, which leaves lots of time to write. His passion now is to promote Biblical principles through his writing. He has authored 13 books and coauthored seven more.

As in the 1960s, today's college environment is rampant with liberal and radical faculty members.

"In the university environment, it's well known that I'm a Christian," Olasky says. Nevertheless, he has, despite some opposition, become tenured and a full professor. While he would be receiving more recognition and making more money with politically correct writings, he prefers to write scholarly works from a distinctly Biblical perspective. He lives out this commitment , at the time of this writing, as a senior fellow with the Acton

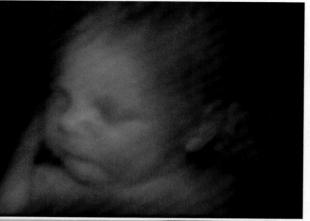

© 2012 by Valentina R.
Used under license of Shutterstock, Inc.

As an offshoot of his Biblical philosophy of compassion, Olasky also has been instrumental in defending unborn children's right to life, championing causes that will change hearts rather than merely legislate.

Institute for Religion and Liberty and as the editor of a Christian news magazine.

The publicity Olasky receives in the somewhat hostile academic environment only adds to his unique role. The student newspaper occasionally takes potshots at him for his conservative views. Sometimes graffiti are scrawled on the Christian posters he places on his office door.

Yet, for the Christian students among the 50,000 on campus, Olasky is a rarity: a professor who doesn't attack them for their beliefs, someone who supports them and advises them.

For the many non-Christian students in his larger lectures, Olasky often shatters the stereotypical perceptions they have of Christianity. Meanwhile, Olasky gained recognition in 1994 when the Republican congressional leadership adapted ideas from his book *The Tragedy of American Compassion* for inclusion in the welfare reform debate. He is known as a formulator of a compassionate social policy that attempts to bring a Biblical perspective into American public life. This philosophy, unlike Social Darwinism, which teaches that society is better off if the poor are ignored, holds that all people have value and should be treated as such because all are created by God in His image.

"We are commanded not to look away from the psychologically and spiritually distressed," Olasky says. The book describes how Americans successfully fought poverty before the government took over with myriad programs. His 1996 book, *Renewing American Compassion*, reiterated the themes that the most efficient poverty programs are religion-based and that churches have a responsibility to care for the helpless, especially widows and orphans.

Thus, Olasky has played a role in the welfare rolls being trimmed in half since 1996 and in more adults finding jobs and working their way up the economic ladder.

"God is changing people's lives," he says. "Instead of growing up with a welfare mentality, kids are able to see their parents working, which makes an enormous impact."

As an offshoot of his Biblical philosophy of compassion, Olasky also has been instrumental in defending unborn children's right to life, championing causes that will change hearts rather than merely legislate. The growth of the abstinence movement, the increasing use of ultrasound, and the promotion of adoption have contributed to the number of abortions dropping to 1.2 million annually from 1.6 million. One of Olasky's most recognized contributions to this trend is his 1992 book, *Abortion Rites: A Social History of Abortion in America*.

The youngest of the Olaskys' four children, Benjamin, is adopted, partly as an expression of Marvin's and Susan's Biblically-grounded convictions. "It is something I recommend to everyone," he says. "The sense of satisfaction from children is great whether they are born to you or whether they are adopted. In a sense they have been rescued." The Olaskys helped to start the Austin Crisis Pregnancy Center.

Now living in North Carolina, Olasky currently advances Biblical compassion and ideals in his role as the editor-in-chief of *World* magazine.

Through it all, Olasky is enormously grateful that God saved him from ideologies that led nowhere.

"God knows what we need and gives us gifts even we don't know enough to ask for them," he says.

>> VICKI CARUANA

An educator addresses her colleagues' spiritual needs.

"What do you want to be when you grow up?" From the time she was six years old, Vicki Caruana's answer to that question was always the same: "A teacher!"

And for good reason.

"Mrs. Robinson was my first grade teacher," Vicki recalls. "Her love for kids permeated the classroom. It was so obvious in how she taught, what she taught, in the way she treated people, in the atmosphere of the class. She made learning fun. I loved school because of her and I loved her. I decided I wanted to be just like her. I wanted to grow up to be the kind of person she was—to make other kids feel the way she made me feel, because it was so precious."

Few of us end up in the careers we aspire to in elementary school, but Vicki's determination never wavered. Growing up, she couldn't wait to inspire young hearts and minds. She longed to create that warm and loving environment in a classroom of her own. Caruana graduated from college with a master's degree in education and got her teaching certificate. She thought she was prepared. She felt she was ready.

But as it is for many beginning teachers, Vicki's first year in the classroom turned out to be a rude awakening. "You find out there's so much you *don't* know," Caruana says. "You feel ill-equipped, very inadequate. You don't know if you can really do this job that you signed up for, because so much of it has nothing to do with what you learned in books. Teaching is more of an art than a skill. So much of it is about dealing with people—not just students, but parents, colleagues, administrators. You're interacting, solving problems, being emotionally invested and then dealing with the repercussions of being emotionally invested. You get hurt, you get disillusioned, you get discouraged, and you don't know where to turn. It happens to almost every teacher that first year. It's a baptism by fire, and you have to decide how much you really love it. The desire to make an impact—is it strong enough to carry you?"

Caruana's first teaching assignment placed her in a troubled inner-city school. Her students had severe learning disabilities. Not one of their parents showed up for Open House night. Vicki's classroom was vandalized repeatedly. She was so worried about the safety of her students that she had constant nightmares. It was a learning experience alright—though not the kind she had dreamed of. Yet somehow, knowing that she was making a difference in the life of one child kept her coming back day after day.

"There was one boy—I knew that every night when he went home, he wasn't sure if he'd be alive the next day, because of the circumstances in which he lived. But he loved being in my classroom because I was able to make it safe for him. He felt accepted there and loved there. He loved being in school and he loved to learn. I didn't know if he would ever make it past the third or fourth grade level—if he'd ever graduate. But he made the effort each and every day in his own limited way. This one little boy kept me going," Caruana reflects. "You just need one. One student who needs what you have to give. God always gave me at least one each year, and that's all it took."

As a young teacher, Vicki found her faith played a vital role in how she saw her career— her calling. Caruana had been raised in a Christian home. She says she always had an awareness of God, a sense of His presence in her life—though it wasn't until she was a teenager that she truly understood the Scriptures she had learned and what her faith was all about. Her relationship with Christ gave Vicki the focus, strength, and determination to take on the challenges she faced in the classroom.

"Being a Christian teacher enabled me to look at my students the way God would— especially the ones who seem the most unlovable and unteachable. I knew that God loved them and I asked Him to love them through me," Caruana says. "I came to understand that it was not a mistake, not a coincidence that these children were in my classroom— it was God-appointed. I was appointed to be their teacher and they were appointed to be my kids. It made such a difference to have that outlook. I also knew that the difficulties I had with parents or the demands of my administrators were opportunities to be a witness—to let them see Christ in me. It wasn't easy. It was such a great responsibility. But it was also a great privilege. I wouldn't have wanted it any other way."

Over the years, as she continued teaching in both public and private (Christian) schools, Caruana realized that her early experiences were not unique. New teachers everywhere face the same problems, challenges, and opportunities. They want to touch the hearts and lives of their students, but they are in desperate need of encouragement and inspiration themselves. Too many of them give up too soon.

In time, encouraging teachers became Vicki's new passion—her new calling. She began looking for ways to reach out to other teachers and minister to them. Today, Vicki travels around the country, speaking to teachers at conferences and conventions. She is the award-winning author of a number of best-selling devotional books for teachers, including *Apples and Chalkdust, One Heart at a Time, Recess for Teachers*, and *Prayers from a Teacher's Heart*. Caruana also serves as adjunct professor at a teachers' college in Southwest Florida, teaching, training, and preparing aspiring teachers for the real-world challenges they will face.

© 2012 by Dmitriy Shironosov.
Used under license of Shutterstock, Inc.

Teaching is more of an art than a skill. So much of it is about dealing with people—not just students, but parents, colleagues, administrators.

As the mother of two teenage boys, Caruana has had the opportunity to reach out to her own sons' teachers as well. She encourages parents to get involved and become a part of their teachers' support team. "Ask how you can volunteer. Be willing to do whatever is needed—drivers on field trips, chaperones for parties, bulletin boards, decorating. Notes of encouragement are invaluable," she says. "I still have a big manila envelope with every one I ever received. They're reminders to me as a teacher that I'm on the right track, that I'm doing what God's called me to do—even though I don't see the fruit of it very often. "Find a teacher you used to have. I recently went online and discovered my fourth-grade teacher in a nursing home, 82 years old. I contacted her and thanked her for what she did for me. She was overwhelmed—to her it meant everything. Write a note or an e-mail or just say 'thank you' every once in a while. It means so much to know that you're appreciated."

A frequent guest on national radio and television programs, Caruana calls the Body of Christ to rally around the nation's teachers—to participate in organizations and events that support educators. She's thrilled to see many churches honor the teachers in their congregation with a "Back to School Sunday" prayer service—commissioning them and sending them out into the mission field that is their classroom.

Says Caruana, "The battle that's going on for the hearts and minds of this next generation is a spiritual battle, and teachers are on the front lines. Sometimes they're with our children more than we as parents are. They spend more waking hours with our kids than we do. They're called to encourage those children, and they can't do a very good job of it when they're discouraged and broken-hearted themselves. They really need us to pray for them, to support them, to encourage them, to build them up. They need prayer for direction and guidance, strength to stand firm and speak the truth in love. Even if you don't have children in school at this stage of your life, you're still called to pray. This next generation will be taking care of us soon. They'll be in charge, making all the decisions. We need to nurture our teachers so that they in turn can be nurturing our kids!"

The walls of Vicki Caruana's classroom have expanded far beyond the local elementary school. Her students now include teachers, parents, grandparents, families, and communities around the world. It's obvious Caruana still loves to learn and make learning fun. She cares deeply for each and every life God has given her the opportunity to touch— she wants to make a difference in each one. That's the heart of a teacher.

EDUCATION

∙∙∙∙∙∙∙∙∙∙∙∙∙∙∙∙∙∙∙∙∙∙∙∙∙

REDEMPTIVE FIELD ANALYSIS 1

HONOR STATEMENT: I, the undersigned student, hereby declare before God, before the school, and before the professor that I have read this chapter in its entirety, that I have completed the following exercise with help from no other sources, except as required by the questions, and that I neither have shared nor will share this work with anyone.

Signature: _____ Date: _____

Analysis 1

1. Using words from the fifth chapter, define the term redemptive communicator.

_____

_____

_____

_____

_____

_____

2. Summarize one of this chapter's profiles in the space below. Include the most important details. Omit unnecessary details.

_____

_____

_____

_____

_____

_____

_____

_____

_____

_____

3. If you were asked to use this story or a specific part of this story to support an idea, one that you could present as its main point to an audience, which idea would you present? State this idea as a single declarative sentence in the space that follows:

_____

_____

_____

_____

_____

4. The fifth chapter states that a redemptive communicator interacts with other people in a way that promotes what God values in this world according to Scripture. Review the chapter's list of things that God values. Then, in the space below, identify the specific God-valued thing that this profilee promotes according to the profile. Be sure to explain both how the profilee promotes this specific thing and why you believe this thing is something God values according to Scripture.

_____

_____

_____

_____

_____

_____

_____

_____

_____

_____

_____

_____

_____

_____

_____

5. Which other God-valued things does this profilee promote? Identify these and explain how he or she promotes them.

_____

_____

_____

_____

_____

_____

_____

_____

_____

_____

_____

_____

EDUCATION

· ·

REDEMPTIVE FIELD ANALYSIS 2

HONOR STATEMENT: I, the undersigned student, hereby declare before God, before the school, and before the professor that I have read this chapter in its entirety, that I have completed the following exercise with help from no other sources, except as required by the questions, and that I neither have shared nor will share this work with anyone.

Signature: _____   Date: _____

Analysis 2

1. Using words from the fifth chapter, define the term redemptive communicator.

_____

_____

_____

_____

_____

_____

_____

_____

2. Summarize another of this chapter's profiles in the space below. Include the most important details. Omit unnecessary details.

_____

_____

_____

_____

_____

_____

_____

_____

_____

_____

_____

_____

_____

_____

_____

3. If you were asked to use this story or a specific part of this story to support an idea, one that you could present as its main point to an audience, which idea would you present? State this idea as a single declarative sentence in the space that follows:

_____

_____

_____

_____

_____

_____

_____

_____

_____

_____

_____

4. The fifth chapter states that a redemptive communicator interacts with other people in a way that promotes what God values in this world according to Scripture. Review the chapter's list of things that God values. Then, in the space below, identify the specific God-valued thing that this profilee promotes according to the profile. Be sure to explain both how the profilee promotes this specific thing and why you believe this thing is something God values according to Scripture.

_____

_____

_____

_____

_____

_____

_____

_____

_____

_____

_____

_____

_____

_____

_____

_____

_____

5. Which other God-valued things does this profilee promote? Identify these and explain how he or she promotes them.

_____

_____

_____

_____

_____

_____

EDUCATION

· ·

REDEMPTIVE FIELD ANALYSIS 3

HONOR STATEMENT: I, the undersigned student, hereby declare before God, before the school, and before the professor that I have read this chapter in its entirety, that I have completed the following exercise with help from no other sources, except as required by the questions, and that I neither have shared nor will share this work with anyone.

Signature: _____   Date: _____

Analysis 3

1. Using words from the fifth chapter, define the term redemptive communicator.

_____

_____

_____

_____

_____

_____

_____

_____

2. Summarize another of this chapter's profiles in the space below. Include the most important details. Omit unnecessary details.

_____

_____

_____

3. If you were asked to use this story or a specific part of this story to support an idea, one that you could present as its main point to an audience, which idea would you present? State this idea as a single declarative sentence in the space that follows:

_____

_____

_____

_____

_____

_____

_____

_____

4. The fifth chapter states that a redemptive communicator interacts with other people in a way that promotes what God values in this world according to Scripture. Review the chapter's list of things that God values. Then, in the space below, identify the specific God-valued thing that this profilee promotes according to the profile. Be sure to explain both how the profilee promotes this specific thing and why you believe this thing is something God values according to Scripture.

_____

_____

_____

_____

_____

_____

_____

_____

_____

_____

_____

_____

_____

_____

_____

5. Which other God-valued things does this profilee promote? Identify these and explain how he or she promotes them.

_____

_____

_____

_____

_____

MEDIA >>

MEDIA

LEE STROBEL

A journalistic doubter becomes a popular Christian apologist.

Lee Strobel felt betrayed and frightened when he discovered his wife, Leslie, the woman he had cherished since his youth, had found a new love. In 1979, Leslie professed her devotion to that new love—Jesus Christ—and committed her life to Him.

"I was very upset she'd decided to take this path. I was afraid it would change our marriage. I felt like she'd switched bait on me," Lee Strobel recalls.

Strobel's fears were realized—the couple's marriage did change—but the transformation in his wife's life forced the then *Chicago Tribune* award-winning journalist to don his reporter's cap and pen and take note.

As he witnessed his wife becoming a more caring, compassionate, and tender-hearted woman, Strobel began to investigate Jesus, undeniably the person most responsible for the subtle changes in her life.

Armed with a Master of Studies in Law degree from Yale Law School, Strobel was skillfully trained in fact finding. The challenge was set before him. He had to discover for himself—was there evidence to support a case for Christianity, or was God, as he suspected, only a myth?

"I knew she did not change as the result of some self-help course. There was something fundamentally changing in her very nature—something very attractive and very beautiful. Leslie had always been beautiful, like a budding rose. But when I saw her in a relationship with Jesus Christ, she was more beautiful than ever, like a fully blooming rose. I asked myself, 'What accounts for this?'" Strobel says.

His first step was to accompany Leslie to Willow Creek Community Church, where he listened as Pastor Bill Hybels taught the fundamentals of Christianity to a crowd of suspicious skeptics.

Strobel left that first service with one pressing thought—"I knew if what Hybels said were true, it had huge implications for my life," he recalls.

Armed with a Master of Studies in Law degree from Yale Law School, Strobel was skillfully trained in fact finding. The challenge was set before him. He had to discover for himself—was there evidence to support a case for Christianity, or was God, as he suspected, only a myth?

For nearly two years following his wife's conversion, Strobel plowed through ancient literature, plodded through archaeology, plucked through the Bible, and purposefully interviewed some of the world's leading scholars, all in an effort to investigate the truth, if there was any, in Christianity.

He began by grilling Dr. Craig Blomberg, author of *The Historical Reliability of the Gospels*, widely considered one of the country's leading authorities on the biographies of Jesus. But Strobel wasn't content with just one man's discoveries.

Relentlessly, he interviewed many other scholarly notables, including Bruce Metzger, author and editor of 50 books regarding New Testament text, and historian Edwin Yamauchi, author of several books focusing on Biblical archaeology. Strobel eventually interviewed more than a dozen scholars, finally culminating his quest with born-again philosopher J. P. Moreland.

His research would ultimately form the structure for his recently published book, *The Case for Christ* (Zondervan 1999). Compared by many to Josh McDowell's *Evidence That Demands a Verdict*, Strobel's book leads the reader on an intellectual trek that unearths the rudimentary evidence in support of Christianity.

It was a trek that led Strobel, himself, to the foot of the cross.

So what was the one discovery that clinched the case for Strobel?

"It was the evidence in support of the resurrection," he says.

The same resurrection that changed the lives of the disciples is still changing the lives of people some 2,000 years later.

"Overall, that one fact had more impact on me than any other," he reports.

As a journalist, Strobel had read account after account of terrorists who were willing to lay down their lives for something they believed to be true. But the disciples didn't just have a hunch about the resurrection, Strobel noted, "they knew for a fact it had occurred."

"I couldn't find any examples in history of someone willing to die for a lie," he adds.

James, the half-brother of Jesus, was the one disciple who had a profound effect on Strobel.

"He was not in Jesus's camp. In fact, Jesus would have been an embarrassment to him. There was no incentive to James to report the resurrection as fact. But we know from secular history that James was put to death for his faith in Jesus. Why? Because after the resurrection, Jesus appeared to his half-brother. It changed James," Strobel says.

Changed him into a man willing to die for his faith, for something he not only believed to be true, but knew to be fact because James had personally encountered the resurrected Christ.

When Strobel, who was logging his discoveries on a yellow legal pad, came across James's testimony, he recognized that to continue in his disbelief meant swimming upstream, against the torrent of evidence to the contrary.

"It was not a huge emotional moment. I was simply surprised and convinced by the truth of who God is. It was the single, most rational thing in my life," Strobel says of his own personal encounter with the resurrected Christ.

Years later, Strobel acknowledges God was orchestrating the entire discovery.

As a journalist, Strobel had read account after account of terrorists who were willing to lay down their lives for something they believed to be true. But the disciples didn't just have a hunch about the resurrection, Strobel noted, "they knew for a fact it had occurred."

"My response to the evidence was not because I was clever, but because God used the evidence to open my eyes to the truth of Who He is and showed me my need for a savior," he says.

Strobel's trek to the cross culminated in November of 1981. But it was only the first stop in the journey God had planned for him. Since 1987, Strobel has served as a teaching pastor at the church that challenged him with the Gospel, where he teaches some 17,000 suspicious skeptics, like he once was, who attend a weekly service for spiritual seekers.

"It's ironic that I teach at the same service where my investigation first began," he observes with a wry smile.

Christians, Strobel says, don't have to be intellectual scholars to be a witness. But, he cautioned, they should be prepared to give an answer when the occasion to discuss spiritual matters arises (2 Peter 3:15).

"Know why you believe," he says.

Then pray for opportunities to share that faith with others. Talk about God in everyday conversations.

"Have the courage to seize the opportunities," he says.

And, perhaps, most importantly, listen to the questions nonbelievers pose.

"Don't think you have to have all the answers; you don't," Strobel adds.

Perhaps there is no better evidence of the resurrected Christ than restored lives. Strobel can testify to this. It was his changed life that convinced his own daughter Alison, at age five, to embrace Christianity.

"For the first five years of her life, she knew me as a drunk and absent father, who was angry over life. It was not a good environment. It was so bad that if I entered the front door, Alison would gather her toys from the living room and head for the bedroom. I'm not proud of that, but it's the truth," he confesses.

But about six months after he became a Christian, Alison began to notice a change in her father's priorities and values.

"Even at her tender age, she could see I was becoming someone who was more loving, more positive, more caring. She thought, 'If God does this for people, why would I not want that for myself?'" Strobel says, recalling his daughter's profession of faith.
It was the same question that confronted Strobel following Leslie's conversion—a question that all sincere seekers address eventually.

Today, the Strobel couple rejoices that both Alison and Kyle were raised in a household that demonstrates God's ability to restore lives.

"All the evidence doesn't matter if it isn't played out in the transformation of people's lives. Without a resurrection, it isn't worth the pursuit," Strobel concludes.

>> CAL THOMAS

A leading syndicated columnist views journalism is his mission field.

Although he has been fired and downsized several times from a television and newspaper career that has spanned nearly five decades, Cal Thomas has become the world's most widely syndicated columnist, appearing in 517 newspapers. As a conservative Christian flourishing in a profession dominated by liberal commentators, Thomas wouldn't mind some company.

He believes too many Christians assume that the mass media are so collectively hostile to their beliefs and worldview that it's not worth engaging the media, even in a constructive way. Thomas knows better. "First you have to stop cursing the darkness," he says. "Nothing gets lighter when you curse the darkness. But if God is big enough to create the world, don't you think He's big enough to [place] a few people of His in various professions?"

According to Thomas, Christians need to rethink the definitions of "mission field" and "full-time Christian service." Believers ought to see themselves as already being in full-time Christian service, because the alternative—part-time Christianity—is clearly non-Biblical. "The mission field is wherever God puts you," Thomas says. "It's not only a foreign country where you live among the natives in a grass shack. If that's where God is calling you, you should go. But it can also be in medicine, in law, in education, in the media."

Thomas long ago began to see his work as a missionary calling. "There was a time in my life when I saw the career as an end, supplying not only my physical needs but my emotional wants," Thomas says. "In the process of living and becoming a disciple of Jesus, I found that like so many other things with God, our ways are not His ways, and my perception has turned around. Now I see career as the means, and the credibility that it gives me to share my faith among my colleagues . . . as the end. It is providing more contentment than I ever had when I was pursuing the elusive goals of what the world offers."

Thomas started working in radio as a news reader at age 16, before joining NBC's news division as a copyboy at 18 and working his way up from there. He didn't sense a need for church as he climbed the career ladder. By age 27 he had become one of the youngest people to have appeared regularly on the NBC radio and television networks.

As a child, Thomas had made a nominal profession of faith. "I did what my parents and grandparents expected of me when I was 12— I walked down an aisle, signed a card, went down dry and came up wet, and had my 'fire insurance policy' in my back pocket so I wouldn't fry when I died," Thomas recalls. Yet he rarely read the Bible while growing up, except for the time when his grandfather offered him a silver dollar if he would memorize the 23rd Psalm.

Despite his success working for NBC News in Washington, Thomas sensed a tremendous emptiness. "The more I got in terms of visibility and money, the less satisfied I was," Thomas says.

But his life changed, beginning with a prayer breakfast where he heard a federal judge testify about having a personal relationship with Jesus Christ. Then at a Bible study he heard pastor and later U.S. Senate Chaplain, Richard Halverson, teaching. "He got me out of religion and introduced me to Jesus," Thomas says of Halverson. Thomas committed his life to Christ at age 30, the night NBC News fired him. "God was working things out in me, including reliance on myself, so He could work Himself into me and fit me for the column He was going to give me," Thomas says. "The firing forced me to make a commitment, which was a very gracious thing."

Thomas's faith deepened through the influence of philosopher-theologian Francis Schaeffer. "Francis Schaeffer renewed my mind and taught me how to think," Thomas says. "He pushed people to the logical conclusions of their presuppositions, which is one of the greatest debate tactics ever created."

Today, Thomas and his wife, Ray, sponsor dinners in their Alexandria, Virginia, home for journalism colleagues. The Thomases, who have four grown children, also hold an annual dinner the night before the National Prayer Breakfast where guests hear about the things of God.

© 2012 by vidguten.
Used under license of Shutterstock, Inc.

Society is suffering, in part, Thomas believes, because too many Christians have segregated themselves from sinners, rather than interacting with them as Jesus did.

Christianity should be evident in the lives of its followers. Thomas asks: "Do we stay married? Are we an example to our children? Are we honest in our financial dealings? Do we humble ourselves? How many of us are clothing the naked, feeding the hungry, caring for widows and orphans, visiting those in prison?" (See Matt. 25.)

Society is suffering, in part, Thomas believes, because too many Christians have segregated themselves from sinners, rather than interacting with them as Jesus did. "The people who really need the medicine—the unsaved, the unwashed—aren't getting it in sufficient numbers because not enough of our people hang out where they hang out. They don't go to our churches, so we have to go into the world to them."

Christian laypeople have a special responsibility to be salt and light in the workplace, says Thomas, who over the years has been a political commentator for CNBC and the Fox Network. In many cases, Christians can be more effective in mainstream careers, he says. He recalls meeting a Florida newspaper reporter frustrated with his working conditions. "He told me, 'I'm the only Christian on the staff, and I hardly ever get my views on the editorial page. I'm thinking of leaving and going into full-time Christian service,'" Thomas recalls. "I said, 'Let me ask you a question: Do you know the name of your boss's wife? Your colleague who sits next to you, have you ever gotten her a cup of coffee in the morning? Could you go out to lunch with some of your buddies here and think that you had had an effective witness if the subject of God never came up? Sure, God will allow you to leave, but He [might not give you] this kind of responsibility again. Or you can get back in there and start loving your neighbor as yourself, being among your peers, and seeing how God wants to work this out.'"

In 1980, Thomas became spokesman for Moral Majority. But by 1985, Thomas became concerned that many well-intentioned Christian conservatives had strayed from the church's spiritual calling after being seduced by political power. He believes spiritual regeneration is the key to the societal transformation that so many Christians desire. "We'll never have trickle-down morality," Thomas says. "In a free society, government reflects the soul of its people."

The Los Angeles Times took a chance on Thomas in 1984 by allowing him to start writing a column that challenged conventional wisdom by promoting a return to Biblical morality. Thomas didn't rely solely on the sales staff to make the syndicate a success. "God doesn't reward slothfulness," he says. "I went out and met editors myself and hung out where they hang out. That's what Jesus did; He came down from heaven and became one of us."

For his outspoken articles, Thomas regularly receives hate mail accusing him of being a hypocrite, coward, liar, and bigot. The ungodly have occupied the territory surrendered by Christians, he believes. "They've intimidated anybody who thinks differently," he says, adding that Christians should be as passionate about truth as their antagonists are in their opposition to it.

In his writings, Thomas skillfully presents Biblical truths without being sanctimonious. While his job is to express opinions and to make judgments, he must be careful not to be judgmental. This proves especially challenging when individual moral crises plague the political atmosphere.

Thomas is the author of many books, including *Occupied Territory, Liberals for Lunch, The Things That Matter Most, Uncommon Sense*, and *Blinded by Might* (coauthored by Pastor Ed Dobson). While writing *Blinded by Might*, Thomas says he became concerned that many Christians who strive to transform society do so without really knowing Scripture. Without a knowledge of Scripture, he contends, we tend to refashion the Gospel, supplanting the Biblical emphasis of a world needful of spiritual redemption with agendas that, however admirable, will never be more important than the salvation of human souls.

"No human, fallen leader is going to save this country," Thomas says. "Only Jesus Christ saves individuals. Nations rise and fall. If America became a totalitarian state tomorrow, it would not change one thing that I am commanded or commissioned to do."

>> JIM ADAIR

Longtime editor and author Jim Adair made a difference

PROFILES IN FAITH

During his more than 50 years of penning writing Christian books and editing inspirational publications like Power for Living, *James Adair (1923-2009) knew more than ever that the Gospel works for today and that there is little so powerful as a story for communicating this vital principle to audiences of all ages. Under Jim's editorial oversight, PFL quickly rose in popularity to become one of the most widespread non-denominational publications of its type, circulating each week to nearly one million readers throughout the United States and Canada. Jim's stories and the reader responses they generated impacted the author of this textbook when he succeeded Jim, years after Jim's departure, as the editor of the same publication. More than any other journalistic colleague, Jim taught the author that one can powerfully communicate Biblical principles through stories about real people whose transformational experiences demonstrate those principles. Part II of this textbook is, to a large degree, an extension of the vision that Jim instilled in the author during their 12-year professional association. In the story that follows, written a couple of years before his death, Jim writes about experience as a journalist who used his craft to promote Gospel awareness and literacy.*

It started with a phone call in 1944 when I was 21. "There's an ad in Carl McIntire's *Christian Beacon* that may interest you," a friend told me. She knew that my mother had been praying that I would get into "Christian journalism." At that time I was a newspaper reporter for the *Asheville* (North Carolina) *Times*. Though I never actually saw the ad, it led me in July 1945 to Scripture Press, then in Chicago. It began an adventure that only God could plan.

Having years earlier placed my faith in Christ, I began as an associate editor of a new Sunday School take-home publication, *Power* (later, *Power for Living*). My assignment: to write and edit articles answering, "Does Christianity work today? And if so, what is the evidence?"

I soon became editor and for almost 30 years traveled from time to time far and wide to interview countless people who had been transformed by Jesus Christ. Their stories, and those by other writers, gave strong evidence that there is "power in the blood," as the old song by that name proclaims. Subjects included the educated and uneducated; the rich and the poor; the young and old; laborers and executives; those from many walks of life—

janitor, plumber, barber, rancher, student, athlete, surgeon, scientist, general, governor, senator, and so on.

I did not have to leave my workplace to find excellent examples of those who had found that there is "power in the blood." Scripture calls those redeemed by Christ "saints," and the couple for whom I worked, the founders of Scripture Press—Victor and Bernice Cory—were excellent examples. In a *Power for Living* article, I told their story. In their early adult years he had worked as an electrical engineer and she had taught high school English. They had prided themselves as being good people, but at Bernice's aunt Jennie Rader's Valentine Party they discovered their righteousness did not qualify them to be members of God's family. Responding to the Gospel at the party, they each laid their sin on Christ, receiving His righteousness, and became "spiritual twins." They quickly became enthusiastic followers of the Saviour, and in time God laid it on their hearts to begin Scripture Press and publish Bible-based teaching materials that eventually impacted Sunday Schools across America and abroad.

One of my early *Power* stories introduced readers to Raymond Lilly, a black man I met at a dinner. In conversation, I discovered he was a brother in Christ. He had once worked for a circus as a trapeze rigging man and later for a steel company. A janitor had witnessed to him, and later in a rescue mission he came to Christ. His life was turned completely around; he left a sinful life and in time became a powerful witness at Chicago's Cook County Hospital. At a time when he was penniless, he walked 70 blocks to bring the Gospel to patients while he ministered to their needs—giving shaves, cutting hair, trimming toe nails, perhaps giving a comb, a hair net, a pencil. Lilly became a close friend, and I rejoiced when he was named the first official black chaplain of the hospital. He was indeed a trophy of grace, and I'm sure his story impacted readers!

Another early *Power* story told of "Lucky Lou" Zamperini's narrow escapes from death. An Olympic hero in 1936 in Berlin, Germany, he had climbed a flag pole to bring down Hitler's private Swastika. Guards fired at him, and he "luckily" escaped with his life. In World War II Japanese fire downed his bomber in the Pacific; he lived 47 days on a life raft, then spent 28 months in prison. God transformed him when he encountered the Gospel in Billy Graham's Los Angeles Crusade in 1949. Lou became a herald of the Good News, even going to Japan in the late 1950s to proclaim Christ.

In the mid-'50s a *Saturday Evening Post* article introduced me to a surgeon who, with his associate, had perfected a revolutionary method of treating hydrocephalus for children. He was a Christian, the article mentioned. I made an appointment to interview him at Children's Hospital, Philadelphia, where he was chief surgeon. My interview with Dr. C. Everett Koop, later to become America's Surgeon General, gave me insight into how his sensitive hands had performed delicate operations on infants and children, to save their lives.

© 2012 by kotomiti.
Used under license of Shutterstock, Inc.

During his more than 50 years of penning writing Christian books and editing inspirational publications like *Power for Living*, James Adair (1923-2009) knew more than ever that the Gospel works for today and that there is little so powerful as a story for communicating this vital principle to audiences of all ages.

And it was thrilling to hear from Dr. Koop that, at age 30, under the preaching of Dr. Donald Grey Barnhouse, he had asked Jesus to be his Saviour. In time he shared his faith with his Jewish associate, Dr. Eugene B. Spitz, bringing him to acknowledge Christ as his Messiah.

Jack Wyrtzen, founder of Word of Life, Schroon Lake, New York, whom I had met before coming to Chicago, tipped me off to several good stories. One involved two hippy generation young people—Vicky Riccardella and Tasos Mahairas. In their drug trips during the 1960s, they reached out for love, peace, and a Supreme Being. Tasos at one point thought he had become an incarnation of Christ, and was committed to a mental hospital. Eventually, both he and Vicky were invited to Word of Life youth camp, and there both encountered the Saviour. They later married and established a Gospel outreach in New York City.

Another trophy of God's grace who stands out in my memory is Maxey Jarman, who at that time was chairman of General Shoe Corporation; today you can buy shoes that bear his name. He had faced the sin question as an 11-year-old boy and trusted Christ. I remember his declaring to an audience: "I believe that Christ should be evident in every phase of my life; so certainly that means in my business. The people with whom we are associated in business are watching us. We want to make sure they see Christ." Through the Jarman Foundation, Maxey Jarman made funds available to foreign missions, Bible institutes, orphanages, and other organizations which were "true to fundamental doctrines of the Bible."

General William K. Harrison, Jr. is one of my favorites subjects. A prominent physician and close friend of the general related the story to *Power*. General Harrison was leader of the United Nations' truce delegation that negotiated with the Reds in Korea before an armistice was signed in July 1953. A stalwart believer, he retired after 44 years of continuous service in the U.S. Army, and declared to a friend, "I have made up my mind that I am going to devote the rest of life in full-time work for God." He became director of the Evangelical Welfare Agency in Chicago and led it through a most difficult period of expansion.

A surprise phone call from an acquaintance in the late '40s put me in touch with a man Americans had reason to hate: "Capt. Mitsua Fuchida, the lead pilot who started bombs falling on Pearl Harbor, is in town. He is now a Christian. Perhaps you would want to meet him and interview him." It was indeed a memorable experience for me to sit down with the man whose command, "Whole squadron, plunge into attack," plunged the USA into World War II. A Gospel tract given to him in Tokyo prompted him to buy a Bible. Fuchida believed the Gospel, became a new creation in Christ, and eventually preached and distributed Pocket Testament League Gospel portions in his homeland.

Indeed, during the many years I've written articles for this publication—a task I've exercised as a freelancer since the 1970s—I have found overwhelming evidence that Jesus saves, that there is "power in the blood," that He can transform a sinner into a saint, as Scripture calls believers. I continue to thank God for giving me the opportunity to meet and write about so many of his choice saints.

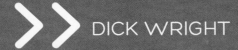

>> DICK WRIGHT

The political cartoonist with a pastoral heart.

Pick up any newspaper in the United States and there's a one-out-of-five chance that your eye will be caught by an editorial cartoon by Dick Wright. (He is syndicated in about 300 of the nation's 1,500 newspapers.) Each cartoon's subject depends on the social and political issues of the date. In December 1998 you might have seen a drawing of the then-U.S. President sitting in a corner he'd painted himself into, surrounded by black paint cans labeled "Lies." In March of 2001 one cartoon depicted the current U.S. President sitting with a donkey in a dilapidated Model-T on blocks. Printed on the jalopy's door: Social Security.

Whether someone agrees or disagrees with Dick Wright's point of view—and many liberal newspaper editors label it too conservative—most admit that he has a witty way of making a point with his pencil. He's been doing it for nearly 40 years.

Drawing Conclusions

When Dick talks about his career, he sometimes mentions his sixth-grade teacher's warnings that he was spending too much time doodling, rather than studying. Her prediction: "If Dickie doesn't quit drawing in class, he'll never amount to anything."

That Pasadena, California, elementary school teacher might be amazed to know that Dickie's doodling evolved into cartoons that are seen by millions of readers four times a week, material that made him a finalist for the Pulitzer Prize in 1983. (He's never been able to reach her to tell her.)

She might not be as amazed to know that her now much older former student, who delivers zingers to politicians, also boldly delivers the eternal truths of Scripture as the pastor of a Bible-believing congregation each Sunday. After all, it was at age 12 that Dick, raised in a devout Christian family (his father has taught Sunday school for 60 years), received Christ as his Savior. "Getting saved that young kept me out of an awful lot of trouble," Dick says. "My focus became the church and the things in the church. My salvation experience was very, very powerful, and it's changed the course of my life."

Dick's devotion to Christ and the authority of Scripture has long been strong. Although the Bible says little of direct relevance to the specific political issues that his cartoons usually address—Social Security reform, education funding, environmental policies, and so forth—Dick turns to Scripture for principles that help guide him to the specific convictions about such issues that he expresses through his editorial cartoons.

His faith in Christ also led Dick, at age 18, to the church where he met the young woman who became the love of his life. When a new family came to church, Dick invited one of the boys to play fast pitch softball. On the field he asked Tim if he had any sisters. Tim replied, "Yes, but you wouldn't want to meet her." Dick chuckles as he says, "I did meet her and I married her." (Dick and Susan Wright have two grown daughters and four grandchildren.)

As a young man, Dick did freelance cartoons for various magazines at night but supported his family through his day job. He was a draftsman at NASA who helped design the fuel system for the Mariner project. That job caused him to decide to go back to college to become an engineer. But, while drawing cartoons for the university newspaper, he dreamed about making drawing cartoons a full-time career. He took his work to local newspapers where editors encouraged him. Eventually he got a job with *The San Diego Union* that launched his cartoonist career. He later became chief cartoonist for the Scripps Howard newspaper chain.

During his career, Dick has worked for several newspapers around the country and moved his family from the West Coast to the East. When it became clear that through syndication he didn't have to work on-site to be a paper's cartoonist, he chose as his home base Gainesville, Virginia, located in the Washington, DC area. It put him close to many of the national events that he addresses via his cartoons.

Wright to the Point

Dick creates four cartoons each week in his basement home office. Each one usually takes four to five hours to get from idea stage to finished product. His ideas come from reading *The Washington Times* and *The Washington Post* early each morning and seeing breaking news on television. The drawing takes shape—and sometimes changes shape—on his 30-year-old draft board as he works with paper, pencils, erasers, and rulers—essentially the same tools he used in sixth grade. After the image is clear, he can use an overhead projector to alter its size. Then he scans it into his computer and sends it on its way to his syndicate editor at Tribune Media and the readers beyond.

On the theory of cartoon drawing, Dick explains the madness behind his method: "There are two schools of thought on editorial cartoons. One is to take current events and to see humor in that and make a light-hearted comment. The other is where I am. I believe an editorial cartoon should have a point to it. You use humor to get your point across. I'm attuned to what's going on and the consequences of the acts of politicians. Many times I'm very upset and do not like what's going on, and I have an opportunity to say that to the reader."

And the readers are able to talk back to him (he puts his e-mail address on each cartoon). Most have positive comments. The negative feedback comes more from newspaper staff members who don't like his politics or, sometimes, his religion.

Like the late Johnny Hart and other cartoonists who are Christians, Dick's faith influences his work in many ways. He isn't afraid to put an explicitly Biblical message in his cartoons or take the flack that comes from it. Holidays give him an easy opening. For example, a cartoon he did in April 2001 showed two Roman soldiers looking back at a hill with three crosses on top and an empty tomb below. One says to the other: "Relax! In a hundred years, who'll care?"

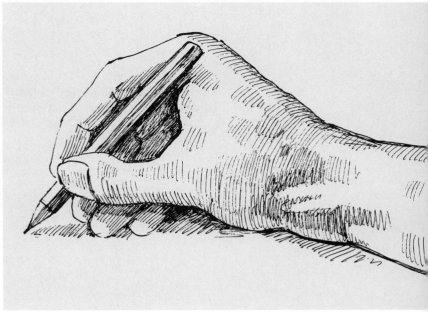

Dick isn't afraid to put an explicitly Biblical message in his cartoons or take the flack that comes from it.

Drawing Near

"I'm longing for the day I check out of this all together and just pastor," Dick Wright says with what sounds like a sigh. That may seem odd coming from a man so successful at what he does. Dick isn't burned out. He's not just tired of 40 years of deadline pressures. He's found a new passion—pastoring a local church.

Dick and some friends founded the Community Christian Fellowship in September 1999. They first began meeting in a home, then moved to a fire hall in New Baltimore, Virginia. The church has purchased five acres on the border of two counties (Faquier and Prince William), bought modular buildings from an army base for temporary space, and is building a sanctuary.

As you would expect from a pastor/cartoonist, things aren't somber in this church. "We're very casual in dress and relaxed," he says. "People are so taken by the fact we can have some fun in church."

The church especially tries to attract unchurched seekers, but Dick sees his congregation as a mixture of types of believers. After the first 18 months of meetings, Dick was grateful that the church had 29 new converts and that many lives had been turned around.

While his political cartoons may be considered polarizing by some, Dick avoids anything divisive in his church. "We don't emphasize our differences. We stick with the main purpose of the church, which is to preach the Gospel, to disciple all people, and to love one another. If you do those things, you're not going to have a whole lot of trouble. . . That's where we're going and it's gone well."

Things have changed for the man who once wanted to do nothing but draw cartoons. "Drawing political cartoons is what I do for a living. I try to do the best job I can, but I'm not consumed by it," Dick says. "My focus has become more and more toward pastoring full-time and taking care of the needs of the church. That is a higher priority to me now than winning Pulitzer Prizes and journalistic awards and getting in more and more newspapers. That's not what drives me."

NAME: _____   DATE: _____

MEDIA

·······················

REDEMPTIVE FIELD ANALYSIS 1

HONOR STATEMENT: I, the undersigned student, hereby declare before God, before the school, and before the professor that I have read this chapter in its entirety, that I have completed the following exercise with help from no other sources, except as required by the questions, and that I neither have shared nor will share this work with anyone.

Signature: _____   Date: _____

Analysis 1

1. Using words from the fifth chapter, define the term redemptive communicator.

_____

_____

_____

_____

_____

_____

2. Summarize one of this chapter's profiles in the space below. Include the most important details. Omit unnecessary details.

_____

_____

_____

_____

_____

_____

_____

_____

_____

_____

_____

_____

3. If you were asked to use this story or a specific part of this story to support an idea, one that you could present as its main point to an audience, which idea would you present? State this idea as a single declarative sentence in the space that follows:

_____

_____

_____

_____

_____

_____

4. The fifth chapter states that a redemptive communicator interacts with other people in a way that promotes what God values in this world according to Scripture. Review the chapter's list of things that God values. Then, in the space below, identify the specific God-valued thing that this profilee promotes according to the profile. Be sure to explain both how the profilee promotes this specific thing and why you believe this thing is something God values according to Scripture.

_____

_____

_____

_____

_____

_____

_____

_____

_____

_____

_____

_____

_____

_____

_____

5. Which other God-valued things does this profilee promote? Identify these and explain how he or she promotes them.

_____

_____

_____

_____

_____

_____

_____

_____

_____

_____

_____

_____

_____

_____

MEDIA

REDEMPTIVE FIELD ANALYSIS 2

HONOR STATEMENT: I, the undersigned student, hereby declare before God, before the school, and before the professor that I have read this chapter in its entirety, that I have completed the following exercise with help from no other sources, except as required by the questions, and that I neither have shared nor will share this work with anyone.

Signature: _____   Date: _____

Analysis 2

1. Using words from the fifth chapter, define the term redemptive communicator.

_____

_____

_____

_____

_____

_____

_____

2. Summarize another of this chapter's profiles in the space below. Include the most important details. Omit unnecessary details.

_____

_____

_____

_____

_____

_____

_____

_____

_____

_____

_____

_____

_____

_____

3. If you were asked to use this story or a specific part of this story to support an idea, one that you could present as its main point to an audience, which idea would you present? State this idea as a single declarative sentence in the space that follows:

_____

_____

_____

_____

_____

_____

_____

_____

_____

_____

4. The fifth chapter states that a redemptive communicator interacts with other people in a way that promotes what God values in this world according to Scripture. Review the chapter's list of things that God values. Then, in the space below, identify the specific God-valued thing that this profilee promotes according to the profile. Be sure to explain both how the profilee promotes this specific thing and why you believe this thing is something God values according to Scripture.

_____

_____

_____

_____

_____

_____

_____

_____

_____

_____

_____

_____

_____

_____

_____

5. Which other God-valued things does this profilee promote? Identify these and explain how he or she promotes them.

_____

_____

_____

_____

_____

_____

MEDIA

....

REDEMPTIVE FIELD ANALYSIS 3

HONOR STATEMENT: I, the undersigned student, hereby declare before God, before the school, and before the professor that I have read this chapter in its entirety, that I have completed the following exercise with help from no other sources, except as required by the questions, and that I neither have shared nor will share this work with anyone.

Signature: _____   Date: _____

Analysis 3

1. Using words from the fifth chapter, define the term redemptive communicator.

_____

_____

_____

_____

_____

_____

_____

_____

2. Summarize another of this chapter's profiles in the space below. Include the most important details. Omit unnecessary details.

_____

_____

_____

_____

_____

_____

_____

_____

_____

_____

_____

_____

_____

_____

_____

3. If you were asked to use this story or a specific part of this story to support an idea, one that you could present as its main point to an audience, which idea would you present? State this idea as a single declarative sentence in the space that follows:

_____

_____

_____

_____

_____

_____

_____

_____

_____

_____

4. The fifth chapter states that a redemptive communicator interacts with other people in a way that promotes what God values in this world according to Scripture. Review the chapter's list of things that God values. Then, in the space below, identify the specific God-valued thing that this profilee promotes according to the profile. Be sure to explain both how the profilee promotes this specific thing and why you believe this thing is something God values according to Scripture.

_____

_____

_____

_____

_____

_____

_____

_____

_____

_____

_____

_____

_____

_____

_____

5. Which other God-valued things does this profilee promote? Identify these and explain how he or she promotes them.

_____

_____

_____

_____

_____

_____

LAW & GOVERNMENT »

LAW & GOVERNMENT

 PHILLIP JOHNSON

A distinguished law professor hammers evolutionary theory.

Shards of morning sunlight sliced through the windows overhead and sent shadows scampering under the pews. A thousand bodies shifted in their seats, a hundred voices whispered, one coughed. Then, into the light stepped a gentleman with white hair, rosy cheeks, and an easy smile. He didn't look like the leader of a revolution. He didn't even look like a lawyer. He looked a little like Santa Claus.

His fingers rested on the lectern. His smile widened. The crowd quieted. The man put a hand to the tie that hung crookedly from his neck. Then, he began to speak. And as he did, the noose of Darwinism that has choked our society for decades seemed to unravel. And that's when I knew that this was no Santa Claus. This was a man who is changing our world.

Phillip Johnson never dreamed that God would call him to spearhead the assault on Darwinism and the naturalistic philosophy that has enslaved our culture with skepticism toward Biblical truth. As a young man, he believed he had life figured out. He graduated with prestige from Harvard and the University of Chicago. He had the rare honor of clerking for the Chief Justice of the United States Supreme Court, then Earl Warren, and later became a law professor at University of California at Berkeley. In the world's eyes, he had it all.

But when he received the Lord as his Savior, Johnson quickly found himself torn between two worlds—the world of academia and the world of the church. "In becoming a Christian, I was accepting as true some things which are assumed throughout the university world to be altogether false," he says. "So the question [of creation] required serious investigation. What was the truth I had accepted? Was it really truth? Or was it all imaginary? It seemed to be something that the really educated people discarded many years ago."

He found the distinction between secular academia and his new beliefs to be particularly acute at church where the pastors and members considered themselves to be a part of the university community. "They believed they were respected and accepted," says Johnson. But he knew the academic world well. He knew that Christians were neither respected nor accepted. "They assume that everything we stand for is false and even ridiculous," he reveals.

That discordance set Johnson on a path of investigation that eventually led to the publication in 1991 of *Darwin on Trial*, a book that rocked the academic world by exposing the flaws of evolutionary naturalism. Rather than primarily defending his own beliefs, Johnson chose, much like Paul at Athens (Acts 17), with this and his other books that have followed to go on the offensive against falsehood by forcing evolutionists to defend their own unquestioned assumptions. *Darwin on Trial*, which has been translated into Chinese, Spanish, French, Polish, Czech, and other languages, created such a ripple that it provoked sharp responses from such leading evolutionary thinkers as the now late Stephen Jay Gould of Harvard.

Why would an accomplished law professor devote the latter years of his life to addressing the creation question? "What else is there?" Johnson replies. How were we created? What is the truth about creation and evolution? To Johnson, these are among the most interesting and significant questions in the world.

Rather than primarily defending his own beliefs, Johnson chose, much like Paul at Athens (Acts 17), with this and his other books that have followed to go on the offensive against falsehood by forcing evolutionists to defend their own unquestioned assumptions.

Every culture, asserts Johnson, has a creation story and a priesthood that has the authority to tell that story. In our culture, Darwinian evolution has become our creation story, with scientists and TV anchors as its priests. They say evolution is real, and creation is not. They say, "In the beginning were the particles . . ." and relegate God to a place next to Tinkerbell and the Toothfairy. But then along comes Johnson, a respected professor from a prestigious university—a man who is one of the academy's own— and catches them off guard by publicly scrutinizing the culture's established creation myth.

"It's very difficult to challenge it," says Johnson. "If you do, you're accused of bringing up 'religion,' that is to say 'imaginary things,' in the viewpoint of the secular world." So, Johnson needed to devise a strategy to, as he says, "batter down the door, to split the log of dogma" that stands in the way of truth. And that is just what he did.

"Johnson's genius was in framing the debate to be about evidence. Not God. Evidence," says James Scott Bell, author of *The Darwin Conspiracy*. Though not a scientist himself, Johnson has shaken the evolutionary establishment by exposing flaws in evolutionary theory itself. Like a true prosecuting attorney, he has put the theory of evolution "on the stand" and has challenged its accuracy based on the facts themselves. He has turned the tables (or in this case, the fossils) on the evolutionary "priests" to show that their position requires more "faith" than that of "Intelligent Design." Much like Paul in Athens, Johnson uses what evolutionists understand—science—to challenge Darwinism. Science, he has found, is not the enemy of creation, but in fact supports the idea of a Creator.

Like a true prosecuting attorney, Johnson has put the theory of evolution "on the stand" and has challenged its accuracy based on the facts themselves.

So, unlike many others before him, Johnson successfully defanged the opposition, approaching the question of origins in a manner that forces them to engage him as someone who is more than a "Bible-thumping religious fanatic."

"If you're going to challenge something as powerfully entrenched as the theory of evolution, you can't just have a strong feeling of 'well, I'm right.' You can't just have arguments that appeal to your own side. You must have an argument which has the capability of breaking through the opposition," says Johnson.

Through Johnson's leadership, this Wedge strategy (getting the wedge of truth into the scientific debate on origins), is making inroads into the once impenetrable realm of evolutionary thinking.

Johnson describes his Wedge strategy as an ax—he is the initial sharp edge, but behind him have now come a number of distinguished scientists and scholars, such as Michael Behe, Bill Dembski, Nancy Pearcey, and Jonathan Wells, who form the thicker part of the ax which is necessary to split the log.

The time is ripe, believes Johnson, to overturn the governing paradigm of the entire thinking world, to shatter the dominant belief that nature alone explains how we (and the universe) came into being.

Just as Johnson felt he was gaining ground, his life and career took a new turn in 2001. On Friday, July 13th, the world blurred, and the thing that Johnson had most relied on in his career and ministry—his brain—failed him. He had a stroke, a serious stroke. "It was the most devastating and frightening thing I could imagine," he shares, "more so than death even." He didn't know if he'd ever walk again, let alone debate evolutionists, or write books, or speak to crowds about his passion for God, the Creator.

Then, into his darkness and fear stepped a Christian friend named Kate. She stood by his bed in the Oakland Kaiser hospital and sang an old hymn: "On Christ the solid rock I stand, all other ground is sinking sand . . ." At that moment, a question whispered through Johnson's mind: "Am I actually standing on the solid rock?" he asked himself. And the answer he found was yes, he was, or at least he knew he had one foot on the solid rock. "But perhaps I was trying to make things a little better by getting an additional foothold on the shifting sand," he relates. "The sand was my brain, the brain that had taken me from a small town in Illinois to Harvard at the age of 17, had made me at the top of the legal profession and a professor at Berkeley—the brain that I thought would get me through any other trouble." This was not a moment of conversion, Johnson is quick to clarify, but of a deepening, solidifying commitment to Christ, and Christ alone.

And so today, with both feet planted firmly on the solid rock of Christ, Johnson stands before a church filled with people, with his tie slightly askew and his shoes tied by his wife, because he still hasn't relearned how to tie them. In the power of God alone, with the sun shining in his hair, he shares the truth about creation and evolution. God has granted him the grace to continue his mission, to keep on fighting, keep on declaring the reality of an Intelligent Designer.

"We may look back at him in a hundred years and say, 'He's the guy that unraveled Darwinism in our culture,'" says James Scott Bell. And I have to agree. But it won't be because of Phillip Johnson's intellect, it will be because he dared, in the power God had given him, to ask the hard questions, the right questions. It will be because he stood up among the secular priests of Darwinism and boldly declared, "The emperor Evolution has no clothes!"

>> MAT STAVER

A leading constitutional lawyer takes the culture war into the courtroom.

Mathew D. Staver is a driven man. He has a bachelor's degree in theology, a master's degree in religion, and a doctorate in law. He heads the Christian defense organization Liberty Counsel, shuttling between offices in Florida, Virginia, and Washington, DC. He is a professor and dean of the law school at Liberty University. He produces a half-hour weekly TV program, *Law & Justice*; a 15-minute daily radio program, *Faith & Freedom*; and a 90-second daily radio program, *Freedom's Call*. Oh, and he's written 11 books.

"The Lord gives me a lot of energy," Staver says. "I work around a lot of talented people." The dynamic and humble Staver models his work ethic after his mother, who as a single mom worked three jobs during his early childhood in rural Florida.

The only memories he has of his father are of a violent alcoholic who physically abused his mother. By the time he reached age 3, Staver's parents had divorced. His dad moved to Illinois with two of his siblings while Mat, the youngest, remained in Florida with his mom and four brothers and sisters. His mother operated a paper route before dawn, worked as a waitress in the day, and as a nurse's aide during the evening.

Staver grew up determined not to follow in the footsteps of his father, who died in middle age of cirrhosis of the liver. Mat became a record-setting placekicker on his Charlotte County high school football team and hoped to make the sport his profession. But a leg injury in his senior year dashed his hopes.

After graduation, Staver attended an evangelistic revival service in Punta Gorda, Florida, an evening that would change the course of his life. Although he had attended church regularly throughout his youth, Staver didn't have a personal relationship with Jesus. At the meeting he committed his life to Christ as Savior. He determined to enter the ministry, and graduated cum laude from Southern University with a theology degree.

He later graduated summa cum laude, first in his class, from Andrews University Seminary with a master's degree in religion. One day in Lexington, Kentucky, where he served as a pastor, Staver attended a meeting with other local clergy. It became another gathering that would change the course of his life. There, the ministers watched a video on abortion. For the first time, Staver saw an unborn child in the womb as well as the graphic aftermath of an abortion.

Immediately, Staver obtained as much information about abortion as he could from a local right-to-life organization. He visited the University of Kentucky law library and for the first time read a legal case—*Roe v. Wade*. At age 25, Staver became active in the pro-life movement.

As he prepared sermons each week at the seminary, Staver kept thinking about what he had learned at the law library across the street. Although he didn't understand why God might be diverting him from full-time ministry, Staver—who reads Hebrew, Greek, and Aramaic—sensed that God wanted him to become involved in the legal and public policy arenas of the sanctity of life movement.

Soon, Staver enrolled in the University of Kentucky Law School. After graduation—and marriage to his wife, Anita—he moved to Orlando, Florida, and went to work for a private practice law firm, still engaged in right-to-life activities in his free time. Two years later, in 1989, Staver formed his own commercial law firm so that he could become more involved in pro-life issues on the side. Income from Staver & Associates financed Liberty Counsel, which initially focused on pro-life and religious liberties cases. Staver, who started out with only a secretary to help him in the Liberty Counsel office, became a pioneer in providing free Christian defense in the religious liberties movement, following John W. Whitehead who started the Rutherford Institute in Charlottesville, Virginia, in 1982.

© 2012 by JustASC.
Used under license of Shutterstock, Inc.

Staver sensed that God wanted him to become involved in the legal and public policy arenas of the sanctity of life movement.

Even working part time for Liberty Counsel, Staver managed to litigate significant cases. In 1994, he argued *Madsen v. Women's Health Clinic*, an important "buffer zone" case for the free-speech rights of pro-lifers, before the U.S. Supreme Court. A judge in Melbourne, Florida, had ordered volunteer sidewalk counselor Judy Madsen and other pro-lifers to keep at least 36 feet away from an abortion facility. In addition, the judge approved a 300-foot zone around the building that would outlaw pro-life speech unless listeners showed an interest.

"In public areas, the Constitution does not require peaceful protesters to first obtain permission from those of the opposing viewpoint to speak," Staver argued. The high court ruled the attempts to silence sidewalk counselors unconstitutional.

Sanctity of life—all life—is important to Staver, whose father committed incest with one of his sisters. The rape resulted in the birth of a baby.

Anita, who had obtained a counseling degree, decided to obtain a law degree after the *Madsen* case so that she could work beside her husband. She has more than 30 published legal opinions.

Within a decade, Staver & Associates, the secular firm that bankrolled Liberty Counsel, had grown to 40 employees and included a branch in Tallahassee. The business law firm attracted statewide clients in the insurance, hotel, restaurant, and hospital industries. But Staver found that the company's success acted as an impediment to Liberty Counsel. Staver had to spend too much of his time tending to commercial law matters, time he believed should have been devoted to Christian cases.

He sought counsel from Liberty Counsel board member Alfred Williams, a London pastor. Williams gave Staver three pieces of advice:

- If he had peace in his heart about God wanting him to devote all his time to defending religious liberties and the sanctity of life, he should pursue it, even if he didn't know where he would obtain funding.
- Satan is a master at delaying and distracting Christians from accomplishing visions God has imparted.
- When God presents a plan of action, He may not speak again until the vision has been fulfilled.

Staver, indeed, had felt directed by God to start Liberty Counsel in 1989. But by 1999, he believed he had failed to completely trust God, instead hoping for a miraculous monetary gift to make the organization fully functional.

"In retrospect, I realized I hadn't been living in full dependence and faith on the Lord," Staver says.

So Mat and Anita took a leap of faith. They figured they would still have each other even if they lost all their possessions in closing Staver & Associates and its lucrative source of income.

God blessed the decision. A recently renovated office building the firm had purchased in Tallahassee had been on the market for 14 months without a single offer. It sold in six weeks. Staver & Associates sold its corporate airplane, two Mercedes Benzes, and several $20,000 copy machines. Outstanding receivables owed to the company were paid at a higher percentage rate than in the history of the firm. Within nine months, the company had paid off all its obligations.

Today, Liberty Counsel is fully funded by donations from individuals, churches, and organizations to provide pro bono legal services.

Staver has continued to argue cases that reach the U.S. Supreme Court. In 2000, he became involved in the history-making decision of *Bush vs. Gore* that cleared the way for George W. Bush to be elected president. Staver represented absentee voters whom candidate Al Gore's campaign attempted to disenfranchise. In 2005, Staver defended a Ten Commandments display in county courthouses in *McCreary County v. ACLU of Kentucky*, but the Supreme Court ruled against him—on the same day the justices determined that a Ten Commandments monument at the Texas State Capitol was constitutional.

In 2004, Staver took another faith step by helping found the Liberty University School of Law in Lynchburg, Virginia. For several years, Staver had written a column in *National Liberty Journal*, a monthly newspaper published by Liberty University founder Jerry Falwell. He also appeared on Falwell's weekly *Listen America* cable television talk show. Staver urged Falwell to start a law school in order to teach religious liberties to a new generation. Falwell didn't need much prodding; he had been thinking about it himself. The school began operation in 2004, headquartered in an 888,000-square-foot complex of buildings on 110 acres adjacent to Liberty University. Hobby Lobby founder David Green paid $10.3 million to a cellular telephone company moving operations overseas for the property.

In 2006, Staver relented to Falwell's persistent request that he become dean of the law school. Staver agreed, provided he could open a Liberty Counsel office on campus. The law school at Liberty University, where Staver also is a professor, serves as a training laboratory for future lawyers who hold a Christian worldview.

Liberty Counsel now also has offices in Texas and Washington, DC. There are hundreds of affiliate attorneys around the country, in all 50 states. Ninety-five percent of Liberty Counsel's legal work is resolved without going to court. In its 20-year existence, Liberty Counsel has won 86 percent of the cases it has litigated, including 92 percent since 2004. Typical suits are filed to ensure that a Good News Club has a right to meet in a public school or to defend a second grader who had been prohibited from giving Bibles to friends at school.

In addition to religious liberties and anti-abortion litigation, a third emphasis of Liberty Counsel for the past decade has been defense of the traditional family, marriage between one man and one woman. In 2008, Staver became the lead lawyer trying to overturn same-sex marriage in California. He needed bodyguards when arguing in court in San Francisco.

"My mission in life is to be a friend of God and to do His will in a Christ-like way, but to be uncompromising on principles of truth," Staver says. "So I'm not a friend of the world. A lot of people disagree with me."

Staver has attracted his most strident opposition from abortion-rights and homosexual-rights groups. He has endured vicious untrue attacks against his character from those who disrespect his Biblical viewpoints.

Meanwhile, Staver is encouraged by the number of students at Liberty University who will be trained in law.

"The biggest legacy we can leave behind is the life of someone who is inspired to follow the will of God," Staver says. "The law school is training men and women in all areas of law—business, education, public policy, public service, ministry. These people will become lawyers, judges, educators, policymakers, and world leaders."

Today, Liberty Counsel has a staff of 28, plus up to 20 student interns at any given time, most of them from Liberty University. During summer, the number of interns swells to 50.

"The synergy with Liberty University has solidified the future of Liberty Counsel," says Staver, now in his upper fifties.

A partnership between Liberty Counsel and Liberty University created the Liberty Center for Law and Policy in Washington, DC, to train legislators. A similar collaboration expanded the Liberty Center for International Human Rights in 2009 after the entity had helped Christians in countries such as Romania, Malaysia, and China.

Of course the main concentration will continue to be on freedoms in the United States.

"Some people don't realize the serious threat against our liberties today, particularly from the homosexual agenda," Staver says. "Our job is to educate, motivate, and equip Christians to be able to engage the culture and advance the Kingdom."

GARY HAUGEN

An accomplished attorney wars against the international slave trade.

When Gary Haugen was growing up in Sacramento, California, he didn't have a care in the world. His father, a physician, provided a comfortable income for the family of eight. At school each morning as he stood to recite the Pledge of Allegiance, he had no idea the implications the phrase "and justice for all" would have on his life in years to come.

"In elementary school I was oblivious to the anti-war movement, the ongoing conflicts in Vietnam, and the racial tensions that marked our nation in the early seventies," Gary admits. "What I read in my textbook about President Lincoln's passion to free the slaves was the only thing I knew about the denial of human rights."

It was not until Gary moved to Boston to begin his studies at Harvard in the fall of 1981 that his eyes were opened to the plight of people struggling to experience the comforts of life he'd always taken for granted.

"I saw homeless families living in alleyways as I went to class," Gary recalls. "It had a profound impact on me. As a member of our local campus Christian fellowship, I worked in a homeless shelter in Cambridge and helped to winterize the homes of the poor in Boston. It was an eye-opening experience for me."

© 2012 by Goran Bogicevic / Shutterstock.com.
Used under license of Shutterstock, Inc.

But Gary's eyes weren't the only part of him that was impacted. His heart was too. By the time he graduated from Harvard in 1985, he felt called to live out his faith and education by investing in a cause bigger than himself. He traveled to South Africa and worked to promote human rights there. The months he spent working with the National Initiative for Reconciliation caused him to see the mandate for Christians to stand against injustice where it is found.

In the late 1980s, after getting a law degree from the University of Chicago, Gary worked for the Lawyers Committee for Human Rights. In that role he investigated police and military misconduct in the Philippines in which civilians were murdered. The miscarriage of justice haunted the young lawyer whose core values were marked by Scripture he'd learned early on.

"According to a recent *National Geographic* article, there are more slaves in the world today than there were in 400 years of trans-Atlantic slave trade," he observes. "My fear is that [we] celebrate what Wilberforce did in 1807 but overlook the far greater situation that exists 200 years later. Too many lives are at stake for Christians not to take action."

"My mom prayed with me to receive Christ as a young boy," Gary acknowledges with a smile. "I'm grateful to her for making sure my siblings and I were in church to hear of God's love. But I'm also grateful for the experiences God has allowed me that have helped me understand His passion for justice in the lives of helpless victims."

Another one of those experiences occurred after Gary went to work for the U.S. Department of Justice in Washington, DC. In the aftermath of the Rwandan genocide in which 800,000 men, women and children were slaughtered in eight weeks' time, Gary was sent to that blood-soaked African nation to investigate. His survey of mass graves and eye-witness accounts caused him to return to the United States determined to do something.

"While some people asked where God was during such a human tragedy, I came home with another question burning in my gut," Gary admits. "I wanted to know where God's people were, [those who]could have stopped the needless slaughter of innocent lives. From the studies I conducted, it was obvious the genocide could have been prevented if certain people had done certain things."

Convinced Rwanda wasn't the only country where inhumane treatment of ordinary citizens was taking place, Gary left the Department of Justice to strike out on his own. In 1997 he founded International Justice Mission (IJM) in suburban Washington with a simple vision. He wanted to work with local authorities to dig up evidence and bring prosecutions against those guilty of abuse and slavery in accordance with local laws.

Gary's vision was not only based on what he'd observed in South Africa, the Philippines, and Rwanda. He was convinced by his reading of the Bible that God's heart beat on behalf of those denied fair treatment by those usurping control over them. A survey he'd conducted of 65 missionary organizations (representing more than 40,000 overseas workers) indicated they were aware of abuses of power but lacked the tools to oppose them. Gary was motivated to provide the tools because of his knowledge of God's Word.

"When you read the Scriptures with an eye for passages related to justice, you see it everywhere," Gary contends. "In Micah 6:8 God tells us that the bottom-line agenda for his people is to do justice and love mercy and walk humbly with him. Through Isaiah God bears His soul. 'Learn to do well; seek judgment, relieve the oppressed, judge the fatherless, plead for the widow' (Isa. 1:17). It's clear that God hates injustice and wants His people to confront it."

As he began IJM, Gary found himself incensed about the trafficking in sex slaves that he observed taking place in Cambodia. IJM's undercover operatives shot video of children being offered for sale in brothels. When authorities were shown how young children were being forced into lurid behavior, brothels were raided and profiteers were arrested.

"We want to speak up for the abused and expose corrupt officials who turn a blind eye and hold out a greedy hand," the founder of IJM explains. "We exist to help missionaries and aid workers who discover criminal abuse but lack the resources or expertise to expose the perpetrators."

While sexual exploitation of women and children are one focus of IJM's agenda, the nonprofit organization also opposes forced labor, illegal land seizures, illegal detention, and police brutality. Its overall purpose is to protect people from violence by securing rescue and restitution for victims and ensuring that public justice systems work for the disadvantaged.

The organization's mission has drawn attention. A steady stream of Christian lawyers and human rights activists have joined IJM's cause, convinced that their service matters more overseas than in a country rich with litigators. Today IJM (which is 95 percent privately funded) has 16 offices in 12 countries and currently employs more than 260 individuals. Gary's passion for his calling has resulted in many volunteer lawyers and investigators who leave their jobs for a few weeks to offer their skills in a country where abuses exist. Chicago-based lawyer Bob Mangan is one of those. When a U.S. Congressman asked Bob to attend a gathering in his home to hear Gary share his vision, Bob had no idea what would result.

"As I heard Gary speak about the plight of young girls being exploited in Peru, I knew I had to get involved," Bob recalls. "When Gary reported that Peru exceeds the rest of South America in its ambivalence towards the sexual abuse of women, I questioned how my involvement would make any difference. But upon going and serving in Jesus's name, I came to believe that any justice served is service to a holy God and is not without effect." Gary's success in inspiring volunteers like Bob is an ongoing joy to him. But the husband and father of four refuses to let a ministry he feels passionate about undermine his effectiveness at home.

"I am very intentional about my work and travel schedule," Gary says without hesitation. "I won't travel more than six nights a month domestically and will not agree to more than three overseas trips a year. Not only do I need to avoid the potential for burnout, I want to be able to coach my kids' teams."

In light of his passion for justice, Gary has been called a modern-day Wilberforce. William Wilberforce, a nineteenth-century British parliamentarian, is credited with bringing an end to his nation's slave trade. Although he does not deny the similarity of their concern, Gary is quick to note that the campaign against modern slavery is far from over.

"According to a recent *National Geographic* article, there are more slaves in the world today than there were in 400 years of trans-Atlantic slave trade," he observes. "My fear is that [we] celebrate what Wilberforce did in 1807 but overlook the far greater situation that exists 200 years later. Too many lives are at stake for Christians not to take action."

LAW & GOVERNMENT

·······················

REDEMPTIVE FIELD ANALYSIS 1

HONOR STATEMENT: I, the undersigned student, hereby declare before God, before the school, and before the professor that I have read this chapter in its entirety, that I have completed the following exercise with help from no other sources, except as required by the questions, and that I neither have shared nor will share this work with anyone.

Signature: _____   Date: _____

Analysis 1

1. Using words from the fifth chapter, define the term redemptive communicator.

_____

_____

_____

_____

_____

_____

2. Summarize one of this chapter's profiles in the space below. Include the most important details. Omit unnecessary details.

_____

_____

_____

_____

_____

_____

_____

_____

_____

_____

_____

3. If you were asked to use this story or a specific part of this story to support an idea, one that you could present as its main point to an audience, which idea would you present? State this idea as a single declarative sentence in the space that follows:

_____

_____

_____

_____

_____

_____

4. The fifth chapter states that a redemptive communicator interacts with other people in a way that promotes what God values in this world according to Scripture. Review the chapter's list of things that God values. Then, in the space below, identify the specific God-valued thing that this profilee promotes according to the profile. Be sure to explain both how the profilee promotes this specific thing and why you believe this thing is something God values according to Scripture.

_____

_____

_____

_____

_____

_____

_____

5. Which other God-valued things does this profilee promote? Identify these and explain how he or she promotes them.

LAW & GOVERNMENT

....

REDEMPTIVE FIELD ANALYSIS 2

HONOR STATEMENT: I, the undersigned student, hereby declare before God, before the school, and before the professor that I have read this chapter in its entirety, that I have completed the following exercise with help from no other sources, except as required by the questions, and that I neither have shared nor will share this work with anyone.

Signature: _____ Date: _____

Analysis 2

1. Using words from the fifth chapter, define the term redemptive communicator.

_____

_____

_____

_____

_____

_____

_____

_____

2. Summarize another of this chapter's profiles in the space below. Include the most important details. Omit unnecessary details.

_____

_____

_____

_____

_____

_____

_____

_____

_____

_____

_____

_____

3. If you were asked to use this story or a specific part of this story to support an idea, one that you could present as its main point to an audience, which idea would you present? State this idea as a single declarative sentence in the space that follows:

_____

_____

_____

_____

_____

_____

_____

_____

_____

_____

_____

4. The fifth chapter states that a redemptive communicator interacts with other people in a way that promotes what God values in this world according to Scripture. Review the chapter's list of things that God values. Then, in the space below, identify the specific God-valued thing that this profilee promotes according to the profile. Be sure to explain both how the profilee promotes this specific thing and why you believe this thing is something God values according to Scripture.

_____

_____

_____

_____

_____

_____

_____

_____

_____

_____

_____

_____

_____

_____

_____

_____

5. Which other God-valued things does this profilee promote? Identify these and explain how he or she promotes them.

_____

_____

_____

_____

_____

LAW & GOVERNMENT

....

REDEMPTIVE FIELD ANALYSIS 3

HONOR STATEMENT: I, the undersigned student, hereby declare before God, before the school, and before the professor that I have read this chapter in its entirety, that I have completed the following exercise with help from no other sources, except as required by the questions, and that I neither have shared nor will share this work with anyone.

Signature: _____   Date: _____

Analysis 3

1. Using words from the fifth chapter, define the term redemptive communicator.

_____

_____

_____

_____

_____

_____

_____

_____

2. Summarize another of this chapter's profiles in the space below. Include the most important details. Omit unnecessary details.

_____

_____

_____

_____

_____

_____

_____

_____

_____

_____

_____

_____

_____

3. If you were asked to use this story or a specific part of this story to support an idea, one that you could present as its main point to an audience, which idea would you present? State this idea as a single declarative sentence in the space that follows:

_____

_____

_____

_____

_____

_____

_____

_____

_____

_____

_____

4. The fifth chapter states that a redemptive communicator interacts with other people in a way that promotes what God values in this world according to Scripture. Review the chapter's list of things that God values. Then, in the space below, identify the specific God-valued thing that this profilee promotes according to the profile. Be sure to explain both how the profilee promotes this specific thing and why you believe this thing is something God values according to Scripture.

_____

_____

_____

_____

_____

_____

_____

_____

_____

_____

_____

_____

_____

_____

_____

5. Which other God-valued things does this profilee promote? Identify these and explain how he or she promotes them.

_____

_____

_____

_____

_____

_____

BUSINESS & FINANCE >>

BUSINESS & FINANCE

>> DAVE RAMSEY

A leading financial counselor shares wisdom from Scripture.

Growing up in the Nashville suburb of Antioch, Tennessee, Dave Ramsey had honest, hardworking parents who made a living as real estate agents. They were more likely to be attending an open house than a house of worship on Sundays.

Ramsey followed in his family's footsteps after graduating from the University of Tennessee in 1982 with a degree in finance and real estate. Soon he and his wife, Sharon, whom he met in college, started buying and selling property with aplomb. By age 26, Ramsey had amassed a $4 million real estate portfolio.

But the Ramseys borrowed too much money. And when another financial institution bought the bank that loaned them all the credit, the couple began to default on short-term loans. Within three years of making $200,000 annually, they filed for bankruptcy protection.

The Ramseys borrowed too much money. And when another financial institution bought the bank that loaned them all the credit, the couple began to default on short-term loans. Within three years of making $200,000 annually, they filed for bankruptcy protection.

The financial turmoil naturally resulted in an emotional rift between the spouses, who by this time had two young children. They stayed together, in part because they didn't have enough money to leave each other.

But more important, the couple had a spiritual walk that kept their marriage intact. At age 24, Ramsey attended a motivational sales-training seminar in which the impressive and credible speaker ended his presentation with a challenge to the audience: "Anyone who really wants to be a success can't leave God out of his life."

Ramsey went home from the seminar and told his wife they needed to start attending church, which they did.

"I met God on the way up the real estate ladder, but I really got to know Him on the way down," says Ramsey, now in his fifties. "Pain and fear and hopelessness always lead you in a special way into the throne room."

Amid his despair, Ramsey devoured the Bible, became keenly aware of God's authority over his life, and asked Jesus to be his Savior. The Ramseys began teaching teenagers at church. Then the pastor asked Ramsey to teach a Sunday school class about money to those in college. By this time, Ramsey already had read all that Christian financial-expert pioneers Larry Burkett and Ron Blue had written. He compiled his own book, the first version of *Financial Peace*, about God's way of handling money based on what he had learned from the mistakes he had made. The class's attendance swelled from 35 to 350.

Ramsey continued to sell real estate and—out of the trunk of his car—copies of *Financial Peace*. "It takes selling a lot of $12 books to eat," he says.

In 1992, Ramsey made a life-changing decision. He agreed to fill in as the host of a one-hour daily show at a radio station in financial straits. That evolved into the national "The Dave Ramsey Show," which continues today with the frank and humorous host serving as a personal money-management expert.

Ramsey is a fast-talking, in-your-face kind of guy whose tough-love guidance over the airwaves from Nashville is connecting with a lot of Americans. Every few minutes on his three-hour weekday afternoon radio program, callers who recently paid off massive amounts of credit card obligations scream, "I'm debt free!"

Unlike most money experts who are Christian, Ramsey gained entrée into secular radio, resonating in a medium that reaches far beyond the evangelical world. He is syndicated on more than 300 radio stations, fewer than 15 of them Christian. He also is on subscription-based satellite radio. He has three million listeners each week.

"I sell a lot of books in Christian settings and speak in a lot of churches, but my calling is in the mainstream marketplace," Ramsey says.

Yet Ramsey, at intentionally strategic times, is overtly Christian and boldly proclaims his faith on the program. For instance, if a caller says he is a Christian and that his car has just been repossessed, Ramsey will quote a Scripture, such as Proverbs 22:7: "The rich rule over the poor, and the borrower is servant to the lender."

Sometimes Ramsey's Biblical paraphrases are more blunt: "If you sow stupid, you reap desperate and broke."

Ramsey doesn't have much patience for Christians looking for God to bail them out of the reckless financial decisions they've made in a society where preapproved credit card applications arrive in the mail virtually every day. Ramsey says too many consumers have fallen prey to the sophisticated marketing schemes of financial institutions.

"We've come to believe debt is a way of life, that the way to prosper is through the use of a credit card, that you can't be a student without a student loan," Ramsey says. "I've cried over this stuff, too. I've done stupid with zeroes on the end. But our Heavenly Father loves us enough to show us the right way to do it, even if the path to get there is a little bit painful."

Ramsey believes he has made inroads into the mainstream market because of the credibility that he gained through the firsthand experience of failing to get a grip on his own finances.

"I went broke a few years ago," Ramsey says. "If somebody's hurting, I can relate. I'm a wounded healer."

In the couple of minutes or so of interaction that Ramsey has with each caller he says he must rely on the Holy Spirit's guidance to decipher whether a tender or brusque response is necessary. Whichever method fits the occasion, he wants the listener to emerge with a plan of action.

"I don't want to jump down the throat of a hopeless person," Ramsey says. "But I don't want to love on somebody too tenderly who is slothful. There are plenty of people who are poor because they are taken advantage of and oppressed, but one of the reasons the Bible says the poor will always be with us is because the lazy won't get up and work."

Still, the Ramseys have formed a program called "Share It," which they finance heavily from their own income. Share It enables disadvantaged people—prisoners, unwed mothers, recovering drug addicts, those in low-income housing, victims of domestic violence—to attend classes for free to learn God's way of handling money.

More than 350,000 people have completed Ramsey's Financial Peace University, a 13-week course that he says enables the average family to pay off $5,300 in debt and save $2,700 in the first 91 days. In addition, 400,000 people have attended live events Ramsey has hosted to promote the rapid eradication of debt, based on his book *The Total Money Makeover*. At the end of his talks he always talks about the importance of the Lord.

"There's not one time in the Bible where God uses debt to bless His people," Ramsey says. "If you're a Christian and you use Scripture as your standard, every time debt is mentioned it's a curse and you're a slave."

Ramsey's no-nonsense approach to money has landed three of his books on *The New York Times* best-seller list. While thousands of Americans have heeded Ramsey's message, many others aren't listening.

"The statistics of pain are getting worse every year," Ramsey says. "We have more people getting behind on credit cards, more people filing bankruptcy, more people in foreclosure right now than we've ever had in this nation."

But numerous families are making better decisions and changing because of Ramsey's advice. And that means more people are saving—and giving money to their churches.

ANNE BEILER

An entrepreneur retains eternal perspective amid remarkable success.

Anne F. Beiler's life went into a tailspin after the death of her 19-month-old daughter Angela, who was run over by a farm tractor in 1975. Beiler, in her mid-twenties at the time, found herself depressed and, more than once, on the brink of suicide.

Despite being a faithful churchgoer, Beiler didn't feel as though she could share her pain with friends or family members. She and her husband, Jonas, whom she had wed at 19, drifted apart. The couple didn't talk about the tragedy and its ramifications. Instead, they remained silent partners who simply lived together. Anne determined to stay with her husband for the sake of their two other daughters. But she contemplated filing for divorce once LaWonna and LaVale grew up.

Seven years into the ordeal, Jonas convinced his wife to go with him for marriage counseling at their church.

"I really didn't want to go, even though my life was falling apart," she says. "But I had a breakthrough and in the process of counseling I saw how God loved me."

As God restored Anne, she and Jonas reconciled with each other. The Lord also revealed to the Beilers that many Christians around them suffered with a great deal of unspoken pain because of various crises in their lives.

After studying at EMERGE Ministries, founded by Dr. Richard Dobbins in Akron, Ohio, the Beilers began providing lay counseling as a way to help such broken people.

In order to make ends meet during those years, Anne relied upon the youthful baking experience she gained growing up on an Amish-Mennonite farm with seven siblings. Because Beiler had asthma as a child, she never ventured outdoors much. Thus, she inherited the role of cook and baker for the family. By age 12, she made as many as 70 pies and cakes from scratch each week for sale at a nearby farmer's market. She didn't skimp on the ingredients, and always carefully made sure the wares looked and tasted great.

"God often uses our history to fulfill His plan," Beiler tells *Power for Living*. "God was preparing me for the future."

As a financial means to supplement the counseling work she did with her husband, Beiler bought a concession stand at a farmer's market in Downingtown, Pennsylvania. She sold everything from pizza to ice cream, but it was the hand-rolled soft pretzels that customers gobbled up the fastest. Because of such demand, Beiler dropped the rest of the products and concentrated full time on the pretzels.

From that modest start she became one of the nation's leading entrepreneurs. Although the family's counseling center in Gap, Pennsylvania, has grown tremendously and today employs 17 people—handling more than 2,300 appointments annually—it's the baking business that has generated a much higher profile.

Auntie Anne's Hand-Rolled Soft Pretzels now rakes in $247 million in sales a year. In 18 years, the company has grown from one outlet in a Pennsylvania farmer's market to more than 850 shops worldwide. Auntie Anne's, which likewise has headquarters in Gap, Pennsylvania, has found a niche among snack-seeking mall shoppers. The company has stores in 44 states.

In 1995, the business also began the process of allowing franchisees to open overseas. There are stores in 13 foreign countries, all because wealthy business people have sought Auntie Anne's out. The company doesn't advertise franchise opportunities, yet applications filter in on a daily basis. Today, the U.S. pretzel company is found in such unlikely spots as Indonesia, Thailand, Venezuela, and Saudi Arabia.

"The pretzel is a bread with a universal language," Beiler says. "The reaction is the same around the world."

The menu has expanded to offer more than pretzels. Customers want to dip their snacks into sauces, so a wide range is available, including cream cheese, marinara, caramel, and sweet mustard. And munching those pretzels can work up quite a thirst, so drinks include old-fashioned lemonade, gourmet coffee, and frozen beverages ranging from wild cherry to mocha.

But it's the pretzels—which are mixed, twisted, and baked in full view of customers—that keep the franchise so popular. There are a dozen varieties, including cinnamon sugar, glazin' raisin, garlic, onion, and sour cream and onion. Yet the unadorned, lightly salted original remains the best seller.

"The pretzel is a bread with a universal language," Beiler says. "The reaction is the same around the world."

Despite the great financial rewards, Beiler, now in her sixties, had no trouble keeping her faith in God at the forefront of her business dealings. She started Auntie Anne's without a high school education, business knowledge, or financial capital.

"My history is one of depending on God," she says. "I know who my Source is. The business is much bigger than I am."

Beiler says she based the company on the Book of Proverbs. The acronym LIGHT forms its statement of purpose: Lead by example; Invest in employees; Give freely; Honor God; and Treat all business contacts with integrity. She believes that God wants Christian men and women to open their own businesses and to find a higher purpose, as she and Jonas did. Jonas went on to found the nonprofit Family Resource and Counseling Center, established in 1992.

"Without the love of my husband and God I wouldn't be here today," Anne says.

In 1999, Auntie Anne's began a foundation that provides funds to groups caring for children and families in need. The Angela Foundation, named after their deceased daughter, contributes money to charities and missionary organizations.

Ignoring early warnings from bankers that they were giving away too much of their profits, the Beilers have consistently donated more than a tenth of their corporate income to ministry causes.

In 2005, founders Anne and Jonas Beiler sold the company to Sam Beiler, a second cousin who had been Auntie Anne's president and chief operating officer since 2001. Anne and Jonas currently are focused on the development of the Gap Family Center to help needy children and families. Anne Beiler's image and likeness continue to be an integral part of the company.

>> DAVID GREEN

A successful entrepreneur promotes eternal values through his creative centers.

The son of a financially strapped pastor, David Green began working in a five-and-dime store at age 15. He learned the ins and outs of merchandising and as a young adult worked his way up to become a supervisor of several stores.

But in 1970, Green and his wife, Barbara, dreamed of owning their own business and they borrowed $600 from a bank to buy a frame chopper and sticks of moldings. In the Oklahoma City family's garage they started a miniature picture frame manufacturing company. Sons Mart and Steve assembled the frames while David and Barbara glued them together.

After a year and a half, they opened their first Hobby Lobby store, which had only 300 square feet of floor space. Although they soon moved into a building with 6,000 square feet, by the fifth year Barbara still couldn't draw a salary and David kept a full-time department store job to make ends meet.

"When you don't have money it takes forever," Green says. In that fifth year, 1974, the company did only $150,000 in sales.

The turning point came in 1975 when Green quit his other job and opened a second, larger store. Revenues in the sixth year totaled $750,000.

By branching out to other markets, Hobby Lobby found its niche. Although local "ma and pa" operations sold similar products, no specialized chain offered arts and crafts supplies, fashion fabrics, baskets, silk flowers, needlework, wearable art, picture framing, greeting cards, party supplies, furniture, and seasonal merchandise under one roof.

Although local "ma and pa" operations sold similar products, no specialized chain offered arts and crafts supplies, fashion fabrics, baskets, silk flowers, needlework, wearable art, picture framing, greeting cards, party supplies, furniture, and seasonal merchandise under one roof.

The company continued to expand and the Greens cultivated a growing clientele among wealthy homeowners looking to furnish their decors. But the 1985 oil bust almost put Hobby Lobby out of business. All of a sudden the upscale product line stopped moving off the shelves. The company lost $1 million. Banks threatened to foreclose.

The Green family spent much focused time in prayer seeking God's direction.

"It was one of the worst times, but also one of the best times in my life," Green says. "We found we had to depend more on God than in our abilities. Talents are of no value without His blessings on our business. God brought us through that time miraculously."

Within a year, Hobby Lobby again was turning a profit. Green has continued to find entrepreneurial success while growing in his faith through regular Bible reading, prayer, and church attendance.

"God has a purpose in all our lives, but that purpose isn't just to gain assets that don't have a purpose for eternity," Green says. "Life is not just to gain riches for ourselves."

Through the years Green has bucked the trend of business owners in secular society who increasingly put profits ahead of God's priorities. In 1999, Hobby Lobby began an 18-month process of closing all its stores on Sundays.

Green figured the company couldn't be true to its statement of purpose if employees missed church and a day with their families because they had to work.

That statement of purpose is unabashedly Christian and includes a section that says the corporation is committed to "serving our employees and their families by establishing a work environment and company policies which build character, strengthen individuals, and nurture families."

At the time, Hobby Lobby did $100 million a year in Sunday revenues.

"I have no regrets," Green says.

The company's statement of purpose concludes: "We believe that it is God's grace and provision that Hobby lobby has endured. He has been faithful in the past, we trust Him for our future."

The company now stocks 60,000 items and is the largest privately held hobby and craft company in the United States. Hobby Lobby has 335 stores in 27 midwestern and southern states. Green intends to keep growing.

"The larger the business, the larger our mission efforts," he says. "We can't get God's blessing unless we use our assets the way God wants us to use them. All that counts is what is eternal, not what's temporal."

Selling decorations for the home is the avenue for the Greens' real goal: spreading the Gospel. Hobby Lobby has purchased millions of dollars worth of real estate and buildings for Christian ministries, schools, and churches.

Its largest undertaking is underwriting an effort to print 180 million copies of *The Book of Hope* so that they may be distributed in more than 100 countries. The publication is a chronological rendering of the four gospels for young people and includes the prayer of salvation at the end. Hobby Lobby also has backed an Every Home for Christ campaign to place the Gospel in more than 40 million homes in Asia.

Part of Green's evangelistic outreach is through Hobby Lobby itself. On Christmas in 1993, Green read the Oklahoma City newspaper and in dismay realized how commercialized the holiday had become.

"I couldn't find any advertisement mentioning the real reason for Christmas," Green recalls. "All the ads said 'Season's Greetings' or 'Happy Holidays.'"

The next year, Hobby Lobby, at a cost of hundreds of thousands of dollars annually, began taking out full-page newspaper ads in every city where it has a store. On Christmas, the ads simply tell about the birth of Jesus and on Easter they explain the resurrection of Christ in succinct, poignant terms. Hundreds of readers have responded to a ministry phone number in the ads and received Christ as Savior.

At this writing, Green remains president of the business. Son Steve is executive vice president of Hobby Lobby. Son Mart is chief executive officer of Mardel Christian, Office, and Educational Supply, a 19-store chain. Daughter Darsee is involved in advertising and product development for Hobby Lobby and its eight affiliate companies.

"We're not planning to branch out to any more companies, but who knows?" Green says.

The corporation has its headquarters in a 2.7 million square-foot manufacturing, distribution, and office complex in Oklahoma City. Hobby Lobby did $1.4 billion in sales during one recent year.

"My response is so what—if we didn't do something of eternal value," Green says.

DAN CATHY

Chick-fil-A continues its Biblical approach to business.

In a sense, Dan T. Cathy has been in the restaurant business his whole life—and then some.

Cathy likes to joke that he has been working at Chick-fil-A since being in the womb of his mother, Jeannette. The chicken chain started by his father, S. Truett Cathy, always has been a family business where everyone helps out. Four years ago Dan became president and chief operating officer of the company his father founded six decades ago.

Dan started his chicken career at age 9 by singing songs for customers at the original diner site, the Dwarf Grill. As a youth he performed a number of menial tasks at that Atlanta diner: picking up trash in the parking lot, washing dirty dishes, extracting chewing gum stuck underneath dining room tables, filling up ketchup and mustard bottles.

When Chick-fil-A began branching out in 1967, it concentrated on retail shopping malls. Over the years, restaurants have been added at locations such as college campuses, hospitals, and airports. Now, the majority are built as freestanding stores. Dan says today's consumers often are incredibly busy, preferring to pick up food from their cars at a drive-through window than going inside a time-consuming mall.

Now in its sixtieth year, staying relevant to an ever-changing marketplace is a challenge for the Atlanta-based Chick-fil-A, which pioneered the boneless breast of chicken sandwich in the quick-service restaurant industry. Chick-fil-A has added fresh fruit and more salad entrees to its menu for a customer base demanding healthier and more nutritional meals. Chicken, of course, remains the staple item, with its preparation being in a multitude of creative ways.

What haven't and won't change are the Biblical principles on which the company is based. They include keeping stores closed on Sundays, a rare decision for a chain in the restaurant trade today. But Chick-fil-A insists that operators and their employees take Sundays off to be with their families, rest, and worship God, if they so choose. Even though that decision has meant a potential loss of 20 percent in business, the chain nevertheless has had 38 straight years of growth, with sales approaching $2 billion annually.

"Our corporate purpose for being is to glorify God by being a faithful steward of all that

He has entrusted to us," Cathy says. "Because of being closed on Sunday, we think our food tastes better on Monday."

Being a privately held corporation not beholden to shareholders is a chief reason Chick-fil-A can remain closed on Sundays.

"We're not answerable to a bunch of Wall Street analysts looking for higher earnings," Cathy says. "That pressure often causes businesses to make short-term decisions that aren't in the best long-term interests of the company."

Cathy credits the stability of the corporation's leadership and operators for keeping Chick-fil-A on course with its corporate purpose. The firm has more than a 96 percent annual stability rate with its franchise operators, and the corporate staff has an even higher retention rate.

In its management style, Cathy says the company focuses more on living out spiritual beliefs than propagating them.

"We aren't hesitant to share our Christian faith and Biblical views, and we're thankful that in the Constitution our forefathers made provision for religious expression, even in the workplace," Cathy says. "However, the most potent way of sharing our faith with others is in the relationships we have in terms of compassion, kindness, and understanding in helping people accomplish their dreams, hopes, and ambitions."

While some other companies founded on Scriptural tenets have stopped being so outspoken in order to not offend an increasingly pluralistic society, Chick-fil-A continues to abide by the Golden Rule.

Chick-fil-A offers several types of enrichment opportunities for its workers, including awarding a $1,000 scholarship to college-bound restaurant employees who have shown leadership, longevity with the chain, and demonstrate school and community involvement. More than $20 million has been awarded since the program started in 1973, resulting in Chick-fil-A scholarship recipients attending more than 1,200 institutions.

In 1984, S. Truett and Jeannette Cathy formed the WinShape Foundation, which provides a variety of services to support youth and marriages. That includes operating a two-week summer camp experience for 1,700 boys and girls every year; providing a loving, stable environment for more than 150 children in 14 foster homes; and sponsoring retreats for couples whose marriages need transformation.

While some other companies founded on Scriptural tenets have stopped being so outspoken in order to not offend an increasingly pluralistic society, Chick-fil-A continues to abide by the Golden Rule.

"Because Jesus Christ died for us all, that gives me the freedom and confidence to share this message of redemption in meaningful ways," Cathy says. "In the complete picture of what's going on, sharing our faith is not only not offensive, it can be incredibly winsome and endearing to others."

For children, Cathy also wants the meal experience to be more than just about food. Rather than a tie-in to the latest Hollywood movie, premiums with kid meals have a more positive, lasting impact with literacy or more values. Recently, a book from the Emmy Award–winning PBS program *Between the Lions* or an audiocassette from the Focus on the Family Adventures in Odyssey series has accompanied kids' meals. In addition to focusing on education and character development, the giveaways are designed to foster conversation between parents and child.

Work doesn't consume all of Cathy's time. Church has been a priority ever since he received Jesus Christ as Lord and Savior at age 12.

He has been playing trumpet for 43 years and he continues to practice nearly every day. He plays occasionally at weddings and sporting events, but every Sunday morning he is on the platform with the rest of the band at New Hope Baptist Church in Fayetteville, Georgia, a suburb of Atlanta.

"I take the responsibility of leading people in worship every seven days very seriously," says Cathy. "There's a difference between playing the notes and playing the music. People worship when the music is played." Jeannette Cathy, who also played the trumpet, instilled a love of the instrument in him as a young boy.

Another passion of Cathy's life is instructing 12th-grade boys in Sunday school every week. He has been a Sunday school teacher for more than 30 years, also a discipline of his father for nearly half a century. Cathy believes that church and Sunday school, unlike local civic organizations, help people develop an eternal outlook on the particulars of everyday life.

"It's a joy to serve the local church," Cathy says. "A local church ministry that impacts the lives of children, young people, and families in a positive way is the greatest community organization that we have."

Chick-fil-A now has more than 40,000 restaurant employees in 1,250 stores in 38 states and Washington, DC. Cathy says putting a franchise in every state isn't a goal; the firm simply wants to be in markets where it makes business sense.

With his customary zeal, S. Truett Cathy, nearly 90 at the time of this writing, continues to work as chairman and chief executive officer at the conglomerate every day. Dan doesn't spend as much time around corporate headquarters because there aren't any chickens or cash registers there. While not home with Rhonda, his wife, he enjoys being with store employees and customers.

BUSINESS & FINANCE

....

REDEMPTIVE FIELD ANALYSIS 1

HONOR STATEMENT: I, the undersigned student, hereby declare before God, before the school, and before the professor that I have read this chapter in its entirety, that I have completed the following exercise with help from no other sources, except as required by the questions, and that I neither have shared nor will share this work with anyone.

Signature: _____   Date: _____

Analysis 1

1. Using words from the fifth chapter, define the term redemptive communicator.

_____

_____

_____

_____

_____

_____

2. Summarize one of this chapter's profiles in the space below. Include the most important details. Omit unnecessary details.

_____

_____

_____

_____

_____

_____

_____

_____

_____

_____

_____

_____

3. If you were asked to use this story or a specific part of this story to support an idea, one that you could present as its main point to an audience, which idea would you present? State this idea as a single declarative sentence in the space that follows:

_____

_____

_____

_____

_____

_____

4. The fifth chapter states that a redemptive communicator interacts with other people in a way that promotes what God values in this world according to Scripture. Review the chapter's list of things that God values. Then, in the space below, identify the specific God-valued thing that this profilee promotes according to the profile. Be sure to explain both how the profilee promotes this specific thing and why you believe this thing is something God values according to Scripture.

_____

_____

_____

_____

_____

_____

_____

_____

_____

_____

_____

_____

_____

_____

_____

_____

5. Which other God-valued things does this profilee promote? Identify these and explain how he or she promotes them.

_____

_____

_____

_____

_____

_____

_____

_____

_____

_____

_____

_____

_____

_____

BUSINESS & FINANCE

....

REDEMPTIVE FIELD ANALYSIS 2

HONOR STATEMENT: I, the undersigned student, hereby declare before God, before the school, and before the professor that I have read this chapter in its entirety, that I have completed the following exercise with help from no other sources, except as required by the questions, and that I neither have shared nor will share this work with anyone.

Signature: _____   Date: _____

Analysis 2

1. Using words from the fifth chapter, define the term redemptive communicator.

_____

_____

_____

_____

_____

_____

_____

_____

2. Summarize another of this chapter's profiles in the space below. Include the most important details. Omit unnecessary details.

_____

_____

_____

_____

_____

_____

_____

_____

_____

_____

_____

_____

_____

_____

3. If you were asked to use this story or a specific part of this story to support an idea, one that you could present as its main point to an audience, which idea would you present? State this idea as a single declarative sentence in the space that follows:

_____

_____

_____

_____

_____

_____

_____

_____

_____

_____

_____

_____

4. The fifth chapter states that a redemptive communicator interacts with other people in a way that promotes what God values in this world according to Scripture. Review the chapter's list of things that God values. Then, in the space below, identify the specific God-valued thing that this profilee promotes according to the profile. Be sure to explain both how the profilee promotes this specific thing and why you believe this thing is something God values according to Scripture.

_____

_____

_____

_____

_____

_____

_____

_____

_____

_____

_____

_____

_____

_____

_____

_____

5. Which other God-valued things does this profilee promote? Identify these and explain how he or she promotes them.

_____

_____

_____

_____

_____

_____

BUSINESS & FINANCE

· ·

REDEMPTIVE FIELD ANALYSIS 3

HONOR STATEMENT: I, the undersigned student, hereby declare before God, before the school, and before the professor that I have read this chapter in its entirety, that I have completed the following exercise with help from no other sources, except as required by the questions, and that I neither have shared nor will share this work with anyone.

Signature: _____   Date: _____

Analysis 3

1. Using words from the fifth chapter, define the term redemptive communicator.

_____

_____

_____

_____

_____

_____

_____

_____

2. Summarize another of this chapter's profiles in the space below. Include the most important details. Omit unnecessary details.

_____

_____

_____

_____

_____

_____

_____

_____

_____

_____

_____

_____

_____

3. If you were asked to use this story or a specific part of this story to support an idea, one that you could present as its main point to an audience, which idea would you present? State this idea as a single declarative sentence in the space that follows:

_____

_____

_____

_____

_____

_____

_____

_____

_____

_____

4. The fifth chapter states that a redemptive communicator interacts with other people in a way that promotes what God values in this world according to Scripture. Review the chapter's list of things that God values. Then, in the space below, identify the specific God-valued thing that this profilee promotes according to the profile. Be sure to explain both how the profilee promotes this specific thing and why you believe this thing is something God values according to Scripture.

_____

_____

_____

_____

_____

_____

_____

_____

_____

_____

_____

_____

_____

_____

_____

_____

5. Which other God-valued things does this profilee promote? Identify these and explain how he or she promotes them.

_____

_____

_____

_____

_____

MUSICAL ARTS >>

MUSICAL ARTS

>> HARRY CAUSEY

Vision becomes reality for the National Christian Choir's founder.

C. Harry Causey began singing while still in the playpen. By age 4 he had learned to play the piano by ear. During elementary school he sang in a children's choir at the Presbyterian church in Rockingham, North Carolina, that his parents attended every week. The young boy loved to talk to his pastor about the Lord and the Bible.

In seventh grade, Causey sensed a calling to the ministry. At an evangelistic crusade conducted by Leighton Ford, Billy Graham's brother-in-law, Causey left his place in the choir and went forward to make a public profession of faith in Jesus Christ as Savior.

"I sought God's guidance as to whether to become a musician or a minister as an adult," Causey remembers. "At that point I never considered the possibility of doing both. I thought I could do only one or the other."

Although he possessed a great deal of musical talent, Causey sought to learn more. That's why he obtained a bachelor of music degree from Davidson College, a master's degree in music composition from Florida State University, and a doctorate in choral conducting from the University of Cincinnati.

During high school, he became the assistant choir director for the adult choir at church, where he also played piano and organ. Yet during the late 1950s and early 1960s, Causey says he learned more about sacred music from his Christian teachers at high school than from church.

"In those days one could be open about faith in school," Causey says. "My teachers were good evangelists in their own way."

Although he possessed a great deal of musical talent, Causey sought to learn more. That's why he obtained a bachelor of music degree from Davidson College, a master's degree in music composition from Florida State University, and a doctorate in choral conducting from the University of Cincinnati.

During his college and postgraduate years, every summer Causey attended choral music workshops conducted by Lara Hoggard, who served as assistant conductor to popular bandleader Fred Waring.

Waring, leading the group called The Pennsylvanians, made choral music popular at the time. Through record albums, radio, television, and concert tours, Waring popularized both secular and sacred music.

Hoggard, a Christian known for his choral conducting, took an interest in Causey, who admired him tremendously. Causey considered the possibility of going into show business—in the hopes of becoming another Fred Waring—or writing music for TV dramas in Hollywood.

But after graduating with his final degree, Causey took a position as a full-time minister of music at a Cincinnati church. Soon after joining the staff at the church in 1969, both Causey and his wife, Elizabeth, reaffirmed their commitment to prioritizing God's call in their lives. Causey determined at that point to remain in music ministry.

Extra summer jobs helped convince him that he had made the right choice. He had been hired to prepare a choir for a Cincinnati Symphony Orchestra concert as well as another choir for a Presbyterian evangelical conference.

"As a newly recommitted Christian, I began to realize how fulfilled the people were who sang for the Lord and how unfulfilled the people were in the secular concerts," Causey says. "In the secular concert the personnel were bickering, complaining, and unhappy. But at the Christian concert they were singing for the Lord, still joyous in the parking lot afterwards."

In the early 1970s, Causey began to dream about forming a national Christian choir, which no one had done in evangelical circles, as a way to exalt Jesus Christ. Despite repeated attempts, he couldn't arrange any financial backing to get such an effort off the ground in Cincinnati.

In 1980, the same year he received his ministerial ordination from the Evangelical Church Alliance, Causey was recruited by Fourth Presbyterian Church minister Richard C. Halverson to become minister of music at that suburban Washington, DC, church.

But a year into Causey's new position, Halverson received an appointment as chaplain of the U.S. Senate. Causey then became a freelance minister of music, starting a workshop and newsletter ministry called Music Revelation to help other music ministers.

"God used the move to Washington, DC, for me to found the National Christian Choir," Causey says. "The nation's capital is the place for this ministry."

In 1983, Christian businessman Ron Doucette contacted Causey about heading up an innovative musical project. Doucette explained that he wanted to honor God by underwriting the expenses of renting Constitution Hall in downtown Washington, DC, if Causey would enlist a choir and orchestra to present an evening of praise and worship. Causey in turn described his vision for the National Christian Choir (NCC) and agreed to conduct the concert if the event served as the birth of the ministry. Doucette consented. Causey convinced Christian radio stations in the area to run free public service announcements for choir auditions. He called his choir director friends around the city and auditions were held at five locations. By the time of the concert, 250 qualified singers had signed up.

"We were extremely diverse when we walked into the room, but within minutes we all realized that God had given us a gift of unity," Causey recalls. "Everyone there was a believer in Christ and we all had the same desire to honor Him."

The January 1984 concert proved to be a great success, and the NCC quickly formed a board of directors. The choir has been going strong ever since, celebrating its silver anniversary this year.

Although Causey is one of five full-time paid staff members, all choir members donate their time. They have weekly Monday night rehearsals at a Baptist church in Rockville, Maryland, during the school year, as well as four practices in the summer. Singers come from a wide geographic area, from Philadelphia in the north to Fredericksburg, Virginia, in the south. Some members drive three hours one way to attend rehearsal.

"They're called by God to this ministry," Causey says. "Every person involved takes commitment seriously."

The NCC performs about a dozen concerts a year around Washington, DC. Once a year, the choir goes on tour for a long weekend somewhere in the United States. Every five years, the NCC goes on an extended trip, to places such as Alaska, Israel, or Eastern Europe. Choir members pay for their own airfare, hotel rooms, ground transportation, and most meals.

Those in the NCC for the most part aren't professional singers but "above average" church choir members, Causey says. They must show a certain amount of proficiency in an audition for reading music, controlling their voice, and blending their voice with others.

Members also must sign a statement of faith. "Even with our different worship styles, churches, backgrounds, traditions, and ages, we all have in common the belief that Jesus Christ is Lord and Savior," Causey says. "We celebrate a great deal of unity in the midst of diversity."

Only five members remain from the first concert 25 years ago, yet the majority has been part of the choir for more than 15 years. Causey says the nearly 200-member choir—which contains singers from 100 regional congregations—has an annual turnover rate of only half a dozen singers.

The choir has made two dozen audio recordings. Causey goes over thousands of new choral releases every year and whittles the list down to a few dozen favorites. In brainstorming sessions with his two accompanists and the rest of his music team, Causey determines what exactly to put on every year's particular compact disc. Each CD has a theme, whether it's hymns, patriotic music, Christmas carols, praise choruses, or inspirational numbers. Causey and his accompanists often arrange the selected pieces for the choir, and they themselves have written a few compositions for the CD recordings. Once the songs are finalized, Causey travels to Indianapolis to record the music in a studio (primarily with musicians from the Indianapolis Symphony Orchestra). Back in Washington, DC, Causey records the choir voices. Then he returns to Indianapolis to mix the voices and instruments for the CD. The entire process—from looking for tunes to pressing a CD—typically takes three years.

The three most popular NCC CDs, with sales approaching 50,000, all deal with providing comfort, peace, and healing: *You are My Hiding Place, Wonderful Peace*, and *Balm in Gilead*. "Those who are sick or who have experienced grief because of the death of a family member find the worshipful music quiets their souls," Causey says.

One of the outreaches of the NCC is a weekly radio program called *Psalm 95*, which began in 2002. Causey came up with the idea of an hour of choir singing interspersed with him offering Scripture readings and inspirational thoughts as host. The worship-laden *Psalm 95* (which starts out "Come, let us sing for joy to the Lord; let us shout aloud to the Rock of our salvation") is the name of the program and helped convince WRBS, a Christian radio station in Baltimore, to carry it. Various choir members put together enough money to put the show on the air for its first 11 weeks. Gradually other radio stations—all of them nonprofits that didn't require payment for commercials—have added the show. Now more than 375 nonprofit stations in all 50 U.S. states and all 13 Canadian provinces carry *Psalm 95*. The program is rebroadcast in 177 foreign countries and on the Armed Forces Network.

Since 1990, the NCC has been sending music (first cassettes and now CDs) to U.S. soldiers overseas. Funds are donated by concertgoers to send the music to troops through the Music for Overseas Military program. More than 50,000 recordings have been sent to military personnel.

Causey says he receives letters frequently from two primary types of audiences who appreciate *Psalm 95*.

"There are elderly people who are unable to get to church or who feel disenfranchised because contemporary music dominates their church," he says. "We also hear from prisoners who tell us over and over that the show gives them hope, peace, and a sense of freedom behind bars."

Psalm 95 still is on WRBS, the only one that charges for airtime. Causey is hoping the NCC can raise funds to expand *Psalm 95* to other commercial stations.

Many choir members have told Causey they are drawn closer to the Lord through the NCC than by their own church.

"We don't want to be a church substitute," Causey says. "But because worship is our priority, we have a lot of worship at rehearsals. Our presentations are more worship service than concert. The purpose of the NCC continues to be to glorify God and draw people into a deeper relationship with Him."

While some NCC music has a contemporary flavor, most of it is in the traditional inspirational style. Most listeners are 65 and older.

"This age group needs someone to preserve the music for them that they love," Causey says. "And I see the pendulum swinging back. There is a renewed interest in choral singing in churches that have abandoned choirs; in liturgical worship among those not liturgically minded; and a discovery of hymns among younger people who never heard hymns before."

Causey knows the day will come when he must pass on his baton.

"But I still have the stamina, health, drive, and desire to stay," he says. "Lord willing, I plan to keep going until I'm at least 75."

By necessity, Causey wears many hats at the NCC. He is music director, executive director, public relations marketing director, and resource development director. Elizabeth, his wife, does volunteer work for the choir, ranging from writing thank you notes to donors to being the orchestra music librarian.

Causey says he may keep some jobs once he can no longer direct.

It's not that Causey is bereft of ideas. He wants to see the NCC acquire a facility for rehearsals. He also wants the NCC to give birth to a national children's choir, youth choir, and adult ensemble.

"I will have to lay it down eventually, but those of us here now hope to leave a legacy," Causey says. "I love my work. I feel called to it."

FERNANDO ORTEGA
An award-winning musician revives a passion for the sacred.

After being challenged by a classmate to pronounce his faith publicly, a young and impassioned Fernando Ortega once stood on top a table and declared for all the art class to hear that Jesus is Lord of his life.

"It wasn't a very orthodox profession of faith," Ortega says, with a chuckle. "But I consider that the moment when I recognized my need for a Redeemer."

Today, this gifted musician seeks to deliver that same message in a less self-serving fashion.

"When I first became a Christian, I told everybody," Ortega recalled. "I was so vocal; it led to some really obnoxious, cringeable moments."

No one is cringing now. This award-winning singer/songwriter is sought after, and his compositions are admired by many. His artistry has been honored with two Dove

Awards—one for Inspirational Album of the Year (2000's *Home*) and one for Bluegrass Recorded Song of the Year for "Children of a Living God" with Alison Krauss. Eight of his singles have reached number one on Christian music charts, and 12 have been nominated for Dove Awards. One of his latest recordings, *The Shadow of Your Wings*, which features the Turtle Island String Quartet, compels listeners to be mindful of God's presence.

Fernando has included at least two hymns on each of his recordings, but nearly half of this latest effort is devoted to hymns and sacred songs. Taking verses from centuries-old Christian liturgy, he aimed to express these classic expressions of worship in music that is suitable for modern audiences. The experience proved to be a faith-building experience for him. Throughout the composition process, he often sensed the hand of God upon the project.

"There was a certain pronouncement, a bending of the knee, an acknowledgement that I can't even worship God unless he gives me breath to do it," he recalls.

For those of us who grew up singing *Holy, Holy, Holy* or *Come, Thou Fount of Every Blessing* every Sunday, it is mind-boggling that many believers have never heard or do not recognize the lyrics of these sacred classics. When Fernando changed the chords and played his musically updated yet worshipful version of *Come, Thou Fount*, many in the congregation where he was leading worship assumed he had written the song. They had never heard the old hymns before.

These congregants were familiar with a more utilitarian style of music, Ortega says; a form of corporate worship involving simple choruses designed to illustrate the speaker's main point. Ortega found such music vacuous. Hymns cover more ground theologically, historically, and lyrically. Ortega defines his own musical style as heavy on the story line. "My hope is that I'm able to take a song about my grandfather, or my wife, or my former landlady, Mildred, and say something about them in a universal way that means something to someone else. I hope I am writing and singing about things that resonate with others, and allows them to see how faith in God can be expressed not only in the most glorious, but even the most mundane moments of our everyday lives."

A musician's life is not all glitz and glamour, and few artists meet with overnight success. Fernando was no child prodigy, but he was unusually talented from a very early age. As an undergraduate at the University of New Mexico, he earned the distinction of being one of the school's most outstanding musicians. "I thought I had a good shot at being a world class pianist if I worked hard enough," he recalls.

His vision abruptly fell short, however, when he auditioned for graduate school.

"As I was walking to the audition I heard one of the pieces I'd chosen to play—one of Chopin's ballades—being played far better than I could play it. I looked into the room and saw that it was being played masterfully by a young Korean girl, 12 to 14 years of age.

"I realized I could practice all I wanted and I would never be able to play like that. My musical gifts were elsewhere—writing music was my gift. That was a real defining moment for me, a moment that changed the course of my life."

Eventually, Ortega went on staff with Campus Crusade for Christ, and led worship for the organization's founder, Dr. Bill Bright. That high-profile position earned him some name recognition and created opportunities for his musical ministry. He even managed to get a record deal with a company that, ironically, ended up going bankrupt.

After that record deal went belly up, Fernando abandoned his quest to make it big with a solo career. He was in his thirties and on staff at the South Coast Community Church in Irvine, California. It was a great place to serve God and others, but it just wasn't the way Ortega envisioned his career unfolding.

A musician's life is not all glitz and glamour, and few artists meet with overnight success. Fernando was no child prodigy, but he was unusually talented from a very early age.

"I experienced a death of a vision. At best, that vision was a pretty empty one," he says now. "Up until that point, my desire to make music was tinged with an ambition to be well known. I hate to think I was that shallow, but playing concerts in front of large audiences was something I longed for. It was a vision that needed to die."

Fernando says he wasn't too upset at God over his failing quest for a musical career, but he was concerned about the fact that he still was single. Why hadn't God sent him the love of his life yet?

"I really wanted to be married. I was sick of living in apartments with roommates."

But before Fernando reached the state of frustration, God moved, as He so often does, in a mighty way. Ortega found the love of his life, literally, right before his nose.

"Margee came in with a friend and sat on the front row in a church where I was worship leader. It was a very social church, with constant chattering during worship, but Margee would be there with her eyes closed, really worshipping God. I found that beautiful." Shortly afterward, they married, and Fernando's recording career took off.

Now that all that professional and personal striving is in his rearview mirror, Fernando devotes his energies to creating songs that minister God's grace. He has a particular compassion for those in mourning. When he first conceived his latest album, he had thought in terms of composing the content of a worship service.

"I wanted to do something liturgical for people who are mourning," Ortega said.

But the songs on *Shadow* go beyond grief. They are about shutting out the noise of the world and turning one's eyes upon Jesus. The songs grew out of Fernando's own heightened sense of frustration over life's clamor.

"This album is like a devotional. It takes concentration and requires you to be quiet and still," he says. "Our culture seems to be getting louder and louder. It's not only loud, it's in your face; indicative, I think, of the influences of television and the Internet. Christian music has followed suit, getting more in your face. It is growing increasingly more difficult to be in a meditative state. I guess that's why I'm drawn to sacred music and hymns."

The other reasons might lie in the musical influences in Ortega's life. Gifted from an early age and raised in a nurturing Christian home, he began to take piano lessons at age 8 from Ralph Berkowitz, of Albuquerque, New Mexico. Berkowitz, an ardent classicist, introduced Ortega to the ballades of Chopin and the concertos of Mozart and Brahms. Add to that, the Mexican and Italian folk songs that are a part of Fernando's Hispanic heritage, and the music education he received at the University of New Mexico, and the result is an enormous talent with eclectic skill. All of which Ortega devotes to serving God.

Now that God has given him the desires of his heart, Ortega says he's learned a few more lessons about what it takes to succeed as an artist.

"It's way more work than I ever imagined, but incredibly fulfilling."

Still, he is keenly aware that all that he has, all that he is, is because of God's faithfulness, not his own.

"People have an elevated expectation of me as a person, as a Christian," he observes. "An expectation that, of course, is beyond my ability to rise to. I find that disappointing, but ultimately, it sends me to my knees and makes me recognize my need for God and my constant dependence on Him."

There's nothing complex about this for any of us—life at its fullest is just an old sweet tune about Jesus and His love.

Rapt silence grips the concert hall. All eyes are riveted on center stage as Christopher Parkening's hands trip masterfully up and down his guitar.

"Wow," whispers one captivated fan. "That's so awesome!" he quietly exclaims, while gleefully plucking his own "air guitar" right there in the plush velour seats of the symphony hall.

You wouldn't normally find such a scene at a classical music concert, listening to Joaquin Rodrigo's "Adagio" from *Concierto de Aranjuez*. But then, Christopher Parkening isn't the typical classical guitarist.

Arguably the world's best, Parkening hasn't just mastered the guitar technically; he *inspires* people with it. At intermission, admirers devour the man's CDs, videos, and method books, and then shift down the table like a herd of cattle to have them signed by the Grammy-nominated virtuoso. Unlike your garden-variety rock star, though, Parkening attracts a wide-ranging demographic. From a budding, slick-haired classical guitarist who wants to take a picture with his hero, to a bespectacled, balding grandfather seeking an autograph, it seems everybody can sense musical greatness in their midst.

Take a closer look, though, and you'll see a classical guitarist who isn't just an inspiring musician. There on the table, prominently arrayed in front of his autograph-signing area, are several CD-sized booklets. With every signature and handshake, Parkening offers one of these unassuming little items, and if you're not careful, you might miss the title that appears on them: "Life Story and Christian Testimony."

Talk to Parkening for five minutes and you quickly discern that his true passion is telling others about his relationship with Jesus Christ. Don't misunderstand: He loves his music. He plays more than 50 concerts a year and has released more than 13 recordings. Yet in many ways his guitar is a means to an end.

"The Lord has opened up a million opportunities for me to share my faith in Christ," Parkening says.

In addition to distributing printed versions of his personal testimony, he delivers his testimony at churches across the country, presents the Gospel to students in his classes, and discusses it with his peers.

The man has a lot to be thankful for: he is a one-in-a-million talent, with droves of adoring fans, and a platform to influence them. Yet there was a time when he almost threw it all away—not for the Gospel, but for a trout stream in southwest Montana.

Mercurial Rise to Fame

A child of the post–World War II era, Parkening grew up in a God-fearing southern California home. His mother and father took him to church regularly, and he learned many basic truths of the Christian faith. "They told me I was a Christian, and I always believed that I was," he recalls.

As a kid Parkening's focus was his guitar. Parkening chose the instrument at age 11 and plunged in head-first.

Yet, as with many who grow up in the church, knowing about Christ didn't affect his life much. He wasn't a rebellious kid. In fact, he was very disciplined, which could help explain his mercurial rise to fame by the age of 19. Yet it could also have fed some self-reliance that kept him from depending on God.

"I believed all the right facts, and I suppose that I even wanted a Savior to save me from hell," Parkening says, "but what I did not want was a Lord of my life that I should follow and trust and be obedient to."

No, as a kid his focus was his guitar. Parkening chose the instrument at age 11 and plunged in head-first. Encouraged by his father, he got up at 5:00 each morning and practiced for an hour and a half before school, then put in another 90-minute session in the afternoon.

Within four years, he had landed a rare spot in a class being taught by Andres Segovia, generally regarded to be the greatest classical guitarist ever. At 15, Parkening was the youngest of only nine students in the select class.

Before he left his teens, the prodigy had been asked to start a guitar department at the University of Southern California, and had signed a six-album recording contract with Capitol Records. Soon he was touring the world, playing roughly 90 concerts a year and wowing audiences with his extraordinary talent.

But Parkening soon realized that the life of a touring solo musician wasn't for him.

"I hated it," he says. "One major city after the next; the monotony of the concerts; the pressure of them; the plane flights; the hotel rooms."

He still loved the music, but he was already burning out from the rigorous schedule of teaching, practicing, recording, and touring that his newfound fame had brought.

"It was a means to an end for me," he says.

Early Retirement

The "end" that Parkening sought was retirement.

"My father had retired at the age of 47, so I thought that 30 would be a very good age to retire," he says. "I thought, *I'll still be in the prime of life.*"

Retirement would give him time to pursue his other passion: fly-fishing. As with his guitar playing, Parkening had become an expert fly-fisherman. It was an escape for him. He loved to wade into the cool water of a stream and enjoy the scenery as he fished for trout. "I thought, *If I could buy a ranch someday with my own trout stream, and not have to work . . . I would be happy,*" Parkening remembers.

It was this dream that helped him endure what had become the drudgery of the concert life.

Come age 30, Parkening had reached his goal. Having made his fortune, he promptly set out to find his trout stream. And he found it, on a ranch in southwestern Montana. Parkening then called his record company, his concert promoter, and his university and told them he was walking away.

For a while, he lived—and loved—"the good life."

It took about a year, but the joy of retirement and fishing-til-you-drop finally began to wear off.

"I started thinking, *This is not what I thought it would be. I'm unfulfilled. I am unhappy,*" he says. "It was without purpose, and I sensed that."

"Lord, Lord"

Whether he realized it or not, his nagging lack of purpose set Parkening on a search for significance in his life. Yet he didn't take the easy road and fall back on his guitar. He stayed retired, for the time being.

During a visit to southern California, a neighbor invited him to church. Having grown up in a church-going family, the decision to go was no big deal. In fact, he still regularly attended church in Montana. But this church—Grace Community Church in Sun Valley—was different from anything he had found.

"I was shocked that everybody had a Bible," Parkening recalls.

He got another jolt as he listened to the sermon that day. Speaking from Matthew 7, Pastor John MacArthur discussed Jesus's warning: "Not everyone that saith unto me, Lord, Lord, shall enter into the kingdom of heaven; but he that doeth the will of my Father which is in heaven." The words hit Parkening squarely between the eyes. He realized immediately that simply going to church and knowing some facts about Jesus wasn't good enough. That night, he recalls, Parkening received Christ as Savior.

Finding Purpose

Parkening knew immediately upon receiving Christ that he had finally found the path to purpose in his life. He devoured MacArthur's sermon tapes, absorbing all the Bible teaching he could find.

Parkening grew so fond of MacArthur that one year he drove three Montana pastors down for a conference MacArthur was leading. When Parkening arrived, the pastor surprised the lapsed guitarist by asking him to perform and give his testimony.

The thought terrified Parkening. "First of all, I hadn't played in public for four years," he recalls. "Secondly, I'd never given my Christian testimony."

Yet he did it, and afterward MacArthur approached Parkening and encouraged him to pick up the guitar again—this time for a different purpose.

A Different Kind of Fishing Pole

Shortly after his talk with MacArthur, Parkening sensed God's call to more actively glorify Him with his life.

"There were only two things I knew how to do," he says. "One was fly-fishing for trout, and the other was playing the guitar. The latter seemed the better option to pursue."

So, in 1981, after four years away from playing professionally, Parkening called his recording and concert-management companies and told them he wanted back in.

There was no doubt Parkening was playing with newfound purpose and energy. With each concert, he sought not just to play with excellence, but to truly "honor the Creator" by playing his music "from the heart."

Yet, as he grew in his faith, he realized God wanted more than just a soulful performance. "I realized that as good a motive as that is, it is incomplete apart from making disciples for Christ," he says.

At first, he wondered how he could possibly share the Gospel as a concert guitarist. He could try preaching from the stage, but he wouldn't be invited back to many places if he did. Yet his heart was willing, and soon God began to open opportunities.

For example, he found that he had an audience whenever he taught a class. After the instruction was over, he frequently had the chance to tell his students what truly motivated him.

Parkening's stature as a musician also has given him an entrée with his peers—such as leading film-score composers John Williams and Elmer Bernstein—to present the Gospel.

Then there were the concerts, with their aspiring guitarists and adoring fans who were eager to soak up whatever wisdom the man has to offer.

"They will listen to anything you have to say," he says.

Now, he uses every occasion he gets to describe to others the life and purpose he has found in Christ, which is undoubtedly why he lingers after each performance to sign autographs and pass out his printed testimony.

It's funny, when you think about it: The gift that a man once gave up so he could fish for trout is now a gift that God uses to fish for men.

DIANE BISH
The First Lady of the Pipe Organ

Fifteen-year-old organist Diane Bish weighed her options. Two churches desired her skills—one boasted a magnificent pipe organ and offered a tempting salary, the other housed a mediocre instrument and paid a lower wage.

God, show me Your will, prayed Bish. *Where do You want to best use the talent You've given me?* The teen recalled Matthew 6:33: "But seek ye first the kingdom of God, and his righteousness; and all these things shall be added unto you." Her passion for God tipped the scale. Bish chose the more menial job.

"It was a difficult decision, but I felt at home in that church," she recalls years later from her home in Bloomington, Indiana. "I felt I could worship wholeheartedly there. I think the Lord has blessed that decision throughout my life."

More than four decades after her humble beginnings, Bish is perhaps the world's most visible organist. Her recordings, compositions, and weekly television appearances on "The Joy of Music" have earned international acclaim. She performs approximately 35 classical concerts (regularly fighting nervous jitters) across North America annually. Critics applaud her performances as "stunning, virtuoso, fiery, and astonishing." In 1989, The National Federation of Music Clubs of America awarded Bish the National Citation— "the highest honor for distinguished service to the musical, artistic, and cultural life of the nation."

Piano lessons at age six began Bish's musical career. She practiced diligently and won numerous competitions, but before long, a different instrument fascinated her. Every Sunday morning, her father's radio brought an organ's rich resonance into the family's home. And every week Bish admired the organ in her church sanctuary. She eyed the "king of instruments" and observed the musician's feet fly across its pedals. She watched her change its settings and listened to its majestic anthems. *Someday I'll play the organ, too*, she thought.

At age 14, her legs finally able to reach the pedals, Bish's dream came true. Her parents purchased an organ to facilitate her practice schedule. Before long she was playing concertos on her school's pipe organ and landed her first church organist position.

Bish continued her studies, winning national organ and composition competitions under Mildred Andrews's tutelage at the University of Oklahoma. She received Fulbright and French government grants for study in Amsterdam and Paris. Upon returning to the United States, Bish received a job offer from Dr. James Kennedy, pastor of Fort Lauderdale's Coral Ridge Presbyterian Church.

"I visited the church, saw its small organ, and declined. I took a teaching position at a university with a strong organ department instead," says Bish. "I worked there for a year, but throughout that entire time I sensed the Lord telling me I belonged at Coral Ridge."

Discovering that the church organist position was still available, Bish made the move. Her decision spawned a 20-year tenure filled with innovative methods for musically presenting the Gospel of Jesus Christ—a vision she'd embraced since receiving Christ as her Savior while attending a revival meeting at the age of five.

"Through grade school, junior high, and senior high, I wanted to spread God's Word," she says. "I witnessed whenever, wherever possible. I wanted to evangelize the world. I still do!"

Bish's extraordinary musical ability is her tool. When Coral Ridge built a bigger facility, she designed its 117-rank Ruffatti featuring 7,000 pipes, considered one of the world's greatest organs today. She then cofounded the largest church-concert series in history. Averaging 14 concerts from November through April, the series draws people who don't normally attend church. Each concert attracts more than 1,000 folks. She clearly presents the Gospel message throughout the program.

Bish also founded the Church Music Explosion, an ongoing, annual, five-day workshop for national church and university musicians. Attendees study various aspects of music ministry: how to lead worship, how to hold a concert series in one's own church, how to use music as an evangelism tool, how to pursue musical excellence, and for church-goers who don't yet have a personal relationship with Jesus—how to become a Christian.

In 1982, Bish's expertise led to yet another evangelism opportunity through the launching of her television program, "The Joy of Music." The weekly show continues more than 20 years later, sponsored by donations totaling $400,000 annually. With satellite broadcasting, it reaches between 150 and 200 million viewers worldwide on both Christian and secular stations.

Bish's mandate? "To provide inspiration through great classical and sacred music and share the Gospel through the testimonies of classical artists who are Christian. I also want to feature famous cathedrals and organs, and tell the stories of faith behind them."

To accomplish that goal, she has produced 400 episodes of "The Joy of Music" in three categories. The first explores the Bible's teachings regarding music—the singing voice, the trumpet, the harp, the pipes, stringed instruments, and more. Outstanding artists sing or play corresponding instruments and tell their salvation testimony. The second category highlights renowned Christian composers' and artists' spiritual lives.

The third category takes viewers on musical journeys to stately palaces, museums, monasteries, and cathedrals around the world. Bish plays the organ, shows the artwork and Biblical paintings, and tells well-researched stories about the massive structures and the faith of those who built them.

"Other documentaries might teach about the world's historic cathedrals, but they don't mention the faith that built them, the faith that resonates from them, or the Creator God and Jesus Christ," says Bish. "'The Joy of Music' always acknowledges God as Creator and Inspirer of great art, of the Church, and the music that flows from it."

The television program regularly whisks its viewers to locations such as Hamburg, Germany, where St. Jacobi Church houses an organ played by musical masters including Bach. It transports them to the Market Church in Halle, Germany, where young Handel played for church services.

It carries them to Bish's favorite—St. Bavo Cathedral in Haarlem, Holland, located around the corner from Corrie ten Boom's father's clock shop. Chatting over breakfast one morning, Corrie told Bish that, as a young girl, she sat in that church and listened to the music being played.

"In my opinion, St. Bavo's 'Great Golden Organ' is the world's finest, rising 90 feet high and dating to 1737," says Bish. "It's an organist's mecca. Even Handel and Mozart made special trips to play this instrument."

At age 14, her legs finally able to reach the pedals, Bish's dream came true. Her parents purchased an organ to facilitate her practice schedule. Before long she was playing concertos on her school's pipe organ and landed her first church organist position.

Historical data fascinates Bish and the program's viewers, but the show offers more than interesting statistics. It reveals a spiritual heritage often wrought through physical suffering. In a typical episode, viewers might see Germany's Ulm cathedral, boasting the highest spire in Europe. Bish tells how the townspeople built it from their own sweat, tirelessly carrying stones and stacking them one atop the other.

"Some folks spent their entire lives building this place of worship in the city's center. They did all the work themselves; they didn't hire engineers or other people to do it. It was an extension of their faith, not just a place to visit once in a while. We dare not forget our fathers' faith that has brought us to where we are today," she says.

Many of her travelogues feature guest artists' testimonies and musical performances celebrating the Christian faith's great hymns. "Our spiritual heritage comes to us through the arts in many ways," says Bish. "We must not lose the great hymns. They're not folk—here today and gone tomorrow. They are statements of faith that flow from our Christian heritage.

"The hymns we've heard over the years often come from Scripture—we must not let them pass away. They're doctrine. They're strong."

Stating that she personally finds much encouragement not only in Scripture but also in hymns, Bish recites lyrics from "How Firm a Foundation," written in the 1700s:

> *Fear not, I am with thee, O be not dismayed,*
> *For I am thy God, I will still give thee aid;*
> *I'll strengthen thee, help thee, and cause thee to stand,*
> *Upheld by My gracious, omnipotent hand.*

On October 30, 2002, these lyrics gripped Bish afresh. That night, fire destroyed her home and consumed nearly every earthly possession—her grand piano and organ, car, clothing, her artist father's paintings, and photos. Devastated, Diane found comfort and hope in the lyrics she knows by heart.

It's her desire that others find the same hope and comfort through the One about Whom the lyrics are written. But not everyone appreciates her evangelistic zeal.

"I've received numerous letters from public TV stations saying that 'The Joy of Music' is a great show, but they don't want Scripture readings. They don't want artists' salvation testimonies or God's name mentioned. I've had to choose between deleting the ministry part and remaining on secular stations or leaving it in and losing my place." True to her passion for God, Bish seeks His kingdom first and maintains the ministry focus.

"I believe we must honor God in the most excellent way possible," says Bish. "We must give Him our best efforts, glorifying Him with the talents He's given us." She's doing exactly that.

MUSICAL ARTS

....

REDEMPTIVE FIELD ANALYSIS 1

HONOR STATEMENT: I, the undersigned student, hereby declare before God, before the school, and before the professor that I have read this chapter in its entirety, that I have completed the following exercise with help from no other sources, except as required by the questions, and that I neither have shared nor will share this work with anyone.

Signature: _____   Date: _____

Analysis 1

1. Using words from the fifth chapter, define the term redemptive communicator.

_____

_____

_____

_____

_____

_____

2. Summarize one of this chapter's profiles in the space below. Include the most important details. Omit unnecessary details.

_____

_____

_____

_____

_____

_____

_____

_____

_____

_____

_____

_____

_____

3. If you were asked to use this story or a specific part of this story to support an idea, one that you could present as its main point to an audience, which idea would you present? State this idea as a single declarative sentence in the space that follows:

_____

_____

_____

_____

_____

_____

4. The fifth chapter states that a redemptive communicator interacts with other people in a way that promotes what God values in this world according to Scripture. Review the chapter's list of things that God values. Then, in the space below, identify the specific God-valued thing that this profilee promotes according to the profile. Be sure to explain both how the profilee promotes this specific thing and why you believe this thing is something God values according to Scripture.

_____

_____

_____

_____

_____

_____

_____

_____

_____

_____

_____

_____

_____

_____

_____

_____

5. Which other God-valued things does this profilee promote? Identify these and explain how he or she promotes them.

_____

_____

_____

_____

_____

_____

_____

_____

_____

_____

_____

_____

_____

MUSICAL ARTS

....

REDEMPTIVE FIELD ANALYSIS 2

HONOR STATEMENT: I, the undersigned student, hereby declare before God, before the school, and before the professor that I have read this chapter in its entirety, that I have completed the following exercise with help from no other sources, except as required by the questions, and that I neither have shared nor will share this work with anyone.

Signature: _____   Date: _____

Analysis 2

1. Using words from the fifth chapter, define the term redemptive communicator.

_____

_____

_____

_____

_____

_____

_____

_____

2. Summarize another of this chapter's profiles in the space below. Include the most important details. Omit unnecessary details.

_____

_____

_____

_____

_____

_____

_____

_____

_____

_____

_____

_____

_____

3. If you were asked to use this story or a specific part of this story to support an idea, one that you could present as its main point to an audience, which idea would you present? State this idea as a single declarative sentence in the space that follows:

_____

_____

_____

_____

_____

_____

_____

_____

_____

_____

_____

4. The fifth chapter states that a redemptive communicator interacts with other people in a way that promotes what God values in this world according to Scripture. Review the chapter's list of things that God values. Then, in the space below, identify the specific God-valued thing that this profilee promotes according to the profile. Be sure to explain both how the profilee promotes this specific thing and why you believe this thing is something God values according to Scripture.

_____

_____

_____

_____

_____

_____

_____

_____

_____

_____

_____

_____

_____

_____

_____

_____

5. Which other God-valued things does this profilee promote? Identify these and explain how he or she promotes them.

_____

_____

_____

_____

_____

_____

MUSICAL ARTS

....

REDEMPTIVE FIELD ANALYSIS 3

HONOR STATEMENT: I, the undersigned student, hereby declare before God, before the school, and before the professor that I have read this chapter in its entirety, that I have completed the following exercise with help from no other sources, except as required by the questions, and that I neither have shared nor will share this work with anyone.

Signature: _____   Date: _____

Analysis 3

1. Using words from the fifth chapter, define the term redemptive communicator.

_____

_____

_____

_____

_____

_____

_____

_____

2. Summarize another of this chapter's profiles in the space below. Include the most important details. Omit unnecessary details.

_____

_____

_____

_____

_____

_____

_____

_____

_____

_____

_____

_____

_____

3. If you were asked to use this story or a specific part of this story to support an idea, one that you could present as its main point to an audience, which idea would you present? State this idea as a single declarative sentence in the space that follows:

_____

_____

_____

_____

_____

_____

_____

_____

_____

_____

4. The fifth chapter states that a redemptive communicator interacts with other people in a way that promotes what God values in this world according to Scripture. Review the chapter's list of things that God values. Then, in the space below, identify the specific God-valued thing that this profilee promotes according to the profile. Be sure to explain both how the profilee promotes this specific thing and why you believe this thing is something God values according to Scripture.

_____

_____

_____

_____

_____

_____

_____

_____

_____

_____

_____

_____

_____

_____

_____

5. Which other God-valued things does this profilee promote? Identify these and explain how he or she promotes them.

_____

_____

_____

_____

_____

_____

PERFORMING ARTS ››

PERFORMING ARTS

>> JOHN DAVID WARE

A filmmaker uses Scripture to help teach his craft.

John David Ware's vocational and spiritual trajectory changed forever in 1997 on the day his car got rear-ended by a vanload of missionaries. Ware had just moved to Los Angeles from Columbus, Ohio. It turned out the missionaries, returning from Mexico, were from the same church he attended in his native Columbus.

Ware and the missionaries began talking, and the missionaries soon discovered that while Ware accepted Jesus intellectually, he really had not made a commitment with his heart. He had tried to believe and to know, but he couldn't. But he was seeking.

"Accepting aspects like the Virgin Birth and the Resurrection had been difficult for me, because I was too logical," Ware recalls. "Actually believing the incredible story of Christ is a gift. He did prove himself to me."

© 2012 by Yuriy Ponomarev.
Used under license of Shutterstock, Inc.

Ware eventually founded the 168 Film Project, a competition that has furthered the careers of many emerging filmmakers.

Ware began attending Bel Air Presbyterian Church, where he cofounded SLATE: Salt and Light Aimed Toward Entertainment. He eventually founded the 168 Film Project, a competition that has furthered the careers of many emerging filmmakers. The faith-based speed program pits teams against each other to create a short film in just one week—that is, 168 hours. The films are shown at a festival, with top scripts vying for cash, prizes, and introductions to veteran Hollywood moviemakers.

Ware knew he was destined for Los Angeles when he graduated with a degree in mass communication and video production at Miami University in Ohio. As the son of two schoolteachers and the brother of two siblings who became psychiatrists, Ware fought the urge to go to Tinseltown. Instead he got a job in Ohio making instructional videos.

But the call to move to L.A. proved irresistible, even though he had no family and no friends there. Nevertheless, Ware quickly found production work on some major projects such as *Independence Day* and then did some screenwriting of his own. But as work on movies dried up, Ware discovered a knack for professional audio/video sales with manufacturer representatives in Los Angeles. In his first year, he sold more than $1 million worth of video and audio gear. More importantly, over seven years, he developed relationships with multiple manufacturers, such as Sony, Arri, and Eiki, which have become sponsors of the 168 Film Project.

Likewise, numerous actors, directors, and producers in the moviemaking business have come to recognize the professionalism and quality of the festival.

"We wanted to give people the chance to do something significant for their career based on God's Word," Ware says. "So we gave them seven days, which is plenty of time to shoot and edit an 11-minute-or-less film. They also get 10 days of preproduction after receiving their foundational Scripture. Giving them time to prepare means that they can walk away with a reel to be proud of, on both sides of the camera."

The first year, participants made 13 films and premiered to a standing-room-only crowd. Word of mouth spread that it could be a tremendous showcase for actors, producers, and directors wanting to break into the business. As of 2010, approximately 6,500 cast and crew have participated, including teams from nearly 30 countries, such as China, Russia,

Israel, Indonesia, and Cameroon. Around 300 Bushmen participated on missionary Greg Yost's team. By April 2011, more than 500 short films will have been made for the 168 Film Project. Contenders pay an entry fee of $168 to $298, depending on when they register.

"We don't allow writing before the verse is given," Ware says. "We want them to fall in love with Scripture over the story, and to take the full opportunity to grow their faith and trust God to deliver a great story in a very short time."

The 168 hours—24 hours times seven days—refers to the actual shooting and editing time available to complete a short film that runs under 11 minutes. Here's how it works: Contestants are randomly assigned one of 70 Bible verses, connected to the year's theme (2010's was "Hearing God"), on which to build their film. While the verse itself doesn't necessarily have to be voiced or read in the picture, the subject matter clearly should reveal the message. Before filming, entrants have 10 days to do the writing and casting, as well as to pick the location and schedule for the one-week shooting. Some studios provide free locations for filming.

"Locally, we help them with a casting session, which speeds up the process," Ware says. "Callbacks are the same day and many productions are cast in just one day. We encourage those out of L.A. to mimic our process."

Many participants hire their own actors. And some wise actors even become producers, thereby creating tailor-made roles for themselves. Producers are responsible for raising their own budgets. Filming budgets range from next to nothing to up to $15,000. Ware encourages prayer throughout the process, pairing teams with prayer partners with the help of local ministry via the Hollywood Prayer Network.

"We tell them they are going to need the prayer and most of them believe it before the contest," Ware says. "All of them believe it afterwards."

While many of those involved in the venture are Christians, it's not a requirement. Indeed, Ware notes that some agnostics have moved closer to the Christian faith upon completing a 168 Film Project. Entrants must follow rules that call for a respectful interpretation of Scripture without gratuitous sex, violence, or obscenity. Blasphemy and heresy aren't permitted. Yet the films aren't to be mere caricatures spouting Bible verses. Screenplays are expected to show authentic characters in redemptive, thought-provoking stories that honor God.

In 2008, *Coppelius* was produced in Germany by Travis, the only Christian on the team. His agnostic film-school crew was excited—until they heard it was a Christian contest. Nevertheless, they went through the process diligently. Nowhere else would a group of agnostics find common ground with Christians studying 1 Peter 2:16 (Live as free men, but do not use your freedom as a cover-up for evil; live as servants for God). Travis's team shot in a bomb shelter, which had been inactive since World War II. After initial meetings, the curators mistakenly thought the filmmakers had written graffiti on the walls. The equation had been there for a long time, like a divine trail of breadcrumbs to these filmmakers: 12 x 14 + 168.

Later, after *Coppelius* won awards at the 168 Film Festival, Travis and the film's director Matthias told Ware that God had revealed himself through several other miracles as they made their film. "After 168, I consider myself a seeker because I can no longer deny the truth of the words of Jesus," Matthias told Ware. The last line in *Coppelius* is, "What is freedom's worth if not used for honoring God?"

Awards at the 168 Film Festival are given in 18 categories including director, actor, actress, screenplay, cinematography, editing, original score, makeup, newcomer, international film, and best Gospel of Jesus presentation.

Some of the greatest prizes in the 168 Film Project are opportunities to interact with some industry players. Those judging in 2010 included producer Ralph Winter (*X-Men Origins: Wolverine* and *Fantastic Four*), writer-producer Luke Schlehaas (*Law and Order* and *Smallville*) and writer-producer Brian Bird (*Touched by an Angel* and *Not Easily Broken*.) "Both Christian and non-Christian filmmakers love story," Ware says. "We're trying to teach them to be in love with Scripture, too, and to experience how a verse can guide their work and improve their art."

The films are shown in a jam-packed two-day festival, with awards announced on the final night. Once made, filmmakers own the rights to the movies. Some have taken them to other film festivals where they have won many awards.

"The films are a calling card to bigger things," Ware says. "We have launched and furthered many careers."

For instance, Robert Kirbyson, who produced two 168 Films, directed his first feature film in 2010, *Snowmen* (MPower Pictures).

Josh Weigel, who won eight awards at the 2008 festival, including best picture, won $100,000 with his film *The Butterfly Circus*, which has been downloaded more than five million times.

In October 2010, the 168 Film Project sponsored its second annual Write of Passage Screenwriting Competition. The mentored competition provides an amazing opportunity for writers to improve as they compete, with the goal of developing redemptive, inspirational stories that honor God. Writers don't have to create overtly Christian characters, but if they do, then authentic Christian characters are encouraged as opposed to one-dimensional caricatures. Writers are directed to create stories that at least hint of redemption, as the whole of the Bible points to Jesus as humanity's redemption. The contest is likewise Scripture-based: a theme, a verse a week.

What's next for Ware? He is working on expanding the 168 Film Project by adding a new film festival called Sermon Story, which targets church production staff. Films produced at any time are eligible, provided they have been made for a church and are no longer than 168 seconds. Winners will be crowned at a new exhibition in Las Vegas at the National Association of Broadcasters Show Convention attended by 80,000 people.

"We know how hard church production staff work every week to entertain and illustrate sermons," Ware says. "We want to reward and recognize their excellence and dedication. The award is long overdue for this previously unheralded genre."

>> TED BAEHR
Transforming Tinseltown

Ted Baehr knows the entertainment industry. Having grown up the child of Robert "Ted" Allen and Evelyn Peirce—who were both successful stage, screen, and television actors—Ted understands it not only as an observer, but as one who functioned as part of the culture, performing as a child in commercials, movies, television, and stage productions.

As others in the industry, Baehr adopted a skeptical view of religion as he grew older. By age 20, Baehr said, "I was pretty footloose and fancy free and slightly anti-Christian." Never did he imagine that one day he would be president of the Christian Film and Television Commission.

Religion was something than angered Baehr during his early years. He had been only 14 when his mother, a lukewarm Christian Scientist who embraced the notion that doctors should be shunned in favor of faith-healing, died.

"That convinced me the whole religion thing was wrong," Baehr recalls. It was this attitude that Baehr packed up and took to Dartmouth College and New York University School of Law, where he earned his law degree.

But Baehr's life changed in 1975. Without an audience to applaud him, or TelePrompTer to lead him, Baehr received the living Christ after responding to a friend's challenge to read the Bible.

Baehr knew he believed the Gospel when he had read "about halfway through the Gospel of Matthew," he recalls. He knows it sounds simplistic, but for a man trained to find evidence, he needed to look no further than the Word of God itself to be persuaded by its message.

Baehr's relationship with Christ impacted his life in a profound way, but it did not take away his passion for the art of acting. Instead of tossing a blanket of condemnation on all things Hollywood, Baehr saw the entertainment industry as needful of God's grace.

© 2012 by Konstantin Sutyagin.
Used under license of Shutterstock, Inc.

The message Hollywood needs to hear is a message of hope.

"I had been involved in financing and producing films," he recalls. "I thought there had to be a way to be redemptive in the film industry."

Setting out to find that way, Baehr learned that prior to 1960 several Protestant churches had maintained their own film offices in Hollywood. A cadre of Christians wielded influence over the kinds of movies being produced.

"The church had been the predominant influence in Hollywood. After the church film offices were closed, the movies went south," Baehr says.

He set out to find a way to rebuild the temple. After consulting George Heimrich, who had been director of the Protestant Film Office, Baehr formed the Christian Film and Television Commission in 1986. Working along with Heimrich and other prominent members of the industry, Baehr continues to serve as a liaison between studio executives and the public at large.

"Our main mission is to redeem the values of media," Baehr said. "The organization's purpose finds its basis in a challenge from Scripture, 'For though we walk in the flesh, we do not war after the flesh: (For the weapons of our warfare are not carnal, but mighty through God to the pulling down of strongholds;) Casting down imaginations, and every high thing that exalteth itself against the knowledge of God, and bringing into captivity every thought to the obedience of Christ'" (2 Cor. 10:3–5).

As a father, Baehr personally understands the need for wholesome family entertainment. So, each year he selects the 10 best family-friendly and 10 best morally-edifying films of the year and gives out awards to the producers, directors, writers, and distribution companies of those films. Baehr also presents the coveted $25,000 Epiphany Prizes for the most inspiring movies and television programs.

"In the past 15 years we have seen the number of programs aimed at families rise from 6 percent to 40 percent. And 95 percent of those have a strong Christian context," Baehr reports. Money talks in Hollywood, so Baehr is careful to phrase his case for morally excellent productions in terms of box office receipts when he talks to industry officials.

Baehr understands that what he does requires a keen sensitivity to the Scriptural challenge of being wise as serpents and harmless as doves (Matt. 10:16). He believes that simply bashing the TV tube and giving up on Hollywood altogether contradicts the example of Christ, who consistently engaged sinners of all stripes, helping them see the truth rather than giving up on them. Recalling a quote from C. S. Lewis, Baehr says, "The problem with evil for us as Christians is that we either become desensitized to it, or hypersensitive to it."

Recalling Paul and Peter's journeys in Acts, Baehr states, "They were driven to some pretty awful places, but God went with them, in order to redeem the people."

The message Hollywood needs to hear is a message of hope, Baehr concludes. "I don't think we are up against an unsolvable problem. [As Lewis observed] 'God's Word inspires us with the tools we need to overcome the world.'"

LARRY POLAND

The Media Master

"Have you ever considered ministering to media people, those in the entertainment industry?" The question put to him in 1980 by a friend caught Dr. Larry Poland by surprise. A former pastor and once president of Miami Christian College, he headed the International Agape ministry of Campus Crusade for Christ, and believed he was in it for the long haul.

"No," he answered. "Why would I want to minister to Americans when so many people overseas are going to hell? Like other Americans, people in the media can hear the Gospel on radio and television, and they can't miss seeing John 3:16 painted somewhere on rocks and signs."

"But," the friend countered, "what about the influence of the media on values that are affecting people everywhere, including Christians? Larry, pray about it. It's a missionary field."

The challenge got to him. "I began to read everything I could get my hands on to understand how the entertainment industry works, who controls it, what the culture is," Larry says.

For six months, he and a team made phone calls to movers and shakers in the entertainment industry to determine how personal beliefs and faith (or the lack of it) affect their lives and decisions. "At the conclusion of the survey," he says, "I had a dramatic, new perspective of Hollywood. I had envisioned dark, smoke-filled rooms with people in black capes dancing around, saying, 'Bubble, bubble, how can we steal the soul of America?' But I found no conspiracy. It would presuppose some kind of organization. And organizing Hollywood would be like herding cats."

He found that people in the entertainment business are "bright, fun people, but most of them are very lost."

He found that people in the entertainment business are "bright, fun people, but most of them are very lost." Hollywood and New York media people, he realized, were in a nearly century-long famine of God's Word and desperately needful of a witness to the Good News of redemption and new life through Jesus Christ. "This," he says, "led to our ministry to media people, mainly those in the film and television industry."

Initially, Poland reached out to Hollywood under the Campus Crusade for Christ umbrella. Then in 1990 he began Mastermedia International, headquartered in Redlands, California, "to start a spiritual revolution in the media." According to its chairman and CEO, the stated mission of Mastermedia is "to build relationships with decision makers for the purpose of sharing Christ and discipling the people who respond, and to encourage and nurture Christians who work within the industry.

"The ultimate objective," he continues, "is to see the industry change, not by external pressure such as anger strategies, protests, boycott, sock-it-to 'em, but by the change of hearts of the people who run the industry." Poland, silver-haired and distinguished in appearance, directs a staff of about 20 people, including reps in Dallas, Chicago, and New York City.

He points out theirs is a classic missionary effort to an unreached people group, the most influential unreached people group in the world, he asserts. "The stuff these people produce," Larry contends, "contaminates every nation in the world. I've seen its effect in 77 countries. American media output has become the foremost moral and cultural pollutant on the planet."

To make contacts, Poland and his Mastermedia reps get appointments with key people—CEOs, presidents, vice presidents. Often many phone calls must be made. They ask for

10 minutes—and usually get more time—to give free "marketing advice" about America's 70 million evangelical Christians. Entertainment executives show appreciation for the counsel and after eight minutes eagerly receive a demographic study. Then, with two minutes of appointment time left, the rep pops the question: "By the way, has there been a time in your life when you personally have prayed and established a personal relationship with Jesus Christ and invited Him to be the central person of your life?"

© 2012 by Benjamin Haas.
Used under license of Shutterstock, Inc.

A senior executive, a believer, in one of the main Hollywood studios told Poland, "I feel so alone. I've never met one person at my level who is a Christian." Larry assured him there are believers in Hollywood who have not "bowed their knees to Baal." He introduced him to some of them.

The question has led to many opportunities to present the Gospel, and some have professed faith in Christ. "I asked that question of the chairman of one of the most influential companies in television," recalls Larry Poland. "He replied, 'Well, I've never done that, but my wife and my mother both think I should.' Two appointments after that, a year and a half later, he prayed with me to receive Christ in his Manhattan office, and he is growing spiritually."

Poland finds women under 30 and men under 40 are "pretty much unreachable." They are buying a pack of lies that money, fame, and sex make for happiness, he says. "But after 30, women begin to realize that isn't true, and men do so after 40," he points out. "Then there are two other hard-to-reach groups—cynical, bitter feminists and in-your-face businessmen. The group easiest to reach is what I call the searchers, those spiritually open through trauma or because other life pursuits have left them unfulfilled."

In contacts, Mastermedia reps have discovered Christians at various levels in the media, and they seek to relate them to one another, so they can pray and network together. These people often refer Mastermedia reps to fellow workers. A senior executive, a believer, in one of the main Hollywood studios told Poland, "I feel so alone. I've never met one person at my level who is a Christian." Larry assured him there are believers in Hollywood who have not "bowed their knees to Baal." He introduced him to some of them.

"The guy came alive," Larry says with glee. "He called me and said, 'I found another one, another senior executive in our studio!' The two of them began a prayer group and Bible study in the board room of that studio. God is indeed at work in the entertainment industry! We have the names of some 2,500 Christians in the film and television business, and we've gotten many of these people together for encouragement and fellowship and strategy."

Some believers have become more bold. One Christian, Larry says, went to the chairman of his studio to discuss a film with sickening bathroom humor and the vulgar promotion that went with it. "It was exciting to realize that a few years ago this man would never have dared go to the chairman of his studio," Larry comments.

Mastermedia reps occasionally influence the content of films or TV programs, though reading and editing scripts is not their calling. A top program executive with a national TV network called. A relatively new Christian, he asked Larry for help. "My network is planning a special series on the subject of talking to God based on the experiences of a man who claims to be able to talk to the spirits of the dead."

"This kind of practice is strictly forbidden in Scripture," Poland responded. "Let me put together the Biblical position and I'll fax it to you." Sometime afterward, the executive gave Larry a thumbs up: "Hey, we killed that project because of you!"

Why aren't we seeing a greater change in content? Over the next few years, Larry believes, the influence of believers within the industry will have a greater impact on TV programming and Hollywood films. "I compare this ministry to that reaching the sports world. They started in the 1960s and early '70s. We've been at it full time less than 20 years. Today, stick a mike in front of a football player and he praises Jesus. That will happen more and more in the entertainment industry.

"I see a spiritual awakening in the media," he says. "Give us a few more years and there will be more good shows and more executives visible as Christians in the industry. We have them coming out of the woodwork and acknowledging that they are Christians, some high-level people."

Most change is visible to people inside the industry, according to Poland. Only little bits of it show on the other side of the screen. But Poland acknowledges the "bad stuff" is getting worse. "We're not saying we can eliminate sin in the media output," he says, "for as long as there's a market for sin they'll produce products that will satisfy the demand for it. But in the future, there's going to be an increasing visibility of Christian people and redemptive content," he predicts.

"The Bible [says] to take the Gospel into the world," Poland says, pointing to the foundation of his ministry. "When the Gospel takes root, it will change people and their lifestyles. It's a change agent, the only one capable of changing the industry."

Crickets are chirping in the rugged, rocky landscape as stars begin to twinkle in the sky. Suddenly, floodlights illuminate a panoramic 550-foot wide, three-story set. A shofar sounds to announce Jesus' triumphal Palm Sunday entry, whisking onlookers back nearly two millennia.

But this isn't Jerusalem; it's the Great Passion Play in the Ozark Mountains of Eureka Springs, Arkansas. About 130 nights each year, outdoor performances at the vast 4,100-seat amphitheater allow audiences to virtually experience the final week of Christ's life on earth, including a graphic flogging, realistic crucifixion, and the ascension, during which Jesus appears to miraculously soar into the trees, sky, and beyond.

The authentic-looking landscape is the equivalent in size of two football fields built into a hillside. As many as six scenes occur simultaneously, all with meticulously costumed actors. For instance, men mingle in the marketplace; women gather water at a well; Pharisees debate in the temple; Roman soldiers gallop on horses to maintain order; young boys chase sheep. In addition to roaring chariots and flying pigeons, the dusty, bustling city streets are filled with camels, horses, mules, and sheep.

Annually around 100,000 people make their way across winding, tree-lined two-lane roads to visit the rural theater tucked away in the northwest corner of Arkansas. Since 1968, more than 7.5 million people have watched the Great Passion Play, which is the nation's most attended outdoor drama event.

Founders Gerald L. K. Smith and Elna M. Smith had been inspired by the passion play in Oberammergau, Germany. The Bavarian drama has been performed since 1634. The Smiths, using Jesus's words of John 12:32 ("And I, if I be lifted up from the earth, will draw all men unto me.") as a guiding principle, figured if Americans could watch a similar play, it could transform their lives.

Although there isn't a formal altar call, officials at the Great Passion Play down through the years have heard various testimonies of how the Gospel presentation has impacted lives.

One such person is Forest "Bobo" Estes. Thirty-five years ago, Estes, then a firefighter in Baton Rouge, Louisiana, drove into Eureka Springs in a drunken stupor, finding little reason to go on living. The alcoholic Estes, separated from his wife, asked a clerk at a local motel what kind of attractions the town had to offer. The clerk told Estes about the Great Passion Play. Estes, thinking something with that title must surely involve pornographic entertainment, headed for the show. As soon as he returned to Louisiana, Estes called a local pastor, who led him in a prayer of salvation.

Estes reconciled with his wife and became involved in Bible studies at his church. He began to bring drug addicts and prostitutes in his nine-passenger station wagon, paying for their tickets to the Great Passion Play, not telling them of its spiritual implications. Eventually he brought hundreds of people to performances in a school bus. Before retiring, Estes organized several mission trips to build churches in Mexico. Estes and his wife celebrated their 50th anniversary in 2006—by attending a Great Passion Play presentation.

It takes 150 paid performers from a multitude of regional churches to make the show a reality. Ninety percent of the cast typically returns from the previous year. Eureka Springs has a population of only 2,300.

As long as there is no danger to the cast or audience, the show continues even if there are 30 mile per hour winds, torrential downpours, or temperatures that dip to near freezing. Prerecorded music plays throughout the performance and nearly all dialogue is directly from Scripture. The two-hour event occurs nearly every night May through October, with the exception of Sundays and Wednesdays, when most performers attend services at their own churches.

About 130 nights each year, outdoor performances at the vast 4,100-seat amphitheater allow audiences to virtually experience the final week of Christ's life on earth.

The two bearded men who alternately portray Jesus are both in their 40s, yet they are hardly carbon copies.

Rick Mann is blond, blue-eyed and 6 feet, 2 inches. He is entering his 10th year depicting the Savior. At his church in nearby Berryville, Mann is worship leader and a Wednesday night Bible study teacher. Mann, who by day is a state housing maintenance mechanic, had theatrical training in high school and quickly adapted to the role of Jesus.

Although the dialogue portion of the performance is prerecorded, Mann initially still had to spend more than two months learning the lines to coordinate his movements. During dress rehearsal before his first performance the lights failed when he emerged from the tomb. During the actual show, the dazzling lights disoriented him and he walked smack into a stone wall.

Mann has learned to go with the flow. Once a pigeon landed on his head as he sat at the Last Supper table. He let the bird remain, reasoning that trying to shoo it away would detract from the character.

An inclement night sparked the most dramatic moment for him. One night as he hung on the cross and cried, "My God, My God, why have You forsaken Me?" thunder loudly clapped right behind him.

Mann is the more expressive of the two Jesus actors, so he holds nothing back when clearing the temple. "I want to show passion in a strong way," Mann says. "Any actor needs to communicate the role so that it's believable."

Joe Smith is the longer-tenured Jesus actor, the dark-haired one and at 6 feet, 7 inches, the taller one. A more soft-spoken, tender Christ figure, Smith has been in the play for more than two decades. It's apparent that this Jesus is a real-life schoolteacher during the week; during a scene teaching at the temple he comfortably interacts with children, placing a toddler on his lap. Smith had no acting experience when he began at the Great Passion Play after college, but he seems born for the role.

"At times I feel the strong presence of the Spirit of God," says Smith, who attends church in Washburn, Missouri. "I pray for that. I want to make a difference and do the best I can for Him."

Five evenings a week before the play, Smith conducts a 20-minute Parables of the Potter demonstration. As he molds a clay pot at his wheel, Smith relates several inspirational and evangelistic Scripture lessons. With his broad smile, piercing blue-gray eyes, calm demeanor, and expressive encouragement, Smith presents what amounts to an effective sermon.

The play provides a concise, direct explanation of the Gospel and it isn't designed just for evangelism, according to Marvin Peterson, the theater's director of operations. "It's not unusual to have discouraged pastors come and be touched by God," Peterson says. "It can be a turning point in a Christian's life."

There is more to the Great Passion Play grounds than the play itself. Visitors have the opportunity to visit a host of Bible-related sites.

The seven-story tall Christ of the Ozarks statue predates the play itself, having been completed in 1966. Emmet Sullivan, who worked on Mount Rushmore, sculpted the statue, which weighs more than two million pounds.

Gerald L. K. Smith and Elna M. Smith commissioned the statue as the first project on the site before they started the play and related attractions.

"In travels across the United States, the Smiths had seen great memorials to war heroes and politicians, but nowhere except in cemeteries had they seen a monument to Jesus Christ," says Peterson, who has been with the Great Passion Play since 1979. "They felt compelled by the Holy Spirit to erect a reminder of God's great love and mercy to all of humanity."

Attractions have been added at the Great Passion Play since its beginning. The New Holy Land tram tour features 30 exhibits recreating the history and culture of the ancient Middle East, including a life-sized reproduction of Moses's Tabernacle in the Wilderness. Along various stops, actors portray everyone from Simon Peter at the Sea of Galilee to Mary at the Bethlehem stable.

The Sacred Arts Center has exhibits dating back 1,200 years showing how artists have expressed their love of God. The Bible Museum contains more than 1,000 Bibles in 625 languages and dialects, several dating back nearly 500 years.

The Museum of Earth History has full-sized dinosaur skeleton displays and exhibits that reveal the scientific facts behind the Bible's historical Genesis account.

"We want to impact lives one at a time," Peterson says. "If we can continue to lift Jesus up as an extension of the church, people will be drawn to Him."

PERFORMING ARTS

· ·

REDEMPTIVE FIELD ANALYSIS 1

Analysis 1

1. Using words from the fifth chapter, define the term redemptive communicator.

_____

_____

_____

_____

_____

_____

2. Summarize one of this chapter's profiles in the space below. Include the most important details. Omit unnecessary details.

_____

_____

_____

_____

_____

_____

_____

_____

_____

_____

3. If you were asked to use this story or a specific part of this story to support an idea, one that you could present as its main point to an audience, which idea would you present? State this idea as a single declarative sentence in the space that follows:

_____

_____

_____

_____

_____

4. The fifth chapter states that a redemptive communicator interacts with other people in a way that promotes what God values in this world according to Scripture. Review the chapter's list of things that God values. Then, in the space below, identify the specific God-valued thing that this profilee promotes according to the profile. Be sure to explain both how the profilee promotes this specific thing and why you believe this thing is something God values according to Scripture.

_____

_____

_____

_____

_____

_____

_____

_____

_____

_____

_____

_____

_____

_____

_____

_____

5. Which other God-valued things does this profilee promote? Identify these and explain how he or she promotes them.

_____

_____

_____

_____

_____

_____

_____

_____

_____

_____

_____

_____

_____

PERFORMING ARTS

....

REDEMPTIVE FIELD ANALYSIS 2

HONOR STATEMENT: I, the undersigned student, hereby declare before God, before the school, and before the professor that I have read this chapter in its entirety, that I have completed the following exercise with help from no other sources, except as required by the questions, and that I neither have shared nor will share this work with anyone.

Signature: _____   Date: _____

Analysis 2

1. Using words from the fifth chapter, define the term redemptive communicator.

_____

_____

_____

_____

_____

_____

_____

2. Summarize another of this chapter's profiles in the space below. Include the most important details. Omit unnecessary details.

_____

_____

_____

_____

_____

_____

_____

_____

_____

_____

_____

_____

_____

_____

_____

_____

3. If you were asked to use this story or a specific part of this story to support an idea, one that you could present as its main point to an audience, which idea would you present? State this idea as a single declarative sentence in the space that follows:

_____

_____

_____

_____

_____

_____

_____

_____

_____

_____

_____

4. The fifth chapter states that a redemptive communicator interacts with other people in a way that promotes what God values in this world according to Scripture. Review the chapter's list of things that God values. Then, in the space below, identify the specific God-valued thing that this profilee promotes according to the profile. Be sure to explain both how the profilee promotes this specific thing and why you believe this thing is something God values according to Scripture.

_____

_____

_____

_____

_____

_____

_____

_____

_____

_____

_____

_____

_____

_____

_____

_____

5. Which other God-valued things does this profilee promote? Identify these and explain how he or she promotes them.

_____

_____

_____

_____

_____

_____

PERFORMING ARTS

· ·

REDEMPTIVE FIELD ANALYSIS 3

HONOR STATEMENT: I, the undersigned student, hereby declare before God, before the school, and before the professor that I have read this chapter in its entirety, that I have completed the following exercise with help from no other sources, except as required by the questions, and that I neither have shared nor will share this work with anyone.

Signature: _____   Date: _____

Analysis 3

1. Using words from the fifth chapter, define the term redemptive communicator.

_____

_____

_____

_____

_____

_____

_____

_____

2. Summarize another of this chapter's profiles in the space below. Include the most important details. Omit unnecessary details.

_____

_____

_____

_____

_____

_____

_____

_____

_____

_____

_____

3. If you were asked to use this story or a specific part of this story to support an idea, one that you could present as its main point to an audience, which idea would you present? State this idea as a single declarative sentence in the space that follows:

_____

_____

_____

_____

_____

_____

_____

_____

_____

_____

4. The fifth chapter states that a redemptive communicator interacts with other people in a way that promotes what God values in this world according to Scripture. Review the chapter's list of things that God values. Then, in the space below, identify the specific God-valued thing that this profilee promotes according to the profile. Be sure to explain both how the profilee promotes this specific thing and why you believe this thing is something God values according to Scripture.

_____

_____

_____

_____

_____

_____

_____

_____

_____

_____

_____

_____

_____

_____

_____

5. Which other God-valued things does this profilee promote? Identify these and explain how he or she promotes them.

_____

_____

_____

_____

_____

VISUAL ARTS >>

VISUAL ARTS

>> MICHAEL SPIELMAN

A graphic artist unmasks America's holocaust.

One of the federally protected liberties Americans have possessed since 1973 is the right to end the life of a baby before its birth, the result of the U.S. Supreme Court's *Roe v. Wade* decision. The debate since then often has devolved into political posturing about "choice." As a result, many people today don't understand what actually constitutes an abortion.

Michael G. Spielman's goal is to explain that grim reality.

Spielman's website, Abort73.com, has been able to accomplish what a lot of arguing elsewhere hasn't: enlightening and changing uninformed minds. With logical, conclusive evidence and graphic images, the site has led to numerous testimonials from readers who say they now comprehend why abortion is wrong.

Spielman, devised the website in response to a transformation in his own thinking. He graduated from Washington State University with a graphic-design degree, then landed a job as a graphic designer at *The Nashville Business Journal*. While he made a good living, Spielman—who received Jesus as his Savior while in the seventh grade—felt he wanted to do something more ministry oriented with his skills, something that would have more eternal significance.

A year into his new job, Spielman attended a seminar presented by Gregg Cunningham of the Center for Bioethical Reform (CBR). That event would be the catalyst he needed to find more meaning. Cunningham persuaded him that abortion isn't a political issue; it's a love-your-neighbor issue (See Matt. 22:38–40).

"I was struck by how clear-cut the case against abortion is from a purely secular standpoint," Spielman recalls. "The overwhelming medical and biological evidence establishes that human life begins at fertilization."

Like many Christians, Spielman had considered himself "pro-life" in his mind but he never really became engaged in the issue with his heart. In fact, he thought involvement in the movement would be a distraction from "real ministry."

In 1999 Spielman began more than five years of full-time work for CBR, fulfilling his longing to meaningfully combine vocation and ministry. Spielman spent a great deal of time on college campuses with CBR's Genocide Awareness Project, which features a huge photo mural exhibit comparing abortion with other crimes against humanity. Most of the posters are from first-trimester abortions, yet those are descriptive enough. The in-your-face encounters energized the low-key, soft-spoken Spielman.

"For the first time in my life I knew what it was to be utterly despised for my faith, and I knew the supernatural thrill of standing in the face of ridicule with nothing but love for the one spewing insults," Spielman says. "As I traveled the country debating the essence of life and death, I found that there are no insignificant conversations and no insignificant people."

Although many students indeed reacted with animosity, Spielman witnessed many others letting go of long-held, unreasonable attitudes about abortion. Still, the process of visiting campus after campus proved to be a labor intensive, expensive, and slow-moving process.

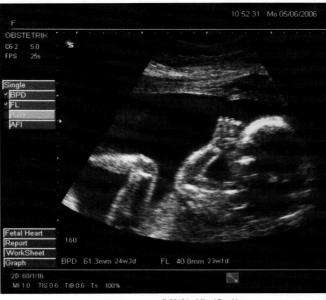

"The overwhelming medical and biological evidence establishes that human life begins at fertilization."

"I wanted a way to simultaneously extend that education to students across the country, and to include high schoolers," Spielman says. "For the project to have a huge cultural impact, more than visits to individual campuses needed to be done."

So he decided to use technology as the means of reaching the masses. He began to devise a website to enable people to see the graphic reality of abortion from their own computers.

"It seemed like the more polished pro-life websites had a lot of details about their particular organization, but were thin when it came to actually educating about abortion," Spielman says. "I wanted a site that took better advantage of the educational opportunities provided by the World Wide Web, while giving pro-life students some practical tools."

Drawing upon his multimedia expertise, Spielman incorporated Loxafamosity Ministries in 2004 and Abort73.com soon followed. He continues to work for CBR part time.

The Abort73.com site has various video, audio, and text arguments against abortion. Reader blogs and message boards show abortion's destruction. Spielman outlines biological, psychological, financial, medical, theological, and other reasons to avoid having an abortion. Along the way, those navigating Abort73.com learn about the Biblical foundation of life and are given opportunity to profess faith in Christ.

Spielman believes the facts about abortion need to be presented explicitly because that's what shook him from his complacency.

"When I went to that CBR seminar it was a graphic video that really hit me hard," Spielman remembers. "It was no longer abstract. The shocking pictures motivated me to get going. I want people to see what abortion does. Then the likelihood that they will go through with it decreases dramatically."

Spielman and his wife, Carrie, whom he married in 2001, live in Rockford, Illinois, and attend Harvest Bible Chapel. They have two children, Seth, 6, and Melanie, 5.
Having children has only reinforced Spielman's fortitude to contest the irrational views he encounters among abortion-rights advocates.

"Over and over I hear some variant of, 'Until a baby can survive on its own, it's not really a person,'" Spielman says. "As any parent knows, however, the smaller and more dependent a child is, the more care and protection we give to the baby."

As young children grow, the amount of direct oversight and provision they need decreases steadily, Spielman notes. But newborns need a great deal of care because they are so vulnerable and needy.

"As it relates to abortion, though, normal parental concern has been turned on its head," Spielman says. "The absolute dependence of unborn children has become the rationale, not for their protection, but for their destruction! The fact that so many mothers think of their child as a parasite is a scary indictment of our society."

Regularly Spielman receives e-mails from guilt-ridden girls confessing to their sin of destroying their offspring. The website has a section that allows women to tell how abortion traumatically affected them, in an effort to prevent others from following the same path.

Typical posted messages read, "Because of your website I chose not to kill my child" or "I showed your website to a lot of my friends and one of them was pregnant and it changed her mind completely."

Most visitors to the site are females of middle school, high school, and college age. In 2007, Spielman purposely began building in more social-networking features on the Abort73.com site for students who are active in doing something about abortion. The site offers everything from digital videodiscs to T-shirts to give students basic tools to get the message out.

Spielman has discovered that the teen years are the best time to convince younger people that abortion is wrong.

"The older people get, the more they are entrenched in their belief system—and the likelier they are to have had a personal involvement in abortion," he says.

As might be expected, not everyone is thrilled with the revelations Spielman presents on the website. He has received angry and threatening e-mails from abortion defenders.

"Spiritual warfare accompanies this work since Satan has an interest in maintaining the abortion status quo," Spielman says. "I've done campus evangelism, but I've never faced such hatred and animosity in sharing the Gospel as I have when talking about abortion."

Spielman takes a great deal of time to address vitriolic remarks with humility and grace, but that often provokes only rage.

"Darkness hates the light," Spielman says "We're not only battling unwitting ignorance, but also chosen ignorance."

Spielman has discovered that the teen years are the best time to convince younger people that abortion is wrong.

>> MATT ANDERSON

A card designer helps Christians encourage each other.

Ask Matt Anderson's children what their daddy does for a living and they'll answer, "He draws little angels with great big noses." But his job goes far beyond sketchbook doodles. The big-nosed angels are the trademark of Matt's greeting cards, Heaven's Unofficial Greetings, and are found in Christian bookstores across North America. Since 1991 Matt's angels have delivered hugs from heaven—mini messages filled with hopeful reminders of Biblical truths; gentle reminders of God's love; humorous tidbits of truth.

"People need encouragement—they can't get enough of it. I want people to be encouraged with the hope that comes from knowing the Lord," says Anderson.

"That goal is accomplished with a clever cover, a Scripture verse inside, and the back message pointing to the Source of hope."

Anderson's cartooning ability was obvious when he was a young boy. Growing up in Seattle, Washington, he spent hours drawing cartoon characters on a roll of butcher paper. Later, in college, he printed and sold several card designs. A crucial element was missing, however. "I could draw funny pictures but I had no message. My cards had no concept of life, truth, and encouragement."

While attending college in Tacoma, Washington, Anderson became sidetracked by mingling with the wrong crowd. "Although I wasn't raised in a Christian home, I'd always lived a clean life," he says. "I wanted to discover what I'd been missing." He found only emptiness.

"As soon as I started making bad choices, I knew I didn't want to live like that. I carried a terrible burden of guilt." He recalls praying, "God, I've really screwed up my life. I know You have the answer but I don't know what it is. Could You please tell me?" Matt bought a one-way ticket to Europe, embarking on a search for that answer.

His prayers continued while hitchhiking through Europe. While touring Spain's northern Basque country, he was suspected of being a foreign terrorist. With a machine gun to his back and soldiers rifling through his belongings, he prayed, "God, get me out of here!" The soldiers released him.

Later in Morocco, Matt suffered from a severe case of food poisoning.

Lying on his bed in a hostel, fearful of dying, he again cried to God for help. He recovered. "God, You must have something for me to do," he acknowledged. He returned home a few weeks later—still searching for spiritual reality, open to whatever it might be.

Upon his return, his parents gave him a Bible. "I read John 14:6 where Jesus says, 'I am the way, the truth, and the life.' Deep inside my soul, something responded, 'Yes. This is the answer.'"

While touring Spain's northern Basque country, he was suspected of being a foreign terrorist. With a machine gun to his back and soldiers rifling through his belongings, he prayed, "God, get me out of here!" The soldiers released him.

The search ended. Weeping, Anderson committed his life to Jesus Christ—"Whatever You want, I'm Yours." He openly shared his newfound faith with his family. One after another, his parents and three siblings received Christ.

"As soon as I became a Christian I realized that, not only did I have peace and purpose, but I had a message to go with my gift for cartooning," says Anderson. "But I still didn't know how to put it all together." He received direction during a year-long tour with the Covenant Players, a Christian drama troupe. While on tour, he stayed in people's homes.

"For the first time I saw Christians not just in church but in their real surroundings. I witnessed the wide variety that exists in the Body of Christ. Through listening to people talk about the struggles in their lives, the Lord showed me their common need for encouragement."

In 1986, one year after graduating from the University of Washington with a bachelor's degree in art, Matt sketched his first angel character. "I drew a little skier skiing off a cliff. His worried expression made me laugh out loud. Be anxious for nothing popped into my thoughts. It was as though the Lord said, 'Matt, this is what I want you to do.'"

Heaven's Unofficial Greetings had been conceived but it would be another five years before its birth. As Matt filled sketch books with ideas, he worked as a youth-pastor intern for a year. One of his favorite cards was modeled after a plaque he made to encourage a boy in his youth group—the only kid in school who didn't receive a year-end award. On it, he sketched the boy's caricature and wrote the words "Masterpiece in Progress." After listing the boy's Christ-like qualities, he added, "God is doing a good work in you." The plaque made such a positive impact that he designed one for the boy's sister as well.

In 1988 he attended Multnomah Graduate School of Ministry in Portland, Oregon, for a year of graduate study in Bible and theology. "If I was going to encourage people with God's word, I wanted to do it accurately," he says.

At Multnomah he met Kris Oman. They married on September 8, 1990. Matt did freelance artwork and custom illustrations while trying to design a card line, but his earnings weren't enough to provide for a family. Kris's job as a dental receptionist provided their main source of income. He was still seeking the secret recipe for the cards when they discovered she was expecting their first child. Their faith faced a major challenge.

"Our prayers became very earnest," Matt admits. "I prayed, 'Lord, You know who You've made me to be and the gifts You've given me. I truly believe You have a purpose. I'm at Your service. I'm tired of trying to make this come together in my brain. You're going to have to do it and You're going to have to do it quickly."

Over the next two weeks, Matt sketched 40 card designs. "It was truly an answer to prayer. It came after releasing myself to what He wanted to do through me instead of what I wanted to do for Him." Anderson showed his cards to friends and family, making necessary changes until he saw the response he'd hoped for—people laughing, saying, "Oh, this is so true. I know someone who needs this!" The artwork and the message were finally working together. He photocopied his cards, hand-painted each design, and sold them in nine local bookstores for several months. He visited each store frequently, keeping accurate sales records.

Kris quit her job at the end of November. Their first child was born in December. After seeing Anderson's sales records, a card company decided to launch Heaven's Unofficial Greetings nationwide in January. Matt was supporting his family within a month.

"I got letters from all across the country. People were hungry for humor and encouragement. I began learning that this business is simply about being a mouthpiece for the Lord to use for speaking encouragement to His people."

In January, 2000, as Matt put the finishing touches on several new card designs, he and his wife found their faith challenged and encouraged again. A doctor's diagnosis gave Kris a 50 percent chance of survival due to stage-three tonsil cancer. One of Matt's new cards read, "God's faithfulness means . . . every storm will pass." Another one read, "When the challenge is God-sized . . . the solution will be, too." "I couldn't believe God's timing," Matt says. "He prepared us through the messages He'd given me for the cards."
As Kris underwent aggressive surgery, chemotherapy, and radiation, "hugs from heaven" embraced them daily in a variety of ways. Encouragement came through God's Word, especially Psalm 20—"The Lord hear thee in the day of trouble; the name of the God of Jacob defend thee." Friends supported them by taking Kris to radiation treatments, homeschooling their three children, doing laundry, housecleaning, and meal preparation. Their help allowed Matt to care for Kris's physical needs and continue working as much as possible in Product Development at DaySpring Cards, the world's largest publisher of Christian greeting cards. Kris completed treatment five months after her diagnosis.

"The byline of my cards is 'Celebrating the Everyday Adventure of Faith,'" says Matt. "Kris's cancer was simply another part of the adventure of walking with Christ. Her illness wasn't about us. It was about Him revealing Himself to us. He was the same the day after her diagnosis as He was the day before. We prayed, 'Lord, just be Who You are. No matter what the outcome is, we can deal with this if You are Who You say You are.'"

Anderson quotes Romans 15:5,6: "Now the God of patience and consolation grant you to be likeminded one toward another according to Christ Jesus: That ye may with one mind and one mouth glorify God, even the Father of our Lord Jesus Christ."

"I love what's revealed in these verses—that God Himself gives encouragement! He often uses another person sharing His Word in love as the bodily form of His own expression of encouragement. The end result is that God is glorified. What an inspiration to me as I work to create products that people can use to encourage one another and ultimately bring glory to our awesome God!"

>> RANDY HOFMAN

A sand sculpture presents the Gospel to Maryland beachgoers.

As a young child, Randy Hofman enjoyed playing in the sand. He and his eight siblings dug around the sandbox in the backyard of their suburban Washington, DC, home. The family also took summer vacations to Ocean City, Maryland, where Hofman could build castles and roads on the white sandy beach. From the age of five, Hofman knew he wanted to be an artist.

Hofman grew up and faced a reality of adulthood: putting away childish dreams and making a living. He began to study advertising design and visual communications at the Pratt Institute in Brooklyn, New York, with plans of becoming a magazine art director. But after a couple of years of classes, Hofman determined such a career path would be too confining.

In 1974, Hofman returned to Ocean City, the site of his childhood summer vacations, to help sand artist Marc Altamar. For seven years, Hofman served as Altamar's apprentice. During that period, Hofman made a commitment to Jesus as his Savior. Since early childhood, Hofman had a head knowledge of the Lord. But at age 25, on the Ocean City beach one night, he agreed to allow Jesus into his heart to guide his daily life.

"I had gone through a party phase in my life and I wanted to be done with that," Hofman says. "I didn't want to just trifle with the Lord anymore."

When Altamar moved to Florida in 1981, Hofman became the sole resident sand-sculpting artist on the Ocean City beachfront, turning it into a full-blown ministry.

These days, Hofman puts in a lengthier workday at the beach. Using only a square shovel and plastic crab-picking knife, he creates sculptures that can extend 40 feet wide and 10 feet tall.

The effort has grown more elaborate in the past quarter century. Initially, Hofman would take a few hours a day to build a sand painting. With overnight winds, it would be indistinguishable by the next day. Since 1990, a glue and water spray mixture has held sculptures intact for up to several weeks—and even months—if the elements or vandals don't damage them.

These days, Hofman puts in a lengthier workday at the beach. Using only a square shovel and plastic crab-picking knife, he creates sculptures that can extend 40 feet wide and 10 feet tall. His most intricate and crowd-pleasing piece, depicting the Last Supper, sometimes takes 17 hours.

Once he begins work, Hofman keeps going until finished, stopping only for dinner and restroom breaks. He never abandons a project to rest and may continue working until dawn.

John and Hale Harrison, Christian brothers who operate the Plim Plaza Hotel in Ocean City, provide free water and electricity to Hofman so he can construct his artwork on a public beach about 25 feet off the boardwalk. The water is essential to make the sand pliable. The lights make the sculptures visible at night. The boardwalk stretches for 2.5 miles as part of the 10 miles of Ocean City beach.

Hofman has a dozen basic Biblical themes for his work, including Noah and the ark, Moses carrying the Ten Commandments, Samson crashing the temple pillars, David fighting Goliath, the Wise Men visiting the newborn Savior, and Jesus praying in the Garden of Gethsemane. Hofman's favorite is an elaborate head of Jesus. A Biblical adage, such as "Wise men still seek Him" often is etched near the top of the carving, giving it the appearance of a newspaper headline.

"I want it to click so that even someone who is spiritually ignorant can understand," Hofman says.

In all, he has completed about 1,000 sculptures, each somewhat different than anything he's done in the past. The artwork and the Bible passage—plus the fact that tens of thousands of tourists are relaxed while on a family vacation—provide an atmosphere for evangelism. "Kids ask their parents what the sculpture is all about," Hofman says.

Sometimes Hofman will create thematic stories side by side, such as Jesus praying in the Garden of Gethsemane, Christ dying on the Cross, and the appearance of the resurrected Lord.

Hofman, who also has been an ordained minister since 1985, engages inquisitive passersby in conversation about God. He sometimes preaches while he's sculpting. He also has distributed more than a million 32-page evangelistic tracts that are available next to his work at the beach.

Although Hofman has a jar beside the sand sculptures for tips, he survives financially by doing oil paintings, primarily individual portraits and landscapes. Hofman and his wife, Marilynne, a registered nurse, live in nearby Berlin, Maryland.

There is room outside his spot near the hotel for four connecting scenes. Youth from a local church group, Son Spot Ministries, excavate the sand piles, digging with shovels to bring moist sand to the top to form a mound. Hofman creates his work at a 45-degree angle so that it's visible from the boardwalk to tourists who flock to Ocean City in the summer. Hofman crafts his designs on the beach from the beginning of April to the end of October.

While Christians usually admire the sculpting mostly for its Biblical storytelling, non-Christians often are drawn by Hofman's craftsmanship. His attention to detail and classical portrayal of the human anatomy frequently impress those who are Biblically illiterate or skeptical.

If a storm or vandal spoils the work, Hofman sometimes takes a day or two to repair it. Few people intentionally destroy the work anymore because the glue makes it difficult to budge.

Still, Hofman occasionally encounters an antagonistic visitor questioning his beliefs—or sanity. "Some people just have a nasty disposition," Hofman says. "The sculptures I choose are about love of God and His generosity. If somebody is crabby about that, they're just crabby."

Although his age, the hot summer sun, and the backbreaking work sometimes take a toll on Hofman, he plans to continue in the artistry that has kept him occupied for more than three decades.

"I see this as the highest calling," says Hofman. "It seems to complete me."

VISUAL ARTS

....

REDEMPTIVE FIELD ANALYSIS 1

HONOR STATEMENT: I, the undersigned student, hereby declare before God, before the school, and before the professor that I have read this chapter in its entirety, that I have completed the following exercise with help from no other sources, except as required by the questions, and that I neither have shared nor will share this work with anyone.

Signature: _____   Date: _____

Analysis 1

1. Using words from the fifth chapter, define the term redemptive communicator.

_____

_____

_____

_____

_____

_____

2. Summarize one of this chapter's profiles in the space below. Include the most important details. Omit unnecessary details.

_____

_____

_____

_____

_____

_____

_____

_____

_____

_____

3. If you were asked to use this story or a specific part of this story to support an idea, one that you could present as its main point to an audience, which idea would you present? State this idea as a single declarative sentence in the space that follows:

_____

_____

_____

_____

_____

_____

4. The fifth chapter states that a redemptive communicator interacts with other people in a way that promotes what God values in this world according to Scripture. Review the chapter's list of things that God values. Then, in the space below, identify the specific God-valued thing that this profilee promotes according to the profile. Be sure to explain both how the profilee promotes this specific thing and why you believe this thing is something God values according to Scripture.

_____

_____

_____

_____

_____

_____

_____

5. Which other God-valued things does this profilee promote? Identify these and explain how he or she promotes them.

VISUAL ARTS

....

REDEMPTIVE FIELD ANALYSIS 2

HONOR STATEMENT: I, the undersigned student, hereby declare before God, before the school, and before the professor that I have read this chapter in its entirety, that I have completed the following exercise with help from no other sources, except as required by the questions, and that I neither have shared nor will share this work with anyone.

Signature: _____   Date: _____

Analysis 2

1. Using words from the fifth chapter, define the term redemptive communicator.

_____

_____

_____

_____

_____

_____

_____

_____

2. Summarize another of this chapter's profiles in the space below. Include the most important details. Omit unnecessary details.

_____

_____

_____

_____

_____

_____

_____

_____

_____

_____

_____

_____

_____

3. If you were asked to use this story or a specific part of this story to support an idea, one that you could present as its main point to an audience, which idea would you present? State this idea as a single declarative sentence in the space that follows:

_____

_____

_____

_____

_____

_____

_____

_____

_____

_____

4. The fifth chapter states that a redemptive communicator interacts with other people in a way that promotes what God values in this world according to Scripture. Review the chapter's list of things that God values. Then, in the space below, identify the specific God-valued thing that this profilee promotes according to the profile. Be sure to explain both how the profilee promotes this specific thing and why you believe this thing is something God values according to Scripture.

_____

_____

_____

_____

_____

_____

_____

_____

_____

_____

_____

_____

_____

_____

_____

_____

5. Which other God-valued things does this profilee promote? Identify these and explain how he or she promotes them.

_____

_____

_____

_____

_____

VISUAL ARTS

....

REDEMPTIVE FIELD ANALYSIS 3

HONOR STATEMENT: I, the undersigned student, hereby declare before God, before the school, and before the professor that I have read this chapter in its entirety, that I have completed the following exercise with help from no other sources, except as required by the questions, and that I neither have shared nor will share this work with anyone.

Signature: _____   Date: _____

Analysis 3

1. Using words from the fifth chapter, define the term redemptive communicator.

_____

_____

_____

_____

_____

_____

_____

_____

2. Summarize another of this chapter's profiles in the space below. Include the most important details. Omit unnecessary details.

_____

_____

_____

_____

_____

_____

_____

_____

_____

_____

_____

_____

3. If you were asked to use this story or a specific part of this story to support an idea, one that you could present as its main point to an audience, which idea would you present? State this idea as a single declarative sentence in the space that follows:

_____

_____

_____

_____

_____

_____

_____

_____

_____

_____

_____

4. The fifth chapter states that a redemptive communicator interacts with other people in a way that promotes what God values in this world according to Scripture. Review the chapter's list of things that God values. Then, in the space below, identify the specific God-valued thing that this profilee promotes according to the profile. Be sure to explain both how the profilee promotes this specific thing and why you believe this thing is something God values according to Scripture.

_____

_____

_____

_____

_____

_____

_____

_____

_____

_____

_____

_____

_____

_____

_____

5. Which other God-valued things does this profilee promote? Identify these and explain how he or she promotes them.

_____

_____

_____

_____

_____

_____

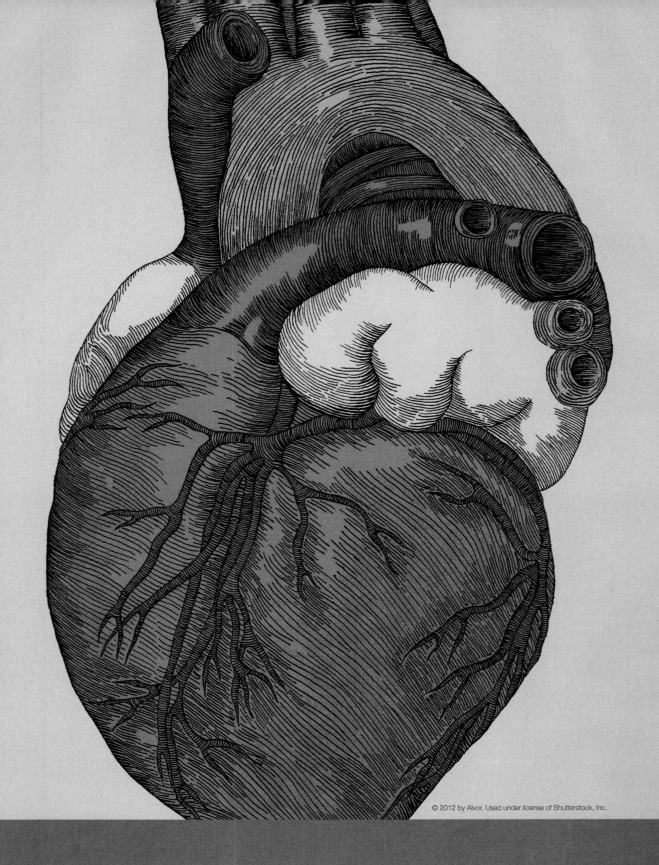

MEDICINE >>

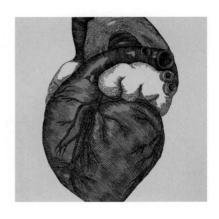

MEDICINE

JILL STANEK

A nurse takes a courageous stand for life.

PART 4 Redemptive Communicators: Profiles from Across the Job Fields

In the end, she actually wanted to get fired. It's true that she had spent the better part of a decade working toward this position, in this unit, in this hospital. And it's true that the job was a dream-come-true, the work both challenging and rewarding.

But Jill Stanek was tired of being whispered about, tiptoed around, and excluded from hallway chatter. Then came the written warnings, the suspension, and the anonymous hate mail.

After all, she was the one who, in 1999, blew the whistle on Chicago's renowned Christ Hospital. She exposed the fact that her employer was performing "live-birth abortions," in which pre-term labor is induced, a fully formed baby delivered intact, and—if still alive—left to die with no medical intervention.

Two years later—two years of constant scrutiny from her bosses and ostracism from her coworkers—Stanek was finally fired.

And, boy, was she relieved.

"I was just so happy and thankful to God," she said. "I was almost laughing."

Even though her job at Christ Hospital had come to an end, though, Stanek was really only beginning her battle for these tiny victims.

Almost immediately, people began to call, offering her writing and speaking engagements. She testified before Congress and dabbled in local politics. And twice she's visited the White House, at President Bush's invitation, to watch him sign pro-life legislation.

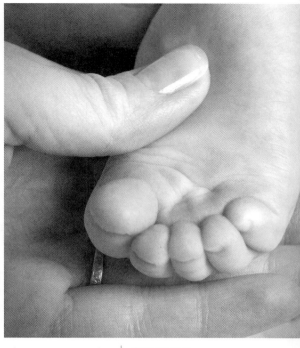

Even though her job at Christ Hospital had come to an end, though, Stanek was really only beginning her battle for these tiny victims.

A Grisly Discovery

A self-described late bloomer, Stanek already had school-aged children when she began working the night shift in labor and delivery section at Christ Hospital in Oak Lawn, Illinois. At first, she wasn't aware that the hospital performed labor-induced abortions; she'd already been there a year when a coworker shared the devastating news.

Stanek learned the hospital had been performing the procedure for more than two decades by the time she came on staff. As sickened as she was by this information, she was even more disturbed by the thought that hundreds—maybe thousands—of hospital employees knew it was going on and had never said a word.

She attributed the silence to fear: fear of losing a job, fear of what others might say, fear of a tarnished reputation. Stanek, too, was frightened into silence, not sure what to do. So for three years she said nothing, until a "crisis of conscience" compelled her to take the risk she'd tried so hard to avoid.

Late one evening, Stanek opened the door that changed her life forever. It was the door to a hospital utility closet, where a coworker—too busy to hold an aborted baby boy until he died—had left the child. By the time Stanek found the Down syndrome boy, abandoned and still breathing, it was too late to provide medical assistance. Huddled in a closet, surrounded by soiled laundry, she cradled him, rocked him—and 45 minutes later, felt his small body go limp in her arms.

Her dream job would never be the same.

"Having to walk by a room where people were aborting and I knew it was going on—not being able to do anything about it was such torture," she said.

Witnessing the devastating effects of late-term abortion was one thing. Knowing a secret the hospital attempted to hide was another. While Christ Hospital officials claimed this procedure was performed only on babies with fatal handicaps, Stanek knew the truth. There were others, perfectly formed, delivered before they had a chance to live.

Because the procedure is so controversial, it's difficult to know how many hospitals perform live-birth abortions, or even who's doing them. At Christ Hospital, Stanek said, they were referred to as "medically indicated" abortions: A pregnant woman was given a drug to dilate the cervix and induce labor. The pre-term babies were often delivered dead—but not always.

True to the procedure's name, some of these babies enter the world with their tiny arms flailing and fragile chests heaving, gasping for air, desperate for help. Yet the doctors and nurses only turn their backs.

Sometimes a nurse will hold them until they die. Sometimes a mother or father will rock their premature son or daughter until death. But many times, these little ones will take their final breaths alone, surrounded only by stark walls and sterile hospital equipment. "You'll find this procedure going on in almost every major city, and people aren't saying anything about it," Stanek says. "They think that it's enough not to participate if you're pro-life. But it's not enough."

So began her one-woman crusade.

Going Public

Like her coworkers, Stanek could have simply looked the other way. But she decided that God had placed her in this position—and that alone was worth risking her job and professional reputation.

"I did want to leave," she said, "but my view was that there is no such thing as a coincidence. God had put me in that place for a reason. So every time I thought about leaving, I thought I was abandoning the position that Christ had put me in."

She handled matters privately at first, writing letters to and meeting with hospital administrators, urging them to change their policy on abortion. But the officials made it clear they had no intention of stopping.

That's when she went public.

Her pastor sent out a letter to about 70 churches and pro-life organizations in Chicago and across the country. The news spread quickly, and before she knew it, Stanek was being interviewed by *The New York Times*, *Newsweek*, and Fox News.

Through it all, she continued to work the night shift at Christ Hospital. Once-friendly coworkers now ignored her, doctors scheduled abortions when she wasn't around, and administrators monitored her every move, watching for any infraction that could merit termination.

For two years, Stanek was on probation for breaking an unspecified rule in her employment contract. And for two years, hospital staff couldn't come up with a compelling reason to fire her.

She knew she was being watched, but she was well past the point of intimidation. She testified twice before Congress about what she saw at Christ Hospital. She campaigned for the federal Born Alive Infants Protection Act, which requires hospitals and doctors to treat all infants who are delivered alive—even those who were aborted—as persons deserving all necessary medical attention.

Stanek's lawyer, Liberty Counsel's Mat Staver, said she wasn't trying to cause controversy; she was just trying to be a good nurse and a good Christian.

"Jill made a decision," Staver says, "and that decision was to stand for principle and to stand for life and the unborn, and she put her entire career literally on the line."

"I Wasn't a Pro-Life Activist"
In August 2001, Stanek returned from vacation to discover that she had indeed been fired. Hospital officials claimed it had nothing to do with her pro-life views or all the negative publicity she brought to Christ Hospital. Yet when they provided Stanek with written reasons for her termination, all pertained to her outspokenness.

Without her nursing career, Stanek devoted herself to full-time activism. Her speaking invitations increased, and she decided to get involved in local politics—running for the Illinois General Assembly against her pro-abortion state representative—only three months after leaving Christ Hospital.

Stanek lost the election, but the experience opened up even more opportunities to share her story. For the last three years, she has spoken extensively about her experiences, been quoted hundreds of times in the national media and currently writes a weekly column on important issues for *The Illinois Leader*.

On August 5, 2002, President Bush invited Stanek to the signing of the Born Alive Infants Protection Act, for which she testified. A year later, she was again in the room when Bush signed long-awaited legislation banning partial-birth abortion. And *World* magazine named her one of the 30 most prominent pro-life leaders of the past three decades.

She testified twice before Congress about what she saw at Christ Hospital. She campaigned for the federal Born Alive Infants Protection Act, which requires hospitals and doctors to treat all infants who are delivered alive–even those who were aborted–as persons deserving all necessary medical attention.

But despite all that, Stanek doesn't see herself as a hero. Rather, she simply lives out the Biblical duty to defend the cause of the helpless.

"I've never tried to open my own door," she said. "God has opened doors I never would have thought possible. I wasn't a pro-life activist, I was just pro-life . . . My home is heaven . . . but as long as I'm here, I have a job to do."

>> JAMES BLESSMAN

A Christian doctor ministers to the physical needs of America's poor.

Tables and chairs are being set up in the waiting area. Ear-probe thermometers, blood pressure cuffs, and tongue depressors are prepared in the screening section. A toy box and children's videos are readied in an overflow room. It's 5:30 p.m. Thursday in the basement of a church in Des Moines, Iowa, and a beehive of active volunteers are transforming Sunday school rooms into a free clinic.

Although patients won't be seen for another half hour, they already are lining up for the first-come, first-served ministry. The church has designated a corner for medical exams and supplies storage. The weekly free clinic is the brainchild of Dr. James L. Blessman. As founder and executive director of the nonprofit Health Care Access Network (HCAN), Blessman has started free weekly clinics in 17 Iowa locations.

HCAN reaches many Iowans who have jobs, but little or no health insurance. With the vision of using volunteers from local churches, Blessman in the past decade has recruited 200 doctors and 1,000 nonphysician volunteers to donate their services. In addition to the free labor, the use of facilities is donated along with most of the equipment and medicines. The state covers malpractice insurance for the doctors providing the free care. The network of clinics provides free primary medical care, no strings attached, to those who likely don't have a regular doctor.

"We're just a tiny piece of the safety net," Blessman says. Many patients who wouldn't set foot in a church for a service don't mind doing so for free health care that is run as efficiently and professionally as commercial clinics. The patients who gather are a mixture, representing the neighborhood in northwest Des Moines: a white elderly woman, an

Hispanic family of five, a black teenager. Typically, three nurses, one doctor, a medical student, and half a dozen nonmedical volunteers will be on hand from 6 to 8 p.m. All likely have put in a full day of work in their regular jobs.

An average of 15 patients are seen each Thursday night, receiving everything from bronchitis medication to measles immunizations. Sometimes a diagnosis and treatment can change a life. At one clinic, a doctor determined that a baby had phenylketonuria, a genetic disorder that results in mental retardation if not caught early and treated with a special diet.

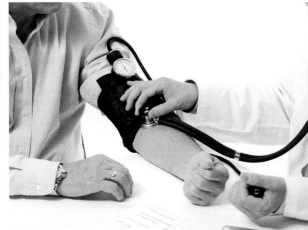

Tonight's on-call physician is Dr. James P. Lovell, a cardiologist who has been volunteering monthly since the clinic opened eight years ago. For a specialist whose career involves the intricacies of the heart, treating a common cold is a bit of a departure.

"I'm just a cardiologist," says Lovell. Recalling Christ's challenge to treat people as if they were Christ Himself (Matt. 25: 31–45), he adds, "Sometimes I wonder if I should be seeing sick babies. But this is a place where God wants me to be. In a sense this is a mission outreach. This is the place where I can make a small contribution."

Blessman grew up attending a church and Sunday school where he never heard about salvation. But as an adult, his pastor asked him the question: If he were to die tonight would he go to heaven? Blessman pondered the question. Unsure of how to answer the question, he soon acknowledged his sinfulness and consequent need of salvation based on someone or something other than himself. He asked God to forgive him of his sins and received Christ, the only Savior, into his life (John 14:6). Although initially motivated to operate the clinics as a social service contribution to the community, Blessman eventually realized that he could serve Christ by serving others. As Jesus himself stated, "Inasmuch as ye have done it unto one of the least of these my brethren, ye have done it unto me" (Matt. 25:40).

Since then, counselors are available at clinics to offer to pray with patients before they leave. Nearly everyone agrees, and almost every week one or two patients decide to receive Jesus as Savior. Those who do, receive a free Bible, discipleship materials, and local church information. Adding a spiritual component to the clinic has meant that the outreach can minister to the physical, emotional, and spiritual well-being of people.

The cost to HCAN for each patient is $21 per visit, one-tenth of the basic cost for a trip to a local hospital emergency room. The entire annual $313,000 HCAN budget comes from private funds and no government money is used. The clinics are dependent upon individuals, congregations, patient donations, and private grants to keep going. Blessman is continually on the hunt for more corporate sponsors. The most ambitious free clinic is La Clínica de la Esperanza (Clinic of Hope), opened by Blessman's group in 1994.

Now there are three local health care providers coordinating services at the facility, which is open every weekday and has three registered nurses on staff. The clinic is located in southeast Des Moines where many poor, undocumented Hispanics work in meat-packing plants. La Clínica is expected to treat 10,000 patients a year.

For years Blessman says he was a workaholic while he practiced family medicine and also operated a pain-relief center in Des Moines. "I spent the first 45 years of my life trusting in my own abilities, power, and influence," Blessman says. "I thought I was very successful and living the best life that I possibly could. Looking back on the decision to turn my finances, work, time, family, and relationships over to the Lord should have been easy, but I had a difficult time letting go of the control I thought I had."

Blessman left the lucrative medical profession in 2001 after overseas short-term missionary health care trips stirred his heart toward poor and spiritually lost people in Third World countries. At 58, he has reached the point in life where most doctors are winding down and looking forward to a comfortable retirement. Instead, he and his wife, Beth, last year became medical missionaries with HealthCare Ministries, based in Missouri. They take 10 annual, two-week, medical-team and disaster-response trips bringing God's love and healing to people around the world.

"On most trips we get to openly share the Gospel," says Blessman, who has provided free medical care in countries such as El Salvador, Vietnam, and Zambia. "Now I know that this is what God wants me to do—reach out to poor people in countries where they might not receive much medical attention otherwise. We can provide medical care, which is temporary, but we can also share [about the Gospel of] Jesus, which is an eternal benefit."

RON HOEKSTRA

A doctor ministers to the families of prematurely born babies.

While growing up in a conservative Christian home, Ron Hoekstra developed a respect for human life that is foundational to the worldview of many believers: All people are created in God's image and have worth, even people whose lives are limited by physical or mental handicaps, or babies who survive only for a few days. As Scripture teaches, "He giveth to all life, and breath, and all things . . . . For in him we live, and move, and have our being (Acts 17:25–28).

A neonatal specialist at Children's Hospital in Minneapolis since 1979, Hoekstra has had the opportunity to put his beliefs in action.

"Any life has tremendous value, no matter how imperfect, no matter how long," says the lifelong Minnesotan. "These [prematurely born] babies, from a human and medical perspective, didn't work out. But they had a tremendous impact on numerous lives. There's no price tag on that."

Hoekstra finished his pediatric residency at the Mayo Clinic in Rochester, Minnesota, in an era when neonatology was not a recognized specialty. But drug and technological advances in the past three decades mean that a baby born at 28 weeks, who previously had little chance of survival, now is likely to live a full and productive life. These days, the medical consensus is that every effort should be made to save a child born at 24 weeks. Hoekstra, 59, goes further. He is willing to take a risk on babies who, if they live, probably will end up with long-term disabilities.

"I feel powerless without faith in God," Hoekstra says. "There's not a day I walk into the neonatal intensive care that I don't ask God for wisdom to know what's right."

At the hospital, Hoekstra and his colleagues have tried to save the lives of 37 babies born at 22 weeks, a time in gestation at which a baby's anatomy has often not developed to a point of being compatible with survival outside the uterus. Before that, a baby's anatomy has not had adequate time to develop properly. Ten 22-week preemies treated by Hoekstra have survived and four of those are severely handicapped. In 2000, Hoekstra cowrote with Daniel Taylor *Before Their Time: Lessons in Living from Those Born Too Soon* (InterVarsity Press). The book details the stories of six premature babies, some who lived and some who did not. A century ago such preemies died. They had no chance.

Many neonatologists won't even consider saving 22-week-old infants, who, if they survive, will typically end up staying in a hospital for three months at a cost of $400,000. They see no reason to hook up a child to expensive machines when the baby is likely to die anyway, or at least have physical handicaps. A *New England Journal of Medicine* study in 2000 found that half of the preemies born before the 26th week are disabled, with problems including seizures, mental retardation, and deafness.

Hoekstra himself has been roundly criticized by other neonatal doctors who view efforts to save extreme preemies as illogical and too expensive. Many physicians argue that medicine is a science dealing with practical logic, not nebulous miracles. Yet Hoekstra, who with his wife, Claudia, a nurse, has three adult sons, sees events from a different perspective. Time and again Hoekstra has seen children survive who had been classified as hopeless. Standard answers in a scientific textbook ignore the reality of flesh and blood struggling for life.

"A lot of lives are saved that might otherwise have slipped into eternity with little notice," Hoekstra says.

While he concedes that those who survive have a much higher likelihood of debilitating problems such as brain damage, chronic lung disease, or vision problems, Hoekstra believes children who enter this world should be given a chance to make it.

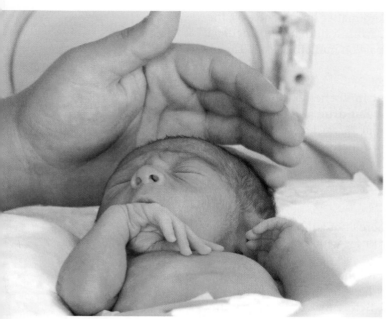

© 2012 by Reflekta.
Used under license of Shutterstock, Inc.

Though he is a gifted pediatric specialist, Hoekstra understands that reliance on God is key to his work in the neonatal intensive care unit.

Though he is a gifted pediatric specialist, Hoekstra understands that reliance on God is key to his work in the neonatal intensive care unit. In his care of a 20-ounce preemie, Hoekstra frankly tells parents that God has more to do with healing than anything he can do medically. Every time he scrubs up before examining a newborn, Hoekstra prays for the child and asks God for wisdom in how to proceed with treatment.

"Sometimes a baby will live or die depending on factors that have nothing at all to do with medicine," Hoekstra says. "Frequently it's not a question of skill, or of medical ethics, but simply a question of how one assesses the possibilities."

Many other doctors inquire starkly as to whether the parents want to save the child, assuming that the little body has no value if it is unwanted and has medical problems. Hoekstra believes that faith, prayer, and praising God have as much to do with survival as medical care. And the hope God offers often is the difference in getting the parents through as well.

For the passing of one crisis usually brings only temporary relief; likely there will be many other critical periods where life and death hang in the balance. The faith—and marriages—of parents is severely tested by such stress. Those who find strength in the Lord learn to pray as never before and they pray more specifically, more confidently, and more boldly. There is little time for the trivial when one is pleading for the life of his or her baby. Just as the saying goes that there are no atheists in foxholes, there don't appear to be any in the neonatal intensive care unit either.

Hoekstra tries to maintain a balance between optimism and realism, a balance rooted in both his faith and medical experience. Even when everything is done for some babies, they still die. Only God creates life and sustains it at such a young age. Hoekstra ultimately asks whether things are being done for the baby or simply to the baby. In nearly all cases, the Lord helps him realize whether it's time to discontinue treatment when a baby has made no effort to respond to medical treatment. There comes a point when the parents must decide to turn the baby over to God. "God is faithful in helping us make agonizing decisions," Hoekstra says.

"But if [people say] it must die because it is flawed, or because it will be difficult to care for or, God forbid, because it is too expensive, then something is wrong," Hoekstra says. "A baby's physical and cognitive life does not have to be perfect to have value and meaning." While such a baby can put the rest of the family under great stress, that child also can be a tremendous blessing and inspiration.

Hoekstra is grateful that God has equipped him to relate to people at the greatest crisis in their lives, for he notes that pain is not meant to be endured alone. God, who sent his Son to die an excruciating death, understands when people cry out in despair.

"I try to never forget that life is sacred," Hoekstra says. "It's a rare privilege to walk through the most critical period of the lives of these parents. To see how they respond to the situation is to learn what it means to have faith."

>> JEAN CHAMBERLAIN-FROESE

A Canadian doctor ministers to Uganda's mothers.

Grief sweeps over Dr. Jean Chamberlain-Froese as she stands in the back hall of the university hospital in Kampala, Uganda. On a metal trolley before her lie five babies—three stillborn infants and two neonatal deaths. The wee bodies are wrapped in thin blankets. Name tags on each blanket identify the children's mothers.

The doctor reads the names and then thinks of another mother—one who died of pregnancy-related complications in the same hospital a few hours ago. Six needless deaths in one day, she thinks. If this happened in North America, authorities would launch an investigation and heads would roll. But here? Nothing happens.

Jean turns from the trolley with increased determination to save the lives of Uganda's mothers and children. A specialist in obstetrics and gynecology, she's committed to using her medical skills and her voice to make necessary changes, and she's succeeding. In 2005, Froese cofounded Save the Mothers, an international organization whose mission is to improve the quality of life for mothers in developing countries. If mothers enjoy good health, their children also benefit, she reasons. She bases her efforts on Proverbs 31:9: "Open thy mouth, judge righteously, and plead the cause of the poor and needy."

"As a follower of Christ, it's my responsibility to speak up for the rights of the destitute, for those who can't defend themselves," says Jean. "Ugandan mothers and children fall into this category." She quotes startling statistics to support her stance:

- A woman in Africa has a 1 in 16 chance of dying from pregnancy-related complications—a stark contrast from the industrialized world where that figure is 1 in 4,000.

- These medical difficulties claim the lives of approximately 17 Ugandan women each day, or 6,000 annually.

- Most of these deaths are from severe bleeding. This could be remedied with a 33-cent medication, less than the price of a cup of coffee.

- On the average, each woman who dies leaves four children behind. Those children are 3 to 10 times more likely to die within two years than those living with both parents.

Jean, an assistant professor at Canada's McMaster University, had practiced medicine in Zimbabwe, Zambia, Pakistan, and Russia before her first rural hospital posting in Uganda in 1998. Nothing had prepared her for the dire need she encountered: water supply was sporadic; forty patients shared one room; flimsy mattresses covered the beds; patients had to supply their own bedding, plastic gloves, and medications; surgical equipment, including anesthesia, was either outdated or nonexistent. Local doctors and nurses were overworked and often didn't want to be there, and their attitudes toward patients reflected their frustration. The combination of poor facilities and ill treatment frightened expectant mothers who, in turn, refused to visit the hospital for prenatal care or for their baby's safe delivery. This jeopardized the mothers' well-being, which in turn placed their babies and other children at risk.

Inadequate facilities and poor treatment contributed to the nation's high maternal mortality rate, but Jean soon discovered a deeper issue. "I realized that the root problem was how women are viewed within their community. If they're properly valued, then their communities will be willing to invest in medical services to ensure their health. Unfortunately, the opposite is usually true."

In this culture, Jean discovered, women are denied the freedom to make decisions about their own health. They must receive permission and money from their husbands before seeking medical care. If a woman needs a Caesarean section to deliver her child safely but her husband is not present to give permission, doctors refuse to operate. This usually results in the woman's death.

She also discovered cultural superstitions that endanger women and children. One myth says that women who need C-sections have been unfaithful to their husbands. That misunderstanding causes expectant mothers to stay far from hospitals. Another belief says that pregnancy is like a battle for each individual woman. She goes in and fights that battle. Some mothers win; some lose.

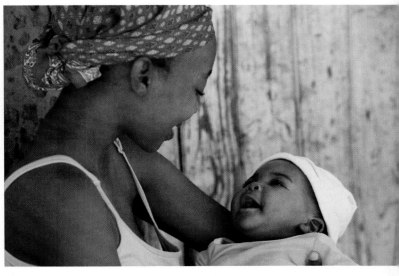

A woman in Africa has a 1 in 16 chance of dying from pregnancy-related complications.

"You don't see the community rally around the woman if she has complications," says Jean. "No one says, 'Let's find transportation and take her to the hospital, and let's make sure the hospital provides decent care.' If the woman dies, it's because she lost her battle and she's considered a failure. Her family will spend one or two hundred dollars for her funeral, but no one donates a few dollars to save her life."

Because taking a rural woman to a hospital requires time, family members are often reluctant to help her. Jean says the common thought is: We can't afford to lose two weeks of work to save this mother's life. "She's not valued as highly important in the family, the one who raises the children and ensures their health. From an economic point of view, it makes sense to invest in a mother's health. It saves money in the long run, but people don't see it that way," she says. "People think short term—I'm going to lose two weeks now; rather than—If we don't commit two weeks now, we'll lose the mother of these children."

Jean cites the story of a mother who hemorrhaged to death after childbirth. A film crew went to the funeral and interviewed the woman's 13-year-old daughter. "I don't know what to do," the girl said. "My mother was everything. She encouraged and comforted me. She taught me how to cook and do other everyday things. Now she's gone. I'll have to leave school to take over her responsibilities."

This scenario is commonplace. In many cases, the father sends his children to live with other families who are already struggling financially to feed and care for their own youngsters. The end result? Children's health is ccompromised, and medications are not affordable if diseases such as pneumonia or malaria strike them. "When the mother dies, the whole family suffers," says Jean, "and when the family breaks down, society follows. Satan loves to see this happen. But we can make a difference by praying intentionally and then doing something about the problem."

Following her own counsel, Jean and Dr. Florence Mirembi, former chair of the OB Gyn department at Uganda's Makerere University, established Save the Mothers. Their strategy is simple but effective: train leaders such as journalists, politicians, health workers, social workers, teachers, and pastors to educate others about the problem. In conjunction with the health program taught at the Ugandan Christian University, professionals earn a master's degree in public health leadership. The course requires them to attend classes for three weeks, three times a year for two years. They must also complete a major project focused on safe motherhood in their own area of work.

"Basically, these leaders are being trained in preventative medicine," says Jean. "They're learning about the essentials needed to save a mother's life. But they're also learning to integrate their new knowledge with their daily lives. As a result of their influence, legislation has been passed to include maternal health care in the nation's budget, and the public is learning about the problem through media coverage. Perhaps most importantly, these professionals are learning about the key to behavioral change— understanding that women are not just objects; they are valued people."

Alex, a student-leader enrolled in Save the Mothers, works for a nongovernmental agency that serves people with HIV/AIDS. Upon completing one module, he returned to his village and met with women's groups to discuss their health issues. "A man meeting with women's groups is far from the norm in this culture; nevertheless, the event was an overwhelming success," recalls Jean. "Alex later testified to being a changed person having taken the course. He said, 'I see women differently now.' That's exactly what I want to hear."

Her role as advocate for Ugandan mothers and children has given Jean a deeper understanding of God's love and concern for people within the context of a fallen world. "God values the poor and destitute, and He's moving people such as national professionals to get involved on their behalf. It's happening in Uganda, and we hope to establish Save the Mothers in Asia as well. But we need more North Americans to come alongside and become advocates, too. Scripture says we're to pray to the Lord of the harvest to send forth laborers, so that's what we're doing. The North American Christian community can engage in this battle by learning more about the problem, praying for improvement, traveling to Uganda and other similar countries to see the struggle firsthand, financially supporting programs that care for the health of mothers and children, and telling others."

"Poor maternal care is a neglected tragedy," says Jean. "Rather than simply lamenting the issue, we, as believers, ought to cast a vision for a solution and then move forward on behalf of the poor and destitute."

>> CHARLES DE HAAN

A physician revives a traditional approach to health care.

Dr. Charles De Haan is a third-generation physician. His grandfather practiced medicine in Michigan in the early 1900s, but felt called to abandon his little black bag to study a big black leather-bound Bible. His grandfather's passion for the study of Scripture (coupled with his intrinsic concern for the spiritual well-being of people) resulted in the founding of Calvary Church in Grand Rapids and a media ministry known as The Radio Bible Class.

While one of Dr. M. R. De Haan's sons followed in his father's ministerial footsteps, another son took up the elder De Haan's medical mantle. It was into the latter son's family that Charles was born.

During the 1950s and '60s, the life of a general practice physician in the western suburbs of Chicago was much like that of Marcus Welby, MD. Charles and his siblings would often accompany their doctor-father as he called on his patients.

"Those occasions impacted me more than I realized at the time," Charles recalls. "Long before I had any interest in studying medicine or becoming a physician, I understood the significance of caring for someone in an environment in which they felt secure."

Still Charles did not grow up dreaming of stethoscopes and scalpels. It wasn't until his sophomore year at Taylor University that he began to think increasingly about a future in medicine. He was surprised at his aptitude for math and science. For the first time in his life, Charles wondered if the Lord might indeed be calling him to practice medicine as a means of ministering to the people's physical and spiritual needs.

After completing his undergraduate degree, the would-be doctor attended Chicago Medical School and then fulfilled his residency requirements at the University of Illinois family practice program in Rockford, Illinois. With a wife and three daughters to provide for, Charles settled in the Rockford area working in emergency medicine at a Swedish American hospital. In addition to working in emergency medicine and becoming board certified, he worked in an occupational medicine program, also in Rockford.

After seven years of providing for the needs of walk-ins and critical-care patients at the ER, Charles began to wonder if there might be a better way of going about the task of doctoring. The discomfort and emotional trauma which required patients to seek urgent care was exacerbated by getting to the hospital. For elderly people in particular, having to wait in a crowded waiting room and then wade through the seemingly endless paperwork before being seen was incredibly stressful.

"In the emergency department where I worked, my colleagues and I saw many patients who would have been more appropriately cared for in their homes," Charles notes. "I couldn't help but think about the pattern my grandfather and my dad observed when meeting patients on their home turf. I wondered if a case couldn't be made for returning to the familiar practice that had been deemed obsolete."

Charles's inclinations led him to do some investigation. The studies he researched validated his hunches. They showed that 85 percent of patients in the ER didn't need to be there. They could just as easily have been treated in the comfort of their own home. Relying on his father's experiences and his own research, he evaluated the strengths and weaknesses of house calls in light of today's portable technology. In 1993, with the courage of a pioneer, Charles devised a new paradigm that he called his "back to the future" approach to home health care.

"In an increasingly impersonal culture, people can easily feel more like a number than an individual," Charles admits. "House calling is much more personal. My patients get to know me better and I get to know them better. What is more, their trust level goes up. They are impressed about doctors who will make the extra effort to care for them in this special way."

© 2012 by Carme Balcells.
Used under license of Shutterstock, Inc.

"Essentially, our practice actually is just like any other primary care practice," Charles explains. "The primary difference is that we see the patients in their home. But there are other differences. We also attempt to bring a spiritual component to our care."

Based in northern Illinois, this unique program is the first full-time house-call practice in the Midwest. It currently covers 10 counties between Chicago and Rockford and primarily serves the elderly, disabled, and those who are housebound. A central office staffed by a full-time nurse and administrative assistants attend to the initial calls for help and schedule visits. In addition, they communicate with the families, dispatch home health care workers, and support the doctors in the field. On average, 600 house calls are made each month.

"Essentially, our practice actually is just like any other primary care practice," Charles explains. "The primary difference is that we see the patients in their home. But there are other differences. We also attempt to bring a spiritual component to our care."

As a responsible physician, Charles insists that the physical health of his patients is his primary concern. But as a committed Christian and active member at Harvest Bible Church in Rockford, he launched the MD at Home program assuming that "in home" care would lend itself to serving the "whole" person. With that assumption, Matthew 25:36 was identified as a theme verse. Jesus's explanation that those who visit the sick and needy are actually ministering unto Him seemed to capture both the physical and spiritual dimensions of the program's nontraditional approach.

"Because we see people who are in such great physical need in their familiar surroundings, we have many opportunities to discuss more than just their health concerns," Charles observes. "Given the informal setting, it is only natural to discuss their spiritual and social concerns with them. We have had many opportunities to pray with our patients and have even prayed with some to receive the Lord."

In the decade since MD at Home began, Charles has become more adept at recognizing the Lord's presence while making house calls. As he's reviewed patients' charts, he's been able to trace the hand of God in unexpected ways. For example, while calling on one patient with Alzheimer's disease, he seized upon a brief lucid period of time and led her to profess faith in the Lord. "This specific example happened as my nurse practitioner was doing the house call in my absence," he recalls. "We found out later that the Christian Medical Society, of which I am a member, had us listed to pray for on the day when the patient professed faith in the Lord." On another occasion, while stopping to check on a patient, he ended up participating in a home Bible study.

In addition to the medical charts Charles and his colleagues keep (there are five physicians who work with MD at Home), they also make mental notes of the more unusual settings in which they've found themselves.

Given the severity of Midwestern winters, MD at Home doctors are often forced to navigate icy roads to reach a patient's home. On more than one occasion they have had to shovel a path from an unplowed driveway to the front door. But that isn't the only shoveling these doctors have been called to do in order to render service.

As might be expected, the homes of elderly house-bound patients are quite unlike a sterile hospital setting where everything is clean and organized. The homes and apartments of those who live alone are often cluttered and impassable. Before tending to the needs of the patient they've driven to see, these "physicians on wheels" have had to clear paths through hallways stacked two feet high with newspapers, magazines, boxes, and litter.

Once while going to see an elderly woman patient in Chicago's inner city, Charles was approached by a rough-looking gang. He nervously told the apparent leader he was a doctor and stated that he was seeing one of the elderly women in the neighborhood. Amazingly, the gang stepped aside and let him pass. As he cautiously made his way to the graffiti-sprayed housing project, he worried about his car on the street. Although it was locked, there was expensive medical equipment that could easily be stolen from it, including an ultrasound and an EKG machine. Charles whispered a prayer as he entered the run-down building and cared for his patient with sensitivity. As he exited the building, Charles noticed the gang was waiting for him.

"My hands were sweaty when I saw them again," Charles recalls. "But I had nothing to worry about. They had hung around just to ask me some medical advice about one of their members who had AIDS. And they had been the means the Lord used to answer my prayer about my car. Without me knowing it, they had been guarding it."

Charles admits that he would not continue with his innovative approach to medical care were it not for his God-given desire to minister to patients' physical as well as spiritual needs. The complexity and inconvenience of the "house call" practice prevents most new doctors from even considering it. But he hopes those who view their medical calling as a ministry will at least look for ways to increase their personal contact with patients.

"Our calling as physicians gives us the privilege of responding to obvious needs of those who look to us," Charles contends. "But that is just the start. A doctor/patient relationship opens the door to share at a more personal level about less obvious needs our patients have. For me, making house calls in Jesus's name provides me with one open door after another."

MEDICINE

·······················

REDEMPTIVE FIELD ANALYSIS 1

HONOR STATEMENT: I, the undersigned student, hereby declare before God, before the school, and before the professor that I have read this chapter in its entirety, that I have completed the following exercise with help from no other sources, except as required by the questions, and that I neither have shared nor will share this work with anyone.

Signature: _____   Date: _____

Analysis 1

1. Using words from the fifth chapter, define the term redemptive communicator.

_____

_____

_____

_____

_____

_____

2. Summarize one of this chapter's profiles in the space below. Include the most important details. Omit unnecessary details.

_____

_____

_____

_____

_____

_____

_____

_____

_____

_____

_____

3. If you were asked to use this story or a specific part of this story to support an idea, one that you could present as its main point to an audience, which idea would you present? State this idea as a single declarative sentence in the space that follows:

_____

_____

_____

_____

_____

_____

4. The fifth chapter states that a redemptive communicator interacts with other people in a way that promotes what God values in this world according to Scripture. Review the chapter's list of things that God values. Then, in the space below, identify the specific God-valued thing that this profilee promotes according to the profile. Be sure to explain both how the profilee promotes this specific thing and why you believe this thing is something God values according to Scripture.

_____

_____

_____

_____

_____

_____

_____

_____

_____

_____

_____

_____

_____

_____

_____

_____

_____

5. Which other God-valued things does this profilee promote? Identify these and explain how he or she promotes them.

_____

_____

_____

_____

_____

_____

_____

_____

_____

_____

_____

_____

_____

_____

MEDICINE

·························

REDEMPTIVE FIELD ANALYSIS 2

HONOR STATEMENT: I, the undersigned student, hereby declare before God, before the school, and before the professor that I have read this chapter in its entirety, that I have completed the following exercise with help from no other sources, except as required by the questions, and that I neither have shared nor will share this work with anyone.

Signature: _____   Date: _____

Analysis 2

1. Using words from the fifth chapter, define the term redemptive communicator.

_____

_____

_____

_____

_____

_____

_____

2. Summarize another of this chapter's profiles in the space below. Include the most important details. Omit unnecessary details.

_____

_____

_____

_____

_____

_____

_____

_____

_____

_____

_____

_____

_____

_____

3. If you were asked to use this story or a specific part of this story to support an idea, one that you could present as its main point to an audience, which idea would you present? State this idea as a single declarative sentence in the space that follows:

_____

_____

_____

_____

_____

_____

_____

_____

_____

_____

4. The fifth chapter states that a redemptive communicator interacts with other people in a way that promotes what God values in this world according to Scripture. Review the chapter's list of things that God values. Then, in the space below, identify the specific God-valued thing that this profilee promotes according to the profile. Be sure to explain both how the profilee promotes this specific thing and why you believe this thing is something God values according to Scripture.

_____

_____

_____

_____

_____

_____

_____

_____

_____

_____

_____

_____

_____

_____

_____

_____

_____

5. Which other God-valued things does this profilee promote? Identify these and explain how he or she promotes them.

_____

_____

_____

_____

_____

_____

MEDICINE

. . . .

REDEMPTIVE FIELD ANALYSIS 3

HONOR STATEMENT: I, the undersigned student, hereby declare before God, before the school, and before the professor that I have read this chapter in its entirety, that I have completed the following exercise with help from no other sources, except as required by the questions, and that I neither have shared nor will share this work with anyone.

Signature: _____   Date: _____

Analysis 3

1. Using words from the fifth chapter, define the term redemptive communicator.

_____

_____

_____

_____

_____

_____

_____

_____

2. Summarize another of this chapter's profiles in the space below. Include the most important details. Omit unnecessary details.

_____

_____

3. If you were asked to use this story or a specific part of this story to support an idea, one that you could present as its main point to an audience, which idea would you present? State this idea as a single declarative sentence in the space that follows:

_____

_____

_____

_____

_____

_____

_____

_____

_____

_____

4. The fifth chapter states that a redemptive communicator interacts with other people in a way that promotes what God values in this world according to Scripture. Review the chapter's list of things that God values. Then, in the space below, identify the specific God-valued thing that this profilee promotes according to the profile. Be sure to explain both how the profilee promotes this specific thing and why you believe this thing is something God values according to Scripture.

_____

_____

_____

_____

_____

_____

_____

_____

_____

_____

_____

_____

_____

_____

_____

_____

_____

5. Which other God-valued things does this profilee promote? Identify these and explain how he or she promotes them.

_____

_____

_____

_____

_____

_____

MATH & SCIENCE >>

MATH & SCIENCE

 DAVID BLOCK

A Jewish astronomer's spiritual odyssey.

The year was 1969. The event had been advertised on the radio again and again. I arose at four o'clock in the morning and watched a blazing comet with utter awe, as its tail stretched across the eastern skies. My love affair with astronomy had begun.

South African astronomer Jack Bennett, who discovered the comet and whose name the heavenly object bore, became my hero. The next day I telephoned him and asked him rather timidly, "May I meet with you?" To my surprise he said, "Yes, do come over." And it was really then that the little hidden flame which had been ignited began burning to understand the universe.

Shortly after this my father bought me a four-and-a-half inch reflector telescope. That was no little thing for a teenager. With that incredible instrument, I could start to look at planets like Saturn and at some of the nebulae in which stars are born.

I wanted to pursue studies in astronomy and my father was my biggest supporter. Leon Block always encouraged me to question things, to look beyond the ordinary and to make up my own mind. After all, we were Jews and that was part of our tradition as well.

I wanted to pursue studies in astronomy and my father was my biggest supporter. Leon Block always encouraged me to question things, to look beyond the ordinary and to make up my own mind. After all, we were Jews and that was part of our tradition as well.

My Jewish Upbringing

Both of my parents' Orthodox Jewish families have their roots in Lithuania. And we certainly kept to all the traditions as well; my mother would light the Sabbath candles and we would have a traditional Sabbath meal together. I went to synagogue both on Friday night and Saturday. We kept Passover. I fasted on Yom Kippur. I was bar mitzvah. We were practicing Jews. And I did all the things expected of a good Jewish boy. Actually, I felt that I was doing the best that I knew how to live out my Jewish faith.

Now this didn't mean that I was unquestioning when it came to the things of God. On the contrary, I'd listen in synagogue as the rabbis expounded how God was a personal God and how God would speak to Moses, to Abraham, to Isaac, and to Jacob, and wonder how I fit into all of it. And by the time I entered university, I became concerned over the fact that I had no assurance that God was indeed a personal God. I did know that He was an historical God and that He did deliver our people from the hands of Pharaoh. But that seemed far removed from me in this scientific age. Those were "stories," as it were.

Where was the personality and the vibrancy of a God Who could speak to David Block? If God is truly God, I reasoned, then why had He suddenly changed His character? The seeds of doubt were sprouting.

University Years

In order to follow my interest in astronomy, I entered the Witwatersrand University in Johannesburg (South Africa). I sought a bachelor of science degree in applied mathematics and computer science. As a professional astronomer, a background in mathematics and statistics would be essential.

While still a student, I was appointed to be a "demonstrator" on the staff—in other words, I would help students with their tutorial problems on a formal basis. And while a student, I also became quite friendly with Lewis Hurst, then professor of genetics and of medicine.

He had a great interest in astronomy, if only from an amateur point of view, and he asked if I would give him individual lessons.

Week by week, Lewis and I would sit around the table and I would discuss the complexities of the cosmos with him and also explain fundamental terms in astronomy such as "black holes" and "quasars." It was a full but private course I was giving him.

The friendship grew and I started sharing my feelings about the cosmos with him—that it is so beautiful, that God is so creative, that He's made this stunning world. I even shared my doubts with him: "Are we, as Shakespeare said, just as a 'fleeting shadow to appear and then disappear'? What is our purpose for living? What's the raison d'etre for being here? Is there a Designer out there?"

Lewis listened thoughtfully and then spoke, "David, there is an answer to all your questions."

"You know, Lewis, what does concern me is that the universe is so large, it's so immense. Do we go anywhere when we die?"

"There's an answer to all the questions you're asking," Lewis repeated. "Would you be willing—I know you come from an Orthodox Jewish family—but would you be willing to meet with a dear friend of mine, the Reverend Mr. John Spyker?"

My parents had taught me to seek answers where they may be found, and so I consented to meet with this Christian minister. Of course, in my heart, when I had put my telescope on Saturn and saw it in all its majesty and splendor—its rings simply encircling that globe—I just knew that there was a Great Designer. In fact, I knew there must be a personal God.

The Reverend Mr. Spyker read to me from the New Testament book of Romans where Paul says that Y'shua (Jesus) is a stumbling block to Jewish people, but that those who would believe in Y'shua would never be ashamed.

Suddenly it all became very clear to me: Y'shua had fulfilled the messianic prophecies in the Hebrew Scriptures, such as where the Messiah would be born and how he was to die. While my people were still waiting for the Messiah, I suddenly knew that I knew that I knew that I knew that Jesus was the Messiah and is the Messiah. And I surrendered my heart and my soul to him that day. That was in October of 1976.

I gave Judaism a chance and I accepted Him who is fully, fully Jewish. Paul, before he believed in Jesus, was a student of the great rabbi, Gamaliel. He was a Hebrew of the Hebrews. He had studied. He had examined. Yet, when Paul met the Master face to face, the Master mastered him. The Master mastered me as well.

Faith and Science

It might seem strange to some that a scientist and a Jew could come to faith in Jesus. But faith is never a leap into the dark. It is always based on evidence. All people believe and all scientists believe. They don't all believe in a personal God, of course, but each one of us uses our own measure of faith. Each one of us has a personal world system, a personal belief system.

As a scientist, I always think logically and I reason things out. That was how my whole search for God began. I looked through my telescope at Saturn and said to myself, Isn't there a great God out there? And when I studied relativity, relativistic astrophysics, cosmology and all these beautiful areas of mathematics, they pointed me to the fact that this whole universe is masterfully made, finely-tuned, and controlled by the Great Designer. The logical next step was to want to meet this Designer face-to-face.

Among astronomers today there is great theistic sentiment; even if scientists don't say Jesus has made the universe, they are coming to the very distinct conclusion that the universe is not an accident. The Big Bang is not viewed as a cosmological firecracker. As the physicist Freeman Dyson put it: The universe seemed to be acting in anticipation for the appearance of mankind.

So it is on the basis of logic that we can understand that we live in a universe made by a personal God. It's logic from start to finish.

When it comes to God, many scientists lean toward assumptions that are philosophically comfortable to them. For example, in the Big Bang universe there is an unverifiable assumption called the "principle of homogeneity," which asserts that on a large scale there is "no preferred center"—each point is equivalent in every sense to every other point. This, then, is a drastic departure from the cozy framework early cosmologists had worked with in their geocentric universe models.

Let me explain: If we go back to the 1500s, before the impact of the work of Copernicus, the worldview of the universe was a geocentric one. The earth was the center and the sun went around the earth as did all the stars, and to many it was a very reassuring idea to adopt. In 1543 Copernicus's De Revolutionibus was published and we perceived ourselves to be living in a heliocentric world, (although Ptolemy's earth-centered system was still taught at Harvard University in the first years after its founding in 1636). Mankind was dethroned from its central position in the universe.

Many astronomers have gone to extremes by saying we are simply a "zero" in this large cosmos. After all, there are 100,000 million stars in our Milky Way galaxy. That can make us feel very lonely and unimportant in the light of all the immensity. Yet a simple study shows the opposite is true.

The universe has not always existed. It had a definite beginning. God expanded our early universe at just the critical rate to avoid recollapse. Galaxies and stars then formed, but one must realize that half the stars in the night sky are members of binary or multiple star systems and are therefore unable to support life. (No stable planetary orbits could exist around such star systems.) Of the remaining half there are about 30 parameters which must be met in order for them to support life. With billions and billions of stars, it is improbable that all the conditions which must be met for the existence of life exist elsewhere. I would not be surprised if we were the only intelligent life species in the entire universe. In fact, leading evolutionists such as Dobzhansky and others have agreed that there has not been enough time for mankind to have assembled spontaneously within the time span of our universe.

We have astronomical evidence that demands a verdict. And I have examined this evidence, not from an emotional point of view, but from a logical point of view. We have historical evidence that Jesus, the Jew, lived and died and rose again from the dead. When Albert Einstein was asked by a reporter whether he accepted the historical existence of Jesus, he responded, "Unquestionably! No one can read the Gospels without feeling the actual presence of Jesus. His personality pulsates in every word. No myth is filled with such life. I am enthralled by the luminous figure of the Nazarene."

To the person who is seriously seeking today, I would say: read the gospels from an objective point of view, as Albert Einstein did, as Isaac Newton did. Don't let your emotions override or cloud your decision. Seek after truth and don't let anyone make up your mind for you. It is far too important. It does matter what you believe.

>> RAYMOND DAMADIAN

His invention revolutionized medicine and punctuated his faith in God.

Raymond Damadian realizes he could not have invented the magnetic resonance imaging (MRI) scanner, which has revolutionized the field of diagnostic medicine, without God's intervention. In a critical juncture in his business and personal life, Damadian chose to follow God's path rather than strike out on his own. The Lord has blessed him for his decision.

Damadian grew up in Queens, one of the five boroughs of New York City, and attended a church that taught virtue but did not emphasize the saving grace of Jesus Christ. It was clear from the beginning that Damadian was intelligent, and it showed in several of his pursuits, including music, sports, and academics. He studied violin at the Juilliard School of Music and received a bachelor of science degree in mathematics from the University of Wisconsin in 1956.

At the invitation of his friend—and future wife, Donna Terry—Damadian attended the Billy Graham Crusade in Madison Square Garden in 1957. At the time he was a tennis pro. But the simple salvation message stirred his heart. "I went forward, and I was profoundly impressed by what Billy Graham had to say," Damadian recalls. At that point Damadian realized that simply being a good person was not a ticket to heaven. "As far as I was concerned, I was doing everything right. I was a good student, I did what I thought I ought to do in terms of being careful about the needs of others, and I didn't have any special greedy ambitions. I thought I was a fine chap, which is maybe the most common failing of all for those who think they are living the Christian life, and that I could satisfy the Master's expectations of me with good works. But Scripture does not teach that."

Damadian and Terry married in 1960, just after he received his medical degree from Albert Einstein College of Medicine in New York. Forgetting about athletics and music, Damadian now focused on inventing a machine that could detect human cancer cells. Damadian rose in the academic world, doing work at Washington University, Harvard, and State University of New York. At such institutions, Damadian came in contact with several strong-minded atheists, and he slowly drifted away from God. His training in medicine and physics led him to develop a new theory of the living cell, the Ion Exchanger Resin Theory. He then desperately pushed to make the MRI scanner a reality as a means of detecting disease. "We were climbing the summit of trying to make magnets scan the human body, which the great majority of the scientific world said was impossible," he says.

"And there were a lot of technological problems to be overcome. So I was working night and day, and at that point, that's all that mattered." Most of his fellow academicians in the secular scientific world had no belief in God. Instead, these university professors believed they fully understood the world, it was under their control, and God didn't play a role—neither in creating the earth nor seeing that it kept going. In short, He was not needed.

Asking God for guidance was not really a priority for Damadian at that point. "I was foolish," he says. "I had been taken in by the arguments of the secular scientific world, and the principal damage was the acceptance of evolution." Looking back, Damadian sees how such thinking could be the linchpin in destroying faith. "Once you destroy the foundation of Genesis, then all the rest of Scripture has to be qualified, and you don't have much left," he says. "Any time you don't like what something says, you write it off as allegorical or symbolical and you skirt the discomfort of confronting it."

By 1977, his life had drifted out of control because of his consuming desire to succeed in inventing the MRI scanner. "Because of the ill-begotten attitudes of the secular scientific world, I drifted away considerably," he remembers, "at one point telling my technician, to

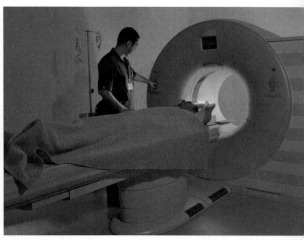

Raymond Damadian realizes he could not have invented the magnetic resonance imaging (MRI) scanner, which has revolutionized the field of diagnostic medicine, without God's intervention.

her horror, that there was no God." At the same time, with typically rebellious teenagers in his house, Damadian felt further alienated from God. "I wasn't the priest of the home that I should've been," he says.

Fortunately for Damadian, his family—his wife and his parents—still believed in God and believed God could redeem circumstances. They continued praying for him to return to the Lord, realizing that his accomplishments would only have lasting value if directed by God. Damadian went to his knees to seek the Lord's direction.

In July 1977, Damadian and his team achieved the first successful MRI scan of the human body. The following year he founded FONAR Corporation in Melville, New York, to manufacture the MRI scanner, which is now used in hundreds of medical institutions around the world. The MRI produces images of the interior of the body that are far more detailed than was possible with X-ray devices.

Since that time, Damadian has prayed and read Scripture every day. At his company, there is a prayer meeting every morning for employees who want to participate. "We try to do what the Lord would have us do in all that we do, which in business is not easy," he says.

Damadian is still facing cutthroat competition over patents. FONAR's rivals are huge, multinational corporations: General Electric, Siemens, Hitachi, and Toshiba. "These are companies we have to go toe-to-toe with or not eat," Damadian says. "We've looked to Malachi 3:11, which says: 'For My people I will stop the devourer, and you will have the fruit of your vine.' That's the problem we've been facing as a small company. We need to be able to use our own seed corn, but the giants eat our seed corn as fast as we produce it."

FONAR now has 650 employees, including Damadian's two sons. Timothy is an executive and Jevan is an electrical engineer. The youngest of his three children, daughter Keira, is in nursing school and plans to use that training in missions. She has been on short-term mission trips to Burundi, Thailand and Mexico.

As he grows older, Damadian sees God's purpose in allowing him to invent the MRI. "I can be a voice within the scientific world and I am in a position to say that the Biblical account of origins is the correct one," he says. "I am in a position to get people to take notice where they would normally not have any exposure at all. It's come to pass that God has made it possible for me to be a witness on an important subject."

Indeed, President Ronald Reagan bestowed the National Medal of Technology upon Damadian. And he has been inducted into the National Inventors Hall of Fame.

Unlike many of his colleagues, Damadian knows that God and science are compatible. "The greatest scientists of the nineteenth century and the early part of the twentieth century were all very godly men," he says. "Unless you have your eye on the Almighty, there's nothing directing you and encouraging you to take the daring steps to think big.

Fear of the unknown is a strong current, especially when the fear of embarrassment is even greater. Only those who can trust in the Lord get beyond these fears to attempt big things. So many of the great accomplishments in science by people like Louis Pasteur, Isaac Newton, and James Clerk Maxwell were made because these men were not turned inward to the shrunken confines of the human mind." Such thinkers, Damadian says, believed, as Johannes Kepler put it, that it was their duty to "think God's thoughts after Him" or, as Newton said, "All of my discoveries came in response to prayer."

>> LEROY DORMINY

A veterinarian reaches people through animal science.

Dr. Leroy Dorminy may not always look like a man on a serious mission. He often wears plaid shirts, blue jeans, and walking shoes—suitable attire for a veterinarian like him who may be called upon to treat a dog with worms one minute and deliver a calf the next. But despite his modest appearance, Dorminy is a man who is serious about his vocation and about his faith in Christ.

Dorminy is the founder and director emeritus of Christian Veterinary Mission (CVM), (www.christianvetmission.org). The purpose of the nonprofit organization is to challenge, empower, and facilitate veterinarians to serve others though their profession, living out their Christian faith on the job. The work is Christ-centered and veterinary focused.

CVM encourages members to be involved in ministry to the people of other countries. They do this through a variety of outreaches that involve evangelism, education, encouragement, modeling, and prayer. As the Lord himself did, the mission seeks to address people's physical and spiritual needs.

So far, the organization has established outreach programs in more than 35 countries, including Haiti, Bolivia, Nepal, Bangladesh, Cambodia, Sudan, and Kenya.

"One of the most amazing places I've gone into is Mongolia," Dorminy says. "It's astounding how CVM has been able to meet the needs in that area. Most of the people there are herders, of one form or another—sheep, goats, horses. They have lots of animals."

By teaching the natives of Mongolia how to better care for their livestock, CVM has been able to establish a broad-based ministry in the region. "Our professional skills have allowed us to minister to these people in a way that I never thought possible," Dorminy says.

By teaching the natives of Mongolia how to better care for their livestock, CVM has been able to establish a broad-based ministry in the region.

There are currently 22 veterinarians serving through long-term missions for CVM, typically via three-year terms. And last year, 125 veterinarians served on short-term overseas missions trips with CVM.

The vision for sending veterinarians into undeveloped countries as lay ministers came to Dorminy in 1975 during an international conference that his denomination held in Stockholm. More than 10,000 people from over 84 different countries were in attendance. Dorminy recalls the moment when the Lord first impressed him with the idea of a Christian veterinary mission.

"We were in a small Bible-study group and our discussion leader asked a woman from an emerging nation in Africa how Christians of the developed world could help her people. She replied, 'Come and teach us your skills that we may do things for ourselves.'"

Dorminy was struck by the profound simplicity of her suggestion.

"I was 53 when I attended that convention. I went looking for something. I wasn't completely satisfied with what I was doing. This lady's comment weighed on me. I was really bothered by it," Dorminy recalls.

The woman's challenge continued to gnaw at him even after he returned to his practice in rural Georgia. In response, he volunteered his services to a mission board for overseas service and soon found himself in the Dominican Republic, where he performed short-term mission work alongside Charley Purtle, an agricultural missionary from Oklahoma. Purtle had requested help from someone with animal husbandry and veterinary skills. Dorminy was apparently God's answer to Purtle's plea. The experience proved to be life-changing for the former.

"That was the most satisfying two weeks I've ever spent, before or since," Dorminy claims. The opportunity to use his professional skills to minister to people in a practical hands-on fashion stirred something deep inside of Dorminy. The idea of getting more veterinarians into the fields as missionaries to needy people became an all-consuming goal—one that would not let him rest.

"I became less and less interested in my practice and more and more focused on CVM," Dorminy says. He wasn't intimidated by the idea of doing something that hadn't been done before.

"I'm a Type-A person. I don't go around many obstacles—I go through them," he says. So he hired another veterinarian to help run his Georgia office. And he spent three or four hours a night on the phone, raising support and interest in his vision.

"Every night I would work these leads. In nine months time, I had 300 people with a real interest in CVM." Some of those original 300 folks continue to support the ministry today, Dorminy, now in his 80s, notes with pride.

"Not all Christians are interested in missions. That I was able to identify 300 people that were, in that short of a time period, is really amazing."

A native Georgian, Dorminy came to know Christ at an early age. "I could go to the exact spot where I was sitting when the preacher was preaching in 1935," Dorminy says, recalling the meeting where he professed faith in Christ.

It was a small country church in Enigma, Georgia, just outside Tifton. The preacher had delivered a fiery sermon.

"He cautioned us that we needed to prepare ourselves for eternity. I remember him asking if we knew how long eternal life is," Dorminy recalls.

Dorminy, then 12, straightened his back when the preacher explained that in the time it would take a bird to move the earth to the moon, flying back and forth carrying one grain of sand at a time, eternity would just be beginning.
"I didn't go down to the altar because I was frightened. I went down because God's Spirit had touched my heart and I wanted to prepare myself for an eternity with Him," Dorminy recalls.

A stint in the Navy during World War II helped nurture Dorminy's desire to work outdoors with the animals he'd loved since boyhood.

"I was so tired of living on a steel ship for two years, I wanted to get outdoors. I liked science. And I had always liked animals. I thought being a veterinarian would enable me to combine those two," he observes.

But he was nourishing another love as well—his relationship with God. He believes God has endowed each of us with a special gift that He intends for us to use for His name's sake.

"One verse I've always utilized is 1 Peter 4:10. Each of us is called upon to use our gifts in dispensing God's grace to others. I've often said every one of us has special skills. I think we are to use those special skills in God's Kingdom, to help others with physical needs and to be a witness through that," Dorminy says.

And, he believes no one is better suited to helping underdeveloped nations and their people than veterinarians.

"Veterinarian medicine is a tough profession," Dorminy explains, "for a lot of reasons. You work with many species of animals—we can't focus on one. It's not very lucrative work, compared to human medicine. Vets have to be practical folks and they have to be problem solvers. I've done Caesarean sections in a stall covered in manure and saved both the cow and the calf. Conditions in veterinary practice are seldom ideal, and that is the same for missionaries overseas. If there is anything that describes missions, that's it— the need and ability to be practical and to utilize what you have. Veterinarians know how to do that."

CVM folks are doing life-saving work around the world, both for animals and for people. Before CVM arrived, Haiti was in dire need of skilled veterinarians, Dorminy says. "They only had about five vets in a country of five million people."

One of the ministry's goals has been to train locals as veterinary technicians. It gives the people a skill and helps the economy of the community, as well as it keeps their livestock healthy.

"These people can fulfill a need and perform useful skills," Dorminy observes, noting that CVM has trained more than a thousand such technicians in Haiti alone.

One day while feasting on a lunch of rice and beans with Keith Flannagan, one of CVM's missionaries, Dorminy asked the natives what they thought of the veterinarians' work in their country. A dark-skinned man put down his bowl and spoke up.

"Well, to be quite truthful with you, it's allowed me to make a living for my family. And more importantly, before I got into this program, I was lost. I didn't know what I was going to do. I'd lost all hope in life. This program has given me hope."

Dorminy has heard similar testimonials in every country in which CVM ministers. "In Nepal, veterinarian Karen Stoffer has been ministering to women. Nepal is one of the most notorious countries in the world for mistreatment of women. They are treated as mere chattel."

Dorminy said many times women are assigned away in marriage, often before they turn 14 years of age. "They are slaves to their own families," he says. "It's horrible to have to be married to a person you don't love and forced to have his children."

Stoffer befriended such a girl. When her husband ran off and left her with two children to care for, Stoffer stepped in to aid the distraught girl. "Karen was able to help this girl gain a skill and knowledge. She taught her how to read and write, which then enabled her to get a job to support her two boys," Dorminy says. "Karen was able to salvage this lady's life and the lives of her two boys by telling her about the hope Christ offers. I seldom read Karen's letters without shedding a tear. She writes the truth of what she encounters," Dorminy says.

It's truly gratifying to use one's professional skills to help people with physical, emotional, and spiritual problems, he adds. "Our profession allows us to minister to people in many ways. It allows us to share hope with the world."

Hope is what Christ gave each of us when He suffered that painful death upon the cross—hope for a life that outlasts suffering, sorrow, or shame; a life that will last far longer than it takes for a bird to fly to the moon and back; a life that will last vastly longer than any of our sufferings; an eternal life.

"Nepal is one of the most notorious countries in the world for mistreatment of women. They are treated as mere chattel."

That's the message that CVM strives to bring to the people of this world whose lives are touched daily by tremendous sorrows. "Everybody needs to have hope," Dorminy says. "It really touches me that we've been a catalyst for change in people's lives. They have some hope because of what CVM has been able to accomplish."

Sometimes people ask Dorminy how it is he's able to motivate veterinarians to leave the United States and devote their lives to working in underdeveloped nations. He gives the same answer every time.

"They don't do it because of me. They do it because of their commitment to the Lord and their tenacity as veterinarians," he says. "Being a vet steels them and makes them persevere. They rise to the challenge that mission work presents."
They've also learned that the best way to minister the love of Christ to another person is one-on-one. "If you are going to witness to somebody, you have to be involved with that person's life," Dorminy remarks. "You have to earn the right to witness to them. CVM does that by helping people with their animals. It allows us to minister in unbelievable ways."

GEORGE BARNA

A statistician aims to make the church more self-aware.

During his childhood in Princeton, New Jersey, George Barna attended Mass every Sunday, served as an altar boy, and went through catechism and confirmation classes. By the time he went to premarital counseling sessions, Barna wondered why his Church believed certain tenets and performed certain rituals. The priest advised him to stop asking such probing questions, to just accept what the Church teaches, and to believe that everything would work out fine.

He didn't realize it at the time, but Barna would go on to make it his life's work to examine the intricacies of Christian belief and behavior, often uncovering that what people claim with their mouths doesn't match how they act.

Barna, in graduate school as he prepared to wed in 1978, didn't think the priest's counsel to turn off his intellect sounded too reasonable. He and his new wife, Nancy, decided to go on their own quest to truly discover God.

They found a small Bible-believing church, where the pastor embarked on a pursuit they never had witnessed before: verse by verse detailed explanation of Scripture.

After a few weeks of the couple's attendance, the preacher came calling to the Barna home. He made a presentation of the Gospel message, ending with an invitation that they receive Jesus as Lord and Savior.

"I said I didn't think so," Barna recalls. "But I told the pastor if Jesus is as great as He claimed, I'd give Jesus a month to prove it." The preacher reluctantly agreed, provided that Barna attend Sunday morning church services, attend Wednesday evening Bible studies, read the Bible daily beginning with the Gospel of John, pray daily that God would reveal Himself, and allow the pastor to visit him weekly.

Before the end of the month, Barna had committed his life to Jesus.

Yet within a few months, Barna learned he needed to adhere to a set of religious rules to be a "real Christian." The minister told Barna he must look like a believer, and that meant shaving off his beard and wearing his hair in a specific style. Barna protested, but his arguments fell on deaf ears.

While many new Christians might have walked away from the faith under such circumstances, Barna determined to find another church.

"I had grown in my relationship with Christ and realized that even if whacky stuff goes on in the way people live and the man-made rituals they practice, Jesus is still real," Barna says.

Meanwhile, after earning two master's degrees from Rutgers University, Barna began working as a pollster for political candidates. Later, as the lone Christian at a Los Angeles media-research marketing firm, Barna received the assignment of helping several television ministries determine what worked and what didn't on the air.

That got Barna to thinking about full-time work in the field of studying Christian attitudes and actions. Although the Gallup Poll had long asked general religious questions, no one, until Barna came along, tracked in-depth responses about evangelical spiritual beliefs and behavior.

In 1984, he opened his own marketing-research firm, The Barna Research Group, then based in Glendale, California. (The company since has expanded and been renamed The Barna Group and relocated to Ventura, California.) In the intervening years he has continued to hone his skills and methods in order to provide current, reliable, and accurate bite-sized information to ministries wanting to make strategic marketing decisions.

Early on, many hailed Barna as an innovative wunderkind, delivering much-needed tell-it-like-it-is research on church health, leadership, and trends. But by the time he wrote his third book, Barna's detractors had grown vociferous, suggesting that relying on research, marketing, and strategic plans to communicate the Gospel amounted to secular selling out.

"Marketing in and of itself has no moral content," Barna notes. "It's just a process in which connections are made with people and each other's needs are met through a transaction." Despite the reservations of skeptics, many more people thought Barna's numbers, guided by Biblical principles, made sense in advancing the work of God's kingdom. They understood that marketing-research figures, if used wisely, could be a tool, just as preaching is. Many recognized that research can help the church, in response to Jesus's words: function in a culture of wolves with the wisdom of serpents (see Matt. 10:16).

Barna's influence continued to grow. His work helped pastors become more realistic and objective about the actual state of affairs their congregations were in, rather than assuming everything would run smoothly perpetually.

Along the way, as he publishes research findings, conducts all-day seminars for church leaders, and writes books, Barna has become a widely quoted authority—both inside and outside the church—on Christianity. His three-dozen books include best sellers such as *The Frog in the Kettle*, *User Friendly Churches*, and *Transforming Children into Spiritual Champions*.

He also has done much to challenge people to scrutinize the depth of their spirituality. While a Christian remnant lives faithfully and behaves ethically, Barna has reams of data showing that a lot of Americans think they are going to heaven even though they have no relationship with the Lord.

"Jesus died on the cross not to make people feel happy or to fill church auditoriums, but so that we can be transformed and completely committed to serve Him and other people," Barna says. "If Christ truly lives in us and the Holy Spirit truly guides us, there should be evidence of progress toward a greater state of holiness. It's a continual journey."

At times Barna becomes disappointed with those who are unwilling to examine whether their practices are truly Biblical. Their criticisms can be disheartening, but Barna continues his work, guided by the belief that calls His people to evaluate themselves and that sometimes, as with the Old Testament prophets, He calls individuals to issue this call to the current culture.

"It's never really concerned me whether people accept what I put out there because I'm doing this for God," Barna says. "Truth and transformation always have been my main focus."

But he still finds a ready audience willing to listen to his warnings. His family often accompanies him when he travels for his busy speaking schedule. He and his wife, Nancy, have several adopted daughters.

Barna continues to keep challenging ministry and institutional leaders, even when they wish he would go away with his challenging forecast for the American church.

"I can't worry about my critics," Barna says. "Jesus expects me to use all the years and the resources He gave me to facilitate transformation."

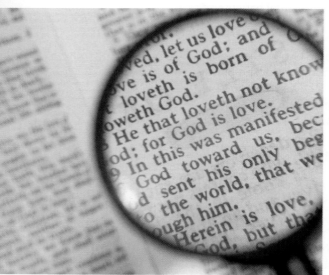

While a Christian remnant lives faithfully and behaves ethically, Barna has reams of data showing that a lot of Americans think they are going to heaven even though they have no relationship with the Lord.

MATH & SCIENCE

....

REDEMPTIVE FIELD ANALYSIS 1

HONOR STATEMENT: I, the undersigned student, hereby declare before God, before the school, and before the professor that I have read this chapter in its entirety, that I have completed the following exercise with help from no other sources, except as required by the questions, and that I neither have shared nor will share this work with anyone.

Signature: _____   Date: _____

Analysis 1

1. Using words from the fifth chapter, define the term redemptive communicator.

_____

_____

_____

_____

_____

_____

2. Summarize one of this chapter's profiles in the space below. Include the most important details. Omit unnecessary details.

_____

_____

_____

_____

_____

_____

_____

_____

_____

_____

_____

3. If you were asked to use this story or a specific part of this story to support an idea, one that you could present as its main point to an audience, which idea would you present? State this idea as a single declarative sentence in the space that follows:

_____

_____

_____

_____

_____

_____

4. The fifth chapter states that a redemptive communicator interacts with other people in a way that promotes what God values in this world according to Scripture. Review the chapter's list of things that God values. Then, in the space below, identify the specific God-valued thing that this profilee promotes according to the profile. Be sure to explain both how the profilee promotes this specific thing and why you believe this thing is something God values according to Scripture.

_____

_____

_____

_____

_____

_____

_____

_____

5. Which other God-valued things does this profilee promote? Identify these and explain how he or she promotes them.

MATH & SCIENCE

· ·

REDEMPTIVE FIELD ANALYSIS 2

HONOR STATEMENT: I, the undersigned student, hereby declare before God, before the school, and before the professor that I have read this chapter in its entirety, that I have completed the following exercise with help from no other sources, except as required by the questions, and that I neither have shared nor will share this work with anyone.

Signature: _____   Date: _____

Analysis 2

1. Using words from the fifth chapter, define the term redemptive communicator.

_____

_____

_____

_____

_____

_____

_____

2. Summarize another of this chapter's profiles in the space below. Include the most important details. Omit unnecessary details.

_____

_____

_____

_____

_____

_____

_____

_____

_____

_____

_____

_____

_____

_____

3. If you were asked to use this story or a specific part of this story to support an idea, one that you could present as its main point to an audience, which idea would you present? State this idea as a single declarative sentence in the space that follows:

_____

_____

_____

_____

_____

_____

_____

_____

_____

_____

_____

4. The fifth chapter states that a redemptive communicator interacts with other people in a way that promotes what God values in this world according to Scripture. Review the chapter's list of things that God values. Then, in the space below, identify the specific God-valued thing that this profilee promotes according to the profile. Be sure to explain both how the profilee promotes this specific thing and why you believe this thing is something God values according to Scripture.

_____

_____

_____

_____

_____

_____

_____

_____

_____

_____

_____

_____

_____

_____

_____

_____

5. Which other God-valued things does this profilee promote? Identify these and explain how he or she promotes them.

_____

_____

_____

_____

_____

_____

MATH & SCIENCE

·······················

REDEMPTIVE FIELD ANALYSIS 3

HONOR STATEMENT: I, the undersigned student, hereby declare before God, before the school, and before the professor that I have read this chapter in its entirety, that I have completed the following exercise with help from no other sources, except as required by the questions, and that I neither have shared nor will share this work with anyone.

Signature: _____   Date: _____

Analysis 3

1. Using words from the fifth chapter, define the term redemptive communicator.

_____

_____

_____

_____

_____

_____

_____

2. Summarize another of this chapter's profiles in the space below. Include the most important details. Omit unnecessary details.

_____

_____

_____

_____

_____

_____

_____

_____

_____

_____

_____

_____

_____

3. If you were asked to use this story or a specific part of this story to support an idea, one that you could present as its main point to an audience, which idea would you present? State this idea as a single declarative sentence in the space that follows:

_____

_____

_____

_____

_____

_____

_____

_____

_____

_____

_____

4. The fifth chapter states that a redemptive communicator interacts with other people in a way that promotes what God values in this world according to Scripture. Review the chapter's list of things that God values. Then, in the space below, identify the specific God-valued thing that this profilee promotes according to the profile. Be sure to explain both how the profilee promotes this specific thing and why you believe this thing is something God values according to Scripture.

_____

_____

_____

_____

_____

_____

_____

_____

_____

_____

_____

_____

_____

_____

_____

5. Which other God-valued things does this profilee promote? Identify these and explain how he or she promotes them.

_____

_____

_____

_____

_____

_____

ENGINEERING >>

ENGINEERING

R. G. LETOURNEAU

A successful engineer's earthly business had a heavenly motive.

DURING MUCH OF HIS LIFE, Robert Gilmour (Bob) LeTourneau was indeed widely known as a "mover of men and mountains." For 25 years he drove or flew across America and flew to several foreign countries, speaking in churches and auditoriums large and small, usually about six times a week.

He called himself "just a mechanic whom the Lord has blessed" and enthusiastically proclaimed to listeners that God needs business people as partners as well as preachers. Many began a partnership with God, especially after LeTourneau helped establish the Christian Business Men's Committee movement flourishing on a national and international basis. In his later years, he kept only 10 percent of his income and gave 90 percent to the Lord's work, and this undoubtedly moved many to tithe.

LeTourneau's eight-wheeled digger could quickly produce work that previously had required thousands of hours in manual labor.

A blue-collar worker in his younger years, he had worked as an iron molder, a brick layer, a gold miner, a stump puller, an irrigation ditch digger, and an auto mechanic. But in his 30s, he began to build earth-moving machines. His firm, R. G. LeTourneau, Inc., built huge earth movers that enabled him to "take part in and contribute to the development of those great, heavy construction machines that have helped produce our twentieth century," he claimed during the late 1950s.

His eight-wheeled digger could quickly produce work that previously had required thousands of hours in manual labor. Instead of men pushing 100-pound wheelbarrow loads to accomplish a task, the operator of the digger would push a button and the machine would pick up the loads of 1,500 wheelbarrows, rolling them off at 15 miles per hour (mph) instead of 2 mph.

When the Allies invaded the beaches of Normandy on June 6, 1944, Le Tourneau earth movers and other machinery accompanied the great invasion force. His equipment constituted about 50 percent of the equipment used in combat during World War II.

"On D-Day, as on islands in the Pacific, the bulldozers wallowed ashore to push aside the tank traps and barbed wire, and then rush, with upraised blades fending off machine gun bullets, to storm pill boxes, burying the fire slits under tons of dirt and smothering the gun crews that refused to flee or surrender," Le Tourneau wrote. "They sliced through hedgerows of Normandy, cut new approaches to bombed-out bridges, plowed through the debris of bombed cities, and had a field day tearing up the dragon's teeth, gun emplacements, and pill boxes of the 'impregnable' Siegfried Line. One bulldozer, we were told, did the work a thousand men did with shovels in World War I," according to his autobiography.

Bob LeTourneau was born November 30, 1888, on a farm near Richford, Vermont, and was named after his father's best friend, Robert Gilmour. He grew to become a "restless, inquisitive, energetic, determined, and ambitious boy" according to his mother. His brothers had less-biased opinions of him, describing him as "destructive, willful, stubborn, and fanatically determined to amount to nothing."

He invented what might be called his first earth-moving machine when he was 12, a heifer-pulled snow plow to ease his job of plowing snow. It was a V-shaped board with curving sides to shove snow to the side and make a path. It might have worked had not the heifer kicked it and him before he could really find out, curing him forever of his reliance on animal power of any kind.

That summer Bob had an accident that revealed what a wild kid he was. He swam out to a rock some 100 yards from shore. To return to shore, he dived off the rock and hit a rock he hadn't seen, and was groggy until the 50-degree water brought him to. He made it to shore before rescuers could reach him, and ran home and collapsed. It took 16 stitches to sew up the gash in his head. His father's comment hurt him: "Only fools jump in where angels fear to tread."

In his early teens, young Bob clashed with his father, and sparks would fly. Dad prayed for Bob and worked on him harder than his brothers and sisters combined, serving to make Bob feel picked on. When he was 13, after his dad became furious with him for cutting up fence posts for firewood, and called him too dumb to recognize a fence post when he saw one, Bob ran away. He spent that cold, fall night in a ravine and wondered how his father would feel when they found his frozen body.

Hunger pangs the next morning sent him a mile away to the home of a widow, Mrs. Spango, for whom he had done chores, and he became her hired man after she talked with his father. She was harder on him than Dad, making him wash until he felt his skin was wearing thin. He began milking cows before sunup and hauled in wood to carry the stove through the night. She pushed him out the door for school despite heavy snow, and he had to walk twice as far as he did while living at home. "There were no dumb Swedes in my family," Mrs. Spango declared, "and I won't have one now even if he does have a French name."

Thanksgiving came and Bob's sister Mattie coaxed him to join the family at the home of an aunt and uncle. While he was there, a heavy snow fell. Bob found himself following his father home as he broke a trail.

"In the morning I helped with chores, and discovered my father could make a fair batch of pancakes," LeTourneau wrote. "That led to my helping him cut wood . . . and on the job I made another discovery. As long as I was an eager and willing worker . . . Dad could be a mighty fine fellow. By noon I saw my running away from home and rebellious stand in all its pettiness, and I was one repentant boy."

He discovered his father's love and it changed his whole attitude.

Chores that he had hated and fought against resentfully, he did cheerfully because he wanted to serve his dad.

"It's like that when you discover the Lord, and you don't grow up," LeTourneau told audiences. "Your heavenly father is with you always and everywhere. If you aren't serving Him now, it's because you don't know Him, like I didn't really know my own father," he would assert. "But when you do know Him, you'll love Him, and when you love Him, you'll serve Him, and find great happiness."

In his early years, Bob attended services in a small, Plymouth Brethren church but recalled that he "heard a lot about God but without learning a thing."

School was a drag until the fifth grade, when he discovered that arithmetic makes sense. And geography became exciting when he learned that pink, green, and yellow areas on the map were real places, perhaps with palm trees instead of the snow that he was so accustomed to in Vermont and Minnesota, where the family resettled in his boyhood. At the same time, he took an interest in reading, enjoying all the fifth-grade books and most of those at sixth-grade level.

His teacher was delighted and his folks stunned, resulting in his skipping sixth grade and being promoted to the seventh. "What a mistake," LeTourneau wrote. "The seventh-graders had put in a long, earnest year on the subjects I had skimmed over so swiftly, and when it came to reciting, I wasn't in their league." At almost six feet tall, he was not only the biggest in the class, but "also the dumbest," he remembered, going on to say it resulted in his developing an inferiority complex. He quit trying and came to hate school.

After his family resettled again to Portland, Oregon, at age 14, he quit school following a heated session with his father. He soon was working as an apprentice molder at East Portland Iron Works, a place that "filled the bill for Dante's Inferno," he recalled facetiously. The boss set him to work with the comment, "It's a job for a strong back and a weak mind. There's a gondola full of sand. Shovel it into a wheelbarrow and bring it in here." He was advised "not to work hard but fast."

When he was 16, friend problems impacted Bob's life. First, the police came to him seeking information about a friend who was wanted for assault and battery. Then in rapid succession three other friends got into trouble with the law.

This sudden accumulation of troubles brought him face to face with himself. "I could tell myself all I was doing with my spare time was making a model steam engine, but I couldn't escape the fact that my closest associates were enrolled with the police," LeTourneau recalled in his autobiography. "'A man is known by the company he keeps,' said Dad."

The week before Christmas 1904, when Bob was 16, a citywide revival stirred Portland. He gave up working on his steam engine and decided to see if the revival could do anything for him. But after a week of concentrated singing and listening to sermons, he "didn't feel even a tremor of response." He told himself he might as well have stayed home and worked on his steam engine. When he confessed this to his mother, the look on her face made him realize he couldn't have hurt her more if he'd "stabbed her with a blunt knife."

"I gave myself a working over that night—no great flash of awareness. I just prayed to the Lord to save me," LeTourneau wrote. "All my bitterness was drained away. I was filled with such a vast relief that I could not contain it all. I ran to my mother. 'I'm saved,' I cried. 'You don't have to worry about me anymore. I have felt the love of our Lord Jesus Christ.'"

After a long silence, followed by a deep sigh, his mother responded, "Robert, we knew it had to happen. Two years ago, when we discovered we couldn't guide you, we left it in God's hands." Then she added, "But He kept us waiting a long time."

Bob entered New Year's Day 1905 with high hopes. At church, he joined the choir but soon quit because his "foundry-trained voice" was deep enough but usually not on tune. At the young people's missionary society, led by his two sisters, he was so painfully inarticulate that he could only squeak when he was called on to pray.

So things were off to a disappointing start for the new year. Then, in the fall, the foundry where he was working burned down. Now he was without a job. He found himself planted at the family table "mooching free meals." He considered himself "big, dumb, unemployed, and unemployable."

It was in May 1921 when Bob LeTourneau, at the age of 32, hung out his sign "R. G. LeTourneau, Inc." at 122 Moss Avenue, Stockton, California, and began what in time became a huge business—manufacturing huge earth-moving machines. The barn became his machine shop and the acre of land his open-air factory. But he joked, "I was in business for five years before I noticed it had started. It was that small." Over the years he put machinery on the market that contractors welcomed: the rooter, hopper wagons, bottom-dump carts, bulldozers, and semi-drag scrapers, to name a few.

However, before that sign went up, Bob had many bumps in the road, along with memorable adventures, that followed his conversion to Christ in late 1904.

A few weeks after that life-changing experience, Bob's father received a letter from a friend saying that a job awaited Bob in San Francisco if he wanted it. And so it was, after several job-related disappointments, he left his family in Portland, Oregon, and began work in San Francisco as an apprentice at Moore and Scott Iron Works. Knowing that San Francisco could gobble up their 16-year-old son, Mom and Dad reminded him they would pray hard for him. He assured them that he knew he couldn't make it without calling on the Lord for help along the way. God was on his side, he asserted, but years later he realized he needed to be on God's side.

On Sundays he attended church and the Young People's Missionary Society. His sisters Sarah and Marie were studying to become missionaries to China, and Bob considered going to China and opening a foundry to make farm equipment. But hearing his sisters try to pronounce Chinese words convinced him he could never learn the language, jesting that not even the Chinese could learn to speak their language.

He thought his life was over when, at 5:12 a.m. on April 18, 1906, an earthquake began to violently shake San Francisco. As buildings crumbled, Bob's bedroom dropped 10 feet and his bed and the bureau swapped places.

Bob covered his head with a blanket and thought, "This is the end of the world. Thank God I am saved and going to heaven." Though fire swept much of San Francisco and destroyed the foundry where he worked, he and his friends were unscathed.

Days later he landed a job with the Pacific Foundry in an unharmed part of the city. But he was let go when contracts expected to come out of reconstruction failed to materialize. Soon he went to work at an Oakland elevator company, but when the need for elevators faded, he was again out of a job. However, the four years of apprenticeship at the foundry made him a journeyman molder. After tromping the streets trying to find another job, Bob returned to Portland and worked for his brother, pulling stumps, using a cable and a steam-powered engine.

By1910 he had settled in Stockton, California, and soon had the reputation as the best mechanic in town. Two years later in an auto race at a county fair, to help sell Regals that he and a partner were selling, LeTourneau suffered a broken neck in an accident. Poor medical care caused him for a time to carry his head on his right shoulder "like a tote sack," resulting in his ear being rubbed raw. Though he got additional medical help, the injury caused him to go through life with a slightly tilted head.

LeTourneau thought his life was over when, at 5:12 a.m. on April 18, 1906, an earthquake began to violently shake San Francisco. As buildings crumbled, Bob's bedroom dropped 10 feet and his bed and the bureau swapped places.

LeTourneau's first successful invention brought in customers both young and old. He had bought a used welding torch and had become an expert welder through a six-month course. With his welding torch, he did tricks to turn automobiles into hotrods and by applying his torch to the muffler he provided drivers an ear-splitting noise when they pulled a wire.

One day at his garage, LeTourneau thought God was calling him home. He was working in his grease pit, juicing up a car for an elderly man. The undercarriage was a mass of oil and grease. He asked Uncle Bob Gilmour, after whom he was named, to stand by with a pail of water in event of a fire as he used his torch on exhaust pipe. Sure enough, the oil-soaked floorboards of the car ignited. Uncle Bob grabbed a bucket that he thought was water and dumped the contents onto the fire. But it was gasoline. The whole pit burst into flames. "How I got out from under the car [without being burned] I have never figured out," LeTourneau wrote. "I knew I had been saved by the Lord Jesus, and my thanks were directed to Him."

The accident served as an illustration for LeTourneau when he answered people who asked what difference a man's religion makes as long as he is sincere. "I say it makes a big difference," he voiced. "The Bible says there is no other name under heaven whereby we can be saved but the name of Jesus. Uncle Bob was just as sincere as he could be, and he wouldn't have hurt me, his namesake, for the world, but his sincerity couldn't stop gas from exploding, nor save me from being in the midst of the explosion."

Finding a wife was an adventure LeTourneau would prefer to have been more traditional. Some years earlier he had boarded with the Oscar Peterson family when their daughter Evelyn was a child in high-buttoned shoes. Now she was wearing pumps and silk dresses, and was "something to behold." He fell in love with her, and her father said yes to his marrying her—if they waited five years. This did not set well with the young couple. Instead of waiting, they eloped in Mexico on an August evening in 1917. She was 16 at the time. Mr. Peterson filed charges of kidnapping against his now son-in-law. Finally he said, "All right, Bob, we're dropping charges, but so help me, don't do it again."

Oscar Peterson didn't speak to Bob for another seven years. Then one day in 1924 he came to Bob and said, "You're all right. I'm the one who's wrong in holding a grudge. Want to shake hands?" In a flash, Bob grabbed his hand. But then Oscar added, "It isn't Christian, and I was wrong for being sore for seven years. But I was right the first three months."

You might guess that the newlyweds lived happily ever after, but the early years were tough going. They began married life living in a room with a gas plate to heat food; a bathroom was down the hall.

Bob offered himself for military service but was turned down because of his neck injury. He went to work for a Navy yard and became an electrical machinist. Evelyn rented an old farmhouse, where she raised her own vegetables. Bob came home often enough to split firewood for the kitchen range.

On October 30, 1918, their first child, Caleb, was born. But during a flu epidemic that swept the country, the child died the next February. It shook Bob to the extent that he reviewed his life and realized he had been "acting like a Christian but really serving myself." As a result, he refocused his life, determined to follow Matthew 6:33, "Seek ye first the kingdom of God and His righteousness, and all these things shall be added unto you." Over the ensuing years, God gave Bob and Evelyn five more children, a daughter and four sons, each of whom went on to serve the Lord.

After joining a Christian and Missionary Alliance church at the invitation of a friend, LeTourneau became a strong supporter of missions and a local rescue mission, where he overcame his fear of speaking in public. He tithed his income, heeding the principle of Malachi 3:10: "Bring ye all the tithes into the storehouse. . . I will pour you out a blessing." Even when debts overwhelmed him, he still managed to keep his financial pledge to his church. Years later when he became wealthy, he and the family lived on 10 percent of his income, and he used 90 percent to further God's work. Evelyn worked as a nursemaid for a time to help Bob get started in his earth-moving business. Once he had so many contracts that he "felt like the little dog that chased freight trains and finally caught one." He built a scraper powered by electric motors that made earth-moving speedier, enabling him to honor his contracts.

In the mid-1930s he opened a manufacturing plant in Peoria, Illinois, and later put factories in Toccoa, Georgia; Vicksburg, Mississippi; and Longview, Texas. Today there are two plants, in Vicksburg and Longview.

To reach employees with the Gospel, he hired chaplains and held chapel services; attendance was voluntary. Plants closed Sundays.

In Toccoa he built a dormitory for Toccoa Falls Bible Institute and established a Christian conference center. In Longview a foundation that he initiated gave birth to what is now LeTourneau University with a current enrollment of some 3,400.

In Liberia and Peru he established missionary projects where his machines cleared land for people to grow food and where the Gospel was preached.

As the years passed, LeTourneau spoke to audiences across the nation. On May 12, 1937, he had a close call as he and his wife were en route to Bob Jones College in Cleveland, Tennessee. A speeding car crashed into the LeTourneau car, killing his veteran driver and another passenger. Both LeTourneau and his wife received severe injuries. He was in a cast "from head to foot" for months. While incapacitated he invented a stretcher that allowed him to be wheeled through his plant in Peoria.

Next he invented the Tournapull, a huge, ugly, diesel-powered machine but "a beauty when it went into action." After the bombing of Pearl Harbor, Tournapulls filled in bomb craters on runways, packing and spreading dirt so swiftly that the U.S. planes that had gone into the air to challenge the attackers were able to return to their own base.

In his 75th year, it became evident, because of declining health, that LeTourneau's traveling and speaking days were behind him. On March 17, 1969, he concluded his earthly ministry when he went to his heavenly home.

Thousands of times to thousands of listeners, R. G. LeTourneau had said, "If you're not serving the Lord, it proves you don't love Him; if you don't love Him, it proves you don't know Him. Because to know Him is to love Him, and to love Him is to serve Him."

The man who moved men and mountains had served the Savior well. He loved Him deeply.

ALLAN MCGUIRL

An inventor's solar-powered radios reach the world's isolated peoples.

THE 62-YEAR-OLD WOMAN sitting in her hut high in the mountains of central Mexico thought she heard an airplane flying low over her village. She went outside and noticed a small parachute with a little box attached dropping close by. Could it be an explosive device? Putting her fears aside, she investigated. Inside the box was a small red plastic radio with a pictorial set of instructions showing her how to operate it. The radio was turned on, broadcasting a Christian program in Spanish. It was preset to hear only KVOH, the Voice of Hope.

Soon she was for the first time in her life hearing the Gospel of Jesus Christ. God had come knocking at her door. For days she enjoyed the Christian music, Bible reading, and Gospel messages. In time she prayed to receive Christ as her Savior, following along on the radio as she invited Jesus Christ into her heart. Later, as a bonus, God healed her of a malady she had suffered for many years.

© 2012 by megainarmy.
Used under license of Shutterstock, Inc.

The woman became so excited that she found a Bible in Spanish and learned to read within nine days by following along with Bible readings. She began inviting relatives and friends to her hut for Bible study. Soon they had begun a house church.

The amazing facts of this story are that no missionary, pastor, or evangelist had ever been up in those rugged mountains to share about the Gospel. It all had happened through the little radio, a Galcom "Go-Ye" radio, dropped out of the sky by a missionary pilot.

Nearly 500,000 "Go-Ye" radios have been sent to some 120 countries by Galcom International, with offices in Hamilton, Ontario, and Tampa, Florida. Approximately 2,000 radios are sent out monthly at a cost of about $36,500. The little radios are manufactured in Hamilton at a cost of just under $20.00 and operate on 700 milliamp industrial batteries that are kept charged by solar power.

"The solar panel on the radio puts out 100 milliamps of current and works off indoor lighting as well as outdoor lighting," explains Allan McGuirl, Galcom's international director. "The radios draw only 30 milliamps of energy and will operate in the sun without batteries. Battery power is used only if a listener has his/her radio on all night." "Go-Ye" radios will operate for as many as 10 years.

"We are really dependent on supporters' prayers as we send out these little, portable missionaries to reach the unreached in AM, FM, and short-wave frequencies," stresses McGuirl.

Galcom International came into being in February 1989 while McGuirl, Harold Kent, and Ken Crowell were attending the National Religious Broadcasters annual convention. The Lord, they attest, had earlier brought them together through friends. All three had independently thought of using radios preset to Christian stations to use in evangelism—McGuirl, in Hamilton, Ontario; Crowell, in Israel; and Kent, in Tampa, Florida.

"We chose the name Galcom International partly based on Psalm 37:5, 'Commit thy way unto the Lord . . .'" McGuirl says. "Commit in Hebrew is gal. Gal is half of a wheel or a wave. Gal is rolling over to God daily. Com is for communications. International means worldwide. So Galcom International indicates our commitment to communicating the Gospel worldwide.

"We decided to call our little radios the 'Go-Ye' radios, based on the great commission, 'Go ye therefore, and teach all nations . . . (Matt. 28:19).'"

Allan McGuirl, an ordained minister, would seem to be an unlikely person to build a solar-powered radio, but he had built one a year or so before he met Kent and Crowell. He is dyslexic, and says that as a boy he struggled with reading and writing, but the Lord gave him a very creative mind.

"As a ten-year-old I rigged up a control so that I could open and close the door to my room from my bed," he reveals. "I had my desk wired up with alarms so no one could take my pens and pencils. I hooked up a radio so I could pick up programming from all over the world. I could look at circuitry and determine the way it should be put together. I look at my affliction as a strength and a weakness, making me totally dependent on the Lord."

As McGuirl traveled widely as Canadian Director of Gospel Recordings, an agency that uses hand-wind cassette players to evangelize in many languages, the idea of using preset radios became increasingly on his mind and heart. After he became acquainted with Crowell and Kent, he and his wife, Florrie, prayed much about it and he agreed to leave Gospel Recordings to reach out with radio.

Ken Crowell, an American pastor and engineer, had gone with his wife, Margie, to Israel in 1978 as "tentmaker missionaries." They established Galtronics Electronics Ltd. in Tiberius, Israel, on the Sea of Galilee, which today produces more than 40 million antennas a year for the worldwide cellular industry. Many employees have come to Christ and worship in three congregations begun by the Crowells.

It was in 1987 that Crowell worked on a fixed-tuned radio for evangelizing, but in his busy life he filed his plans away. Then in 1988 he ran across the folder and felt the Lord moving him to do something with the radio idea. A few days later a friend phoned him to come to Florida to meet Harold Kent, "a person who has a proposal that might interest you."

"It just happened that I was to fly to the United States that following week on business," recalls Crowell. "This is an example of the Lord's leading."

Harold Kent, head of a chain of feed mills who came to Christ at age 40, sat in an assembly at a Christian camp in 1966 with his wife, Jo Ann. "It was shortly after I received Jesus as Lord of my life," he says. "As I listened to a message, I saw [in my mind] the world as a deep blue globe. I saw a dot of light appear, then another dot, until the whole earth was filled with dots of light. I [came to realize the symbolism] of this many years later," he recalls.

In 1988 he listened to a Christian radio broadcaster speak of desiring to broadcast radio programs on short wave so that the Gospel could be heard in unreached parts of the world. "The thought crossed my mind, 'How do you know if anyone is listening?'" Crowell recalls. "In many parts of the world people do not have electricity or access to a radio, and even those who have a short-wave receiver must by chance tune into a Gospel program. It was at that moment the Lord seemed to say, 'Make fix-tuned radios and distribute them around the world to people who have no other way of hearing the Gospel.'" He thought of the image he had envisioned years before and associated each dot of light with people reached with the Gospel by radio.

In organizing Galcom International, the three men decided that Crowell would finish engineering the radio and manufacture them, Kent would begin funding the project, and McGuirl would distribute the radios around the world. Production of the radios is now in Hamilton, as mentioned.

Many stories of the effectiveness of the radio ministry are chronicled in the paperback book He Who Has Ears to Hear by Gary Nelson, president of Galcom International USA. Included are stories from Central and South America, Africa, and the Middle Eastern Muslim lands.

In Haiti a missionary group heard the testimony of a man who had come to Christ through a Galcom radio; then he shared the radio with a friend, a witch doctor. The witch doctor also received the Lord. As the father gave his testimony to the missionary group, other village people gathered and 17 professed faith in the Lord. Later, the visitors heard the testimony of the witch doctor, who said he was out of business as the village witch doctor. Twelve of his 13 children had received Christ.

A missionary pastor in Ecuador, Felix Lician, relates the following:

A few weeks ago [a pastor] returned from a mission trip with young people from his church. They went to a village where they intended to do mission work; 98 percent of the villagers were professing Christians. Earlier someone had given them one Galcom fix-tuned radio and they had attached it to an external speaker so that the entire village could listen to the Gospel programming. They have been and continue to be discipled in Christ by that one missionary radio.

A similar story derives from a village in Panama. A villager asked a missionary he encountered to come to the village to serve communion to the Christians of the community. The Christian worker asked if any missionary, pastor, or evangelist had been to the village. The villager said no but that there was a large number of Christians in the village. They had come to Christ through a radio tuned to HCJB and now wanted someone to come and serve communion to them.

In Estonia, some 600 hardened prisoners shared 120 radios that a pastor distributed. A couple of months later the warden called. "I've got good news: you've changed the atmosphere of this prison. The bad news is I've got 262 men who want to be baptized and I don't know what to do."

In Iraq, Christian radio stations, called The Voice of Peace, have a potential listening audience of 1,250,000 Kurds. Thousands of Galcom fix-tuned radios have been distributed to the people in the country's northern region.

In Iraq, a 16-year-old married Muslim woman received the Lord after listening to a radio broadcast, and her husband put her in prison with her infant son. That month she had lost her mom and only brother in a car accident. The local church stood by her in prayer. In court the judge asked her if she had become a Christian and she acknowledged she had come to Christ. The judge divorced her and allowed her to keep her child.

Zewar, a Christian taxi driver living in Zakho, in northwest Iraq, made a practice of giving Galcom radios to customers. In February 2002 a customer demanded that he renounce his faith, and when Zewar refused, the customer shot him 28 times, killing him. "It is our prayer that Zewar will be the last Christian martyr in Iraq," writes Gary Nelson, a highly decorated combat fighter pilot who served 29 years in the U.S. Air Force before joining Galcom.

For more than 10 years Galcom has established "suitcase radio stations," stations that technicians set up in remote areas to reach out as far as 80–100 miles. Some can download from satellites in English and Spanish programming. "The cost for these stations is about $10,000, including studio, transmitter, tower, and antenna," according to Allan McGuirl. "We have about 70 now, 90 percent of them being FM."

By the time you read this article Pygmies—the Bakas—will be hearing the Gospel via Galcom radios in such countries as The Republic of Congo, Gabon, and Cameroon. They live in small jungle villages, and when the area becomes depleted of food, they move on, making it difficult to evangelize them. Suitcase radio stations will reach out to them, likely operated by Campus Crusade for Christ.

In a sense, Galcom International is doing a work like the angel in Revelation 14:6: "And I saw another angel fly in the midst of heaven, having the everlasting Gospel to preach unto them that dwell on the earth, and to every nation, and kindred, and tongue, and people." All with little "Go-Ye" radios.

>> DON SCHOENDORFER

A PhD from MIT helps bring dignity to the world's destitute crippled masses.

SEVERAL YEARS AGO, Don Schoendorfer was a 49-year-old husband and father who had achieved what many people associate with success. This mechanical engineer with a PhD from MIT had a great marriage, three beautiful daughters, and lived in Orange County, California. In addition, Don had a number of patents with his name attached to them.

"I had tasted the flavors of worldly success, but really wasn't satisfied," Don admits. "I had an inner hunger for more. I wanted a life that was marked by significance more than success."

Don's search for significance began with an honest confession. His nominal Christianity did not equate to having a personal relationship with Christ.

"The Lord got my attention when one of my daughters admitted to having an eating disorder," Don admits. "My world spun out of control, and I realized I needed Him to bring order out of chaos. I credit that crisis with my openness to surrender my life and my family to Jesus."

Don and his wife, Laurie, began to attend church regularly. Seeing how God was working in their lives, they gradually surrendered to Him. It was about this time that Don's pastor gave a message on the rich fool from Luke 12. He realized he was like the man in Jesus's parable by waiting until he had everything before using his gifts for God. The Lord reminded Don of something he had seen 20 years previously while on vacation in Morocco. A paraplegic woman in blood-soaked and torn clothing clawed her fingers into the dirt in an attempt to gain traction. Her daring goal was to pull her lifeless legs across a road. The image of that woman kept surfacing in his thoughts.

"Sensing that my purpose in life was now to serve Jesus by helping others, I determined to do something for people like that poor woman in North Africa," Don acknowledges. "I was obsessed with finding a way to provide the gift of mobility that every person created in the image of God deserves."

Don's goal was to design a lightweight wheelchair that would be durable yet inexpensive. He started with a white, plastic lawn chair seen on most Americans' patios. Sawing off the chair legs, he then attached two 24-inch mountain bike tires. For several months Don tinkered with a prototype in his garage before and after work. After countless hours of redesign and tweaking, Don was pleased with the result.

In February 2001 Don was given an opportunity to travel with a ministry team from his church to India. Since he had assembled 100 wheelchairs in his garage, he got excited about taking all of them to distribute. Because of travel restrictions, though, he was allowed to take only four.

Initially Don was disappointed to have only a few chairs to give away. But as he got to Chennai and saw the reaction of the crippled people who were given the chairs, he knew all his months of work were in keeping with God's purposes. Something inside him told him the other chairs would eventually find a home.

While Don was gone, the company for which he worked went bankrupt. Don was faced with a life-changing decision.

"I had a choice," Don admits. "If I looked for a new job, I would have to give it my full attention and have to give up on making wheelchairs. But after returning from India, all I could think about was the reaction of the people who were granted dignity by sitting in a chair instead of crawling on the ground."

In spite of the financial challenges it would mean for his family, Don knew the Lord was calling him to dedicate himself fully to the wheelchair project. He emptied his savings account, leased a warehouse, and established a nonprofit ministry. Since the wheelchairs would be given away to those in need of one at no charge, he chose to call the new outreach Free Wheelchair Mission (FWM).

In spite of the financial challenges it would mean for his family, Don knew the Lord was calling him to dedicate himself fully to the wheelchair project.

"I came to realize there are 100 million people in the world like that woman in Morocco," Don soberly admits. "That's mind-boggling. Our goal as an organization is to distribute 20 million wheelchairs."

Another of Don's goals is to keep the cost of manufacturing and distributing each chair under $50. Thanks to using components that are produced in high volume, inexpensive labor in China, and distribution networks already in place, the price tag for each wheelchair is only $48.35.

In the summer of 2005, Don received a call from the White House indicating that President Bush wanted to meet him. After seeing the chair and hearing how Don's mission began, the president praised his ingenuity and dedication.

In the summer of 2007, Don and a member of his board, Dr. Michael Bayer (the ministry's medical director), rode their bikes from coast to coast as a way of publicizing his organization. The 3,500-mile trek began in New York City with an appearance on The Early Show on CBS television and concluded with a celebration at Mariners Church near the Pacific Ocean. The six-week adventure achieved Don's dream. Donations to FWM for the year increased by 40 percent.

Now in his 60s, Don confesses amazement at how God has blessed his efforts. To date Free Wheelchair Mission has provided more than 335,000 wheelchairs to people with disabilities in more than 75 countries, all given free of charge to them.

In March of 2008, Don was one of three individuals chosen from across the nation to receive the Above and Beyond Citizens Award. The honor was presented by the Congressional Medal of Honor Committee at Arlington National Cemetery.

"I know that there are others more deserving an award like that than me," Don says humbly. "But I am honored to know that being obedient to what God asks you to do can be recognized on such a public platform. Because Free Wheelchair Mission is solely dependent on donations and grants, I am grateful for whatever means the Lord uses to get the word out."

ENGINEERING

· ·

REDEMPTIVE FIELD ANALYSIS 1

HONOR STATEMENT: I, the undersigned student, hereby declare before God, before the school, and before the professor that I have read this chapter in its entirety, that I have completed the following exercise with help from no other sources, except as required by the questions, and that I neither have shared nor will share this work with anyone.

Signature: _____   Date: _____

Analysis 1

1. Using words from the fifth chapter, define the term redemptive communicator.

_____

_____

_____

_____

_____

_____

2. Summarize one of this chapter's profiles in the space below. Include the most important details. Omit unnecessary details.

_____

_____

_____

_____

_____

_____

_____

_____

_____

_____

_____

3. If you were asked to use this story or a specific part of this story to support an idea, one that you could present as its main point to an audience, which idea would you present? State this idea as a single declarative sentence in the space that follows:

_____

_____

_____

_____

_____

_____

4. The fifth chapter states that a redemptive communicator interacts with other people in a way that promotes what God values in this world according to Scripture. Review the chapter's list of things that God values. Then, in the space below, identify the specific God-valued thing that this profilee promotes according to the profile. Be sure to explain both how the profilee promotes this specific thing and why you believe this thing is something God values according to Scripture.

_____

_____

_____

_____

_____

_____

_____

_____

_____

_____

_____

_____

_____

_____

_____

_____

5. Which other God-valued things does this profilee promote? Identify these and explain how he or she promotes them.

_____

_____

_____

_____

_____

_____

_____

_____

_____

_____

_____

_____

ENGINEERING

·························

REDEMPTIVE FIELD ANALYSIS 2

HONOR STATEMENT: I, the undersigned student, hereby declare before God, before the school, and before the professor that I have read this chapter in its entirety, that I have completed the following exercise with help from no other sources, except as required by the questions, and that I neither have shared nor will share this work with anyone.

Signature: _____   Date: _____

Analysis 2

1. Using words from the fifth chapter, define the term redemptive communicator.

_____

_____

_____

_____

_____

_____

_____

2. Summarize another of this chapter's profiles in the space below. Include the most important details. Omit unnecessary details.

_____

_____

_____

_____

_____

_____

_____

_____

_____

_____

_____

_____

_____

_____

3. If you were asked to use this story or a specific part of this story to support an idea, one that you could present as its main point to an audience, which idea would you present? State this idea as a single declarative sentence in the space that follows:

_____

_____

_____

_____

_____

_____

_____

_____

_____

_____

_____

4. The fifth chapter states that a redemptive communicator interacts with other people in a way that promotes what God values in this world according to Scripture. Review the chapter's list of things that God values. Then, in the space below, identify the specific God-valued thing that this profilee promotes according to the profile. Be sure to explain both how the profilee promotes this specific thing and why you believe this thing is something God values according to Scripture.

_____

_____

_____

_____

_____

_____

_____

_____

_____

_____

_____

_____

_____

_____

_____

_____

5. Which other God-valued things does this profilee promote? Identify these and explain how he or she promotes them.

_____

_____

_____

_____

_____

ENGINEERING

....

REDEMPTIVE FIELD ANALYSIS 3

HONOR STATEMENT: I, the undersigned student, hereby declare before God, before the school, and before the professor that I have read this chapter in its entirety, that I have completed the following exercise with help from no other sources, except as required by the questions, and that I neither have shared nor will share this work with anyone.

Signature: _____   Date: _____

Analysis 3

1. Using words from the fifth chapter, define the term redemptive communicator.

_____

_____

_____

_____

_____

_____

_____

2. Summarize another of this chapter's profiles in the space below. Include the most important details. Omit unnecessary details.

_____

_____

_____

_____

_____

_____

_____

_____

_____

_____

_____

_____

_____

_____

3. If you were asked to use this story or a specific part of this story to support an idea, one that you could present as its main point to an audience, which idea would you present? State this idea as a single declarative sentence in the space that follows:

_____

_____

_____

_____

_____

_____

_____

_____

_____

_____

4. The fifth chapter states that a redemptive communicator interacts with other people in a way that promotes what God values in this world according to Scripture. Review the chapter's list of things that God values. Then, in the space below, identify the specific God-valued thing that this profilee promotes according to the profile. Be sure to explain both how the profilee promotes this specific thing and why you believe this thing is something God values according to Scripture.

_____

_____

_____

_____

_____

_____

_____

_____

_____

_____

_____

_____

_____

_____

_____

5. Which other God-valued things does this profilee promote? Identify these and explain how he or she promotes them.

_____

_____

_____

_____

_____

_____

MILITARY >>

MILITARY

DANIEL HARDIN

A military officer's wound prepared him to help traumatized soldiers.

JUST BEFORE THE DEPLOYMENT of his Alaska-based airborne parachute infantry regiment to Iraq, Chaplain Capt. Daniel W. Hardin learned he needed surgery to repair torn knee cartilage. Hardin was disheartened when his unit, known as the Geronimos, left without him in October 2006.

After a couple of months of recuperation, Hardin was well enough to go to Iraq. On Christmas Eve he stood in front of U.S. troops, preached, and served Communion. Twelve hours later two of the paratroopers from Hardin's forward operating base were dead. Their truck had struck an improvised explosive device (IED).

© 2012 by Maxim Petrichuk.
Used under license of Shutterstock, Inc.

Dealing with death and its aftermath, Hardin quickly learned, was part of the assimilation process in Iraq with the 1st Battalion, 501st Parachute Infantry Regiment, 4th Brigade Combat Team (Airborne), 25th Infantry Division.

On February 4, 2007, Hardin accompanied a convoy to an outpost to conduct a worship service and offer grief counseling for a platoon that had lost a paratrooper to sniper fire. At approximately 8:30 p.m. on a road west of Baghdad outside Fallujah, the truck in which Hardin rode struck a pressure plate–detonated IED. The blast knocked the driver unconscious, wounded the front-seat passenger-commander in the leg, and tore a hole in the firewall of the crew compartment—where Hardin sat.

At approximately 8:30 p.m. on a road west of Baghdad outside Fallujah, the truck in which Hardin rode struck a pressure plate-detonated IED. The blast knocked the driver unconscious, wounded the front-seat passenger-commander in the leg, and tore a hole in the firewall of the crew compartment–where Hardin sat.

"It felt like the right side of my face was on fire," recalls Hardin.

Hardin exited the truck stunned, groping to find his way onto the night-time roadway. Spc. Jemell Garris, an infantryman assigned to the battalion as the chaplain's assistant—with the primary duty of providing security for the unit ministry team—found Hardin.

The 6-foot-2-inch Garris carried Hardin to a medic and returned to extract other wounded soldiers from the burning vehicle. No one died or suffered permanent injuries in the explosion, despite extensive damage to the vehicle.

Hardin suffered facial burns, eyelid and chin cuts, and a punctured outer ear. After stitches and the removal of gravel embedded in his face, he returned to his duties within three days. Outward appearances indicate that Hardin mended quickly. But healing emotionally proved to be arduous.

Suddenly the textbook theology Hardin learned in the classroom didn't jibe so smoothly with real-life experience. The nagging hurt, the shattering of his notions about God, feeling alone and helpless, and wondering what others thought of him plagued him.

As the only chaplain for his base, Hardin sensed soldiers with no faith background were checking to see if he still believed in God. Some questioned what he had done to make God so mad. Others thought if God didn't bother to protect the chaplain from harm, how could the Almighty care about the rest of them?

For the first two months after the attack, Hardin wanted to escape the war as memories of the attack loomed. Regularly he broke out in cold sweats when he heard outgoing mortar fire. Sleep did not come easily and he imagined something or someone was going to smack him in the face.

Hardin began to doubt if he had the fortitude to last as a chaplain.

Compounding Hardin's turmoil was his struggle with homesickness and news his mother had breast cancer. His workload also required him repeatedly to conduct memorials for troops killed by IEDs or sniper fire. Other duties included counseling soldiers dealing with everything from crumbling marriages to thoughts of suicide. All of it left Hardin sullen.

Via e-mail, retired U.S. Army Col. Scott McChrystal, who spent seven years as senior chaplain at the U.S. Military Academy at West Point, persuaded Hardin to talk about the trauma with someone in person.

"People who are impacted by IEDs and live to tell about it will never forget," says McChrystal, who witnessed the horror of fellow soldiers dying from bamboo-shard booby traps as an infantry platoon leader in Vietnam. "The Lord helps in the healing process." Hardin laid bare his innermost thoughts with other chaplains. They told him he didn't have to put on a game face.

"I was afraid if they knew the real me with all my wounds, fears, inadequacies, and sins I would be rejected," Hardin says.

McChrystal explained to Hardin that if he didn't take care of himself, if he didn't acknowledge his vulnerability, he would quickly burn out.

"How a chaplain recovers from psychological trauma is extremely important," McChrystal says. "When a chaplain gets wounded, other soldiers take notice."

McChrystal says it's no shock that clergy in a prolonged war might be temporarily racked with disillusionment. Emotional healing is a process, and there can be times of discouragement.

"David, the warrior king after God's own heart, shows God can handle us being real and transparent about our weaknesses," explains McChrystal.

While recovering from surgery, Hardin opened a free coffeehouse for soldiers in Iraq. The Anchorage Daily News sent newspapers for free distribution, plus provided a professional-grade espresso machine and 100 pounds of specialty coffee. Congregations in the United States raised $6,000 to sustain the supply of beverages.

The Drop Zone Café opened in March 2007, dispensing coffee, cappuccino, lattes, and snow cones to about 55 soldiers daily.

The café featured two decked-out MacBook computers connected with wireless Internet that allow soldiers to e-mail family, watch movies, or listen to music.

Many paratroopers wandering into the coffeehouse sought spiritual counseling or prayer. Because of the sheer number of casualties and the nature of those deaths, U.S. troops in Iraq have a heightened sense of mortality. This creates within them an increased focus on spiritual matters, and soldiers typically view a chaplain as God's representative in camp.

Still, recovery proved to be a long process for the man of God dispensing Biblical counsel.

Hardin returned to Alaska in November 2007. Within 40 days of the beginning of 2008, Hardin's two grandmothers and an uncle died; he endured another knee surgery; and he was diagnosed with post traumatic stress disorder (PTSD). Many soldiers have PTSD, which is related to surviving the threat of death or serious injury. Hardin's symptoms were typical: insomnia, being easily provoked to anger, lack of motivation, and a general mental fog.

A downcast Hardin attended a church workshop in March 2008, which further helped him heal psychologically from the trauma. Hardin, for the first time, began to speak in front of small groups of paratroopers suffering from the physical and psychological wounds of war. He frankly explained his struggles and victories.

At the urging of his superiors, Hardin documented his experiences by putting together a program to help soldiers understand and normalize trauma and how to position themselves for healing. The work was published in The U.S. Army Chaplaincy Journal in 2009.

In December 2008, Hardin was transferred to Fort Benning, Georgia, where he oversees small groups that specialize in bringing healing and comfort to those who struggle with the effects of trauma.

Ironically, Hardin believes the best part of deployment was that he and Ann, his wife, grew closer. They stayed connected with letters, e-mails, instant messaging, and the occasional phone call (which is expensive because soldiers must pay international rates). The couple prayed for each other in their almost daily contact. Still, the couple experienced separation anxiety as Ann, living on the Army post, tried to raise four children 12 time zones away from her husband. She taught their teenage son Matthew to drive and potty trained toddler Katherine. The couple has two other children, Elizabeth and Joshua.

Today, Hardin has a renewed zeal to pray and read the Bible. The psalms of lament and grief offer him special consolation. The lengthy recovery process reshaped Hardin's theology of pain and evil, which in turn has helped him aid others.

"God is near even when I don't sense him." Hardin says. "He is not so much interested in keeping us from harm as He is in helping us through it. All people, including spiritual leaders, will experience pain and suffering because they are human and live in a broken world."

Hardin believes his Iraq deployment and the aftermath taught him a great deal about life, marriage, and ministry.

"As long as my family can handle this vocation, I will serve as a chaplain in the Army," he says. "I was made for this."

CLEBE MCCLARY

A wounded veteran helps wounded military personnel overcome despair.

FIRST LIEUTENANT CLEBE MCCLARY clips off platitudes like he's ordering take-out from Sonny's Barbecue. He's picked his remarks from the menu of hardship, and he's got his favorites memorized: FIDO. "Forget about it and drive on," McClary explained.

That's the advice he gives to new recruits and old veterans on how to cope with the unpacked baggage they bring home from the battlefield. McClary knows what's inside those duffel bags—survivor's guilt, flashbacks, nightmares, lost limbs, fallen friends, the should'ves, could'ves, and would'ves.

In September 1967, McClary boarded a jet airliner out of Charleston, South Carolina. Two days later, the then 26-year-old lieutenant arrived in DaNang, Vietnam. Attached to the First Marine Recon, McClary fought at DaNang, Quang Tri, and in the Tet Offensive. He was wounded twice in December 1967, but not badly enough to leave the battle.

Yet, the day did come—March 3, 1968—when McClary's squad was overrun. Eight out of 13 squad members were wounded, and another three were killed. McClary recalled the moment when he was severely wounded.

"I was leading a patrol of 13 men into a valley where very few of our troops had been. We stopped for the night on the top of a hill. Three men dug a foxhole to my right. I got into a punji pit and another eight men were in a large bomb crater about 50 meters behind me."

Sometime around midnight, McClary heard the whistle of incoming fire. He climbed out of the pit to see if the guys in the nearby foxhole had heard anything when a grenade exploded, striking him in the neck and shoulder. McClary grabbed his radio and began calling for artillery support, when he saw a suicide squad of about 10 North Vietnamese fighters, charging the hill, with grenades strapped to their waists and in their hands. Their sole mission—to destroy the patrol of U.S. Marines.

McClary aimed his 12-gauge and fired. An enemy soldier fell on McClary, knocking them both into the punji pit, where the Vietnamese's satchel charge exploded, blowing them back out of the hole.

"I reached back for my shotgun and that's when I realized my left arm had been blown off. Bone hanging there. Nothing else," McClary recalled.

McClary began to crawl to the foxhole, but was stopped by yet another grenade. This one blew out his left eye and much of his teeth. He jumped up, running for the bomb crater where eight of his comrades were fighting, but another explosion knocked McClary's feet out from under him. He wasn't sure if he would live to see another day.

His radio man and medic were nearby, dead. Another grenade explosion followed. The three fellows in the foxhole were hit. Private First Class Ralph Johnson was dead. Johnson had thrown himself on a grenade to save the lives of the other two Marines.

McClary began to crawl to the foxhole, but was stopped by yet another grenade. This one blew out his left eye and much of his teeth. He jumped up, running for the bomb crater where eight of his comrades were fighting, but another explosion knocked McClary's feet out from under him. He wasn't sure if he would live to see another day.

McClary thought of his young bride, Deanne, and how badly he wanted to see her again. They were supposed to meet in Hawaii soon for some much-deserved rest and relaxation. That isn't going to happen now, McClary thought as he lay in a pool of blood.

A North Vietnamese soldier shoved the enemy flag into the ground about 15 feet from McClary's head. And one other walked up to him and shot him in the right arm at point-blank range.

"I thought it was all over," he said. But then, he heard the voice of a young private calling out, "Lieutenant! Lieutenant!"

An 18-year-old Marine had come to rescue him. McClary urged the boy to call for choppers. The chopper crew said they couldn't get in till daybreak, another hour away, at least.

"Tell them to forget it then," McClary said, disgusted. "We won't last that long. We are out of grenades."

The chopper showed up within minutes.

"They put my two dead men, the four wounded, and me on the first bird. The last seven men jumped on the next bird. As it lifted off, about 150 or more of the enemy swarmed over the top of the hill. A few more minutes there and not a one of us would have gotten off that hill alive."

As it is, three of the men who were rescued that day have since taken their own lives. Private Johnson, the only other South Carolinian on the patrol, was posthumously awarded the Medal of Honor, the nation's highest award for heroism.

"Ralph came from a family of 18 brothers and sisters. His mother was a cleaning lady. He didn't know his own daddy," McClary said, then pausing, added, "He was one of my closest friends."

Friendships forged in the fire of war retain their incandescent glow over the years, growing sharper even as memory dims.

If he had died that day, McClary says he would have "split the gates of hell wide open." Raised on a 10,000-acre plantation outside Georgetown, South Carolina, McClary had grown up in the church.

"Like a lot of Americans, I went to church. I had a lot of religion in my head but nothing in my heart. I didn't smoke, drink, or cuss. I was so good, I was good for nothing."

Still, McClary said that if he had returned home in a casket, everyone would have assumed he was saved.

"The church would've been packed out because of Mama and Daddy. And 90 percent of 'em would've said if anyone's in heaven, Clebe is. But I wouldn't have been. I didn't have a personal relationship with Jesus. I could not claim him as my Savior."

Flown from DaNang to Japan for medical treatment, McClary began a grueling recovery. He'd lost an arm and an eye, and doctors warned him that he'd never walk again. There were times when McClary despaired.

"The doctors wouldn't let me look in the mirror because my injuries were so extensive. I was married to a beauty queen. I knew if I died she could do a lot better than me. I was in a lot of pain. I wanted to die."

But on one of those dark days, McClary received a visit from a pro-golfer, Billy Casper. McClary overheard the chaplain tell Casper not to bother because "He's not going to make it." But Casper walked over to McClary, and in all sincerity told him, "Marine, I love you. I'll be praying for you."

That one act of kindness gave McClary the will to live.

When he was well enough to travel, he was taken to Bethesda Naval Hospital for more surgery, more recovery—months worth. Deanna would drive up from South Carolina to sit by his side, and to map out new dreams. Sometimes he would leave with Deanna for day trips; sometimes weekend trips.

During one of those trips home to South Carolina, McClary discovered that New York Yankee Bobby Richardson would be making an appearance at the local football stadium. "C'mon, get in the car! Let's go," McClary, a long-time sports buff, told his wife.

The two didn't know Billy Zeoli of Gospel Films would be preaching, too.

"He preached a sermon I'll never forget," McClary said. "He started off talking about Joshua and his troops, marching around the city of Jericho, shouting. Zeoli said if someone did that today we'd think they had a heat stroke.

"But Joshua was a fool—a fool for Christ. Zeoli said there are two kinds of fools in this world: either you're a fool for Christ or a fool for others. What kind of fool are you?"
McClary said there was no question in his heart whose fool he had been. "I had gone to Sunday school and church all my life because my father and mother made me. I had a lot of religion but I still needed a Savior."

At that stadium, with his wife praying beside him, McClary asked Jesus into his heart.
"I found the real joy, real life, and real peace of a living Savior. I didn't change much on the outside, but my heart was different. Jesus filled up the hole that was leaking inside me."

McClary reads five psalms and one proverb every day, and has ever since he was saved. "The Psalms teach us about our relationship with God and Proverbs teach us about our relationship with others," he explained. McClary believes that clean living and a disciplined lifestyle are necessary components for healing from any battle wounds.

Citing Roman 5:3–5, McClary said he is in pain everyday but that he's learned to put his suffering into perspective: "But we glory in tribulations also: knowing that tribulation worketh patience; and patience, experience; and experience, hope: and hope maketh not ashamed; because the love of God is shed abroad in our hearts by the Holy Ghost which is given unto us."

McClary knows, despite the platitudes he's so fond of quoting, that a soldier who has been in battle and watched his buddy exhale his last breath, will never ever forget it.

"I will take the memory of that to my grave. But I don't dwell on it," he said. "I learn from it because I have another war to fight."

This time he's fighting for his fellow soldiers. McClary devotes much of his time to working with veterans returning from Iraq and Afghanistan, sharing the lessons he's learned with a whole new generation of people broken by war. His message is simple, "They can find healing in Christ."

JEFF STRUECKER

An officer's spiritual passion for his fellow Army Rangers.

"GET READY!" Sixty-four rigged soldiers on the C-130 recheck their equipment—straps, harnesses, and buckles.

One soldier's heart starts to pound. Thump thump, thump thump.

Two more commands are yelled over the roaring engines of the plane. Everyone stands.

"Hook up!" The soldier reaches, hooking his static line. What if the chute doesn't open? Thump thump, thump thump.

"Sound off for equipment check!" The relay starts. His shoulder is grabbed. "OK!" he yells. His hand lands on the shoulder in front of him. With the last OK, the ramp lowers. The screaming wind whips by at 130 mph. Thump thump. Thump thump.

"Stand by!" Twenty seconds left. Thump thump. First guy's in the doorway. Thump thump. Thump thump. Now they must trust the jumpmaster—the one who checked all the parachutes back on the ground.

The plane approaches the drop zone. Thump thump. Thump thump. Thump thump.

"Go!"

Silence. The hard part is over.

Capt. Jeff Struecker is a jumpmaster for the 82nd Airborne Division. If one soldier dies in this maneuver, he has failed.

His responsibilities as a chaplain carry the same weight. With the souls of 650-plus soldiers on the line, Jeff longs for each of them to have a personal relationship with Jesus Christ. And timing is everything.

Jeff's battalion maintains a two-hour recall status—they must stay within two hours of Fort Bragg, North Carolina.

"Within 18 hours we could be lifting off of Pope Air Force Base flying anywhere in the world," says Jeff. "But what my soldiers don't understand is they may never come back alive. I understand that all too well."

A decorated Army Ranger, Jeff served in Panama and Desert Storm and received a Bronze Star for Valor for his role in Mogadishu, Somalia, featured in the book and film Black Hawk Down. When he signs copies, Jeff describes the 1993 event as the most intense 24 hours of his life with Jesus Christ.

"It could happen in 50 other places in the world—like Kandahar, Saudi Arabia, or the Philippines," says Jeff, "and it could be tomorrow. Once my soldiers get on those airplanes I may never have a chance to share Christ with them again."

After experiencing the spiritual openness of the soldiers in Somalia, Jeff decided to become a chaplain. "I want to see soldiers in love with Christ. I want to see Him make the difference in their lives that He made in mine."

But Jeff is also known for being tough, hence his nickname: Evil Christian. In a real combat situation, he wants his soldiers to survive. One told Jeff's pastor, "Sir, he is the meanest Christian I know."

Jeff pushes soldiers to the brink of their limitations, never over.

Once, at an obstacle course, specialist Bucky Harris froze 30 feet above the ground. "I can't do it," Bucky said, staring at the rope just out of reach. "If I grab it I am gonna fall."

Immediately, Jeff climbed the obstacle course. Oh no, here he comes, Bucky thought. Jeff surprised Bucky by coaxing him to sit down next to him.

"Just look out across the horizon. Let everyone go ahead," Jeff continued. Fifteen minutes later Bucky completed the course.

"There are times when I am in a tough situation," Bucky says with a Southern drawl, "and I think, What would Jeff do?"

Serving on active duty as a chaplain, the father of Aaron, Jacob, Joseph, Abigail, and Lydia, sleeps less than most. Up at exactly 4:35 a.m. to spend time in prayer and Bible study yet make it to the office by 6:00, Jeff completes his required PT (physical training) on the base.

"He is one of the most mentally and physically tough soldiers I've ever met," says his commander, Lt. Col. Richard Clarke. Jeff runs longer than most soldiers, then crams in sit-ups, push-ups, and pull-ups. Just two days after starting to lead his battalion's PT he was asked to quit; the troops were too worn out.

In his afternoons, Jeff may visit a soldier in the hospital, plan a marriage seminar, or research Sunday's sermon. But when he visits his battalion on the field, he sheds his office-quality battle-dress uniform for another with frayed edges and faded camouflage green. With his unit out sweating and crawling in the dirt, Jeff explains that they will resent him if he shows up neatly pressed. One soldier told him he was the dirtiest chaplain he's ever seen. Jeff considered it a compliment.

With one glance at his badges, a serviceman or woman immediately knows Jeff's credentials; to most soldiers, those badges are the goal of their career.

Sitting in his office at a drab metal desk, he points to the chaplain's badge with a cross on his shoulder. "When I stand before God He's not going to be impressed by this or this or this," indicating his other badges. "Right here [the cross that represents Jesus Christ] is all that is going to matter."

Before you begin your topic research, make sure you know the parameters of the speech assignment.

"He is not looking for notoriety or acknowledgment of what he has done or where he is," says Gen. Joe Gray, national director of Campus Crusade for Christ's Military Ministry. "He wants to pass it on to someone else who will maybe go through the same experience."

Once unwelcome, the publicity of the Black Hawk Down book and subsequent film now provides Jeff opportunities to recount that experience and the message of Jesus Christ. With hundreds of requests during the past year from churches and from Congress, Jeff takes advantage of this fleeting platform whenever possible. The urgency of Christ's message motivates him.

"I can share Christ with my soldiers 24/7 and not get through all 650 before half of them leave," says Jeff, "and another 300 show up." This is where Military Ministry's influence is vital.

"I don't have the budget or the personnel, and [other than] the Holy Spirit at work, it is an impossibility to adequately minister to this battalion," laments the brown-haired, blue-eyed Ranger. His role in the military assigns him all the responsibilities of a pastor. "But I praise God that the Holy Spirit is at work, and Military Ministry has products and resources just for chaplains."

One Military Ministry resource essential to him is the Rapid Deployment Kit (RDK). Inside a sandwich bag, a New Testament with Psalms and Proverbs, a devotional booklet, and a Gospel tract fit compactly enough for soldiers to put the RDK in their pocket. Since the September 11, 2001 attacks on the United States, more than 250,000 RDKs have been given away by 375 military chaplains.

When his unit entered the desert for a two-week training, Jeff handed each person an RDK. He told them to read the Bible, read the Gospel tract, then think and pray about it. "In the middle of their firing missions and shooting howitzers," Jeff beams, "I just pulled a couple of them aside and said, 'Let's have a field chapel service.'" Throughout those weeks at least 13 men received Christ.

Soldiers also seek Jeff for counseling—often for their marriages. Dana Greenly found himself frequently yelling at his family and generally unhappy since his father's death. He came to Jeff's office hoping baptism would make a difference.

As the two men sat face to face behind a closed door, Jeff pulled out a Gospel tract. "You know what?" Jeff asked. "You can go down in the water with sin in your life, and when you come back out, all you are is a sinner that just got wet."

Dana agreed: "You're right; you're absolutely right."

"What you need to do," Jeff continued, "is get your heart right first." He explained about receiving Christ by faith through prayer, but with an intense voice, Jeff warned Dana not to make the mistake of saying that prayer and not meaning it.

"I can make that commitment," Dana replied, "but I'm not going to be like you."

"I am not the standard by which you need to measure yourself," Jeff said. That day, Dana trusted Christ.

With every life that Jesus changes, Jeff gets fired up to keep going. But with the responsibilities of a large family and being husband to Dawn as his priority, the souls of his soldiers a close second, and constant speaking requests, Jeff struggles to find balance. "I have not had a day yet where I felt like I got it right," he says.

Throughout his career of leadership in the Army, and currently as a jumpmaster, his job is to prepare soldiers for combat—to prevent death. As a chaplain, he explains the purpose of life—to love Jesus Christ: "Every morning when I roll out of bed I think there's another soldier that I can see come to Christ."

Soon enough, Jeff knows each soldier will face the silence. They will all have to jump.

MILITARY

....

REDEMPTIVE FIELD ANALYSIS 1

HONOR STATEMENT: I, the undersigned student, hereby declare before God, before the school, and before the professor that I have read this chapter in its entirety, that I have completed the following exercise with help from no other sources, except as required by the questions, and that I neither have shared nor will share this work with anyone.

Signature: _____   Date: _____

Analysis 1

1. Using words from the fifth chapter, define the term redemptive communicator.

_____

_____

_____

_____

_____

_____

2. Summarize one of this chapter's profiles in the space below. Include the most important details. Omit unnecessary details.

_____

_____

_____

_____

_____

_____

_____

_____

_____

_____

_____

3. If you were asked to use this story or a specific part of this story to support an idea, one that you could present as its main point to an audience, which idea would you present? State this idea as a single declarative sentence in the space that follows:

_____

_____

_____

_____

_____

_____

4. The fifth chapter states that a redemptive communicator interacts with other people in a way that promotes what God values in this world according to Scripture. Review the chapter's list of things that God values. Then, in the space below, identify the specific God-valued thing that this profilee promotes according to the profile. Be sure to explain both how the profilee promotes this specific thing and why you believe this thing is something God values according to Scripture.

_____

_____

_____

_____

_____

_____

_____

_____

_____

_____

_____

_____

_____

_____

_____

5. Which other God-valued things does this profilee promote? Identify these and explain how he or she promotes them.

_____

_____

_____

_____

_____

_____

_____

_____

_____

_____

_____

_____

MILITARY

....

REDEMPTIVE FIELD ANALYSIS 2

HONOR STATEMENT: I, the undersigned student, hereby declare before God, before the school, and before the professor that I have read this chapter in its entirety, that I have completed the following exercise with help from no other sources, except as required by the questions, and that I neither have shared nor will share this work with anyone.

Signature: _____   Date: _____

Analysis 2

1. Using words from the fifth chapter, define the term redemptive communicator.

_____

_____

_____

_____

_____

_____

_____

_____

2. Summarize another of this chapter's profiles in the space below. Include the most important details. Omit unnecessary details.

_____

_____

_____

_____

_____

_____

_____

_____

_____

_____

_____

_____

_____

_____

_____

3. If you were asked to use this story or a specific part of this story to support an idea, one that you could present as its main point to an audience, which idea would you present? State this idea as a single declarative sentence in the space that follows:

_____

_____

_____

_____

_____

_____

_____

_____

_____

_____

_____

_____

4. The fifth chapter states that a redemptive communicator interacts with other people in a way that promotes what God values in this world according to Scripture. Review the chapter's list of things that God values. Then, in the space below, identify the specific God-valued thing that this profilee promotes according to the profile. Be sure to explain both how the profilee promotes this specific thing and why you believe this thing is something God values according to Scripture.

_____

_____

_____

_____

_____

_____

_____

_____

_____

_____

_____

_____

_____

_____

5. Which other God-valued things does this profilee promote? Identify these and explain how he or she promotes them.

_____

_____

_____

_____

_____

NAME: _____   DATE: _____

MILITARY

....

REDEMPTIVE FIELD ANALYSIS 3

HONOR STATEMENT: I, the undersigned student, hereby declare before God, before the school, and before the professor that I have read this chapter in its entirety, that I have completed the following exercise with help from no other sources, except as required by the questions, and that I neither have shared nor will share this work with anyone.

Signature: _____   Date: _____

Analysis 3

1. Using words from the fifth chapter, define the term redemptive communicator.

_____

_____

_____

_____

_____

_____

_____

2. Summarize another of this chapter's profiles in the space below. Include the most important details. Omit unnecessary details.

_____

_____

_____

_____

_____

_____

_____

_____

_____

_____

_____

_____

_____

_____

3. If you were asked to use this story or a specific part of this story to support an idea, one that you could present as its main point to an audience, which idea would you present? State this idea as a single declarative sentence in the space that follows:

_____

_____

_____

_____

_____

_____

_____

_____

_____

4. The fifth chapter states that a redemptive communicator interacts with other people in a way that promotes what God values in this world according to Scripture. Review the chapter's list of things that God values. Then, in the space below, identify the specific God-valued thing that this profilee promotes according to the profile. Be sure to explain both how the profilee promotes this specific thing and why you believe this thing is something God values according to Scripture.

_____

_____

_____

_____

_____

_____

_____

_____

_____

_____

_____

_____

_____

_____

5. Which other God-valued things does this profilee promote? Identify these and explain how he or she promotes them.

_____

_____

_____

_____

_____

APPENDIX 1

HISTORIC CHRISTIAN CREEDS

THE APOSTLE'S CREED

I believe in God, the Father Almighty,
the Maker of heaven and earth,
and in Jesus Christ, His only Son, our Lord:
Who was conceived by the Holy Ghost,
born of the virgin Mary,
suffered under Pontius Pilate,
was crucified, dead, and buried;
He descended into hell.
The third day He arose again from the dead;
He ascended into heaven,
and sitteth on the right hand of God the Father Almighty;
from thence he shall come to judge the quick and the dead.
I believe in the Holy Ghost;
the holy catholic church;
the communion of saints;
the forgiveness of sins;
the resurrection of the body;
and the life everlasting.
Amen.

THE NICENE CREED

I believe in one God, the Father Almighty, Maker of heaven and earth, and of all things visible and invisible.

And in one Lord Jesus Christ, the only-begotten Son of God, begotten of the Father before all worlds; God of God, Light of Light, very God of very God; begotten, not made, being of one substance with the Father, by whom all things were made.

Who, for us men and for our salvation, came down from heaven, and was incarnate by the Holy Spirit of the virgin Mary, and was made man; and was crucified also for us under Pontius Pilate; He suffered and was buried; and the third day He rose again, according to the Scriptures; and ascended into heaven, and sits on the right hand of the Father; and He shall come again, with glory, to judge the quick and the dead; whose kingdom shall have no end.

And I believe in the Holy Ghost, the Lord and Giver of Life; who proceeds from the Father and the Son; who with the Father and the Son together is worshipped and glorified; who spoke by the prophets.

And I believe in one holy catholic and apostolic Church. I acknowledge one baptism for the remission of sins; and I look for the resurrection of the dead, and the life of the world to come. Amen.

THE WESTMINSTER CATECHISM (SHORTER)

Q. 1. What is the chief end of man?
Man's chief end is to glorify God, and to enjoy him forever.

Q. 2. What rule hath God given to direct us how we may glorify and enjoy him?
The word of God, which is contained in the scriptures of the Old and New Testaments, is the only rule to direct us how we may glorify and enjoy him.

Q. 3. What do the scriptures principally teach?
The scriptures principally teach what man is to believe concerning God, and what duty God requires of man.

Q. 4. What is God?
God is a spirit, infinite, eternal, and unchangeable, in his being, wisdom, power, holiness, justice, goodness and truth.

Q. 5. Are there more gods than one?
There is but one only, the living and true God.

Q. 6. How many persons are there in the godhead?
There are three persons in the Godhead; the Father, the Son, and the Holy Ghost; and these three are one God, the same in substance, equal in power and glory.

Q. 7. What are the decrees of God?
The decrees of God are his eternal purpose, according to the counsel of his will, whereby, for his own glory, he hath foreordained whatsoever comes to pass.

Q. 8. How doth God execute his decrees?
God executeth his decrees in the works of creation and providence.

Q. 9. What is the work of creation?
The work of creation is God's making all things of nothing, by the word of his power, in the space of six days, and all very good.

Q. 10. How did God create man?
God created man male and female, after his own image, in knowledge, righteousness and holiness, with dominion over the creatures.

Q. 11. What are God's works of providence?
God's works of providence are his most holy, wise and powerful preserving and governing all his creatures, and all their actions.

Q. 12. What special act of providence did God exercise toward man in the estate wherein he was created?

When God had created man, he entered into a covenant of life with him, upon condition of perfect obedience; forbidding him to eat of the tree of the knowledge of good and evil, upon the pain of death.

Q. 13. Did our first parents continue in the estate wherein they were created?

Our first parents, being left to the freedom of their own will, fell from the estate wherein they were created, by sinning against God.

Q. 14. What is sin?

Sin is any want of conformity unto, or transgression of, the law of God.

Q. 15. What was the sin whereby our first parents fell from the estate wherein they were created?

The sin whereby our first parents fell from the estate wherein they were created was their eating the forbidden fruit.

Q. 16. Did all mankind fall in Adam's first transgression?

The covenant being made with Adam, not only for himself, but for his posterity; all mankind, descending from him by ordinary generation, sinned in him, and fell with him, in his first transgression.

Q. 17. Into what estate did the fall bring mankind?

The fall brought mankind into an estate of sin and misery.

Q. 18. Wherein consists the sinfulness of that estate whereinto man fell?

The sinfulness of that estate whereinto man fell consists in the guilt of Adam's first sin, the want of original righteousness, and the corruption of his whole nature, which is commonly called original sin; together with all actual transgressions which proceed from it.

Q. 19. What is the misery of that estate whereinto man fell?

All mankind by their fall lost communion with God, are under his wrath and curse, and so made liable to all miseries in this life, to death itself, and to the pains of hell forever.

Q. 20. Did God leave all mankind to perish in the estate of sin and misery?

God having, out of his mere good pleasure, from all eternity, elected some to everlasting life, did enter into a covenant of grace, to deliver them out of the estate of sin and misery, and to bring them into an estate of salvation by a redeemer.

Q. 21. Who is the redeemer of God's elect?

The only redeemer of God's elect is the Lord Jesus Christ, who, being the eternal Son of God, became man, and so was, and continueth to be, God and man in two distinct natures, and one person, forever.

Q. 22. How did Christ, being the Son of God, become man?

Christ, the Son of God, became man, by taking to himself a true body and a reasonable soul, being conceived by the power of the Holy Ghost in the womb of the virgin Mary, and born of her, yet without sin.

Q. 23. What offices doth Christ execute as our redeemer?

Christ, as our redeemer, executeth the offices of a prophet, of a priest, and of a king, both in his estate of humiliation and exaltation.

Q. 24. How doth Christ execute the office of a prophet?

Christ executeth the office of a prophet, in revealing to us, by his word and Spirit, the will of God for our salvation.

Q. 25. How doth Christ execute the office of a priest?

Christ executeth the office of a priest, in his once offering up of himself a sacrifice to satisfy divine justice, and reconcile us to God; and in making continual intercession for us.

Q. 26. How doth Christ execute the office of a king?

Christ executeth the office of a king, in subduing us to himself, in ruling and defending us, and in restraining and conquering all his and our enemies.

Q. 27. Wherein did Christ's humiliation consist?

Christ's humiliation consisted in his being born, and that in a low condition, made under the law, undergoing the miseries of this life, the wrath of God, and the cursed death of the cross; in being buried, and continuing under the power of death for a time.

Q. 28. Wherein consisteth Christ's exaltation?

Christ's exaltation consisteth in his rising again from the dead on the third day, in ascending up into heaven, in sitting at the right hand of God the Father, and in coming to judge the world at the last day.

Q. 29. How are we made partakers of the redemption purchased by Christ?

We are made partakers of the redemption purchased by Christ, by the effectual application of it to us by his Holy Spirit.

Q. 30. How doth the Spirit apply to us the redemption purchased by Christ?

The Spirit applieth to us the redemption purchased by Christ, by working faith in us, and thereby uniting us to Christ in our effectual calling.

Q. 31. What is effectual calling?

Effectual calling is the work of God's Spirit, whereby, convincing us of our sin and misery, enlightening our minds in the knowledge of Christ, and renewing our wills, he doth persuade and enable us to embrace Jesus Christ, freely offered to us in the gospel.

Q. 32. What benefits do they that are effectually called partake of in this life?

They that are effectually called do in this life partake of justification, adoption and sanctification, and the several benefits which in this life do either accompany or flow from them.

Q. 33. What is justification?

Justification is an act of God's free grace, wherein he pardoneth all our sins, and accepteth us as righteous in his sight, only for the righteousness of Christ imputed to us, and received by faith alone.

Q. 34. What is adoption?

Adoption is an act of God's free grace, whereby we are received into the number, and have a right to all the privileges of, the sons of God.

Q. 35. What is sanctification?

Sanctification is the work of God's free grace, whereby we are renewed in the whole man after the image of God, and are enabled more and more to die unto sin, and live unto righteousness.

Q. 36. What are the benefits which in this life do accompany or flow from justification, adoption and sanctification?

The benefits which in this life do accompany or flow from justification, adoption and sanctification, are, assurance of God's love, peace of conscience, joy in the Holy Ghost, increase of grace, and perseverance therein to the end.

Q. 37. What benefits do believers receive from Christ at death?

The souls of believers are at their death made perfect in holiness, and do immediately pass into glory; and their bodies, being still united to Christ, do rest in their graves till the resurrection.

Q. 38. What benefits do believers receive from Christ at the resurrection?

At the resurrection, believers being raised up in glory, shall be openly acknowledged and acquitted in the day of judgment, and made perfectly blessed in the full enjoying of God to all eternity.

Q. 39. What is the duty which God requireth of man?

The duty which God requireth of man is obedience to his revealed will.

Q. 40. What did God at first reveal to man for the rule of his obedience?

The rule which God at first revealed to man for his obedience was the moral law.

Q. 41. Where is the moral law summarily comprehended?

The moral law is summarily comprehended in the ten commandments.

Q. 42. What is the sum of the ten commandments?

The sum of the ten commandments is to love the Lord our God with all our heart, with all our soul, with all our strength, and with all our mind; and our neighbor as ourselves.

Q. 43. What is the preface to the ten commandments?
The preface to the ten commandments is in these words, I am the Lord thy God, which have brought thee out of the land of Egypt, out of the house of bondage.

Q. 44. What doth the preface to the ten commandments teach us?
The preface to the ten commandments teacheth us that because God is the Lord, and our God, and redeemer, therefore we are bound to keep all his commandments.

Q. 45. Which is the first commandment?
The first commandment is, Thou shalt have no other gods before me.

Q. 46. What is required in the first commandment?
The first commandment requireth us to know and acknowledge God to be the only true God, and our God; and to worship and glorify him accordingly.

Q. 47. What is forbidden in the first commandment?
The first commandment forbiddeth the denying, or not worshiping and glorifying the true God as God, and our God; and the giving of that worship and glory to any other, which is due to him alone.

Q. 48. What are we specially taught by these words before me in the first commandment?
These words before me in the first commandment teach us that God, who seeth all things, taketh notice of, and is much displeased with, the sin of having any other god.

Q. 49. Which is the second commandment?
The second commandment is, Thou shalt not make unto thee any graven image, or any likeness of anything that is in heaven above, or that is in the earth beneath, or that is in the water under the earth: thou shalt not bow down thyself to them, nor serve them: for I the Lord thy God am a jealous God, visiting the iniquity of the fathers upon the children unto the third and fourth generation of them that hate me; and showing mercy unto thousands of them that love me, and keep my commandments.

Q. 50. What is required in the second commandment?
The second commandment requireth the receiving, observing, and keeping pure and entire, all such religious worship and ordinances as God hath appointed in his word.

Q. 51. What is forbidden in the second commandment?
The second commandment forbiddeth the worshiping of God by images, or any other way not appointed in his word.

Q. 52. What are the reasons annexed to the second commandment?
The reasons annexed to the second commandment are, God's sovereignty over us, his propriety in us, and the zeal he hath to his own worship.

Q. 53. Which is the third commandment?
The third commandment is, Thou shalt not take the name of the Lord thy God in vain: for the Lord will not hold him guiltless that taketh his name in vain.

Q. 54. What is required in the third commandment?
The third commandment requireth the holy and reverent use of God's names, titles, attributes, ordinances, word and works.

Q. 55. What is forbidden in the third commandment?
The third commandment forbiddeth all profaning or abusing of anything whereby God maketh himself known.

Q. 56. What is the reason annexed to the third commandment?
The reason annexed to the third commandment is that however the breakers of this commandment may escape punishment from men, yet the Lord our God will not suffer them to escape his righteous judgment.

Q. 57. Which is the fourth commandment?
The fourth commandment is, Remember the sabbath day, to keep it holy. Six days shalt thou labor, and do all thy work: but the seventh day is the sabbath of the Lord thy God: in it thou shalt not do any work, thou, nor thy son, nor thy daughter, thy manservant, nor thy maidservant, nor thy cattle, nor thy stranger that is within thy gates: for in six days the Lord made heaven and earth, the sea, and all that in them is, and rested the seventh day: wherefore the Lord blessed the sabbath day, and hallowed it.

Q. 58. What is required in the fourth commandment?
The fourth commandment requireth the keeping holy to God such set times as he hath appointed in his word; expressly one whole day in seven, to be a holy sabbath to himself.

Q. 59. Which day of the seven hath God appointed to be the weekly sabbath?
From the beginning of the world to the resurrection of Christ, God appointed the seventh day of the week to be the weekly sabbath; and the first day of the week ever since, to continue to the end of the world, which is the Christian sabbath.

Q. 60. How is the sabbath to be sanctified?
The sabbath is to be sanctified by a holy resting all that day, even from such worldly employments and recreations as are lawful on other days; and spending the whole time in the public and private exercises of God's worship, except so much as is to be taken up in the works of necessity and mercy.

Q. 61. What is forbidden in the fourth commandment?
The fourth commandment forbiddeth the omission or careless performance of the duties required, and the profaning the day by idleness, or doing that which is in itself sinful, or by unnecessary thoughts, words or works, about our worldly employments or recreations.

Q. 62. What are the reasons annexed to the fourth commandment?

The reasons annexed to the fourth commandment are, God's allowing us six days of the week for our own employments, his challenging a special propriety in the seventh, his own example, and his blessing the sabbath day.

Q. 63. Which is the fifth commandment?

The fifth commandment is, Honor thy father and thy mother; that thy days may be long upon the land which the Lord thy God giveth thee.

Q. 64. What is required in the fifth commandment?

The fifth commandment requireth the preserving the honor, and performing the duties, belonging to every one in their several places and relations, as superiors, inferiors or equals.

Q. 65. What is forbidden in the fifth commandment?

The fifth commandment forbiddeth the neglecting of, or doing anything against, the honor and duty which belongeth to every one in their several places and relations.

Q. 66. What is the reason annexed to the fifth commandment?

The reason annexed to the fifth commandment is a promise of long life and prosperity (as far as it shall serve for God's glory and their own good) to all such as keep this commandment.

Q. 67. Which is the sixth commandment?

The sixth commandment is, Thou shalt not kill.

Q. 68. What is required in the sixth commandment?

The sixth commandment requireth all lawful endeavors to preserve our own life, and the life of others.

Q. 69. What is forbidden in the sixth commandment?

The sixth commandment forbiddeth the taking away of our own life, or the life of our neighbor unjustly, or whatsoever tendeth thereunto.

Q. 70. Which is the seventh commandment?

The seventh commandment is, Thou shalt not commit adultery.

Q. 71. What is required in the seventh commandment?

The seventh commandment requireth the preservation of our own and our neighbor's chastity, in heart, speech and behavior.

Q. 72. What is forbidden in the seventh commandment?

The seventh commandment forbiddeth all unchaste thoughts, words and actions.

Q. 73. Which is the eighth commandment?

The eighth commandment is, Thou shalt not steal.

Q. 74. What is required in the eighth commandment?

The eighth commandment requireth the lawful procuring and furthering the wealth and outward estate of ourselves and others.

Q. 75. What is forbidden in the eighth commandment?

The eighth commandment forbiddeth whatsoever doth or may unjustly hinder our own or our neighbor's wealth or outward estate.

Q. 76. Which is the ninth commandment?

The ninth commandment is, Thou shalt not bear false witness against thy neighbor.

Q. 77. What is required in the ninth commandment?

The ninth commandment requireth the maintaining and promoting of truth between man and man, and of our own and our neighbor's good name, especially in witness-bearing.

Q. 78. What is forbidden in the ninth commandment?

The ninth commandment forbiddeth whatsoever is prejudicial to truth, or injurious to our own or our neighbor's good name.

Q. 79. Which is the tenth commandment?

The tenth commandment is, Thou shalt not covet thy neighbor's house, thou shalt not covet thy neighbor's wife, nor his manservant, nor his maidservant, nor his ox, nor his ass, nor anything that is thy neighbor's.

Q. 80. What is required in the tenth commandment?

The tenth commandment requireth full contentment with our own condition, with a right and charitable frame of spirit toward our neighbor, and all that is his.

Q. 81. What is forbidden in the tenth commandment?

The tenth commandment forbiddeth all discontentment with our own estate, envying or grieving at the good of our neighbor, and all inordinate motions and affections to anything that is his.

Q. 82. Is any man able perfectly to keep the commandments of God?

No mere man since the fall is able in this life perfectly to keep the commandments of God, but doth daily break them in thought, word and deed.

Q. 83. Are all transgressions of the law equally heinous?

Some sins in themselves, and by reason of several aggravations, are more heinous in the sight of God than others.

Q. 84. What doth every sin deserve?

Every sin deserveth God's wrath and curse, both in this life, and that which is to come.

Q. 85. What doth God require of us that we may escape his wrath and curse due to us for sin?

To escape the wrath and curse of God due to us for sin, God requireth of us faith in Jesus Christ, repentance unto life, with the diligent use of all the outward means whereby Christ communicateth to us the benefits of redemption.

Q. 86. What is faith in Jesus Christ?

Faith in Jesus Christ is a saving grace, whereby we receive and rest upon him alone for salvation, as he is offered to us in the gospel.

Q. 87. What is repentance unto life?

Repentance unto life is a saving grace, whereby a sinner, out of a true sense of his sin, and apprehension of the mercy of God in Christ, doth, with grief and hatred of his sin, turn from it unto God, with full purpose of, and endeavor after, new obedience.

Q. 88. What are the outward and ordinary means whereby Christ communicateth to us the benefits of redemption?

The outward and ordinary means whereby Christ communicateth to us the benefits of redemption, are his ordinances, especially the word, sacraments, and prayer; all which are made effectual to the elect for salvation.

Q. 89. How is the word made effectual to salvation?

The Spirit of God maketh the reading, but especially the preaching, of the word, an effectual means of convincing and converting sinners, and of building them up in holiness and comfort, through faith, unto salvation.

Q. 90. How is the word to be read and heard, that it may become effectual to salvation?

That the word may become effectual to salvation, we must attend thereunto with diligence, preparation and prayer; receive it with faith and love, lay it up in our hearts, and practice it in our lives.

Q. 91. How do the sacraments become effectual means of salvation?

The sacraments become effectual means of salvation, not from any virtue in them, or in him that doth administer them; but only by the blessing of Christ, and the working of his Spirit in them that by faith receive them.

Q. 92. What is a sacrament?

A sacrament is an holy ordinance instituted by Christ; wherein, by sensible signs, Christ, and the benefits of the new covenant, are represented, sealed, and applied to believers.

Q. 93. Which are the sacraments of the New Testament?

The sacraments of the New Testament are baptism and the Lord's supper.

Q. 94. What is baptism?

Baptism is a sacrament, wherein the washing with water in the name of the Father, and of the Son, and of the Holy Ghost, doth signify and seal our ingrafting into Christ, and partaking of the benefits of the covenant of grace, and our engagement to be the Lord's.

Q. 95. To whom is baptism to be administered?

Baptism is not to be administered to any that are out of the visible church, till they profess their faith in Christ, and obedience to him; but the infants of such as are members of the visible church are to be baptized.

Q. 96. What is the Lord's supper?

The Lord's supper is a sacrament, wherein, by giving and receiving bread and wine according to Christ's appointment, his death is showed forth; and the worthy receivers are, not after a corporal and carnal manner, but by faith, made partakers of his body and blood, with all his benefits, to their spiritual nourishment and growth in grace.

Q. 97. What is required to the worthy receiving of the Lord's supper?

It is required of them that would worthily partake of the Lord's supper, that they examine themselves of their knowledge to discern the Lord's body, of their faith to feed upon him, of their repentance, love, and new obedience; lest, coming unworthily, they eat and drink judgment to themselves.

Q. 98. What is prayer?

Prayer is an offering up of our desires unto God, for things agreeable to his will, in the name of Christ, with confession of our sins, and thankful acknowledgment of his mercies.

Q. 99. What rule hath God given for our direction in prayer?

The whole word of God is of use to direct us in prayer; but the special rule of direction is that form of prayer which Christ taught his disciples, commonly called the Lord's prayer.

Q. 100. What doth the preface of the Lord's prayer teach us?

The preface of the Lord's prayer, which is, Our Father which art in heaven, teacheth us to draw near to God with all holy reverence and confidence, as children to a father able and ready to help us; and that we should pray with and for others.

Q. 101. What do we pray for in the first petition?

In the first petition, which is, Hallowed be thy name, we pray that God would enable us and others to glorify him in all that whereby he maketh himself known; and that he would dispose all things to his own glory.

Q. 102. What do we pray for in the second petition?

In the second petition, which is, Thy kingdom come, we pray that Satan's kingdom may be destroyed; and that the kingdom of grace may be advanced, ourselves and others brought into it, and kept in it; and that the kingdom of glory may be hastened.

Q. 103. What do we pray for in the third petition?

In the third petition, which is, Thy will be done in earth, as it is in heaven, we pray that God, by his grace, would make us able and willing to know, obey and submit to his will in all things, as the angels do in heaven.

Q. 104. What do we pray for in the fourth petition?
In the fourth petition, which is, Give us this day our daily bread, we pray that of God's free gift we may receive a competent portion of the good things of this life, and enjoy his blessing with them.

Q. 105. What do we pray for in the fifth petition?
In the fifth petition, which is, And forgive us our debts, as we forgive our debtors, we pray that God, for Christ's sake, would freely pardon all our sins; which we are the rather encouraged to ask, because by his grace we are enabled from the heart to forgive others.

Q. 106. What do we pray for in the sixth petition?
In the sixth petition, which is, And lead us not into temptation, but deliver us from evil, we pray that God would either keep us from being tempted to sin, or support and deliver us when we are tempted.

Q. 107. What doth the conclusion of the Lord's prayer teach us?
The conclusion of the Lord's prayer, which is, For thine is the kingdom, and the power, and the glory, forever, Amen, teacheth us to take our encouragement in prayer from God only, and in our prayers to praise him, ascribing kingdom, power and glory to him. And in testimony of our desire, and assurance to be heard, we say, Amen.

THE LAUSANNE COVENANT (1974)

INTRODUCTION
We, members of the Church of Jesus Christ, from more than 150 nations, participants in the International Congress on World Evangelization at Lausanne, praise God for his great salvation and rejoice in the fellowship he has given us with himself and with each other. We are deeply stirred by what God is doing in our day, moved to penitence by our failures and challenged by the unfinished task of evangelization. We believe the Gospel is God's good news for the whole world, and we are determined by his grace to obey Christ's commission to proclaim it to all mankind and to make disciples of every nation. We desire, therefore, to affirm our faith and our resolve, and to make public our covenant.

1. THE PURPOSE OF GOD
We affirm our belief in the one-eternal God, Creator and Lord of the world, Father, Son and Holy Spirit, who governs all things according to the purpose of his will. He has been

calling out from the world a people for himself, and sending his people back into the world to be his servants and his witnesses, for the extension of his kingdom, the building up of Christ's body, and the glory of his name. We confess with shame that we have often denied our calling and failed in our mission, by becoming conformed to the world or by withdrawing from it. Yet we rejoice that even when borne by earthen vessels the gospel is still a precious treasure. To the task of making that treasure known in the power of the Holy Spirit we desire to dedicate ourselves anew.

(Isa. 40:28; Matt. 28:19; Eph. 1:11; Acts 15:14; John 17:6, 18; Eph 4:12; 1 Cor. 5:10; Rom. 12:2; II Cor. 4:7)

2. THE AUTHORITY AND POWER OF THE BIBLE

We affirm the divine inspiration, truthfulness and authority of both Old and New Testament Scriptures in their entirety as the only written word of God, without error in all that it affirms, and the only infallible rule of faith and practice. We also affirm the power of God's word to accomplish his purpose of salvation. The message of the Bible is addressed to all men and women. For God's revelation in Christ and in Scripture is unchangeable. Through it the Holy Spirit still speaks today. He illumines the minds of God's people in every culture to perceive its truth freshly through their own eyes and thus discloses to the whole Church ever more of the many-colored wisdom of God.

(2 Tim. 3:16; 2 Pet. 1:21; John 10:35; Isa. 55:11; 1 Cor. 1:21; Rom. 1:16, Matt. 5:17, 18; Jude 3; Eph. 1:17,18; 3:10,18)

3. THE UNIQUENESS AND UNIVERSALITY OF CHRIST

We affirm that there is only one Saviour and only one gospel, although there is a wide diversity of evangelistic approaches. We recognise that everyone has some knowledge of God through his general revelation in nature. But we deny that this can save, for people suppress the truth by their unrighteousness. We also reject as derogatory to Christ and the gospel every kind of syncretism and dialogue which implies that Christ speaks equally through all religions and ideologies. Jesus Christ, being himself the only God-man, who gave himself as the only ransom for sinners, is the only mediator between God and people. There is no other name by which we must be saved. All men and women are perishing because of sin, but God loves everyone, not wishing that any should perish but that all should repent. Yet those who reject Christ repudiate the joy of salvation and condemn themselves to eternal separation from God. To proclaim Jesus as "the Saviour of the world" is not to affirm that all people are either automatically or ultimately saved, still less to affirm that all religions offer salvation in Christ. Rather it is to proclaim God's love for a world of sinners and to invite everyone to respond to him as Saviour and Lord in the wholehearted personal commitment of repentance and faith. Jesus Christ has been exalted above every other name; we long for the day when every knee shall bow to him and every tongue shall confess him Lord.

(Gal. 1:6–9; Rom. 1:18-32; 1 Tim. 2:5,6; Acts 4:12; John 3:16–19; 2 Pet. 3:9; 2 Thess. 1:7–9; John 4:42; Matt. 11:28; Eph. 1:20,21; Phil. 2:9–11)

4. THE NATURE OF EVANGELISM

To evangelize is to spread the good news that Jesus Christ died for our sins and was raised from the dead according to the Scriptures, and that as the reigning Lord he now offers the forgiveness of sins and the liberating gifts of the Spirit to all who repent and believe. Our Christian presence in the world is indispensable to evangelism, and so is that kind of dialogue whose purpose is to listen sensitively in order to understand. But evangelism itself is the proclamation of the historical, biblical Christ as Saviour and Lord, with a view to persuading people to come to him personally and so be reconciled to God. In issuing the gospel invitation we have no liberty to conceal the cost of discipleship. Jesus still calls all who would follow him to deny themselves, take up their cross, and identify themselves with his new community. The results of evangelism include obedience to Christ, incorporation into his Church and responsible service in the world.

(1Cor. 15:3,4; Acts 2: 32–39; John 20:21; 1 Cor. 1:23; 2 Cor. 4:5; 5:11,20; Luke 14:25–33; Mark 8:34; Acts 2:40,47; Mark 10:43–45)

5. CHRISTIAN SOCIAL RESPONSIBILITY

We affirm that God is both the Creator and the Judge of all people. We therefore should share his concern for justice and reconciliation throughout human society and for the liberation of men and women from every kind of oppression. Because men and women are made in the image of God, every person, regardless of race, religion, colour, culture, class, sex or age, has an intrinsic dignity because of which he or she should be respected and served, not exploited. Here too we express penitence both for our neglect and for having sometimes regarded evangelism and social concern as mutually exclusive. Although reconciliation with other people is not reconciliation with God, nor is social action evangelism, nor is political liberation salvation, nevertheless we affirm that evangelism and socio-political involvement are both part of our Christian duty. For both are necessary expressions of our doctrines of God and man, our love for our neighbour and our obedience to Jesus Christ. The message of salvation implies also a message of judgment upon every form of alienation, oppression and discrimination, and we should not be afraid to denounce evil and injustice wherever they exist. When people receive Christ they are born again into his kingdom and must seek not only to exhibit but also to spread its righteousness in the midst of an unrighteous world. The salvation we claim should be transforming us in the totality of our personal and social responsibilities. Faith without works is dead.

(Acts 17:26, 31; Gen. 18:25; Isa. 1:17; Psa. 45:7; Gen. 1:26, 27; Jas. 3:9; Lev. 19:18; Luke 6:27, 35; Jas. 2:14–26; John 3:3, 5; Matt. 5:20; 6:33; 2 Cor. 3:18; Jas. 2:20)

6. THE CHURCH AND EVANGELISM

We affirm that Christ sends his redeemed people into the world as the Father sent him, and that this calls for a similar deep and costly penetration of the world. We need to break out of our ecclesiastical ghettos and permeate non-Christian society. In the Church's mission of sacrificial service evangelism is primary. World evangelization requires the whole Church to take the whole gospel to the whole world. The Church is at the very centre of God's cosmic purpose and is his appointed means of spreading the gospel. But a church which preaches the cross must itself be marked by the cross. It becomes a stumbling block to evangelism when it betrays the gospel or lacks a living faith in God, a genuine love for people, or scrupulous honesty in all things including promotion and finance. The church is the community of God's people rather than an institution, and must not be identified with any particular culture, social or political system, or human ideology.

(John 17:18; 20:21; Matt. 28:19,20; Acts 1:8; 20:27; Eph. 1:9,10; 3:9-11; Gal. 6:14,17; 2 Cor. 6:3,4; 2 Tim. 2:19–21; Phil. 1:27)

7. COOPERATION IN EVANGELISM

We affirm that the Church's visible unity in truth is God's purpose. Evangelism also summons us to unity, because our oneness strengthens our witness, just as our disunity undermines our gospel of reconciliation. We recognize, however, that organisational unity may take many forms and does not necessarily forward evangelism. Yet we who share the same biblical faith should be closely united in fellowship, work and witness. We confess that our testimony has sometimes been marred by a sinful individualism and needless duplication. We pledge ourselves to seek a deeper unity in truth, worship, holiness and mission. We urge the development of regional and functional cooperation for the furtherance of the Church's mission, for strategic planning, for mutual encouragement, and for the sharing of resources and experience.

(John 17:21, 23; Eph. 4:3,4; John 13:35; Phil. 1:27; John 17:11–23)

8. CHURCHES IN EVANGELISTIC PARTNERSHIP

We rejoice that a new missionary era has dawned. The dominant role of western missions is fast disappearing. God is raising up from the younger churches a great new resource for world evangelization, and is thus demonstrating that the responsibility to evangelise belongs to the whole body of Christ. All churches should therefore be asking God and themselves what they should be doing both to reach their own area and to send missionaries to other parts of the world. A reevaluation of our missionary responsibility and role should be continuous. Thus a growing partnership of churches will develop and the universal character of Christ's Church will be more clearly exhibited. We also thank God for agencies which labor in Bible translation, theological education, the mass media, Christian literature, evangelism, missions, church renewal and other specialist fields. They too should engage in constant self-examination to evaluate their effectiveness as part of the Church's mission.

(Rom. 1:8; Phil. 1:5; 4:15; Acts 13:1–3, 1 Thess. 1:6–8)

9. THE URGENCY OF THE EVANGELISTIC TASK

More than 2,700 million people, which is more than two-thirds of all humanity, have yet to be evangelised. We are ashamed that so many have been neglected; it is a standing rebuke to us and to the whole Church. There is now, however, in many parts of the world an unprecedented receptivity to the Lord Jesus Christ. We are convinced that this is the time for churches and para-church agencies to pray earnestly for the salvation of the unreached and to launch new efforts to achieve world evangelization. A reduction of foreign missionaries and money in an evangelised country may sometimes be necessary to facilitate the national church's growth in self-reliance and to release resources for unevangelised areas. Missionaries should flow ever more freely from and to all six continents in a spirit of humble service. The goal should be, by all available means and at the earliest possible time, that every person will have the opportunity to hear, understand, and to receive the good news. We cannot hope to attain this goal without sacrifice. All of us are shocked by the poverty of millions and disturbed by the injustices which cause it. Those of us who live in affluent circumstances accept our duty to develop a simple life-style in order to contribute more generously to both relief and evangelism.

(John 9:4; Matt. 9:35–38; Rom. 9:1–3; 1 Cor. 9:19–23; Mark 16:15; Isa. 58:6, 7; Jas. 1:27; 2:1–9; Matt. 25:31–46; Acts 2:44,45; 4:34,35)

10. EVANGELISM AND CULTURE

The development of strategies for world evangelization calls for imaginative pioneering methods. Under God, the result will be the rise of churches deeply rooted in Christ and closely related to their culture. Culture must always be tested and judged by Scripture. Because men and women are God's creatures, some of their culture is rich in beauty and goodness. Because they are fallen, all of it is tainted with sin and some of it is demonic. The gospel does not presuppose the superiority of any culture to another, but evaluates all cultures according to its own criteria of truth and righteousness, and insists on moral absolutes in every culture. Missions have all too frequently exported with the gospel an alien culture and churches have sometimes been in bondage to culture rather than to Scripture. Christ's evangelists must humbly seek to empty themselves of all but their personal authenticity in order to become the servants of others, and churches must seek to transform and enrich culture, all for the glory of God.

(Mark 7:8, 9, 13; Gen. 4:21,22; 1 Cor. 9:19–23; Phil. 2:5–7; 2 Cor. 4:5)

11. EDUCATION AND LEADERSHIP

We confess that we have sometimes pursued church growth at the expense of church depth, and divorced evangelism from Christian nurture. We also acknowledge that some of our missions have been too slow to equip and encourage national leaders to assume their rightful responsibilities. Yet we are committed to indigenous principles, and long that every church will have national leaders who manifest a Christian style of leadership in terms not of domination but of service. We recognise that there is a great need to improve theological education, especially for church leaders. In every nation and culture there should be an effective training programme for pastors and laity in doctrine, discipleship, evangelism, nurture and service. Such training programmes should not rely on any stereotyped methodology but should be developed by creative local initiatives according to biblical standards.

(Col. 1:27, 28; Acts 14:23; Tit. 1:5, 9; Mark 10:42–45; Eph. 4:11,12)

12. SPIRITUAL CONFLICT

We believe that we are engaged in constant spiritual warfare with the principalities and powers of evil, who are seeking to overthrow the Church and frustrate its task of world evangelization. We know our need to equip ourselves with God's armour and to fight this battle with the spiritual weapons of truth and prayer. For we detect the activity of our enemy, not only in false ideologies outside the Church, but also inside it in false gospels which twist Scripture and put people in the place of God. We need both watchfulness and discernment to safeguard the biblical gospel. We acknowledge that we ourselves are not immune to worldliness of thoughts and action, that is, to a surrender to secularism. For example, although careful studies of church growth, both numerical and spiritual, are right and valuable, we have sometimes neglected them. At other times, desirous to ensure a response to the gospel, we have compromised our message, manipulated our hearers through pressure techniques, and become unduly preoccupied with statistics or even dishonest in our use of them. All this is worldly. The Church must be in the world; the world must not be in the Church.

(Eph. 6:12; 2 Cor. 4:3, 4; Eph. 6:11, 13–18; 2 Cor. 10:3–5; 1 John 2:18–26; 4:1–3; Gal. 1:6–9; 2 Cor. 2:17; 4:2; John 17:15)

13. FREEDOM AND PERSECUTION

It is the God-appointed duty of every government to secure conditions of peace, justice and liberty in which the Church may obey God, serve the Lord Jesus Christ, and preach the gospel without interference. We therefore pray for the leaders of nations and call upon them to guarantee freedom of thought and conscience, and freedom to practise and propagate religion in accordance with the will of God and as set forth in The Universal Declaration of Human Rights. We also express our deep concern for all who have been unjustly imprisoned, and especially for those who are suffering for their testimony to the Lord Jesus. We promise to pray and work for their freedom. At the same time we refuse to be intimidated by their fate. God helping us, we too will seek to stand against injustice and to remain faithful to the gospel, whatever the cost. We do not forget the warnings of Jesus that persecution is inevitable.

(1 Tim. 1:1–4, Acts 4:19; 5:29; Col. 3:24; Heb. 13:1–3; Luke 4:18; Gal. 5:11; 6:12; Matt. 5:10–12; John 15:18–21)

14. THE POWER OF THE HOLY SPIRIT

We believe in the power of the Holy Spirit. The Father sent his Spirit to bear witness to his Son; without his witness ours is futile. Conviction of sin, faith in Christ, new birth and Christian growth are all his work. Further, the Holy Spirit is a missionary spirit; thus evangelism should arise spontaneously from a Spirit-filled church. A church that is not a missionary church is contradicting itself and quenching the Spirit. Worldwide evangelization will become a realistic possibility only when the Spirit renews the Church in truth and wisdom, faith, holiness, love and power. We therefore call upon all Christians to pray for such a visitation of the sovereign Spirit of God that all his fruit may appear in all his people and that all his gifts may enrich the body of Christ. Only then will the whole church become a fit instrument in his hands, that the whole earth may hear his voice.

(1 Cor. 2:4; John 15:26;27; 16:8–11; 1 Cor. 12:3; John 3:6–8; 2 Cor. 3:18; John 7:37–39; 1 Thess. 5:19; Acts 1:8; Psa. 85:4–7; 67:1–3; Gal. 5:22,23; 1 Cor. 12:4–31; Rom. 12:3–8)

15. THE RETURN OF CHRIST

We believe that Jesus Christ will return personally and visibly, in power and glory, to consummate his salvation and his judgment. This promise of his coming is a further spur to our evangelism, for we remember his words that the gospel must first be preached to all nations. We believe that the interim period between Christ's ascension and return is to be filled with the mission of the people of God, who have no liberty to stop before the end. We also remember his warning that false Christs and false prophets will arise as precursors of the final Antichrist. We therefore reject as a proud, self-confident dream the notion that people can ever build a utopia on earth. Our Christian confidence is that God will perfect his kingdom, and we look forward with eager anticipation to that day, and to the new heaven and earth in which righteousness will dwell and God will reign forever. Meanwhile, we rededicate ourselves to the service of Christ and of people in joyful submission to his authority over the whole of our lives.

(Mark 14:62; Heb. 9:28; Mark 13:10; Acts 1:8–11; Matt. 28:20; Mark 13:21–23; 1 John 2:18; 4:1–3; Luke 12:32; Rev. 21:1–5; 2 Pet. 3:13; Matt. 28:18)

CONCLUSION

Therefore, in the light of this our faith and our resolve, we enter into a solemn covenant with God and with each other, to pray, to plan and to work together for the evangelization of the whole world. We call upon others to join us. May God help us by his grace and for his glory to be faithful to this our covenant! Amen, Alleluia!

APPENDIX 2

"GOD THE COMMUNICATOR"

"GOD THE COMMUNICATOR"
BY REV. DR. ARNE H. FJELDSTAD

THE GOD OF THE BIBLE is the God who communicates with the human being. As Johannes Henrici points out: 'Communication is deeply rooted in God's nature and it is this nature he imparted to humanity when he created us in his own image [1].

Communication is a God-given capability given to the created human being and is "the only way to be fully human"[2]. In principle, to be a human is to be a communicator. Communication—the ability to express oneself—remains God's gift to humanity.

This basic understanding of communication as a result of God's creating act in history deepens our understanding of God's own desire for a relationship with His created beings. God wants us to communicate with Him and He with us. Throughout history, as reported in the Bible, we can see how God has communicated through His prophets and then through His Son and how He calls us to respond. Hearing the Good News, living by it and witnessing to it, is the basic calling for all Christians.

The reformer Martin Luther underlines this fundamental link between creation and communication: "he claims that to be created in God's image has to do with relationship and communication …That means I am created for dialogue: God's communication with me takes the form of a conversation. This is the basic theme in all of Scripture: God is continually seeking man (sic) out to talk with him, from the story of Eden until the proclamation of the new heavens and the new earth. In the same way the concept of covenant is based on two-way communication"[3].

God moves into the receptor's frame of reference, namely, the culture and the language. "He goes beyond the predictable and the stereotype in his communicative efforts"[4]. He uses the language and thought patterns of those with whom He speaks.

I have been a journalist in mainstream media for more than 30 years. I do think journalists oftentimes in a special way can understand the issue of Gods passion for communication. News reports, articles, presentations or audio/video programs demand a lot of work and oftentimes becomes a "baby" for many journalists. There is an act of "creation" in the very process of communicating a message, directing a program or writing a story.

God has revealed His passionate heart by choosing a significant method of communication, namely incarnation. The almighty, supreme God is really a "God who bends down and, lowering himself, speaks that we might hear and understand This 'bending down' means that all God's communications are incarnational: God reveals

Himself in and through the ordinary situations of human life…. And that leads us into history and culture, into created life as well as its vulnerability and brokennes."[5].

God's heartfelt desire to communicate His eternal message of love and redemption has profound consequences for the basic understanding of every Christian's calling to communicate—in any way possible—the good news of salvation. We are called to be "ambassadors of Christ" (2 Corinthians 5:20). Paul's life and work are significantly marked by his skills as a highly effective and successful communicator. Paul's success as a communicator not only in preaching and teaching the gospel, but also in manifesting the truth in daily life brought him into persecution, imprisonment and torture. His methods were dynamic, focused, pastoral and passionate. The apostle related to the needs of people in a particular place and situation. He never lost track of the essential message, the gospel.

All of this comes together in the fact that Paul lived out a holistic theology in his ministry. "Paul showed in many ways and in various situations that he was concerned with people in their total life, and with the effect that the gospel could have on the whole of life. He was, before everything else, the evangelist, calling for the heart and mind to be put right with God. … practical application of Christian truth was more important to Paul than apprehension of all the content"[6].

Communicating the gospel in today's world also needs to be carried out in a holistic way, with an evangelistic focus, and a pastoral heart authentically caring for people to be reconciled with God. As Christians the Lord Jesus has commissioned us to be his communicators. Our task is to communicate the good news about Jesus Christ in any way possible to every human being (Matthew 28:18–20, John 20:21). This task was given both to the Church as a whole and to every Christian, to the craftsman as well as the journalist.

This understanding of every Christian as a communicator is based upon God as the Creator of the universe. Yet, it is organically woven together with our commission to share the good news of the gospel with other people. Dr. Charles Kraft reminds us "the messenger himself/herself is the major component of the total message. … We are a major part of the message that we seek to communicate"[7]. Our challenge is to "embody Christ" in our lives, so that not only our words but also our deeds may converge into a holistic testimony of our Lord and Savior Jesus Christ.

In other words, our testimony is our story, our life is our story, and our story must be woven together with God's story. Dr. Leighton Ford has pointed out, the story of God "… goes on forever, weaving its way through countless human lives, countless human stories. We are all part of that great narrative, as we join our stories to His. And we expand that narrative as we call others to join their stories to His"[8].

The heart of all communication is that it takes place in a person-to-person encounter. It is never only a "transmission" of messages. Communication is to be involved, and must "result in Christ becoming flesh and blood in ever new settings. It is the very nature of the Good News that it will sound differently in Addis Ababa and in London, because it is the Good News about the Word that became a human being. The gospel is the same, but its form will differ according to the situation"[9].

This "holistic" and "organic" view of every Christian as a communicator and inevitably a "missionary" is a result of "the two mandates of creation and mission." Dr. Vinay Samuel writes, "As humans made in God's image we are empowered with stewardly responsibility for the earth and for the gospel of the kingdom. It is in the exercise of that stewardship we affirm our identity as God's children and also fulfill our humanity"[10].

Yet, we need to keep in mind that communication is an intrinsic part of the Trinity—Father, Son and Holy Spirit. Some comments have already been made, but let us just note also how God in the Old Testament uses signs to remind His people about the relationship and the covenant: the rainbow for Noah, the blood on the doorframe at Passover, the circumcision to set apart Abraham's descendants.

Jesus Christ is proclaimed as the essence of communication. He is the Word. "In the beginning was the Word, and the Word was with God, and the Word was God. He was with God in the beginning. Through him all things were made; without him nothing was made that has been made. In him was life, and that life was the light of men… The Word became flesh and made his dwelling among us. We have seen his glory, the glory of the One and Only, who came from the Father, full of grace and truth" (John 1:1–14).

Again, we need to keep in mind a holistic approach: Jesus is not only the spoken Word, but the Word in action. The Kingdom of God is near, He said—and it truly was and is today, through the Holy Spirit. Not only because Jesus Himself was dwelling among us, proclaiming the gospel, but equally so because He acted to heal, feed, comfort and even restore to life.

The Holy Spirit is the Communicator as well. The Bible calls Him "the Counselor" and "the Spirit of truth" who will convince of sin and "guide you into all truth. He will not speak on his own; He will speak only what He hears, and He will tell you what is yet to come. He will bring glory to me by taking from what is mine and making it known to you."

Even more so, to enable us to carry out the task of communicating the Gospel, we have been promised the power of the Holy Spirit. It is this Spirit that can change the Babel of confusion into the Pentecost of genuine understanding. Martin Luther is taking this even further when he explains the 3rd Article of faith in this way: "I believe that I cannot by my own reason or strength believe in Jesus Christ, my Lord, or come to Him; but the Holy Ghost has called me by the Gospel, enlightened me with His gifts, sanctified and kept me in the true faith; even as He calls, gathers, enlightens, and sanctifies the whole Christian Church on earth, and keeps it with Jesus Christ in the one true faith"[11].

Our challenge is to work in the power of the Holy Spirit to reach out to the human heart. We are called to be Spirit-filled communicators linking our personal stories to God's ongoing story in this world. We are called to be humble, honest and transparent communicators always ready to listen, to answer questions and to share the most important story ever told—the real story of our Lord Jesus Christ that can change a life—forever.

END NOTES

[1] Johannes Henrici, "Towards an Anthropological Philosophy of Communication." *Communication Resource*. March 1983. 1.

[2] Viggo Søgaard, *Research In Church and Mission*, Pasadena, CA: William Carey Library, 1996, 11.

[3] Knud Jørgensen, "Christian Communication: Remote Control or Incarnation?" *World Evangelization*. December 1996/January 1997, 5.

[4] Charles Kraft, *Communicating the Gospel God's Way*, Pasadena, CA: William Carey Library, 1983, 11.

[5] Jørgensen, ibid.

[6] Dean S. Gilliland, *Pauline Theology & Mission Practice*, Grand Rapids, MI: Baker Book House, 1983, 15.

[7] Kraft, ibid., 31.

[8] Leighton Ford, *The Power of Story. Rediscovering the Oldest, Most Natural Way to Reach People for Christ*, Colorado Springs, CO: NavPress, 1994, 179.

[9] Jorgensen, ibid., 7.

[10] Vinay Samuel, "Journalism and the Two Mandates: The news profession as vocation. The role of journalism in creation and mission." Available at http://www.gegrapha.org/VinaySamuel.asp

[11] Martin Luther's explanation to the 3rd article of faith. Available at http://cat41.org/WhoWhat/Confessions/SC.htm

Taken from The Oxford Centre for Religion & Public Life. Used by permission.

APPENDIX 3

WHAT GOD VALUES:
A BASIC BIBLICAL CATALOG

1. God values His rightful authority over all things, including our bodies (Ezek. 18:4; 1 Cor. 3:16-19; 6:18-20; 2 Cor. 6:16-17), our minds (Isa. 55:7; Rom. 12:2; 2 Cor. 10:5), and His creation (Ex. 9:29; 19:5; Deut. 10:14; 1 Chron. 29:11-12; Job 41:11; Pss. 24:1; 50:10-12; 89:11; 95:4-5; 1 Cor. 10:26).

2. God values truth as that which actually is the case (Num. 23:19; Pss. 31:5; 33:4; 89:14; 111:7; 119:160; Isa. 65:16; Micah 7:20; John 8:31-32; 14:6; 17:17; 2 Cor. 4:2; 2 Thes. 2:10-12; 2 Tim. 2:15; Titus 1:2; 3 John 4; Rev. 15:3). Truth sometimes can be legitimately applied in a variety of ways (Rom. 14; 1 Cor. 8; Gal. 5:13-14).

3. God values His exclusive right to our worship (Ex. 20:3-5; 34:14; Deut. 4:24; 5:9; 6:14-15; Isa. 43:21; 44:22-23; 45:5-6; Jer. 13:11; Matt. 21:12-13; 1 Pet. 2:9; Rev. 4:8-11; 15:3-4).

4. God values human life. (Gen. 1:26-27; 9:6; Ex. 20:13; 21:12, 22-25; Deut. 5:17; Prov. 6:16-17; 24:11-12; Amos 1:13; Acts 17:28-29; Rom. 1:29; James 2:11). This includes preborn human life (Isa. 44:24; 49:1-5; Jer. 1:5; Gal. 1:15-16), older human life (Lev. 19:32; Job 12:12; Prov. 16:31; Isa. 46:3-4), and impaired human life (Matt. 14:14; 15:30; 20:34; Luke 4:18; 7:22).

5. God values animal life, albeit less than he values human life. (Gen. 1:28, 31; 9:8-13; Ex. 23:5 and 12; Deut. 5:14; 25:4, Job 12:10; Pss. 36:6; 37:5-6, 28; 104:10-14 and 24-25; Prov. 12:10; 27:23; Jer. 12:4; Matt. 6:26; 10:29-31; Luke 12:6; 1 Cor. 3:16-17).

6. God values the earth (Gen. 1:31; Deut. 10:14; Job 26:7-9, 11-14; Pss. 24:1; 89:11; 145:9; 1 Cor. 10:26; Col. 1:16-17). He values humans' care of the earth (Gen. 2:15; Ex. 23:10-11; Lev. 18:26-28; 25:2-5; Deut. 20:19).

7. God values justice (Deut. 10:17-18; 2 Chron. 19:7; Pss. 9:8; 10:17-18; 11:7; 36:6; 45:6-7; 67:4; 75:2; 89:14; 97:2; 98:9; Prov. 21:3; Isa. 61:8-11; Amos 5:14-15, and 24; Micah 6:8; Matt. 5:6; Acts 17:31; 2 Thes. 1:5-6).

8. God values mercy (Num. 14:18; Neh. 9:27; Job 20:19-20; Pss. 106:1; 107:1; 136:1-26; Isa. 54:7; Lam. 3:32; Amos 8:4-7; Micah 7:18; Matt. 5:7; 9:13; 12:7; 18:23-35; Eph. 2:4-7; 4:32; James 2:13; 1 Pet. 1:3)

9. God values humility (Pss. 18:27; 147:6; Prov. 3:34; 27:2; Isa. 5:21; 66:2; Micah 6:8; Matt. 18:3-4; Luke 1:52; 14:7-11; 18:9-14; 22:24-27; Mark 9:35; Rom. 12:3; 1 Cor. 3:19; 13:4; 2 Cor. 11:30; 12:6-10; Gal. 6:14; Eph. 4:2; Phil. 2:1-11; Col. 3:12; James 4:6; 1 Pet. 5:2-6). This humility shows, among other ways, when a person limits his or her freedom out of respect for another person's sensitivities (Rom. 14; 1 Cor. 8; Gal. 5:13-14).

10. God values peace (Ps. 34:14; 133; Isa. 2:1-5; 26:3; 55:12; Matt. 5:9; Rom. 12:18; 14:17-19; 2 Cor. 13:11; Gal. 5:22; Phil. 2:1-2; 2 Tim. 2:22; James 3:16-18), although there are times when He authorizes war (Deut. 20:1-4; Josh. 8:1-29; 2 Chron. 20:13-21; Ps. 144:1; Eccl. 3:8). He loathes interpersonal discord (Prov. 6:19; 18:6; 22:10; James 3:14-18).

11. God values honesty (Lev. 19:13, 35-37; Deut. 25:13-16; Prov. 11:1-5; Micah 6:10-13; 7:2-4; Luke 3:12-14; 1 Cor. 6:10; Eph. 4:28; 1 Thes. 4:6)

12. God values self-control (Prov. 16:32; 25:28; 1 Cor. 6:10; 9:24-27; Gal. 5:23; 1 Thes. 4:4-5; 1 Tim. 3:2, 11; Titus 1:8-9; 2:2, 12; 1 Pet. 1:13; 2 Pet. 1:6).

13. God values family (Psalms 127 and 128; Prov. 20:6-7; 31:10). He values reproduction (Gen. 1:22-28; 9:1-7; Deut. 7:12-14; Ps. 113:7-9; 127:3-5).

14. God values monogamous, heterosexual marriage (Gen. 2:22-24; Deut. 24:5; Prov. 5:18-19; 18:22; 19:14; Matt. 19:4-6; Mark 10:6-9; 1 Cor. 7:1-16; Eph. 5:22-23; Col. 3:18-19; Heb. 13:4). He loathes divorce (Matt. 5:32).

15. God values sexual purity. He loathes sexual activity that is premarital (Matt. 19:19; Rom. 1:29; 1 Cor. 7:1-5), adulterous (Ex. 20:14; Matt. 5:18; Heb. 13:4), homosexual (Lev. 18:22; 20:13; Rom. 1:23-28; 1 Tim. 1:10), or perverse (Lev. 18:23; Rom. 1:23-28; 1 Cor. 5:1-8; 6:9-10; Gal. 5:19-21; Eph. 5:3; 1 Thes. 4:3-5; Jude 7). This includes lust (Job 31:1-12; Matt. 5:28-29; 1 Cor. 7:9; Col 3:5; 2 Tim. 2:22; 2 Pet. 2:14-16).

16. God values the church as an equipper of believers for doing God's redemptive work in the world (Matt. 16:18; 1 Cor. 10:31-33; 12:12-26; Eph. 1:22-23; 2:19-22; 4:4-16; 5:25-32; Col. 1:17-20; 3:14-16; 1 Pet. 2:9-10).

17. God values government as an executor of His righteousness (1 Kings 10:9; 2 Chron. 9:8; Amos 5:15-24; Rom. 13:1-7; 1 Tim. 2:1-4; Titus 3:1; 1 Pet. 2:13-17). He values His authority over government (Col. 2:10, 15; Eph. 1:20-22).

18. God values personal property rights (Ex. 20:15; Lev. 6:1-7; 19:11-13; Deut. 5:19; Judg. 11:15; Prov. 22:28; Eccl. 5:19; Amos 3:10; Zech. 5:3-4; Matt. 19:18; 25:14-30; 1 Cor. 6:10; Eph. 4:28).

19. God values our faith in Him (Gen. 15:6; Hab. 2:2; Matt. 17:20; 23:23; Mark 11:22; Luke 18:17; Rom. 1:17; 3:27-5:2; 10:6-10; Gal. 3:6-23; Heb. 11; James 2).

20. God values our love for others (John 13:34-35; 15:12-17; Rom. 12:10; 16:16; 1 Cor. 16:20; 2 Cor. 13:11-12; Gal. 5:13-15; Eph. 4:2, 16; Phil. 1:9; Heb. 10:24; 1 Thes. 3:12; 4:9; 5:13; 2 Thes. 1:3; Heb. 13:1; 1 Pet. 1:22; 4:8; 5:14; 1 John 2:7; 3:10-11, 18; 4:7-21; Rev. 2:4).

21. God values our compassion for others. This includes the poor and oppressed (Job 18:7; Isa. 58:7; Jer. 5:28; 22:16; Mal. 3:5; Matt. 4:23-25; 8:1-3; 9:1-8; 25:35; 1 Tim. 5:10; John 3:17), children (Matt. 18:1-14; 19:13-15; Luke 17:1-3; James 1:27; 2:6-9), , employees (Isa. 58:6); prisoners (2 Chron. 28:15; Matt. 25:39), widows and the fatherless (Job 31:16-22; Jer. 5:28; Mal. 3:5; 1 Tim. 5:1-12); strangers (Mal. 3:5; Matt. 25:31-46), the sick (Matt. 25:31-46).

22. God values our hospitality to others (Lev. 19:34; Job 31:32; Isa. 58:7; Matt. 25:35, 38; Luke 10:30-37; 14:12-14; Rom. 12:13; Heb. 13:2; James 2:15-17; Titus 1:7-8; 1 Pet. 4:9).

23. God values our impartiality (Acts 10:34; Rom. 2:11; Eph. 6:9). He loathes prejudice against the poor (Ex. 23:6; Job 18:8; James 2:2-9), against employees (Eph. 6:9; Col 4:1), against foreigners (Lev. 19:33; Deut. 10:17-19), against people of different races/ethnicities (Numbers 12; Rom. 3:9, 29-30; Gal. 2:11-16; 3:28), or against the opposite sex (Gen. 5:1-2; Gal. 3:26-29; Col. 3:18-19). This does not disregard the fact, in the case of opposite sex relations, that God assigns unique roles to males and females (Gen. 3:16-19; 1 Cor. 11:3-10; Eph. 5:21-30).

24. God values human creativity that expresses truthful or righteous principles (Ex. 31:1-6; 35:30-35; Psalm 150; 1 Cor. 14:26; Eph. 5:19-20; Col. 3:16).

25. God values sound reasoning that expresses truthful or righteous principles (Isa. 1:18; Matt. 22:37; Mark 12:30; Luke 10:27; John 20:30-31; 2 Tim. 3:16-17; 1 Peter 3:15-16).

26. God values our attempts to liberate the wrongly oppressed via speech (Ps. 82:3-4; Prov. 24:11-12; 31:8-9; Isa. 1:17; Jer. 22:3; Ezek. 33:8).

27. God values our attempts to communicate His gospel of forgiveness and redemption to those who do not know Him (Pss. 67:1-2; 96:2-3; Isa. 49:6; 52:7; Matt. 5:14-16; 28:18-20; Mark 13:9-10; 16:15; Acts 1:8; Rom. 10:14-15).

28. God values our attempts to help others in their efforts to promote the things God values according to Scripture (John 13:1-17; 1 Cor. 12:12-31; Gal. 5:13; Eph. 4:12; 6:2-22; Col. 4:7-8).

INDEX